SEMANTICS FOR LATIN

SEMANTICS FOR LATIN

AN INTRODUCTION

A. M. DEVINE

LAURENCE D. STEPHENS

OXFORD
UNIVERSITY PRESS

OXFORD
UNIVERSITY PRESS

Oxford University Press is a department of the University of Oxford. It furthers the University's objective of excellence in research, scholarship, and education by publishing worldwide.

Oxford New York
Auckland Cape Town Dar es Salaam Hong Kong Karachi
Kuala Lumpur Madrid Melbourne Mexico City Nairobi
New Delhi Shanghai Taipei Toronto

With offices in
Argentina Austria Brazil Chile Czech Republic France Greece
Guatemala Hungary Italy Japan Poland Portugal Singapore
South Korea Switzerland Thailand Turkey Ukraine Vietnam

Published in the United States of America by
Oxford University Press
198 Madison Avenue, New York, NY 10016

Library of Congress Cataloging-in-Publication Data

Devine, A. M. (Andrew M.)
Semantics for Latin : an introduction / A.M. Devine and Laurence D. Stephens.
pages. cm.
Includes bibliographical references and index.
ISBN 978-0-19-996952-4
1. Latin language--Grammar. 2. Semantics. I. Stephens, Laurence D. II. Title.
PA2071.D49 2013
470.1'43—dc23 2012043543

1 3 5 7 9 8 6 4 2

Printed in the United States of America on acid-free paper

PREFACE

The advent of the new discipline of Formal Semantics around forty years ago has resulted in a vast expansion in our knowledge and theoretical understanding of grammatical meaning. In this book we collect together this new material, apply it to Latin and make the results accessible to a Classical audience. The issues confronted by Formal Semantics are mostly those that comprise the core subject matter of Latin grammar. But Formal Semantics is not just a new way of doing an old subject: the richness and explanatory depth of its analyses, together with their striking elegance and precision, go way beyond anything that was achieved by the typically rather vague notional semantics used in our classroom textbooks and in the standard German reference grammars.

It has been said of philology (by one of the characters in Christopher Hampton's play 'The Philanthropist') that it combines the boredom of the sciences with the uselessness of the humanities. Whether you think that semantics is a branch of philology or that philology is a tool of semantics, this introduction to the subject aims to persuade you that semantics is not boring at all, but in fact intellectually as exhilarating as it is challenging, going to the very essence of what is being communicated when people talk and authors write. It is not useless either, at least not for Classicists, who spend a great deal of time first learning and then teaching the meaning of the Latin grammatical inflections and of the constructions in which they are used. So apart from its intrinsic interest, we hope that the material in this book will be of real practical value to students and teachers of Latin and, more generally, to scholars engaged in any discussion of Latin textual meaning.

In conformity with the usual introductory textbook style, we have refrained from giving point-by-point bibliographical references. (Nonspecialist readers, we felt, would not be particularly interested in our sources, and specialist readers would readily recognize most of them without the need for Quellenforschung.) The bibliography is limited to a few suggestions for further reading. So it is important for us to take this opportunity to issue a general acknowledgement of our systematic indebtedness to the already rather extensive body of published and unpublished work in semantic theory, the existence of which made it both possible and desirable for this book to be written. We would also like to thank Susan F. Stephens for her kind help with the proofs and Helen Devine for a great deal of very smart and prompt IT service.

A.M.D., L.D.S.

CONTENTS

ABBREVIATIONS

Acad	Cicero *Academica*
Ad Att	Cicero *Epistulae ad Atticum*
Ad Brut	Cicero *Epistulae ad Brutum*
Ad Fam	Cicero *Epistulae ad Familiares*
Ad Qfr	Cicero *Epistulae ad Q. fratrem*
Aen	Vergil *Aeneid*
Amp	Ampelius
Apic	Apicius
Apul Apol	Apuleius *Apologia*
Apul Flor	Apuleius *Florida*
Apul Met	Apuleius *Metamorphoses*
Apul Mun	Apuleius *De Mundo*
Apul Plat	Apuleius *De Platone*
Asc Ped Pis	Asconius Pedianus *In Pisonem*
Asc Ped Sc	Asconius Pedianus *Pro Scauro*
BAfr	*De Bello Africo*
BAlex	*De Bello Alexandrino*
BC	Caesar *De Bello Civili*
BG	Caesar *De Bello Gallico*
BHisp	*De Bello Hispaniensi*
Brut	Cicero *Brutus*
Cat	Cicero *In Catilinam*
Cato	Cato *De Agri Cultura*
Catull	Catullus
Cels	Celsus *De Medicina*
CIL	Corpus Inscriptionum Latin.
Col	Columella *De Re Rustica*
Col De Arb	Columella *De Arboribus*
Comm Ant	*Commodus Antoninus*
De Amic	Cicero *De Amicitia*
De Div	Cicero *De Divinatione*
De Dom	Cicero *De Domo Sua*
De Fat	Cicero *De Fato*
De Fin	Cicero *De Finibus*
De Har Resp	Cicero *De Haruspicum Respons.*
De Inv	Cicero *De Inventione*
De Leg Agr	Cicero *De Lege Agraria*
De Leg	Cicero *De Legibus*

De Off	Cicero *De Officiis*
De Or	Cicero *De Oratore*
De Part Or	Cicero *De Partitione Oratoria*
De Prov	Cicero *De Provinciis Consular.*
De Rep	Cicero *De Republica*
De Sen	Cicero *De Senectute*
Orat	Cicero *Orator*
Div Caec	Cicero *Divinatio in Caecilium*
Enn Ann	Ennius *Annals*
Flor	Florus *Epitome*
Frontin	Frontinus *Strategemata*
Fronto Aur	Fronto *Ad Aurelium*
Fur Ant	Furius Antias
Gaius Inst	Gaius *Institutiones*
Gall	*Gallieni Duo*
Gell	Aulus Gellius
GL	*Grammatici Latini* Keil
Hist Aug	*Historia Augusta*
Hor Ep	Horace *Epistles*
Hor Epod	Horace *Epodes*
Hor Od	Horace *Odes*
Hor Sat	Horace *Satires*
In Pis	Cicero *In Pisonem*
In Vat	Cicero *In Vatinium*
Juv	Juvenal
Luc	Cicero *Lucullus*
Lucr	Lucretius
Mart	Martial
Mela	Pomponius Mela
ND	Cicero *De Natura Deorum*
NH	Pliny *Naturalis Historia*
Ov Am	Ovid *Amores*
Ov Ars Am	Ovid *Ars Amatoria*
Ov Ex Pont	Ovid *Ex Ponto*
Ov Fast	Ovid *Fasti*
Ov Her	Ovid *Heroides*
Ov Met	Ovid *Metamorphoses*
Ov Rem	Ovid *Remedia Amoris*

Ov Trist	Ovid *Tristia*
Parad	Cicero *Paradoxa Stoicorum*
Pers Sat	Persius *Satires*
Petr	Petronius *Satyricon*
Phaedr	Phaedrus
Phil	Cicero *Philippics*
Pl Amph	Plautus *Amphitruo*
Pl Asin	Plautus *Asinaria*
Pl Aul	Plautus *Aulularia*
Pl Bacch	Plautus *Bacchides*
Pl Capt	Plautus *Captivi*
Pl Cas	Plautus *Casina*
Pl Cist	Plautus *Cistellaria*
Pl Curc	Plautus *Curculio*
Pl Ep	Plautus *Epidicus*
Pl Men	Plautus *Menaechmi*
Pl Merc	Plautus *Mercator*
Pl Mil	Plautus *Miles Gloriosus*
Pl Pers	Plautus *Persa*
Pl Poen	Plautus *Poenulus*
Pl Pseud	Plautus *Pseudolus*
Pl Rud	Plautus *Rudens*
Pl Stich	Plautus *Stichus*
Pl Trin	Plautus *Trinummus*
Pl Truc	Plautus *Truculentus*
Pliny Ep	Pliny *Epistles*
Pliny Paneg	Pliny *Panegyricus*
Pompon Dig	Pomponius in *Digest*
Post Red Pop	Cicero *Post Reditum ad Popul.*
Post Red Sen	Cicero *Post Reditum in Senatu*
Pro Arch	Cicero *Pro Archia*
Pro Balb	Cicero *Pro Balbo*
Pro Caec	Cicero *Pro Caecina*
Pro Cael	Cicero *Pro Caelio*
Pro Clu	Cicero *Pro Cluentio*
Pro Flacc	Cicero *Pro Flacco*
Pro Font	Cicero *Pro Fonteio*
Pro Lig	Cicero *Pro Ligario*
Pro Leg Man	Cicero *Pro Lege Manilia*
Pro Marc	Cicero *Pro Marcello*
Pro Mil	Cicero *Pro Milone*
Pro Mur	Cicero *Pro Murena*
Pro Planc	Cicero *Pro Plancio*
Pro Quinct	Cicero *Pro Quinctio*
Pro Rab Perd	Cicero *Pro Rabirio Perduell.*
Pro Rab Post	Cicero *Pro Rabirio Postumo*
Pro Reg Deiot	Cicero *Pro Rege Deiotaro*
Pro Rosc Am	Cicero *Pro Roscio Amerino*
Pro Rosc Com	Cicero *Pro Roscio Comoedo*
Pro Scaur	Cicero *Pro Scauro*
Pro Sest	Cicero *Pro Sestio*
Pro Sull	Cicero *Pro Sulla*
Pro Tull	Cicero *Pro Tullio*
Prop	Propertius
Publ Syr	Publilius Syrus
Quadrig	Quadrigarius
Quint	Quintilian *Institutio Oratoria*
Quint Decl	Quintilian *Declamationes*
Res Gest	*Res Gestae Divi Augusti*
Rhet Her	*Rhetorica ad Herennium*
Rutil Lup	Rutilius Lupus
Sall Cat	Sallust *Catilina*
Sall De Rep	Sallust *De Republica*
Sall Jug	Sallust *Jugurtha*
Sall Hist	Sallust *Histories*
Scrib Larg	Scribonius Largus
Sen Apoc	Seneca *Apocolocyntosis*
Sen Con	Seneca *Controversiae*
Sen De Ben	Seneca *De Beneficiis*
Sen De Brev	Seneca *De Brevitate Vitae*
Sen De Clem	Seneca *De Clementia*
Sen De Vit Beat	Seneca *De Vita Beata*
Sen Ep	Seneca *Epistulae Morales*
Sen NQ	Seneca *Naturales Quaestiones*
Sen Med	Seneca *Medea*
Sen Suas	Seneca *Suasoriae*
Sil Ital	Silius Italicus
Suet	Suetonius *De Vita Caesarum*
Suet Gramm	Suetonius *De Grammaticis*
Suet Plin Sec	Suetonius *Vita Plinii Secundi*
Tac Agr	Tacitus *Agricola*
Tac Ann	Tacitus *Annals*
Tac Dial	Tacitus *Dialogus*
Tac Ger	Tacitus *Germania*
Tac Hist	Tacitus *Histories*
Ter Ad	Terence *Adelphi*
Ter Andr	Terence *Andria*
Ter Eun	Terence *Eunuch*
Ter Haut	Terence *Hauton Timorumenos*
Ter Hec	Terence *Hecyra*
Ter Phorm	Terence *Phormio*
Tib	Tibullus
Top	Cicero *Topica*
Tusc	Cicero *Tusculan Disputations*
Val Max	Valerius Maximus
Varro LL	Varro *De Lingua Latina*
Varro RR	Varro *Res Rusticae*
Vell Pat	Velleius Paterculus
Verg Georg	Vergil *Georgics*
Verg Ecl	Vergil *Eclogues*
Verr	Cicero *In Verrem*
Vitr	Vitruvius

SEMANTICS FOR LATIN

INTRODUCTION

A note to the student

One of the things that is sort of quirky about Classics is that our standard language textbooks and grammars are all over a hundred years old. Even the more recent ones are firmly rooted in the nineteenth-century philological tradition. Noone nowadays would dream of teaching a course in, say, physics or neuropsychology using a nineteenth-century textbook, and, unless you're rather heavily into steam punk, you will surely agree that it is not healthy for this practice to continue on in our discipline indefinitely. To put things in context, take Bradley's Arnold as an example, probably the most famous textbook in Classics, and rightly so. Here is a book with a truly venerable pedigree. It first came out in 1839, the year in which Queen Victoria became engaged to Prince Albert. This was 35 years before the arrival of set theory and 40 years before the invention of predicate logic. Dean Bradley's revision appeared in 1884, the year in which Gordon was besieged in Khartoum. Mountford's further revision, which we use today, dates back to the eve of the second world war, and it would be another thirty years or so before the advent of formal semantics, which is now the standard way to talk about grammatical meaning. So when people complain, as they sometimes do, that the English in the exercises of Bradley's Arnold is quaint and antiquated, they are missing the real issue that the theoretical framework of the grammatical explanations themselves is also very dated.

Grammar is like a software programme that Classicists rely on for their everyday research and teaching activities. Most of us regularly update our software, so it is evidently high time, in view of what has just been said in the preceding paragraph, for us to update that part of our grammatical software that deals with the meanings of inflections and constructions, in other words to "download" a current version of semantic theory. At this point you're probably thinking: "If formal semantics is the standard theory of semantics in use today, what exactly is it and what does it achieve that traditional semantics did not achieve?" A definition of formal semantics broad enough to encompass the varieties and styles in which it is currently practised might be "the application of formal languages such as set theory, the propositional calculus, the predicate calculus, higher order and intensional logics, aspects of abstract algebra such as lattice theory, and model theory to achieve a rigorous elucidation of meaning in natural languages." From a disciplinary perspective, both in its nature and in its origins, formal semantics lies at the confluence of linguistics with the philosophy of logic, the philosophy of language and the philosophy of mathematics. The present work represents a further interface of formal semantics itself with Classics. Formal semantics is more precise than the notional semantics of traditional grammars because it gives well-defined expressions for the meanings of syntactic constituents and a mathematically exact account of how the meanings of individual words combine to form those constituents and how those constituents themselves combine to form intermediate and sentence level meanings in terms of their denotations. So it is not just a new way of saying old things about grammatical meaning, it is also a way of saying a lot of new things that serve to correct, render precise, enhance and enrich the formulations of traditional grammar. It is more complicated than traditional grammar, and you may find its technical machinery a bit intimidating at first; but given the importance of grammar for understanding texts, you should find it well worth the effort. At least, we did, and we hope you will too. This book collects together the main theoretical concepts needed to analyze the meaning of the Latin simple sentence; the material is presented from the perspective of the Latin student and in a format that emphasizes the linguistic applications of the theory over its logical underpinnings. The analyses are, in the words of the wellknown saying, made as simple as possible but no simpler. Examples are given to illustrate how you could apply the concepts being presented to actual sentences in Latin texts you might be studying. The chapters can be read in any order, but the first three are perhaps a bit less technical than the others, as well as dealing with some of the most basic topics. There is a highly selective list of further reading at the end of each chapter, in case you wish to pursue the subject further.

Now that we have said why the book is needed and what it is designed to do, perhaps we should briefly note what it is not designed to do. First, it is about the semantics of grammar, not about lexical semantics (except in so far as the latter influences the former, which is quite a bit): you will not find a discussion of the difference between 'cat' and 'dog,' but you will find a discussion of the difference between singular and plural (Chapter 6) and between perfect and imperfect (Chapter 2). Secondly, it does not provide an Auseinandersetzung of currently available competing analyses with an evaluation of their respective pros and cons. Most of the time we just present a single analysis, the one that we like best. We are no more responsible for creating this analysis than your grammar book is responsible for inventing the ablative absolute: we claim no credit for its merits and take no responsibility for its deficiencies. But we do grant ourselves the freedom to merge features of different analyses and to adapt and modify their form or substance as necessary in order to reduce complexity and meet the specific requirements of the Latin language. The scope of the book is limited to the simple sentence; subordinate clauses are not analyzed except incidentally.

The book is not intended to be either a Latin textbook/grammar or a terminological dictionary. In fact it is designed to be used in conjunction with a Latin grammar and with dictionaries of linguistic and philosophical terms, either in print or online. The aim is to offer a supplement to our standard textbooks and grammars that will bridge the gap between the semantic concepts available to traditional grammar and the much richer theoretical framework of semantics as it is today.

Elements of set theory

A set is a collection of distinct entities. These entities are called members or elements of the set. They may be any sort of thing at all, abstract, concrete or fictional; they may even be other sets. The symbol ∈, adapted from Greek ε, the first letter of ἐστί 'is,' stands for 'is an element/member of,' 'belongs to.' Lower case italic letters are used for the elements of a set, upper case italics for sets, and, when the distinction is important, bold upper case italics for sets of sets. Thus $a \in B$ means 'object *a* is a member of set *B*.' A set is completely defined by its members. For sets with a finite number of members, it is, at least theoretically, possible to list them. When we list the members of a set, they are separated by commas and enclosed in braces: {C. Julius Caesar, M. Calpurnius Bibulus} is the set of consuls in 59 B.C. The order in which the elements are listed is irrelevant. A set can also be defined by a description that specifies a property or properties that each member of the set has. In this predicate notation, a variable symbol such as *x* is followed by a colon, and the description; the whole is then enclosed in braces: {*x*: *x* is consul in 59 B.C.}.

For two sets to be identical, their membership must be the same. This is known as the principle of extensionality: $X = Y \leftrightarrow \forall x. x \in X \leftrightarrow x \in Y$. Sets *X* and *Y* are identical if and only if everything that belongs to *X* also belongs to Y and everything that belongs to *Y* also belongs to *X*. From the principle of extensionality it follows that there is only one set with no members: the empty set is unique. The empty set points up very clearly that set theory is not concerned with the intensional meanings of the predicates that define set membership. Intensionally 'priests or augurs during the reign of Romulus' (see Livy 4.4.2) means something quite different from 'four-sided triangles,' yet the set of the former is identical to the set of the latter; they are each the empty set. There is a special symbol, ∅, for the empty set. ∅ should be clearly distinguished from {∅}: the latter is the singleton set of which the empty set is a member. The membership relation, ∈, is not reflexive, because generally no set is a member of itself. The set of consuls is not itself a consul. Nor is ∈ symmetric. Caesar is a member of the set of consuls, but the set of consuls is not a member of the individual Caesar. Nor is ∈ transitive. If it were, then it would be the case that whenever $x \in X$ and $X \in \boldsymbol{Y}$, then $x \in \boldsymbol{Y}$. But this is not necessarily the case: for if $X = \{a, b\}$ and $\boldsymbol{Y} = \{\{a, b\}, \{c, d\}\}$, neither *a* nor *b* is a member of ***Y***, because neither *a* nor *b* is a set and only sets are members of ***Y***.

If every member of X is a member of Y, X is included in Y and is said to be a subset of Y. The symbol $\subseteq$ is used for the subset relation. Formally $X \subseteq Y \equiv \forall x.x \in X \rightarrow x \in Y$. By this definition every set is a subset of itself: $\subseteq$ is reflexive. $\subseteq$ is not symmetric, for if there are elements in Y that are not in X, Y cannot be a subset of X. $\subseteq$ is, however, transitive: if $X \subseteq Y$ and $Y \subseteq Z$, then $X \subseteq Z$. When X is a subset of Y but not identical to Y, X is called a proper subset of Y, and the symbol $\subset$ is used instead of $\subseteq$. Formally, $X \subset Y \equiv X \subseteq Y \wedge X \neq Y$. We can look at the inclusion relation between sets the other way around. Instead of saying that X is a subset of Y, we can say that Y is a superset of X. The symbol is $\supseteq$ or $\supset$, depending on whether the relation is that of superset or proper superset. Set inclusion and set membership are very different types of relations and should be carefully distinguished. The subset relation is a relation between two sets. The membership relation can be between individuals and sets or between sets and sets of sets. Consider the set $X = \{a, b, \{c, d\}\}$. Neither a nor b nor c nor d nor $\{c, d\}$ is a subset of X. $a, b,$ and $\{c, d\}$ are elements of X, but c and d are elements of $\{c, d\}$, not of X. Examples of subsets of X are $\{a\}$,$\{b\}$, $\{\{c, d\}\}$, $\{a, b\}$ and $\{a, \{c, d\}\}$. It follows from the definition of subset that the empty set is a subset of every set, for if there were some set X of which $\varnothing$ was not a subset, $\varnothing$ would have to have some member that was not a member of X, but that is impossible since $\varnothing$ has no members.

Cardinality refers to the number of elements in a set. The symbol for the cardinality of a set X is $|X|$. For finite sets, cardinality is just a natural number: 1, 2, 3... So if $X = \{a, b, c\}$, $|X| = 3$. Infinite sets have cardinalities as well, but these cannot be natural numbers. There is an infinite sequence of transfinite cardinal numbers, beginning with the cardinal of the set of natural numbers, $\aleph_0$, $2^{\aleph_0}$..., but the theory of transfinite numbers is not crucial for our purposes.

In Generalized Quantifier Theory, theories of plurality and elsewhere in semantics, it is necessary to consider the set of subsets (including $\varnothing$) of a given set (including U, the universe of discourse); this is called its powerset. The powerset of a generator set X is symbolized $\mathcal{P}(X)$. For example, if $X = \{a, b, c\}$, $\mathcal{P}(X) = \{\varnothing, \{a\}, \{b\}, \{c\}, \{a, b\}, \{a, c\}, \{b, c\}, \{a, b, c\}\}$. The term 'power' in 'powerset' comes from its mathematical sense of exponent. If a generator set has cardinality n, then the cardinality of its powerset is 2^n.

Operations on sets are functions which map two or more sets onto another set. The intersection of two sets is the set of all the elements that belong to both. The symbol for the intersection operator is $\cap$. The formal definition of set intersection is $X \cap Y \equiv \{x: x \in X \wedge x \in Y\}$. If X is the set of Roman consuls between 105 and 62 B.C. and Y is the set of people born in Arpinum, $X \cap Y$ is the set of consular Arpinates in this period, that is Marius and Cicero. If two sets X and Y are mutually exclusive, $X \cap Y = \varnothing$. Intersection is analogous to logical conjunction ($\wedge$ 'and'). The union of two sets X and Y is the set of elements that belong to one or the other or both sets, that is the set of elements that belong to at least one of the two sets. The symbol for the union operator is $\cup$. Formally set union is defined as $X \cup Y \equiv \{x: x \in X \vee x \in Y\}$. Union is analogous to logical (nonexclusive) disjunction (∨ 'or'). The binary operations of union and intersection can be generalized to apply to any number of sets. The symbol for generalized intersection is $\bigcap$ (large $\cap$). Let $\boldsymbol{Z}$ be a set of sets $X_1, X_2\ldots$; then $\bigcap \boldsymbol{Z} \equiv \{x\text{: } \forall X_i \in \boldsymbol{Z} \rightarrow x \in X_i\}$. Generalized union, $\bigcup \boldsymbol{Z}$, gives the set of the elements that belong to at least one of the sets in $\boldsymbol{Z}$.

The difference between two sets X and Y is the set of members of X that are not members of Y. Set difference is symbolized either as $X-Y$ or as X/Y. Formally it is defined as $X-Y \equiv \{x\text{: } x \in X \wedge x \notin Y\}$. If X and Y are mutually exclusive, then taking the difference $X-Y$ leaves X unchanged, since there are no members of Y that are in X; so nothing is subtracted from X. Set difference is not symmetric: the set of shirts that are not white is not the same as the set of white things that are not shirts. $X-Y$ is also called the relative complement of Y in X. The complement (simpliciter) of a set X, symbolized X', is everything in the universe of discourse that is not a member of X. So the complement of a set is always taken relative to U: $X' = U-X$. Taking the complement of the complement of a set returns the original set: $(X')' = X$. The complement of the empty set is the universe of discourse: $\varnothing' = U$. The union of a set and its complement is also the universe of discourse: $X \cup X' = U$. Finally, if X is a subset of Y, then the complement of Y is a subset of the complement of X and vice versa: $X \subseteq Y \leftrightarrow Y' \subseteq X'$. Consuls are a subset of senators ($C \subseteq S$) and nonsenators are a subset of nonconsuls ($S' \subseteq C'$), because the set of nonconsuls includes both everyone who is not a senator (S') and every senator who is not a consul ($S - C$), and clearly $S' \subseteq (S' \cup (S - C))$.

The principle of duality states that if you take any true subset relation or equation and interchange $\subseteq$ and $\supseteq$, $\subset$ and $\supset$, $\cup$ and $\cap$, X and X', and $\varnothing$ and U pairwise everywhere they occur, you will get another true relation or equation. The principle of duality means that the fundamental laws of set theory come in pairs, as can be seen in the following list of the most helpful laws of the algebra of sets: (1) Idempotent Laws: $X \cup X = X$ and $X \cap X = X$. Everything which is in a set or in itself is in itself, and everything which is in a set and in itself is in itself. (2) Commutative Laws: $X \cup Y = Y \cup X$, and $X \cap Y = Y \cap X$. Everything that belongs to X or, respectively and, Y is the same as everything that belongs to Y or, respectively and, X. (3) Associative Laws: $X \cup (Y \cup Z) = (X \cup Y) \cup Z$, and $X \cap (Y \cap Z) = (X \cap Y) \cap Z$. The order in which three sets are combined by union, respectively intersection, is immaterial. (4) Distributive Laws: $X \cup (Y \cap Z) = (X \cup Y) \cap (X \cup Z)$, and $X \cap (Y \cup Z) = (X \cap Y) \cup (X \cap Z)$. The set of elements which are either in X or in both Y and Z is the same as the set of elements which are both in either X or Y and either X or Z. The set of elements which are both in X and in either Y or Z is the same as the set of elements which are either in both X and Y or in both X and Z. (5) Identity Laws for the Empty Set and the Universal Set: $X \cup \varnothing = X$ and $X \cap U = X$. $X \cup U = U$ and $X \cap \varnothing = \varnothing$. (6) De Morgan's Laws: $(X \cup Y)' = X' \cap Y'$ and $(X \cap Y)' = X' \cup Y'$. The complement of the union is the intersection of the complements, and the complement of the intersection is the union of the complements.

Relations and functions

The denotation of a simple one-place predicate, written $[[P]]$, is the set of things in the universe of discourse which the predicate describes: $[[P]] \equiv \{x: P(x)\}$. To say that an individual c has property P is equivalent to saying that c is an element of the set of things that have property P. $P(c) \equiv c \in \{x: P(x)\}$. Relations hold between two or more things: binary relations between two, ternary between three, n-ary between n. Simple predication can be regarded as a unary relation. The order in which the elements of that set are listed is irrelevant. Order, however, is crucial for relations. The denotation of a relation is not just the set of all the entities that enter into it. Those entities have to be in the correct position or order. Cicero is older than Tullia; Tullia is not older than Cicero. The denotation of the relation 'Older than' is the set of ordered pairs $<x,y>$ in which the first element is older than the second: $[[F]] \equiv \{<x,y>: F(x,y)\}$. The notation $R(x,y)$ and the notation xRy are both used to mean x bears the relation R to y. So in general the denotation of a binary relation is a set of ordered pairs, that of a ternary relation a set or ordered triples, that of an n-ary relation a set of ordered n-tuples. Two ordered pairs are identical if and only if the first members are identical and the second members are identical: $<w,x> = <y,z> \leftrightarrow (w = y \wedge x = z)$. n-tuples can be reduced to recursively embedded ordered pairs. The ordered triple $<a,b,c>$ is an ordered pair the first element of which is an ordered pair $<<a,b>,c>$. The ordered quadruple $<a,b,c,d> = <<<a,b>,c>,d>$, and so on.

The Cartesian product of two sets A and B is the set of all the ordered pairs the first member of which comes from A and the second member of which comes from B: $A \times B \equiv \{<x,y>: x \in A \wedge y \in B\}$. The A set is called the domain of the relation, the B set the range. The domain and the range can be the same set: $A \times A$. Let H be the set of humans and M be the set of males; if we form the Cartesian product $H \times M$, the set of ordered pairs will include pairs of a sister and her brother, a man and himself, a child and its father, and so on. It follows that the relation 'having as father' is a subset of the Cartesian product of the set of humans and the set of males. In general, any relation R from set A to set B is a subset of the Cartesian product $A \times B$: $R \subseteq A \times B$. Equivalently R is an element of the powerset of the Cartesian product: $R \subseteq \mathcal{P}(A \times B)$. The complement of a relation, R^-, is the set of ordered pairs in the Cartesian product that do not stand in the relation R: $R^- \equiv (A \times B) - R$. The inverse of a relation, $\check{R}$, reverses the order of the first and second elements: $<x,y> \in R \leftrightarrow <y,x> \in \check{R}$.

There are four properties of relations which are particularly important and from combinations of which further useful properties can be defined. These properties apply only to relations from a set to itself, $A \times A$, not $A \times B$, $A \neq B$. (1) Reflexivity: a relation R is reflexive if and only if every member of its domain bears the relation to itself: $\forall x.R(x,x)$. 'As old as' and 'equal to' are reflexive relations. A relation is irreflexive if no member of its domain bears the relation to itself: $\forall x.\neg R(x,x)$. 'Older than' and 'not equal to' are irreflexive. A relation that is neither reflexive nor irreflexive is called nonreflexive. 'Satisfied with' is nonreflexive. (2) Symmetry: a relation is symmetric if, whenever it holds between two elements x and y, it also holds in the opposite direction: $\forall x \forall y.R(x,y) \rightarrow R(y,x)$. 'Cousin of' is symmetric, while 'brother of' is nonsymmetric. A relation is asymmetric if it never holds in the opposite direction: $\forall x \forall y.R(x,y) \rightarrow \neg R(y,x)$. 'Father of' is asymmetric. A relation is antisymmetric if it holds between x and y only when x and y are identical; for example in the set of numbers if x is greater than or equal to y, then y is greater than or equal to x if and only if $x = y$: $\forall x \forall y.R(x,y) \wedge R(y,x) \rightarrow x = y$. As we have seen, the subset relation $\subseteq$ is antisymmetric. (3) Transitivity: a relation is transitive if, whenever it holds between x and y and between y and z, it holds between x and z: $\forall x \forall y \forall z.R(x,y) \wedge R(y,z) \rightarrow R(x,z)$. If this is never the case, the relation is intransitive. 'Greater than' and 'brother of' are transitive. 'Father of' is intransitive, because the father of a father of someone is that person's grandfather. 'Acquainted with' and 'resemble' are nontransitive. (4) Connectedness: a relation is connected if and only if every pair of distinct elements ($x \neq y$) stands either in the relation $R(x,y)$ or $R(y,x)$: $\forall x \forall y.x \neq y \rightarrow R(x,y) \vee R(y,x)$. 'Less than' and 'greater than' are connected in the set of natural numbers. 'Father of' is not connected in the set of humans.

Relations that are reflexive, symmetric and transitive are called equivalence relations. Equivalence relations are 'as P as' relations, for instance 'as great as,' 'as good as.' An equivalence relation defines equivalence classes, sets of things that are the same as each other according to the relations: $S(a) = \{x: R(a,x)\}$. Equivalence classes are mutually exclusive, and their union is the domain of the relation that defines them. Relations that are reflexive, transitive and antisymmetric are called partial orders. 'Subset of,' $\subseteq$, is a partial order. Relations that are irreflexive and transitive are called strict partial orders. 'Proper subset of,' $\subset$, is a strict partial order. A relation that is (strict and) connected is called a (strict) total, or linear, order. 'Less than' and 'greater than' are strict total orders in the set of natural numbers. In a powerset the subset relation is not a total order, because it does not hold between pairs of sets the first of which is not included in the second.

Functions are a subtype of relations. A function is a relation in which each element of the domain is assigned to a unique element of the range. So the relation 'having as father' is a function since it assigns to each person his or her unique father. Functions apply to their arguments to give a value. The arguments belong to the domain, the values to the range. The term 'map' is also used: a function maps its domain to its range. Functions from A to B are called 'into B' if the range of the function is a subset of B, and 'onto B' (surjections) if the range is equal to B, that is if every element of B is the value of the function for some member of A. For example, the function that maps child onto father is into but not onto M, the set of males, because not every male is a father. Functions that map distinct elements of their domains onto distinct elements of their ranges are called 'one-to-one' (injections). Functions which are both one-to-one and onto are called one-to-one correspondences (bijections). A function that maps an organism onto its DNA is a bijection from the domain of organisms onto the domain of DNA molecules. Bijective functions have inverses that are also functions. The domain of the inverse function, f^{-1}, is the range of the original function f, and the range of f^{-1} is the domain of f. For example 'immediately precede' is the inverse of 'immediately succeed.' Functions may take other functions as their arguments and have functions as their values. Examples likely to be familiar are the derivative and the (indefinite) integral of calculus. We will encounter a couple of these in the next section. A particularly useful function is the characteristic function of a set. It maps entities onto 1 if they are members of the set and onto 0 if they are not: $\chi_A(a) = 1$ iff $a \in A$ and $\chi_A(a) = 0$ iff $a \notin A$. Accordingly there is a one-to-one correspondence between sets and their characteristic functions. So sets may be identified with their characteristic function and vice versa. This identification allows us to switch between formulas in settheoretic terms and formulations in terms of functions and arguments.

Truth conditions and semantic composition

Formal semantics is truthconditional. It assumes that the necessary conditions for an adequate account of the meaning of a sentence include the specification of the conditions under which it would be true, whether in the actual or some possible world. For every sentence S in the object language (the language being analyzed) we need to spell out in the metalanguage (the language in which the object language is being analyzed) the conditions Φ, such that "S is true iff Φ," where Φ is the set of truth conditions. Sentences of this form are called T-sentences after Alfred Tarski, who pioneered truthconditional semantics starting in the 1930's. Consider the sentence 'Alcibiades was brought up in the household of Pericles' (cp. Nepos 7.2.1). To spell out Φ for this sentence we have to know, among much else, what entities in Nepos' domain of discourse the names Alcibiades and Pericles and the definite noun phrase 'the household of Pericles' pick out and what entities the predicate 'brought-up' applies to. The domain of discourse and the context of utterance are crucial for determining the truth of a sentence. This is obvious for anaphoric expressions, deictics, and indexicals in general, but it is also true for sentences without any of these elements. Take the sentence 'Caesar wrote about the role of analogy in language.' If the domain of discourse includes the Romans of the first century B.C., the sentence is true, but if the domain is twenty-first century linguists and their pets and 'Caesar' picks out a black Labrador, the sentence is false. What makes the precise formulation of truth conditions possible is the model-theoretic nature of formal semantics. A model is an ordered pair $M = \langle D, I_M \rangle$. D is the domain of discourse, the set of all the individual entities in the context. I_M is the interpretation function. Since the interpretation function depends on the model, and hence will vary from one model to another, we index it with M. It is I_M that determines the denotation of the primitive (atomic, noncomposite) terms of the object language. For any constant term (such as a proper name) a, $I_M(a)$ is the referent of a in D. The denotation of 'Caesar' is the individual who is called Caesar in the model. For any one-place predicate P, $I_M(P)$ is the set of entities in D to which P applies. The denotation of the predicate 'laugh' is the set of individuals in the model who laugh; the denotation of the predicate 'dog' is the set of individuals in the model that are dogs. For any n-place predicate (relation) R, $I_M(R)$ is a set of ordered n-tuples. If R_2 is a two-place predicate like 'stab,' $I_M(R_2)$ is a subset of the Cartesian product $D \times D$; if R_3 is a three-place predicate like 'give,' $I_M(R_3)$ is a subset of the Cartesian product $D \times D \times D$, and so on. The denotation of the predicate 'stab' is the set of pairs of stabbers and stabbees in the model; Brutus and Caesar, and Cassius and Caesar, might be members of that set. Note that the denotation does not tell you anything about what dogs are like or what happens when you laugh: it just gives you a list of dogs and a list of individuals who laugh in the model. The model is, therefore, purely extensional: it says nothing about the concepts or cognitive representations that may be correlated with these extensions. This makes formal semantics a theory of grammatical (compositional) meaning much more than a theory of lexical meaning (which is just fine if you are studying Latin grammar). Typetheoretical definitions are similarly purely combinatorial. It is just this avoidance of intrinsic meaning that makes formal semantics work so successfully. All the denotations of syntactically complex expressions are constructed settheoretically from just the set D, the domain of individuals. It follows that predication is defined as set membership: $P(a)$ is true iff $I_M(a) \in I_M(P)$. For example 'Cicero was consul' is true in model R (ancient Rome) iff I_R(Cicero) $\in$ I_R(Consul). This is a T-sentence with 'Cicero was consul' replacing S and I_R(Cicero) $\in$ I_R(Consul) replacing Φ. From this perspective, a sentence denotes the set of its truth conditions. But the lefthand side of a T-sentence 'S is true' can be analyzed in terms of functor plus argument: $V_M(S) = 1$, where V_M is the function that assigns truth values to a sentence according to the model M. V_M maps S to 1 (true) iff its truth conditions are satisfied in M, otherwise it maps S to 0 (false). The sentence 'Atticus was consul' is assigned the truth value 0, because its truth conditions are not satisfied in the model R. Since the logical connective 'iff' asserts the identity of the expressions on its left and on its right, a sentence having a truth value 1 is the same thing as the satisfaction of its truth conditions in the model. So sentences can be said to denote their truth values, and it is traditional in logic and formal semantics to take the denotation of a sentence to be its truth value. We have built up the truth conditions settheoretically, but the result is neither an element nor a subset of D. It is an expression that has a truth value. There are only two truth values: true and false. Since truth values are not entities in the domain of discourse, we need to recognize two basic types. The type of individuals is denoted by <e> (entity), the type of sentences by <t> (truth-bearing expression).

Formal semantics is also compositional. Sentences denote truth values; a list of words in a sentence does not. The meaning of a sentence and the meaning of each syntactic constituent of a sentence is a function of the meaning of their parts and the way those parts are combined. Compositionality makes possible a semantic analysis of syntactic structure such that to every step in the syntactic derivation of a sentence there is a corresponding semantic step: syntax and semantics work in tandem. How does compositionality work and how does it interface with the settheoretic analysis of denotation? For instance, how does 'Cicero' (an entity) combine with 'is consul' (a predicate) to yield the sentence 'Cicero is consul'? The property of being consul is an unsaturated meaning, it needs an individual to saturate it: settheoretic representation does not show this. But since sets and their characteristic functions are interchangeable, we can treat 'is consul' as a function that maps 'Cicero' onto the truth value 1. A property acts like a functor applying to an entity, the argument that saturates its meaning. In general simple one-place predication is the application of a property's characteristic function to an entity to give a truth value: $P: a \rightarrow t$. Familiar mathematical functions like square root or division look different from the functions we encounter in natural language because their domains and ranges are numbers, and in the case of functions onto truth values because their range is not limited to two values. Functional application is the general principle of saturating unsaturated meanings and is not restricted to simple predication. We could say that any expression needing something else to complete its meaning to become another expression needing something else to complete its meaning, and so on, is a sequence of functional applications to arguments, each saturating the need of each in the sequence. Functional application like this has the great advantage that it works in parallel with the computation of semantic types. There is a recursive rule for generating derived, functional types: "if <a> is a type and <b> is a type, then <a, b> is a type, the function from type <a> expressions to type <b> expressions." This rule will generate an infinity of types, but only a few are needed for the analysis of natural language (including types that map functions onto functions). Since the type of *a* is <e> and the type of *P*(*a*) is <t>, *P* must be a function that maps an entity onto a truth value. Therefore its type must be <e, t>; the convention is that the type of the domain of the function is given to the left, the type of the range of the function to the right. The type deduction for simple predication is <e><e, t> → <t>. Further advantages of functional application emerge when we consider two-place predicates like 'stab.' In the predicate calculus, the denotation of 'Stab' is the set of ordered pairs <stabber, stabbee>. The predicate calculus has no way to represent the hierarchical structure of the sentence 'Brutus stabbed Caesar.' 'Stab' has a characteristic function which maps the pair <Brutus, Caesar> (technically the denotations of those names in the model) onto 1, because that pair is a member of the set of pairs that 'stab' denotes in the model. So we can take 'stab' as the functor and the pair <Brutus, Caesar> as the argument to which it applies. This is how 'Brutus stabbed Caesar' is analyzed in the predicate calculus. But syntactically 'Brutus stabbed Caesar' has a hierarchical internal structure. We want answers to the following questions: How does 'stab' combine with 'Caesar,' what does 'stabbed Caesar' mean, and how does 'stabbed Caesar' combine with 'Brutus' to make a sentence? 'Stabbed Caesar' means the property of having stabbed Caesar, a property that belongs to Brutus inter alios. It works like a one-place predicate to combine with 'Brutus' to make a sentence. So we deduce it must have the type

<e,t>. 'Stabbed Caesar' has the same type as an intransitive verb like 'laugh,' but it differs in having internal structure; it is a derived property. 'Caesar' has the type <e>, so 'stab' needs to be a function that applies to 'Caesar' to give a function that applies to 'Brutus' to make a sentence. Using the rule for derived types, we get <e,<e,t> for the type of 'Stab,' but we now need a formal device to construct derived properties. This is where the λ-operator comes in.

The λ-operator is the indispensable formal means for representing expressions of natural language in terms of functor and arguments. Before the two arguments of 'stab' have been saturated by (filled up with) constants, its representation in the predicate calculus is in terms of free variables, Stab(*x*, *y*), which is of type <t>. The λ-operator binds a free variable like the quantifiers 'some' and 'all' do, but, unlike the quantifiers, it changes the type of the expression: λ*y*.Stab(*x*, *y*) has the type <e,t>. This operation is called λ-abstraction. Two applications of λ-abstraction give λ*y*λ*x*.Stab(*x*,*y*), which has the type <e,<e,t>>. The two applications of λ-abstraction have opened up a binary relation into a sequence of two unary functions. This is an example of the process called 'currying,' after the logician Haskell Curry. In general, a function of type <<a,b>,<c>>, i.e. a function that takes a complex argument of type <a,b> and returns a value of type <c>, can be curried to the type <<a>,<b,c>>, a function that takes an argument of type <a> and returns another function that takes an argument of type <b> and returns a value of type <c>. <a>, <b> and <c> can each be complex types to which currying can apply recursively. The result of currying is to reduce complex semantic computations to a series of binary steps.

λ-reduction (also called λ-conversion) is the name for the combination of a λ-expression with an argument (argument saturation) with the result that the argument replaces the variable bound by the λ. The rule is that the outermost λ is saturated first and the first argument to be absorbed is written first after the λ-expression. Here is a derivation of 'Brutus stabbed Caesar' in tandem with its type deduction:

> λ*y*λ*x*.Stab(*x*,*y*)(Caesar)(Brutus): <e,<e,t>>
> λ*x*.Stab(*x*,Caesar)(Brutus): <e,t>
> Stab(Caesar, Brutus): <t>.

Every λ-reduction has a corresponding type deduction and vice versa. This principle is called the Curry-Howard correspondence, and it lies at the very basis of formal semantics. Let's look at the second line more closely: λ*x*.Stab(*x*,Caesar) denotes the set of everyone who stabbed Caesar. Our model theoretic formalism shows why: I_R(λ*x*.Stab(*x*,Caesar)) = {*a*: <*a*,I_R(Caesar)> ∈ I_R(Stab)}, the set of individuals, *a* of *D* which form the ordered pairs <*a*,Caesar> that are elements of the denotation of 'Stab.' Brutus is an element of this set.

It is much easier to represent λ-reduction by binary trees in which type deduction and λ-reduction proceed in tandem. The (nonterminal) nodes of the tree are labeled according to their syntactic constituency. The trees we use in this book are a species of logical form representation, although they are often isomorphic to surely syntactic, binary, X-bar trees: an example is given below. Tree representation makes it clear that semantic computations are local in the sense that the denotation of any branching node is computed entirely from the denotations of its two daughter nodes. It also makes clear that semantic computation is type-driven. V° combines with the noun phrase (NP) on its right and the verb phrase with the noun phrase on its left by one and the same rule of functional application. The hierarchical relations of the lexical items in the terminal nodes as articulated in the tree and the semantic types of the nodes together drive the computation. Functional application, while not the only mode of semantic computation, is the most general. In a tree representation it takes this form: if *B* and *C* are the two daughter nodes of a node *A*, and [[*B*]] (the denotation of *B*) is a function of type <c,a>, and [[*C*]] is of type <c>, then the denotation of *A* is the result of applying the function [[*B*]] to the argument [[*C*]]: [[*A*]] = [[*B*]]([[*C*]]) and is of type <a>.

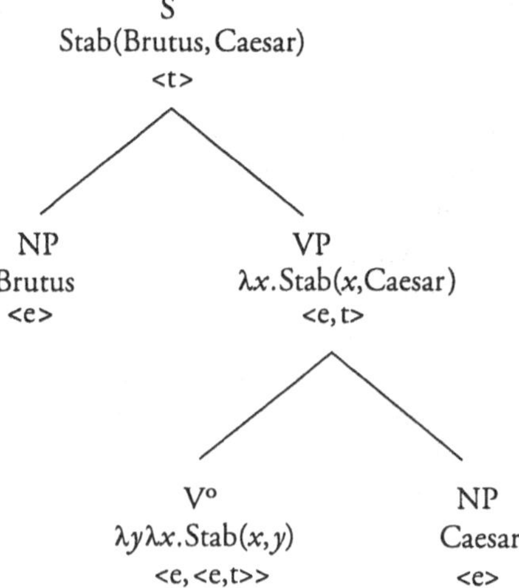

FURTHER READING

Allwood, Andersson & Dahl (1995); Cann (1993); Cann, Kempson & Gregoromichelaki (2009); Detlefsen, McCarty & Bacon (1999); Heim & Kratzer (1998); Partee, ter Meulen & Wall (1990); Portner & Partee (2002); Sider (2010).

1 | TENSE

Ontology of time

Time is a central element of the way in which we experience the world around us and of the way in which we think about it; so it is not surprising if many languages have systematic grammatical mechanisms for encoding temporal information. Every finite verb in Latin (as well as many nonfinite forms) includes temporal information as part of its inflectional ending. In some languages which encode tense by particles or auxiliaries, tense can optionally be omitted when it is redundant and otherwise available from the context or the rest of the sentence. But this could not happen in Latin, since the inflectional ending is fused with the verb stem and cannot be dropped (although the present tense form is sometimes used in subordinate clauses as an unmarked tense).

Our intuition of time is Janus-faced. On the one hand it sees time as dynamic, moving from past to present to future

(1) fugit inreparabile tempus (Verg Georg 3.284)
id dividitur in tempora tria: praeteritum, instans, consequens (Rhet Her 2.8).

This view motivates the etymology of 'moment' (*momentum temporis*) from *moveo* 'move'

(2) deinde momento temporis repressus est imber (Curt Ruf 8.13.24).

On the other hand it sees time as static, like a line on which we can mark points (*puncta temporis*), which stand in an unchanging order

(3) omnia postremo quae puncto tempore cernis diffugere ut fumum (Lucr 2.456)
temporis ut puncto nil existet reliquiarum (Lucr 1.1109).

(1) Time is passing quickly and irretrievably (Verg Georg 3.284). This is divided into three times: anterior to, simultaneous with and posterior to the crime (Rhet Her 2.8).

(2) Then in a moment of time the rain stopped (Curt Ruf 8.13.24).

(3) Finally, everything that you see dispersing in a moment of time, like smoke (Lucr 2.456). So that in a moment of time there would be no trace left (Lucr 1.1109).

If we press this distinction

(4) siquidem tempus movetur, perennitatis fixa et immota natura est (Apul De Plat 1.10),

we arrive at what has come to be called the A-theory and the B-theory of time. The A-theory takes the notions of past, present and future as basic: as time goes by, future events become present events and then past events. It readily accommodates the concept of change, something that the B-theory does not do. The ontology of the A-theory is parsimonious; it does not quantify over instants or intervals of time. It treats past and future as properties of propositions, and transfers the indexical nature of tensed statements from natural language into formal semantics. In this way only the present is spoken of de re, and past and future things are spoken of only de dicto. The B-theory, in contrast, does quantify over instants and intervals: events are ordered relative to one another, but there is no time flow. Everything expressible in A-theory can be translated into B-theory, but not vice versa. Since quantification over time is crucial for the explanation of many semantic phenomena of natural language (for instance the account of *dum* licensing negative polarity items in Chapter 8), we adopt the richer ontology of B-theory. But what are instants of time? When we formalize the metaphor of time as a line, we treat instants like points in geometry

(5) punctum esse quod magnitudinem nullam habeat... lineamentum sine ulla latitudine (Luc 116: app. crit.).

Instants of time are isomorphic to the real numbers. They are everywhere dense on the time line: between any two instants, no matter how close they are to each other, there is always another instant. The time line is continuous. There are no gaps or jumps, so there is no place on the time line where there is no instant. (The rational numbers are dense, but not continuous; the integers are neither continuous nor dense, but discrete.) Instants of time are ordered by the relation of temporal precedence. Temporal precedence is a strict linear order: it is irreflexive (no instant is before itself), asymmetric (if $t^1 > t^2$, then not $t^2 > t^1$), transitive (if $t^1 > t^2$ and $t^2 > t^3$, then $t^1 > t^3$) and connected (every instant is either before or after every other instant).

However, we need more than just instants. States persist for periods of time, events evolve over time, accomplishments reach end points in time. Periods are modeled as intervals. Intervals are bounded substretches of the time line. They are convex subsets of the set of instants. 'Convex' means that intervals are not interrupted; they contain all the instants between their initial and final bounds or endpoints. They may be closed on both sides, or they may be open on both sides, or they may be closed on one side and open on the other. To describe the difference between open and closed intervals it is necessary to distinguish between endpoint and bound. The closed side of an interval has an endpoint;

(4) Since time moves, while the nature of eternity is fixed and immobile (Apul De Plat 1.10).
(5) A point is that which has no magnitude; a line is without width (Luc 116).

the endpoint is part of the interval. The open side of an interval does not have an endpoint, but if it gets closer and closer to some point without ever reaching it, it has a bound. If you were to add that point to the interval, it would become an endpoint and the interval would become closed on that side. Subintervals of the time line which stretch infinitely far into the past or future have neither endpoints nor bounds in the past/future respectively. It is one of the advantages of modeling instants by the real numbers that every finite interval will have either an endpoint or a bound on each side, and every infinite interval formed by cutting the time line at just one place will have an endpoint or a bound at the cut point. This would not be true if instants were treated as rational numbers, because the rational numbers take up a vanishingly small part of the line (they have measure zero), whereas almost all real numbers are irrational. So almost anywhere you might cut the time line would be an irrational point, and there would not be a rational point to function as endpoint or bound. Intervals have additional useful properties that make it easier to work with them directly, rather than always working up from instants. Intervals are related by a strict, linear order of complete temporal precedence. An interval I completely precedes an interval I' if and only if every instant in I precedes every instant in I'. Additionally intervals have the mereological relations of overlap and inclusion. An interval I overlaps an interval I' if and only if I and I' have a subinterval in common, that is $I \cap I' \neq 0$. An interval I is part of an interval I' if and only if every interval overlapping I also overlaps I'. It turns out that there are just 13 basic relations in which two intervals can stand to each other: two of inclusion (I includes I' or vice versa), two of overlap ($I \circ I'$ and I starts before I' or vice versa), two of starting together (the initial point of I = the initial point of I' and either I ends before I' or vice versa), two of ending together, one of identity, and two of abutting (the final point of I = the initial point of I' or vice versa).

Times that contribute in one way or another to the temporal location of an eventuality are the event time ($\tau(e)$), the utterance time (t^u), the reference time (t^{ref}), and the time denoted by an adverbial (t^{adv}). We will discuss each one in turn, since it is not immediately obvious exactly how they differ from one another and how each contributes to the location of an eventuality in time.

Event time

In the theory presented here, events (and states) are part of the semantic ontology. This is not the case for all semantic theories. For instance events might also be taken to be properties of times: then the denotation of an event like 'Caesar invades Britain' is the set of times at which that is true in the actual world. But there are many features of language that seem to call for a more direct representation of events. Nominalizations like 'invasion' are on the face of it eventive entities. Just like physical objects, events can be counted, anaphorically referred to and modified ('Caesar invaded Britain. It happened twice. The Britons resisted immediately'). 'Invade(x,y)' is a predicate of events, just as 'sword' is a predicate of objects. Any particular invasion is a member of the set of invasion events (an instantiation of the property), just as any particular sword is a member of the set of sword entities. In context, a specific invasion has a referent, just as a specific sword does. There are many problems relating to event identification. To start with, we need to be clear whether we are talking about identity of event referents or identity of event descriptions. Both invasions of Britain by Caesar were invasions (same event description), but they were different events (referentially distinct), most obviously because they occurred at different times (August 55 and July 54 B.C.). This does not mean that everything that happens at the same time and in the same place is the same event. For instance, if you listen to Bach happily and read Tertullian painfully at the same time and in the same place, those are two events with a single spatiotemporal location: it is perfectly possible for one to occur without the other. But just as the same physical object can often be described in different ways, so there may be various different ways of describing one and the same event. There are also part-whole problems. Are sailing ten miles across the Channel and sailing an additional five miles two separate sailing events or two subevents of a single event of sailing fifteen miles? What about events with plural participants ('Caesar's soldiers drew their swords')? There is a sword-drawing subevent for each soldier, and each of these subevents consists of various parts like lowering the hand and grabbing the handle. The term 'eventuality' is used as a cover term for events and states, although 'event' can also be used less precisely to include states. Some theories admit events into their semantic ontology while excluding some or all states; events would then be individual entities but states would just be properties of times. States are less complex than events, so it is not surprising if they sometimes behave differently from events. For instance permanent states are not easily locatable in space and time (*'I am tall this year/in Rome'), and because they are not agentive they resist modification by manner adverbs (*'I am carefully tall').

Events are taken to be arguments of the verb. So a transitive verb has the type <e,e,εt> rather than just <e,et>. As the types indicate, events are here assumed to be the last argument to be composed with the verb. Since events take place in space and time, we can map an event onto the space that it occupies and onto the time through which it evolves. The former is done by the spatial trace function σ (which is in principle three-dimensional), the latter by the temporal trace function τ (which is one-dimensional): less formally we can speak of the path function and the run time function. These give, respectively, the run space and the run time for the event. The run time function is a function from an event to an interval (possibly an instant): this can be written $\tau(e,t)$ or $\tau(e) = t$, where t is an interval. We will usually use $\tau(e)$ to represent the value of the function, that is the interval occupied by the event. Run times are intervals, not durations: but an interval can be measured to give its duration (just as a path can be measured to give its length), so there is a function from a temporal interval to a point on a scale using units of measurement like hours and minutes. Since the run time is an interval on the time line, it is definitionally one-dimensional. While space is three-dimensional, the run space of an event can be one-dimensional if it is idealized as a line. The participants of a motion event are then treated as a single (zero dimension) point; as this point traces out a path, you get a line. The line is one-dimensional (although it is still located in three-dimensional space).

Consider again the momentous occasion of Caesar's first invasion of Britain in August of 55 B.C.

(6) *tertia fere vigilia* solvit... *hora circiter diei quarta* cum primis navibus Britanniam attigit atque ibi in omnibus collibus expositas hostium copias armatas conspexit... montibus angustis mare continebatur (BG 4.23).

The run space of Caesar's voyage ($\sigma(e)$) was the twenty-five miles or so of English Channel between Boulogne and Dover. The run time of his voyage ($\tau(e)$) was roughly from midnight to nine o'clock in the morning. Both mappings are in principle homomorphic: for each amount of the event completed there is a corresponding amount of sea traversed and a corresponding amount of time elapsed. So the two mappings can be combined into a single spatiotemporal path, any point on which is defined by a pair of values, one spatial and one temporal. A phrase such as *saltare in convivio* 'dance at a party' (cp. Verr 2.3.23) denotes a set of events of someone dancing at a party, each one with its own run time: $\lambda x \lambda t \lambda e.\text{Salt}(e,x) \wedge \tau(e) = t$. Since each run time is an interval, it is situated somewhere on the time line; it covers a slice of history. We don't know which slice of history: the possibilities only begin to get narrowed down when the event is existentially quantified and embedded in a discourse context. Functions have unique values, so $\tau(e)$ (the value of the run time function for an event e) is a definite interval. But $\tau(e)$ is not a constant in the above expression, since it is not the case that all dancing events occupy the same interval; rather it is a type of dependent definite that shifts in a pointwise fashion as the value of the event variable shifts. We will call this type of dependent definite a pointwise definite. Dancing is a human activity; it has to start at some point and end at some point, so it occupies an interval of time. Not all eventualities occupy a (nonminimal) interval. Some are instantaneous like *copias armatas conspexit* in (6). Others are permanent states, like *montibus angustis mare continebatur* in (6), with indeterminate bounds.

Utterance time

The contextual location of a speech event is obviously liable to influence its content, but it is also a basic factor in how the message is encoded and how its truth is evaluated. References to time, space and participants in the conversation are anchored to the time of utterance, and the location and identity of the speaker. The world is viewed from the standpoint of the speaker. Certain expressions, known as deictic expressions, can only be correctly interpreted rel-

(6) Around the third watch he weighed anchor... about the fourth hour of the day he himself reached Britain with the first ships and saw there the enemy forces drawn up armed on all the hills; the sea was closely hemmed in by cliffs (BG 4.23).

ative to those anchors, which are constantly changing as different participants take successive turns in the conversation. So for instance the reference of pronominal forms like *ego* 'I,' *vos* 'you,' *illi* 'they' depends on the identity of the speaker. The interpretation of demonstrative pronouns like *hic, iste, ille* is computed relative to the location of the speaker: *hos digitos meos* (Pro Rosc Com 1) 'these fingers of mine,' *ista subsellia* (Cat 1.16) 'the benches near you,' *illis temporibus* (Brut 315) 'at that time.' The same applies to locative pronouns, for instance *hinc* 'from where I am,' *istinc* 'from where you are,' *illinc* 'from over there.' Temporal information is likewise interpreted relative to some anchor, the default value for which is the time of utterance: this applies for instance to adverbs like *nunc* 'now,' *tunc* 'then,' and to tense. Although the run time of the utterance is an interval, the time of utterance used in the computation of tense and consequently in the evaluation of tensed propositions is conceived as an instant. The utterance time t^u is the value of the utterance time function, which is a function from the event of utterance to an instant, namely the conceptual now included in the utterance run time. A different function is needed when tense is computed relative to some temporal anchor other than the time of utterance.

Reference time

Reference to individuals, as we know, can be indefinite (*aliquis*), specific indefinite (*quidam*) or definite (*ille*). Like individuals, times are entities, and reference to times can likewise be indefinite (*aliquando*), specific indefinite (*quondam*) or definite (*tunc*). The times at which events are contextually situated are called reference times. The reference time t^{ref} is the value of the reference time function, which is a function from topical subject matter in the discourse to an interval. The time of the utterance is uniquely identifiable; so the present time can only be definite and present tense events have definite reference times. But past times are not restricted in this way

(7) *vidi* in alvariis apium satam (NH 12.98)
Decrevit quondam senatus uti L. Opimius consul videret ne quid res publica detrimenti caperet (Cat 1.4)
Quid *fecisti*? "Pecuniam," inquit "*dedi.*" (Quint Decl 345.8)
postridie... hora quarta... eodemque tempore... in oppidum *introiit* Terentia (Ad Fam 16.9.2).

Vidi in the first example (NH 12.98) is an experiential perfect: Pliny is saying that there exists an event (or events) in which he saw the plant in question sown among beehives and that this event is now part of his experience; the run time of the event is some indefinite interval in Pliny's lifespan prior to the time of

(7) I have seen it planted among beehives (NH 12.98). The senate once decreed that L. Opimius the consul should see to it that the republic come to no harm (Cat 1.4). "What did you do?" "I gave money," he says (Quint Decl 345.8). On the next day at the fourth hour... and at the same time Terentia entered the town (Ad Fam 16.9.2).

writing. Indefinite times are also found in examples with a contextually independent past tense

(8) Cur Plato Aegyptum *peragravit...*? Cur ipse Pythagoras et Aegyptum *lustravit* et Persarum magos *adiit*? (De Fin 5.87).

The events described happened at some point or other in the past during the lifespans of Plato and Pythagoras, not at some particular point in time that the writer is referring to. On the other hand, in the second example in (7) (Cat 1.4) Cicero is talking about a specific decree passed at a specific time. He is referring to one particular time at which the event is situated. It can be a point or an interval. In the third example (Decl 345.8) the rich man is being interrogated about the event of tyrannicide which he has financed. The context provides a definite reference time (the time when the tyrant was killed). *Quid fecisti?* does not mean 'Tell me your life history' but 'Tell me what you did at the contextually relevant reference time.' *Pecuniam dedi* does not refer to one of the many other occasions on which the rich man paid for some service but to the definite occasion in question (on which he paid for the killing of the tyrant). The reference time is the time for which the truth of the sentence is evaluated: once the reference time is entered into the compositional semantics, *Pecuniam dedi* is true for the tyrannicide payment and false for all the other payments. As often, the temporal restriction of the reference time is covert: it has to be recovered from the context, but it is nonetheless there. The same applies to spatial restrictions: *pluet... hodie* (Pl Curc 132) 'it will rain today' is normally understood to apply to the location of the utterance (Epidaurus), not to some village in Northern Pannonia. Although covert reference times and reference locations are implicit adverbials, it does not follow that you can map directly from the run time of the event $\tau(e)$ to the adverbial time t^{adv}: without a contextually situated reference time, you would not know which adverbial time to choose. In fact, when it is difficult to find an appropriate context (for instance at the very outset of a conversation), a past tense can be hard to interpret and consequently infelicitous. The reference time is less likely to be specific in the future. We know when a present event is taking place by definition, we can often be fairly certain when a past event took place, but we often cannot predict exactly when a future event will take place. Probably for this reason too, metrical tense systems tend to be less complex in the future than in the past.

In the last example in (7) above the time of Terentia's entrance into Brindisi is also definite and its reference (10 a.m. on November 24th) can be recovered anaphorically from the preceding text, just as the identity of an anaphoric pronoun is established from the context. Anaphoric update of the reference time is a key element in the interpretation of narrative text. Consider the following passage from the beginning of the same letter of Cicero

(8) Why did Plato travel all over Egypt? Why did Pythagoras himself both tour Egypt and visit the magi of the Persians? (De Fin 5.87).

(9) *discessimus* a.d. iv Non. Novembr.; Leucadem *venimus* a.d. viii Idus Novembr.; a.d. vii Actium... inde a.d. quintum Idus Corcyram bellissime *navigavimus*... A.d. xv Kalend. Decembr. in portum Corcyraeorum ad Cassiopen stadia cxx *processimus*. (Ad Fam 16.9.1).

The sentences are ordered iconically according to the serial order of the events. Each perfective past tense in the narration advances the reference time by at least the event time of the preceding event. In this passage each reference time update is overtly registered by the dates, but in most narratives it is implicit, as for instance in the sequence of events in the poisoning charge against Caelius

(10) *quaesivit* venenum, *paravit... attulit* (Pro Cael 31: app.crit.)

This is illustrated in Figure 1.1. In nonnnarrative text the reference time does not necessarily shift forward with each new past tense

(11) qua in legatione *duxit* exercitum, signa *contulit*, manum *conseruit*, magnas copias hostium *fudit*, urbes partim vi partim obsidione *cepit* (Pro Mur 20).

Here the events are listed in some sort of descriptively logical order but do not represent a single sequential narrative. In narrative too, reference time update is not automatic: even if a following sentence contains a perfective verb, it can be an explanation or elaboration of the previous sentence, or just a simultaneous event. If these discourse coherence relations are not overtly expressed by tense or aspect (pluperfect, imperfect), the listener has to use the context to track reference time advancement correctly.

Adverbial time

The most important classes of temporal adverbials are positional (*hodie* 'today,' *abhinc annos quattuordecim* 'fourteen years ago'), frequency (*cotidie* 'every day,' *quinto quoque anno* 'every fifth year'), duration (*diu* 'for a long time,' *per trien-*

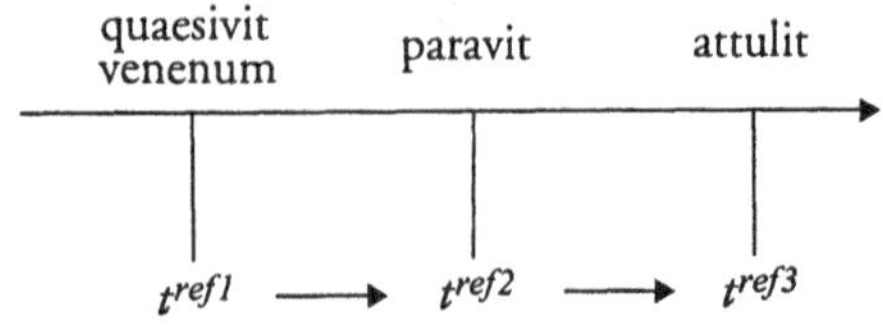

Figure 1.1
Narrative reference time update
Quaesivit venenum, paravit... attulit (Pro Cael 31)

(9) We left on November 2; we reached Leucas on November 6th and Actium on the 7th. From there we had a very nice voyage to Corcyra on the 9th. On the 16th we proceeded 120 stades to the Corcyrean port of Cassiope (Ad Fam 16.9.1).

(10) He obtained poison, prepared it and delivered it (Pro Cael 31).

(11) In this command he led an army, fought battles, took part in combat, routed large enemy forces, captured cities partly by storm and partly by siege (Pro Mur 20).

nium 'for three years') and container *paucis diebus* 'in a few days,' *intra paucos annos* 'within a few years').

The reference of positionals may be fixed in calendar or clock terms (*anno quingentesimo quinquagesimo primo ab urbe condita, P. Sulpicio Galba C. Aurelio consulibus* 'in 200 B.C., during the consulship of P. Sulpicius Galba and C. Aurelius,' *a.d. iv Non. Novembr.* 'on November 2,' *hora tertia* 'at the third hour'), or relative to a deictic point (socalled indexicals, *heri* 'yesterday,' *cras* 'tomorrow,' on the day before/after the day containing the utterance time) or anaphorically (*paucis post diebus* 'a few days after that'). Inner positional adverbials modify the event time, outer ones modify the reference time, and the two types are accordingly attached at different positions in the logical form. Many examples are ambiguous in this regard, but nominalizations and nonfinite forms clearly involve inner adverbials: *nocturno impetu* 'by a night attack' is the temporal counterpart of a locatively modified expression like *maritima oppugnatio* 'naval attack.' On the other hand initial and presumably dislocated temporal expressions are typically outer adverbials

(12) *Postero die* Caesar promota turri perfectisque operibus... magno coorto imbre... arbitratus est (BG 7.27).

Just as a locative adverbial like *in Gallia* 'in Gaul' serves to limit the possible locations of the event to the set of places in Gaul and means 'somewhere in Gaul,' so a positional temporal adverbial like *postero die* limits the possible reference times for the event to the set of times included in the day after the day including the reference time of the preceding sentence and means 'some time on the next day.'

Positional adverbials introduce relations between two times: $\lambda t'\lambda t.R(t, t')$. The simplest relation is identity (AT, $t = t'$): the positional adverbial is a function from a set of events with run time or reference time t to a set of events with run time or reference time at t'

(13) *Media nocte* in Algidum perveniunt (Livy 3.27.8).

The reference time, which is the time of the event of the Romans reaching Algidus (t) was midnight (t'). The ablative ending encodes a covert prepositional head which takes the two times as its arguments. The whole phrase *media nocte* out of context denotes the set of events whose reference times are at midnight, in context the set of events whose reference time is that particular midnight in 458 B.C. (of which the event *in Algidum perveniunt* is a member). The ablative can also express a relation of inclusion between two intervals (DURING, $t \subseteq t'$)

(14) Itaque *proxima nocte*... castra ab Ticino mota festinatumque ad Padum est (Livy 21.47.2)

(12) The next day, after a tower had been moved forward and the siege-works completed, it began to rain heavily and Caesar decided... (BG 7.27).

(13) At midnight they arrived at Mt. Algidus (Livy 3.27.8).

(14) So the next night he moved camp from the Ticinus and marched quickly to the Po (Livy 21.47.2).

(15) *Eodem anno* Anxur trecenti in coloniam missi sunt (Livy 8.21.11).

The reference time that the event comes to be associated with (t) is contained in the interval denoted by the adverbial (t'). Both examples are outer positionals, but inner positionals also occur

(16) qui nuntiarent adventum percontarenturque... *interdiu* an *noctu* venire sese vellet (Livy 27.45.12)
An *noctu* tamquam furtiva in aerarium deportabuntur? (Livy 45.39.5).

Noctu means that the event is nocturnal, not that it happens on some particular night. Anteriority ($t < t'$) and posteriority ($t > t'$) require an overt preposition

(17) *ante occasum solis* urbem ingressi sunt (Livy 29.7.7)
is *post proelium* se ad hominem necessarium, A. Plautium, in Bithyniam contulit (Ad Fam 13.29.4).

Durative adverbials measure the run time of atelic predicates (including secondary atelics like habituals and iteratives without frequency adverbs), that is the interval of time occupied by the temporal trace of the event

(18) Signis conlatis iusto proelio *per quattuor horas* pugnatum (Livy 23.40.10)
numquam *diu* eodem vestigio stare fortunam (Curt Ruf 4.5.2)
Quinque dies aquam in os suum non coniecit, non micam panis (Petr 42).

The first example (Livy 23.40) says that the run time of the fighting event was an interval of at least four hours (starting with the reference time) and that in every subinterval of that four hours the fighting was ongoing (roughly $\lambda e.\text{Pugnatum}(e) \wedge \mu^h(\tau(e)) \geq 4 \wedge \forall t.t \subseteq \tau(e) \rightarrow \text{Pugnatum}(t)$). The run time of the event is measured in hour-long degrees on a scale. Zero on the scale is aligned with the left boundary of the temporal trace, and the value given by the measure function is the maximal degree on the scale reached by the run time of the event, therefore its right boundary. Universal quantification over subintervals is fine for states, but needs some qualifications for activities: gaps (insignificant intermissions in the fighting) are discounted, because it is recognized that when the fighting starts up again it is a continuation of the preceding event, not a new and independent event (so the same battle, not a different battle). It is also understood that at extremely small intervals the ongoing activity may not be recognizable as fighting. There is also an iterative reading ('They fought fre-

(15) In the same year three hundred people were sent to Anxur to form a colony (Livy 8.21.11).

(16) To announce their arrival and ask whether he wanted them to come during the day or during the night (Livy 27.45.12). Are they going to be transported to the treasury during the night like stolen goods? (Livy 45.39.5).

(17) They entered the city before sunset (Livy 29.7.7). He went to Bithynia after the battle to an old friend of his, A. Plautius (Ad Fam 13.29.4).

(18) They fought a regular pitched battle for four hours (Livy 23.40.10). That fortune never stays put very long (Curt Ruf 4.5.2). For five days he put no water in his mouth nor a scrap of bread (Petr 42).

quently for three years') and a cumulative reading that sums up independent nonadjacent fighting intervals and gives the total time they occupy (like 'He worked on his paper for thirty-two hours'). The other two examples illustrate negative scope with durative adverbials. In the second example (Curt Ruf 4.5) the adverbial is inside the scope of the negative: it never happens that there is an event of fortune staying in the same spot for a long time; the interval *diu* starts with the point at which fortune occupies a new spot. In the last example (Petr 42) the adverbial is outside the scope of the negation: throughout an interval of five days there was no event of Chrysanthus eating or drinking anything. Note that lower negation licenses a durative adverbial with the telic phrase *coniecit in os suum*, because it creates a state of failure or abstention, and states are divisive and atelic (see Chapter 2). It is probably necessary to distinguish inner duratives (which measure the duration of the eventuality) from outer duratives (which define a reference interval), but many examples seem ambiguous.

While durative adverbials occur with atelic predicates, container adverbials occur with telic predicates. Duratives tell you how long an event continued, container adverbials tell you the interval within which the event or some phase of an event is completed. So while duratives measure the interval between the endpoints of $\tau(e)$, container adverbials create a bound for an event-related time. They locate some point of the run time of the event inside an interval, exactly which point (the onset, an internal point or the endpoint) depends on the eventuality type, the viewpoint aspect, the tense and the context (see Chapter 2). Here we will consider the simplest type, which uses the complete event including its telos. Inner container adverbials modify the run time of the event by locating it within an interval: they are functions from a set of events with run time t to a set of events with run time $t \subseteq t'$, so the event time is a subinterval of the adverbial interval

(19) Facile id dicemus quod... *quam brevissimo tempore* confici potest (De Inv 2.169)
paucis diebus exercitum fecit (Phil 5.23)
duobus *paucis diebus* amissis filiis (Tusc 3.70).

The interval starts with the beginning of the event and ends after the achievement of the telos or the termination of the event. Outer container adverbials measure an interval starting at the reference time and continuing at least until the onset or completion of the event

(20) Perscribam ad te *paucis diebus* omnia (Ad Att 5.17.2)
Itaque video *paucis diebus* nos in armis fore (Ad Att 16.8.1).

Container adverbials can be used for iterated events with frequency adverbs

(19) We will call easy that which can be achieved in the shortest possible time (De Inv 2.169). Within a few days he formed an army (Phil 5.23). Who lost two sons within a few days (Tusc 3.70).

(20) I will send you an account of everything within a few days (Ad Att 5.17.2). So I see that within a few days we will be in arms (Ad Att 16.8.1).

(21) Quater *intra paucos annos* primum pilum duxi. (Livy 42.34.11).

Container adverbials also differ from duratives in their direction of entailment among quantifiers. While there is nothing wrong with the durative *multos annos* 'for many years,' if you change *paucis diebus* in the above examples into *multis diebus*, the result is infelicitous: 'I will write to you in a few/*many days time.' Durative *quattuor dies* entails *tres dies*, but container *quattuor diebus* entails *quinque diebus*. Since the entailments go in opposite directions, so do the implicatures: discounting the effects of approximation, durative adverbials give the maximum interval the speaker can truthfully claim for the duration of the event, container adverbials give the minimum interval within which the speaker can truthfully claim that the event is included. So durative *quattuor dies* means 'for exactly four, or possibly more than four, days,' container *quattuor diebus* means 'in exactly four, or possibly less than four, days.' The 'exactly' reading is cancelled by spelling out the covert numerical modifiers in the alternative floor and, respectively, roof readings

(22) *amplius semihora* tubicines imitatus est (Petr 69).
castella facere coepit atque ea *minus semihora* effecit (BAfr 38: app. crit.).

The four time system

At this point you may be wondering whether we really need all these different times, and whether the system couldn't be simplified by deriving one from another. The answer is no. The time denoted by an adverbial is not necessarily the same as the run time of the event; it can be a larger interval in which the run time of the event is included, as in the case of *postero die* (t^{adv}) versus the time of *arbitratus est* ($\tau(e)$) in (12) above; or it can be a smaller interval as with the progressive

(23) *simul* castra *oppugnabantur*, simul pars exercitus ad populandum agrum Romanum missa (Livy 3.5.2).

Nor is the time denoted by an adverbial necessarily the same as the reference time; it can be larger, as in the example in (12) again, where all four events described in the sentence (*promota, perfectis, coorto, arbitratus*) are included in the time of the adverbial *postero die*, although each has a different reference time. Finally the reference time is not necessarily the same as the run time of the event. In the case of nonperfective present tenses, this is automatically the case, since the reference time is the same as the utterance time (conceptually an instant)

(21) I was chief centurion four times within a period of a few years (Livy 42.34.11).

(22) He imitated trumpet-players for more than half an hour (Petr 69). He began to build forts and finished them in less than half an hour (BAfr 38).

(23) At one and the same time the camp was being attacked and a part of the army was sent to lay waste the Roman fields (Livy 3.5.2).

(24) Quid istic *facitis*? (Ad Fam 8.17.2).

As the use of the progressive in English indicates ('What are you doing?'), the event time overlaps the reference time and unavoidably spills over into the past and normally into the future. But even with nonpresent tenses it can happen that the assertion is limited to a reference time that is shorter than the run time of the eventuality, as in the following examples with statives

(25) Hunc (collem)... palus difficilis... *cingebat* (BG 7.19)
montibus angustis mare *continebatur* (BG 4.23)
illim assumes quae ad hunc locum *pertinebunt* (De Off 1.151)
verebar ne ita caderet, quod etiam nunc vereor (Ad Fam 2.19.1).

In the first two examples (BG 7.19; 4.23) the verbs are interpreted as individual level (permanent) rather than stage level (transient) properties, but the past tenses do not trigger the inference that the nominal referents no longer exist ('Jack was tall'). It is not being asserted (nor implied or presupposed) that by the time Caesar published his work the marsh near Bourges had been drained or the cliffs of Dover had been significantly eroded. The situation is described from the perspective of the actors at the time of the narrative; the assertion is simply limited to the reference time, which is included in the time of the eventuality (see Figure 1.2), and is noncommittal about other times. The facts are communicated as part of the descriptive and causal background of the narrative, not as independent items of geographical information. The third example (De Off 1.151) shows the same effect outside a narrative context and in future rather than in past time. The fourth example (Ad Fam 2.19) does involve a stage level predicate: Cicero says that he became afraid and still is afraid, without a contradictio in adiecto. The usual implicature that the state has lapsed

(26) quod modo *verebar* tibi gratias agere, nunc plane ago (Ad Fam 13.18.2)

is cancelled by *etiam nunc vereor*.

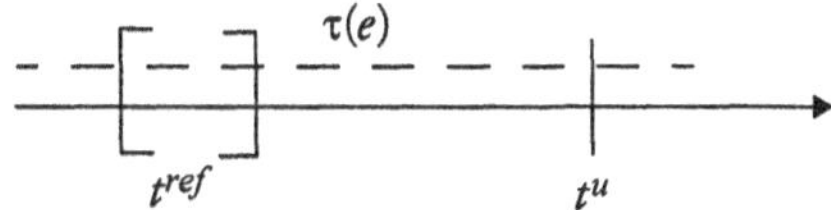

Figure 1.2
Imperfect tense for currently true state
$t^{ref} < t^u \wedge \tau(e) \supset t^u$

(24) What are you doing there? (Ad Fam 8.17.2).

(25) A difficult marsh surrounded this hill (BG 7.19). The sea was hemmed in by narrow cliffs (BG 4.23). You will find there the material that pertains to this issue (De Off 1.151). I was afraid, as I still am afraid, that it would turn out to be the case that... (Ad Fam 2.19.1).

(26) Although I was previously afraid to thank you, I now do so plainly (Ad Fam 13.18.2).

Tense

So, given all these times, which are the ones that tense relates to? Tense is computed relative to an anchor, which in the default case is the time of utterance. The other time used in the computation of tense is the reference time, not the event time nor the adverbial time. For instance, if the event time overlaps the time of utterance but the reference time precedes it, the past tense is used, not the present; this was the case with the examples in (25) above. If the adverbial time overlaps the time of utterance but the reference time follows it, the future tense is used, not the present

(27) *Hodie* igitur me *videbit* (Ad Att 13.7a.1).

So we can understand the future tense here as a property of the reference time, namely the property of being posterior to the utterance time. While adverbials can specify times quite precisely

(28) *illo die ab hora diei tertia ad octavam* (Livy 8.38.10)
postridie (id erat *a.d. vii Kal.Dec.*) *hora iiii* Brundisium venimus (Ad Fam 16.9.2),

tense is restricted to the very simple relations of anteriority, coincidence and posteriority for past, present and future respectively. These are the same as those expressed in adverbials like *ante proelium* 'before the battle,' *in proelio* 'during the battle,' and *post proelium* 'after the battle,' which are the temporal counterparts of locative adverbials like *ante aciem* 'in front of the line,' *in acie* 'in the line,' and *post aciem* 'behind the line.' The following examples

(29) castra *oppugnavit* (Livy 26.13.10)
me *oppugnat* (Div Caec 23)
castra *oppugnabimus* (Livy 42.61.7)

are illustrated in Figure 1.3. Some languages (like Latin) have different inflectional paradigms for all three tenses, others distinguish only past from nonpast

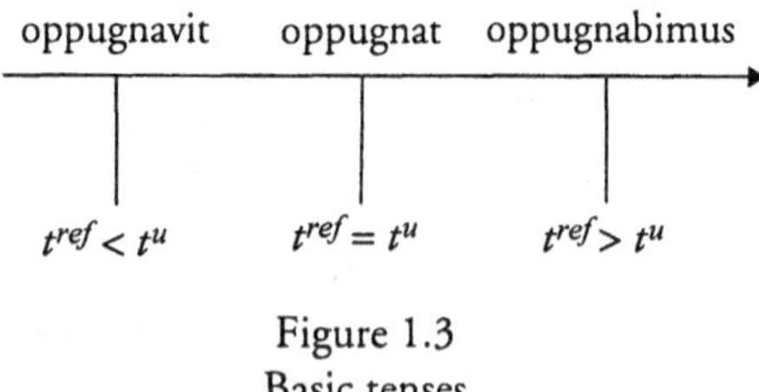

Figure 1.3
Basic tenses

(27) So today he will see me (Ad Att 13.7a.1).
(28) On that day from the third hour of the day to the eighth (Livy 8.38.10). The next day (which was the 24th November) at the fourth hour we arrived at Brundisium (Ad Fam 16.9.2).
(29) He attacked the camp (Livy 26.13.10). He is attacking me (Div Caec 23). We will attack their camp (Livy 42.61.7).

(present and future) or future from nonfuture (present and past). There are also languages that subdivide the past and the future into a number of different metrically defined tenses. For instance the Bantu language Mituku has the following metrical past tenses: hodiernal past, hesternal past, recent past, intermediate past (more than a week ago), remote past. Most of these systems use a hodiernal past for events on the same day as the utterance but anterior to the utterance time, not a simple hodiernal for any past, present or future hodiernal event.

As we already noted, in narrative the reference time is continuously updated with each successive (perfectively presented) event. This applies to future narrative as much as to past narrative

(30) hanc... *evertes,... deligere* iterum consul... Numantiam *exscindes... offendes* rempublicam consiliis perturbatam nepotis mei. (De Rep 6.11).

For the present tense the reference time is tied to the utterance time; since the utterance time is continuously updated with each successive utterance, in an eventive sequence of present tenses like a sportscast, the reference time is updated along with the utterance time. The difference is that for past and future narrative, the updating process is anaphorically based, whereas for present tense it is deictically based. If during the conversation you are taking a walk down a basilica, the spatial location of the utterance is continuously updated too.

From event to proposition

Now we have to consider how tense (and aspect) are added onto event descriptions to create propositions. Although tense and aspect are encoded by the morphology as verbal inflections, semantically they scope over the event description and so the inflections have to be semantically interpreted higher in the tree in positions approximating those of the English auxiliaries like *have* and *will.* In the theory presented here, tense and aspect are relations between two times: tense is a relation between the reference time and the utterance time and aspect is a relation between the event time and the reference time. The details are presented in Figure 1.4, using an example with an imperfect (past tense with imperfective aspect)

(31) *Oppugnabant* Athenienses Chium (Nepos 12.4.1),

'(the situation was that) the Athenians were attacking Chios.' The diagram is not quite as complicated as it seems at first sight. It is a logical form with the structure of a syntactic tree containing a tense projection and an aspect projection. As just noted, the Tense head and the Aspect head each take two arguments, one in the complement position and one in the specifier position. Each head takes as its complement an event description that includes a time and

(30) You will overthrow it, you will be chosen as consul for a second time, you will destroy Numantia, you will find the republic disturbed by the political plans of my grandson (De Rep 6.11).

(31) The Athenians were attacking Chios (Nepos 12.4.1).

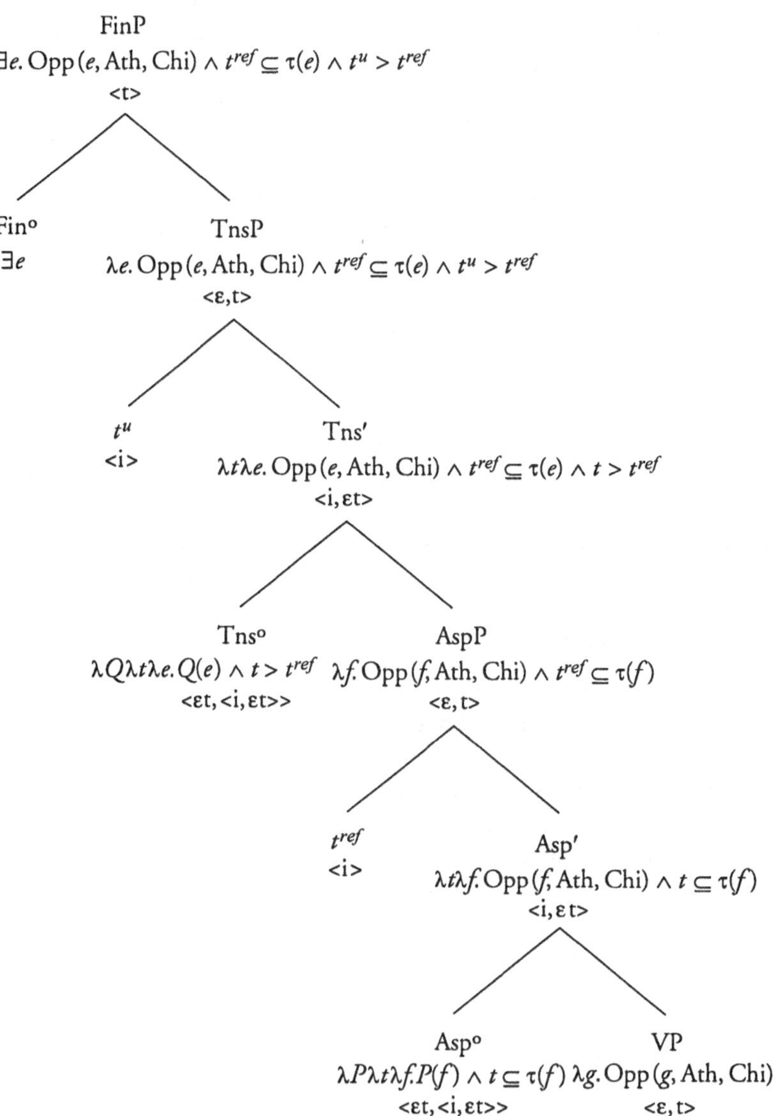

Figure 1.4
Tense and aspect
Oppugnabant Athenienses Chium (Nepos 12.4.1)

adds a restriction on that time (its relation to the time in the specifier). This is a bit like the nominal suffix *-ic-* in e.g. *accusatrix* 'female prosecutor,' which takes an agent noun predicate and adds the restriction that it is female (or grammatically feminine). Starting at the bottom right hand corner, the (subject internal) VP node is an event description, the set of events *g* of the Athenians attacking Chios: $\lambda g.$Opp$(g,$ Ath, Chi)). The verb has an event argument (not represented structurally) but not a time argument; time is introduced indirectly by the event argument. The aspectual head is a rather heavy-duty head. It composes with the event description: when the latter is substituted for *P* in the expression $\lambda P_{<\varepsilon,t>}.P(f)$, we get λg [Opp$(g,$ Ath, Chi)](f), which reduces to Opp$(f,$ Ath, Chi); as the subscript type indicates, *P* is a property of events, not of individuals. It also modifies *P* by activating the value of the event run time function and intersecting *P* with the set of events having an inclusion relation between the reference time and the run time. The reference time in this example is a contextually supplied free variable, so referential (pronominal) rather than existentially quantified, namely the narrative time at the beginning of the story of Chabrias' death. The result of this initial compositional step is Asp′, a function that takes the reference time to give AspP, a set of events *f* for which the reference time is included in the run time: $t^{ref} \subseteq \tau(f)$. The Tense head works in the same way: it takes the resulting Aspect Phrase (an aspectually restricted event description, $Q_{<\varepsilon,t>}$) as its complement and adds the further restriction that the reference time contained therein is anterior to the utterance time in the specifier position, which is again a contextually determined free variable: $t^u > t^{ref}$. The denotation of the resulting Tense Phrase is the set of events of the Athenians attacking Chios in which the run time of the event frames the reference time and the reference time is anterior to the utterance time: $\lambda e.$Opp$(e,$ Ath, Chi) $\wedge\ t^{ref} \subseteq \tau(e) \wedge t^u > t^{ref}$. This set of events is then existentially quantified by an operator in a higher projection, which we have located in the Finite Phrase, changing a property of events (type (<ε,t>) into a truth value (type <t>) or into a proposition in an intensional framework (type <s,t>). The order of the functional heads (Finite – Tense – Aspect) tends to be the mirror image (inverse) of the order in which the inflectional suffixes are added to the verb in any particular language (to the extent that they are not fused). This order reflects the computation of semantic scope from the left edge of the sentence inwards towards the verb and from the right edge of the verb inwards towards the root. Figure 1.5 is a little diagram to illustrate this. Since we are using a lexicalist theory of morphology, we do not posit any lowering of a tense-aspect morpheme onto the verbal root (such a lowering might in any case be quite local, since the arguments are probably raised to the left of the Tense and Aspect operators).

Future

Event descriptions like *Caesar castra oppugn-* 'Caesar attack- camp' don't have truth conditions until they are located in time (and place). Once an event

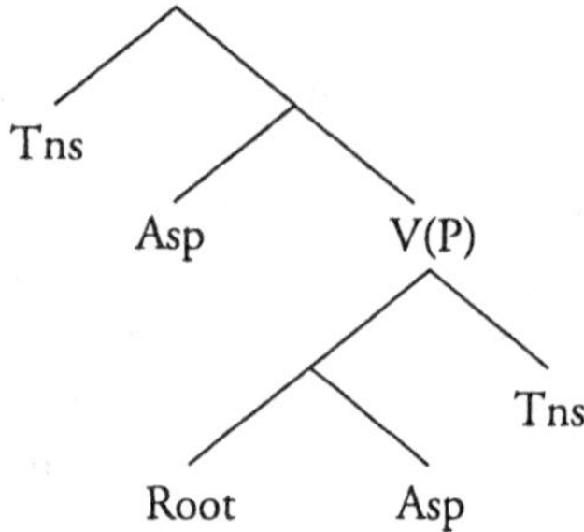

Figure 1.5
Inverse ordering of syntactic and morphological elements

description is equipped with (aspect and) tense, it can be verified against the facts in the actual world. This immediately raises a problem about the future: how can one verify an event that has not yet taken place? Latin tense morphology is structured in such a way as to suggest that the future is simply a mirror image of the past, yet we know that in many languages future tense morphology is derived from volitional or deontic modal expressions (like English *will* and *shall* respectively), and it is often claimed that the future is not a tense but a mood. In considering this question, we need to separate our linguistic concerns from the preliminary philosophical issues of determinism and scepticism. To what extent can a proposition about the future be true at all at the present, and to what extent can we actually know at the present that an eventuality will obtain in the future? The former question is objective and relates to circumstantial modality; the latter question is subjective and relates to epistemic modality. So our discussion will need to use some of the modal concepts presented in Chapter 9.

Let's start with determinism. The status of the future depends on whether we adopt a deterministic or an indeterministic perspective. If the course of events is determined, then an assertion about a future event is already either true or false at the time of utterance, we just don't know which until the event occurs and the facts can be verified (although we often know enough to make predictions with the future tense). The event may be an epistemic possibility but objectively it is a necessity (or an impossibility), since the domain of worlds is limited to a single world, the actual world. So we can use the traditional single time line to represent this approach: there are many moments of time to consider but just one world. The history of this world as it develops through time has a linear representation in both the past and the future, and the future is indeed a mirror image of the past (tense in a deterministic perspective is represented as in Figure 1.3). If we adopt an indeterministic perspective, things are quite different. Now there is no single future world, rather there are many possible future worlds. A proposition about a future event can be true at the present if it is inevitable (true in all possible future worlds, however else they may differ from one another), and false if it is impossible (true in none). Otherwise it will be a contingent future, which has no truth value at the present. Contingent futures are undefined at the present; their truth values will be determined by the future course of events. Contingent futures require not only epistemic indeterminism but also circumstantial indeterminism. We can continue to use a linear representation of the past (the past is unique because there is only one actual world), but we will need a branching representation for the future in which each branch represents a possible world (see Figure 1.6). If each world has its own complete history, then the branches are merged (or run parallel) in the past, since each branch has the same past. For some histories the future proposition is a true prediction, for others it is false. Clearly, on this perspective the future is not a mirror image of the past: the past is actual, the future is modal. As the course of events progresses into the future, either the event takes place or it does not, so at some point in the future the proposition does become verifiable and take on a truth value. But if we project this latter truth value back to the original time of utterance and say that the prediction turned out to be true, that is a retrospective evaluation, which is something quite different. Any proposition can be retrospectively re-evaluated in the light of new evidence, also those with a past tense. In fact the future tense can be used for a future event that leads to verification of a present state

(32) Nummi sescenti hic *erunt* (Pl Pers 437; cp. Frag Inc 6).

The money is in the purse at the time of utterance, and when Dordalus takes the purse and opens it, he will be in a position to verify the sum. The proposition is known by the speaker to be true at the time of utterance and verifiable by the addressee at a future time. This is related to the inferential future (see Chapter 9), which is used when the speaker too cannot verify the assertion at the time of utterance.

Now when we look at the way speakers actually use the future indicative, we see that neither their personal philosophical opinions *De Fato* nor the general assumptions of the language community about how the world works (socalled natural language metaphysics) are sufficient to account for the data. Future indicatives are not equivalent to circumstantial modals (nor for that matter to

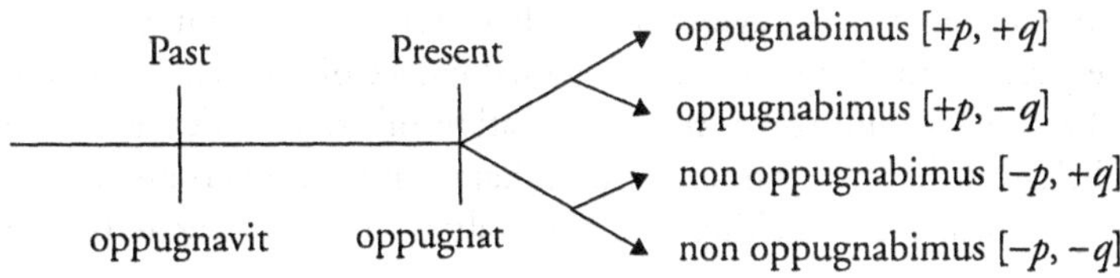

Figure 1.6
Tense in a nondeterministic perspective

(32) You will find that there are six hundred coins here (Pl Pers 437).

epistemic modals): (It has gone up, so) 'it will come down' is not the same thing as 'it may come down' (existential quantification over circumstantially accessible worlds) or 'it will have to come down' (universal quantification over circumstantially accessible worlds). On the face of it, the speaker adopts an indeterministic perspective for the modals (quantifying over future possibilities) and a deterministic one for the future indicative (talking about a single definite future).

Turning now to the subjective side of things, speakers regularly make assertions of all sorts that come nowhere near the high epistemic standards of absolute truth that even a modest sceptic might demand. It is understood by the conversational participants that in representing himself as believing the proposition 'Caesar will attack' to be true, the speaker has excluded a number of far-fetched worlds, for example those in which there is a flood or an earthquake and those in which Caesar has a heart attack or even just changes his mind. He has excluded from the domain of quantification worlds in which the course of events does not proceed in a stereotypically predictable fashion but is interrupted by some unpredictable contretemps. His assertion is true in all the inertially accessible worlds that form the basis for ordinary conversation. It would be unreasonable to reply 'That's not true: there might be a meteor strike'; you would have to say 'Technically/strictly speaking that's not true, because there might be a meteor strike' (not a very helpful contribution, because the epistemic standard has been inappropriately raised too high). Assertions about the future use an inertial ordering source: they are true in all worlds accessible via this ordering source. If one wanted to represent this situation explicitly, one could use a covert assertion operator. Although we have just talked about them in modal terms, (as already noted) future assertions are not just another type of modality but have a special status as factually presented claims about how the actual world will develop. In this sense they are extensional (unlike modals, which are intensional). They take the future course of events to be settled in much the same way that the past course of events is settled, making the future indicative the mirror image of the past indicative. In fact, assertions about the present and the past are likewise filtered by an ordering source reflecting such things as the reliability of our information. (Some languages encode the type of evidence used by well developed systems of evidential marking; certain Latin uses of the subjunctive are evidential in character.) Assertion in general defaults to rather weak knowledge standards: global choice of a pedantically high epistemic threshold would force the modalization of pretty much every sentence. Nevertheless, if the issue is not settled in their minds, speakers are not willing to take responsibility for making assertions about a future event but resort to modalization.

The settledness of future events that we have just been talking about is not identical with that of the socalled futurate (present for planned, scheduled or predetermined future events), which like the prospective (*-turus sum*) has the more complicated NX temporal structure analyzed in Chapter 2

(33) Deinde me *expedio* ad Drusum, inde ad Scaurum (Ad Att 4.15.9)
Is hodie apud me *cenat* et frater meus (Pl Stich 415)
Hodie uxorem *ducis*? (Ter Andr 321).

Although the event time of the futurate is future, the reference time is present ('I am now flying to Paris tomorrow')

(34) Lentulus Spinther hodie apud me, cras mane *vadit* (Ad Att 14.11.2)
Cras tamen mane domum ad te *veniam* (Fronto Aur 5.25)

GEL. *Ibisne* ad cenam foras? PAMPH. Apud fratrem *ceno* in proxumo. GEL. Certumnest? PAMPH. Certum. (Pl Stich 612)

Cras *est* mihi iudicium (Ter Eun 338)
Sulla... cras *erit* hic cum Messalla (Ad Att 11.22.2).

The departure of Spinther the next morning (*cras mane*) is planned or scheduled at the time of writing (*hodie*). Since the reference time is the present, this is part of the assertion. The adverbs *cras mane* in the first example (Ad Att 14.11) modify the event time: if a future event time is not specified, it should be recoverable from the context (or, as in the case of *ceno* in the third example, from the lexical semantics of the verb); otherwise the sentence would default to a present rather than a futurate reading

(35) Sed quam mox *coctum est* prandium? (Pl Rud 342)
Coctumst prandium? (Pl Bacch 716).

Present time adverbs on the other hand are redundant and infelicitous with futurates unless they are contrastive ('We are NOW leaving tomorrow'). In the second example in (34) (Fronto 5.25) the reference time of the visit of Fronto to Marcus Aurelius is in the future, so the future tense is used. The visit is still planned, but this is an implicature and not part of the assertion. Similarly in the third example (Stich 612) the future in the question (*Ibisne*) is answered by a present (*ceno*) indicating a scheduled future event. *Certum* shows that the scheduled event is treated as a settled fact of the actual world, not a quantification over possible worlds. Present tense refusals are negative futurates

(36) MEN. Perge porro. PEN. Non *pergo* hercle (Pl Men 150)
TRACH. Audi. GR. Non *audio* (Pl Rud 946).

(33) Then I am going to prepare for Drusus and after that for Scaurus (Ad Att 4.15.9). He is having dinner at my place today along with my brother (Pl Stich 415). Are you getting married today? (Ter Andr 321).

(34) Lentulus Spinther is staying with me today; he leaves tomorrow morning (Ad Att 14.11.2). Tomorrow morning however I will come over to your house (Fronto Aur 5.25). GEL. Are you going out to dinner? PAMPH. I'm having dinner at my brother's next door. GEL. Is that fixed? PAMPH. Yes (Pl Stich 612). I'm in court tomorrow (Ter Eun 338). Sulla will be here tomorrow with Messalla (Ad Att 11.22.2).

(35) But how soon is lunch ready? (Pl Rud 342). Is lunch ready? (Pl Bacch 716).

(36) MEN. Go on. PEN. I'm sure as hell not going on (Pl Men 150). TRACH. Listen. GR. I won't listen (Pl Rud 946).

As a consequence of their different temporal structures, futurates and futures tend to convey different degrees of immediacy and of epistemic commitment. Events that are hard to predict and cannot be scheduled make bad futurates in some languages including English (*'Caesar defeats the Gauls tomorrow'; *'The snow melts tomorrow'). Conversely certain verbs of motion, particularly verbs of departure and return, have an inbuilt prestate at which an imminent event is planned but not yet actuated (see Chapter 2). So they are particularly common in the first person futurate and do not require an adverbial specifying the event time

(37) Ego in aedem Veneris *eo*. (Pl Poen 190)
Redeo intro. (Pl Cist 704)
Ego ad anum *recurro* rursum. (Pl Cist 594).

The event time is not obligatorily expressed since it is lexically recoverable in context as the immediate future (which is not the case for verbs of other classes). If it is not the most immediate event, the event time requirement resurfaces

(38) Deos salutabo modo, poste ad te continuo *transeo* (Pl Stich 623)
Ego abeo... iam ego *recurro* huc (Pl Asin 379).

Note that in the first example (Stich 623) both events are in the immediate future: the earlier event is a nonmotion verb and in the future tense (*salutabo*), the later event is a motion verb and in the futurate (*transeo*). Nonfuturate forms of these verbs of motion too can access the prestate

(39) Quid mihi *discedens* mandaris memini (Ad Fam 8.6.2)
hoc litterularum exaravi *egrediens* e villa ante lucem (Ad Att 12.1.1).

We have said that future tense assertions are sensitive to an inertial ordering source. Let's take a concrete example

(40) Mago locum *monstrabit* quem insideatis (Livy 21.54.3).

Call this proposition p. Hannibal asserts that p will be true in the future history of the actual world and presupposes that the actual world is a member of the set of worlds whose future histories are locally inertial, that is inertial with respect to p (it doesn't matter whether, also, it rains in Tasmania or not). In open conditionals the inertial worlds are added into the restriction

(41) Si *egebis*, tibi dolebit, non mihi (Caecilius in Pro Cael 37);

(37) I'm going to the temple of Venus (Pl Poen 190). I'm going back inside (Pl Cist 704). I'm rushing back to the old woman (Pl Cist 594).

(38) I'll just salute the gods, then I'll come right over to you (Pl Stich 623). I'm off; I'll hurry back here straight away (Pl Asin 379).

(39) I remember the instructions you gave me as you were leaving (Ad Fam 8.6.2). I wrote these few lines as I was leaving my country house before dawn (Ad Att 12.1.1).

(40) Mago will show you where to lie in ambush (Livy 21.54.3).

(41) If you become impoverished, you will regret it, not me (Pro Cael 37).

all worlds in which you are poor and which are inertial worlds are worlds in which you will be miserable. In the simplest case, inertiality depends on the stereotypical application of the laws of nature

(42) olea... celeriter *concalescet* (Col 12.52.17)
sparsaque caelesti rore *madebit* humus (Ov Fast 1.312).

Agentive futures are more complicated because agency introduces additional modal components of meaning: capability, opportunity, and choice or commitment. Bouletic modality is also typical, but not all desires are achievable and not all agentive events are desired. Let's use Cicero's own examples to illustrate

(43) Et si tum non esset vera haec enuntiatio "Capiet Numantiam Scipio," ne illa quidem eversa vera est haec enuntiatio "Cepit Numantiam Scipio." (De Fat 27).

The future assertion presupposes that Scipio has the capability to capture Numantia (quite reasonably, given the superiority of the Roman forces), that he has the opportunity (he was made commander in Spain), that he chooses to initiate such action and is committed to carrying it out; it also implicates that he desires to do so and is not just carrying out orders of which he personally disapproves. All these conditions can be conjoined with inertiality in the description of the set of worlds in whose futures the assertion is true: for instance $\{w: R^{Inert}(w^*, w) \wedge R^{Dyn}(w^*, w) \wedge R^{Boul}(w^*, w) = 1\}$. If all this is the case for agency in the future, then obviously it is also the case for agency in the past. But since the past is settled, the modal components of agency don't really matter any more for the past. In fact the past event may not even have been inertial at all: it could have been a pure fluke. For a past assertion we know whether the event was inertial or not, for a future assertion we presuppose that it will be. Without the inertial restriction on the domain of future assertions, we cannot avoid Cicero's paradox. Predictably, the future in the past must be settled true

(44) Non tu, Pyrrhe ferox, nec tantis cladibus auctor Poenus *erit* (Lucan 1.30)
Quintius dictaturam properat pervadere? Ab aratro *revocabitur* (Sen De Brev 17.6).

The meaning of the future is also sensitive to pragmatic conditions involving person. Agents generally know perfectly well what they intend to do (even if they may not be aware of all the consequences of their proposed action), so first person interrogative agentive futures and second person declarative agentive

(42) The olives will quickly heat up (Col 12.52.17). And when the ground is wet, sprinkled with dew from the sky (Ov Fast 1.312).

(43) And if the assertion "Scipio will capture Numantia" had not been true then, neither is the assertion "Scipio took Numantia" true now that it has actually been overthrown (De Fat 27).

(44) Neither you, fierce Pyrrhus, nor the Carthaginian will be responsible for so great disasters (Lucan 1.30). Does Quintius hasten to complete his dictatorship? He will be recalled from the plough (Sen De Brev 17.6).

futures can be infelicitous (depending on the informational structure of the sentence), causing such futures to default to marked readings

(45) dominum legata *rogabo* multaque mandatis oscula mixta feram (Ov Her 3.127)
Quid faciam? Roger anne rogem? Quid deinde *rogabo*? (Ov Met 3.465)
"Quid *facies*?", inquis. Quid *faciam*? Veniam. (Mart 6.51.4)
si quid acciderit novi, *facies* ut sciam (Ad Fam 14.8).

Interrogative *rogabo* in the second example (Met 3.465) gets a deliberative (deontic) reading. Interrogative *faciam* in the third example (Mart 6.51) is an echo question. Declarative *facies* in the last example (Ad Fam 14.8) gets a deontic/imperative reading. Marked readings of this type occur not only with interrogative first person futures

(46) Quid viro meo *respondebo*? (Ter Hec 516)
Quid *negabo* aut quid *fatebor*? (Pl Capt 535)

but also with futurates

(47) Utrubi *accumbo*? (Pl Stich 747)
PAR. *Addone*? DIAB. Adde (Pl Asin 755).

Nonagentive futures like unaccusatives and passives do not behave in this way

(48) in occulto *iacebis* (Pl Trin 664)
Medio *iugulaberis* ense (Ov Met 12.484),

although they can be coerced into agentives with imperative readings

(49) Sed *valebis* meaque negotia *videbis* (Ad Fam 7.20.2).

Valebis is roughly equivalent to *fac valeas* and *videbis* to *cura*. All the examples so far have been episodic sentences with definite (first or second person) subjects. Gnomic futures, by contrast, are based on universal quantification over future situations with arbitrary or generic subjects (animate or inanimate). If a situation will always be the case in a contextually given context in the future, it is easy to extrapolate from this that it is also the case at the present and has always been the case in the past. This in turn allows it to be interpreted as a dispositional property

(45) As an envoy I will ask my master and I will bring many kisses mixed in with my message (Ov Her 3.127). What am I to do? Am I to be wooed or to woo? And why should I woo at all? (Ov Met 3.465). "What will you do?" you say. What will I do? I will come (Mart 6.51.4). If anything new happens, make sure I know about it (Ad Fam 14.8).

(46) What answer am I going to give my husband? (Ter Hec 516). What will I deny or what will I admit (Pl Capt 535).

(47) Which side shall I lie? (Pl Stich 747). PAR. Shall I add that? DIAB. Yes (Pl Asin 755).

(48) You will lie hidden (Pl Trin 664). You will be killed by the sword's edge (Ov Met 12.484).

(49) Stay well and look after my business (Ad Fam 7.20.2).

(50) ab occasu brumali Africus *flabit* (NH 18.336)
Iuga Romanica optima *erunt* (Cato 135.2)
prudens agricola... Pingui et uberi *dabit* agro gracilem vitem (Col 3.1.5)
Animo *imperabit* sapiens, stultus *serviet* (Publ Syr A40).

Dispositional modality in its turn often induces overtones of teleological or deontic modality, particularly in the presence of adjectives of evaluation (such as *optima, prudens, sapiens, stultus* in the examples just given).

Pluperfect

We have already discussed the iconic sequencing of events in narrative: the most famous example is *Veni. Vidi. Vici.* (Suet Jul 37.2). If sequencing fails, this can be indicated by use of the pluperfect (*Vidi. Veneram. Vici.*)

(51) Quarto die qui *missus erat* Lunam venit; paucis ante diebus Calpurnius *profectus erat* (Livy 39.21.5)
Tarenti ludi forte erant cum illuc venit. Mortales multi... *convenerant* (Pl Men 29)
Erant minori illi adulescenti fidicina et tibicina; peregre *advexerat* (Pl Stich 542).

In the first example (Livy 39.21) we have three events, all in the past relative to the time of Livy's writing. Furthermore both the sending of the messenger from Rome and Calpurnius' departure are past relative to the reference time, which is the messenger's arrival in Luna. For the simple past (*venit*), the event time is included in the reference time (a subinterval of the fourth day); for the pluperfects (*missus erat, profectus erat*), the event time is anterior to the reference time. Use of the pluperfect to express anteriority to a past reference time is not obligatory; it can sometimes lapse when the reference time is recalibrated

(52) Superioribus diebus nona Caesaris legio... castra eo loco *posuit* (BC 3.66)
Cum Hannibal ad portas esset (Nolam enim rursus a Nuceria *movit* castra)... Marcellus... intra muros se recepit (Livy 23.16.2)

and in relative clauses like English 'She lost the ring she got for Christmas'

(53) eos quos *misit*, quod ire noluerunt, in vincla coniecit (Pro Reg Deiot 23)
Ab eis Caesar haec facta cognovit qui sermoni *interfuerunt* (BC 3.18).

(50) The African wind blows from the south west (NH 18.336). Roman yokes are the best (Cato 135.2). The wise farmer will assign a slender vine to rich and fertile land (Col 3.1.5). The wise man is a master of his feelings, the foolish man is a slave to them (Publ Syr A40).

(51) The man who had been sent arrived at Luna on the fourth day; Calpurnius had set out a few days before (Livy 39.21.5). There happened to be a festival going on at Tarentum when he got there. Many people had gathered (Pl Men 29). The younger man had a girl lyre-player and a girl pipe-player; he had brought them from abroad (Pl Stich 542).

(52) On the preceding days Caesar's ninth legion pitched camp in that spot (BC 3.66). When Hannibal was at the gates (for he again moved his camp from Nuceria to Nola), Marcellus withdrew inside the walls (Livy 23.16.2).

(53) He threw those whom he sent into prison because they refused to go (Pro Reg Deiot 23). Caesar learned of these events from those who took part in the conversation (BC 3.18).

Although the pluperfect develops into a simple remote past tense in some languages, it is not a remote past in Latin. Very remote events in Roman history are expressed by a simple past tense

(54) ille qui hanc urbem *condidit* Romulus (Cat 3.19).

The pluperfect would be no more correct here than it would for remote events in English history (*'Caesar had invaded Britain many years ago'). The pluperfect is used if the event is anterior to the reference time

(55) emissique captivi quos Philippus tamquam in tutissimam custodiam *condiderat* (Livy 31.23.9).

Conversely the pluperfect can be used for events that are quite recent relative to the time of utterance or writing, so long as they are anterior to the current reference time

(56) ubi Caesaris statuam *consecraverant* (BC 3.105)
domum mei fratris *incenderat* (Pro Mil 87).

But in some languages the pluperfect is used instead of the simple past for a cancelled resultant state ('Who had built this house?' of a collapsed building). Latin can use the pluperfect for unfulfilled commands or simply the reprise of an earlier incomplete item of discourse

(57) embasicoetan *iusseras* dari (Petr 24)
At nunc adulescentuli nostri deducuntur in scholas... Sed, ut dicere *institueram*, deducuntur in scholas (Tac Dial 35.1)
quae libro quinto leviter in transitu *attigeram* (Quint 7.3.27)
"Hic est," inquam, "pater quem vobis *laudaveram*" (Sen Con 1.7.7).

Many Plautine examples seem to fall into this category

(58) heri iam *edixeram* omnibus *dederamque* eas provincias (Pl Pseud 148).

The imperfective counterpart of this pluperfect is the imperfect type *dicebam* 'I was/kept trying to tell you.'

When a temporal adverbial is used with the pluperfect, it can modify either the time of the event described by the pluperfect or the reference time relative to which the pluperfect is past

(54) Romulus who founded this city (Cat 3.19).

(55) The captives, who Philip had put there in high security detention, were released (Livy 31.23.9).

(56) Where they had dedicated a statue of Caesar (BC 3.105). He had set fire to my brother's house (Pro Mil 87).

(57) You had ordered me to be given a nightcap (Petr 24). But now our boys are taken to schools... But, as I began to say, they are taken to schools (Tac Dial 35.1).Which I had briefly touched on in passing in Book Five (Quint 7.3.27). "This," I say, "is the father whom I praised so highly to you" (Sen Con 1.7.7).

(58) I already issued instructions and assigned your tasks to all of you yesterday (Pl Pseud 148).

(59) Cephalio mihi a te litteras reddidit a.d. viii Id. Mart. vespere. Eo autem die *mane* tabellarios miseram (Ad Att 11.12.1)
Pyrrhi temporibus iam Apollo versus facere desierat (De Div 2.116).

In the first example (Ad Att 11.12) the reference time is *vespere*, the event time is *mane* on the same day; so it is the event time that is modified. In the second example the reference time is *Pyrrhi temporibus*, the event time is the time when Apollo ceased issuing oracles, which is anterior to the period of Pyrrhus.

We probably need to distinguish between two types of pluperfect, which we can call past perfect and past aorist respectively. The past perfect has the same sort of "extended now" (XN) semantics as the present perfect (see Chapter 2), except that its reference time is in the past rather than at the present. So we find examples with a resultant state obtaining at the past reference time

(60) *Operuerat* Ascyltos pallio caput (Petr 20)
desiluerant in parva navigia (Curt Ruf 4.3.3)
flagrantes onerarias quas *incenderant* milites... videbatis (De Div 1.69),

as well as experiential pluperfects

(61) Numquam epulum *videras*? (In Vat 32)
Conflixerat apud Rhodanum cum P. Cornelio Scipione consule... cum hoc eodem Clastidi apud Padum decernit (Nepos 23.4.1).

The event time is in the XN relation to the reference time, which is anterior to the utterance time: $\exists e.\textsc{lb}(\tau(e)) < t^{ref} \wedge P(e) \wedge \tau(s^{e}) \supset t^{ref} \wedge t^{u} > t^{ref}$ (see Chapter 2 for details). However, this semantics will not work for all examples. As we have seen, there are some pluperfects with an adverbial specifying the time of the past anterior event (not the primary past reference time)

(62) Id... vitium quod tu iam Kalendis Ianuariis futurum esse *provideras* et tanto ante praedixeras (Phil 2.83)
ut Lacedaemonii, qui paulo ante victores *viguerant*, perterriti pacem peterent (Nepos 7.5.5)
Capitonem in Germania cum similia coeptaret... legati legionum *interfecerant* (Tac Hist 1.7).

(59) Cephalio delivered to me a letter from you on the 8th March in the evening. That same day I had sent letter-carriers in the morning (Ad Att 11.12.1). At the time of Pyrrhus Apollo had already ceased making verses (De Div 2.116).

(60) Ascyltos had covered his head with his cloak (Petr 20). They had jumped into the small boats (Curt Ruf 4.3.3). You saw the merchant ships in flames which the soldiers had set fire to (De Div 1.69).

(61) Had you never seen a funeral banquet? (In Vat 32). He had already fought with P. Cornelius Scipio at the Rhone... He battled with that same man at Clastidium on the Po (Nepos 23.4.1).

(62) That defect that you had already foreseen there would be on the 1st January and had predicted so long before (Phil 2.83). That the Lacedaemonians, who shortly before had been flourishing as victors, sought peace in terror (Nepos 7.5.5). The commanders of the legions had killed Capito in Germany when he embarked on a similar course of action (Tac Hist 1.7).

These do not fit with the resultative or experiential XN semantics of the perfect, which licenses an adverbial for the (present) reference time but not as a rule for the past event time. Similarly the present counterpart of

(63) eodem loco sepultus <est> ubi vitam *posuerat.* (Nepos 4.5.5);

is not 'He is being buried where he has lost his life,' since locatives should not modify the process subevent of a perfect. There are also anterior states that terminate prior to the past reference time

(64) ubi rex Tullus *habitaverat* (De Rep 2.53)
Pythian... meliorem fideliоremque habuit quam *habuerat* antequam offenderet (Frontin 4.7.37).

This second type of pluperfect, the past aorist, probably needs a subsidiary reference time for the anterior event. This secondary reference time can be expressed adverbially, as we have seen, and it would also be needed to compute aspect; this would be particularly clear for the progressive (e.g. 'they had been fighting'), of which the following may be an example

(65) iugum ex quo *pugnaverant* dum per proclive pulsos insequuntur tradiderant hosti (Livy 33.9.11).

Normally the secondary reference time includes the event time and is anterior to the primary reference time, which in turn is anterior to the utterance time: $t^{ref'} \supseteq \tau(e) \wedge t^{ref} > t^{ref'} \wedge t^{u} > t^{ref}$. Neither type of pluperfect allows both the reference time and the event time to be modified by adverbials in the same sentence ('On the Ides of March they had captured the city on the Nones of March'). In the case of the past perfect this follows from the general rule excluding event time adverbials in perfects (*'I have broken my arm yesterday'). For the past aorist it may just be redundant (*'Yesterday I saw you on Tuesday').

Although multiple pluperfects can appear in a random (list) or even anti-iconic order

(66) parietes quorum ornatus tot saecula *manserant*, tot bella *effugerant* (Verr 2.4.122)
Miserat hunc ill Therses, *fabricaverat* Alcon (Ov Met 13.683),

both types can also appear in iconic sequence

(63) He was buried in the same place where he had lost his life (Nepos 4.5.5).

(64) Where King Tullus had lived (De Rep 2.53). He had in Pythias a better and more faithful subject than he had had before he had given him offence (Frontin 4.7.37).

(65) They had yielded to the enemy the ridge from which they had been fighting while they were pursuing the soldiers who had been driven down the hill (Livy 33.9.11).

(66) The walls whose decorations had lasted for so many centuries and which had escaped so many wars (Verr 2.4.122). Therses had sent it to him, Alcon had crafted it (Ov Met 13.683).

(67) quos... equites... ex hibridis, libertinis servisque *conscripserat*, *armaverat* equoque uti frenato *condocuerat* (BAfr 19)
Producit servos quos in pabulatione paucis ante diebus *exceperat* et fame vinculisque *excruciaverat* (BG 7.20).

The first example (BAfr 19: see Figure 1.7) looks like a past perfect; the second (BG 7.20), with its adverbial specifying the event time, looks like a past aorist.

Future perfect

The future perfect has the same structure as the pluperfect but with the reference time posterior to the utterance time rather than anterior to it

(68) Simulac *constituero*, ad te scribam (Ad Att 12.40.5; cp. 16.11.6)
Quos *nominavero* arcesse (Livy 40.9.14)
Cum tu haec leges, ego illum fortasse *convenero* (Ad Att 9.15.3).

While the event time is often posterior to the utterance time too, that is not part of the meaning of the future perfect; the event time could also be present or past. This can happen in examples involving deadlines, when the speaker does not know whether an event has already occurred (or is now occurring) but asserts that it will have occurred by some future date (at which point it will also be verified). If you say 'Caesar will have invaded Britain by the end of August,' the invasion could be future, currently going on or already achieved. All that is being asserted is that the event time is prior to the future reference time (the bound introduced by the container adverbial), just as, if you say 'Hilary will marry a president,' the time of the presidency could be past, present or future. This does not apply to the pluperfect, because the pluperfect is not the mirror image of the future perfect. (The mirror image of the future perfect is the past prospective.) Consider the following excerpts from Cicero's Philippics

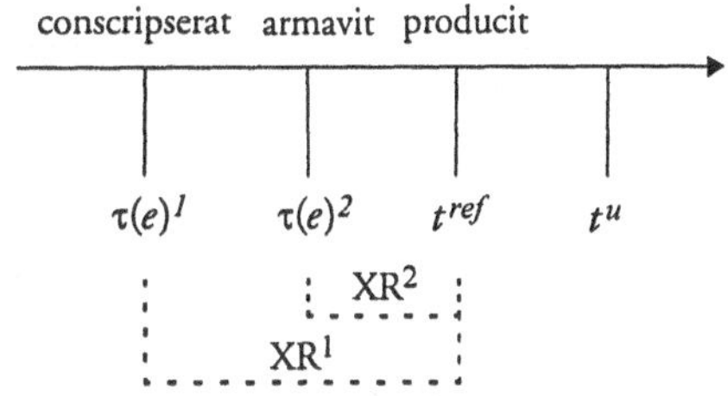

Figure 1.7
Sequential Pluperfects (cp. BAfr 19, BG 7.20)

(67) Cavalry which he had conscripted from half-castes, freedmen and slaves, armed and taught to use a bridled horse (BAfr 19). He produced slaves whom he had captured foraging a few days before and tortured with food deprivation and chains (BG 7.20).
(68) As soon as I decide, I will write to you (Ad Att 12.40.5). Summon those who I name (Livy 40.9.14). By the time you read this, perhaps I will have met him (Ad Att 9.15.3).

(69) Cum enim legati *renuntiarint*, quod certe renuntiabunt, non in vestra potestate... esse Antonium, quis erit tam improbus civis qui illum civem habendum putet? (Phil 6.16).
Quid enim legati egerint, nondum scimus... Haec si *fecerit*, erit integra potestas nobis deliberandi; si senatui non *paruerit*... populo Romano bellum *indixerit* (Phil 7.26).

The first example (Phil 6.16) represents the default situation: we know that the envoys to Antony have not yet returned to Rome from Modena and reported Antony's response; when the report has been delivered ($\tau(e) > t^u$), everyone will agree on Antony's behaviour ($\tau(e) < t^{ref}$, discounting the XN component). In the second example (Phil 7.26) we know that the meeting between Antony and the envoys has already taken place (*legati egerint*), but we do not know what happened at the meeting: in some epistemically accessible worlds Antony has agreed to the senate's ultimatum, in others he has not (*non paruerit*, consequently *bellum indixerit*: $\tau(e) < t^u$); the reference time is the time when the envoys deliver their report, at which point Antony's response can be verified ($\tau(e) < t^{ref}$). If Antony has accepted the terms of the senate, we do not know whether he has already implemented them and desisted from military action in Cisalpine Gaul as required (*haec fecerit*: $\tau(e) < t^u$), is now in the process of doing so $\tau(e) \supset t^u$), or has not yet done so but will do so at some point between now and the return of the envoys ($\tau(e) > t^u$). See Figure 1.8 for this difference between the pluperfect and the future perfect. (The mostly preclassical use of morphologically future perfect forms for aspectually perfective simple future tense is discussed in Chapter 2.) Like multiple pluperfects, multiple future perfects can be iconically serialized

(70) Cum autem Karthaginem *deleveris*, triumphus *egeris*, censorque *fueris* et *obieris* legatus Aegyptum, Syriam... (De Rep 6.11).

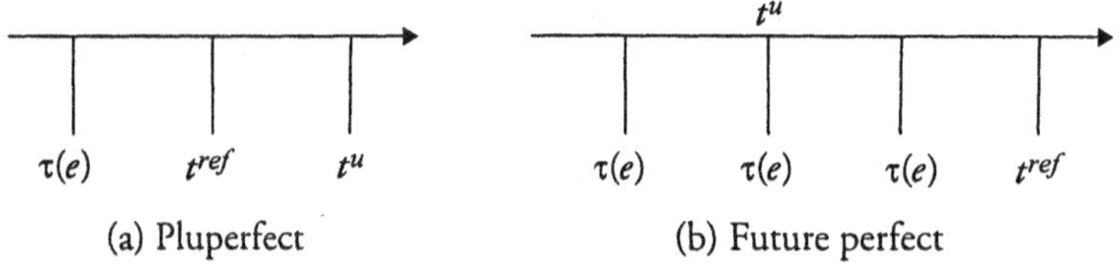

Figure 1.8
Pluperfect (a) and Future perfect (b)

(69) For when the envoys report, as they certainly will, that Antony is not under your power, who will be so wicked a citizen as to think that he ought to be considered a citizen? (Phil 6.16). We don't yet know what the envoys have achieved. If he does these things, we will have the freedom to deliberate; if he does not obey the senate, he will have declared war on the Roman people (Phil 7.26).
(70) When you have destroyed Carthage, celebrated a triumph, been censor and visited Egypt and Syria as an envoy (De Rep 6.11).

Relative tense

The pluperfect and the future perfect are often called relative tenses (as opposed to absolute tenses like the past, present and future). Let's take the pluperfect. In its past perfect reading, it has XN semantics, so its reference time is the right-hand boundary of the XN interval. In the pluperfect this is anterior to the utterance time (rather than equal to the utterance time as it is in the simple perfect): the pluperfect is computed relative to this past reference time. In its past aorist reading the (secondary) reference time of the pluperfect is not simply anterior to the utterance time but anterior to the primary reference time (which is itself anterior to the utterance time). In both cases, the default rule by which tense is computed directly from the utterance time is overridden, and the utterance time is replaced by a past time in the computation. Tense in nonfinite verb forms like participles and infinitives is also relative

(71) Extemplo M. Geganius consul cum exercitu *profectus* tria milia passuum ab hoste locum castris cepit (Livy 4.9.12)
Castra *vallantem* Fabium adorti sunt (Livy 9.41.16)
cum perfecto Africo bello exercitum eo *traiecturus* sacrificaret (Livy 21.1.4).

All three participles (past: *profectus,* present: *vallantem,* and future: *traiecturus*) denote events in the past relative to Livy's time of writing. The past participle *profectus* in the first example (4.9) denotes an event whose time is anterior to the reference time established by the main verb *cepit* (we will get to the XN semantics in a moment). The present participle *vallantem* in the second example (9.41) denotes an event whose time includes the reference time established by the main verb *adorti sunt.* The future participle *traiecturus* in the third example (21.1) denotes an event whose time is posterior to the time of the verb *sacrificaret.* Similarly a present participle with a future main verb

(72) et ego fortasse *discedens* dabo ad te aliquid (Ad Att 10.8.10)

denotes an event (the prestate of) which includes the future time of *dabo,* not the present time of the utterance. A past participle with a future verb means that the time of the participial event is anterior to the future time of the main verb

(73) se... aedemque Matutae Matris *refectam* dedicaturum (Livy 5.19.6)
Hanc igitur partem *relictam* explebimus (De Off 3.34).

No relation to the time of utterance is entailed; so *refectam* in the first example (Livy 5.19) is posterior to the time of utterance, *relictam* in the second example

(71) Immediately the consul M. Geganius, having set out with an army, took a position three miles from the enemy for his camp (Livy 4.9.12). They attacked Fabius while he was fortifying his camp (Livy 9.41.16). When after the completion of the African war he was sacrificing prior to taking his army across there (Livy 21.1.4).

(72) And maybe I will send you some news as I leave (Ad Att 10.8.10).

(73) That he would restore and rededicate the temple of Mater Matuta (Livy 5.19.6). So I will complete this part which was passed over (De Off 3.34).

(De Off 3.34) is anterior to the time of utterance. Similarly a future participle is posterior to a past main verb, but can be anterior, overlapping or posterior to the time of the utterance, as illustrated in Figure 1.9.

Like the pluperfect and the future perfect, the past and future participles commonly have XN/NX semantics. One would then say that for present participles the time of the event includes the reference time, for past participles the poststate of the event includes the reference time, and for future participles the prestate of the event includes the reference time. However, as before not all examples fit this description

(74) binis postridie *amissis* castris (Livy 23.5.6)
media nocte silentio *profectus* ad hostium castra mane pervenit (BG 7.18.2);

the positional temporal adverbials here point to a simple past rather than a perfect ('*He has set out at midnight'). The past participle often has a circumstantial, causal or concessive connotation, and the future participle a modal (teleological) connotation

(75) Marcellus *perterritus* conviciis a sua sententia discessit (BC 1.2)
ipse per agrum Campanum mare inferum petit *oppugnaturus* Neapolim (Livy 23.1.4).

Here is a set of examples illustrating relative tense for infinitives in oratio obliqua

(76) istum bona sua... ex aedibus suis *eripuisse* dixit (Verr 2.2.13)
Quaestorem se... *exspectare* dixit (Verr 2.1.99)
Is mihi dixit se Athenis me *exspectaturum* (Ad Att 6.3.9).

Notice again that the future relative tense after a past verb like *dixit* can denote an event that is past, present or future relative to the time of utterance of the

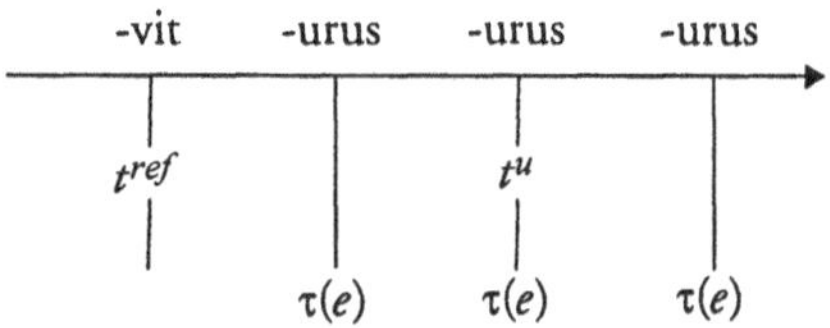

Figure 1.9
Future participle with past verb

(74) When two camps were lost the next day (Livy 23.5.6). Having set out silently at midnight he reached the enemy camp in the morning (BG 7.18.2).

(75) Marcellus, since he was frightened by the harsh criticism, gave up his proposal (BC 1.2). He himself made for the Tuscan Sea across the Campanian territory in order to attack Naples (Livy 23.1.4).

(76) He said that Verres had stolen his property from his house (Verr 2.2.13). He said that he was waiting for his quaestor (Verr 2.1.99). He told me that he would wait for me at Athens (Ad Att 6.3.9).

whole sentence; all that is required is that it be future relative to the time of *dixit*: 'Maharbal said that in four days Hannibal would dine in the Capitol, and so he did/is/will.'

Epistolary tense

The time a message is uttered by the speaker and the time it is received by the hearer pretty much coincide (although transcontinental news interviews have a characteristic time lag). However under exceptional circumstances the two times may be different: you can leave a message on your telephone answering machine saying 'I am in Tahiti' or you can write a suicide note saying 'I am dead.' In that case you would be using the time of the message reception rather than the time of the message production as the anchor time for the computation of tense. In Cicero's letters it is not infrequent for the time of reception of the letter to be chosen as the anchor time; this is not obligatory and the choice between production anchor time and reception anchor time depends on contextual factors. Reception anchor time is particularly frequent in sentences relating to the writing and sending of the letter: the imperfect is used for events that are ongoing at the time of writing, the perfect sometimes for events whose completion is related to the writing of the letter, the past prospective for events that are posterior to the time of writing, and the pluperfect for events that are anterior to the time of writing or for states resulting from an event anterior to the time of writing

(77) Pompeius *erat* apud me cum haec scribebam (Ad Fam 16.10.2)
Exspectabantur litterae tuae (Ad Fam 1.8.7)
Ego has pr. Nonas Quinctiles proficiscens Athenis *dedi* (Ad Att 5.11.4)
Prid. Id. Febr. haec *scripsi* ante lucem. Eo die apud Pomponium in eius nuptiis *eram cenaturus* (Ad Qfr 2.3.7)
Ego, ut ad te pridie *scripseram*, Nonis *constitueram* venire in Puteolanum. (Ad Att 15.28.1)
Unam adhuc a te epistulam *acceperam* (Ad Att 7.12.1).

This is illustrated in Figure 1.10. For instance in the second example (Ad Fam 1.8) the time of production is the same as the reference time ($t^u = t^{ref}$), but the time of reception is later than the reference time ($t^{uR} > t^{ref}$), hence the imperfect is used (*exspectabantur*) rather than the present. Contextual clues are needed to tell which anchor time is being used where there is potential ambiguity ('I'm dead. I'm really sorry I won't get to see you before jumping off a cliff')

(77) Pompey is staying at my house while I write this (Ad Fam 16.10.2). I am waiting for your letter (Ad Fam 1.8.7). I am sending this letter on July 6 as I leave Athens (Ad Att 5.11.4). I have written this letter before dawn on February 12. Today I am going to dine with Pomponius at his wedding party (Ad Qfr 2.3.7). As I wrote to you yesterday, I have decided to go to my house at Puteoli on the seventh (Ad Att 15.28.1). Up to now I have received one letter from you (Ad Att 7.12.1).

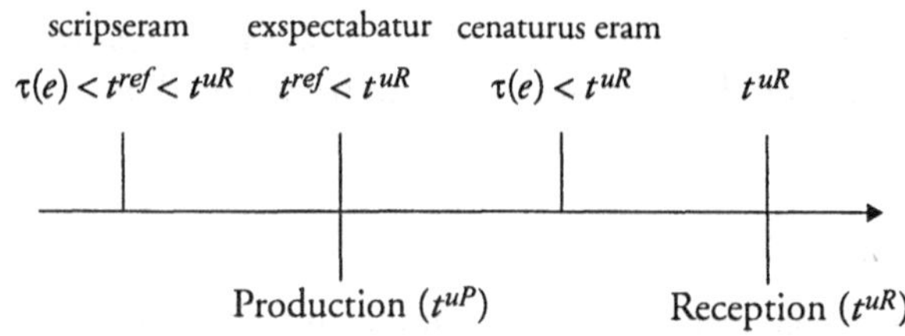

Figure 1.10
Epistolary tenses (cp. Ad Att 15.28, Ad Fam 1.8, Ad Qfr 2.3)

(78) *Nunc* iter *conficiebamus* aestuosa et pulverulenta via. *Dederam* Epheso pridie: has *dedi* Trallibus. In provincia mea fore me putabam Kal. Sextilibus... *Habes* epistulam plenam festinationis et pulveris. (Ad Att 5.14.1)

Hanc epistulam *dictavi* sedens in raeda cum in castra proficiscerer, a quibus *aberam* bidui. Paucis diebus *habebam* certos homines quibus darem litteras... Sed *nunc propero*: *perscribam* ad te paucis diebus. (Ad Att 5.17.1)

The second person present tense *habes* (Ad Att 5.14) has reception anchor time, while the first person present tense *propero* (Ad Att 5.17) has production anchor time. Certain other deictic elements like locative and temporal adverbials can also vary between production and reception deixis

(79) *eo die* cogitabam in Anagnino, *postero* autem in Tusculano (Ad Att 12.1.1)
Cras igitur ad me fortasse veniet (Ad Att 10.10.8)
senatus *hodie* fuerat futurus, id est Kal. Octobribus: iam enim luciscit (Ad Att 4.17.4).

Narrative tense

We have seen that the function of the past tense in narrative is somewhat different from that of the past tense in nonnarrative text. On the one hand there is the additional requirement for reference time update, on the other hand the past tense relation, once established, tends to become redundant. In some languages, a narrative may start with a regular past tense and continue either with

(78) Right now I am travelling on a hot and dusty route. I wrote from Ephesus yesterday; this letter is from Tralles. I think I will be in my province on August 1. The letter you have is all dust and haste (Ad Att 5.14.1). I have dictated this letter sitting in a carriage on my way back to camp, from which I am two days away. In a few days I will have reliable men to give a letter to. But right now I'm in a hurry. I will write fully to you in a few days (Ad Att 5.17.1).

(79) I am thinking of spending today at my place at Anagnia, and tomorrow at my villa at Tusculum (Ad Att 12.1.1). So tomorrow he will perhaps come to me (Ad Att 10.10.8). The senate is going to meet today, that is October 1: for it is already growing light (Ad Att 4.17.4).

forms unmarked for tense, a special narrative past tense, or simply with the present tense. The latter is often called the historical present.

Latin seems to have two slightly different types of historical present. In one type the present can be taken as a semantically tenseless form that picks up its past tense from an associated past tense verb in the syntactic or narrative context. This type has Indo-European origins; it may survive in cases where a historical present is conjoined with a past tense

(80) Caesar... in deditionem Suessiones *accepit* exercitumque in Bellovacos *ducit.* (BG 2.13).

The socalled historical present in some subordinate clauses may also be tenseless in this way. If the past tense picked up by the historical present is definite, it is the past reference time of the narrative. But there is also an existential historical present, in which the past time is indefinite. In the existential historical present, all that is asserted is the occurrence at some point in the past of the event: this seems to be the case in inscriptions on gravestones and monuments and for eventualities occurring in works of literature

(81) aliter enim Naevianus ille *gaudet* Hector... aliter ille apud Trabeam (Tusc 4.67)

(which is perfective on the evidence of English: 'Macbeth kills Duncan in Shakespeare's play').

The other type of historical present is used more consistently throughout a section of narrative. Since use of the historical present is optional, it can cooccur with the past tense. Narratives typically begin and often end with a past time marker, and past tenses can be interspersed among historical presents. The pragmatic conditions for the alternation of historical presents with past tenses have been studied in a number of different languages. In the historical present a copy of the speech time ($t^{\Leftarrow u}$) is transferred to the past situation at the relevant point in the narrative, and tense is computed relative to this transferred anchor, as illustrated in Figure 1.11. It is not the case that the whole discourse context is transferred to the past situation

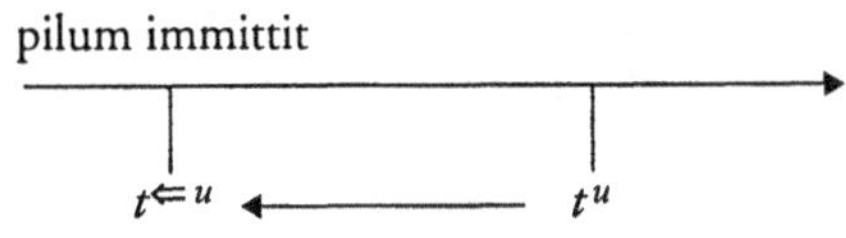

Figure 1.11
Historical present
Pullo pilum in hostes immittit (BG 5.44)

(80) Caesar accepted the surrender of the Suessiones and led his army into the territory of the Bellovaci (BG 2.13).

(81) For Hector rejoices one way in Naevius' play and differently in Trabea's (Tusc 4.67).

(82) *Postridie* homines mane in contionem veniunt (Verr 2.1.68)
Postridie in castra ex urbe ad nos veniunt flentes principes (Pl Amph 256)
Abeo iratus *illinc* (Pl Aul 377: app. crit.).

We find *postridie* rather than *cras* and *illinc* rather than *hinc*. The narration takes the same form as a simultaneous sportscast, with each sequential past event located at the continuously updated anchor point (as in Figure 1.1). Telic events are construed perfectively ($\tau(e) \subseteq t^{ref}$).

(83) Pullo pilum in hostes *immittit* (BG 5.44)
Caesar vallo castra *communit* (BC 1.42),

which is why we use the English simple present rather than the continuous present to translate the Latin historical present: 'Pullo hurls his javelin at the enemy,' 'Caesar fortifies his camp with a rampart,' not 'Pullo is hurling,' 'Caesar is fortifying.' This perfectivity is due to the narrative sequencing of events; it reappears in joke telling ('The Englishman walks over to the Irishman'). Contrast slide shows, where the past is transferred to the present rather than vice versa, the event includes the instant of the snapshot and the imperfective is used ('In this one Churchill is smoking a cigar').

Like regular past tense narrative, narrative structure with historical presents may be more complex than a simple sequence of individual events. There may be plural events where the historical present is overall imperfective (corresponding to an iterative imperfect)

(84) Signa nunc resistentia *deseruntur* ab antesignanis, nunc inter suos manipulos *recipiuntur* (Livy 4.37.11).

Or contiguous sentences may have the same reference time

(85) Tota Italia delectus *habentur*; arma *imperantur*; pecuniae a municipiis *exiguntur*, e fanis *tolluntur* (BC 1.6).

For the historical present, a past time is used as an anchor relative to which present tense is computed. The same shifted anchor in principle licenses use of the future tense for events that are future relative to the anchor but past relative to the unshifted utterance time (future in the past or historical future, see (44) above: $\lambda P \exists e \exists t. P(e) \wedge t \supseteq \tau(e) \wedge t > t^{ref} \wedge t^{ref} < t^{u}$)

(82) On the next day in the morning the people met in an assembly (Verr 2.1.68). The next day the leaders came from the city to our camp weeping (Pl Amph 256). I left there angrily (Pl Aul 377).

(83) Pullo hurled his javelin at the enemy (BG 5.44). Caesar fortified his camp with a rampart (BC 1.42).

(84) Sometimes the standard-bearing soldiers held their ground but were deserted by the front rank troops, sometimes they would fall back among their own maniples (Livy 4.37.11).

(85) Levies are held throughout Italy, arms are requisitioned, funds are exacted from towns and carried off from shrines (BC 1.6).

(86) Annus hic *erit* insignis novi hominis consulatu (Livy 7.1.1)
Turno tempus *erit* magno cum *optaverit* emptum intactum Pallanta (Aen 10.503).

The future in the past is particularly used in verse, where the historical present is a standard narrative tense

(87) Crastina dira quies... undique funestas acies *feret* (Lucan 7.26)
Gentes Mars iste futuras *obruet* (Lucan 7. 389).

A perfect in the past is a narrative pluperfect and a negated perfect in the past can be a narrative future

(88) Respicio et quae sit me circum copia lustro: *deseruere* omnes defessi (Aen 2.564)
Cum venit, aulaeis iam se regina superbis aurea *composuit* sponda mediamque *locavit* (Aen 1.697)
nondum *attigit* arcem (Lucan 7.593).

Time in nominals

Although noun and adjectival predicates tend to be less transient in nature than verbal predicates, in principle all predicates are located in time, that is they may be true of an entity at one time but not at another. For instance, event denoting nouns like *pugna* 'fight,' *mors* 'death' are true of the event at the time of the event ($\tau(e)$), object denoting nouns like *arbor* 'tree,' *pilum* 'javelin' are true of the object throughout its lifespan ($\tau^l(x)$). This can trigger lifetime inferences, which are particularly clear with adjectives

(89) *Tristis* erat (Curt Ruf 6.11.27)
L. Catilina... fuit... *ingenio malo* pravoque (Sall Cat 5.1)
luscus Phryx erat (Mart 6.78.2)
ollam *novam* sumito (Col 12.8.1).

Tristis as used in the first example (Curt Ruf 6.11) is a transient state true for a comparatively short period of time (although it can also be a permanent property): $\tau(e) \subseteq \tau^l(x)$. *Ingenio malo* in the second example (Cat 5.1) is a permanent property true of Catiline throughout his life. *Luscus* (Mart 6.78) is typically a

(86) This year will be notable for the consulship of a *novus homo* (Livy 7.1.1). The time will come for Turnus when he wishes he had paid a great price for the safety of Pallas (Aen 10.503).

(87) Tomorrow his dreams will be frightening, filled with visions of fatal battle (Lucan 7.26). This battle will destroy future peoples (Lucan 7.389).

(88) I looked back and observed what forces were around me; everyone had deserted in exhaustion (Aen 2.564). When he arrived, the queen had already reclined on the golden couch among the sumptuous tapestries and taken her place in their midst (Aen 1.697). He had not yet reached the pinnacle of power (Lucan 7.593).

(89) He was sad (Curt Ruf 6.11.27). L. Catilina had an evil and depraved character (Sall Cat 5.1). Phryx was blind in one eye (Mart 6.78.2). Take an unused pot (Col 12.8.1).

permanent property starting with an event of going blind in one eye; the mirror image of this is *novam* in the last example (Col 12.8) which is a property that is true of the pot from the time it comes into existence until the time it is first used. These distinctions account for the different lifetime inferences associated with different nominal predicates: from 'he was sad' we do not infer that he was dead, but from 'he had an evil character' and 'he was blind in one eye' we infer either that he is dead or that our perspective on his state of blindness/evil-character is limited to the time of the narrative. From 'it was a new pot' we do not infer that it is necessarily broken, but from 'it was a pot' we do infer that it is now broken. An exception arises when the material in an object lives on in a new object fabricated out of the old one

(90) ubi iste post *phasellus* antea fuit comata *silva* (Catull 4.10).

There are also predicates that do not trigger lifetime inferences because they can be true of an individual also (or even only) after his death

(91) L. Brutus patriam liberavit, *praeclarus* auctor nobilitatis tuae (Tusc 4.2).

In most cases the default is for a noun phrase to be interpreted at the reference time of the clause. Typically the time at which the noun phrase is true includes the reference time of the clause ($t^N \supseteq t^{ref}$, but contrast 'He created an explosion'), so part of the noun phrase time equals the clausal reference time (for simplicity $t^N = t^{ref}$)

(92) Paulum *consulem* occidit et aliquos praeterea *consulares* (Nepos 23.4.4)
illud signum conlocandum *consules* illi locaverunt (Cat 3.20).

Paulus was consul at the time he was killed by Hannibal and the others were exconsuls. The consuls in the second example (Cat 3.20) are Cotta and Torquatus, the consuls at the time the contract was made for the new statue of Jupiter. In quantified examples this applies to each event in the set of events

(93) persaepe seditisosis atque improbis *tribunis* plebis boni et fortes *consules* obstiterunt (De Leg Agr 2.14).

In each event of resistance the consuls and the tribunes were in office at the time of the event ('the then consuls'). However there are also examples in which the noun phrase is interpreted at the deictic moment of the utterance instead

(94) Id facio quod *pater meus* fecit cum iuvenis esset (Sen Con 2.6.11)
Quod confido equidem *consules designatos*, simul ut magistratum inierint, esse facturos (Phil 3.2; cp. Livy 43.11.12).

(90) Where what was afterwards this yacht was formerly a leafy forest (Catull 4.10).

(91) L. Brutus, the famous originator of your noble status, liberated the country (Tusc 4.2).

(92) He killed the consul Paulus as well as several exconsuls (Nepos 23.4.4). The consuls at the time put out a contract for setting up that statue (Cat 3.20).

(93) Good and brave consuls have very often resisted seditious and evil tribunes of the people (De Leg Agr 2.14).

(94) I am doing what my father did when he was young (Sen Con 2.6.11). I am sure that the consuls elect will do this as soon as they enter office (Phil 3.2).

The individual who is my father now was not yet my father when he was a young man ($t^N = t^u$, $t^N > t^{ref}$); when the consuls elect enter upon their magistracy, they will no longer be future consuls but current consuls ($t^N = t^u$, $t^N < t^{ref}$). The relationship between the time of the nominal property and the time of interpretation of the noun phrase (either the clausal reference time or the utterance time) need not be inclusion, it may also be anteriority or posteriority; in other words the noun can be interpreted with a covert modifier changing a current property into a past or future property

(95) Scribonius Aphrodisius, Orbili *servus* atque *discipulus*... docuit quo Verrius tempore. (Suet Gramm 19)
Cum haec leges, habebimus *consules* (Ad Att 5.12.2).

Aphrodisius was an exslave and expupil of Orbilius at the time he taught; he was manumitted by Scribonia ($t^N < t^{ref}$). In the second example (Ad Att 5.12) the consuls will actually be *consules designati* at the time Atticus reads the letter ($t^N > t^{ref}$). Note that the temporal interpretation of each noun phrase has to be established independently

(96) Horum *consulum* ruinas vos *consules* vestra virtute fulsistis (Post Red Sen 18).

At the reference time Gabinius and Piso (*horum consulum*) are exconsuls (they were consuls at the time the *ruinae* were created) and Metellus and Lentulus (*vos consules*) are current consuls. In fact noun times can even be mixed in a single plural set

(97) Unus furiosus gladiator... contra quattuor *consules* gerit bellum (Phil 13.16).

The members of the set *quattuor consules* are Hirtius and Pansa (the consuls in 43 B.C.: $t^N = t^{ref}$) and Plancus and D. Brutus (the consuls elect: $t^N > t^{ref}$). A third possibility is for the noun phrase to be interpreted neither at the reference time nor at the utterance time but at some third independent time

(98) Ateius Philologus *libertinus* Athenis est natus. (Suet Gramm 10)
cum *pater familiae* inlustriore loco natus decessit (BG 6.19).

Ateius was not a freedman at the time of his birth nor at the time Suetonius was writing (long after his death), but during his scholarly career ($t^N < t^u$, $t^N > t^{ref}$, $t^N = t'$); he was also an exslave during his scholarly career ($t^N < t'$). The temporal counterpart, so to speak, of the freedman was born at Athens. The second example (BG 6.19) is a quantified version of this: the aristocratic Gauls were fathers

(95) Scribonius Aphrodisius, slave and pupil of Orbilius, taught at the same time as Verrius (Suet Gramm 19). By the time you read this, we will have consuls (Ad Att 5.12.2).

(96) You, the present consuls, propped up the ruins created by these previous consuls through your courage (Post Red Sen 18).

(97) One crazy gladiator is waging war against four consuls (Phil 13.16).

(98) Ateius Philologus, a freedman, was born at Athens (Suet Gramm 10). When a father of aristocratic birth has died (BG 6.19).

at the time they died but not at the time they were born. While nominal event times can be indefinite (existentially quantified: a *consularis* is someone who has been consul at some time in the past), they can also be linked to definite reference times

(99) Si Caesar *vicit*, celeriter me exspecta (Ad Fam 15.19.4)
Uticenses animo addito ex Caesaris *victoria* lapidibus fustibusque equites reppulerunt (BAfr 87).

The victory in the second example (BAfr 87: nominal *victoria*) has to be understood as Caesar's victory at Thapsus, not any of the many other victories in Caesar's career, just as the clausal reference time in the first example (Ad Fam 15.19: verbal *vicit*) anticipates Caesar's victory at Munda.

The denotation of the noun phrase is the set of individuals that has (or had or will have) the property in question at the time of interpretation. Different times of interpretation (t^{ref}, t^u, t') and different temporal relations (=, <, >) potentially give different sets

(100) Trecenti ab hoste *captivi* ad portas nocte venerunt (Sen Con 5.7.pr).

The captives are no longer captives once they escape (whether *ab hoste* is adnominal or adverbial), so the nominal predicate is true at a contextually determined time t^N anterior to the clausal reference time t^{ref}. If all the captives escaped and no new captives were taken, interpreting *captivi* as a property that is current at rather than anterior to the reference time will give the empty set. If some of the captives refused to join the escape, interpreting *captivi* at some time t' during the captivity will likewise give a different set. Then whether 'All the captives reached the gates' or 'Not all the captives reached the gates' is true depends on which time of interpretation is chosen, since the domain of quantification varies with time; similarly for 'The three boldest captives reached the gates.' If some of the escaped captives perished en route to the city, then they have to be thrown out of the denotation of *captivi* (at t^{ref}) too: only live individuals can walk, but dead individuals can be famous, so 'the excaptives are reaching the gates' and 'the excaptives are famous' can have different sets. A similar observation can be made for 'They chained the captives' and 'They buried the captives' at the same reference time.

Anterior and posterior readings are much more difficult to get in predicative nominals and in presentational sentences

(101) Hodie *captivus* essem (Sen Con 1.6.2)
Captivi erant Graeci ad iiii milia fere, quos Persae... volentes regi occurrere non prohibuerant (Curt Ruf 5.5.5).

(99) If Caesar has won, expect me to come soon (Ad Fam 15.19.4). The inhabitants of Utica, encouraged as a result of Caesar's victory, drove back the cavalry with stones and clubs (BAfr 87).

(100) Three hundred captives came from the enemy to the gates at night (Sen Con 5.7.pr).

(101) I would be a captive today (Sen Con 1.6.2). They were up to four thousand Greek captives, whom the Persians had not prevented from going to meet the king when they desired to do so (Curt Ruf 5.5.5).

The first example naturally means 'I would be a captive today.' However in the second example (Curt Ruf 5.5) the Greek captives had been released by the Persians and so were excaptives at the reference time.

So far we have been talking about covert temporal marking on nominals. But it is also possible for precedence relations to be overtly expressed on nominals (while the interpretation time remains covert). This can be done by derivational morphology (*consularis* 'ex-consul') or by modification (*consul designatus* 'consul designate,' *priores et futuri principes* (Tac Hist 1.40) 'past and future emperors'). A famous English example is 'current future ex-boyfriend'; the following Latin examples include purely temporal, deictic and modal modifiers

(102) Est enim narratio aut *praeteritarum* rerum aut *praesentium*, suasio autem *futurarum*. (De Part Or 13)
a verecundia simul *pristinae* dignitatis ac misericordia *praesentis* fortunae (Livy 33.16.8)
ne prius *hesternae* fugae quam *hodiernae* victoriae fama Romam perveniat (Livy 27.13.12)
etsi magis *partam* quam *speratam* gloriam amplecteris (Livy 28.41.5: app. crit.).

FURTHER READING

Copley (2009); Kamp & Reyle (1993:483-689); Klein (1994); Landman (1991: 70-233); Tonhauser (2006).

(102) For narrative involves either the past or the present, but persuasion involves the future (De Part Or 13). Both out of respect for their former high position and out of pity for their present misfortune (Livy 33.16.8). So that the news of yesterday's flight did not reach Rome before the news of today's victory (Livy 27.13.12). Even if you prefer glory that you have already won to glory that you are hoping for (Livy 28.41.5).

2 | ASPECT

While tense is concerned with the temporal location of an eventuality relative to some anchor (by default the utterance time), aspect is concerned with the temporal properties of eventuality structure. Is the eventuality instantaneous or does it have duration? Does it have boundaries? Does it involve a change of state? How does one talk about its initial, medial and terminal phases? Information of an aspectual order surfaces at various linguistic levels. In Latin we may distinguish three layers, defined grosso modo as follows: lexical aspect (eventuality types), syntactic aspect (compositional eventuality types) and morphological aspect (viewpoint aspect). Lexical aspect is the aspectual meaning of verbal roots, independent of their syntactic arguments and adjuncts and independent of their inflectional endings (but including derivational suffixes and prepositional prefixes). Syntactic aspect is the aspectual meaning of a verbal projection (typically the surface or underlying verb phrase) after the verb has been composed with the arguments and adjuncts therein. Morphological aspect comprises the contribution of the verbal inflections to the aspectual meaning of the sentence. Basically the same properties of temporal structure are involved at each layer, but the functions and mechanisms of aspect vary from one layer to another. We will consider each one in turn.

Eventuality types

According to the standard lexicalist analysis, verb roots can be classified into four eventuality types: states, activities, accomplishments and achievements. This classification is nonexclusive, since some verbs can belong to more than one class; so it is not difficult to find contexts in which verbs do not belong to the class to which they are assigned below. States include verbs such as *aegroto* 'be ill,' *albeo* 'be white,' *areo* 'be dry,' *careo* 'be without,' *fulgeo* 'shine,' *gaudeo* 'be happy,' *madeo* 'be wet,' *maneo* 'remain,' *vereor* 'fear,' *vivo* 'live.' States have no internal eventuality structure: they contain no repeated cyclic subevents (contrast *n(at)o* 'float' with *n(at)o* 'swim') and no stages. They do not evolve through time, they are not scalar (increasing and decreasing intensities are processes rather than states), and they have no inbuilt endpoint (telos): contrast *madeo* 'be wet' with *madefacio* 'make wet'; similarly *liqueo* 'be liquid,' *liquefacio* 'make liquid.' States share certain properties with mass nouns: they are strongly homogeneous. A predicate is homogeneous if it is cumulative (upward homogeneous) and divisive (downward homogeneous). A predicate is cumulative if, when it applies to x and y, it also applies to the combination of x with y: $\forall x \forall y . P(x) \wedge P(y) \rightarrow P(x \cup y)$. States are cumulative: if you combine two stative eventualities P, you can just get a larger single state P. A predicate is divisive (on the strongest definition) if, when it applies to x, it also applies to y, any part of x: $\forall x \forall y . P(x) \wedge y \subseteq x \rightarrow P(y)$. States are continuously divisible into identical smaller states. In temporal terms, when a state holds of an interval it also holds of any subinterval of that interval, all the way down to an instant

(1) eos... *punctum temporis* frui vita... non putat oportere (Cat 4.7);

this is known as the subinterval property. States can be seen as the iteration of a predicate applying at an instant. So a period of wetness consists of an infinite number of shorter periods of wetness, and combining two contiguous periods of wetness can give you a larger period of wetness (so long as the result is construable as a single eventuality). In the same way in the nominal domain both parts and sums of wine are wine (see Chapter 6). States may be permanent or temporary, and the same verb can vary according to its argument

(2) *arentem... Libyen* (Lucan 1.687)
aret pellis (Verg Georg 3.501).

Temporary states can be place sensitive as well as time sensitive (your skin may be dry in Libya but not in Norway), while permanent states like being smart or blonde travel with their owners. The boundaries of permanent states are not well defined. Temporary states are bounded and can be explicitly delimited by durative adverbials

(3) aliquot dies *aegrotasse* (Pro Clu 168)
multos annos *quievit* (Brut 16);

they can also be counted

(4) aegrotas uno *decies* aut saepius anno (Mart 12.56.1)
qui *ter* consul fuerat (Livy 3.12.2),

which might be an argument for treating at least some states as autonomous entities like events rather than simply as properties of times. An important related (nontemporal) property of states is that they are not energized: they just obtain, no input of energy is required to be in a state, so states tend to persist. You don't have to do anything to be ill, or tall or blonde, that's just the way you are. A change of state may require energy input and may depend on the volition

(1) He does not think that they ought to enjoy life for an instant of time (Cat 4.7).
(2) To desert Libya (Lucan 1.687). Its skin is dry (Verg Georg 3.501).
(3) That he was ill for a few days (Pro Clu 168). It has lain fallow for many years (Brut 16).
(4) You are ill ten or more times in a single year (Mart 12.56.1). Who had been consul three times (Livy 3.12.2).

and control of an agent, but a change of state is not part of the state. Because of their relative permanence and their nonenergization, it is more difficult, but not impossible, for states to contain gaps (insignificant pauses) than it is for activities.

Activities include verbs such as *cano* 'sing,' *curro* 'run,' *frico* 'rub,' *laboro* 'work,' *latro* 'bark,' *ludo* 'play,' *pugno* 'fight,' *quatio* 'shake,' *rideo* 'laugh,' *salio* 'jump,' *salto* 'dance,' *scrutor* 'scrutinize,' *serpo* 'crawl,' *spargo* 'scatter,' *verbero* 'beat.' Some activities, like *vomerem traho* 'drag the ploughshare,' are both divisive and cumulative just like states: a predicate that is true at an instant iterates with no intrinsic endpoint. The difference is that activities are energized: they start with the onset of the input of energy and terminate with its cessation. Consequently they progress through time, and the rate of progression can be specified adverbially

(5) se *sensim* referebant (Livy 8.8.11: app. crit.)
sensim referre pedem (Livy 22.29.5).

States on the other hand do not progress and do not allow such modification; one can hardly say *sensim in fuga esse.* Other activities consist of repeated minimal cyclic subevents, and so are divisible only down to those minimal subevents. It is these subevents that iterate, so 'walk' is an iteration of steps and 'swim' is an iteration of swim strokes. This is the case for *salio, curro, verbero.* Like states, activities have no inbuilt telos. The energy source does not have to be animate: *undo* and *aestuo* in the sense of 'surge, flood, seethe' are probably activities; activities with an inanimate energy source are sometimes termed processes. Since energy input is not normally permanent, activities can contain gaps and are typically delimited, that is they are instantiated in bounded episodes. The bounds can be overtly specified by durative adverbials

(6) *Tres ferme horas* pugnatum est (Livy 22.5.8)
totum diem oppugnarunt (Livy 40.25.6)

or they can remain implicit

(7) Pugnatum est utrimque fortissime atque acerrime (BC 1.57).

Bounded activities are countable events and as such can appear with container adverbials

(8) sinistra manu sola *quater* pugnavit (NH 7.104)
quater *intra paucos annos* primum pilum duxi (Livy 42.34.11).

An interesting effect of the presence of gaps is that an activity verb sentence need not be literally true at the reference time: *pugnatur* 'fighting is going on'

(5) They would withdraw gradually (Livy 8.8.11). They retreated slowly (Livy 22.29.5).

(6) They fought for about three hours (Livy 22.5.8). They attacked for the whole day (Livy 40.25.6).

(7) They fought with great bravery and vigour on both sides (BC 1.57).

(8) He fought four times with his left hand alone (NH 7.104). I was senior centurion four times within the period of a few years (Livy 42.34.11).

asserts that at the moment of utterance a fight is in progress, not that at the moment of utterance there is literal sword to shield contact.

Accomplishments include verbs such as *aedifico* 'build,' *cingo* 'surround,' *coquo* 'cook,' *deleo* 'destroy,' *inanio* 'empty,' *iungo* 'yoke, join,' *onero* 'load,' *orno* 'equip,' *purgo* 'clean,' *rado* 'shave,' *sepelio* 'bury.' Subjects of transitive accomplishments need not be animate (*frigus gelat aquas* 'the cold freezes the waters'), and subjects of intransitive accomplishments need not be agentive (*sol occidit* 'the sun sets'). Accomplishments consist of a dynamic phase that culminates at some point in a clearly definable resultant state: for instance *navem onero* 'load a ship' involves an activity phase in which cargo is progressively transferred from the shore to the ship and a culmination phase in which the ship is fully loaded. This culmination point is the inbuilt telos; the property of telicity distinguishes accomplishments from activities. Accomplishments are internally complex events in that they contain these two phases; consequently they are not divisive (they have the "antisubinterval" property), and they are not cumulative. Part of an event of building a ship (*quinque naves aedificavi* Petr 76) is not building a ship, and two events of building a ship is building two ships. The boundaries of accomplishments are well defined: the initial boundary coincides with the onset of energy for the activity phase and the terminal boundary coincides with the change of state. However in any particular instantiation of an accomplishment, the input of energy may continue up to the culmination point or it may cease prior to the culmination point. In the latter case the telos is not reached and the accomplishment is effectively reduced to an activity. This becomes explicit with a durational adverbial ('They loaded the ship for three days'), but, even when it is implicit, the distinction can sometimes be recovered from the context

(9) *Legi* tuum nuper quartum De Finibus (Tusc 5.32)
Liber tuus *et lectus est et legitur* a me diligenter (Ad Fam 6.5.1).

In the first example (Tusc 5.32), on the most likely interpretation, the reading of the book was completed, in the second (Ad Fam 6.5) it was not. The ambiguity can be resolved by using a derived verb with a telicizing prefix (see the end of this section) to mark the culmination explicitly (*pellego* 'read through').

What distinguishes the class of accomplishments from the class of achievements is that with achievements a change of state is treated as instantaneous, whereas with accomplishments it is gradual. For canonical accomplishments like verbs of construction (*aedifico, exstruo*) and destruction (*deleo, destruo*), and for verbs of consumption (*comedo, ebibo*), it is typically the case that the direct object is incrementally affected by the verbal action as the event progresses. (We assume that transitive 'build' and 'eat' are intrinsic accomplishments rather than activities that get their telicity from their themes, although when detransitivized they are activities.) If you eat a pea, the event is only minimally gradual, but eating an

(9) I have recently read the fourth book of your *De Finibus* (Tusc 5.32). Your book has been and is being read carefully by me (Ad Fam 6.5.1).

apple is normally incremental: you start off with a whole apple and gradually whittle it down. Similarly if you build a tower (*turrim aedifico* Vitr 5.12.6) or a villa on your farm

(10) Villam urbanam pro copia *aedificato* (Cato 4.1),

you start at the bottom and gradually raise the edifice. Not only does the event progress along with the timeline, but there is a homomorphic mapping from the physical dimensions of the edifice to the temporal progression of the event and vice versa: the mereological structure of the one corresponds to that of the other. Each part of the event of building the tower corresponds to a part of the tower itself; so the tower is called an incremental theme. This is illustrated in Figure 2.1. The details of the correlation can vary according to the noun and the context. One normally assumes a correlation between the progression of the event and the height of the tower as well as its mass, although this would not apply if all the floors of the tower were built separately and then mounted at the end. Incremental structure joins parts together differently from plural structure. Plural structure allows a join to be formed from any two atoms: for instance, if one says 'I built two floors of the tower,' that could mean the second and the fourth floor. By contrast, incremental structure cannot join noncontiguous parts; the second floor can only be joined with the first or third floor. Paths too are incremental

(11) ab urbe proficiscitur *Brundisiumque* pervenit (BC 3.2)
Larisam contendit... ad mare pervenit (BC 3.96).

Each part of the event of a journey from the city to Brindisi and from Larisa to the sea can be mapped onto a corresponding part of the route from one to the other, as illustrated in Figure 2.2. Backtracking and coffee breaks are not relevant in this computation.

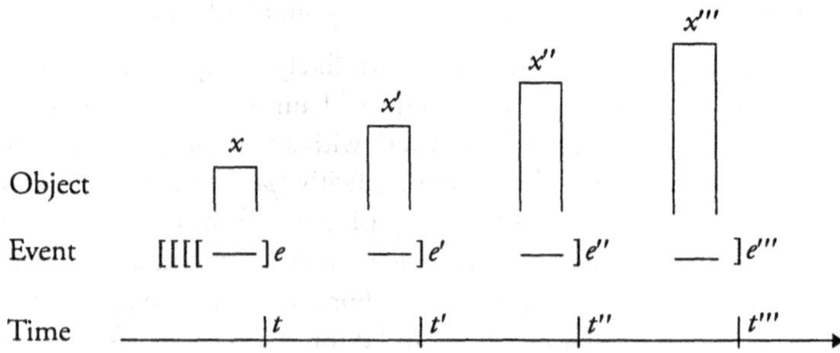

Figure 2.1
Incremental theme
Turrim aedificare (cp. Vitr 5.12.6)

(10) Build the living quarters according to your means (Cato 4.1).
(11) He left the city and went to Brundisium (BC 3.2). He hurried to Larisa; he reached the sea (BC 3.96).

Path	${}_{\text{Urbs}}[[[[\text{—}]\pi$	$\text{—}]\pi'$	$\text{—}]\pi''$	$\text{—}]\pi'''_{\text{Brundisium}}$
Event	$[[[[\text{—}]e$	$\text{—}]e'$	$\text{—}]e''$	$\text{—}]e'''$
Time	$\vert t$	$\vert t'$	$\vert t''$	$\vert t''' \rightarrow$

Figure 2.2
Incremental path
Ab urbe proficiscitur Brundisiumque pervenit (BC 3.2)

Just as not all telic events are incremental (achievements are not), so not all incremental events are telic: *augeo* 'increase' is incremental but not telic, since there is no inbuilt point at which it culminates; the verb is based on an open scale. Other scalar verbs like 'heat, warm, melt, freeze, cook,' etc. are based on a closed scale but can vary between telic and atelic readings, with the telic reading enforced by a telicizing prepositional prefix

(12) prius abis quam lectus ubi cubuisti *concaluit* locus (Pl Amph 513)
dolium *calfacito* minus quam si picare velis... lenibus lignis facito *calescat* (Cato 69.2).

In the first example (Amph 513) prefixed *concaleo* means 'become fully warm'; in the second example (Cato 69.2), as the context shows, both verbs are atelic; warming needs to stop before the jar is fully warm. In general these verbs denote iterated changes of state from lower to higher degrees along the scale in question.

Achievements, according to the definition adopted here, are (more or less) punctual versions of any of the three above classes. States can hardly be punctual, but punctual changes of state are fine. These include verbs such as *aspicio* 'notice,' *conticeo* 'fall silent,' *intellego* 'realize,' *morior* 'die,' *perio* 'perish,' *sentio* 'become aware of.' Like English 'touch,' *attingo* can be used either as a change of state (achievement, eventive) or as a state. Punctual versions of activities include verbs such as *contingo* 'touch,' *emico* 'shoot out,' *nicto* 'blink,' *nuto* 'nod,' *sternuo* 'sneeze.' Some of these verbs vary between achievement and activity readings: the semelfactive reading of 'cough' ('give a cough') is an achievement, the iterative reading ('do coughing') is an activity. Punctual versions of accomplishments include *findo* 'split,' *frango* 'break,' *ignosco* 'pardon,' *neco* 'kill,' *nubo* 'marry,' *pungo* 'prick,' *rumpo* 'burst,' *trado* 'hand over.' What constitutes punctuality is not quite the same for each class of achievement. For states it is the instantaneous change of state, which can be thought of as occurring at an instant or at the transition from one instant to another. For activities it is a momentary

(12) You are leaving before the part of the bed where you lay has got warm (Pl Amph 513). Heat the jar less than if you wanted to coat it with pitch; let it warm over a slow wood fire (Cato 69.2).

act; so semelfactives have the duration of the minimal cyclic event of the activity in question, which is obviously much longer than an instant. For accomplishments, any duration there may be in the activity phase is disregarded, so all that remains is the instantaneous change of state. A verb can vary between achievement and accomplishment depending on its direct object or even on specifics of the physical context. For instance *frango* is probably an achievement in *crustallinum frango* 'break a glass' (Sen De Ira 3.40.2) and an accomplishment in *fores frango* 'break down the door' (Pl Amph 1022).

It is also common for unprefixed verbs to belong to one class and prefixed verbs to another: *eo* 'go,' *transeo* 'cross,' *ineo* 'enter,' *obeo* 'meet'; *pugno* 'fight,' *expugno* 'take by storm'; *bello* 'wage war,' *debello* 'subdue.' In these examples the unprefixed verb is atelic (activity) and intransitive, the prefixed verb is telic (accomplishment or achievement) and transitive. The prefixed verbs may have opaque, lexically idiosyncratic meanings. Not all cases involve a change in valency: *dormio* 'sleep,' *obdormisco* 'fall asleep.' (In other cases an unprefixed verb is lexically telic and addition of the prefix serves as an explicit marker of complete culmination: *morior* 'die,' *emorior* 'perish.') The unprefixed forms may allow both telic and atelic readings, as in (9) above, while the prefixed forms enforce the telic reading. This distinction can then be exploited, particularly in earlier Latin, to encode viewpoint aspect, as happens systematically in Slavic and some other languages. The telicizing function of the prefix is comparable to that of English verbal particles in 'pick, pick up; chew, chew up; run, run down; polish, polish off.' These English particles are distinct from prepositions ('pick it up, *pick up it; climb up it, *climb it up') and the meaning of the verb plus particle combination is not necessarily transparent ('polish off'). Like the English particles, the Latin telicizing prefixes lexicalize the resultant state subevent (see Chapter 3).

Compositional eventuality types

So far in our classification of verbs according to their eventuality type, we have considered verbs in isolation, without taking account of ways in which arguments or adjuncts might influence the classification: we were working with an idealized or default version of the predicate meaning. This is particularly true for verbs taking incremental themes (*urbem deleo* 'destroy the city') or goal of motion complements (*curro ad praetorium* 'run to the governor's house'). Consider first the following sets of examples with incremental themes

(13) Legi *orationes duas tuas* (Ad Brut 3.4)
orationes scripsit *aliquot* (Brut 286)
iam *tres libros* absolverat (Pliny Ep 5.5.3)
orationes eum scribere aliis coepisse (Brut 48)

(13) I have read your two speeches (Ad Brut 3.4). He wrote some speeches (Brut 286). He had already finished three books (Pliny Ep 5.5.3). That he began to write speeches for others (Brut 48).

(14) eos *quorum urbes* barbari delessent (Curt Ruf 5.7.3)
ignobilia oppida Lucanorum aliquot expugnavit (Livy 25.1.5)
Celtiberi... *tria oppida* vi expugnant (Livy 22.21.7)
castra urbesque primo impetu rapere (Livy 6.23.5)

(15) *id vinum* condito in dolia lauta (Cato 112)
cum *vinum* biberint (NH 30.149).

In the first example of each set (Ad Brut 3.4; Curt Ruf 5.7; Cato 112) the direct object is definite. In the second example of (13) and (14) (Brut 286; Livy 25.1) it has an indefinite quantifier (*aliquot*), while in the third example (Pliny 5.5; Livy 22.21) it is a cardinal (*tres*). In the last example of (13) and (14) (Brut 48; Livy 6.23) it is a nonspecific indefinite plural, corresponding to an English bare plural ('speeches,' 'cities'); in the last example of (15) (NH 30.149) it is a mass noun ('wine'). In each set the last example is atelic ('write speeches,' 'sack cities,' 'drink wine' are activities), while the other examples are either telic like the corresponding singular ('read your two speeches,' 'destroy their cities,' 'bottle that wine' are accomplishments) or a delimited sequence of telic events ('finish three books,' 'storm three towns'). If you storm three towns, then there is a set of subevents each of which contains a point at which the town is destroyed, the telos of the subevent is reached, and you can move on to the next one. This is the event-distributive reading. There is an iteration of telic events but the macroevent is not an unbounded activity because it is delimited by the cardinal numeral. There is also a collective reading. If you destroy two contiguous cities all together in one fell swoop (collective reading), then there is a single telic event of destruction, and when the incremental theme is fully destroyed, the event has culminated: this might happen in an earthquake

(16) Illa vasta concussio quae *duas* suppressit *urbes*, Helicen et Burin (Sen NQ 6.25.4).

But a bare plural ('destroy cities') does not specify any particular cities or any particular number of cities that got destroyed; and a mass noun ('drink wine') does not specify any particular wine or any particular quantity of wine that got drunk. There is no inbuilt telos to reach, the object is not independently referential ('the cities') nor is there any delimiting quantifier ('three cities'). Destroying cities, like shooting ducks or guzzling gas, describes an activity; the nonreferential bare plural or mass noun (type <e, t>) is probably just incorporated into the verb (type <et, et>), giving a complex predicate, rather like the compounds 'duckshooting' and 'gasguzzling.' The relevance of independent reference and quantification is confirmed by occasional leakages from these categories: 'wash the dishes' and 'wash some (sm) dishes' are activities when the object is not interpreted as ref-

(14) Those whose cities the barbarians had destroyed (Curt Ruf 5.7.3). He stormed some minor Lucanian towns (Livy 25.1.5). The Celtiberi took three towns by storm (Livy 22.21.7). To storm camps and cities on the first assault (Livy 6.23.5).

(15) Store that wine in washed jars (Cato 112). When they have drunk wine (NH 30.149).

(16) That huge earthquake, which wiped out two cities, Helice and Buris (Sen NQ 6.25.4).

erential or as a countable set. So for these incremental theme verbs the eventuality type depends on the meaning of the whole verb phrase predicate, not just on the meaning of the verb. One could say that these verbs are basically telic, but that they get detelicized if they take bare plural or mass noun objects. (The alternative is to say that these verbs are basically atelic, or are unmarked (neutral) for telicity, and pick up their telicity from their theme arguments.) *Urbes delevit* meaning 'he destroyed cities' and *vinum biberunt* meaning 'they drank wine' are temporally delimited activities, not culminated accomplishments. In fact bare plural accomplishments do not necessarily entail any telic culmination: you can say 'Jack wrote papers all last week without finishing a single one,' whereas 'Jack wrote some papers' does entail his finishing them. *Aliquot* like *multi* is a vague quantifier: it denotes a countable set of entities, even if the cardinality of the set is not specified, just as *aliquantum* and *multum* denote a mass that is delimited rather than unbounded.

Punctual telic verbs (achievements) with bare plurals can also become atelic, like 'pop balloons' where the iteration of a telic achievement gives an atelic activity; the effect even extends to transitive subjects ('Guests noticed the spot on the carpet all evening'). This iteration of events in a macroevent can be compared to the iteration of minimal subevents in an activity event like 'swim.' However in other cases a single episode (existential) reading is easier ('He noticed spots on the carpet'). Certain case distinctions can also cue activity versus accomplishment status

(17) *duo tresve cyathos...* bibant (Cels 1.8.3)
hoc eodem poculo quo ego bibi (Pl Cas 933).

In the first example (Cels 1.8) the accusative direct object is the incremental theme of an accomplishment, in the second example (Cas 933) the ablative is the source phrase of an activity.

We have seen that a bare plural makes the event atelic (*urbes... cepit* 'he captured cities' Pro Mur 20), whereas a quantifier adds a bound to an event plurality (*aliquot urbes... cepit* Livy 9.42). Note that with some qualifications *aliquot urbes capere* is both cumulative and divisive: *aliquot urbes* + *aliquot urbes* = *aliquot urbes* (although at some point there will be pragmatic pressure for *multas* or *omnes*) and *aliquot urbes* – *aliquot urbes* = *aliquot urbes* (excluding the singular). Although homogeneity is an inherent property of activities, the quantifier is able to override it: there just has to have been a countable set of cities captured, it doesn't matter if you don't know the exact number. The only way for *aliquot urbes capere* to get a (noniterative) atelic interpretation would be if it could have a reading where it is a prescribed activity or task, like 'write some papers for a few days.' In the same way, cardinals that are upward entailing relative to other cardinals like *ducenti amplius* 'more than two hundred' (Livy 44.31.9) are cumulative, and downward entailing cardinals like *minus centum*

(17) Should drink two or three cups (Cels 1.8.3). From the same cup that I drank from (Pl Cas 933).

'less than a hundred' (Livy 39.18.9) are divisive, but as themes both serve to delimit eventualities; so a general rule licensing durative adverbials with cumulative and/or divisive predicates would not apply to these cases.

A similar change working in the opposite direction is found with goal of motion complements, which have the effect of telicizing basically atelic verbs

(18) Ibam forte *Via Sacra* (Hor Sat 1.9.1)
cum *Sacra Via* descenderem (Ad Att 4.3.3)
ibat *in Graeciam* (Ad Att 8.8.1)
in pacatum Soranum agrum pabulatores ibant (Livy 10.33.7)

(19) qui *per Assorinorum agros* fluit (Verr 2.4.96)
is *inter montes...* fluit (Livy 32.5.11)
si lacus Albanus... *in mare* fluxisset (De Div 2.69)

(20) *per maria* manaret (ND 1.40)
in mare manare (Livy 5.16.8).

The first two examples in (18) (Sat 1.9; Ad Att 4.3) include a path (*Via Sacra* 'along the Sacred Way') but no goal, the other two examples (Ad Att 8.8, Livy 10.33) have a goal of motion argument (*in Graeciam* 'into Greece,' *in Soranum agrum* 'into the territory of Sora'). Similarly in (19) (which involves the motion of a fluid mass rather than a solid bounded object) and (20) *per agros* 'through the fields,' *inter montes* 'between the mountains,' *per maria* 'through the seas' are path expressions, while *in mare* 'into the sea' is a goal expression. The simple path expression has no effect on the eventuality type, which remains an activity ('walk along the Sacred Way,' 'flow between the mountains'). But the addition of a goal of motion argument changes the activity into an accomplishment by providing a specific telos. If and when Pompey gets to Greece and the overflowing Alban Lake reaches the sea, the event culminates and terminates at that point. Note that for the accomplishment reading to click in there has to be an actual goal of motion; a simple direction like 'northwards' is not sufficient, since it does not include a telos

(21) Pompeiani... universi iugis eius *Larisam versus* se recipere coeperunt (BC 3.97)
equites cedere seque *in castra* recipere iubet (BG 5.50).

In the first example (BC 3.97) we have an activity ('retreat in the direction of Larisa'), in the second (BG 1.25) an accomplishment ('retreat into camp'). Events having paths that end in a goal are telic, but they are not necessarily non-

(18) I was walking by chance on the Sacred Way (Hor Sat 1.9.1). When I was going down the Sacred Way (Ad Att 4.3.3). He is making for Greece (Ad Att 8.8.1). The foragers went to the peaceful territory of Sora (Livy 10.33.7).

(19) Which flows through the territory of the people of Assorus (Verr 2.4.96). It flows between the mountains (Livy 32.5.11). That if the Alban Lake flowed into the sea (De Div 2.69).

(20) It flows through the seas (ND 1.40). To flow into the sea (Livy 5.16.8).

(21) All the Pompeians began to retreat towards Larisa on its ridges (BC 3.97). He ordered the cavalry to yield and to withdraw into camp (BG 5.50).

divisive. Consider again the journey from Rome to Brindisi in the first example in (11). An event of travelling from Venosa to Brindisi is a proper part of an event of travelling from Rome to Brindisi (given that you would use the Via Appia). It is in the denotation of the predicate 'travel' and also of the predicate 'travel to Brindisi,' but not of the predicate 'travel from Rome to Brindisi.' So whether 'travel to Brindisi' is divisive or not depends on whether there is an open beginning or an implicit specific starting point for the path, which in most contexts there would be. Similar qualifications apply to temporal delimitation. A shorter running event included in a longer one is itself a running event (similarly for 'run till midnight'), but an event of running for two minutes included in an event of running for four minutes is not itself an event of running for four minutes.

The atelic and telic versions of verbs of motion have different event structures. The atelic version is a simple activity (unergative, nonoriented motion), the telic version additionally projects a resultant state subevent for the goal and so is a change of location verb (unaccusative, oriented motion). Latin (like English but unlike some other languages) also allows goal phrases with some agentive manner of motion verbs

(22) *in portu Syracusano* piraticus myoparo navigavit (Verr 2.3.186)
his navibus Flaccus ex Asia *in Macedoniam* navigavit (Pro Flacc 32)
vacua volat altus *in aura* spiritus (Ov Trist 3.3.61)
Caere vulturium volasse *in aedem Iovis* (Livy 27.23.3).

The first example in each pair has a simple place-where locative, the second has a goal. The goal examples look like genuine change of location structures ('a vulture flew into the temple of Jupiter'), rather than activities with adjunct goals ('a vulture flew around until it got inside the temple of Jupiter'), so they may be unaccusative rather than unergative like the first examples.

Delimitation and containment of eventualities

As already noted, a durative (time-how-long) adverbial can explicitly delimit an activity

(23) *per quattuor horas* pugnatum (Livy 23.40.10)
Hic *paulisper* est pugnatum (BC 3.67).

No telos is introduced, and the activity remains an activity; it does not change into an accomplishment, but just becomes temporally bounded. States can be delimited by a durative adverbial in the same way

(22) The pirates' ship sailed around in the harbour of Syracuse (Verr 2.3.186). Flaccus sailed from Asia to Macedonia in these ships (Pro Flacc 32). The spirit flies on high in the empty air (Ov Trist 3.3.61). That at Caere a vulture had flown into the temple of Jupiter (Livy 27.23.3).

(23) They fought for four hours (Livy 23.40.10). They fought here for a short time (BC 3.67).

(24) Ille vult diu vivere, hic *diu* vixit (De Sen 68)
Naxium *diu* placuit ante alia (NH 36.54).

Because they are divisive, activities and states satisfy the subinterval clause in the quantificational definition of durative adverbials given in Chapter 1. Telic eventuality types are not compatible with durative adverbials because the delimitation conflicts with the intrinsic telos: the event is over not when the agent feels like stopping but when the telos is attained. Duratives can occur with telic eventualities only to the extent that secondary readings are available. In the case of accomplishments this would mean that the durative modifies not the whole event but either the process subevent ('He unloaded the truck for half an hour, but didn't finish the job') or the resultant state ('He took the dog to the park for half an hour'). Change of state achievements are instantaneous and so the process subevent is not compatible with duratives ('I noticed the spot on the carpet in / *for a second'), but semelfactive achievements are compatible with duratives ('The spark flashed for a second'). Iteratives create a macroevent which is atelic, so outer durative adverbials are licensed with telic events in iterative contexts ('He unloaded the truck for several days'): iterated telic events are delimitable activities.

Now let's consider container (time-within-which) adverbials. When these are used with a perfective verb (as they normally are), on their inner reading they serve to specify the maximum time taken to attain the telos: they provide a right bound for the interval including the event but not an endpoint. This reading is definitionally unavailable for atelic eventualities (states and activities): activities have to be coerced into accomplishments ('The gladiator fought in five minutes'). It is available for accomplishments but not for achievements (since they have minimal or no duration)

(25) Numidae *paucis diebus* iussa efficiunt (Sall Jug 24.1)
Marius... in Africam profectus *paucis diebus* Uticam advehitur (Sall Jug 86.4)
paucis diebus... quinqueremes v confecerunt (BAlex 13).

Negation expresses failure of the event to occur with the specified interval

(26) quae *intra quinquennium* non peperit (Sen Con 2.5.15).

In their outer reading container adverbials with a perfective verb express the interval from the reference time to the onset of an eventuality or its complete occurrence. They are compatible not only with telic events

(24) The former wants to live for a long time, the latter has already lived for a long time (De Sen 68). The Naxian one was for a long time prized above the others (NH 36.54).

(25) The Numidians carried out his commands in a few days (Sall Jug 24.1). Marius having set out for Africa reached Utica in a few days (Sall Jug 86.4). They built five quinqueremes in a few days (BAlex 13).

(26) She who has not borne children within five years (Sen Con 2.5.15).

(27) Perscribam ad te *paucis diebus* omnia (Ad Att 5.17.2)
Et ipse *paucis diebus* eodem profectus est (Sall Jug 35.9)
paucisque diebus interiturum Alexandrum (De Div 1.53),

but also with states, expressing the interval from the reference time to the onset of the state

(28) Fracta classis, et *intra paucos dies* natavit nova (Sen De Ben 6.32.3)
alterum... necesse est *paucis diebus* paeniteat audere (De Prov 15)
video nos *paucis diebus* in armis fore. (Ad Att 16.8.1).

Negation of this type expresses cessation of the state before the end of the interval in question

(29) neve quis... in urbe... *intra certam diem* maneret (Livy 26.34.7).

Outer container adverbials are again difficult with activities, but they are quite common with a future progressive in English ('In a few days he will be fighting in Gaul').

Both telic and delimited events are countable ('They captured the city three times,' 'They fought for four hours three times'), and both types of plural events can be used with container adverbials ('They captured the city three times in a year,' 'They fought for four hours three times in a year'). Nevertheless it is probably inadvisable to conflate telicity with delimitation (and both need to be kept distinct from perfectivity). Delimitation (temporal or spatial) just measures the bounds of an activity ('He marched for five minutes/a mile'), while a telos is an inbuilt endpoint of the event. The endpoint of a (goal-free) running event depends on a decision of the runner, the endpoint of reading the first Eclogue is line 83. The difference surfaces clearly with the progressive (in its more usual noncommensurate reading). You can say 'He was capturing the city' or 'He was travelling to Brindisi,' but 'He was fighting for four hours (at that time)' and 'He was marching a mile' do not make sense in a simple delimitative reading, only if the duration and the extent are part of a prescribed or preplanned task. Likewise 'He was capturing three cities' is infelicitous unless it is presupposed that the number of cities to be captured is three. This is because you do not know how far someone is going to march until they finish marching, unless the march has preassigned temporal or spatial limits, and you do not know how many cities someone is going to capture until he has captured the last one, so long as they are being attacked sequentially rather than collectively. Delimitation just measures, telicity entails a predictable point at which the event culminates. You can locate the reference time either at some point during a process or

(27) I will let you know everything in a few days (Ad Att 5.17.2). A few days later he himself set out for the same place (Sall Jug 35.9). And that Alexander would die within a few days (De Div 1.53).

(28) His fleet was wrecked and in a few days a new one was afloat (Sen De Ben 6.32.3). The other is bound to regret daring to do so within a few days (De Prov 15). I see that within a few days we will be under arms (Ad Att 16.8.1).

(29) And that noone should remain in the city beyond a certain date (Livy 26.34.7).

at its termination/culmination, but you cannot locate it at both points simultaneously.

Viewpoint aspect

Up to this point we have been looking at eventualities in the abstract, unhitched from any discourse context. But when we use predicates in actual discourse, they are located in space and time; everything happens somewhere and at some time. So the various eventuality types have to be linked to a reference time (and a reference location) in order to be interpreted in a real discourse context. Viewpoint aspect comprises the different ways in which eventualities can be linked to reference times. The two basic viewpoint aspects are perfective and imperfective. For the perfective aspect the run time of the event is included in or coincides with the reference time, $\tau(e) \subseteq t^{ref}$: the event is seen as a bounded whole occurring within or at the reference time

(30) Eo anno rex Prusia *venit* Romam cum filio Nicomede (Livy 45.44.4)
Celtiberi inde nocte proxima *moverunt* castra (Livy 39.21.7).

The arrival of King Prusias at Rome occurs at a reference time included in the adverbial time of that year; the Celtiberi move camp at a reference time included in the adverbial time of the following night. The perfective aspect is encoded by use of the simple past tense (*venit, moverunt*). This is illustrated in Figure 2.3; compositionally, the perfective is a function that takes the lexical verb phrase meaning $\lambda e.P(e)$ and returns a perfective verb phrase $\lambda e.P(e) \wedge \tau(e) \subseteq t^{ref}$. Conversely for the imperfective aspect the reference time is included in or commensurate with the run time of the event, $t^{ref} \subseteq \tau(e)$: consequently it can be located at one of the internal stages into which the event is structured

(31) Thaumacos eo tempore Philippus summa vi *oppugnabat* (Livy 32.3.7)
Coracesium eo tempore Antiochus operibus *oppugnabat* (Livy 33.20.4).

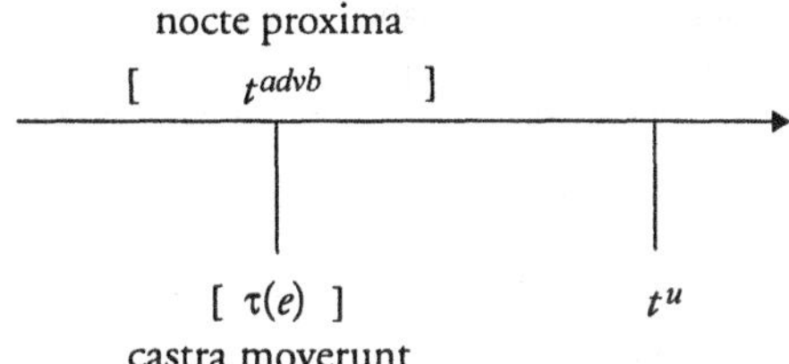

Figure 2.3
Perfective aspect
Celtiberi nocte proxima moverunt castra (Livy 39.21.7)
$\exists e.\text{Mov}(e, \text{Celt}, \text{Castra}) \wedge \tau(e) \subseteq t^{ref} \wedge t^{ref} \subseteq t^{advb} \wedge t^{ref} < t^{u}$

(30) In this year King Prusias came to Rome with his son Nicomedes (Livy 45.44.4). The Celtiberi moved their camp from there the next night (Livy 39.21.7).

(31) At that time Philip was besieging Thaumaci with maximum force (Livy 32.3.7). At that time Antiochus was besieging Coracesium with siege-works (Livy 33.20.4).

Philip's siege of Thaumaci and Antiochus' siege of Coracesium are in progress at the reference time, which coincides with the adverbial time (*eo tempore*), so that the run time of the event frames the reference time. The imperfective aspect is encoded by use of the imperfect tense (*oppugnabat*). This is illustrated in Figure 2.4. In the examples in (30) and (31) the reference time is overtly given in the text. If, as is often the case, it is not explicitly stated, then it has to be derived from the discourse context, for instance on the basis of the most recent event in a narrative sequence. In narrative, perfectively presented past eventualities usually (but not always) advance the reference time, imperfectively presented eventualities (progressives, most states, habituals) do not. Just like tense, viewpoint aspect cannot be interpreted without a reference time (whereas lexical and syntactic aspect are in principle independent of the reference time).

The definition of the aspects given above overlaps when event time and reference time are commensurate, but there is a slight difference. With the perfective an adverbial (temporal clause) delimits the interval occupied by an atelic eventuality, with the imperfective it expresses an interval at all points during which the eventuality is asserted to be ongoing. The definition of perfective aspect ($\tau(e) \subseteq t^{ref}$) ensures that, although the event time may be commensurate with the reference time, it does not spill over the boundaries of the reference time (see Figure 2.5): an event *P* cannot start before the left hand boundary of the reference time nor terminate after its right hand boundary (if it does, some form of corrective amplification will be required to include this fact in the assertion)

(32) pro tua in me observantia, quam penitus *perspexi* quamdiu Brundisii *fuimus* (Ad Fam 13.50.1)
quoad *potuit*, fortissime *restitit* (BG 4.12)
quoad *vixit*, virtutum laude *crevit* (Nepos 24.2.4)
Romani et Eumenes, quoad sufficere remiges *potuerunt*... satis pertinaciter *secuti sunt* (Livy 36.45.2).

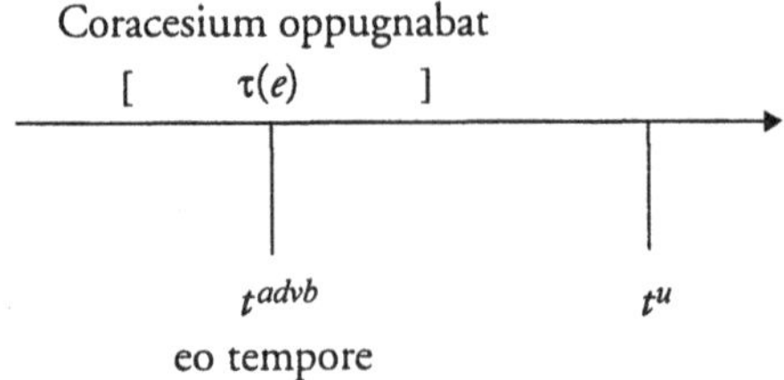

Figure 2.4
Imperfective aspect
Coracesium eo tempore Antiochus oppugnabat (Livy 33.20.4)
$\exists e.\text{Opp}(e,\text{Ant},\text{Cor}) \wedge t^{ref} \subseteq \tau(e) \wedge t^{ref} = t^{advb} \wedge t^{ref} < t^{u}$

(32) In accordance with your respect for me, which I saw clearly the whole time I was at Brundisium (Ad Fam 13.50.1). He resisted very bravely for as long as he could (BG 4.12). His reputation kept growing for as long as he lived (Nepos 24.2.4). The Romans and Eumenes pursued quite resolutely so long as the rowers' strength lasted (Livy 36.45.2).

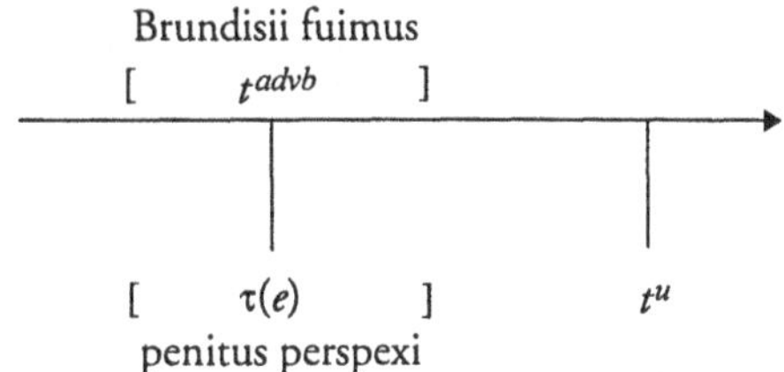

Figure 2.5
Commensurate intervals in perfective aspect
Penitus perspexi quamdiu Brundisii fuimus (Ad Fam 13.50.1)
$\exists e.\text{Persp}(e, \text{Ego}, \text{Obs}) \wedge \tau(e) = t^{ref} \wedge t^{ref} = t^{advb} \wedge t^{ref} < t^u$

The definition of the imperfective aspect ($t^{ref} \subseteq \tau(e)$) permits, but does not require, the event time to extend beyond the initial and/or final moments of the reference time: the event time may (but need not) overlap or include the reference time. We find the imperfect for commensurate intervals mostly with iteratives and distributives, habituals and the activity subevent of accomplishments, but also with states that can easily spill over the endpoints of the reference time

(33) cum *exhauriebas* aerarium, cum *orbabas* Italiam iuventute... si triumphum *contemnebas* (In Pis 57)
is exitus quem vir fortissimus, M. Antonius, iam tum *timebat* cum tantum instare malorum *suspicabatur* (Ad Fam 6.2.2).

Although in principle each of the four eventuality types can be used either perfectively or imperfectively, different eventuality types may be more or less compatible with one or the other viewpoint aspect, and particular nuances of meaning can result from the way in which the temporal structure of an eventuality type interfaces with a viewpoint aspect. If a regular interpretation is difficult, a secondary reading may become available through coercion. Since states extend through time, they are often used imperfectively, but completed states can also be seen from a perfective viewpoint

(34) et illam ducere *cupiebat* et *metuebat* absentem patrem (Ter Phorm 117)
Iure tum *florebat* populi Romani nomen (Div Caec 69)
in Graecia musici *floruerunt* (Tusc 1.4)
Amavi curam et sollicitudinem tuam (Pliny Ep 5.6.1).

(33) When you were exhausting the treasury and robbing Italy of its youth, if you despised a triumph (In Pis 57). That outcome which the excellent M. Antonius already feared when he suspected that so great a calamity was looming (Ad Fam 6.2.2).

(34) He both desired to marry her and was afraid of his absent father (Ter Phorm 117). At that time the name of the Roman people was justifiably renowned (Div Caec 69). Musicians flourished in Greece (Tusc 1.4). I appreciated your care and concern (Pliny Ep 5.6.1).

The second example (Div Caec 69) is imperfective, the third (Tusc 1.4) perfective, and the last is episodic perfective (as in 'I liked that movie'). Perfectivity in Latin is quite compatible with durational extension of a state

(35) nonaginta *vixit* annos (Luc 16)
complures annos Sueborum vim *sustinuerunt* (BG 4.4).

As already noted, delimited states can be counted, with the plural events expressed by cardinal adverbs or vague quantifiers

(36) ter omnino per quattuordecim annos *languit* (Suet 6.51.1)
Interdum *timui* ne... mersa foret cana naufraga puppis aqua (Ov Her 2.15)
Homines maritimi Syracusis, qui saepe istius ducis nomen audissent, saepe *timuissent* (Verr 2.5.65).

Perfective states can also get an inceptive-like reading (cp. Italian *ho conosciuto* 'I got to know')

(37) cum *amaverunt*, iudicant (Sen Ep 3.2)
prudentiam novi dictatoris extemplo *timuit* (Livy 22.12.6: app. crit.).

Similarly perfect participles of deponents like *veritus* 'fearing,' *ratus* 'thinking' denote the state resulting from an anterior change of state. Delimited states are still states (the terminal change of state is an implicature), while true inceptives are changes of state, therefore telic. Activities too are commonly used both imperfectively and perfectively

(38) Missilibus enim Lacedaemonii *pugnabant* (Livy 34.39.2)
Pedites ab dextro cornu egregie *pugnavere* (Livy 3.70.3).

In the first example (Livy 34.39) the fighting frames the reference time: this type of imperfective is called the progressive. (Other types of imperfective will be discussed later.) For the event to be in the progressive aspect, it must already be underway and not yet terminated, although the reference time may turn out to be the final instant in the event if the event is interrupted at that point. While the progressive requires some degree of durativity, durational extension is no obstacle to a perfective viewpoint

(35) He lived for ninety years (Luc 16). They withstood the attacks of the Suebi for several years (BG 4.4).

(36) He was ill no more than three times in fourteen years (Suet 6.51.1). Sometimes I feared that your ship had gone down wrecked in the foaming waters (Ov Her 2.15). The seafaring people at Syracuse, who had often heard the name of this leader and often feared it (Verr 2.5.65).

(37) When they have made friends, they form a judgement (Sen Ep 3.2). He was immediately worried by the prudence of the new dictator (Livy 22.12.6).

(38) For the Lacedaemonians were fighting with missiles (Livy 34.39.2). The infantry on the right wing fought exceptionally well (Livy 3.70.3).

(39) summa vi totum diem *oppugnarunt* (Livy 40.25.6)
aequis viribus per aliquot horas *pugnarunt* (Livy 31.33.9)
diu pugnam ancipitem Poeni... *fecerunt* (Livy 23.40.10).

The adverbial serves to quantify the activity by delimiting it, which induces a perfective viewpoint.

Since accomplishments are telic, they have a natural affinity with the perfective viewpoint, but they can be used progressively too

(40) ibique hiberna *aedificavit* (Livy 23.48.2)
Galli... oppidum in agro qui nunc est Aquileiensis *aedificabant*. Id ut eos prohiberet... praetori mandatum est. (Livy 39.45.6)
cohortes v... pontem fluminis *interrumpebant*... a ponte repulsi se in oppidum receperunt (BC 1.16).

When an accomplishment is used in the progressive, it denotes only some part of the activity subevent of the event and does not include the telos. This follows from the interface of the meaning of the progressive with the temporal structure of the accomplishment. In the second example (Livy 39.45) the Gauls were engaged in the activity phase of building a town, but the event was not culminated and no town was completed (*oppidum aedificare... coepisse* Livy 39.54.5; *oppidumque... aedificare conati sint* Livy 39.54.10). The prefixed form *exaedifico* is not necessary for the phrase to be telic: the Gauls successfully engaged in the activity of town-building but tried unsuccessfully to bring this activity to its culmination. In the normal course of events, townbuilding culminates in a completely built town, but that is not part of the meaning of the progressive, which is compatible with the event being interrupted prior to its telos. Attainment of the telos is entailed by the perfective, as in the case of the consul's winter quarters in the first example (Livy 23.48), but not by the progressive. The normal implication of 'I was crossing the bridge' is that I did get across, but it is also possible to say 'I was crossing the bridge when it collapsed.' In the same way in the third example (BC 1.16) Domitius' cohorts were breaching the bridge and would have succeeded had they not been driven back into the town by Caesar's troops. What is required is a recognizable partial token of the event type of town-building (or bridge-busting) and a reasonable expectation that the event would reach successful completion if not interrupted. A couple of Gallic shepherds building overnight huts does not qualify as a subevent of town-building, and if the Gauls knew from the start that there was only enough building material to build two or three blocks, that would not qualify either.

(39) They attacked all day with the utmost force (Livy 40.25.6). They fought on equal terms for several hours (Livy 31.33.9). The Carthaginians made the outcome of the battle uncertain for a long time (Livy 23.40.10).

(40) And there he built his winter camp (Livy 23.48.2). The Gauls were building a town on the land that now belongs to Aquileia. The praetor was instructed to prevent them from doing this (Livy 39.45.6). Five cohorts were breaking down the bridge over the river. Driven back from the bridge they withdrew into the town (BC 1.16).

The senate tells Lucius Julius the praetor 'The Gauls are building a town. You are instructed to stop them' (Livy 39.45). The activity subevent (that part of it that precedes and includes the reference time, which is the same as the utterance time) meets the requirements set out in the preceding paragraph: the activity subevent of townbuilding is factual and extensional. But the rest of the event is potential and intensional: perhaps the Romans will fail to stop the Gauls and the town will actually be built; perhaps, as in fact turns out to be the case, they will successfully stop the Gauls and the town will not get built. It depends whether the building event proceeds inertially the way most building events do, without running into any obstacle fatal to its completion. We have already used the modal concept of inertially accessible worlds in our discussion of the future in Chapter 1. But while the future asserts that actual world is one of the worlds in which the event is successfully completed (so the proposition 'The Gauls will build a town' is true for the actual world), the progressive just implicates this, leaving wide open the possibility that the actual world is not one of the worlds in which the event is successfully completed: see Figure 2.6. (As in the case of the future, inertiality has to be interpreted relative to the continuation of the event in question, not relative to the continuations of all events in the world.) Note that the worlds may have begun to diverge far earlier than the reference time of the progressive: arguably the building of the town was a lost cause from the moment the Romans found out about it. An inertial ordering source is not the same as an epistemic ordering source (you need not expect the event to culminate), nor the same as a circumstantial ordering source (facts of the world, unknown to the agent, may preclude culmination of the event). In addition to the inertial worlds implicature, the progressive also has a bouletic worlds implicature, which is sensitive to person in the same way as happens with the future. The Gauls have every intention of building a town, so they can say 'We are building a town' (in all worlds compatible with the wishes of the Gauls, a town gets built), but M. Claudius Marcellus, who stopped them, could have said 'That may be your intention, but the fact of the matter is: you are not building a town, you are only building four blocks.' The modal component in the meaning of the progressive explains how the progressive of a telic verb can be licensed in the apodosis of past unfulfilled conditionals

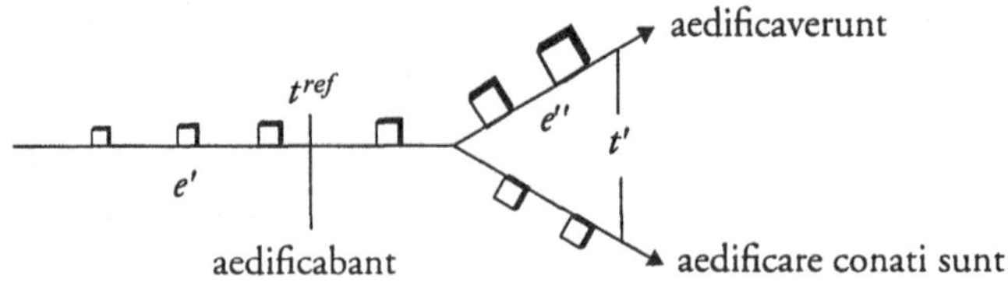

Figure 2.6
Progressive accomplishment
Galli oppidum aedificabant (Livy 39.45.6)

(41) Caecina... suffosso equo delapsus *circumveniebatur*, ni prima legio sese opposuisset (Tac Ann 1.65)
trudebanturque in paludem... ni Caesar productas legiones instruxisset (Tac Ann 1.63).

While it is fine to say 'Trimalchio was building five ships' if they were being collectively built in a single shipbuilding macroevent, noncollective quantified objects are difficult in progressive accomplishments, as already noted. 'Appius Claudius was taking six cities by storm' is not very felicitous, unless it is understood as a preassigned task. In the perfective there is no problem

(42) Ap. Claudius... sex praeterea oppida eorum *expugnavit* (Livy 39.32.4).

A similar clash can sometimes arise between the progressive and a telicizing prefix, as it can with telicizing particles in English ('Jack was eating up an apple'). Hence the preference, particularly marked in early Latin, for verbs without a telic prefix in the progressive and verbs with a telic prefix in the perfective. Here is an example with a goal of motion accomplishment

(43) pallam ad phrygionem... *ferebat* (Pl Men 564)
pallam... et spinter quod ad hanc *detulerat* (Pl Men 807).

Pallam ad phrygionem ferebat is a compositional accomplishment in the imperfective aspect. Even accomplishments in which the resultant state is just lexically salient (like 'obliterate,' 'eliminate') can be more difficult to use in the progressive.

Since true achievements consist of just an instantaneous change of state, achievements are in principle incompatible with the progressive reading of the imperfective. They occur mostly in the perfective (although they can of course be used imperfectively with an iterative, distributive or habitual reading)

(44) e vestigio eo *sum profectus* prima luce (Ad Fam 4.12.2)
postero die... Dyrrachium *profectus est* (BC 3.41).

A true progressive of *proficisci* would require some form of slow motion reading ('The bomb was exploding just at that moment'). What we actually find when this verb is used in the progressive is a prestate reading

(45) quod in Ciliciam *proficiscebar* (Ad Fam 2.18.3)
Capuam tamen *proficiscebar* haec scribens (Ad Att 7.19.1).

(41) Caecina fell with his horse stabbed and would have been surrounded if the first legion had not intervened (Tac Ann 1.65). They would have been driven into the marsh, if Caesar had not brought forward the legions and drawn them up (Tac Ann 1.63).

(42) Appius Claudius also took six of their towns by storm (Livy 39.32.4).

(43) He was carrying the coat to the embroiderer (Pl Men 564). The coat and the bracelet that he had taken to her (Pl Men 807).

(44) I left for the place on the spot at daybreak (Ad Fam 4.12.2). On the next day he set out for Dyrrachium (BC 3.41).

(45) Since I am setting out for Cilicia (Ad Fam 2.18.3). As I write this I am setting out for Capua (Ad Att 7.19.1).

This means that 'at the time of writing I was in the prestate of setting out'; it does not refer to the initial phase of the journey itself. Some achievements have a near punctual activity prephase (or a related accomplishment variant) and license a progressive reading when the reference time is included in this activity prephase

(46) in ipso maleficio vox illius qui *occidebatur* audita (Rhet Her 4.53).

Other examples (*occidebatur* Sen Con 9.6.17; *cum interficeretur Caesar* Phil 2.34) involve a more extensive prephase. Interruptions (failure of culmination) are far more difficult with achievements in the progressive ('He was reaching the top but he didn't make it') than with accomplishments in the progressive. The (broad scope) negation of an achievement is not an achievement but a state; consequently durational adverbials are licensed with negated achievements, although they would be impossible in the corresponding sentence without negation

(47) *per biduum* nemo hominem homo agnosceret (ND 2.96)
Agnovit Tryphaena verum Gitona (**per biduum*) (Petr 110).

Similarly in English we can say 'Noone punctured the balloon for two days' but not 'Someone punctured the balloon for two days' (if we discount the scenario of an iterated puncture and repair cycle).

Up to now our examples of viewpoint aspect have been confined to past tense, where we found the imperfect used for imperfectives and the simple past for perfectives. Distinctions of viewpoint aspect are more productive in the past than in the present and future. Consequently they are more likely to be morphologically marked in the past than in the other tenses, as is indeed the case in Latin. This in turn makes it easier to base an analysis of viewpoint aspect on past tense examples. Nevertheless viewpoint aspect also has a role to play in the present and future tenses. Progressives are less common in the future than in the past. A sentence like 'This time yesterday I was drinking coffee in Paris' depends for its verification only on a past event, planned or unplanned. But 'This time tomorrow I will be drinking coffee in Paris' normally implies some degree of planning or predetermination. Telic eventuality types probably have a default perfective reading in the future (providing that this is not disturbed by the non-actuation of future events in the way that negation can interfere with perfectivity, i.e. provided the perfective is not factive)

(48) *Properabo* ad forum (Pl Men 666)
Ibis litoreas, Macer, Salonas (Mart 10.78.1)
participes omnes meos praeda *onerabo* (Pl Pseud 588).

(46) During the actual commission of the crime the voice of the man being killed was heard (Rhet Her 4.53).

(47) For two days no man recognized another man (ND 2.96). Tryphaena recognized the real Giton (Petr 110).

(48) I will hurry to the forum (Pl Men 666). You will go to Salonae by the sea, Macer (Mart 10.78.1). I will load all my comrades with booty (Pl Pseud 588).

But imperfective readings are available for states and progressive readings for activities (and presumably accomplishments)

(49) scribes aliquid si *vacabis* (Ad Att 12.38.2)
An cum *vexabuntur* urbes, tecta *ardebunt*, tum te non existimas invidiae incendio conflagraturum? (Cat 1.29).

In the first example (Ad Att 12.38) Atticus' state of being at leisure frames the event of his writing (deontic future). In the second example (Cat 1.29) Cicero's unpopularity is framed by or commensurate with the state of roofs being on fire and the activity of cities being plundered. These examples seem to be future versions of structures like the following

(50) quos tum scripsimus cum gubernacula rei publicae *tenebamus* (De Div 2.3)
tum cum res publica vim et severitatem *desiderabat*, vici naturam (Pro Mur 6)
cum varices *secabantur* C. Mario, dolebat (Tusc 2.35).

The imperfect forms here point to a corresponding imperfective reading for the italicized futures in (49). There is also morphological evidence for aspectually distinct future readings, since the Classical future perfect originates as a perfective future and is still quite commonly used as a simple future (rather than a future perfect) in main clauses in comedy

(51) breve quod vitae relicuomst voluptate, vino et amore *delectavero* (Pl Merc 548: app. crit.)
Ego *emero* matri tuae ancillam viraginem aliquam non malam... ea molet, coquet (Pl Merc 413).

These forms tend to occur in recognizably perfective contexts: telic expressions (like the second example (Merc 413); contrast the habitual activities *molet*, *coquet*), temporally delimited states, temporally delimited activities, quantified objects (like the first example (Merc 548)). Quite subtle nuances of perfective meaning can come into play, for instance temporary resultant state (*concessero* 'I'll step aside for a while' vs. *concedam* 'I'll step aside') or immediate completion (*abibo* 'I'll go away' vs. *abiero* 'I'm out of here'), so that it can be hard to find objective proof of a difference between minimal pairs

(49) Write me a line if you have time (Ad Att 12.38.2). Or when the cities are devastated, the buildings are on fire, don't you think that then you will burn in a fire of unpopularity? (Cat 1.29).

(50) Which I wrote at the time when I held the reins of political power (De Div 2.3). When the political situation demanded force and severity, then I overcame my natural instincts (Pro Mur 6). When Marius' varicose veins were being cut, he was in pain (Tusc 2.35).

(51) I will enjoy the short time I have left to live with pleasure, wine and love (Pl Merc 548). I will buy as a slave for your mother some virago, not a bad person; she will grind flour and cook (Pl Merc 413).

(52) alium *adlegavero* qui vendat (Pl Pers 135)
alium ego isti rei *allegabo* (Pl Amph 674).

After all, the simple future forms could just be unmarked for aspect (aspectually neutral). In any case, in Classical prose the morphological simple future is regularly used to express almost all the perfective meanings for which these perfective forms were used in the earlier language. The perfective forms survive, but aspectual perfectivity has been reanalyzed as temporal anteriority (with or without XN).

In the present tense, the reference time is the utterance time, conceptualized as instantaneous. Consequently the reference time is automatically included in any event that is ongoing at the moment of utterance, and the default viewpoint aspect is imperfective

(53) tribus locis *aedifico*, reliqua concinno (Ad Qfr 2.5.1)
Tuas nunc epistulas a primo *lego* (Ad Att 9.6.5).

These examples translate into the English continuous (progressive) present: 'I am building,' 'I am now reading.' Perfective presents are limited to marked contexts. One type is the performative ('With this ring do I thee wed')

(54) ego te... manum consertum *voco* (Pro Mur 26)
Per ego te... quaecumque iura liberos iungunt parentibus *precor quaesoque* (Livy 23.9.2)
Illud tamen tibi *polliceor* (Ad Fam 6.22.3).

Unlike the examples in (53), these translate into the English simple present: 'I hereby summon you,' 'I beg and beseech you,' 'I promise you.' As already noted in chapter 1, the historical present is typically perfective, since it presents the events as whole bounded entities occurring at the continuously updated reference time

(55) primo impetu *pellit*, fugientis *persequitur*, multos *interficit*, castra hostium *capit*. (Nepos 14.6.7).

Activities and states can be perfective too when they are delimited

(56) diu immobiles *silent*... deinde castra propter aquam vallo circumdant (Livy 9.2.11)
nec diu *manet* superstes filio pater (Livy 1.34.3)
Pugnatur aliquamdiu pari contentione (BG 8.19).

(52) I'll give someone else the job of selling her (Pl Pers 135). I'll give this job to someone else (Pl Amph 674).

(53) I am building in three places and fixing up the others (Ad Qfr 2.5.1). I am now reading your letters from the beginning (Ad Att 9.6.5).

(54) I summon you to contest ownership (Pro Mur 26). By whatever rights join children to their parents, I beg and beseech you (Livy 23.9.2). But I promise you (Ad Fam 6.22.3).

(55) He routs them on the first attack, pursues those who are fleeing, kills many, and captures the enemy camp (Nepos 14.6.7).

(56) For a long time they remain silent without moving. Then they surround a camp with a rampart near the water (Livy 9.2.11). The father does not survive his son for very long (Livy 1.34.3). They fight for a while on equal terms (BG 8.19).

Some examples are open to an inceptive reading (although that is not required)

(57) Consulatus uterque apud patricios *manet* (Livy 7.19.6)
Pugnatur una omnibus in partibus (BG 7.67),

but others are probably just imperfective

(58) Urbs hostibus impletur. Omnibus locis *pugnatur.* Deinde... senescit pugna (Livy 5.21.13)
Totum sudor *habet* corpus multumque *laborat* (Enn Ann 15.396)
Quisque ut steterat *iacet* (Pl Amph 241)
cruor undique *manat,* detectique *patent* nervi, trepidaeque sine ulla pelle *micant* venae (Ov Met 6.388).

Pugnatur in the first example (Livy 5.21) seems to have a continuative as well as an inceptive phase but no terminative phase, in which case it would mean 'fighting is going on everywhere' rather than 'fighting breaks out everywhere' or 'fights occur everywhere.'

Iteration

Verbal plurality is initially classified as internal or external. Internal plurality involves the repetition or incrementation of subevents inside a single event, as for instance in intensives or perseveratives. External plurality can involve the repetition of an event, either a single repetition (*iterum* 'again') or multiple repetitions (*identidem* 'repeatedly'); but it can also involve the distribution of subevents of a single event over multiple participants. Finally it is important to distinguish between event pluralization and quantification over events, because they have quite different semantics.

Let us start with examples of an event which has a number of subevents distributed over different participants or groups of participants (for instance object distributivity, subject distributivity, subject and object distributivity)

(59) Ap. Claudius... belli auctores tres et quadraginta securi *percussit.* (Livy 39.32.4)
Octo elephanti *capti,* tres *occisi.* (Livy 24.42.8)
ibi multos Uticenses *interfecerunt* domosque eorum *expugnaverunt* ac *diripuerunt* (BAfr 87)
quas singulas scaphae adversariorum complures adortae *incendebant* atque *expugnabant* (BAfr 21).

(57) Both consulships remain with the patricians (Livy 7.19.6). There is fighting at one and the same time in all areas (BG 7.67).

(58) The city is filled with the enemy. There is fighting in all areas. Then the fighting begins to diminish (Livy 5.21.13). Sweat covers his entire body and he is under great stress (Enn Ann 15.396). Each one lies as he had stood (Pl Amph 241). Blood flows everywhere, his uncovered sinews lie bare and his veins quiver throbbing without any skin (Ov Met 6.388).

(59) Ap. Claudius beheaded forty-three captives who had been responsible for the war (Livy 39.32.4). Eight elephants were captured and three were killed (Livy 24.42.8). There they killed many inhabitants of Utica and captured and plundered their houses (BAfr 87). They were set on fire and captured after being attacked individually by several enemy boats (BAfr 21).

In the second example (Livy 24.42) there was an event of eight elephants getting captured; the plural passive subject triggers a plurality of elephant capturing subevents. These subevents do not have to be sequential: two elephants can get captured at the same time, though not necessarily collectively. Iteration proper involves multiple events that are separate in time and/or space and can be counted by frequency adverbs

(60) Veliterni coloni... agrum Romanum aliquotiens *incursavere* (Livy 6.36.1)
sacrificantem mane haruspex identidem *admonuit* caveret periculum (Suet 7.19.1)
Adversae Hannibalis factionis homines principibus Romanis, hospitibus quisque suis, identidem *scribebant* (Livy 33.45.6).

Notice that the first two examples (Livy 6.36; Suet 7.19.1) are perfective, while the last (Livy 33.45) is imperfective. Iteration of the event gives a macroevent. Apart from the existence of gaps between the iterated events, the macroevent is structurally comparable to an activity having cyclically repeated subevents, and like activities these macroevents are atelic eventuality types: they are unbounded and do not inherently refer to a specific number of events. So at any particular reference time an iterated event can be ongoing (even during gaps between instantiating events), just as a single episodic event is ongoing in the progressive. However, again like activities, they can also be delimited. Since an iterated event can be included in the reference time or ongoing at the reference time, both the perfective and the imperfective are licensed. (This is one of the ways in which achievements can get to be used imperfectively.) As illustrated by the last example (Livy 33.45), this type of imperfective is entirely compatible with vague frequency adverbs

(61) Camillus identidem omnibus locis *contionabatur* (Livy 5.25.4)
Recitabatur identidem Pompei testimonium (Pro Rab Post 34)
Iumenta *secabant* interdum etiam infimam ingredientia nivem et... penitus *perfringebant* (Livy 21.36.8: app. crit.).

But as already remarked with reference to the progressive, imperfectives are difficult with exact numerals: cardinal frequency adverbs count the number of events in the macroevent

(62) qui bis Italiam obsidione... *liberavit* (Cat 4.21)
Ter *depugnavit* Caesar cum civibus (Phil 2.75).

If the exact total number of events is known, the macroevent must be complete. This makes the progressive unsuitable, although events with a progressive plus

(60) The colonists of Velitrae invaded Roman territory several times (Livy 6.36.1). As he was sacrificing in the morning a priest repeatedly warned him to beware of danger (Suet 7.19.1). The members of the party opposed to Hannibal wrote repeatedly to the Roman leaders, each one to his own hosts (Livy 33.45.6).

(61) Camillus repeatedly gave speeches everywhere (Livy 5.25.4). The evidence of Pompey was repeatedly read out (Pro Rab Post 34). As they advanced the baggage animals sometimes cut even the lowest layer of snow and broke right through it (Livy 21.36.8).

(62) Who twice freed Italy from invasion (Cat 4.21). Caesar fought with his fellow-citizens three times (Phil 2.75).

inverse *cum* can be counted: 'Spring was approaching three times when Hannibal moved from his winter quarters'. Durative adverbials are licensed with unbounded frequency adverbs but not with bounded ones: you can say 'Jack phoned Sheila repeatedly for an hour' but not 'Jack phoned Sheila nine times for an hour.' The event pluralization associated with iteration is inside the scope of aspect. It must be very low in the structure, perhaps the counterpart in the verbal domain of plurality in the nominal domain, since even singular indefinite objects scope higher than verbal plurality; only bare nouns scope lower. 'He shot arrows for an hour' involves different arrows, but 'He shot an arrow for an hour' can only mean that he shot the same single arrow over and over. A narrow scope reading for singular indefinites is possible with a cardinal frequency adverb ('He shot an arrow three times') and readily available if the sentence contains an expression that introduces restricted quantification over events ('He shot an arrow at every enemy for an hour'). We have to conclude that simple pluralization of events and restricted quantification over events do not work in the same way at all: distributivity fails for the former but is natural for the latter.

In the examples cited so far, the quantifiers have all been vague or exact frequency adverbs, which have weak (bipartite, unrestricted) semantics, unless they are coerced into a strong quantifier reading: it is simply asserted that there exists a plural event with property P and cardinality n ($\exists E.|E| = n \wedge \forall e \in E \rightarrow P(e)$). For instance, in the second example in (62) (Phil 2.75) there exists an iterated event of Caesar fighting with citizens and its cardinality is three. Strong quantifiers by contrast are tripartite and have an overt or covert restriction

(63) frumentum ex agris *cotidie* in castra conferebat (BG 4.31)
equestribus proeliis inter se *cotidie* dimicabant (BAfr 61).

The quantifier *cotidie* divides the iteration into equal daylong intervals and distributes an event to an appropriate time in each interval. So the second example (BAfr 61) says that for each interval (quantifier) of the iteration that was a day long (restriction) there was one or more cavalry battles (nuclear scope). Strong quantification is also found when iterated events are paired off without any claim of habituality

(64) Pepulit ergo, *quotienscumque* congressus est, multo maiores adversariorum copias (Nepos 17.3.6)
legem istam nullam esse, *quotienscumque* de me senatus sententiam dixit, totiens iudicavit (De Dom 69)
quotienscumque... volemus, facile... consequemur (Rhet Her 3.34).

(63) He brought corn from the fields into the camp every day (BG 4.31). They fought with each other in cavalry battles every day (BAfr 61).

(64) So whenever he engaged in battle, he routed far larger enemy forces (Nepos 17.3.6). Every time the senate pronounced an opinion about me, it thereby judged that law to be invalid (De Dom 69). Whenever we wish, we will easily succeed (Rhet Her 3.34).

The first example (Nepos 17.3) says that all events in which Agesilaus engaged the enemy were matched one for one with events in which he routed far superior enemy forces and vacuously vice versa: $\forall e'.\mathrm{Congr}(e', \mathrm{Ag}) \rightarrow \exists e.\mathrm{Pell}(e, \mathrm{Ag}, \mathrm{copias}) \wedge \mathrm{M}(e', e)$. In this construction, the frequency of the asserted event (*pepulit*) is expressed by quantifying over another event (*congressus est*) which also contributes the basis for the reference times of the asserted event. Some form of matching mechanism (M in the formalism) is necessary, so you don't connect the start of one battle with the outcome of a completely different battle.

Habitual

The present tense is used for the expression of general truths, definitions, proverbs and the like

(65) Centies vicies duceni quadrageni *fiunt* viginti octo milia et octingenti (Col 5.2.3)
Stadium... *habet* passus CXXV, id est pedes DCXXV, quae mensura octies *efficit* mille passus (Col 5.1.6)
ipsa holera olla *legit* (Catull 94.2).

Habet in the second example (Col 5.1) is a state, but *efficit* is telic. The aspect is imperfective, since the time of the general truth frames the reference time (the time of utterance), but a progressive reading ('Two plus two is making four') is not appropriate since the event time is not bounded, but unbounded like a state. A similar parallelism between states and processes is found with geographical descriptions

(66) ad meridiem *spectat* (BG 5.13)
Aegyptum Nilus *inrigat* (ND 2.130).

Spectat in the first example (BG 5.13) is a state, *inrigat* in the second (ND 2.130) is a process. The Nile has the permanent property of irrigating Egypt (by flooding the fields during the summer and then receding). In much the same way generic sentences (narrowly defined) can predicate characteristic or salient actions of kinds ('dogs bark')

(67) gallinae avesque reliquae... nidos... *construunt* (ND 2.129)
feminae pavones quae non *incubant* ter anno fere partus *edunt* (Col 8.11.10),

and habitual sentences predicate characteristic actions of individuals ('Jack smokes')

(65) 120 times 240 equals 28,800 (Col 5.2.3). A stadium contains 125 paces, that is 625 feet, eight times which equals a thousand paces (Col 5.1.6). A pot gathers its vegetables itself (Catull 94.2).

(66) It faces south (BG 5.13). The Nile irrigates Egypt (ND 2.130).

(67) Hens and the other birds build nests (ND 2.129). Female peacocks that do not sit on their eggs usually produce offspring three times a year (Col 8.11.10).

(68) Noctu *ambulabat* in publico Themistocles (Tusc 4.44)
Idem poemata *renuntiabat* et Graece et Latine (Nepos 25.4.1)
battuebat pugnatoriis armis (Suet 4.54.1)
Tingit cutem Charinus (Mart 1.77.5).

Noctu ambulabat in the first example (Tusc 4.44) does not mean that at a certain reference time during the night Themistocles was walking (progressive reading) but that at all times during some interval of his life he was a night walker. Similarly *tingit cutem* does not entail (or preclude) that Charinus is colouring his skin now; it just says that he has the habit of doing so and that this habit is instantiated on various occasions by a colouring event. As in the case of iteratives, the events that are instantiations of the habit comprise an unbounded macroevent, specifically the state of having the habit in question, for instance of being a night walker. In this case the adverb *noctu* modifies the time of the instantiating event, not the time of the interval comprising the habit. A past habitual is true during a certain interval covering at least the time from its first instantiation to its final instantiation, for instance the professional career of an orator. Like states in general, habituals can be viewed imperfectively or perfectively, as illustrated in the following examples with a lexically habitual verb

(69) Fannius... causas *defensitavit* (Brut 100)
cuius quidem sententiam Carneades... studiose *defensitabat* (Luc 139).

The same absence of a narrow scope reading for singular indefinites that we saw with iteratives reappears with habituals: *causam defensitavit* would mean that he habitually defended the same case, so long as it was a simple habitual and there was no quantificational expression to license distributivity. So simple habituals, like simple iteratives, are nonquantificational. They are built out of plural events. The difference is that while iteratives are episodic macroevents, habituals get an attributive interpretation; this is somewhat analogous to the difference between individuals and kinds in the nominal domain. The frequency of instantiation depends on the nature of the habit and other contextual factors, for instance singing as a professional occupation versus singing as a hobby

(70) Valerius *cotidie* cantabat; erat enim scaenicus... At Numerius Furius...
cum est commodum cantat, est enim paterfamilias (De Or 3.86).

In fact habituals have the potential to be only rarely instantiated

(71) Nam *perraro* praesidere... consueverat (Suet 6.12.2).

(68) Themistocles used to walk around in public at night (Tusc 4.44). He also recited poems in both Latin and Greek (Nepos 25.4.1). He used to fence with real weapons (Suet 4.54.1). Charinus colours his skin (Mart 1.77.5).

(69) Fannius regularly defended cases in court (Brut 100). Whose opinion Carneades used regularly to defend enthusiastically (Luc 139).

(70) Valerius used to sing every day, for he was a performer. But Numerius Furius sings when it suits him, for he is the father of a family (De Or 3.86).

(71) For he very rarely used to preside at the games (Suet 6.12.2).

Habituals do not have to be lifetime properties; they may apply over only a limited period of time ($\tau(e) \subset \tau'(x)$)

(72) *Substringebat* caput loro... verberibus *cogebat* exsultare... qui motus... sudorem *excutiebat* (Nepos 18.5.5)
Ad natalicias dapes *vocabar*, essem cum tibi, Sexte, non amicus (Mart 7.86.1)
Argenti libram *mittebas*; facta selibra est (Mart 10.57.1).

The first example (Nepos 18.5) describes Eumenes' temporary method of exercising his horses during the siege of Nora. Note that the habit can be temporary without the aspect being perfective.

The relationship between the habit and its instantiations requires some form of modality to cover exceptions in which instantiation fails. Given a habit, there is a likelihood that it will be instantiated under normal circumstances; and conversely, given a repetitive event, a generalization may be drawn as to its habituality. While iterations can arise by accident, habits are properties of individuals. Suppose someone says 'Themistocles walks at night.' Consider what this claims about the behaviour of Themistocles at some time t in the future: let t be during the night, because the habit says nothing about the daytime. Simplifying a bit, we can envision two sets of worlds at t: a set w' of accessible worlds in which the habit is instantiated, and a set w'' of inaccessible worlds in which the habit is not instantiated because some circumstance supervenes to block it (inclement weather, say, or a high fever). The weather belongs to the circumstantial modal base, and Themistocles' habit is the norm in the ordering source (see Chapter 9). Then the sentence says that at all worlds accessible from the actual world w^* on the basis of Themistocles' habit, he walks at t. We cannot be sure which set of worlds the actual world will be a member of. In fact there are clear examples of habits, or at least dispositions, that are never instantiated, typically involving machinery that is never used or professional occupations that are assigned but never undertaken ('Prof. Jones teaches the Aeolic Verse Composition class').

It is quite common for habituals to include some type of adverbial quantifier like *saepe* 'often' or *raro* 'rarely.' The quantifier changes the sentence from a simple statement of the habit into one which spells out the frequency of its instantiation

(73) *Plerumque* iumenta morbos concipiunt lassitudine et aestu, nonnumquam et frigore (Col 6.30.3)
Equestribus proeliis *saepe* ex equis desiliunt ac pedibus proeliantur (BG 4.2)
vinum aegrotis... prodest *raro*, nocet saepissime (ND 3.69).

(72) He would raise up its head with a thong and force it to jump by beating it; this movement caused it to sweat (Nepos 18.5.5). When I was not your friend, Sextus, I used to get invited to your birthday parties (Mart 7.86.1). You used to send a pound of silver; it has become half a pound (Mart 10.57.1).

(73) Horses usually get ill from fatigue and heat, sometimes also from the cold (Col 6.30.3). In cavalry battles they often jump down from their horses and fight on foot (BG 4.2). Wine is rarely helpful and very often harmful to the sick (ND 3.69).

Unlike simple habituals, these are properly quantificational structures, but it is not quite clear whether the quantification is over events, over individuals or (unselectively) over pairs of events and individuals. Specifically the last example (ND 3.69) could be analyzed with quantification over events, meaning few events in which there is a sick person and wine is given to him are events in which the wine helps him: FEWe. $\exists x$.Sick(x) $\wedge$ Give(e,y,x,wine). Help(e,wine,x). Or it could be analyzed with quantification over individuals, meaning few people who are sick are helped by wine: FEWx. Sick(x). Help(wine,x). Or it could be analyzed with quantification over both, meaning few sick people in events of being given wine are helped: FEWe,x. Sick(e,x) $\wedge$ Give(e,y,x, wine). Help(e, wine,x). Similarly the first example (Col 6.30) means that on most occasions that horses and mules fall ill from some cause, they fall ill from fatigue and heat. The restriction and the nuclear scope involve one and the same event (the wine and the heat are causative participants): this is most clear in the second example (BG 4.2: *proeliis proeliantur*). On the other hand when the restriction is overtly spelled out by a temporal clause, there are typically two separate events, an event e in the restriction and a related event e' in the nuclear scope

(74) cum ver esse *coeperat...* *dabat* se labori atque itineribus (Verr 2.5.27)
Legionibus Romanis cedebant in urbem; ubi abductas *senserant* legiones, agros *incursabant* (Livy 2.48.6)
gravis enim armaturae miles simul atque ab eis insectatus *constiterat* in eosque impetum *fecerat,* illi veloci cursu periculum facile *vitabant* (BAfr 71).

In the second example (Livy 2.48) for instance, each event of (their noticing the) withdrawal of the Roman legions is followed by an event of incursion into the fields. Each event of Roman withdrawal in the domain is mapped onto a related event of Veians raiding the fields in the range, the mapping being one to one. The imperfect in the main clause is a habitual (cp. *solebat* Verr 2.4 in (77) below), the pluperfect in the subordinate clause is an XR type, as is clear when the same structure appears in present time

(75) gubernatores cum exsultantis lolligines *viderunt...* tempestatem significari *putant.* (De Div 2.145).

There is a variant in which the anteriority is encoded in the linear order of two main clauses, both in the imperfect

(76) Consul in aciem *exibat,* hostes pugnam *detrectabant* (Livy 35.4.2).

(74) When spring began, he would dedicate himself to hard work and travel (Verr 2.5.27). They would retreat into the city before the Roman legions; when they perceived that the legions had been led away, they would make raids on the fields (Livy 2.48.6). For as soon as the heavily armed infantry they were pursuing made a stand and attacked them, they easily avoided the danger by their speed of movement (BAfr 71).

(75) When pilots see cuttle-fish jumping, they think that it means the approach of a storm (De Div 2.145).

(76) The consul would march out to battle, the enemy would decline to fight (Livy 35.4.2).

The mapping may involve an indefinite pronoun or a distributive quantifier in the subordinate clause: in such cases both the event variable and the individual variable are explicit in the syntax

(77) si *qui* graviore vulnere accepto equo deciderat, circumsistebant (BG 1.48)
Messanam ut *quisque* nostrum venerat, haec visere solebat (Verr 2.4.5)
quocumque aspexisti... tuae tibi occurrunt iniuriae (Parad 18)
Ut *quisque* istius animum aut oculos offenderat, in lautumias statim coniciebatur (Verr 2.5.143)
Ut *quisque* acciderat, eum necabam ilico (Pl Poen 485).

Each event in which a Roman citizen annoyed Verres was quickly followed by a related event of that citizen being thrown into gaol: $\forall ex.\text{Offend}(e,x,\text{Verres}) \rightarrow \exists e'.\text{Go-to-gaol}(e',x) \wedge \text{M}(e',e)$. x is a covert "donkey" pronoun; the last example (Poen 485) has an overt one (*eum*). Progressives and temporary states can appear inside the scope of the quantifier

(78) Gellius *aedificat* semper: modo limina ponit, nunc foribus claves aptat (Mart 9.46.1)
socer in ore semper Graecos versus de Phoenissis *habebat* (De Off 3.82).

At all times t during this period of his life Gellius is building at t, or on all occasions e that someone meets Gellius in e, Gellius is building in e', where the run time of e' includes that of e.

Extended now (XN)

If you say 'I lost my umbrella,' you are asserting a past event; if you say 'I have lost my umbrella,' you are asserting a present state arising out of a past event. The former uses the simple past tense, the latter the present perfect tense. The simple past tense involves a reference time in the past, but the temporal structure of the present perfect is more complex: it involves two times, the reference time (for the present perfect this is the utterance time) and an indefinite time anterior to the reference time (the event time). Taken together, these two times create an interval stretching back from the present to some point in the past; hence the term 'extended now' (XN for short). While the right boundary of the XN interval is fixed at the reference time, the left boundary is nonspecific. Just as adverbial times can include the reference time, so adverbially defined XN intervals can be container intervals for the eventively defined XN

(77) Any time anyone fell from his horse with a serious wound, they would surround him (BG 1.48). Whenever any of us went to Messana, he would visit these statues (Verr 2.4.5). Wherever you look, your sins meet your eyes (Parad 18). Whenever any one of them offended his thoughts or his eyes, he was immediately thrown into gaol (Verr 2.5.143). As each one fell, I killed him straight away (Pl Poen 485).

(78) Gellius is always building: one moment he is laying down thresholds, another he is fitting keys to doors (Mart 9.46.1). His father-in-law always had on his lips the Greek verses from the Phoenissae (De Off 3.82).

(79) Nam equidem *postquam gnatus sum* numquam aegrotavi unum diem (Pl Men 959).

The adverbial XN is the interval from Menaechmus' birth to the time of utterance, the eventively defined XN is the interval from the beginning of an illness of Menaechmus (LB($\tau(e)$)) to the time of utterance ($t^{ref} = t^u$; the durative adverbial *unum diem* measures the event time). There are three main different XN readings, depending on how the XN interval maps onto the event structure of the eventuality type. These are the continuous perfect ('I have been working all morning'), the experiential perfect ('I have seen the queen'), and the resultative perfect ('I have broken my leg'). The continuous type is also called the universal perfect and the experiential type the existential perfect, but this terminology tends to obscure the basic identity of the XN readings by substituting quantificational terms for aspectual terms. Part or all of the XN interval is universally filled in all readings: the difference lies in what fills it (see Figure 2.7). Since Latin does not have a morphological present perfect paradigm distinct from the simple past and present tenses (syntactic evidence exists, but it is rare), the issue is not "What is the semantics of the Latin present perfect?" but "What semantics are we imputing to a Latin verb form by translating it with an English present perfect?". The assumption is that whatever triggers use of the present perfect form in English can trigger a reading with perfect semantics in Latin, although it is often impossible to exclude an alternative reading with simple past semantics.

In the continuous reading of XN, a state or an event is ongoing throughout the XN interval. Latin uses the present tense for this reading

(80) Iamdudum *splendet* focus (Hor Ep 1.5.7)
mihi ieiunitate iam dudum intestina *murmurant* (Pl Cas 803)
Verbi enim controversia iam diu *torquet* Graeculos homines (De Or 1.47)

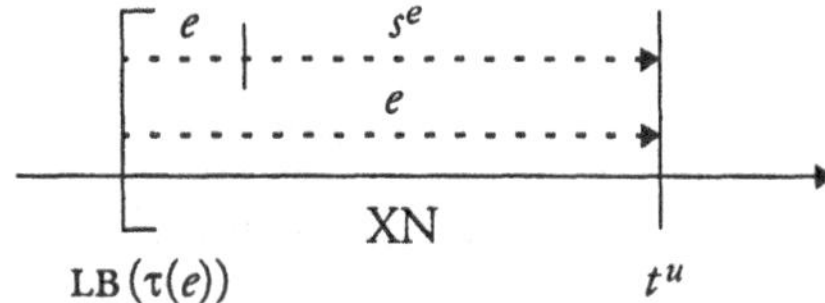

Figure 2.7
Continuous, experiential and resultative perfect

(79) I have never been ill for a single day since the time I was born (Pl Men 959).
(80) My hearth has been bright for a long time now (Hor Ep 1.5.7). My insides have been rumbling from lack of food for a long time now (Pl Cas 803). For controversy about the meaning of words has been tormenting the Greeks for a long time (De Or 1.47).

(81) siccas insana canicula messes iam dudum *coquit* (Pers 3.6)
Hic annus sextust postquam ei rei operam *damus* (Pl Men 234)
Cum iam tot horas... de istius nefaria crudelitate *dicam* (Verr 2.5.159).

The present tense encodes the reference time; the rest of the XN interval is taken care of by the adverbial (*iam dudum, iam diu, iam tot horas*), which in these examples measures the XN interval and thereby contributes the onset time of the progressive or stative eventuality. The XN reading depends on the adverbial: without the adverbial the default would be an ordinary present tense. The last example (Verr 2.5) says that there is an event of Cicero's speaking about Verres' cruelty, that the onset (left boundary) of that event is some time anterior to the reference time (same as the utterance time), that the event continues through the utterance time, and that the duration of the XN interval is many hours: $\exists e.\text{LB}(\tau(e)) < t^{ref} \wedge P(e) \wedge \tau(e) \supset t^{ref} \wedge \mu^h\text{XN} \geq tot.$ Without the durative adverbial this would just be a redundant expression for the present tense, since any eventuality that is ongoing at the utterance time has its left boundary before the utterance time. This explains why many languages including Latin use the present tense for the continuous perfect. The onset time of the event is indefinite; it is not fixed at some reference time but just has to be anterior to the reference time. The duration of the XN interval is not necessarily the same as the duration of the event, since the event can continue after the reference time. But the event has to be ongoing at the present: if the event time abuts the time of utterance rather than overlapping it, the perfect is used since the eventuality is delimited

(82) quem ego... usque adhuc *quaesivi* quemque ego esse inventum gaudeo (Pl Men 1133)
ego vitam duram quam *vixi* usque adhuc... omitto (Ter Ad 859).

When there is an implicature that the past eventuality does continue through the present, this can be overtly spelled out

(83) et bonos et aequos et faventes vos *habui* dominos et adhuc *habeo* (Suet 3.29.1).

What has always been the case will usually be the case at the present too

(84) hanc... mercaturam... alienam dignitate populi Romani *semper putavi* (De Leg Agr 2.65),

(81) The summer sun has been baking the crops dry for a long time now (Pers 3.6). This is the sixth year that we have been occupied with this matter (Pl Men 234). Since I have already been speaking about his wicked cruelty for so many hours (Verr 2.5.159).

(82) Whom I have been looking for up to now and who I am happy has been found (Pl Men 1133). I am giving up the hard life that I have lived up to now (Ter Ad 859).

(83) I have regarded you, and continue to regard you, as good, fair and well-disposed masters (Suet 3.29.1).

(84) I have always considered this type of commerce to be incompatible with the dignity of the Roman people (De Leg Agr 2.65).

but again that is only an implicature, so it can be asserted without redundancy

(85) *Amo* autem et *semper amavi* ingenium studia mores tuos (Orat 33)
is in causis patronus... et *sum* et *semper fui* (Pro Planc 75).

While English has a progressive perfect, the Latin perfect is perfective: it denotes delimited or completed events, and so is unsuitable for the continuous perfect

(86) *Dixi.* (Verr 1.1.56)
Dixi ad id tempus quod mihi... praestitutum est (Pro Rab Perd 38).

The first example (Verr 1.1) amounts to 'I am just past the endpoint of my speech.' Whereas states are normally free of gaps (*splendet focus*), activities do not have to be literally continuous; they can be iterated, giving a derived pluractional macroevent

(87) Querendum est ergo et deplorandum, id quod iam dudum *facio*, de omni accusationis iniquitate (Pro Flacc 23).

If you say 'I have been complaining about this for a long time now' (*iam dudum deploro*), that allows for gaps between episodes of complaining during the XN interval. The continuous XN reading can be used with any eventuality type. Like all XN readings, it makes no sense with permanent states ('I have been tall since last week'). Achievements are literally incompatible with the continuous reading, since achievements are momentary and XN is an interval; consequently an iterated reading is coerced

(88) iam dudum *sputo* sanguinem (Pl Merc 138).

Accomplishments either get an iterated reading ('I have been building sandcastles all afternoon'), or they are detelicized ('I have been unloading the truck all afternoon'); in the following example the XN interval is the resultant state

(89) Quam dudum in portum *venis*? (Pl Stich 528).

In the experiential reading, an event occurs one or more times during the XN interval; since experiences cannot be cancelled, this becomes a fact of someone's experience or of history from the time of the event up to the right hand boundary of the XN interval, i.e. the present time. Latin uses the perfect for experiential XN. We give examples containing a frequency adverbial, because they are less open to an alternative simple past reading

(85) I love, and I have always loved, your intellect, your pursuits and your character (Orat 33). I am and have always been the sort of lawyer (Pro Planc 75).

(86) This completes my case (Verr 1.1.56). I have spoken for the time period fixed for me (Pro Rab Perd 38).

(87) Therefore I must protest and deplore, as I have been doing for a long time now, the overall unfairness of the accusation (Pro Flacc 23).

(88) I have been spitting blood for a while now (Pl Merc 138).

(89) How long have you been in port? (Pl Stich 528).

(90) tuum est, Caesar, qui pro multis saepe *dixisti* (Pro Reg Deiot 7)
ter iam homo stultus *triumphavit* (In Pis 58)
In nubibus numquam *animadvertisti* leonis formam aut hippocentauri? (De Div 2.49)
vidi ego dis fretos saepe multos decipi (Pl Cas 349).

At the time of utterance Caesar has had many experiences of speaking in defence of men (and in (79) Menaechmus has had no experience of being ill). For each of these there is an event of Caesar's speaking for the defence, the onset (left boundary) of that event is some time anterior to the reference time (same as the utterance time) and the poststate of that event (not just any event) continues through the utterance time: $\exists e.\textsc{lb}(\tau(e)) < t^{ref} \wedge P(e) \wedge \tau(s^e) \supset t^{ref}$. The poststate of the event is lexically defined by the event but it is a very weak version of a poststate, since it amounts to just the experience of the event. The experiential reading is compatible with all eventuality types, although, as before, it makes no sense with permanent states (*'I have been tall three times'). Since the reference time is the present, the person having the experience must be alive at the present time (lifetime inferences apply): you can't say 'Henry the Eighth has had many wives' (although that would have been fine in 1545). The experience must be replicable; so neither of the following examples

(91) *Mutavere* meas Itala regna comas (Mart 10.103.10)
Psittacus Eois imitatrix ales ab Indis *occidit* (Ov Am 2.6.1)

can have an experiential reading: one's hair only grays once, and, while cats may have nine lives, Corinna's parrot had only one. Furthermore the experience must not only be replicable in absolute terms but also replicable at the present time, as though the sentence contained a covert 'already.' Cicero cannot ask someone 'Have you been to Murena's games?' if he is well aware that the games are over, nor 'Have you seen Murena?' if he knows that Murena left the week before for his province in Gaul. (In some languages the perfect marker is a morpheme meaning 'already.') This seems to be the eventive correlate of the lifetime inference in existential sentences for individuals ('Is there a cat/*dodo in the garden?'). The scope of the existential quantifier over events extends to the entire event description. So while container temporal adverbials are fine (see the example in (79)), properly past positional temporal adverbials are not unless they are low adverbials and part of the event description

(92) Quemne ego *heri* vidi ad vos adferri *vesperi*? (Ter Andr 769).

(90) It is your duty, Caesar, who have often spoken on behalf of many men (Pro Reg Deiot 7). The idiot has already had three triumphs (In Pis 58). Have you never made out the shape of a lion or a hippocentaur in the clouds? (De Div 2.49). I have often seen many who trust in the gods being disappointed (Pl Cas 349).

(91) I have grown grey in the land of Italy (Mart 10.103.10). The parrot, winged mimic from the eastern land of India, has died (Ov Am 2.6.1).

(92) The one I saw yesterday being brought to you in the evening (Ter Andr 769).

While *vesperi* is a low adverbial and so permits an experiential perfect in the appropriate context ('I have seen the baby in the evening, although I usually visit in the morning'), *heri* is not and forces a past tense reading ('I saw/*have seen the baby yesterday'). A perfect reading is only possible if *heri* is outside the event description, adjunct material anaphorically modifying the specific past instance of the event description that is introduced by the experiential perfect ('I have seen the baby. It happened yesterday'). Negative experientials with indefinite subjects can be gnomic

(93) Nemo nisi victor pace bellum *mutavit* (Sall Cat 58.15)
non aeris acervus et auri aegroto domini *deduxit* corpore febris (Hor Ep 1.2.48).

There is a type of perfect that is similar to the experiential perfect, called the recent past perfect ('I have been ill (twice), but I'm OK now'). In this type the present relevance (s^e) comes not from the experience itself ('I've been ill before'), but from its recency. 'I've been working a lot' is probably the progressive version of this.

In the resultative reading of XN, the interval between a singular event and the present time is filled by a continuation of the state arising from a change of state entailed by a telic event

(94) mi *excivisti* lacrimas (Pl Cist 112).

Selenium has caused Gymnasium's eyes to change from the state of being dry into the state of being full of tears at some time anterior to the reference time (same as the utterance time), and their tearful state continues through the reference time. The semantics is the same as that given above for the experiential perfect ($\exists e.\text{LB}(\tau(e)) < t^{ref} \wedge P(e) \wedge \tau(s^e) \supset t^{ref}$), except that the poststate s^e is interpreted as the lexically defined resultant state that is the lowest subevent of the event structure. Consequently only telic eventuality types (verb phrase accomplishments and achievements) can have resultative perfects: *expugnavi* 'I have captured' can have a resultative or an experiential reading, but *pugnavi* 'I have fought' can only have an experiential reading within the family of XN readings (apart from the rather marginal reading in which there is the successful completion of a specific fighting task). As in the case of the experiential perfect, it is often a matter of some subjectivity whether a Latin perfect form is a resultative perfect or a simple past tense. However, when the present component is particularly strong, Latin can use primary sequence of tenses with the resultative perfect, which provides us with an empirical indication that we have a perfect and not a simple past tense. English has primary sequence with the resultative perfect and historical sequence with the experiential perfect (where the past

(93) Only a victor has ever exchanged war for peace (Sall Cat 58.15). No heap of bronze or gold has ever relieved the sick body of a master of its fevers (Hor Ep 1.2.48).
(94) You have made me cry (Pl Cist 112).

event is more salient); so historical sequence does not necessarily prove that only the simple past reading is available. Here are some examples

(95) quibus rebus adductus ad causam accesserim *demonstravi* (Div Caec 10)
ipsi enim venerunt, ipsi publicas litteras deportaverunt, *docuerunt* vos quid lucelli fecerit... Apronius (Verr 2.3.106)
Sed tamen ne me totum aegritudini dedam, *sumpsi* mihi quasdam tamquam θέσεις (Ad Att 9.4.1)
Etiamne ad subsellia cum ferro ac telis *venistis*, ut hic aut iuguletis aut condemnetis Sex. Roscium? (Pro Rosc Am 32).

Take the last example (Pro Rosc Am 32): if *venistis* had simple past tense semantics ('you came here'), the resultant state ('you are here now') would just be a pragmatic inference (on a par with 'you are not suffering from typhoid fever'; see the next paragraph), and there would be nothing in the meaning of the verb form to trigger primary sequence. The time of the actuation of the event in the purpose clause, if it is actuated, is apparently not relevant: 'You have come/came to kill Roscius, and you have done/will do so.'

While experiential poststates are permanent (experiences cannot be undone), resultative poststates are easily changed. Once that has happened, the resultative perfect can no longer be used (although an experiential reading may still be available), since its semantics require the resultant state to be true at the present time. Once Gymnasium's eyes are dry again, she can no longer say 'You have brought tears to my eyes'; she needs to use the simple past and say 'You brought tears to my eyes.' Negation cannot apply to just one subevent (alternative denial: $\exists e$ NAND $\tau(s^e) \supset t^{ref}$), it has to apply to both the event and its resultant state (joint denial: $\exists e$ NOR $\tau(s^e) \supset t^{ref}$). There cannot be a resultant state of a nonoccurring event, and even when the state exists for some other reason the perfect is difficult ('I haven't painted the wall red: it's always been that colour'). Cancellation of the resultant state does not entail nonoccurrence of the event, but the joint denial requirement means that Selenium cannot reply 'I haven't brought tears to your eyes: they are dry now.' Futurate uses of the present perfect

(96) Si te in platea offendero hac post umquam... *periisti* (Ter Eun 1064)
Interii si non invenero ego illas viginti minas (Pl Asin 243)
Si... animum... eundem mox... habueritis, *vicimus*, milites (Livy 21.43.2)

(95) I have set out the reasons for my getting involved in the case (Div Caec 10). They have come themselves, they have brought official letters, they have informed you of the little bit of profit Apronius made (Verr 2.3.106). So as not to surrender completely to depression, I have chosen some topics (Ad Att 9.4.1). Have you come into the courtroom with weapons and arms with the intention of either killing or securing the condemnation of Sex. Roscius here? (Pro Rosc Am 32).

(96) If I ever run into you on this street again, you're toast (Ter Eun 1064). If I don't find those twenty minae, I'm toast (Pl Asin 243). If you show the same enthusiasm in the future, we have already won, soldiers (Livy 21.43.2).

express the resultant state of a future event: since the future event is predetermined at the present time, so is its resultant state. Note that what is entailed by the resultative perfect is the lexically defined resultant state; pragmatically relevant resultant states are not part of the meaning of the resultative perfect. 'I have broken my arm' entails that at the time of utterance my arm is still in a broken state and not healed. It may (or may not) also be the case that it hurts or I can't play soccer or I can't finish my paper on Statius, but those are pragmatically relevant consequences, not lexical entailments. Atelic eventualities too can have pragmatic consequences, but only telic ones have resultant states. Lifetime inferences again apply:

(97) Clodius insidias *fecit* Miloni? (Pro Mil 60)

cannot be a resultative perfect ('Has Clodius laid an ambush for Milo?'), nor indeed any other type of perfect, because Clodius is dead at the time of utterance. Apparent exceptions turn out actually to be presentational sentences with a currently existing subject ('Statius has left us some fine poems' = 'There are some fine poems left to us by Statius'). Properly past temporal positional adverbs are again illicit

(98) Linguam quoque etiam *vendidi* datariam (Pl Stich 257)
vina quae heri *vendidi* vinario Exaerambo (Pl Asin 436)

Venisti huc ubi mures ferrum rodunt (Sen Apoc 7.1)
is heri in portum navi *venit* vesperi (Pl Poen 114).

The first example in each pair can be translated with the present perfect ('I have sold,' 'You have come'), but the second example cannot because of the past adverbs (*'I have sold the wine yesterday,' *'He has come into port yesterday'). The past adverbial in the illicit perfect readings is an adjunct outside the scope of the existential description of the past event, as well as being incompatible with the present reference time for the resultant state. Since the resultative perfect is an existential assertion about a past event and its current resultant state, sentences in which the event is presupposed are infelicitous. This emerges clearly in questions

(99) Spem teneo, salutem *amisi*; redeat an non nescio (Pl Merc 592)
Qua ratione *amisisti*? (Ter Eun 322).

In the first example (Merc 588) a resultative perfect reading is very natural ('I have lost my wellbeing'); in the second example (Eun 322) it is excluded by being in the presupposition of a question (*'How have you lost her?'). An exis-

(97) Did Clodius ambush Milo? (Pro Mil 60).

(98) I've even sold my tongue, the one I use for acts of generosity (Pl Stich 257). The bottles of wine which I sold to the wine merchant Exaerambus yesterday (Pl Asin 436). You have come here to the place where mice nibble iron (Sen Apoc 7.1). He came into harbour on his boat yesterday evening (Pl Poen 114).

(99) I still have hope, but I have lost my well-being; whether it will return or not I don't know (Pl Merc 592). How did you lose track of her? (Ter Eun 322).

tentially asserted event is indefinite, a presupposed event is definite. Similarly, a resultative reading is fine for 'Has Pompey defeated the pirates?', but only an experiential reading (if any) is available for questions that pertain to the process subevent (e^p in Chapter 3): 'Where has Pompey defeated the pirates?', 'With whom has Pompey defeated the pirates?', 'How quickly has Pompey defeated the pirates?', 'Who has defeated the pirates?'. Contrast 'Why/How fully has Pompey defeated the pirates?' and 'Who has been defeated?', which are fine because the queried modifiers and argument (respectively) belong to the resultant state subevent (e^s).

Extended reference time (XR)

The final moment of the XN interval is its reference time. In the present perfect, as its name implies, this is the time of utterance. However it is also possible for XN-like intervals to appear with a past reference time (and with a future reference time); we will call this XR (extended reference time). The semantics is the same as for the XN perfects in the previous section, but the reference time is anterior to the utterance time rather than including it. A continuous type XR in the past appears with an imperfect tense in Latin

(100) te... libidinosam atque improbam matrem... iam diu *diligebat* (Pro Scaur 8)
pater grandis natu iam diu lecto *tenebatur* (Verr 2.5.16)
illis, quod iam diu *cupiebant*, novandi res occasio data est (Livy 24.29.3).

In the first example (Pro Scaur 8) Aris had loved Bostar's mother over an interval (XR) stretching from a long time before up to the reference time. Experiential and resultative XR readings in past time are encoded by the pluperfect, as already noted in Chapter 1. Here are a few more examples. Frequency adverbs point to an experiential reading

(101) bis consul *fuerat* (De Fin 2.65)
Quod si ego qui trinos ludos aedilis *feceram* tamen Antoni ludis commovebar (Pro Mur 40)
at ille, qui saepius eiusmodi ludos *spectaverat* (Petr 36).

In the second example (Pro Mur 40), at the reference time (the time of Antonius' games) Cicero had put on three sets of earlier games. The following examples contain verbs whose meaning predisposes them to a resultative reading

(100) He had for a long time been in love with you, a lustful and immoral mother (Pro Scaur 8). His elderly father had been confined to bed for quite a while (Verr 2.5.16). The former got an opportunity for revolution, something they had long desired (Livy 24.29.3).

(101) He had been consul twice (De Fin 2.65). But if I, who had given three sets of games as aedile, was nevertheless moved by Antonius' games (Pro Mur 40). But he, who had seen performances of this sort quite often (Petr 36).

(102) Sullae dominatione agros bonaque omnia *amiserat* (Sall Cat 28.4)
omnes Eburonum et Nerviorum quae *convenerant* copiae discedunt (BG 5.58)
L. Caesar... pedibus Hadrumetum *perfugerat.* Id oppidum C. Considius Longus... tuebatur. (BC 2.23).

In the third example (BC 2.23) at the reference time Considius was guarding Hadrumetum and L. Caesar was there as a result of having previously fled on foot.

Now extended (NX), reference time extended (RX)

XN is an interval that stretches back from the present to some point in the past; the present is the right hand boundary of the XN interval. The mirror image of XN is an interval that stretches forward from the present to some point in the future. We will call this interval NX. The present is the left hand boundary of the NX interval. While the resultative and experiential perfects are used to express the poststate of a past event, the prospective is used to express the prestate of a future event: for instance the result of an event fills out XN, while the plan for an event fills out NX. s^e is the prestate of *e* (*e* will occur at an indefinite time in the future): $\exists e.\tau(e) > t^{ref} \wedge P(e) \wedge \tau(s^e) \supset t^{ref}$. In Latin the prospective is encoded by the future participle (representing the right boundary of NX and possibly a preceding subinterval) with the present auxiliary (representing the left boundary of NX)

(103) faber cum quid *aedificaturus est* non ipse facit materiam (ND 3.frag. 2)
de praeda mea praeter quaestores urbanos... teruncium nec attigit nec *tacturus est* quisquam (Ad Fam 2.17.4).

The present component in the meaning of the prospective indicates that the event is already intended, decided, predetermined, etc. at the present time

(104) Bellum *scripturus sum* quod populus Romanus cum Iugurtha rege Numidarum gessit (Sall Jug 5.1)
sin una *est interiturus* animus cum corpore (De Sen 81).

In the first example (Jug 5.1) the prospective expresses the intention of Sallust to write the history of the war with Jugurtha, in the second (De Sen 81) it expresses the idea that the soul is predestined to perish along with the body. We

(102) During the rule of Sulla they had lost all their lands and property (Sall Cat 28.4). All the forces of the Eburones and the Nervii that had assembled departed (BG 5.58). L. Caesar had fled on foot to Hadrumetum. C. Considius Longus was guarding this town (BC 2.23).
(103) A builder when he is going to build something does not make the timber himself (ND 3.frag. 2). Noone apart from the urban quaestors has touched or is going to touch a penny of my booty (Ad Fam 2.17.4).
(104) I am going to write the history of the war which the Roman people waged with Jugurtha, king of the Numidians (Sall Jug 5.1). But if my soul is going to perish along with my body (De Sen 81).

will not repeat the remarks already made in Chapter 1 about modal components in the meaning of the future and of agency, which also apply to the prospective. Although upcoming events are perhaps more likely to be decided or predetermined than distant events, there is in principle no metrical constraint on the extent of the NX interval

(105) ille in balineas *iturust,* inde huc veniet postea (Pl Asin 357)
qui fuerunt quique *futuri sunt* posthac stulti (Pl Bacch 1087).

So the Latin prospective corresponds more closely to English 'is going to' than 'is about to, is on the verge of.' The prospective differs from the perfect in allowing event time positional temporal adverbials

(106) si in senatum non est *Kal. Iuniis* venturus (Ad Att 14.18.4)
Ille abducturus est mulierem *cras.* (Pl Pseud 82).

In this too it is more like English 'is going to' than 'is about to' (which has an inbuilt NX measure): "I am going to / *about to take care of this tomorrow at 3 o'clock.' Although the speaker often has a choice whether to encode an event with the future or with the prospective, their meanings remain distinct

(107) *fiet* tamen illud quod *futurum est* (De Div 2.21)
si *est* bellum civile *futurum,* quod certe erit (Ad Att 14.13.2).

Fiet in the first example (De Div 2.21) is an assertion about an event in the future, *futurum est* is an assertion about the present and the following NX interval; if there were no difference, the sentence would be a tautology. In conversation the future is more appropriate when it expresses a decision made by the speaker in response to what the other interlocutor has just said (e.g. 'I will do what you suggest,' $t^{ref} > t^{u}$), while the prospective is more appropriate when it expresses a pre-existing decision on the part of one of the interlocutors (e.g. 'I have already decided/am already scheduled to do what you suggest,' $t^{ref} = t^{u}$, left boundary of NX)

(108) TOX. Hoc si *facturu's* face. SAT. *Faciam* equidem quae vis (Pl Pers 146)
PER. Quin tu eloquere, quid *faciemus?...* EP. Tum tu igitur calide quidquid *acturu's* age (Pl Ep 274, 284)
LACH. I ergo intro... dixi. SO. Ita ut iubes *faciam.* (Ter Hec 612)
SAT. *Futura es* dicto oboediens an non patri? VIR. *Futura* (Pl Pers 378).

(105) He is going to go to the baths and from there he will come here afterwards (Pl Asin 357). Past and future idiots (Pl Bacch 1087).

(106) If he is not going to come to the senate on June 1st (Ad Att 14.18.4). He's going to take the woman away tomorrow (Pl Pseud 82).

(107) What is going to happen will happen (De Div 2.21). If there is going to be a civil war, which there certainly will be (Ad Att 14.13.2).

(108) TOX. If you're going to do this, do it. SAT. I'll do what you want (Pl Pers 146). PER. Tell me: what shall we do? EP. Then quickly do whatever you are going to do (Pl Ep 274), 284). LACH. So go inside: those are my instructions. SO. I'll do as you say (Ter Hec 612). SAT. Are you going to obey your father or not? VIR. I am (Pl Pers 378).

We have seen that XN intervals can appear with past and future reference times (right hand boundaries), which we called XR intervals. The mirror images of XR intervals are NX intervals with past and future reference times (left hand boundaries); we call these RX intervals. The following examples combine an instance of past XR (pluperfect tense) with an instance of past RX (past prospective tense)

(109) quem neque umquam ante *videram* nec *eram* postea *visurus* (Livy 42.41.4)
is id quod *erat aedificaturus* iis rebus ornare quas *ceperat* noluit (Verr 2.4.123).

In the first example (Livy 42.41) at no time during an XR interval stretching back from the past reference time nor during an RX interval stretching forward from the past reference time had/would Perseus see(n) Rammius. Where the narrative structure does not require a past prospective, it is more straightforward to substitute a simple past tense. Instead of saying 'I was going to fly to Paris yesterday' you would simply say 'I flew to Paris yesterday,' if that is what you did. However the past prospective would have to be retained if the prospective event did not materialize ('I was going to fly to Paris yesterday, but my flight was cancelled')

(110) iam arietem muris *admoturus erat.* Ceterum incepto absistere eum coegit subitus Aetolorum adventus (Livy 32.4.1)
iam lituus pugnae signa *daturus erat,* cum raptae veniunt inter patresque virosque (Ov Fast 3.216).

This explains how past prospectives can be licensed in the apodosis of past unfulfilled conditionals

(111) *Relicturi* agros omnes *erant,* nisi ad eos Metellus Roma litteras misisset (Verr 2.3.121).

That is not to say that all past prospectives involve cancelled events

(112) Nam Ariminum ad exercitum *erat iturus*; et statim iit. (Ad Fam 8.4.4)
Silva erat vasta... qua exercitum *traducturus erat.* (Livy 23.24.7)
Scipio... omnia de industria in eum diem quo *pugnaturus erat* mutavit (Livy 28.14.6).

(109) Whom I had never seen before and was never going to see again (Livy 42.41.4). He was unwilling to adorn what he was going to build with the objects that he had captured (Verr 2.4.123).

(110) He was already about to move his battering ram up to the walls. But the sudden arrival of the Aetolians forced him to desist from his endeavour (Livy 32.4.1). The trumpet was already about to give the signal for battle, when the ravished women interposed themselves between their fathers and their husbands (Ov Fast 3.216).

(111) They would all have abandoned their fields, if Metellus had not sent a letter to them from Rome (Verr 2.3.121).

(112) For Pompey was about to go to his army at Ariminum; and he did go immediately (Ad Fam 8.4.4). There was a very large forest, through which he was going to lead his army (Livy 23.24.7). Scipio on purpose changed everything for the day on which he was going to fight (Livy 28.14.6).

In the second example (Livy 23.24) Postumius did lead his army through the forest and was consequently defeated and killed. In the third example (Livy 28.14) Scipio did go on to fight on that day. In both these examples a relative clause contains a predetermined event later than the reference time.

Future RX intervals stretch from a future time to another later future time

(113) ne quem exercitum qui cum populo Romano sociisve bellum *gesturus erit* rex per fines regni sui... transire sinito (Livy 38.38.2)
Quem ramum *insiturus eris* praecidito (Cato 40.2).

In the second example (Cato 40.2) the cutting event is in the future and the grafting event is predetermined at the reference time of the cutting event and occurs later than the cutting event; the interval between the cutting and the grafting is the RX interval.

Encoding aspect

In the analysis of aspectual meaning we have just given, you will have noticed that sometimes a distinction in aspectual meaning was morphologically encoded, sometimes it was not. Most importantly, the basic distinction between perfective and imperfective aspect is encoded by distinct inflections in the past tense but not in the present or the future; this is illustrated in Figure 2.8. The perfectivity distinction is more important and productive in the past tense, but it is not absent in the present and future tense, just morphologically neutralized. Languages may differ in their inventories of aspectual morphemes, but it does not necessarily follow that there are corresponding differences in the range of aspectual meanings that they can access. The imperfective (*-ba-*) and perfective (e.g. *-vi-*) inflectional endings are portmanteau morphemes encoding both aspect and past tense. They are not purely aspectual morphemes (with default tense associations): *-ba-* is not used for imperfective meanings in the present and future, and *-vi-* is not used for perfective meanings in the present and future. On this approach past forms are not marked for aspect and unmarked for tense, but rather present and future

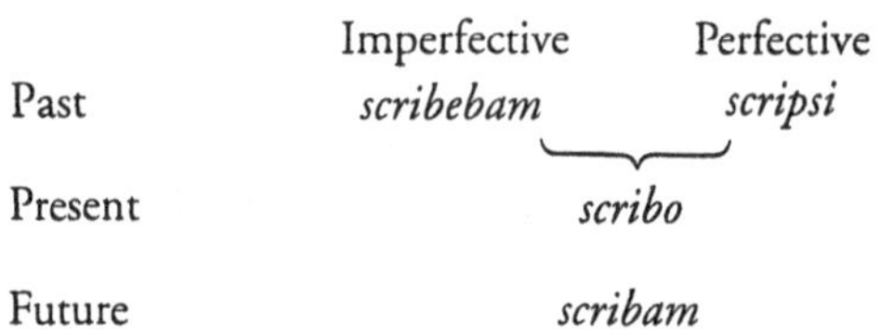

Imperfective
Perfective
Past
scribebam
scripsi
Present
scribo
Future
scribam

Figure 2.8
Morphological encoding of perfectivity

(113) The king is not to allow any army that is going to make war with the Roman people or its allies to cross through the territory of his kingdom (Livy 38.38.2). Cut off the tip of the branch you are going to graft (Cato 40.2).

forms are marked for tense and unmarked for aspect. However there are a number of exceptional usages that do not conform to the general tense system and that point to an earlier more aspectually oriented system. We list them in the following paragraphs.

Even in Classical Latin the future perfect is sometimes used instead of the simple future, i.e. for an event which is included in a future reference time rather than anterior to a future reference time

(114) Atque huiusce rei coniecturam de tuo ipsius studio, Servi, facillime *ceperis* (Pro Mur 9)
Nusquam facilius hanc miserrimam vitam vel sustentabo vel, quod multo est melius, *abiecero.* (Ad Att 3.19.1)
ego certe meum rei publicae atque imperatori officium *praestitero* (BG 4.25).

The presence of adverbs denoting the degree of facility with which the action is completed suggests that this use of the perfective can have the connotation of successful completion (cp. *videro* 'I'll see to it,' *videbo* 'I will see'). The verbs are mostly telic; contrast the use of the simple future for atelic *sustento* in the second example (Ad Att 3.19). If you succeed in doing something, you are in the poststate of doing it, so this usage could conceivably have received some synchronic support from reanalysis in terms of the regular (nonaspectual) meaning of the future perfect. In a number of examples the future perfect in a main clause expresses the automatic consequence of the eventuality in a related clause

(115) Qui enim M. Antonium *oppresserit*, is bellum *confecerit* (Ad Fam 10.13.2)
Tolle hanc opinionem, luctum *sustuleris* (Tusc 1.30).

The perfect subjunctive is used quite regularly in prohibitions with reference to future time

(116) Deus siquidem nobis consulebat, 'Hoc facito, hoc ne *feceris*' diceret (De Div 2.127)
Ne vos quidem, iudices ii qui me absolvistis, mortem *timueritis* (Tusc 1.98).

In positive commands the perfective entails the imperfective, but negation reverses the direction of entailment; so in negative commands the imperfective entails the perfective (what you don't even start you can't possibly complete). Imperfective negative commands are stronger than perfective ones and weaker than prestate ones ('don't even think about it'). Some (but not all) Slavic lan-

(114) You can easily get an idea of what I mean from the analogy of your own profession, Servius (Pro Mur 9). Nowhere will I find it easier to either continue this wretched life of mine or, preferably, put a definite end to it (Ad Att 3.19.1). I at least will be sure to do my duty to the republic and the general (BG 4.25).

(115) The man who crushes M. Antonius is the man who will effectively bring the war to an end (Ad Fam 10.13.2). Take away this belief and you will effectively abolish grief (Tusc 1.30).

(116) If god looked after our interests, he would say "Do this, don't do that!" (De Div 2.127). Don't you fear death either, judges who voted for my acquittal (Tusc 1.98).

guages grammaticalize the perfective for nonvolitional negative commands, so it is interesting that the competing *noli(te)* construction in Latin etymologically presupposes volitional control over the activity subevent. But a perfective complement infinitive is fine after *ne velis/t* in examples like the following

(117) Nequid *emisse* velit insciente domini, neu quid dominum *celavisse* velit. (Cato 5.4)
Interdico ne *extulisse* extra aedis puerum usquam velis. (Ter Hec 563).

The perfective present infinitive is much exploited in Augustan verse poets

(118) cum cupiam dominae *tetigisse* papillas et laevam tunicis *inseruisse* manum (Ov Am 2.15.11)
Talia Milanion Atalantes crura fugacis optavit manibus *sustinuisse* suis. (Ov Am 3.2.29).

When a potential subjunctive is used to attenuate the speaker's responsibility for an assertion, it is sometimes in the perfect

(119) ego istis *censuerim*... novam istam... orationem fugiendam (Brut 288)
Hoc vero sine ulla dubitatione *confirmaverim*... rem unam esse omnium difficillimam (Brut 25).

This perfect subjunctive refers to future time, not past time; contrast the perfect subjunctive in discourse concessions

(120) *induxerit* eum L. Saturnini familiaritas ut amicitiam patriae praeponeret (Pro Rab Perd 23)

which is a real past tense and triggers historical sequence of tenses.

In consecutive clauses a perfect subjunctive is common for past events in apparent violation of the sequence of tenses

(121) Equites hostium essedariique acriter proelio cum equitatu nostro in itinere conflixerunt, ita tamen ut nostri... eos in silvas collesque *compulerint* (BG 5.15)
tantum tamen consilio atque auctoritate valuit ut se... novis opibus copiisque *renovarit*. (Pro Mur 33).

(117) He must not buy anything without the knowledge of the master or hide anything from the master (Cato 5.4). I forbid you to take the child anywhere outside the house (Ter Hec 563).

(118) When I desired to touch the breasts of my mistress and to slip my left hand into her dress (Ov Am 2.15.11). Your legs are like those of the speedy Atalanta that Milanion desired to make love holding up with his hands (Ov Am 3.2.29).

(119) I am inclined to think that they should not adopt this new style of oratory (Brut 288). But I am inclined to assert without any doubt that it is the one most difficult thing of all (Brut 25).

(120) Granted that his intimacy with L. Saturninus induced him to put friendship ahead of country (Pro Rab Perd 23).

(121) The enemy cavalry and charioteers fought fiercely with our cavalry on the march, but the outcome was that our men drove them into the woods and the hills (BG 5.15). He still had such ingenuity and influence that he recovered with new resources and troops (Pro Mur 33).

These subjunctives cannot be interpreted as resultative perfects: the Britons were no longer in the woods at the time Caesar was writing and by the time of Cicero's defence of Murena the war was over and Mithridates was dead. They are perfective, often again with a connotation of successful completion.

The range of evidence for nonpast uses of perfect forms points to some degree of layering in the Latin verbal system. It is basically a tense system, but there is an underlying layer of older aspectual usages that emerges in certain more marked constructions. We have already noted above that there is a tendency to use forms with a telicizing prefix for the perfective and forms without a prefix for the imperfective, and that this tendency is said to be stronger in early Latin.

Speakers often need to refer to the different phases that an event passes through as it is enacted. Such phases include the prestate, inceptive, conative, progressive, perseverative, terminative, poststate; they are illustrated in Figure 2.9. Phasal distinctions can be encoded lexically or by derivational and inflectional morphology. Lexical encoding is done by socalled aspectualizer verbs

(122) cum pluere *incipiet* (Cato 155)
flumen transire *coeperunt* (BG 7.11)

Punice *pergam* loqui (Pl Poen 983)
si malle obsideri *pergat* (Livy 25.30.3)

cum *desierit* pluere (Cato 155)
orationes aliis *destitisse* scribere (Brut 48)
finem fecimus et ambulandi et disputandi (De Fin 2.119).

The first set of examples illustrates inceptive aspectualizer verbs, the second set perseveratives, the third set terminatives. In the following example a modal verb is used temporally to express a prestate

(123) cretatam praetor cum *vellet* mittere mappam (Mart 12.28.9).

If phase is encoded inflectionally, it represents a stage of the eventuality; if it is encoded derivationally, it is lexicalized as an independent eventuality with its own phases. In this sense phase structure is hierarchical. Inflectional coding has

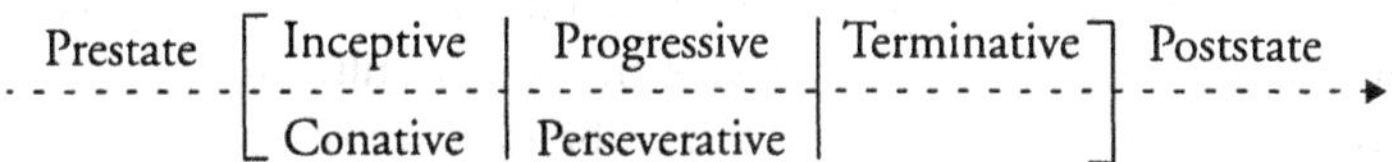

Figure 2.9
Phasal structure of events

(122) When it begins to rain (Cato 155). They began to cross the river (BG 7.11). I'll keep talking Punic (Pl Poen 983). If he continues to prefer to be besieged (Livy 25.30.3). When it has stopped raining (Cato 155). He stopped writing speeches for others (Brut 48). We came to the end of our walk and our discussion (De Fin 2.119).

(123) When the praetor was about to give the start signal with his white flag (Mart 12.28.9).

already largely been covered by the analysis in this chapter. A prestate phase is denoted by NX-forms like the prospective (*futurum est* 'is going to happen') and by use of the futurate (*cras mane vadit* 'He's leaving early tomorrow'). Since the imperfective excludes the terminative phase of an event, it can take on an inceptive or conative connotation (*dabat* 'offered') when the initial phases of the event are salient, and a progressive or perseverative connotation when the nuclear phases are salient. A conative connotation is not possible with atelic eventuality types once the event has initiated: the initial phase of an event of running or fighting is itself a successfully enacted event of running or fighting. A perseverative connotation is found when the eventuality might be expected to terminate but does not

(124) et nihilominus sordidatus divitem *sequebatur* (Sen Con 10.1.Pref)
cum Sextium audiret, nihilominus *declamitabat* (Sen Con 2.Pref.4).

Both examples are habituals. Perfective forms include the terminative phase of the event for both atelic and telic eventualities, while resultative perfects denote the poststate of telic events.

Now we will give some examples of the derivational encoding of phase by prefixes and suffixes. A prestate phase is denoted by desideratives like *esurio* 'desire to eat, be hungry,' *empturio* 'desire to shop,' *micturio* 'desire to urinate.' An ingressive (or more precisely nonterminative) phase is denoted by verbs like *lucesco* 'grow light, dawn,' *plumesco* 'become feathered,' *condormisco* 'fall asleep,' which are incremental: each stage in the progression of the event corresponds to a degree on the scale of the property described. Verbs with a telicizing prefix indicate that the terminative phase is included in the denotation of the verb: *ebibo* 'drink up,' *transfigo* 'pierce through,' *emorior* 'perish.' The prefix *per-* can have a perdurative or perseverative connotation, meaning that a goal is reached although the event might have been expected to stop earlier (thereby making the nuclear phase of the event salient and presupposing that it has already commenced): *perdormisco* 'sleep on to,' *pervigilo* 'stay awake all night.' Intensives also highlight the nuclear phase of the event: *curro* 'run,' *curso* 'run around,' *cursito* 'keep running around'; *volo* 'fly,' *volito* 'fly around.' While the intensive relates to the strength or rate of occurrence of the event, the iterative relates to its repetition. Although distinct in principle, these notions are affinite, since they can represent different strategies for achieving the same result. Consider for instance *pulso* 'strike repeatedly, beat up,' which is the iterative of *pello* 'strike': beating someone (or something) repeatedly is tantamount to beating him intensively.

In Latin tense and aspect are mostly fused into a single portmanteau morpheme attached to the verb; so the meaning components contributed by an inflectional ending have to be disentangled, raised out of the nuclear verb phrase, and arranged in some order suitable for the composition of meaning.

(124) And notwithstanding continued to follow the rich man in mourning clothes (Sen Con 10.1.Pref). Although he was a student of Sextius, he nevertheless continued declaiming (Sen Con 2.Pref.4).

Crosslinguistic analysis of languages from all over the world indicates that when tense and aspect are encoded by separate morphemes (whether those are affixes, auxiliaries or particles), aspect is regularly closer to the verb than tense. So the order is T(ense) Asp(ect) V(erb) for preverbal morphemes and V Asp T for postverbal morphemes. Evidently the linear order reflects the compositional order of the morphemes: the verb phrase (VP) is the locus of eventuality type meaning; aspect dominates (scopes over) VP and tense dominates [Asp [VP]]. Aspect functions as an interface between the temporal information contributed by the verb phrase and the temporal information contributed by tense. In very general terms, first the event time $\tau(e)$ is computed from the verb combined with other material in the verb phrase; then Asp accesses the reference time t^{ref} and establishes a relation of inclusion between $\tau(e)$ and t^{ref}; finally T accesses the utterance time t^{u} and establishes a relation between t^{ref} and t^{u}. The compositional details of all this were already presented in Chapter 1.

FURTHER READING

Giorgi & Pianesi (1997); Kempchinsky & Slabakova (2005); Rothstein (2004); Smith (1997).

3 | ARGUMENT STRUCTURE

We saw in the previous chapter that there are a few main ways in which eventualities can unfold through time. Grammar does not see each eventuality as unique but is sensitive to certain general temporal properties of eventualities which repeat from one eventuality to another. This allows eventualities to be classified into the four main classes of eventuality types: state, activity, accomplishment, achievement. But eventualities are not purely temporal objects: apart from anything else, they have both internal and external causal and consequential structure. Eventualities have aptly been compared to little scenes in the drama of life, and, like scenes in a drama, eventualities contain not just (states or) events but also the participants in those events. In this respect too, eventualities are not unique; they can be classified on the basis of generalizations about the number and roles of their participants. Furthermore, the two bases of classification are not independent: eventuality type and participant structure can be integrated into a single unified account of event structure. On this approach events are not atomic but can be built up by combining more simply structured subevents into a single complex event. Different eventuality types can have different subevent structures: for instance telicity requires the projection of an additional subevent. Each subevent has its own predicational structure. Not only is there a connection between the complexity of an event and the number of its participants, but participants playing different roles can be typically associated with different subevents in a complex event or with different structural positions within a single subevent. There are rules for mapping or linking positions and properties of event structure to grammatical relations, case morphology and syntactic structure.

Argument structure and thematic roles

Argument structure, as used in predicate logic, and thematic roles are convenient grammatical devices for stating the morphosyntactically relevant properties of event structure. Argument structure gives the set of arguments associated with a predicate and the hierarchical relationship among them. *Interfecit* (*x*, *y*) means that two participants, *x* and *y*, are involved in a killing relationship and *x* is hierarchically superior to *y*; so *x* is the subject and *y* is the object. Since one and the same verb can be used in different event structures, a single verb can have more than one argument structure. Even if it is not entirely predictable which verbs can be used with which event structures (they have to be learned for each language), it is by no means random either, because the lexical meaning of a verb is compatible with certain event structures and incompatible with others.

Thematic roles allow one to make additional generalizations about the semantic properties of the different arguments of classes of verbs, for instance *x* is the agent of a killing event and *y* the patient. Here are some of the more important ones, with informal definitions

AGENT: volitional, energized initiator of an action

(1) Patrem occidit Sex. *Roscius* (Pro Rosc Am 39)

EXPERIENCER: one undergoing an involuntary mental state arising from some external sensory, cognitive or affective stimulus

(2) *Quis* vocem praeconis audivit? (Phil 2.103)

PATIENT: one undergoing and being affected or changed by an action

(3) *Patrem* occidit Sex. Roscius (Pro Rosc Am 39)

STIMULUS: nonvolitional source of a mental state in an experiencer

(4) Quis *vocem praeconis* audivit? (Phil 2.103)

CAUSE: entity responsible for a change of state; not necessarily animate or volitional

(5) saxaque interfluens *unda* medium opus rupit (Curt Ruf 4.3.6)

INSTRUMENT: something used by the agent in an action

(6) ne cum improbis boni *ferro* dimicarent (De Dom 5)

THEME: spatially located or displaced entity or, more generally, undergoing entity

(7) *tela* intra vallum coniciebant (BG 5.57)

POSSESSOR: one who possesses some property

(8) Fundum habet in agro Thurino M. *Tullius* paternum (Pro Tull 14)

(1) Sex. Roscius killed his father (Pro Rosc Am 39).
(2) Who heard the voice of the auctioneer? (Phil 2.103).
(3) Sex. Roscius killed his father (Pro Rosc Am 39).
(4) Who heard the voice of the auctioneer? (Phil 2.103).
(5) The water flowing between the stones broke right through the earthwork (Curt Ruf 4.3.6).
(6) So as to avoid having good men come into armed conflict with wicked men (De Dom 5).
(7) They hurled weapons inside the rampart (BG 5.57).
(8) M. Tullius possesses a farm inherited from his father in the territory of Thurium (Pro Tull 14).

POSSESSED: property possessed

(9) *Fundum* habet in agro Thurino M. Tullius paternum (Pro Tull 14)

RECIPIENT, DEPRIVEE: one involved in the transfer of property

(10) arma *Satricanis* ademit (Livy 9.16.10)

BENEFACTIVE, MALEFACTIVE: one benefiting or being injured by the action of another

(11) Neque enim solum *nobis* divites esse volumus sed liberis, propinquis, amicis, maximeque rei publicae (De Off 3.63)

COMITATIVE: spatially associated with the agent or participating with the agent in the action

(12) Cursare iste homo potens *cum filio* blando et gratioso circum tribus (Verr 1.25)

LOCATIVE: static location

(13) *suo* stare *loco* (Livy 9.37.3)

GOAL: location towards which

(14) Mancinus *domum* revenisset (De Or 1.181)

SOURCE: location from which

(15) quem numquam incursiones hostium *loco* movere potuerunt (Pro Rab Perd 36).

The information conveyed by both argument structure and semantic roles is directly derivable from the event structures to be presented in the next section, specifically from the structural position occupied by the participant argument and the semantics of the associated subeventual head.

Event structure

With these preliminaries out of the way, we start our analysis with a set of morphologically related verbs to illustrate the basic mechanics of event structure

(16) dum aestivis serenitatibus ager *aret* (Col 2.8.5)
Padi fons mediis diebus aestivis... semper *aret* (NH 2.229)

(9) M. Tullius possesses a farm inherited from his father in the territory of Thurium (Pro Tull 14).

(10) He deprived the Satricans of their arms (Livy 9.16.10).

(11) For we don't desire to be rich only for ourselves, but also for our children, our relatives, our friends, and above all for the state (De Off 3.63).

(12) This powerful man rushed around the tribes with his charming and obliging son (Verr 1.25).

(13) They stayed in their positions (Livy 9.37.3).

(14) Mancinus had returned home (De Or 1.181).

(15) Who the attacks of the enemy were never able to shift from his position (Pro Rab Perd 36).

(16) When the ground is dry during the clear summer weather (Col 2.8.5). The source of the Po is always dry at noon during the summer (NH 2.229).

(17) herba cum... aestu *arescit* subsecari falcibus debet et quaad *perarescat* furcillis versari; cum *peraruit*... vehi ad villam (Varro RR 1.49.1)
in qualo ubi *arescant* componito; ubi *arebunt*... (Cato 76.1)
cito enim *arescit* lacrima (De Part Or 57)
cum argilla *exaruit* (Col 12.46.5)

(18) Murtam nigram *arfacito* in umbra; ubi iam passa erit... (Cato 125.1)
(dolium olearium novum) *arfacito*; ubi *arebit*... (Cato 69.2).

The event structure illustrated by the examples of *areo* 'be dry' in (16) is that of a monadic (one-argument) state. The event comprises a single subevent: $e = e^S$. This is formalized by the simple logical form in Figure 3.1. We use the term logical form to mean a syntactically structured semantic representation: it is not intended to be an abstract syntactic structure. We are using a version of event semantics in which all eventualities, including states, are assigned event arguments; tense and viewpoint aspect are outside the scope of the figure. The bottom right hand node P is a scalar property of individuals, equivalent to the adjective *aridus* 'dry.' The ground is understood as being located at a point (degree) on the scale of humidity that qualifies as dry. This is represented by the symbol $d^>$, which can be read in two ways, either as the maximum degree on the inverse scale of humidity or as some degree within the scalar interval that

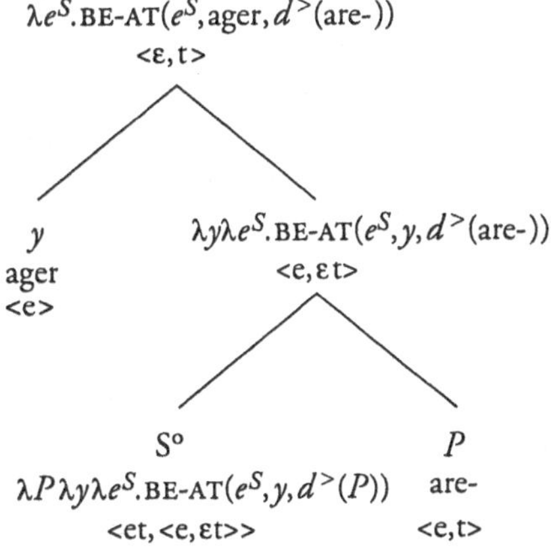

Figure 3.1
Monadic state
Ager aret (Col 2.8.5)

(17) When the grass becomes dry from the heat, it should be cut off with sickles; it should be turned with pitchforks until it becomes completely dry; when it is completely dry, it should be brought to the farmhouse (Varro RR 1.49.1). Arrange them in a basket for them to dry there; when they are dry... (Cato 76.1). For a tear dries quickly (De Part Or 57). When the clay has dried (Col 12.46.5).

(18) Dry black myrtle in the shade; when it is dry... (Cato 125.1). Let the new oil jar dry. When it is dry... (Cato 69.2).

qualifies as dry. As its type indicates, the (sub)event head S° is a function from a property of individuals to a function from an individual to a property of events. It composes with P to give a function from an individual to a property of events. This in turn composes with y (*ager*, a definite description, the theme of the state) in the specifier position to give the meaning of the top node, which denotes a set of eventualities in which the field is in a state of dryness.

Aresco 'become dry' in (17) belongs to a class of verbs known as incremental change of state verbs or inchoative degree predicates. *Aresco* has two readings, an atelic reading and a telic reading. The atelic reading is a simple process, that is an unenergized activity: (y BECOME-MORE). In the first example (RR 1.49) the grass before it is cut undergoes a series of changes of state, each one from a state of being less dry into a state of being more dry (not represented in the figure): each change of state is an achievement, but iteration turns the series into a process with repeatable subevents. This gives a scalar progression down a metaphorical path of dehumidification (whose starting point need not be the maximal degree of wetness). Although it is true that there is a point of maximal dryness beyond which the process cannot continue, that point is not part of the conceptualization of the event (and is actually specifically excluded by the following context in the Varro example). The scalar progression can be delimited (broken off) at any stage

(19) cum deinde modice *aruerint*, in vasa nova... reponito. (Col 12.16.2),

but there is no inbuilt telos: that is why you can say 'My shirt dried for over an hour, at which point it was still quite wet.' Compare the incremental path in atelic 'drive towards Oxford' with the goal in telic 'drive to Oxford.' The simple process event structure is illustrated in Figure 3.2: e^P means process (sub)event. Once again the y argument has the thematic role of theme and is the subject of the sentence.

The telic reading, on the other hand, has a complex event structure that combines the process with its resultant state: (y GO-TO e^S), where e^S is *areo*, as before. The telic reading is indicated by the context in the second example in (17) (Cato 76.1) and by the rate or time-within-which adverb *cito* in the third (Part Or 57), and is explicitly encoded by the telic prefixes in *perarescat* 'dry thoroughly' (RR 1.49) and *exaruit* 'has dried out' (Col 12.46). The unprefixed form just denotes attainment of a scalar degree corresponding to a state that qualifies as *aret*, which is not necessarily the state of maximum possible dryness; the prefixed forms not only induce the telic reading but also serve to indicate that a point at the high end of the scale of dryness is effectively attained. (Remember that we are talking about eventuality types, not viewpoint aspect: viewpoint aspect does not change telicity, it just tells you whether the telos has been reached at the reference time in any particular situation.) In achievement change of state verbs like *obstupesco* 'be struck dumb' the process subevent is instantaneous. The event structure of a resultative process is illustrated in Fig-

(19) Then when they have become moderately dry, store them in new jars (Col 12.16.2).

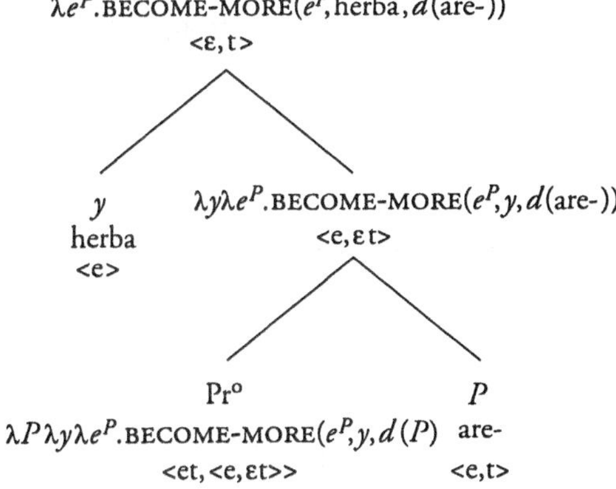

Figure 3.2
Monadic process
Herba arescit (cp. Varro RR 1.49.1)

ure 3.3. According to the analysis adopted here, GO-TO, the metapredicate in Pr° (the head of the process subevent), is a relation between a theme (y) and an eventuality (e^S). The latter is the same as the state depicted in Figure 3.1. GO-TO picks up the scalar dimension lexicalized in the verbal root. So the decomposition paraphrases as 'the set of events in which the clay progresses along a scale of decreasing humidity to a state in which it is dried out.' The resultant state subevent is now an argument of GO-TO. In order to create a single structure, we need to glue the subevents together somehow. One way of doing so is to treat the lower subevent as an indefinite event description. So it is shifted from a set of events <ε,t> into an indefinite individual event of type <ε> (not a quantifier); this is effected in the figure by insertion of a determiner branch informally labelled 'an' (omitted in other figures to reduce complexity). Since the process and its resultant state have the same theme y, the whole complex predicate e^{PS} is still monadic. For the sake of simplicity, we have not abstracted over y, but just lexically inserted it twice (assuming identity), and we have not carried the descriptive content of the stative subevent up the tree. The decomposed predicate λe^P.GO-TO(e^P, argilla, an e^S.BE-AT (e^S, argilla, exare-)) and the undecomposed predicate λe.Exarescit(e, argilla) denote the same characteristic function and consequently the same set of events in all worlds, so we can use the undecomposed version as input to the aspect and tense operators in Chapter 1, since they are not sensitive to the decomposed structure.

Arefacio 'make dry' in (18) adds a superimposed causative subevent with its own participant to any of the change of state structures analyzed so far. The addition of a participant changes the event structure from monadic (intransitive) to dyadic, in this case transitive. That a causative subevent can be added to atelic processes (e^P, illustrated in Figure 3.2) is indicated by examples like

$\lambda e^P.\text{GO-TO}(e^P, \text{argilla}, (\text{an})e^S) = \lambda e.\text{Exarescit}(e, \text{argilla})$
<ε,t>

y
argilla
<e>

$\lambda y \lambda e^P.\text{GO-TO}(e^P, y, (\text{an})e^S)$
<e,εt>

Pr°
$\lambda e^S \lambda y \lambda e^P.\text{GO-TO}(e^P, y, e^S)$
-scit
<ε,<e,εt>>

$(\text{an})e^S$
<ε>

an
$\lambda Q[\text{an}(e).Q(e)]$
<εt,ε>

$\lambda e^S.\text{BE-AT}(e^S, \text{argilla}, \text{exare-})$
<εt>

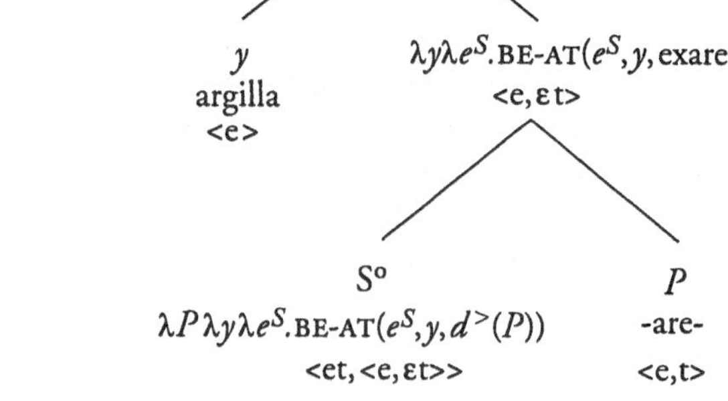

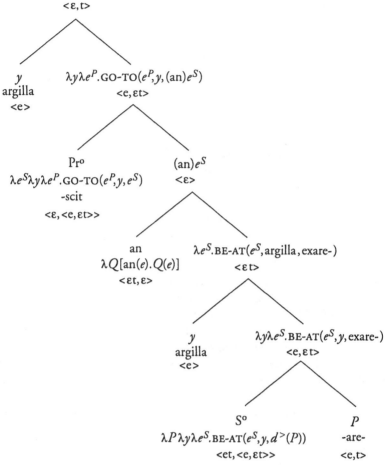

Figure 3.3
Development
Argilla exarescit (cp. Col 12.46.5)

(20) Postea dolium *calfacito* minus quam si picare velis (Cato 69.2)
paulum *pavefactus* (Gell 19.1.9)
parum *patefaciunt* (Cels 7.26.2I),

where the degree modifiers show that the process, while incremental, has not reached an intrinsic telos. That a causative subevent (e^C) can be added to telic processes (e^{PS}, illustrated in Figure 3.3) is indicated by causatives with telic

(20) After that heat the jar less than if you were going to apply pitch to it (Cato 69.2). A bit scared (Gell 19.1.9). They make too small an opening (Cels 7.26.2I).

prefixes like *perfrigefacio* 'chill out,' *excal(e)facio* 'warm up,' although the latter also allows scalar modification

(21) Vetus autem *magis* excalfacit corpora (NH 23.82)

('warms you up more'). The context shows that both examples of *arefacio* in (18) are telic: the telos supplies the reference time for the following temporal clauses with *ubi*. The event structure for these examples is (x CAUSE (y GO-TO e^S)): it is set out in Figure 3.4 for a simplified version of the first example (Cato 125.1), *murtam arefacit* 'he dries the myrtle' (with an indicative verb and a definite object). Like GO-TO, CAUSE is here a relation between an individual and an event, namely the covert pronominal subject x and the process (e^P). The latter is again converted from a set of events into an individual event by the addition of a determiner-like operator of type <εt, ε> (not represented by a separate branch in the diagram). The state subevent is an argument of the process subevent, and the process subevent in its turn is an argument of the cause subevent. In English we get nested relative clauses: 'the set of causative subevents in which he causes a process subevent in which the myrtle goes down a path of dehumidification to a state subevent in which it is dry.' As before, the decomposed predicate and the undecomposed predicate denote the same characteristic function and consequently the same set of events in all worlds. To keep things simple, we have again not carried the descriptive content of the subevents and their combinations up the tree, but just used e^S, e^P and e^{PS} as abbreviations. For an atelic causative, the resultant state subevent (e^S) has to be deleted from the diagram, leaving just e^{CP}. Once again the change of state can be instantaneous: this is hardly applicable to *arefacio* (outside the area of flash-drying technology), but it typically applies to *obstupefacio* 'stun.' According to the terminology adopted here, a causer is a causative agent (whether acting intentionally or unintentionally); nonagentive causes are inanimate. It is also possible to treat the metapredicates as relations between subevents, since it is what the causer does that actually causes the process, and the process culminates in the resultant state.

It is clear that the event structures just analyzed have an autonomous semantic existence. They are not simply idiosyncratic structures projected by individual lexical items. The derivational processes involved are highly productive with events involving scalar properties: so beside *areo – aresco – arefacio*, we find *madeo – madesco – madefacio* 'wet,' *candeo – candesco – candefacio* 'whiten,' *frigeo – frigesco – frigefacio* 'cool,' *rubeo – rubesco – rubefacio* 'redden,' *caleo – calesco – calefacio* 'heat,' *tumeo – tumesco – tumefacio* 'make swollen,' *putreo – putresco – putrefacio* 'rot.' It follows that the argument and event structures involved are generally and independently available, and the lexical semantics of the verb is matched with and integrated into an appropriate event structure, modifying and enriching the bleached-out meanings of the metapredicates in the event structure. The different subevents posited in the analysis are morpho-

(21) It warms the body up more when it is old (NH 23.82).

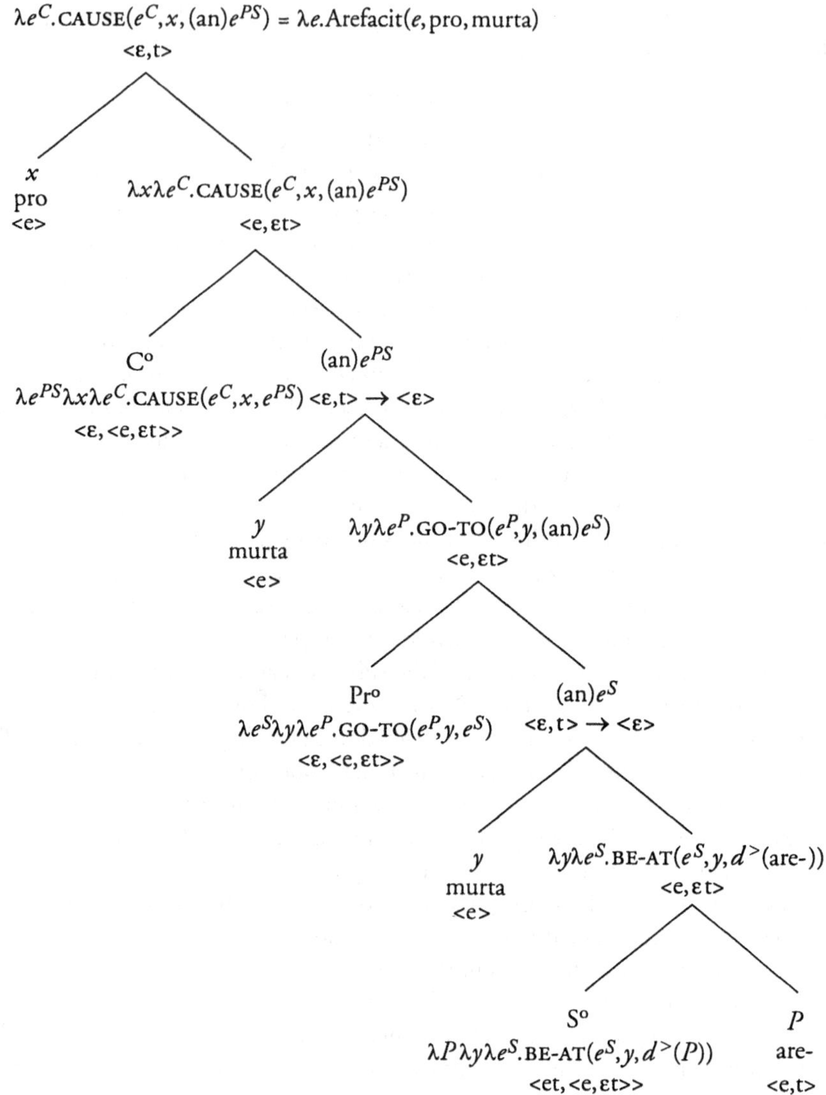

Figure 3.4
Causative
Murtam arefacit (cp. Cato 125.1)

logically transparent: the causative subevent is encoded by the suffix *-faci-*, the process subevent by the suffix *-sc-* (omitted in e^{CPS}), and the stative by the suffix *-e-*; telicity is also encoded by prefixes.

The value of a decompositional analysis is further illustrated by the association of telicizing prefixes with socalled unselected objects, a topic that was briefly mentioned in Chapter 2. Consider the following examples

(22) Aethiopes ultra *sedent* (Mela 3.85)
insident verticem Pisidae (NH 5.94)

et ducit remos illic ubi nuper *arabat* (Ov Met 1.293)
Qui publicos agros *arant* (Verr 2.5.53)
lupinum... pro stercore *inarare* solent (Varro RR 1.23.3)

cursant per urbem (Tac Ann 2.82)
Hercules... modo huc modo illuc *cursabat* (Sen Apoc 9)
Volsinienses... agros Romanos *incursavere* (Livy 5.31.5).

In each set of examples the prefix adds a new locative subeventual structure with its own arguments, thereby either transitivizing the unprefixed verb or modifying its argument structure. (In the first set the unprefixed verb is a state, in the other two it is an activity.) In the prefixed verbs, the verbal root is interpreted as a separate event that lexicalizes one of the metapredicates of the new event structure containing the locative subevent. For instance, in the second set *inarare* (RR 1.23) means to cause by ploughing to go to a state of being in (the earth). The activity *arare* acts as a manner modifier of the process subevent. The predicate of the resultant state subevent is the prefix *in-*; it has two arguments, the lupins (its specifier) and the earth (its covert complement). Note that while the direct object (*lupinum*) is the specifier of the locative subevent in this example, in the last example (Livy 5.31) the direct object (*agros Romanos*) is the complement: the Volsinians are in the Roman territory. Prefixed verbs show considerable constructional variability; the verbs in our examples could potentially develop into simple transitives. For instance *incursare* in the last example might develop from a change of location verb into a change of state verb meaning something like 'occupy by force'

(23) querentes agrum suum ab accolis Gallis *incursari* ac vastari (Livy 28.11.10).

Just as parts of entities can be selectively modified by adjectives ('the red apple'), so subevents other than the causative subevent are independently modifiable by some types of adverbials

(24) *paulisper* obstupuit (Petr 19)
cito rumor percrebuit (Sen Apoc 13)
paulisper recruduit pugna (Livy 10.19.20).

(22) Beyond there live the Ethiopians (Mela 3.85). The Pisidae occupy the mountains (NH 5.94). He rows where he recently ploughed (Ov Met 1.293). Those who farm public lands (Verr 2.5.53). They often plough lupins under in place of manure (Varro RR 1.23.3). They ran through the city (Tac Ann 2.82). Hercules was running this way and that (Sen Apoc 9). The people of Volsinii invaded the Roman territory (Livy 5.31.5).

(23) Complaining that their land was being raided and laid waste by neighbouring Gauls (Livy 28.11.10).

(24) He was struck dumb for a short time (Petr 19). The rumour quickly spread (Sen Apoc 13). The battle flared up again for a short time (Livy 10.19.20).

In the first example (Petr 19) *obstupesco* is presumably an achievement, so the process subevent lacks duration and the adverb has to modify the resultant state. In the second example (Apoc 13) the adverb expresses the rate of the process subevent; it cannot modify the resultant state since states do not have a rate. In the third example the adverb does modify the resultant state: the meaning is not that the battle took a short time to flare up again (assuming a nonachievement reading), but that it stayed flared up for a short time. The same thing happens in English: 'The drug numbed him slowly/for a while,' 'The battle flared up again quickly/for a while.' Note that while 'flare up' contains a telicizing particle encoding the resultant state, 'numb' is not morphologically transparent at all (apart from being de-adjectival): the three subevents (causative, process and resultant state) are lexicalized as an unanalyzable word (in contrast to Latin *obstupefacio*, where the initial and final subevent are separately encoded). But this does not block the adverbials from accessing the different subevents. It follows that the subevent structures depicted in the figures are needed just as much for morphologically unanalyzable (or partially analyzable) verbs as they are for morphologically transparent verbs, as illustrated by examples with durational adverbials like the following

(25) *coquito* paulisper (Cato 156.7)
diu in medio *caesi* milites (Livy 5.8.12)
orcites... sale *confriato* dies v;... in sole *ponito* biduum (Cato 7.4).

In the first two examples (Cato 156.7; Livy 5.8) the durational adverb applies to the process (consisting of a single event of cooking and of plural events of killing, respectively); only a magician can cook an egg, keep it in a cooked state for a while and then uncook it, or kill a girl for a while and then bring her back to life. In the last example (Cato 7.4) the durational expressions apply to the resultant state; we are being told how long the olives need to stay covered in salt and how long they have to be left in the sun, not how long the process of getting the salt onto them and laying them out in the sun should last. When the verb has a telic prefix (like *confriato* just cited), the durational adverbial can refer to the state subevent expressed by the prefix or to the process subevent expressed by the verb, just as in English 'turn the light out for a few minutes' the durational adverbial can modify the state expressed by the particle ('the light is out') or, less felicitously, either the activity subevent expressed by the verb 'turn' or an iteration of complete turning events

(26) Paulisper domini doctos *sepone* libellos (Mart 7.29.5)
lectica paulisper *deposita* (Verr 2.4.53)
detersis paulisper oculis (Petr 22).

(25) Cook it for a short time (Cato 156.7). For a long time the soldiers were cut down between the two armies (Livy 5.8.12). Sprinkle orcite olives with salt for five days; put them in the sun for two days (Cato 7.4).

(26) Put aside for a while the learned books of your master (Mart 7.29.5). Setting down his litter for a while (Verr 2.4.53). Rubbing their eyes for a while (Petr 22).

The *-pono* examples as before have modification of the resultant state, but in the third example (Petr 22) it is an activity that is modified; the difference is schematically illustrated in Figure 3.5. Less felicitously, multiple adverbials can modify different subevents of the same event: 'At six o'clock slowly turn the light on for a few minutes.' Clearly, we will need access to lexical decomposition in order to give an adequate account of event structure. At least some adverbials are able to get inside the meaning of simple verbs that lexicalize complex events and find the appropriate subevent to modify. Not all scopal positions are available for all modifiers, but those that are can hardly be explained without decomposition. Pretty much the same complex event structure can be encoded by a simple verb, by a de-adjectival verb, by a causative compound or by a syntactic phrase

(27) *coquito* sub dio caelo (Cato 95.2)
in umbra *exsiccato* (Col 5.12.5)
in sole *arefacito* (Col 12.30.2)
exarescent faxo (Pl Rud 578).

Unlike drying, cooking is not lexically related to a scalar adjectival property, but the event is similarly incremental: it progresses down a path in which the theme has decreasing degrees of rawness until it reaches a resultant state in which it qualifies as cooked. So the subeventual structures illustrated for scalar verbs in Figures 3.1-4 can be generalized to events with incremental themes: 'BE-cooked' means 'BE-AT the telic point (culmination) of the cooking process.' Syntactic phrases may be less strict in the matter of temporal integration of the subevents and directness of causation: for these distinctions, compare 'A centurion killed Rubellius Plautus' with 'Nero killed Rubellius Plautus.' Since we subscribe to

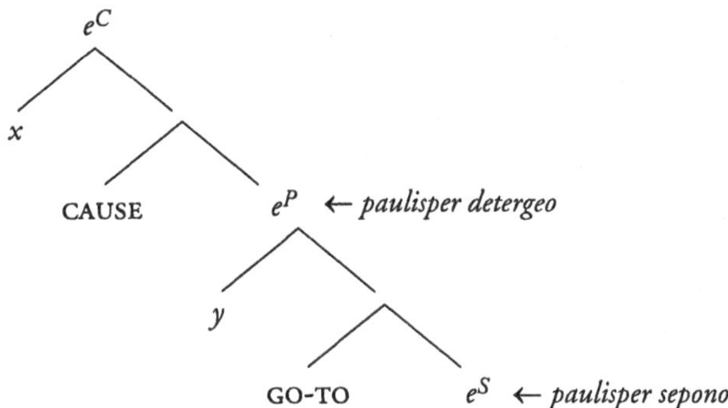

Figure 3.5
Subevent modification by temporal adverbs
Paulisper detergeo/sepono (cp. Mart 7.29, Petr 22)

(27) Boil it in the open air (Cato 95.2). Dry it in the shade (Col 5.12.5). Dry them in the sun (Col 12.30.2). I will get them nice and dry (Pl Rud 578).

the principle of lexical integrity (words are formed in the morphology and arranged in the syntax), we assume that the complex event structure is part of the semantics and is not projected into the syntax, although a lot of valuable work on argument structure is done in a nonlexicalist framework.

Further transitive structures

All the telic verbs we have analyzed so far have belonged to the class of change of state verbs: intransitive process change of state verbs like *exaresco* 'dry out' and transitive causative change of state verbs like *arefacio* 'dry out.' Other change of state verbs involve material integrity (*frango* 'break,' *rumpo* 'burst,' *flecto* 'bend'), cooking (*asso* 'roast,' *frigo* 'roast, fry,' *torreo* 'roast, bake') and assorted other processes (*aperio* 'open,' *claudo* 'close,' *duplico* 'double,' *solvo* 'loosen, thaw'). All transitive change of state verbs are assumed to project both causative and resultative subevents in their event structure, even when they are simple verbs with no transparent morphological derivation: just as *portas patefacio* 'open the gates' projects a resultant state subevent *patefactae sunt portae* 'the gates are open,' so *portas aperio* 'open the gates' projects a resultant state subevent *apertae sunt portae* 'the gates are open' (similarly for *torreo* and *torrefacio* 'roast'). The resultant state can be further spelled out

(28) aperiuntur *in duas partes* (Apic 7.8.1).

However there are many telic verbs or eventuality types which do not express such a salient change of state or even any change of state at all in the entity expressed by the direct object

(29) versus duo tresve *legantur* (Mart 12.2.17)
Caesaris Augusti lascivos... versus sex *lege* (Mart 11.20.1)
Patrae, quas supra *memoravi* (NH 4.13)
ceterisque quos supra *memoravi* (Sall Cat 57.1).

Quantization of the verses in the Martial examples makes the eventualities bounded and therefore accomplishments; *memoro* 'mention' with a singular definite direct object is typically an achievement. Yet there is no change of state to verses when they are read nor to conspirators or towns when they are mentioned. With other verbs the situation is less clear. Consider for instance verbs of ingestion like *edo* 'eat.' Their primary function is not to indicate that the food has gone from a pre-existing state of being whole to a resultant state of being ingested; rather they are verbs with a salient activity component which, like *lego* 'read' in the examples in (29), typically get their boundedness from a quantized object ('eat an orange,' 'drink two beers'). The type of subject they allow is also more constrained for simple agents than it is for causative agents or

(28) They are cut open into two parts (Apic 7.8.1).

(29) Let two or three verses be read (Mart 12.2.17). Read six dirty verses of Caesar Augustus (Mart 11.20.1). Patrae, which I have mentioned above (NH 4.13). And the others whom I have mentioned above (Sall Cat 57.1).

causes. A causative verb like *madefacio* 'wet' can be used with either an animate, volitional, agentive causer or with an inanimate, nonvolitional, nonagentive causer

(30) sunt *qui* micas alii tepido *madefaciunt* oleo (Col 8.5.21)
cum post longas siccitates levis *pluvia* superiorem partem glaebarum *madefecit* (Col 2.4.5).

But reading and eating typically require agentive subjects directly involved in and controlling the event. (If Claudius eats a poisoned mushroom, his choice of food is unintentional but his act of eating is intentional.) On the other hand a causer may have no control over the resultant state caused by his action (intended actions can have unintended consequences), or even over the process subevent if he just sets the stage for the event. Particularly in prose *edo* is not much used metaphorically, while prefixed *exedo* 'eat up' seems less constrained in this regard

(31) ne te tantus *edit* tacitam dolor (Aen 12.801)
quos... nullae aegritudines *exedunt* (Tusc 5.16)
exesis posterioribus partibus versiculorum (Tusc 5.66)
Multa in ea regione monumenta... vetustas *exederat* (Curt Ruf 3.4.10)
nec ulla tam firma moles est quam non *exedant* undae (Curt Ruf 4.2.8).

The same effect is discernible in English: compare 'Sorrow is eating me *(up)' with the first example (Aen 12.801) and 'The waves are eating *(away) the earthwork' with the last (Curt Ruf 4.2). In its literal meaning, eating requires an animate subject and a comestible object, while either or both requirements may be absent in the metaphorical uses (which are easier with the prefixed form in Latin and the telic particle in English). As we have seen, addition of a telicizing prefix brings with it a causative initial subevent and a resultative final subevent: while *edo* means (*x* ACT-ON *y*) by eating, *exedo* means (*x* CAUSE (*y* to GO-TO the resultant state (*y* BE-*ex*-))) by eating. *x* and *y* are not as integrated into the eating activity in the prefixed verb as they are in the simple verb, because in the more complex structure of the prefixed verb *x* is the subject of the subevent predicate CAUSE and *y* of the subevent predicate BE: *y* ends up in the state *ex*-, not necessarily in the state 'eaten.' This suggests that, even when telic, verbs of ingestion have a simpler event structure containing just the process subevent (*x* ACT-ON *y*), which is a relation between two entities (agent *x*, theme *y*), as opposed to the process subevent of a causative which is a relation between an entity and a subevent (causer *x*, resultant state e^S). In the simpler structure, initiation and termination of the event are entailed by its occurrence (just as the existence of an

(30) Some people moisten pieces of garlic with warm oil (Col 8.5.21). When after a long drought a light rain has wetted the upper layer of the clods (Col 2.4.5).

(31) So that this great grief does not consume you in silence (Aen 12.801). Who are not consumed by distress (Tusc 5.16). The latter parts of the verses had worn away (Tusc 5.66). The passing of time has wiped out many monuments in that region (Curt Ruf 3.4.10). No earthwork is so strong that the waves do not wash it away (Curt Ruf 4.2.8).

initial state is entailed by a change of state). If initiation and termination are projected as separate subevents, they will have to be of a different "flavour" from those associated with change of state verbs, that is their metapredicates will have to be differently defined. An atelic simple process structure is independently required for transitive activity verbs like *mulceo* 'caress,' *palpo* 'stroke.' If the agent of such verbs is taken to be a causer, it will be the causer of a process, not the causer of a resultant state.

If the process phase is not instantaneous, it has to involve some sort of development through time. This can be manifested on the argument of the process phase in various ways

(32) quae pumiceas *versat* asella molas (Ov Fast 6.318)
urbemque *delerent* (BC 2.12)
Caesar... cohortes montem *ascendere*... iubet (BG 8.43)
quem librum *legimus* biduo proximo superiore (Gell 17.2.2)
hieme in totum *inarescunt* fontes (NH 31.51).

In the first example (Fast 5.318) the movement is not so much incremental as round and round in a circular path. In the second example (BC 2.12) the city is an incremental theme, as explained in Chapter 2. The mountain in the third example (BG 8.43) is a path that the cohorts cover incrementally. The book in the fourth example (Aul Gell 17.2) can be taken either as an incremental theme or as a path. The last example (NH 31.51) involves a scale of dryness along which the theme progresses (see above).

As already noted, it is perfectly possible for verbs to have meanings which fit nicely into more than one event structure. Some transitive verbs can be used both in a simple process event structure and in a change of state structure. For instance verbs of pushing and pulling (*trudo, traho*) need not have an affected object (*frustra... trudentes* Verg Georg 3.373); when used as activities they are atelic, but they become telic with the addition of a goal, which is the endpoint of a change of location along some path

(33) vili asello... *vomerem* trahente (NH 17.41)
lupos, cum sint nancti *sues*, trahere *usque ad aquam* (Varro RR 2.4.5).

The plough in the first example (NH 17.41) is not affected by being dragged and the path of the dragging ('across the field') is implicit and not part of the argument structure; in the absence of an overtly expressed endpoint, *vomerem trahere* is a simple process. The second example (RR 2.4) is generic, but it is simpler to work with an instantiating episode. The addition of the goal expression *usque ad*

(32) The female donkey that turns the pumice millstones (Ov Fast 6.318). And destroying the city (BC 2.12). Caesar ordered the cohorts to climb the mountain (BG 8.43). The book which I had read on the two previous days (Gell 17.2.2). Springs dry up completely in winter (NH 31.51).

(33) With just a donkey pulling the plough (NH 17.41). Wolves, when they have caught pigs, drag them to water (Varro RR 2.4.5).

aquam turns the activity into an accomplishment by adding a telos: the pigs change location from their place of capture to the water. The object of *trahere* is an E-type pronoun ('them,' i.e. the pigs that they have caught). If the object had been bare plural *sues* 'pigs,' the telicity conferred by the goal would have been neutralized by the bare plural, since 'drag pigs to the (local) water' is an activity. Similarly for *volvo* 'roll'

(34) *Saxum* ingens volvunt alii (Aen 6.616)
oppidani *in proxumos saxa* volvere (Sall Jug 57.5);

note that causing to change location by dragging or rolling uphill requires force to be applied throughout the process phase, while causing to change location by rolling downhill requires just an initial impulse.

Verbs of creation (*librum scribo* 'write a book,' *navem aedificare* 'build a ship') are not selfevidently change of state verbs, since the created object does not exist prior to the event. But some verbs can be used either as verbs of creation or as change of state verbs

(35) curavi... cena *cocta* ut esset (Pl Stich 680)
diequinti Romae in Capitolio curabo tibi cena sit *cocta* (Gell 10.24.6)
Iamne exta *cocta* sunt? (Pl Stich 251)
Coquitur sarda et exossatur (Apic 9.10.2).

The first pair of examples (Stich 680; Gell 10.24) involves making dinner from scratch, the second pair (Stich 251; Apic 9.10) involves the cooking of a pre-existing uncooked entity.

In addition to their regular eventive readings, some change of state verbs like *cingo* 'surround,' *munio* 'fortify,' *claudo* 'close off,' *adorno* 'embellish' also have purely stative readings in which the copresence of an inanimate entity causes some state (without the usual process subevent)

(36) Collis erat... Hunc ex omnibus partibus palus difficilis... *cingebat* (BG 7.19)
(urbem) hinc amnis *munit*, hinc tumuli (Livy 38.4.4)
insula ea sinum ab alto *claudit* in quo sita Carthago est (Livy 30.24.9)
(Scipionem) *adornabat* promissa caesaries (Livy 28.35.6).

The existence of the river causes the city to be naturally fortified (Livy 38.4); Scipio's long hair keeps him looking good (Livy 28.35).

(34) Some roll a huge rock (Aen 6.616). The inhabitants of the town rolled rocks onto the nearest ones (Sall Jug 57.5).

(35) I have made sure that dinner has been cooked (Pl Stich 680). I will see to it that you have dinner cooked for you at Rome in the Capitol in five days time (Gell 10.24.6). Is the liver cooked yet? (Pl Stich 251). The sardine is cooked and deboned (Apic 9.10.2).

(36) There was a hill, which was surrounded on all sides by a difficult marsh (BG 7.19). The river protected the city on one side and the hills on the other (Livy 38.4.4). That island closes the bay on which Carthage lies from the sea (Livy 30.24.9). His long hair made Scipio more attractive (Livy 28.35.6).

Intransitive structures

If we delete the object *y* from the structure (*x* ACT-ON *y*) posited in the previous section, we get the simple agentive intransitive structure (*x* ACT), which is the appropriate structure for the class of socalled unergative verbs. These include verbs of sound emission like *clamo* 'shout,' *latro* 'bark,' *rideo* 'laugh,' *susurro* 'whisper,' *hinnio* 'neigh,' *cano* 'sing,' and verbs of bodily movement and undirected manner of motion like *laboro* 'work,' *ludo* 'play,' *pugno* 'fight,' *salto* 'dance,' *curro* 'run,' *nato* 'swim,' *ambulo* 'walk.' Since they are agentive, it is easy for them to form agent nouns in *-tor*: *clamator, latrator, risor, susurrator, cantor, lusor, pugnator, saltator, cursor, natator, ambulator.* Many unergatives are activities and so atelic, but some have a lexically built-in telos like *ceno* 'dine.' The other class of intransitive verbs is the class of unaccusatives, verbs which have a stative component in their meaning. These include simple statives like *lateo* 'be in hiding,' *frigeo* 'be cold,' *langueo* 'be sluggish,' *vivo* 'live,' *maneo* 'remain'; verbs of change of state like *morior* 'die,' *nascor* 'be born,' *cresco* 'grow,' *evanesco* 'vanish,' *putesco* 'rot,' *rubesco* 'redden'; and verbs of directed motion and change of location like *discedo* 'depart,' *pervenio* 'arrive,' *redeo* 'return,' *perfugio* 'escape,' *emano* 'flow out,' *surgo* 'rise,' *occido* 'fall, set.' The alternation between atelic unergative and telic unaccusative manner of motion verbs was discussed in Chapter 2. The event structure for the simple statives (*y* BE) is illustrated in Figure 3.1; that for the atelic change of state (*y* BECOME) is illustrated in Figure 3.2, and that for the telic change of state and change of location verbs (*y* GO-TO e^S) in Figure 3.3. Some change of location verbs, particularly unaccusative verbs, may have a more complex event structure, since they can be volitionally initiated

(37) At ille... *sua sponte* ad exercitum rediit (Nepos 4.3.1)
si *sua sponte* venisset (Verr 2.2.26)
advenere Samnitium legiones *tanta ferocia* (Livy 8.38.2),

but they are not agentive (their arguments are some type of theme). So it is less natural for them to form agent nouns in *-tor*: the iterative reading of the agent noun has to make an agentive activity out of a nonagentive event, as in *adventor* 'visitor, customer,' *circitor* 'one who does the rounds,' *remansor* 'one who keeps going AWOL.' Conversely in a few middle participles the addition of a covert bound telicizes the event, adds a stative component and changes an unergative activity into an unaccusative accomplishment

(38) Adde inscitiam *pransi, poti,* oscitantis ducis (Pro Mil 56)

('having eaten and drunk himself to satiety').

(37) But he returned to the army of his own accord (Nepos 4.3.1). If he had come of his own accord (Verr 2.2.26). The legions of the Samnites approached with such great ferocity (Livy 8.38.2).

(38) Consider also the ineptitude of a leader who was yawning after a good lunch with a lot to drink (Pro Mil 56).

The distinction between unergative and unaccusative verbs is familiar from the rules for past tense auxiliary selection in a number of European languages; for instance, in Italian unergatives take an auxiliary derived from Latin *habeo* and unaccusatives an auxiliary derived from Latin *sum*. (There is some variation between languages in the definition of the classes, and English, Spanish and Portuguese do not make the distinction at all.) A few examples have been found of the accusative being used to mark the subject of an unaccusative verb in late Latin, and in fact there are languages that regularly use different (pro)nominal forms for the arguments of unergative and unaccusative verbs: the distinction between the two classes is not watertight, and verbs like 'belch,' 'slip,' and 'get drunk' can vary according as they represent a volitionally controlled or an involuntary action. Some verbs, like *trepido* 'act fearfully, be in a fearful state,' have both unergative and unaccusative meanings. There is also variation between languages in the classification of noncore verbs.

Intransitive verbs can sometimes be used in a transitive argument structure. For instance, verbs of nonverbal expression and sound emission can take not only an internal accusative

(39) oculi *vinum* lacrimantes (Rutil Lup 2.7)
sonat *vitium* (Pers Sat 3.21)

but also a direct object representing the stimulus

(40) Tum gemimus *casus* urbis (Juv 3.214)
flens meum et rei publicae *casum* (Pro Sest 60)
Risi *nivem* atram (Ad Qfr 2.12.1).

Psych verbs

Verbs of physical state like *frigeo* 'be cold,' *aegroto* 'be ill' and verbs of physical change of state like *perfrigesco* 'catch cold,' *aegresco* 'get ill' are typically monadic; you don't have to mention the source of the coldness or illness, so they are not part of the argument structure of the verb even though they are part of the eventuality. But most verbs of mental (or psychological) state like *timeo* 'fear,' *terreo* 'frighten,' also known as psych verbs, are obligatorily or at least optionally dyadic: one mentions the person affected by the mental state, called the experiencer, and the entity from which the mental state emanates, called the stimulus. Some verbs of physical state like *esurio* 'be hungry,' *sitio* 'be thirsty,' *tremo* 'tremble' can be used transitively as well as intransitively ('hunger for,' 'thirst for,' 'tremble at'), and they can also be used metaphorically as psych verbs, in which case the object is the mental stimulus. (Verbs of possession are another class of statives that are dyadic.) Psych verbs involve a mental state and so are distinct

(39) With tears of wine coming from their eyes (Rutil Lup 2.7). It sounds flawed (Pers Sat 3.21).

(40) That's when we lament the disasters of the city (Juv 3.214). Grieving over my misfortune and that of the republic (Pro Sest 60). I laughed about your "black snow" (Ad Qfr 2.12.1).

from verbs of mental process like *cogito* in the sense of 'think actively about'; verbs of mental process can be used in the progressive in English ('I'm deliberating about the issue'), while verbs of mental state cannot ('I'm afraid of the Parthians,' *'I am fearing the Parthians'). Although psych verbs can be syntactically transitive, the relationship between the arguments is more symmetrical than it is with agent-patient verbs. The latter regularly lexicalize a relationship in which the agent is the subject and the patient is the object; beside *caedit (x, y)* '*x* kills *y*' there is no simple verb **daecit (x, y)* '*x* gets killed by *y*'; you have to use the passive to get the patient as subject. (A verb like *vapulo* 'get beaten' has the patient as subject but not the agent as object.) Psych verbs are quite different in this regard. Some of them like *timeo* 'fear' take the experiencer as subject and the stimulus as object, others like *terreo* 'frighten' take the stimulus as subject and the experiencer as object. Many psych eventualities can be seen either from the perspective of the stimulus having an effect on the experiencer or from the perspective of the experiencer being sensitive to the stimulus; consequently they can be lexicalized in both directions.

Subject experiencer verbs can be simple states like *amo* 'love,' *contemno* 'despise,' *odi* 'hate,' *timeo* 'fear,' *paveo* 'fear,' or change of state verbs like *expavesco* in the sense of 'become frightened (of),' *concupisco* 'conceive a desire for.' The simple states require a single subevent state structure with two arguments: (*x* BE-IN-PSYCH-STATE-TO *y*). The change of state type requires a process subevent (*x* GO-TO e^S) and a resultant state subevent (e^S), which is the same as the simple state just described, namely (*x* BE-IN-PSYCH-STATE-TO *y*). The stative analysis is confirmed by paraphrases in which the state and, respectively, the change of state are not lexicalized in a single word

(41) *in metu esse* hunc (Ter Haut 199, cp. *metuit*)
Iacet in maerore meus frater (Ad Att 10.4.6, cp. *maeret*)
ne... *in metum redeas* (Pliny Ep 8.11.1)
magnusque *incesserat timor* sagittarum (BC 3.44, cp. *extimescunt*).

In the first two examples (Haut 199; Ad Att 10.4) we have the stative verbs *sum, iaceo*, in the other two examples (Ep 8.11; BC 3.44) we have the change of state verbs *redeo, incedo*; *in metu* is a place-where locative, *in metum* a goal accusative. Subject experiencer psych verbs appear in a number of different constructions. They can be conceptualized as involving a transitive relationship with the experiencer as a metaphorical agent and the stimulus as a metaphorical patient

(42) Ulmus amat *vitem* (Ov Am 2.16.41)
Odistis hominum novorum *industriam*, despicitis eorum *frugalitatem*, *pudorem* contemnitis... *Verrem* amatis (Verr 2.3.7).

(41) That he is afraid (Ter Haut 199). My brother is desolate (Ad Att 10.4.6). That you will become afraid again (Pliny Ep 8.11.1). A great fear of arrows had come over them (BC 3.44).
(42) The elm loves the vine (Ov Am 2.16.41). You hate the hard work of new men, you look down on their self-restraint, you despise their modesty, you love Verres (Verr 2.3.7).

This is particularly appropriate with socalled active emotions like *odi* 'hate,' (*ad*)*miror* 'admire.' With other verbs the stimulus appears in the dative, indicating that the subject is seen as less properly agentive and the object as less directly affected

(43) graviter irasci *inimicis* (BC 1.8)
si *mihi* nemo invideret, si omnes... faverent (Ad Att 2.1.7),

or as an oblique

(44) neque ipse abhorrebat talibus *studiis* (Tac Ann 1.54)
Qui enim poterit aut corporis *firmitate* aut fortunae *stabilitate* confidere? (Tusc 5.40).

The choice of construction does not vary freely according to the semantics of the situation described by the sentence but is fixed by lexical rule for each psych verb. Nevertheless some verbs can license more than one construction: for instance *confido* 'have confidence in' can take either the dative or the ablative. Since an experiencer is not an agent, it is not a prototypical subject role; so it can also be mapped onto the object of an impersonal construction, usually a pronoun

(45) ut me non solum *pigeat* stultitiae meae sed etiam *pudeat* (De Dom 29)
quia *taedebat* populum omnium magistratuum eius anni (Livy 9.7.14)
miserebatque non poenae magis homines quam sceleris (Livy 2.5.6).

These sentences are a type of existential; the subject is a covert argument representing the locative context of the situation ('There affects me displeasure at my stupidity'). Although the experiencer is the object, the impersonal construction is not an object-experiencer construction, because the stimulus is not the subject (unless it is pronominal or clausal). The stimulus is still lower in the event structure than the experiencer, so the impersonal construction is actually a variant of the subject-experiencer type. That is why a reflexive can be bound by the object argument

(46) ut tanto magis *sui* delicias pudeat (NH 22.118)
quos libidinis infamiaeque *suae* neque pudeat neque taedeat (Verr 1.1.35)
num... senectutis eum *suae* paeniteret (De Sen 19).

(43) To become very angry with his enemies (BC 1.8). If noone envied me, if everyone supported me (Ad Att 2.1.7).

(44) He didn't disapprove of this type of activity himself either (Tac Ann 1.54). For how will he be able to be confident of either bodily health or continued material wellbeing? (Tusc 5.40).

(45) With the result that I am not only upset but also ashamed of my stupidity (De Dom 29). Because the people were dissatisfied with all the magistrates of that year (Livy 9.7.14). Men pitied them as much for their crime as for their punishment (Livy 2.5.6).

(46) So that luxury may be all the more ashamed of itself (NH 22.118). Who are neither ashamed nor upset by their own licentious behaviour and wicked reputations (Verr 1.1.35). He would not be regretting his old age, would he? (De Sen 19).

The genitive coding of the stimulus also reflects the nonagency of the experiencer and the unaffected status of the stimulus; it is related to the genitive after verbs of remembering and forgetting. (Finnish and Estonian use the partitive not only with psych verbs but also for unaffected or partially affected objects in eventive sentences.) But the impersonal construction can be coerced into nonstative readings

(47) Verum ego liberius altiusque processi, dum me civitatis morum *piget* taedetque. (Sall Jug 4.9)
Unum te obsecro ut ted huius *commiserescat* mulieris (Pl Rud 1090).

In the first example (Jug 4.9) Sallust is a volitional agent engaged in the activity of expressing his sense of displeasure at the moral standards of the country; the second example (Rud 1090) involves an event under the control of the addressee: Daemones is being asked to take pity on the woman.

Object experiencer psych verbs include *agito* 'distress,' *ango* 'distress,' *commoveo* 'upset,' *delecto* 'delight,' *percutio* 'strike,' *sollicito* 'vex,' *terreo* 'frighten,' *vexo* 'trouble.' Many of these are more or less transparent metaphors of verbs with a literal physical meaning. (Verbs of pleasing like *placeo, iuvo, libet* have a more basically unenergized character and are not metaphors of physical activities.) Object experiencer psych verbs, like their subject experiencer counterparts, can represent a state or a change of state, but unlike subject experiencer verbs they are causatives. When they are stative, the stimulus is copresent with the experiencer throughout the state

(48) se... nec dolore nec paupertate *terreri* (Tusc 5.30)
quem neque pauperies neque mors neque vincula *terrent* (Hor Sat 2.7.84).

When they express a change of state, the stimulus is just the initiator of the psychological state

(49) Repens adventus consulis... *exterruit* Umbros (Livy 9.41.14)
Trepidam urbem... novus insuper de Vitellio nuntius *exterruit* (Tac Hist 1.50).

The same distinction applies to nonpsych causatives, as already illustrated in (36)

(50) sol habitabiles *illustrat* oras (Hor Od 4.14.6)
Postera lux radiis latum *patefecerat* orbem (Ov Met 9.795).

(47) But in writing about my disapproval and dissatisfaction with our standards of morality I have strayed too freely and too far from my subject (Sall Jug 4.9). I beg one thing of you, that you take pity on this woman (Pl Rud 1090).

(48) That they are not frightened either by pain or by poverty (Tusc 5.30). Who neither poverty nor death nor chains frighten (Hor Sat 2.7.84).

(49) The sudden arrival of the consul terrified the Umbrians (Livy 9.41.14). The city, already in a state of alarm, was further terrified by the new report about Vitellius (Tac Hist 1.50).

(50) The sun shines on inhabitable lands (Hor Od 4.14.6). The next day's light had laid open the wide world with its rays (Ov Met 9.795).

Just as the sun keeps the world in a state of illumination (Od 4.14) and the dawn causes it to change from a state of darkness to one of illumination (Met 9.795), so the wise man is not in a state of fear from poverty or death (Tusc 5.30) and the sudden arrival of the consul caused the Umbrians to go from a state of equanimity into a state of terror (Livy 9.41). It is also possible for the cause to be agentive

(51) vi lacessere et *terrere* coepit (Pro Sest 88)
me... Afrorum fremitu *terrere* conere? (Pro Scaur 17).

However not all animate causes are agentive

(52) *Angit* unus Milo. (Ad Qfr 3.7.2)
Sed me maxime *angit* avunculus (Ad Att 13.42.1).

That the various readings are all causative is demonstrated by examples with verbs containing an overt causative element

(53) vos opes... *obstupefaciunt* (Sen De Vit Beat 26.2)
Britannos... visa classis *obstupefaciebat* (Tac Agr 25.2)
Alcides... Lernam *tremefecerit* arcu (Aen 6.803).

The first example (De Vit Beat 26.2) is stative, the second (Agr 25.2) is a change of state, the last (Aen 6.803) agentive. Phrasal paraphrases also have causative verbs

(54) elephantorum magnitudo multitudoque animos militum *detinebat in terrore* (BAfr 72)
Quod factum omnibus maximum *timorem iniecit* (Nepos 10.7.1)
ut arte aliqua *terrorem* hostibus *incuteret* (Livy 7.14.6).

As before, the first example (BAfr 72) is stative, the second (Nepos 10.7) is a change of state, and the last (Livy 7.14) is agentive. The different readings of object experiencer psych verbs could be associated with different event structures. An agentive change of state presumably has the same complex structure as a nonpsych causative (illustrated in Figure 3.4): (*x* CAUSE (*y* GO-TO (*y* BE-afraid scil. of *x*))). For the stative on the other hand the cause may be added to the event structure without an intervening change of state subevent: (*x* CAUSE (*y* BE-afraid scil. of *x*)).

(51) He began to provoke him with violence and to terrify him (Pro Sest 88). Are you to try and terrify me with the shouting of Africans? (Pro Scaur 17).
(52) My one problem is Milo (Ad Qfr 3.7.2). But my biggest worry is my uncle (Ad Att 13.42.1).
(53) Your wealth paralyzes you (Sen De Vit Beat 26.2). The sight of the fleet struck awe into the Britons (Tac Agr 25.2). Hercules made Lerna tremble at his bow (Aen 6.803).
(54) The size and number of the elephants held the minds of the soldiers in terror (BAfr 72). This deed caused the greatest fear among everyone (Nepos 10.7.1). To strike fear into the enemy by some stratagem (Livy 7.14.6).

Obliques

Obliques can appear as arguments or as adjuncts. Source arguments provide a good illustration of obliques in the former function. The following set of examples with an ablative of separation further illustrates how a telicizing prefix can introduce an additional argument into the event structures established above (which is not to say that all prefixes are telicizing or introduce an additional argument)

(55) *Verre* pavimentum (Juv 14.60)
Me memini iratum dominae *turbasse* capillos (Ov Ars Am 2.169)

eo die ex aede Vestae stercus *everritur* (Varro LL 6.32)
Volscos vallo *deturbat* (Livy 3.22.7).

The verbs in the first pair of examples (Juv 14.60; Ars Am 2.169) are simple accomplishments ('sweep clean,' 'dishevel'); for instance, the servants perform a sweeping activity on the floor until it is clean. In the second pair (LL 6.32; Livy 3.22) a directional prefix (*ex-*, *de-*) introduces a third argument and thereby recasts the event structure. Someone performs a sweeping activity on the dung until it is outside the temple: (*x* CAUSE (*y* GO-TO (*y* BE-out-of *z*))), where *y* is the dung and *z* is the temple. The prefix lexicalizes the path of the directed motion (*ex aede*) and the separation predicate of the resultant state (*stercus est extra aedem*); similarly for *vallo deturbat* in the last example. The roots of the verbs (*verr-*, *turb-*) lexicalize the manner of the process (activity) subevent: the dung is removed by sweeping and the Volscians are removed by upsetting. It is also possible for an ablative of separation to shift a verbal root from an activity reading into a directed motion reading, and for a stative root to lexicalize the notion of separation

(56) Nusquam te vestigio *moveris* (Livy 21.44.6)
lapidibus optimos viros foro *pellis* (De Har Resp 39)
suburbano facile *careo* (Ad Att 4.2.7).

The first two examples (Livy 21.44; De Har Resp 39) are causatives; *moveo* is semantically light, while *pello* lexicalizes the manner of the process as above. The last example (Ad Att 4.2) is stative. When the event structure has more than one argument, source ablative arguments do not appear at the high end of the tree (see the examples just cited). However it is possible for the event to be reconceptualized so that a source is treated as an effector (inanimate agent), allowing the theme to be a direct object

(55) Sweep the floor (Juv 14.60). I remember that in anger I dishevelled my mistress' hair (Ov Ars Am 2.169). On that day dung is swept out of the temple of Vesta (Varro LL 6.32). He dislodged the Volsci from the rampart (Livy 3.22.7).

(56) Do not move anywhere from where you are now (Livy 21.44.6). You drive excellent men from the forum with stones (De Har Resp 39). I can easily do without a house outside town (Ad Att 4.2.7).

(57) sincerus (iuncus) in confricando odorem rosae *emittit* (NH 21.120)
sol intercursu lunae vetetur omnes radios *effundere*... exsolutus impedimentis lucem suam libere *mittet* (Sen De Ben 5.6.5).

Instead of saying that a smell of roses comes from the rushes and that light comes from the sun, you can say that the rushes emit a smell of roses and that the sun radiates light.

Instrumental arguments are likewise typically low in the tree

(58) ille... vota facit cumulatque altaria *donis* (Aen 11.50)
alto cinere cumulabo domum (Sen Med 147)
equosque dum *praeda* onerant (Livy 8.38.15: app. crit.)
inventa... vestire atque ornare *oratione* (De Or 1.142).

The event structure for the first two examples is (*x* CAUSE (*y* GO-TO (*y* BE-heaped-WITH *z*))). The instrumental argument is in the resultant state subevent. Although this entails that it is also part of the process subevent, it does not mean that he used gifts to cause the altars to be in a heaped state. Instrumental adjuncts, on the other hand, can appear higher in the tree. They can occur with atelic processes

(59) corvos... radebat *pedibus* terram et *voce* crocibat *sua* (Pl Aul 625)
scabiei locus *nitro* et *aceto* fricatur diutius (Scrib Larg 253).

If we posit a single process subevent, then the instrumental modifies e^P: the crow uses his feet to scratch the earth; the possessor argument of an instrumental body part noun is bound by the subject under normal circumstances, so the feet belong to the crow. There is no resultant state for the instrumental to modify. While causatives do have a resultant state, the adjunct instrumental still probably applies to a higher subevent

(60) inde librum *scalpro* eximito (Cato 42.1)
Munatius Flaccus proximum *gladio* traicit lictorem (BAlex 52).

The first example (Cato 42.1) presumably means 'use a knife to remove the bark,' not 'cause the bark to be removed by a knife' (which is entailed by the former). Similarly in the second example (BAlex 52) Munatius Flaccus takes his sword and uses it to run through the nearest lictor. Although the instrumental

(57) The real one emits a rose scent when rubbed (NH 21.120). The sun is prevented from projecting all its rays due to the intervention of the moon; freed from obstructions it will emit its light freely (Sen De Ben 5.6.5).

(58) He is offering vows and heaping the altars with gifts (Aen 11.50). I will heap his home deep with ashes (Sen Med 147). While they are loading their horses with booty (Livy 8.38.15). To clothe and adorn his ideas with oratory (De Or 1.142).

(59) A raven was scratching the ground with its claws and croaking with its voice (Pl Aul 625). The area with the eczema is rubbed for quite a while with soda and vinegar (Scrib Larg 253).

(60) Remove the bark from it with a knife (Cato 42.1). Munatius Flaccus ran the closest lictor through with his sword (BAlex 52).

predicate BE-BY introduces a new (usually inanimate) participant, it does not create its own new subevent but amplifies an existing subevent (e^{PS}). At this point we are presented with some analytical choices. We could say that the instrument, while inanimate, is still a participant in the event and so should be treated like an argument: after all, you can't run someone through without using a weapon of some sort. On this approach introduction of the instrument is done by arity expansion, that is by increasing the number of the verbal arguments. The event description includes an implicit existentially quantified instrumental: this is activated by removing the existential quantifier, thereby adding its variable to the arguments of the verb. For instance the verb *traicit* in the second example is now no longer $\lambda y \lambda x. P(x,y)$ (plus event argument) but $\lambda y \lambda z \lambda x. P(x,z,y)$, where z represents the sword. This is illustrated in Figure 3.6. The instrumental ending represents a relation between a set of events (those in which the lictor gets run through) and an entity (the sword). Composition is by functional application. The first step gives a set of events in which the lictor gets run through by some entity, the second step supplies the sword as the entity in question. On the alternative approach we would treat the instrument as an adjunct and therefore a modifier, not an argument: *gladio* is a now a predicate of events (the set of events in which a sword is used) and it modifies the verb phrase (the set of events in which the nearest lictor gets run through). This is illustrated in Figure 3.7; note that the event is the subject of the modifier phrase and the event argument is not saturated or existentially quantified, so the denotation of the modifier phrase is a predicate, not a truth value. Composition by

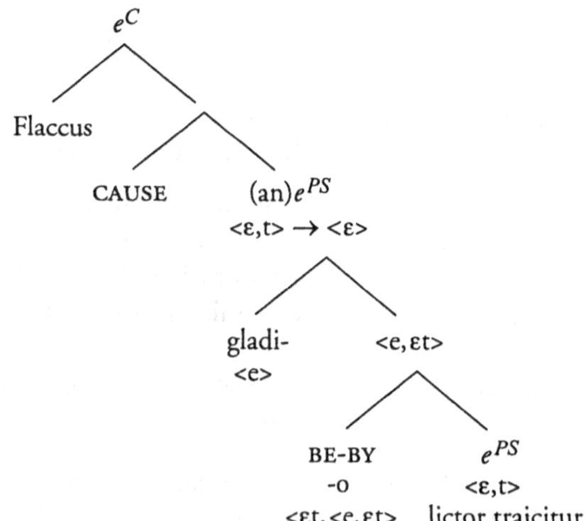

Figure 3.6
Instrumental as arity expander
Flaccus gladio traicit lictorem (BAlex 52)

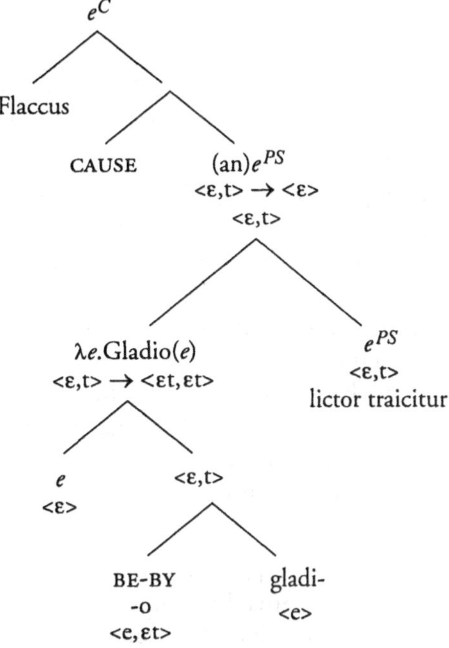

Figure 3.7
Instrumental as event modifier
Flaccus gladio traicit lictorem (BAlex 52)

functional application forces the type of the modifier (<ε,t>) to be raised from predicate of events to a function from a predicate of events to a predicate of events (<<ε,t>,<ε,t>>). This can be avoided by using a specially designed modifier compositional rule that intersects two sets of events to give a set of events.

In English it is possible for the event to be reconceptualized with the instrument as effector: 'An arrow killed King Harold,' 'A pebble broke the window.' When this happens, the instrument is not an adjunct but an argument. This shift is not allowed when the sentence also includes the agent argument: *'An arrow killed King Harold by an archer.' Subject instrumentals are easier with contextual support, and some languages do not allow them at all; they are said to be avoided in Latin prose.

Indirect objects

Indirect objects too can be introduced by prepositional prefixes, but since prepositions do not take the dative, indirect objects are best not analyzed as complements of the stative metapredicate in the same way as the source arguments at the beginning of the previous section

(61) Antonium, qui ei legioni *praeerat* (BC 3.46)
legatisque quos singulis legionibus *praefecerat* (BG 7.45)
Foco virenti *suberat* amphorae cervix (Mart 12.32.14)
cum exceperunt ova generosarum, vulgaribus gallinis *subiciunt* (Col 8.2.12).

The first example in each pair (BC 3.46; Mart 12.32) is stative, and the prepositional prefix adds an argument to monadic *sum*: (*x* BE-prae/sub relative to *y*). The other two examples are causative: (*x* CAUSE (*y* GO-TO (*y* BE-prae/sub) relative to *z*)). Here an argument is added to dyadic *facio, iacio*. The availability and suitability of the indirect object construction and the degree to which it competes with other constructions depend on the semantics of the prepositional prefix and the verbal root that combine to form the compound verb, the need to avoid a double accusative and the details of the context in which the construction is to be used. In simple verbs of transfer of property the predicate of the resultant state subevent is lexicalized in the verbal root (rather than by a prefix as in (61))

(62) pecuniam Staieno *dedit* Oppianicus (Pro Clu 84)
qui de balneis soleas hesterna die mihi *furatus* es (Apul Met 9.21)
nisi lenoni munus hodie *misero* (Pl Pseud 781);

likewise for simple verbs of joining together

(63) quoniam Syphax se Romanis *iunxisset* (Livy 24.49.2)
fletumque cruori *miscuit* (Ov Met 4.141).

Oppianicus causes the money to go to the state of being with Staienus; Myrmex causes the shoes to be in a state of being away from me; Syphax causes himself to get to the state of being with the Romans. If, as in the sending of gifts (Pseud 781 in (62)), giving and receiving can be separated by a significant interval of time, it is possible for the transfer to be incomplete: what is entailed by the resultant state subevent is that the gift is on its way, not that it has necessarily reached its intended recipient. This introduces an intensional component similar to what we found with the progressive in Chapter 2. The gift will reach its recipient in all inertially accessible worlds: $\forall w.R^{Inert}(w^*, w) \rightarrow$ BE-AT (munus, leno, *w*). The transfer of property can be abstract too, as in the case of the perception of a visual or auditory stimulus

(61) Antonius, who was in command of that legion (BC 3.46). The lieutenants whom he had put in command of the individual legions (BG 7.45). The neck of a jar was underneath a stove covered with verdigris (Mart 12.32.14). When they have collected the eggs of the noble hens, they put them under the ordinary hens (Col 8.2.12).

(62) Oppianicus gave Staienus the money (Pro Clu 84). You who stole my shoes from me yesterday at the baths (Apul Met 9.21). Unless I send the pimp a gift today (Pl Pseud 781).

(63) Since Syphax had joined the Romans (Livy 24.49.2). She mixed her tears with his blood (Ov Met 4.141).

(64) Sed quis illas tibi *monstrabit*? (Pl Poen 1149)
nuntiaret senatui ac populo victoriam (Suet 6.1.1).

Now we need to look briefly at verbs that take indirect objects as their only object (possibly competing with other constructions). Some of these have unaccusative semantics

(65) *cedat*... stilus gladio, umbra soli (Pro Mur 30)
domui eius... ignis *propinquaret* (Tac Ann 15.39)
haereret nigro fuligo Maroni (Juv 7.227).

The theme slot in the event structure is used up by the subject and consequently not available for any other argument. The verb in the second example (Ann 15.39) incorporates the meaning of the adjective *propinquus* derived from the preposition *prope* 'near'; the event structure is (*x* GO-TO (*x* BE-near-to *y*)). Other verbs of this class are stative or ingressive subject experiencer psych verbs which incorporate a theme noun in much the same way as *frondeo* 'have leaves (*frons*),' *ignesco* 'catch fire (*ignis*),' pruning the resulting empty argument slot

(66) nec duci milites nec militibus dux satis *fideret* (Livy 10.18.6)
nostrae laudi dignitatique *favisti* (Ad Fam 1.7.8)
et potet caldam qui mihi *livet* aquam (Mart 6.86.6)
se patriae *irasci* nefas esse duceret (Nepos 15.7.1).

The underlying meaning is 'there is in *x* trust/favour/envy/anger towards *y*'; the meaning of the noun is lexicalized in the verbal root giving a dyadic predicate '*x* is in a state of N to *y*.' Verbs of social interaction like *minari* 'threaten,' *gratulari* 'congratulate' are mostly eventive and can license an internal accusative specifying the nature of the threat and the reason for the congratulation

(67) *Minari* Siculis (Verr 2.2.12)
idem supplicium minatur optimis civibus (Phil 3.18)
mihi *gratulatur* (Ad Att 7.2.7)
mihi *gratulatus* es illius diei *celebritatem* (Ad Att 5.20.1).

This class of verbs differs from the prepositional prefix class discussed above in that the accusatives are theme-like hyponymous internal accusatives ('sing an

(64) But who will show them to you? (Pl Poen 1149). To announce a victory to the senate and the people (Suet 6.1.1).

(65) Let the pen yield first place to the sword, study in the shade to fighting in the sun (Pro Mur 30). The fire was getting close to his house (Tac Ann 15.39). Soot sticks to your blackened copy of Virgil (Juv 7.227).

(66) The soldiers did not have enough confidence in the general nor the general in the soldiers (Livy 10.18.6). You have favoured my reputation and position (Ad Fam 1.7.8). May he who is envious of me drink warm water (Mart 6.86.6). He thought it wrong to be angry at his country (Nepos 15.7.1).

(67) They threatened the Sicilians (Verr 2.2.12). He threatens the best citizens with the same punishment (Phil 3.18). He congratulates me (Ad Att 7.2.7). You congratulated me on my enthusiastic reception that day (Ad Att 5.20.1).

aria'), not patient-like regular affected direct objects ('kill a Gaul'). Both agentive (eventive) and nonagentive (possibly stative) readings are available for verbs like *noceo* 'cause harm to, be harmful to' and *opitulor* 'bring help to, be helpful to'

(68) Non meus est error: *nocuit* librarius illis (Mart 2.8.3)
posse *nocere* animis carminis omne genus (Ov Trist 2.264)
naufragus... navi quod potuit est *opitulatus* (De Inv 2.154)
nihil Fregellanis morum et sermonis societas *opitulata* est (Rhet Her 4.37).

Both readings are probably causative; we have already met causatives of statives with object experiencer psych verbs. An interesting difference arises with negation

(69) Pythagoraeque ferunt *non nocuisse* Numam (Ov Ex Pont 3.3.44)
Manlio... cui *non nocuit* et filium et victorem occidere (Sen Con 9.2.19).

The first example (Ex Pont 3.3) is agentive and negates the occurrence of any harmful event. In the second example (Con 9.2) the subject is an event: this event did occur but had no harmful effects on Manlius. The underlying theme that is lexicalized in *nocere* can surface as an internal accusative in the legal phrase *nox(i)am nocere*, which is eventive and telic: *nocere* is like a light verb and lexicalizes CAUSE only, while *nox(i)am* lexicalizes the process plus resultant state subevents (e^{PS}). So for many indirect object verbs it is reasonable to posit an event structure containing a theme position that is either occupied by another argument or just empty. For instance *ignosco* 'forgive' can occur with the offence as direct object and the offender as indirect object, or with one of these positions empty, that is with only the indirect object position filled (offender or offence) or with only the direct object position filled (offence only)

(70) ut *eis delicta* ignoscas (Pl Bacch 1185)
etiam *hostibus* eum ignovisse (Livy 28.25.13)
ignosce *timori* (Prop 2.6.13)
Hoc... ignoscere (Ad Att 16.16c.1).

It is fairly clear that these indirect object verbs form a semantically affinite class: the events they express can be conceptualized as not having a theme or a fully affected patient or a purely locative goal. The nonsubject participant is more like the target entity at which the event is directed. Just the same class of verbs can take dative rather than accusative objects in various other languages, some of them quite unrelated to Latin. (In Icelandic a number of verbs take the

(68) It's not my fault: the copyist introduced the flaws into them (Mart 2.8.3). Every kind of poem is potentially morally dangerous (Ov Trist 2.264). The shipwrecked sailor did what he could to save the ship (De Inv 2.154). The customs and language they shared with us were of no help to the people of Fregellae (Rhet Her 4.37).

(69) They say that Numa did not harm Pythagoras (Ov Ex Pont 3.3.44). Manlius who was not harmed by killing one who was both a victor and his own son (Sen Con 9.2.19).

(70) Forgive them their misdeeds (Pl Bacch 1185). That he had even pardoned enemies (Livy 28.25.13). Pardon my anxiety (Prop 2.6.13). To forgive this (Ad Att 16.16c.1).

accusative for an inanimate object and the dative for an animate object.) Verbs that share semantic properties with the indirect object verbs can be attracted into the indirect object class, as happens with *iubeo* 'order' (cp. *impero* 'order')

(71) propius eum *iussit* accedere (Curt Ruf 6.11.36)
Britannico iussit exsurgeret (Tac Ann 13.15).

Ordinary transitive verbs with affected patients are not susceptible to this sort of class shift. It follows that speakers of Latin were able to make generalizations about the semantic properties of the indirect object class and use them as a basis for extending the membership of that class. At the same time, whether or not a particular verb belongs to the indirect object class depends on the conventions of what is accepted as grammatically correct in a language, and consequently has to be marked in the lexicon. Verbs that are, at least synchronically, near synonyms (like *laedo* and *noceo* 'harm') can belong to different classes in the same language, and synonymous, even etymologically related, verbs in different languages can belong to different classes. Sometimes a language allows both constructions

(72) eos autem qui comitari *eum* solebant (Curt Ruf 9.8.3)
cetera quae comitantur *huic* vitae (Tusc 5.100).

Since the different constructions assign the object participant to different slots in the event structure, as just explained, it is possible for subtle differences in meaning to appear

(73) Quid? ego *Fundanio* non cupio? (Ad Qfr 1.2.10)
Mars videt hanc *visamque* cupit (Ov Fast 3.21).

Cicero does not desire Fundanius in the way Mars desires Silvia, he desires success for him.

Alternative event structures

Multiple arguments can get differently assigned according to different conceptualizations of the event. The most familiar instance of this involves verbs like 'spray' and 'load'

(74) adspergit *sanguine mensas* (Ov Met 5.40)
pecorique adspergere *virus* (Verg Georg 3.419)
(cunila) *sativa... in potione* aspersa (NH 20.173).

(71) He ordered him to come closer (Curt Ruf 6.11.36). He ordered Britannicus to get up (Tac Ann 13.15).

(72) Those who were accustomed to accompany him (Curt Ruf 9.8.3). Everything else that goes with this lifestyle (Tusc 5.100).

(73) Don't I wish the best for Fundanius? (Ad Qfr 1.2.10). Mars saw her, and on seeing her he desired her (Ov Fast 3.21).

(74) He sprinkled the table with his blood (Ov Met 5.40). To sprinkle poison on the cattle (Verg Georg 3.419). The cultivated type, sprinkled on a drink (NH 20.173).

To the extent that there is a difference between the first two constructions in any particular instance, when the goal is in the accusative, like *mensas* in the first example (Met 5.40), it is potentially more fully and directly affected than when the goal is in the dative, like *pecori* in the second example (Verg Georg 3.419). At least, that is what is predicted by the different event structures: (CAUSE (the tables GO-TO (BE-sprinkled WITH blood))) versus (CAUSE (the poison GO-TO (BE-sprinkled ON the flock))). That is also the difference that emerges from comparable constructions in English: 'spray the table with blood' (complete coverage), 'spray blood on the table' (partial coverage). In the former the table changes state, in the latter blood changes location. There is a potential distinction between the dative and the locative too. The dative in the second example (*pecori* Verg Georg 3.419) suggests that the ill effects of the poison are directed at the flock (the flock is an indirect object malefactive), while the locative in the last example (*in potione* NH 20.173) just denotes the place where the substance is sprinkled. Animates make better malefactives than inanimates: in (74) the animate is an indirect object, the inanimates are a direct object and a locative respectively.

Body parts (unsevered ones, any way) and items of military equipment are typically relational nouns. A sword in a sword factory may be a simple entity (λx.Gladius(x)), since the owner of the sword factory is not contextually salient. But a sword in a battle context normally has an additional covert possessor argument ($\lambda y \lambda x$.Gladius(x,y)). The sword is inanimate but the possessor is animate; similarly for body parts. This sets the stage for alternative structures. While the possessor can appear in the genitive, it is also possible for the possessor to be conceptualized as an affected participant in the event (indirect object), appearing therefore in the dative. The latter structure is known as possessor raising. Apart from the anglocentric perspective of this term, note that possessors do not necessarily carry a lifetime inference ('my mother's brooch'), but recipients do ('gave my mother a brooch'). Here are some examples of this alternation in which the relational noun appears as direct object or prepositional goal

(75) Haec *dicentis* latus hasta transfixit (Curt Ruf 8.1.52)
Crispinus supra scutum sinistrum umerum *Badio* hasta transfixit (Livy 25.18.13)

Sub haec dicta ad genua *Marcelli* procubuerunt (Livy 25.7.1)
procumbunt *omnibus Gallis* ad pedes Bituriges (BG 7.15)

cum extorquere arma posset e manibus *iratorum civium* boni civis auctoritas (Brut 7)
quod *ei* ferrum e manibus extorsimus (Cat 2.2).

(75) He pierced his side with the spear as he spoke these words (Curt Ruf 8.1.52). Crispinus pierced Badius' left shoulder above his shield with his spear (Livy 25.18.13). After this speech they fell at Marcellus' knees (Livy 25.7.1). The Bituriges fell at the feet of all the Gauls (BG 7.15). When the authority of a good citizen could have wrested arms from the hands of angry citizens (Brut 7). Because we have wrested his sword from his hands (Cat 2.2).

The relational noun can also appear as the subject of an unaccusative or passive verb with possessor raising

(76) Caput arsisse *Servio Tullio* dormienti quae historia non prodidit? (De Div 1.121)
Transfigitur scutum *Pulloni* (BG 5.44).

The event structures for the two constructions are quite different. For instance in the first example in (75) (Curt Ruf 8.1) the genitive construction has the regular causative event structure (as illustrated in Figure 3.4 and more schematically in Figure 3.5), except that the direct object includes the possessor argument of the noun: *x* CAUSE (*y* of *z* to GO-TO the resultant state (*y* BE *s*)), so Alexander causes Clitus' side to go to the state of being pierced. The second example (Livy 25.18) with possessor raising has the structure illustrated in Figure 3.8: *x* CAUSE (*z* to BE-WITH (*y* GO-TO the resultant state (*y* BE *s*))), so Crispinus causes Badius to have his shoulder go to the state of being pierced. In this structure the dative (*Badio*) binds the possessor argument of the relational noun, which is null in Latin but would surface as 'his' in non-prodrop English; it can't be anyone else's left shoulder that gets pierced.

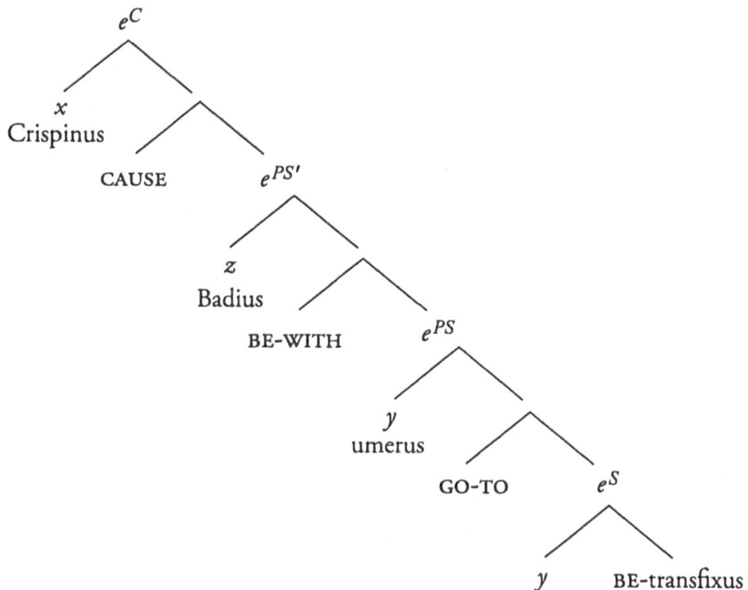

Figure 3.8
Possessor raising
Crispinus umerum Badio transfixit (Livy 25.18.13)

(76) What history has failed to record that Servius Tullius' head burst into flames while he was sleeping? (De Div 1.121). Pullo's shield was pierced (BG 5.44).

Benefactives

Benefactives are adjuncts that introduce a sort of secondary indirect object. Different types of benefactives modify different parts of the event structure. Low benefactives typically occur with verbs of creation or preparation where the benefactive is the intended recipient of the created entity. Low benefactives add or augment a resultant state

(77) Cur igitur me *tibi* iussisti coquere dudum prandium? (Pl Men 388)
si cenam *tibi* facerem (Pliny Ep 7.3.5).

The benefactive adds a resultant state predication to the effect that the meal that has been prepared is intended to go to the beneficiary: BE-FOR (dinner, you). The meaning is not that *x* cooks dinner for *y*'s entertainment or edification (as in a cookery class where the food then goes to charity), but that *x* cooks dinner for *y* to eat it. In all teleologically accessible worlds, *y* does eat the dinner, so the additional resultant state predication could be reformulated as a modalized possessive predicate: $\forall w. R^{Tel(x)}(w^*, w) \rightarrow$ BE-AT $(w, \text{dinner}, \text{you})$. Mid-level benefactives are inserted below the subject

(78) ut *sibi* poenam magistri equitum dictator remitteret (Livy 8.35.1)
quod *aliis* coluit (praedia), non *sibi* (Pro Rosc Am 49).

In the second example (Pro Rosc Am 49) Roscius is engaged in the cultivation of the fields for the benefit of others, not for his own benefit. In the first example (Livy 8.35) the dictator is being asked to remit the punishment of the master of the horse; it is the remission of the punishment (an event) and not the punishment itself (an entity) that is for the benefit of the people. The socalled ethic dative is a type of high benefactive that attaches to the proposition

(79) At *tibi* repente paucis post diebus, cum minime exspectarem, venit ad me Caninius mane (Ad Fam 9.2.1)
Hic *tibi* in rostra Cato advolat (Ad Att 1.14.5).

The writer solicits extra involvement from the reader by suggesting that he will benefit from paying attention to a significant or surprising proposition. Figure 3.9 illustrates the different levels of benefactive insertion; the semantic mechanisms involved are similar to those used above for the introduction of an instrumental adjunct, but the details are not always clear.

(77) So why did you tell me a short while ago to cook lunch for you? (Pl Men 388). If I were making dinner for you (Pliny Ep 7.3.5).

(78) That the dictator should remit for them the punishment of the master of the horse (Livy 8.35.1). That he cultivated the farms for others and not for himself (Pro Rosc Am 49).

(79) But, what do you know, suddenly a few days later, when I was least expecting it, Caninius comes to me in the morning (Ad Fam 9.2.1). At this point, what do you know, Cato rushes onto the platform (Ad Att 1.14.5).

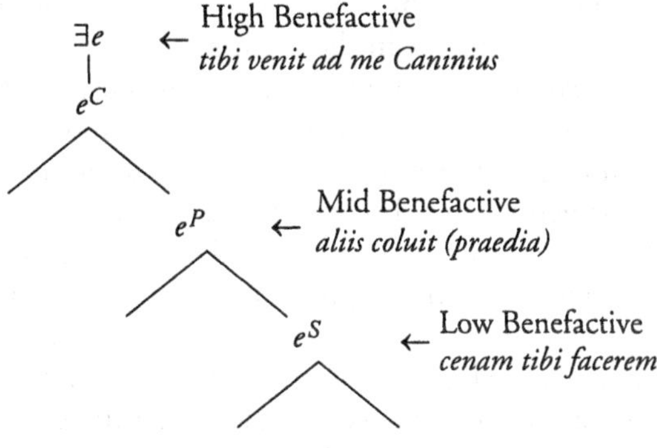

Figure 3.9
Benefactive insertion points
(cp. Ad Fam 9.2.1, Pro Rosc Am 49, Pliny Ep 7.3.5)

Linking rules

According to the theory being presented here, the event structures are abstract semantic decompositions, so rules are needed to map them onto the concrete syntactic structures that we actually get in Latin texts. These rules are usually called linking rules; we will discuss them in this section, sometimes repeating examples from our analysis above for the sake of illustration. Since the event structures are set up with one eye on the syntax, the linking rules are fairly straightforward (and the syntactic facts do not constitute independent evidence for the posited event structures). The details of the linking rules depend on how the event structures are set up, so different theories of event structure may require different linking rules (or none at all, for those which take event structures to be a sort of abstract syntax).

First a few words about lexical insertion. In the event structures the same participant can appear in more than one subevent, and each subevent has its own predicate. Lexical insertion involves collapsing multiple occurrences of any argument into a single occurrence of the corresponding noun phrase, and collapsing the various metapredicates into a single verbal head, although the latter may be transparently morphologically complex like *aresco* and *arefacio*. So in a simple causative sentence like

(80) boves... vites... frangunt (Col De Arb 12.2)

the two occurrences of the variable *y* in the event structure (*x* CAUSE (*y* GO-TO (*y* BE-broken))) are collapsed into a single occurrence of the noun phrase *vites*, and the three metapredicates CAUSE, GO-TO and BE are collapsed into the single predicate *frangunt*.

(80) The oxen break the vines (Col De Arb 12.2).

The main function of the linking rules is to assign grammatical relations and inflectional case to the arguments in the event structure. Although the inflectional case endings serve (directly or indirectly) to encode the information contained in the metapredicates, there is no simple one-to-one mapping from semantics to morphology. Since every sentence is a predication, one of the arguments of the event structure has to become the subject of predication in the syntax. So nominative case is associated with a predication function that lies above the event structure. The argument mapped to the subject grammatical function is the highest argument in the event structure. An argument is higher than another argument if it is in a higher subevent or if it is the specifier of a subevent of which the other argument is the complement. (Participants introduced by adjuncts, like instruments, are excluded from this computation.) If the predicate is monadic, the single argument has to be the subject. It doesn't matter whether it is an agent like the sole argument of an unergative verb

(81) agni *ludunt* (Lucr 2.320)

or a theme like the sole argument of an unaccusative verb, as in the following examples repeated from (16) and (17)

(82) ager *aret* (Col 2.8.5)
herba... *arescit* (Varro RR 1.49.1)
herba... *peraruit* (ibid.).

The first two examples (Col 2.8; RR 1.49) have a single subevent, the last has two subevents sharing the same argument. When the predicate is dyadic, the higher of the two arguments is mapped to subject, whether it is in a separate subevent like the causer in *boves vites frangunt* in (80) or in the same subevent like the experiencer in *ulmus amat vitem* in (42). Adding a causative subevent to a process means that the subject of the process is not the subject of the sentence, because it is no longer the highest argument in the event structure: *herba arescit* but *herbam arefacit.* The lower argument of a dyadic predicate is mapped to direct object if it is the subject of the process subevent like *vites* in (80), and often also if it is the complement of a subevent like *vitem* in (42). This includes in addition to regular themes and patients also nominalized events (*repentinam eruptionem* 'sudden sally'), internal accusative events (*pugnam pugnare* 'fight a fight'), and products of events (*capitis eruptionem* 'head rash'). However the case of the lower argument depends on the metapredicates required by the semantics of the verb, so it can also be an indirect object or an oblique

(83) tanta autem inerat comitas *Scipioni* (Livy 28.18.6)
suburbano facile careo (Ad Att 4.2.7).

(81) Lambs play (Lucr 2.320).

(82) The ground is dry (Col 2.8.5). The grass becomes dry (Varro RR 1.49.1). The grass is completely dry (ibid.).

(83) Scipio had such graciousness (Livy 28.18.6). I can easily do without a house outside town (Ad Att 4.2.7).

Both examples have unaccusative verbs, so the subjects would occupy the theme position in the event structure. If the predicate is triadic, the third argument is typically an indirect object or an oblique, again depending on the lexical semantics of the verb

(84) pecuniam *Staieno* dedit Oppianicus (Pro Clu 84)
ova... *gallinis* subiciunt (Col 8.2.12)
ille... cumulat... altaria *donis* (Aen 11.50),

but an accusative is also possible with double accusative verbs like *rogo* 'ask,' *doceo* 'teach' as well as with some prepositional prefix verbs (*trans-* 'across,' *circum-* 'around'), where the accusative marks the complement of the resultant state subevent. Oblique cases in general depend more on the preposition-like semantics of the metapredicate and less on structural position, while the cases of the grammatical relations (subject, direct object, indirect object) depend more on the latter and less on the former. Oblique cases can often be said to directly lexicalize the meaning of their metapredicate, while nonoblique cases only do so indirectly relative to their structural rank. (Some theories seek to capture this by distinguishing socalled structural case from morphological case.) For instance, the primary function of the nominative ending is to direct the noun to the specifier position of the highest subevent in the structure (whence its subject status), whereas the primary function of the instrumental ending is to define the metapredicate of the instrumental adjunct, as indicated in Figures 3.6 and 3.7.

If every sentence is a predication, and every predication has a subject, what do we do about impersonal verbs (which seem to have no subject) and about symmetrical verbs (which seem to have two equipollent candidates for subject)? Weather verbs are typically impersonal: if we include a causing supernatural entity, they have a maximal structure in which x causes y to go down from v to be at z. Default values are predictable for all the variables, so it is superfluous to require them to be overt arguments. x is the god typically responsible for the weather event; y is the theme (the substance that falls), which is lexicalized in the verb (*ninguit* 'snows' – *nix* 'snow') and does not need to be repeated as an overt argument; v is the source, which is usually the sky and again predictable; z is the goal, typically the discourse location. Any of these variable slots can be filled with an overt argument, particularly when it has an atypical or unpredictable value

(85) *Iove* enim tonante (Phil 5.7)
Lapides pluere (Livy 28.27.16)
Veiis *de caelo* lapidaverat (Livy 27.37.1)
in Remulum fulmina missa ferunt (Ov Fast 4.50).

(84) Oppianicus gave Staienus the money (Pro Clu 84). They put the eggs under the hens (Col 8.2.12). He is heaping the altars with gifts (Aen 11.50).

(85) During a thunderstorm (Phil 5.7). That there are showers of stones (Livy 28.27.16). Stones had rained down from the sky at Veii (Livy 27.37.1). They say that bolts of lightning struck Remulus (Ov Fast 4.50).

The substance can also appear as an instrumental adjunct or take a modifier as an internal accusative

(86) in Aventino *lapidibus* pluit (Livy 35.9.4)
tonuit *laevum* (Ennius in De Div 2.82).

It is reasonable to think that impersonally used weather verbs have a covert subject of predication, and that that subject is the discourse location ('<Here> is <snow> snowing').

The class of symmetrical verbs includes both statives and eventives

(87) Maritima Avaticorum stagno *assidet* (Mela 2.78)
...Anquillaria: hic locus *abest* a Clupeis passuum xxii milia (BC 2.23)
qui rex... se Oceanum cum Ponto... *coniuncturum* putaret (Pro Mur 32)
P. Fabius nuper *emit* agrum de C. Claudio (Pro Tull 14).

From a purely semantic perspective, if *x* lies alongside *y*, then *y* lies alongside *x*; if *x* is twenty-two miles away from *y*, then *y* is twenty-two miles away from *x*; if Mithridates joins the Atlantic to the Black Sea, then he joins the Black Sea to the Atlantic; and if *P. Fabius nuper emit agrum de C. Claudio*, then *C. Claudius nuper vendidit agrum P. Fabio* (assuming equal degrees of enervation and involvement in the transaction by both parties). Evidently the semantics allows the relation to be conceptualized in either direction and the pragmatics governs the choice made by the writer. For instance in the second example (BC 2.23) the topic is Anquillaria, as indicated by anaphoric *hic*, and not Clupea; in the last example (Pro Tull 14) the present owner (Fabius) is a discourse topic, the previous owner (Claudius) is more incidental information.

In addition to mapping the arguments of an event structure onto grammatical relations and inflectional case, the linking rules also map the event structure onto syntactic constituent structure; this is what gives us the basic word order of a Latin sentence. Although Latin word order seems at first sight to be free and unconstrained, there is actually a fixed default order, and variations from the default order are due to a specific set of pragmatically licensed syntactic rules. The default order of arguments is pretty much the same as it is in English

(88) *Baebius exercitum M. Pinario...* tradiderat (Livy 40.25.8)
Saepe enim *nostri imperatores... scribas suos anulis aureis* in contione donarunt (Verr 2.3.185)
Amynander Philippum... insulae praefecit (Livy 36.31.12)
P. Decius... exercitum obsidione liberavit (De Div 1.51)
Metropolitae... muros... armatis compleverunt (BC 3.81).

(86) On the Aventine there were showers of stones (Livy 35.9.4). There was thunder on the left (De Div 2.82).

(87) Maritima Avaticorum adjoins a lagoon (Mela 2.78). ...Anquillaria. This place is 22 miles from Clupea (BC 2.23). The king who thought that he would link the Atlantic with the Black Sea (Pro Mur 32). P. Fabius recently bought the land from C. Claudius (Pro Tull 14).

(88) Baebius had handed over his army to M. Pinarius (Livy 40.25.8). For our generals have often presented their scribes with golden rings in the assembly (Verr 2.3.185). Amynander put Philippus in charge of the island (Livy 36.31.12). P. Decius saved the army from being cut off (De Div 1.51). The Metropolitans filled the walls with armed men (BC 3.81).

Although the verb is at the end in Latin and comes after the subject in English, the order of the arguments is the same: 'Baebius handed the army over to Pinarius,' 'Our generals presented their scribes with gold rings in the assembly,' 'Amynander put Philip in charge of the island,' 'Decius freed the army from siege,' 'The Metropolitans filled the walls with armed men.' The order of arguments also corresponds to their height in the event structure tree, so the linking rule couldn't be simpler: it just says that if argument *x* is higher than argument *y* in the event structure, it c-commands it in the syntactic structure. The complicating factor is the position of the verb in Latin: you can't just compose the verb with its arguments working backwards from right to left. For instance, in the second example (Verr 2.3) the locative adjunct would have to be composed with the verb before the other arguments, which makes no sense: the adjunct locates the whole event described by the verb phrase, not just the verbal activity. If you shoot ducks in the forest, in a neutral pragmatic context you are duck-shooting in the forest, not forest-shooting ducks. (This is because the neutral order of compounding reflects the order in which arguments are composed with the verb for the semantic interpretation of the verb phrase, and adjuncts are composed after arguments.) So it seems that the arguments are lined up as discourse referents in their left-to-right compositional order and linked to post-verbal variables, as illustrated in Figure 3.10. Adjuncts do not move to the left, so they appear at the end of the string of arguments, directly scoping over the remnant verb phrase

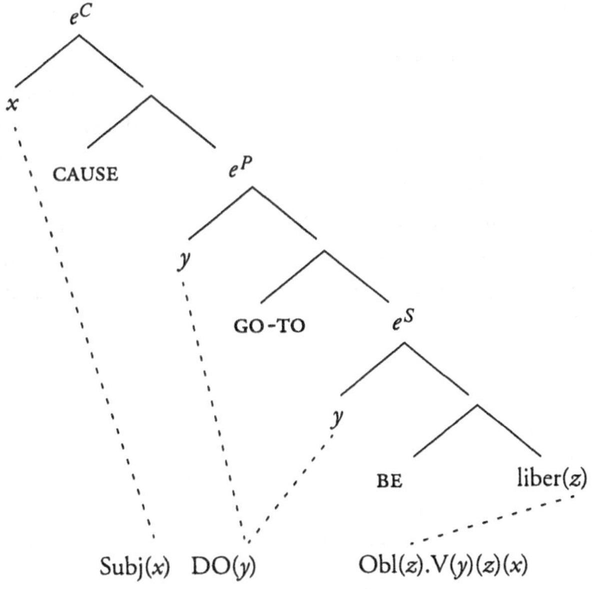

Figure 3.10
Argument order linking rule
P. Decius exercitum obsidione liberavit (De Div 1.51)

(89) brachia *ferro* exolvunt (Tac Ann 15.63)
mulierem *veneno* interfecit (Pro Clu 31).

Directional phrases also stay next to the verb

(90) Pompeium ferro *domum* compulit (De Har Resp 58)
medias vites vinclis *in terram* defigito (Cato 41.4).

Finally, as in some other languages, nonreferential objects do not move to the left but stay attached to the verb

(91) ferro *viam* facientem (Livy 7.33.10)
vi *viam* faciunt (Livy 4.38.4).

Nonreferential objects are not event participants and do not refer independently of the verb. A phrase like *impetum fecerunt* 'they made an attack' answers the question 'What did they do?', not the question 'What did they make?'. While the rules linking the event structure to the syntactic tree are semantically based, they can be disturbed by pragmatically driven modifications. Like a number of other verb final languages, Latin has scrambling, which in its most typical manifestation moves a nonfocal argument to the left of one or more preceding arguments and out of the domain of focus

(92) Ob id *Aelium* Thurini statua et corona aurea donarunt (NH 34.32)
Hannibali Locros tradiderat (Livy 29.6.5)
(Lucustae) *examinibus suis* agros late operirent (Livy 42.10.7)
timens... ne *navibus* nostri circumvenirentur (BC 3.63).

In the first example (NH 34.32) the direct object is scrambled to the left of the subject without being topicalized; in the second example an indirect object is moved to the left of the direct object; both represent discourse established referents. In the last two examples (Livy 42.10; BC 3.63) a discourse established instrumental is moved to the left out of the domain of focus. The effect of scrambling is to change the compositional level at which an argument or adjunct is entered into the semantic computation; this serves to align the syntactic constituency with the constituents of pragmatic meaning at the expense of constituency based on the semantics of the event structure.

(89) They opened the veins in their arms with a weapon (Tac Ann 15.63). He killed the woman with poison (Pro Clu 31).

(90) He drove Pompey to his house at sword-point (De Har Resp 58). Fix the middle of the vines into the ground with fasteners (Cato 41.4).

(91) Fighting my way forward (Livy 7.33.10). They fight their way forward (Livy 4.38.4).

(92) On account of this the Thurini presented Aelius with a statue and a gold crown (NH 34.32). They had handed over Locri to Hannibal (Livy 29.6.5). They covered the fields far and wide with their swarms (Livy 42.10.7). Fearing that our men would be surrounded by the ships (BC 3.63).

Passive

One of the crimes of Oppianicus, Cicero tells us in the Pro Cluentio, is the murder of his brother's wife Auria (cp. (89))

(93) (Oppianicus) mulierem veneno interfecit (Pro Clu 31).

The event described involved a number of participants including Oppianicus (the agent), Auria (the patient), and the poison (the instrument). The agent and the patient are arguments: they cannot be omitted without creating an ungrammatical sentence. The instrument is not obligatory; if it is included, it adds to the number of linguistically encoded participants, but that does not change the basic valency of the predicate *interficio*, which remains dyadic. The passive, on the other hand, subtracts from the set of obligatorily encoded participants, so it is a valency reducing operation

(94) Mithridates... matre sua veneno interfecta (Sall Hist 2.75)
Ex Afranianis interficiuntur T. Caecilius... et praeter eum centuriones iiii (BC 1.46).

While *interficio* is dyadic ($\lambda y \lambda x. V(x,y)$, ignoring the event argument), *interficior* is monadic ($\lambda y. V(y)$). The first example (Hist 2.75) is an ablative absolute and the covert agent argument is supplied by the subject of the main clause (Mithridates). In the second example (BC 1.46) the covert agent is recoverable from the context (unidentified members of Caesar's army): the expression $\lambda y \exists x. V(x,y)$ would capture the semantic accessibility of the suppressed argument. In active sentences the field of view of the linking rules encompasses the whole event structure; so whichever argument is topmost in the event structure gets mapped to subject. Passive morphology serves to limit the field of view of the linking rules, suppressing access to the topmost argument; the linking rules now map to subject the topmost argument in that portion of the event structure that falls within their field of view. This is illustrated in Figure 3.11 for a causative structure based on the following examples

(95) Fregerisne in carcere cervices ipsi illi Vettio? (In Vat 26)
Cervices in carcere *frangebantur* indignissime civium Romanorum (Verr 2.5.147).

Latin has little if any constraints either on the semantic role or on the event structural position of the suppressed argument: all that is required is that it be the topmost argument in the structure. So in addition to the suppression (or demotion) of the agent argument of a change of state predicate

(93) He killed the woman with poison (Pro Clu 31).

(94) Mithridates... after the poisoning of his mother (Sall Hist 2.75). From the troops of Afranius T. Caecilius and besides him four centurions were killed (BC 1.46).

(95) I ask whether you had this same Vettius strangled in prison (In Vat 26). Roman citizens were outrageously strangled in prison (Verr 2.5.147).

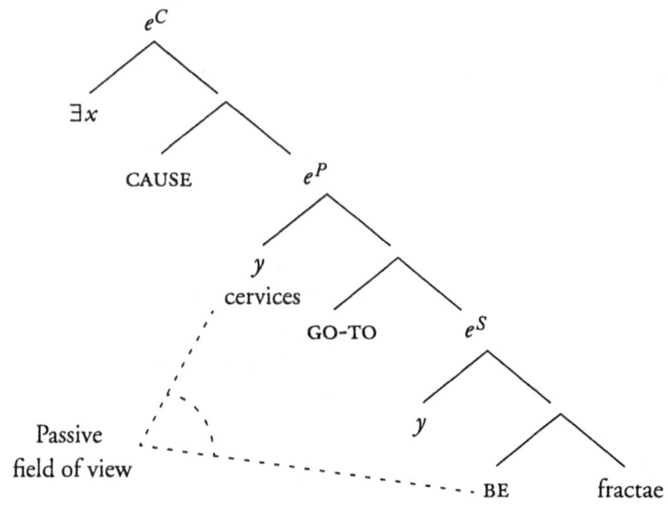

Figure 3.11
Passive field of view in causative structure
Cervices frangebantur (Verr 2.5.147)

(96) M. Marcellum... a P. Magio Cilone... pugione percussum esse (Ad Fam 4.12.2),

we find suppression of the agent of a simple process predicate

(97) vectabulum etiam quod adiunctis pecoribus trahebatur (Gell 20.1.28)
equorum pars magna nantes loris a puppibus trahebantur (Livy 21.27.9).

A causer too can be suppressed as in (95), or an experiencer

(98) amatus est a multis more Graecorum (Nepos 7.2.2)
timebatur non minus quam diligebatur (Nepos 7.7.3),

or an inanimate cause

(99) ferrum robigo consumit (Curt Ruf 7.8.15: cause subject)
Teritur robigine mucro ferreus (Prop 2.25.15: patient subject),

or even a patient

(100) Cum haec accepta clades est (Livy 2.51.1)
multa volnera accepta (Livy 10.1.5).

(96) That M. Marcellus had been stabbed with a dagger by P. Magius Cilo (Ad Fam 4.12.2).
(97) Also a vehicle that was drawn by yoked animals (Gell 20.1.28). A large part of the horses swam across while being pulled by their reins from the sterns of the boats (Livy 21.27.9).
(98) He was loved by many in the Greek manner (Nepos 7.2.2). He was feared no less than he was loved (Nepos 7.7.3).
(99) Rust consumes iron (Curt Ruf 7.8.15). The iron blade is worn away by rust (Prop 2.25.15).
(100) When this disaster was suffered (Livy 2.51.1). Many wounds were received (Livy 10.1.5).

When passivization applies to a transitive predicate, the result is an intransitive predicate: the sentence is detransitivized but still categorical. However passivization can also apply to intransitive predicates, both unergative

(101) *Conclamatur* ad arma (BC 1.69)
Tali dum *pugnatur* modo (BC 1.80)
luditur in castris (Ov Fast 2.724)

and (unlike in some other languages) quite a number of prima facie unaccusatives

(102) in silvam *venitur* et ibi... *considitur* (De Or 3.18)
ita sine vadimonio *disceditur* (Pro Quinct 23)
nec sine periculo *maneatur* (BG 5.31)
de utraque *siletur* (Sall Cat 2.8).

Passivization of an intransitive predicate produces an impersonal structure that is thetic: the subject of predication is the event argument or the location of the event: $\lambda x \lambda e. V(e,x) \rightarrow \lambda e. V(e)$. There is a default bias towards understanding that the suppressed subject is human: *pugnatur* does not denote a cat fight without additional context. However *latratur* (cp. Ov Trist 2.459) denotes a basically nonhuman activity and so has a default nonhuman suppressed agent (contrast English 'One barks when a stranger is outside').

While we have just seen that suppression of the topmost argument is not constrained by its semantic role or event structural position, there are constraints on which other argument can be promoted to subject under passivization. The first rule is that when the topmost argument is suppressed, only the highest remaining argument is mapped to subject; the same linking rule as in active sentences applies, only in the narrower field of view used by the passive. Consequently only the higher of the two remaining arguments of a double accusative verb can become subject under passivization

(103) Motus doceri gaudet Ionicos *matura virgo* (Hor Od 3.6.21)
dignos a quibus causam *diserti* docerentur (Quint 6.2.3)
quisquis alimenta a mendico rogatus est (Sen Con 1.1.10)
Ceteri populi Achaeorum cum sententias perrogarentur (Livy 32.23.1).

Promotion to subject depends on event structural position: in the structure (x CAUSE (y GO-TO (y BE-aware-of z))), y (the patient) is higher than z (the theme).

(101) There was a call to arms (BC 1.69). When there is this style of fighting (BC 1.80). They had fun in the camp (Ov Fast 2.724).

(102) We went into the wood and sat down there (De Or 3.18). They parted without setting a court date (Pro Quinct 23). It was dangerous to stay (BG 5.31). There is silence about both (Sall Cat 2.8).

(103) Teenage girls enjoy being taught Ionian dancing (Hor Od 3.6.21). The sort of people eloquent advocates should be taught the facts of the case by (Quint 6.2.3). Whoever has been asked for support by the beggar (Sen Con 1.1.10). The other peoples of the Achaeans, when they were asked their opinions (Livy 32.23.1).

It does not depend on case (both arguments are in the accusative), and *z* can become subject when *y* is absent

(104) ad sensus, *qui* non docentur (Quint 6.5.2).

The same rule accounts for the promotion to subject of accusatives rather than datives in triadic structures with indirect objects (unlike in some other languages)

(105) Huic... *corona* a populo data est (Nepos 8.4.1)
ista omnis pecunia huic adulescentulo... reddita est (Pro Flacc 89),

and of accusatives rather than ablatives in triadic structures with obliques

(106) Vidi ego pampineis oneratam vitibus *ulmum* (Ov Trist 2.143)
quattuor simul locis *praesidia* Macedonum expulsa (Livy 38.1.9).

However indirect objects and obliques are also semantically unsuitable for promotion to subject under passivization, since they are not promoted in dyadic structures either: only the impersonal passive is licensed

(107) non modo non *invidetur* illi aetati verum etiam favetur (De Off 2.45)
sapienti non *nocetur* a paupertate (Sen Ep 85.37)
cum praesidio earum *indigetur* (NH 10.75).

Some of the exceptions may be passivizations of an alternative transitive event structure

(108) *Larix*... ab carie aut tinea non nocetur (Vitr 2.9.14).

By contrast accusative internal arguments and argument (but not adverbial) measure phrases can be promoted to subject

(109) *Hac pugna* pugnata (Nepos 23.5.1)
si statim *bina stadia* ambulentur (NH 23.26).

While unaccusative subjects can be suppressed, oblique objects cannot be promoted: this supports the idea that dyadic event structural configurations with obliques have empty higher positions that block passivization.

Although the topmost argument is out of the field of view for the passive linking rules, it can reappear overtly as an adjunct *by*-phrase; this applies not only to agents but also to nonagentive arguments like experiencers and also in impersonal passive sentences

(104) To the senses, which are not taught (Quint 6.5.2).

(105) A crown was given him by the people (Nepos 8.4.1). All this money was given to this young man (Pro Flacc 89).

(106) I have seen an elm covered with vine leaves (Ov Trist 2.143). The garrisons of the Macedonians were expelled from the four places at the same time (Livy 38.1.9).

(107) That time of life does not only not meet with hostility but is actually favoured (De Off 2.45). The wise man is not harmed by poverty (Sen Ep 85.37). When their protection is needed (NH 10.75).

(108) The larch is not harmed by rot or maggots (Vitr 2.9.14).

(109) When this battle had been fought (Nepos 23.5.1). If a four hundred yard walk is taken immediately after (NH 23.26).

(110) Sed meus... *a rigido* teritur *centurione* liber (Mart 11.3.2)
quantum *a me* Lesbia amata meast (Catull 87.2)
Pugnabatur *a nobis* ex ponte... ab illis ex navibus (BAlex 19),

even apparently unaccusative ones

(111) *Ab omnibus* in eandem sententiam itur (Sen Ep 66.41)
ut una *ab omnibus*... in colloquium veniretur (Sall Jug 112.3).

It may be relevant that the initial subevent of these unaccusatives is volitional. Inanimate *by*-phrases do not use the preposition

(112) Postea aliquanto ipsos quoque *tempestas* vehementius iactare coepit (De Inv 2.154: active with inanimate subject)
Aquila *tempestate* iactatus promunturium superare non potuit (BAfr 62)

Inanimate *by*-phrases need to be distinguished from instrumentals and causal adjuncts, which are used just as they are in the corresponding active sentences

(113) quamdiu *missilibus* pugnatum est (Livy 34.14.9)
peritia locorum ab Hiberis melius pugnatur (Tac Ann 6.36).

There is someone using the missiles in Livy 34.14 in (113), but noone is using the tempest in BAfr 62 in (112). Manner adverbs and adverbial phrases can be oriented towards the *by*-phrase participant rather than the passive subject

(114) Liber tuus... legitur a me *diligenter* (Ad Fam 6.5.1)
et sum a vobis *benigne ac diligenter* auditus (Phil 1.39).

Significantly, this applies also when the *by*-phrase is not overt, which means that although it is suppressed for the purposes of the passive linking rules and consequently absent from the syntax, it is not eliminated from the semantic computation

(115) *diligenter* defenditur (Pro Rosc Am 148)
haec omnia *summa cura sollertiaque* explicata sunt (Vitr 5.8.1)
Nimium indulgenter nutritus est (Sen Con 2.3.3).

(110) My book is thumbed by tough centurions (Mart 11.3.2). As my Lesbia has been loved by me (Catull 87.2). The fight was conducted by us from the bridge and by them from the ships (BAlex 19).

(111) The same proposal is adopted by everyone (Sen Ep 66.41). That there should be a conference attended by everyone (Sall Jug 112.3).

(112) A little while later a storm began to toss them too rather violently (De Inv 2.154). Aquila, tossed by a storm, was unable to get past the promontory (BAfr 62).

(113) As long as the battle was fought with missiles (Livy 34.14.9). The fight was conducted more successfully by the Iberians due to their experience of the area (Tac Ann 6.36).

(114) Your book is being carefully read by me (Ad Fam 6.5.1). I have been kindly and carefully listened to by you (Phil 1.39).

(115) He is being vigorously defended (Pro Rosc Am 148). All these things have been set out with the greatest care and diligence (Vitr 5.8.1). He was brought up without enough discipline (Sen Con 2.3.3).

The rule covers arbitrary agents of generic sentences, as in the following examples with a modal reading

(116) opercula *diligenter* pice opturantur (Col 12.45.2)
bacae myrti... *diligenter* conteruntur (Col 12.38.2),

as well as impersonal passives with suppressed referential subjects

(117) *modico gradu* ad castra hostium perventum est (Livy 30.5.3)
carpendi *studio* paulatim longius itur (Ov Fast 4.443)

and suppressed arbitrary subjects

(118) Si aliquando *concitate* itur, numquam non *frigide* reditur (Quint 11.3.133)
posita sed luditur arca (Juv 1.90).

The individual in Fast 4.443 in (117) who has *carpendi studium* is the same as the contextually salient individual who *longius it*, namely Proserpina. The Juvenal example in (118) is generic: it means that for every individual *x* such that *ludit* (*x*), *posuit arcam* (*x*). The covert subjects of a sequence of impersonals can be the same, or partially identical as in the first example (Quint 11.3): but a covert *by*-phrase is not anaphorically accessible to a pronoun in the next clause, whereas an overt *by*-phrase is

(119) cum esset cruentus gladius ab accusatore prolatus quo *is* hominem probabat occisum (Quint 6.1.48).

If the *by*-phrase *ab accusatore* is removed from this example, there is no antecedent available for the pronoun *is*.

Some verbs like *frango* 'break' are inherently eventive, others like *timeo* 'fear' are inherently stative, and these properties carry over into the passive

(120) *frangitur* armatum conliso pectore pectus (Lucan 4.783)
timetur inopia, *timentur* morbi (Sen Ep 14.3).

There is an event of one armoured breast getting crushed by another one; people are in a state of fear of diseases. Other verbs like *munio* 'fortify' and *claudo* 'close off' vary between eventive and stative readings, as shown by the examples in (36), and both readings carry over into the passive. Consequently we find these verbs used in the present and imperfect tense to denote ongoing present and past states (as well as ongoing events)

(116) The lids are carefully sealed with pitch (Col 12.45.2). The myrtle berries are carefully crushed (Col 12.38.2).

(117) At a moderate pace they reached the enemy camp (Livy 30.5.3). In her eagerness to pick flowers she gradually went further away (Ov Fast 4.443).

(118) If sometimes the outward trip seems to carry emphasis, the return always looks weak (Quint 11.3.133). People gamble with their entire wealth (Juv 1.90).

(119) When a bloody sword was produced by the prosecutor with which he argued that the man had been killed (Quint 6.1.48).

(120) Armoured breasts are fractured, crushed against each other (Lucan 4.783). Poverty is a source of fear and disease is a source of fear (Sen Ep 14.3).

(121) non enim portu illud oppidum *clauditur*, sed urbe portus ipse *cingitur* (Verr 2.5.96)
idque natura loci... *muniebatur* (BG 1.38).

The harbour of Syracuse is in the state of being surrounded by the city.

When used with the auxiliary in the past passive and the perfect passive, the perfect participle passive of an eventive verb like *frango* covers the same field of view in the event structure as do the finite forms; consequently it is eventive

(122) Quisquis autem pampinus... in exputando vel alligando *fractus est* (Col 5.6.32).

'Any tendril that is in the state of having undergone an event of getting broken during an event of pruning or tying...'. But past passive participles of eventive verbs can also be used with the copula as predicative adjectives and attributively. In that case they have only the resultant state of the event structure in their field of view (see Figure 3.12)

(123) Saepe enim in quibusdam... spes amplificandae fortunae *fractior* (De Amic 59)
fractis sacrum Vadaveronem montibus (Mart 1.49.6).

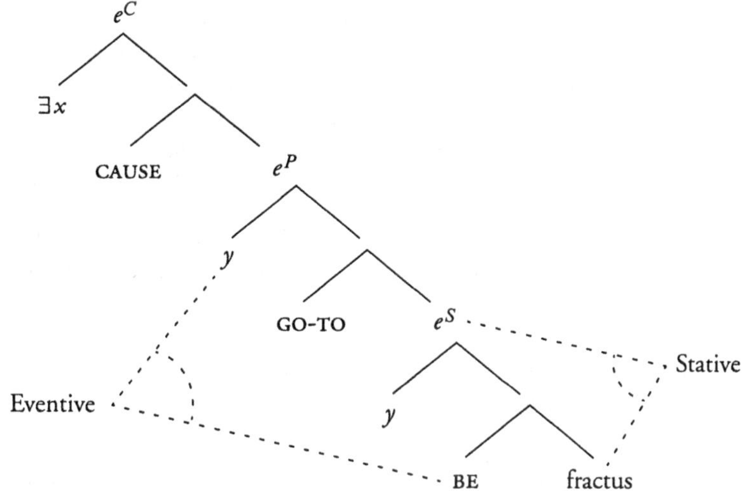

Figure 3.12
Past participle: eventive and stative fields of view
(cp. Col 5.6.32, De Amic 59)

(121) For that town is not bounded by its harbour but the harbour itself is surrounded by the city (Verr 2.5.96). It was fortified by its natural position (BG 1.38).

(122) But any tendril that has been broken in the process of pruning or tying (Col 5.6.32).

(123) For often in certain people the hope of bettering their lot is too weak (De Amic 59). And sacred Vadavero in its rugged hills (Mart 1.49.6).

The first example (De Amic 59) can only be adjectival because events are not gradable (there is no comparative or superlative of an event; it either took place or it didn't). The second example makes no reference to any causing tectonic event but merely describes the current state of the mountains. Another diagnostic for the adjectival reading is the negative prefix *in-*

(124) non solum doctus *indoctum* sed etiam doctior doctum in rhetorices opere superabit (Quint 2.17.43).

Further diagnostics for the eventive reading are event-oriented adverb(ial)s like *nuper* 'recently' and in most cases a *by*-phrase (apparently restricting the field of view to the resultant state subevent suppresses access to the topmost argument)

(125) Hylaeusque ferox *nuper* percussus *ab apro* (Ov Met 3.213).

Consequently verbs that have both eventive and stative readings have two ways of expressing the present passive, with a finite form as in (121) or with the perfect participle and the copula as in the following

(126) *Munitaeque* sunt palpebrae tamquam vallo pilorum (ND 2.143)
aliae coriis *tectae* sunt, aliae villis *vestitae* (ND 2.121)
sinus retrahens... oras usque ad ima montis Idae. Is primo parvis urbibus *aspersus* est (Mela 1.91).

Agentive-eventive readings would give nonsense in all examples.

The passive is a valency-changing operation located in the linking rules, which are at the interface between the semantics of event structure and its morphological and syntactic actuation. It is a convenient mechanism for speakers to use under certain pragmatic conditions, while in others its use is infelicitous. For instance, unknown agents do not make good topics, and this can trigger the passive

(127) Nam vitiumst *oblatum* virgini olim a nescioquo improbo (Ter Hec 383)
Fores ecfregit, *restituentur*; discidit vestem, *resarcietur* (Ter Ad 120).

The same is true for arbitrary subjects in generic sentences

(128) Commoratio est cum in loco firmissimo... *manetur* diutius et eodem saepius *reditur* (Rhet Her 4.58)

(124) In the activity of rhetoric those who have training will surpass those who do not, and further those who have training will themselves be surpassed by those who have better training (Quint 2.17.43).

(125) And fierce Hylaeus, recently gored by a boar (Ov Met 3.213).

(126) And the eyelids are equipped with, so to speak, a palisade of hairs (ND 2.143). Some of them are protected by hides, others are clothed in fur (ND 2.121). A bay extending its shores up to the foot of Mount Ida. It is initially sprinkled with small cities (Mela 1.91).

(127) An outrage was inflicted on the girl by some scoundrel (Ter Hec 383). If he breaks open a door, I will have it fixed; if he tears a jacket, I will have it mended (Ter Ad 120).

(128) Dwelling on the point is when one remains on the strongest argument for a rather long time and keeps returning to it (Rhet Her 4.58).

(129) proinde ut diu *vivitur*, bene *vivitur* (Pl Trin 65)
in foro aut vico quamdiu paucitas est, sine tumultu *ambulatur* (Sen NQ 5.2.1).

Such sentences often have a modal (deontic) reading

(130) Hae herbae diligenter *purgantur* et sub umbra *expanduntur* (Col 12.13.2)
fissura diligenter subacto luto *linitur* (Col 4.29.8).

See (116) for two further examples. Positive polarity focus, also called verum focus, ('Brutus DID stab Caesar') can trigger the passive

(131) COC. Nempe me hinc abire vis. LYS. Volo inquam. COC. *Abibitur.* Drachmam dato. LYS. *Dabitur.* (Pl Merc 775).

Nonspecific indefinite objects (as in 'Jack drank a beer') are unindividuated and make bad topics, which constrains passivization ('A beer was drunk by Jack'). Unaffected entities also sometimes make bad passive subjects: 'This glass was used by Jack' tends to be infelicitous without contrastive focus on the agent, while 'This glass was used by Queen Victoria' is fine. Discourse participants, on the other hand, are strongly topical, which discourages passivization with a *by*-phrase. In a neutral context one says 'I have washed the car' rather than 'The car has been washed by me.' But verum focus can license the passive with a strongly topical *by*-phrase ('The car has been and will be washed by me')

(132) Liber tuus et lectus est et legitur *a me* diligenter (Ad Fam 6.5.1)
reliqua sic *a me* aguntur et agentur (Ad Att 1.20.2).

The passive can also be exploited to maintain continuity of a topic

(133) Fuit eodem ex studio vir eruditus... Q. Tubero. Is... *rogatus est* a Maximo ut triclinium sterneret... stravit pelliculis haedinis lectulos Punicanos (Pro Mur 75).

Maximus eum rogavit would have broken topic continuity in the narrative. Addition of a *by*-phrase (which is actually illicit in some languages) can be necessary to avoid vacuity (and consequently infelicity) when the remainder of a passive sentence is presuppositional material

(129) Living long is living well (Pl Trin 65). As long as only a few people are in a square or a street, one can walk without disturbance (Sen NQ 5.2.1).

(130) There herbs are carefully cleaned and spread out in the shade (Col 12.13.2). The spot where it is cut is carefully spread with kneaded clay (Col 4.29.8).

(131) COC. You want me to leave. LYS. Yes I do. COC. I'll leave. Give me a drachma. LYS. I will (Pl Merc 775).

(132) Your book has been and is being carefully read by me (Ad Fam 6.5.1) My current and future actions will be such that... (Ad Att 1.20.2).

(133) There was a learned man from the same philosophical school, Q. Tubero. He was asked by Maximus to provide cushions for the couches at the funeral dinner. He covered simple Punic couches with goat skins (Pro Mur 75).

(134) Plinius Secundus... Periit clade Campaniae... vi pulveris et favillae oppressus est, vel ut quidam existimant *a servo suo* occisus (Suet Plin Sec).

Occisus does not by itself contribute enough new information to make the addition of the disjunct quite felicitous (since *occido* can be used with an inanimate subject).

Other valency operations

We have seen that the passive involves suppression of an argument and is used at the discretion of the speaker. Other valency operations are not optional in this way: they involve facts about the identity of the participants, and they do not change the number of arguments. In a default event all the participants are nonidentical; so a transitive verb typically has the structure $\lambda y \lambda x. V(x,y) \wedge x \neq y$. In a reflexive sentence, on the other hand, the structure is $\lambda y \lambda x. V(x,y) \wedge x = y$, which reduces to $\lambda x. V(x,x)$

(135) ut ne minus *amicos* quam *se ipsos* diligant (De Fin 1.70)
Pompeianus miles *fratrem suum*, dein cognito facinore *se ipsum* interfecit (Tac Hist 3.51).

Each example illustrates the default structure in the first clause and the reflexive structure in the second. Reciprocalization involves a bidirectional relation, in the case of a dual $\lambda y \lambda x. V(x,y) \wedge V(y,x)$. A few verbs are symmetrical and therefore lexically reciprocal

(136) si palpebrae dormientis non *coeunt* (Cels 2.8.25),

others allow both a reciprocal and a nonreciprocal reading, with the former predominating

(137) nil cessarunt ilico *osculari* atque *amplexari* inter se (Pl Mil 1433);

the nonreciprocal reading (in which Philocomasium and her lover are both kissing and hugging a nonresponding third party) is contextually unavailable and directly excluded by *inter se*. For most verbs the nonreciprocal reading is predominant

(138) cum duo ligna inter se diutius *fricta* sunt (Sen NQ 2.22.1)
conger et murena caudam inter se *praerodentes* (NH 9.185).

(134) Plinius Secundus died in the Campanian disaster. He was overcome by the force of the dust and the ash, or, as some think, was killed by one of his slaves (Suet Plin Sec).

(135) That they should not love their friends less than themselves (De Fin 1.70). A soldier of Pompey killed his own brother and then, realizing what he had done, killed himself (Tac Hist 3.51).

(136) If his eyelids are not closed as he sleeps (Cels 2.8.25).

(137) They went right ahead and kissed and embraced on the spot (Pl Mil 1433).

(138) When two pieces of wood have been rubbed together for a while (Sen NQ 2.22.1). The conger and the moray eel, which gnaw at each other's tails (NH 9.185).

The pieces of wood are not each rubbed against some other unspecified surface but against each other; the two types of eel do not chew the tails of some other unspecified fish but each other's tails.

Another type of valency variation occurs when causative verbs are used in the absence of an external causer, because the process is seen as arising spontaneously in the undergoing entity; as in many other languages, this type of middle use can be marked by the passive or by a reflexive

(139) Nilus.... in plura *scinditur* flumina (Sen NQ 4a.2.8)
Himera... dividuas *se scindit* in oras (Sil It 14.234).

The passive is not a true passive: you can't say 'Caesar was stabbed of his own accord,' but *sua sponte* can be used with these middles

(140) sua sponte *movetur* (ND 2.32)
Ianus geminus sua sponte *apertus* est (Hist Aug Comm Ant 16.4).

Conversely the passive can be used with a *by*-phrase, as illustrated (110), but the middle cannot: an event can have an internal cause or an external cause, but not both at the same time. The reflexive is not a true reflexive either but like English prefixed *self-* ('My old Fiat is self-destructing/*destroying itself'). Sometimes the causative verb is simply used intransitively with no overt mark of the change in valency

(141) securibus galeas loricasque *perrumpere* (Tac Hist 2.42: e^{CPS})
iam in vestibulum *perruperant* templi (Livy 3.18.8: e^{PS}).

The e^{CPS} version expresses a violent change of state caused by an external agent, the e^{PS} version simply expresses a violent change of location; this is the regular meaning of *erumpere*

(142) Catilina... *erupit* ex urbe (Cat 3.3);

passive and reflexive forms are also found. *Verto* 'turn,' *moveo* 'move,' *(con)gelo* 'freeze,' *declinare, inclinare* 'incline' and *deflectere* 'divert' likewise show the whole range of possibilities

(143) in fugam *vertit* equum (Livy 37.43.6)
Aeneadae... Libyae *vertuntur* ad oras (Aen 1.158)
Verti igitur *me*... Arpinum versus. (Ad Att 16.10.1)
Caesar... *vertit* ad Rhenum (Tac Ann 1.56).

(139) The Nile splits into many rivers (Sen NQ 4a.2.8). Himera splits into separate channels (Sil It 14.234).

(140) It moves spontaneously (ND 2.32). The twin gates of the temple of Janus opened spontaneously (Hist Aug Comm Ant 16.4).

(141) They broke through helmets and breastplates with axes (Tac Hist 2.42). They had already broken through into the vestibule of the temple (Livy 3.18.8).

(142) Catiline bolted out of the city (Cat 3.3).

(143) He turned his horse to flight (Livy 37.43.6). The followers of Aeneas turn towards the coast of Libya (Aen 1.158). So I am turning towards Arpinum (Ad Att 16.10.1). Germanicus turned towards the Rhine (Tac Ann 1.56).

Transitive verbs of motion have a quite predictable middle meaning, as do verbs of grooming: one says 'I'm shaving' rather than 'I'm shaving myself.' In fact, 'The barber is shaving' and 'The barber is shaving himself' are not only pragmatically but also semantically distinct, since the latter has a "self-as-other" reading. The simple use of the active form with middle meaning is quite productive, particularly in colloquial Latin. The use of reflexive morphology for semantically middle verbs can be motivated: the participant does not simply undergo the event, as would be the case with a purely patient/theme argument, for instance the argument of an unaccusative verb like *morior* 'die' or *cado* 'fall.' Rather the participant additionally spontaneously causes itself to undergo the event. The use of passive morphology for middle meanings reflects the fact that the causative argument is not lacking but has been suppressed, as happens with the passive.

The last valency changing operation we will consider is object drop. As its name implies, object drop suppresses the direct object from the field of view of the linking rules (in contrast to the passive, which suppresses the subject). So it detransitivizes the verb: $\lambda y \lambda x. V(x,y) \rightarrow \lambda x. V(x)$, as illustrated in Figure 3.13. Object drop has nothing to do with object pro-drop, that is use of a null object pronoun as in *amat* 'he loves her.' (Pro-drop does not detransitivize the verb: it does not suppress the object from the field of view of the linking rules, and is limited to situations where an anaphoric antecedent is contextually available to provide a value for the free variable that is passed through to the syntax.) In one type of object drop, the dropped object is a definite entity directly supplied by the context (but not an anaphoric antecedent)

(144) Romani inde *oppugnabant* (Livy 26.26.3: scil. Anticyram)
Macedones cuniculis *oppugnabant* (Livy 36.25.4: scil. Lamiam)
Hinc Venus, hinc contra *spectat* Saturnia Juno (Aen 10.760: scil. pugnam).

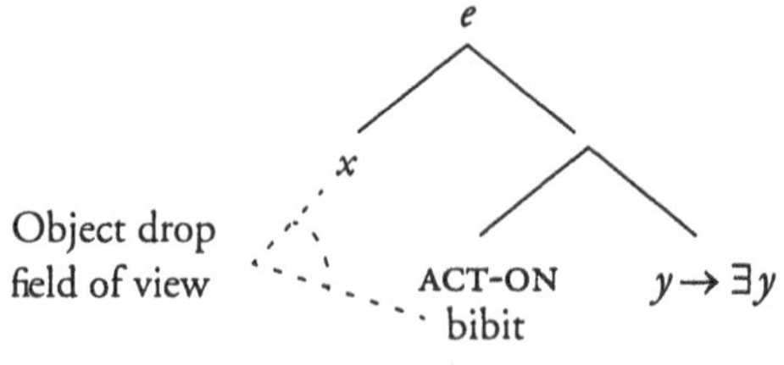

Figure 3.13
Object drop
Bibit (Ad Att 13.52.1)

(144) The Romans were attacking from that side (Livy 26.26.3). The Macedonians were attacking with tunnels (Livy 36.25.4). On one side Venus looks on, on the opposite side Saturnian Juno (Aen 10.760).

The object is a free variable which is not available in the syntax but is present in the event structure (*y* in Figure 3.13). More commonly the dropped object is a nonspecific indefinite count noun or mass noun that is the prototypical object of a verb denoting a recognized common activity, like eating (food), reading (text), sowing (seeds), ploughing (fields) or boarding (a ship)

(145) Itaque et *edit* et *bibit* ἀδεῶς (Ad Att 13.52.1)
Ubi *bibisti*? (Pl Amph 575)
Permisisti mihi ut *sererem* in fundo tuo... *sevi*, nec pateris me fructus tollere (Pompon Dig 19.5.16)
Epheso *conscendentes* hanc epistulam dedimus L. Tarquitio (Ad Att 6.8.4).

In this case the free variable is closed by existential closure ($y \rightarrow \exists y$). It is not anaphorically transparent (*'I'm shooting: they have green feathers'), but it is accessible for adverbial modification: compare 'I'm cooking in the oven' (the food is in the oven) with simple intransitive 'I'm walking in the oven' (I am in the oven). If the verb doesn't have a prototypical object (like 'shake' for instance), then object drop is not licensed. If the object is not the verb's prototypical object but a hyponym of it, then it cannot be dropped

(146) Edunt *cauliculos* decoctos (NH 27.73)
Is... *venenum* bibit (Asc Ped Sc 20).

Even dropping the predicative participle in the first example (NH 27.73), 'they eat' cannot be understood to mean 'they eat stalks of the drabe plant' (except in an esoteric context where for some reason they are the default food). Object drop is easier if the event is iterated, habitual or generic, since this tends to deindividuate the object

(147) filio senis, quicum ego *bibo*, quicum *edo* et *amo* (Pl Bacch 646)
ideo quia mensam, quando *edo*, detergeo (Pl Men 77)
Aut *scribo* aut *lego* (Ad Fam 9.20.3)
boves qui *arant* (Col De Arb 12.2).

If the subject too is suppressed, an impersonal results

(148) *bibitur, estur* quasi in popina (Pl Poen 835)
Amatur atque egetur acriter. (Pl Pseud 273);

(145) So he ate and drank freely (Ad Att 13.52.1). Where did you go drinking? (Pl Amph 575). You allowed me to sow on your farm. I sowed, and you do not permit me to remove the crop (Pompon Dig 19.5.16). I am giving this letter to L. Tarquitius while embarking from Ephesus (Ad Att 6.8.4).

(146) One eats the stalks boiled (NH 27.73). He drank poison (Asc Ped Sc 20).

(147) The old man's son, with whom I eat and drink and love (Pl Bacch 646). Because when I eat I wipe the table clean (Pl Men 77). I either write or read (Ad Fam 9.20.3). The oxen that are used to plough (Col De Arb 12.2).

(148) There is eating and drinking as if in a bistro (Pl Poen 835). I'm badly in love and badly in need of cash (Pl Pseud 273).

object drop applies first, then passivization (not the other way around). Object drop in causative verbs, as opposed to the activity verbs illustrated above, is more difficult

(149) Propino magnum poclum: ille *ebibit* (Pl Curc 359)
Ego illi iam tres cardeles occidi et dixi quia mustella *comedit* (Petr 46);

both examples need a null pronoun for proper interpretation (as also required by the context). The reason why object drop is difficult with these telic verbs is that it would remove the subject of the resultant state subevent predication associated with the prefix. This effect can be overridden by contrastive verb focus, which tends to deindividuate the object

(150) Hic *effringit*, hic *transilit* (Sen De Ben 7.27.2).

The iteration effect just described also tends to widen the range of verbs that license object drop. This is clear if we consider dispositional properties and professional activities. 'I'm biting' is hardly grammatical without an object (except, significantly, at the dentist), but 'Spiders bite' is fine

(151) cum apri *percutiant*, feminae sues *mordent* (NH 11.161)
Minuta quaedam animalia... cum *mordent* non sentiuntur (Sen Ep 94.41)
sic ut scorpio *laedit* dum manu tollitur (NH 32.148).

The first example (NH 11.161) has contrastive focus, while the last two examples (Ep 94.41; NH 32.148) have overt quantification over events, which places the dropped indefinite object in the restrictor of a tripartite structure, the default location of presuppositional material. Genericity and iteration often combine with contrastive focus in licensing object drop

(152) non tanta studia assequuntur eorum quibus *dederunt* quanta odia eorum quibus *ademerunt* (De Off 2.54)
summa Saturni *refrigeret*, media Martis *incendat* (ND 2.119)
Si cotidie *fraudas, decipis, poscis... aufers, eripis* (Parad 43)
animalia... alia *sugunt*, alia *carpunt*, alia *vorant*, alia *mandunt* (ND 2.122).

Here are some examples with professional activities

(149) I proposed a large toast; he drank it all (Pl Curc 359). I recently killed three of his goldfinches and said that a weasel had eaten them (Petr 46).

(150) One breaks down doors, another jumps over walls (Sen De Ben 7.27.2).

(151) While boars gore, sows bite (NH 11.161). The bite of certain tiny animals is not felt (Sen Ep 94.41). When it is lifted by hand, it stings like a scorpion (NH 32.148).

(152) The support they get from those to whom they have given is not as great as the hostility they arouse in those from whom they have taken (De Off 2.54). The highest one, that of Saturn, cools, the middle one, that of Mars, heats (ND 2.119). If every day you cheat, deceive, demand, carry off, plunder (Parad 43). Some animals suck, some graze, some swallow and some chew (ND 2.122).

(153) (Apollonius) mercede *doceret* (De Or 1.126)
is qui *defendit* (De Part Or102)
Quare dicit venenum esse qui *accusat*? (Quint Decl 246.3).

'I'm defending' is an incomplete sentence when uttered in a cinema, but a complete sentence when uttered in a courtroom; 'I'm eating' on the other hand is fine in both. Indirect objects and oblique complements can be dropped under the same conditions as the direct objects just illustrated

(154) se cum posset perdere *pepercisse* quam cum *parcere* potuerit perdidisse (Pro Quinct 51)
Uter igitur est divitior... qui *eget* an qui *abundat*? (Parad 49).

FURTHER READING

Arsenijević (2006); Borer (2005); Levin & Hovav 2005; Matellán (2010); Ramchand (2008).

(153) He taught for profit (De Or 1.126). He who is the defendant (De Part Or 102). Why does he who is the prosecutor say that it is poison? (Quint Decl 246.3).

(154) That although he had the power to ruin he spared rather than that although he could have spared he ruined (Pro Quinct 51). Who therefore is richer, he who is in need or he who has plenty? (Parad 49).

4 | LOCATION

Our intuitions about space seem to fall into two complementary classes. On the one hand, there are the geometrical concepts of points, lines, angles, distances, planes, solids and the three orthogonal axes corresponding to up–down, left–right and back–front. On the other hand, there are the mereological and topological concepts which take regions as basic and work with the fundamental relations between regions: part, proper part, overlap, connection, contact, exterior and interior. This duality of spatial ontologies mirrors the duality of temporal ontologies, one taking the instant of time as basic, the other taking the interval of time as basic. But the dualities are not contradictory. Each can be defined in terms of the other. Points and instants can be defined as ultrafilters on sets of overlapping regions and intervals respectively. This approach is the same as that used in generalized quantifier theory (see Chapter 5), where individuals are defined as the set of all their properties: Sulla = $\lambda P.P$(Sulla). On the other hand, a region can be defined as a set of points which are connected by paths, and intervals can be defined as time lines. Our treatment of location and direction assumes a semantic type of points <p>. Regions are sets of points <p, t>, but it is sometimes convenient to treat regions as a type <r>. Vectors are sets of ordered pairs of points, but it is also convenient to treat them as a type, <v>.

In Latin, locational and directional expressions are encoded primarily by prepositions. The locative case is largely restricted to the names of towns and small islands of the first and second declensions and a few of the third. The locative case also survives in a few common nouns that occur frequently in locational expressions: *domi* 'at home,' *belli* 'in war,' *ruri* 'in the country,' *humi* 'on the ground,' *militiae* 'in the field.' The use of the bare accusative to express goal of motion and bare ablative to express source is similarly restricted to names of towns, small islands and a few common nouns such as *domus*, *rus*, and adverbial expressions like *foras*, *foris* 'outside.' When the same noun is used both in the locative and with the preposition *in*, there is a distinction between viewing the object as a point (*domi* 'at home') and viewing it as an extended region (*in domo* 'in the house'). The same distinction applies to the bare accusative and the preposition *ad* with the names of towns, for instance *Mutinam* 'to Modena,' *ad Mutinam* 'to the neighbourhood of Modena.'

The size of islands seems an odd semantic category, and in fact the rule turns out to be sensitive not only to physical size but also to cognitive size and cultural distance. In Old Latin the bare accusative is used regularly in goal expressions for towns in Italy and familiar cities such as Carthage, but for distant cities like Ephesus Plautus uses both the preposition *in* and the bare accusative; a similar variation occurs with lesser known towns in the De Bello Hispaniensi. In the case of islands, variation with Cyprus is found from Plautus and Terence to Cicero. Variation between locative and the preposition *in* is found with Crete and Lemnos in contrast to islands close to Italy. Also if an island has the same name as its capital city (which is more likely for small islands than for large ones), it follows the analogy of cities and takes the locative and bare accusative. There is a similar rule in Italian, where the preposition *a* 'at' is used with the names of cities and small islands, while *in* 'in' is used with countries and large islands: a smaller island near Italy such as Corsica can be linguistically larger than a larger island farther away such as Cyprus, not to mention extra-mediterranean ones such as Sumatra and Formosa.

The locative case and prepositional phrases of location denote places, not entities. They do not answer questions with 'what' but questions with 'where'

(1) *Ubi* Charinus est erus? *domin* an *foris*? (Pl Merc 131)
SOS. *Ubi* patera nunc est? MER. Est *in cistula*. (Pl Amph 420)
LYC. *Ubi* id est aurum? STROB. *In arca* apud me. (Pl Aul 823).

Similarly the relative locative *ubi* may have a prepositional phrase as its antecedent

(2) Hic *in aedibus ubi* tu habitas. (Pl Amph 699).

The relation between the box and the bowl in the second example in (1) (Amph 420) is not a direct one between two entities, but a relation between the space occupied by the bowl and the interior space of the box. We need to assume a preliminary function σ that maps objects onto the space they occupy. This is the same space function σ that we used for tracing the paths of events in Chapter 1, only now applied to objects. For every object in its domain, σ maps that object onto its eigenspace (the space that it occupies): this is a space or region that is made up collectively of a set of points. So the sigma function $\lambda x.\sigma(x)$ has the type <e,pt>. Consider the last example in (1) (Aul 823). As illustrated in Figure 4.1, the prepositional head is complex: first it goes to the σ function and finds the values for its arguments (these are $\sigma(x)$ and $\sigma(y)$), then it locates the former relative to the latter: the gold is a member of the set of entities whose eigenspaces are internal to the eigenspace of the box. We need the σ function for the subject as well as the object: in the case of a compressible entity like a sponge, it is not the entity but the space that it occupies that determines its location relative to another object. Since the application of the σ function is

(1) Where is my master Charinus? Is he at home or out? (Pl Merc 131). SOS. Where is the bowl now? MER. It is in a box (Pl Amph 420). LYC. Where is that gold? STROB. In a box at my house (Pl Aul 823).

(2) Here in the house where you live (Pl Amph 699).

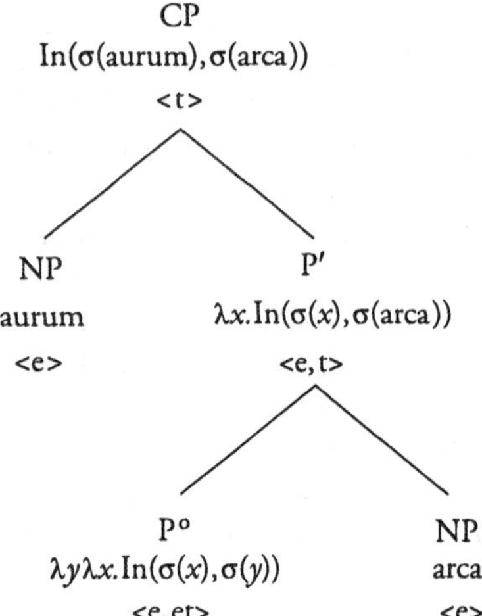

Figure 4.1
Prepositional phrase predication
Id aurum est in arca (cp. Pl Aul 823)

built into the definition of the prepositional head, the preposition can keep its simple type <e,et>.

The tree structure in Figure 4.2 gives a conceptual typology of locative and directional expressions. Figure 4.3 illustrates the locative expressions relative to a cube. The locative expressions denote spatial relations independent of time. They are classified as static because they do not denote change of location. When used as predicates they denote stative situations

(3) Ipse autem Caesar... erat *ad portas* (Pro Sest 41)
Habes hortos *ad Tiberim* (Pro Cael 36).

In the first example (Pro Sest 41) the prepositional phrase is a primary or overt predicate, in the second example (Pro Cael 36) it is a secondary or covert predicate. The directional prepositions are dynamic. They denote change of location, implicating movement from source to goal along a path. Source (motion from which) prepositional phrases may obtain a static reading from implied or hypothetical motion

(4) Zama quinque dierum iter *a Carthagine* abest (Livy 30.29.2)
is est *ab oppido* circiter milia passum decem (Nepos 1.4.2: app. crit.).

The goal of motion preposition *ad* is very commonly stative as in the examples in (3). This static reading of the prepositional phrase derives from the stative

(3) Caesar himself was at the gates (Pro Sest 41). You have a property by the Tiber (Pro Cael 36).

(4) Zama is a five days' march away from Carthage (Livy 30.29.2). This is about ten miles from the city (Nepos 1.4.2).

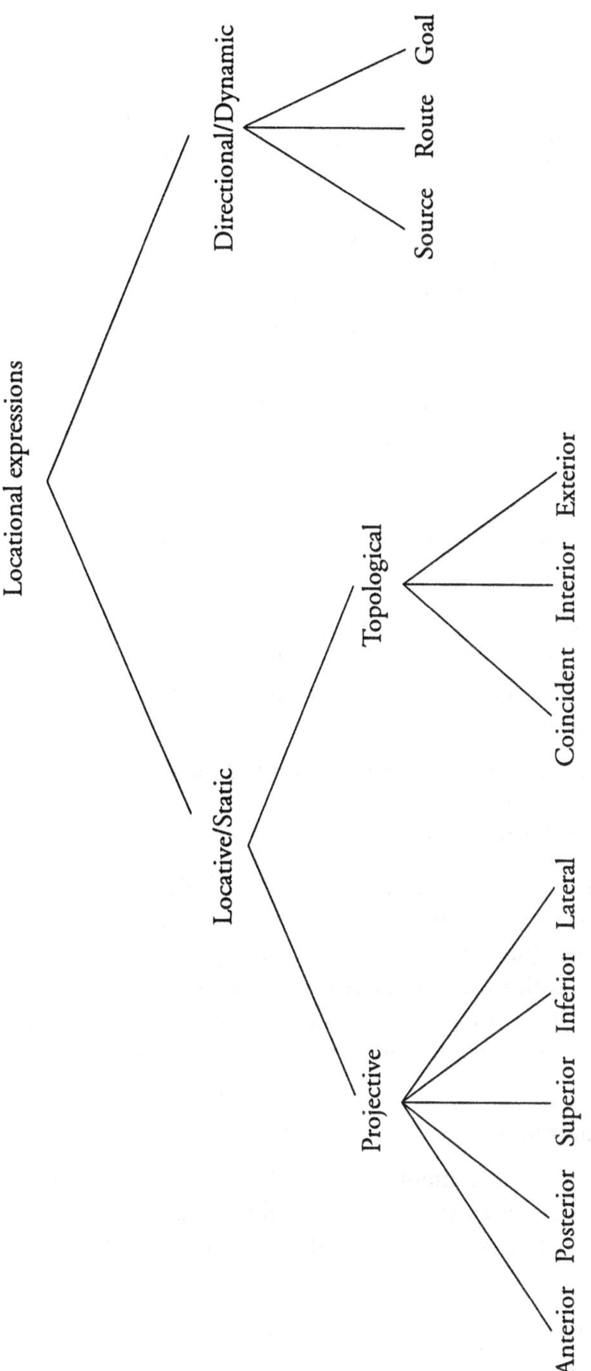

Figure 4.2
Conceptual typology of locatives and directionals

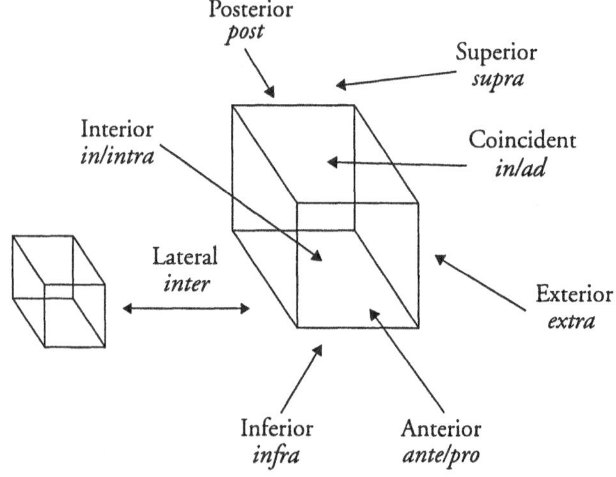

Figure 4.3
Cube representation of locative expressions

component of the resultative perfect reading, which is made available to motion verbs in the perfect by the telicizing effect of the goal of motion prepositional phrase. We can see this in dialogue when a resultative perfect answers a present tense locative question

(5) CHAER. et scis ubi siet? PAR. Huc *deductast* ad meretricem Thaidem (Ter Eun 351)
Sed ubi illest? Intro edepol *abiit*, credo ad uxorem meam (Pl Amph 1045).

Locative prepositions are further classified according as they are independent of or dependent on the frame of reference projected by the speaker or conventional to the reference object (nonprojective and projective prepositions, respectively). Nonprojective prepositions are also known as topological, because they denote locational relations which are invariant under changes of size, shape, etc. of the located object and reference object or of the viewpoint of the speaker.

Nonprojective prepositions

There are three topological relations: (1) coincidence or close proximity according to the degree of granularity appropriate to the context, (2) interiority, and (3) exteriority. Here are some examples of the coincidence relation

(5) CHAER. And do you know where she is? PAR. She has been brought here to the courtesan Thais (Ter Eun 351). But where is he? Heck, he has gone inside, to my wife I imagine (Pl Amph 1045).

(6) Ipse autem coronam habebat unam *in capite*, alteram *in collo* (Verr 2.5.27)
Atque eum vident sedere *ad latus* praetoris (Verr 2.5.107)
caedem *in via Appia* factam esse (Pro Mil 14).

The contact or proximity of the located object or event and the reference object does not depend on the position from which they are viewed or on properties of their shapes.

Subtypes of coincidence are distinguished according to the way the located object and the reference object are conceived in terms of extension, boundedness, genericity and animacy. For example locative *ad* implicates the idea of point of contact or proximity, abstracting away from the physical extension of the reference object

(7) naviculam deligatam *ad ripam* (BG 1.53)
pontem qui erat *ad Genavam* (BG 1.7).

Because mass nouns are unbounded, they do not regularly occur as reference object or located object unless rendered bounded by a determiner or pluralization

(8) *ad summam* iam *aquam* (De Fin 4.64)
quamdiu *ad aquas* fuit (De Or 2.274).

Extended contact between the located and the reference objects such that the contact between them is one or two dimensional and the reference object physically supports the located object is strongly associated with the use rather than the omission of the preposition *in* 'on.' Similarly, interiority or physical containment of the located object inside the reference object promotes the use rather than the omission of *in* 'inside'

(9) Si *in terra* et tabulato olea nimium diu erit (Cato 3.4)
hostili in terra turpiter iacuit insepultus (De Inv 1.108)
Nam et ipsa Peloponnesus fere tota *in mari* est (De Rep 2.8)
quae se *in mari* mergerent (ND 2.124).

When the reference object is generic however, the bare noun in regularly used. For example *mari* 'at/by sea,' *terra* 'on land' and *terra marique* 'by land and sea' are always generic. Perhaps abstracting from particular seas to a dimensionless, generic sea is cognitively akin to viewing an object as a dimensionless point. The factor of animacy is seen in the distinction between *apud* and *ad*. For the

(6) He himself had one garland on his head and another around his neck (Verr 2.5.27). Then they saw him sitting at the side of the praetor (Verr 2.5.107). That there had been a deadly incident on the Via Appia (Pro Mil 14).

(7) A small boat moored to the bank (BG 1.53). The bridge that was at Geneva (BG 1.7).

(8) Already... to the surface of the water (De Fin 4.64). As long as he stayed at the spa (De Or 2.274).

(9) If the olives stay too long on the ground and on the floor (Cato 3.4). He lay shamefully unburied in a hostile land (De Inv 1.108). For the Peloponnesus itself is almost entirely surrounded by the sea (De Rep 2.8). Which dive in the sea (ND 2.124).

coincidence of bounded entities, *apud* is largely restricted to human reference objects

(10) *apud Germanos* ea consuetudo esset (BG 1.50)
apud paucos agricolas et raro contingit (Col 4.10.2),

as also in its forensic use

(11) *apud* bonorum *emptores* ipsos (Pro Rosc Am 72)
apud eosdem iudices reus est factus (Pro Clu 59).

Islands, towns and nations may be viewed as either human collectives or non-human places, and *apud* and *ad* are both licensed

(12) illam pugnam navalem *ad Tenedum* (Pro Mur 33)
incredibilis *apud Tenedum* pugna illa navalis (Pro Arch 21)
Marcelli *ad Nolam* proelio (Brut 12)
specie dedicandi templa apud Capuam Iovi, *apud Nolam* Augusto (Tac Ann 4.57).

With human reference objects *ad* can indicate the home of an individual

(13) *ad M'. Lepidum* te habitare velle dixisti (Cat 1.19)
fuit *ad me* sane diu (Ad Att 10.4.8).

The other two topological locational relations, interiority and its converse, exteriority, are not directly encoded in Latin by basic (proper) prepositions. *In* plus ablative can mean either 'on' (see the first example in (6) (Verr 2.5.27)) or 'in, inside,' depending on context

(14) *in equo* sedentem (Verr 2.5.25)
in dolio aut in seria (Cato 162.1)
homines *in piscina* inventi sunt (Pro Clu 180).

The last two examples have the interiority meaning.

In 'inside,' *intra* 'inside' and *extra* 'outside' are semantically unique among prepositions in their entailment properties. (The last two function as adverbs as well as locative prepositions.) Specifically, *in/intra* is the only locative preposition that is upward entailing with respect to the size or extent of its object, and *extra* is the only one which is downward entailing with respect to the extent of its object

(10) It was the custom among the Germans (BG 1.50). It happens with few farmers and only rarely (Col 4.10.2).

(11) Before a jury of the buyers of the property themselves (Pro Rosc Am 72). He was tried before the same jury (Pro Clu 59).

(12) The famous naval battle at Tenedus (Pro Mur 33). That incredible naval battle at Tenedus (Pro Arch 21). The battle fought by Marcellus at Nola (Brut 12). Under the pretext of dedicating temples to Jupiter at Capua and to Augustus at Nola (Tac Ann 4.57).

(13) You said that you were willing to live at M'. Lepidus' house (Cat 1.19). He stayed at my place a really long time (Ad Att 10.4.8).

(14) Sitting on a horse (Verr 2.5.25). In a large or small jar (Cato 162.1). The bodies of the men were found in the fish pond (Pro Clu 180).

(15) Caesar ad oppidum Avaricum, quod erat maximum munitissimumque in finibus Biturigum atque agri fertilissima regione, profectus est (BG 7.13)
extra forum (Brut 302)
extra curiam (Livy 3.39.6).

If Caesar is in the town of Avaricum, then he is in a very fertile district and that district is in turn in the territory of the Bituriges. Conversely, if the senate convenes outside of the city of Rome, it also meets outside of the forum and consequently outside of the curia. *Procul* 'far away' and *penitus* 'deep inside' are also downward and upward entailing respectively, but they are basically adverbs rather than locative prepositions

(16) ut *procul* tela coniciant nec propius accedant (BG 5.34)
penitus in Lusitania legiones in hibernis conlocaram (Ad Fam 10.33.3).

Contrast *iuxta* 'close to,' which is a fully licensed locative preposition but neither upward nor downward entailing with respect to the extent of the reference object: if you are close to the citadel, you are not necessarily close to the city wall nor vice versa. Further entailment properties of prepositions are discussed below. *In/intra* and *extra* are the only locative prepositions that can be wholly defined settheoretically. *Extra* A denotes the complement of the set of points occupied by A, and *intra* A just that set of points occupied by A (and its boundary). Every other locative preposition restricts the meaning of *extra* in one way or another. So for all other prepositions, A P(B) implies A *extra* B. For instance

(17) *iuxta murum* castra posuit (BC 1.16):

if Caesar pitched camp close to the wall, he still pitched camp outside the wall, not inside the wall itself. The exclusion of prepositions that restrict the meaning of *in/intra* correctly predicts that *penitus* would be an adverb, not a preposition.

Projective prepositions

In contrast to the invariant denotations of the topological prepositions, the denotations of the projective prepositions depend on a frame of reference, which may be absolute, that is determined by stable environmental features independent of the speaker or viewer, reference object or located object

(18) spectant *in septentrionem* et orientem solem (BG 1.1)
ab oriente ad occidentem (ND 2.164)

(15) Caesar set out for the town of Avaricum, which was the largest and best fortified one in the territory of the Bituriges and in a region very rich in agricultural land (BG 7.13). Outside the forum (Brut 302). Outside the curia (Livy 3.39.6).

(16) To throw their weapons from a distance and not to close in (BG 5.34). I had put my legions in their winter quarters deep in Lusitania (Ad Fam 10.33.3).

(17) He pitched camp close to the wall (BC 1.16).

(18) Their territory is oriented towards the north and the east (BG 1.1). From east to west (ND 2.164).

(19) et liquidissimus aether atque levissimus aerias *super* influit *auras* (Lucr 5.500),

or intrinsic to the reference object, based on inherently or conventionally ascribed attributes of the reference object (houses have fronts and backs, mountains have tops and bottoms)

(20) *in radicibus* Caucasi (Tusc 2.52)
mons est *in altitudinem ingentem* cacuminis editi (Livy 28.5.17)
frons aedis doricae... dividatur... *in partes* XXVII (Vitr 4.3.3)
dormiente illo epistulam *super caput* in pulvino temere positam sumit (Sall Jug 71.4),

or deictic, that is projected from a speaker's or viewer's point of view

(21) *Post me* erat Aegina, *ante me* Megara, dextra Piraeus, sinistra Corinthus (Ad Fam 4.5.4).

In the example in (19) (Lucr 5.500) Lucretius uses the absolute, gravitationally determined frame: since air is inherently unbounded, it has no canonical orientation. The gravitational frame therefore is the only one available. The cloudless part of the atmosphere occupies a higher altitude than the cloudy, stormy part. In the last example in (20) (Jug 71.4) Nabdulsa is asleep, more or less horizontal on a bed; part of his head actually extends above the letter as measured on the absolute, gravitationally determined vertical axis, but in the intrinsic frame defined by the canonical orientation of the human body anything at the end of vectors projected perpendicularly from the top surface of his head is above his head regardless of its momentary orientation. In the example in (21) (Ad Fam 4.5.4), if Cicero had been sailing from Megara to Aegina, rather than in the opposite direction, 'in front' and 'behind' would have been interchanged, as would 'left' and 'right.'

It is often assumed that there are only two projective frames of reference for anteriority, the one projected from the speaker/viewer and the one from the reference object; or it is claimed that properties of the located object are marginal at best. In Latin however the orientation of the located object is a crucial part of the denotation of *pro*, which means 'located in front of the reference object and facing away from the reference object: $\lambda x \lambda y.\text{In-front-of}(y, x) \wedge \text{Behind}(x, \text{Back}(y))$

(22) nonne audiente populo sedens *pro aede Castoris* dixit...? (Phil 3.27)
praesidia quae *pro templis omnibus* cernitis (Pro Mil 2)

(19) And ether, the most fluid and the lightest, flows above the airy breezes (Lucr 5.500).

(20) At the foot of the Caucasus (Tusc 2.52). This is a mountain whose peak rises to a great height (Livy 28.5.17). The front of a Doric temple should be divided into 27 parts (Vitr 4.3.3). He took the letter that had been carelessly placed above his head on the cushion as he was sleeping (Sall Jug 71.4).

(21) Behind me was Aegina, in front of me Megara, to my right the Piraeus, to my left Corinth (Ad Fam 4.5.4).

(22) Did he not say while sitting in front of the temple of Castor with an audience of the people...? (Phil 3.27). The guard which you see in front of all the temples (Pro Mil 2).

(23) reliquas sex legiones *pro castris* in acie constituit (BG 2.8)
Caesar... legiones in acie *pro castris* constituit (BG 4.35).

In the first example in (22) (Phil 3.27) Mark Antony is sitting with his back to the temple, facing the people in the Forum. In the second example (Pro Mil 2) the guards are facing into the Forum with their backs to the temples. In the two examples in (23) (BG 2.8; 4.35) the camps are in the rear of the battle lines; the soldiers are not drawn up in battle array facing their own camps. *Ante* in contrast is always projected from the reference object or the frame of reference of the speaker/viewer; it does not inherently denote the orientation of a located object's frontality

(24) In foro L. Antoni statuam videmus sicut illam Q. Tremuli... *ante Castoris.* (Phil 6.13)
postero die mane copias *ante frontem castrorum* instruit (BC 3.37)
Instrui deinde utrimque acies coeptae, Romanorum *pro moenibus Nolae,* Poenorum *ante castra sua* (Livy 23.16.4).

In the first example (Phil 6.13) the statue would have faced into the Forum with its back to the portico of the temple of Castor and Pollux. Cicero uses *ante* rather than *pro* because he is describing the statue as seen by people in the Forum: he and they are facing the front of the statue and the front of the temple. In the second example (BC 3.37) Caesar is presenting the scene from Scipio's viewpoint facing the camp of Domitius. In the last example (Livy 23.16) Livy is not switching frames of reference nor using *ante* for *pro* with reference to the orientation of the located object (the Carthaginian battle line); rather his viewpoint is consistently that of the Roman battle line with the walls of Nola in its rear (so *pro*) and the Carthaginian battle line between it and the Carthaginian camp (so *ante*). *Post* and the rarer *pone* are the converse of *ante*

(25) *post tergum* clamore audito (BG 4.15)
repente *post tergum* equitatus cernitur (BG 7.88).

In regard to the preference for projecting the frame of reference intrinsically from the reference object, it should be noted that in Latin the projective locative prepositions are only used harmonically. Therefore *pro* and *ante* are not combined with object nouns referring to the back or side of the reference object, such as *tergum* 'back,' *posticum* 'back door, rear portico' or *latus* 'side.'

(23) He placed the remaining six legions in line in front of the camp (BG 2.8). Caesar placed his legions in battle line in front of the camp (BG 4.35).

(24) In the forum we see the statue of L. Antonius like that of Q. Tremulus in front of the temple of Castor (Phil 6.13). On the next day in the morning he drew up his forces before the front of the camp (BC 3.37). Then on both sides the battle lines began to be drawn up, that of the Romans before the walls of Nola, that of the Carthaginians in front of their camp (Livy 23.16.4).

(25) Hearing the noise to the rear (BG 4.15). Suddenly the cavalry was noticed to the rear (BG 7.88).

The collocation *post frontem* (with the further qualification of the topological adverb *intra*) occurs in the following example

(26) *Post frontem* horologii intra conlocetur castellum (Vitr 9.8.11),

but this passage is an exception that proves the rule. *Frontem* here is a technical term for the dial of a water clock, which is understood to be powered from behind, on the inside. Consequently *post frontem* here is a harmonic semantic composition meaning 'behind (the back of) the dial.'

Next we will consider affordances and alignment. Inferiority and superiority are expressed by the converse pairs *infra*, *sub* and *supra*, *super*. Our English distinction between 'over' and 'above,' and 'under' and 'below,' does not exist in the Latin lexicon

(27) *super lateres* coria inducuntur (BC 2.10)
tunicaeque pictae insigne dedit et *super tunicam* aeneum pectori tegumen (Livy 1.20.4)
Galli *super umbilicum* erant nudi (Livy 22.46.6)
ea circum terras *infra lunam*... versantur (ND 2.56)
supra lunam sunt aeterna omnia (De Rep 6.17).

In the first example (BC 2.10) the hides extend over a surface. In the second (Livy 1.20) the bronze breastplate is over the embroidered tunic: it affords protection as a covering. This affordance activates the reference frame intrinsic to a covered object in which the surface covered is the salient one, in this case superseding the frame intrinsic to the canonical orientation of the human body. It is in this reference frame that the meaning 'over' is appropriate. In the third example (Livy 22.46) the Gauls are naked above the navel in the frame intrinsic to the human body. In the fourth example (ND 2.56) Cicero does not mean only when the moon is overhead, but below its orbit. When we abstract away from the effect of the affordances of objects on the appropriateness of one preposition over another, the English 'over/above' contrast raises the issue of alignment. If the top branch of a tree that is many yards away from a house is higher than the roof of the house, that branch may be described as 'above' the house but not as 'over' it. 'Over' implicates vertical alignment: a plumb line dropped far enough from some point on the branch would touch some point of the roof. Vertical alignment is not a necessary condition for the appropriateness of *super/supra*, although it is a sufficient one

(28) tabula in aede Iovis... *supra valvas* fixa est (Livy 40.52.7)
montes... *supra Massiliam* incolebant (BC 1.34).

(26) Inside behind the dial of the clock a water tank should be placed (Vitr 9.8.11).

(27) Hides are drawn over the bricks (BC 2.10). He gave them the insignia of the tunica picta and over it a bronze breastplate (Livy 1.20.4). The Gauls were naked from the navel up (Livy 22.46.6). Those things are located around the earth below the moon (ND 2.56). Above the moon all things are eternal (De Rep 6.17).

(28) A tablet was attached above the doors in the temple of Jupiter (Livy 40.52.7). They inhabited the mountains above Massilia (BC 1.34).

In the first example (Livy 40.52) the tablet is aligned over the temple doors, not merely affixed on the wall to the left or right of the doors at a higher level than their top. In the second example (BC 1.34) the mountains are not floating in the air over Marseille. We will see that a vector space semantics for prepositions makes it easy to represent the alignment of reference and located object and to relate it to the affordances of the objects in the context. *Infra* and *supra* also offer an extreme case of the influence of customary practices on the projection of the frame of reference. They are used to locate diners on the Roman banqueting couch: *infra* ≡ 'on the right of,' *supra* ≡ 'on the left of'

(29) et quidem *supra me* Atticus, infra Verrius (Ad Fam 9.26.1)
infra Eutrapelum Cytheris accubuit (Ad Fam 9.26.2)
illam *infra eum* accubantem negasse umquam vidisse quenquam securi ferientem (Livy 39.43.3).

The frame of reference has been transferred from the inferiority-superiority axis to the laterality axis. Such a transference is more easily accommodated in a language like Latin which has no basic prepositions for laterality. *Apud, circa, circum, iuxta* and other prepositions sometimes translated by English 'beside' or 'on both sides,' do not minimally denote a horizontal reference axis orthogonal to the front-back axis of the reference object or speaker/viewer.

Vector space semantics

An intuitively appealing way to model location and direction is by means of vectors. Vectors are the simplest mathematical objects that capture the notions of length and direction, and their start points and end points define locations. The mathematics behind them is relatively simple, but they permit precise formalization of linguistic expressions of location and direction at just about any level of granularity. This in turn makes it easier explicitly to formulate semantic generalizations over various classes of spatial expressions, such as patterns of inference and constraints on possible denotations of prepositions and enables a compositional analysis of the modification of prepositional phrases.

Vectors are equal if they have the same direction and the same length. In Figure 4.4(a) the vectors **a** and **b** are equal as are **c** and **e**. The norm of a vector, $|\cdot|$, determines its length, which is a scalar quantity (a number without direction). There are two operations that apply to vectors, scalar multiplication and vector addition. Scalar multiplication by a positive number, $s > 1$, lengthens the vector in its original direction. If s is positive but less than 1, it shortens the vector. If s is negative, $s < 0$, it reverses the direction of the vector. See Figure 4.4(b). Vectors are added together by putting them head to tail. Intuitively the starting point of one vector is moved to coincide with the end point of the other vector, while keeping their lengths and directions unchanged. The vector sum, also

(29) To my left is Atticus and to my right Vettius (Ad Fam 9.26.1). To the right of Eutrapelus reclined Cytheris (Ad Fam 9.26.2). The lady reclining to his right said that she had never seen anyone beheading someone (Livy 39.43.3).

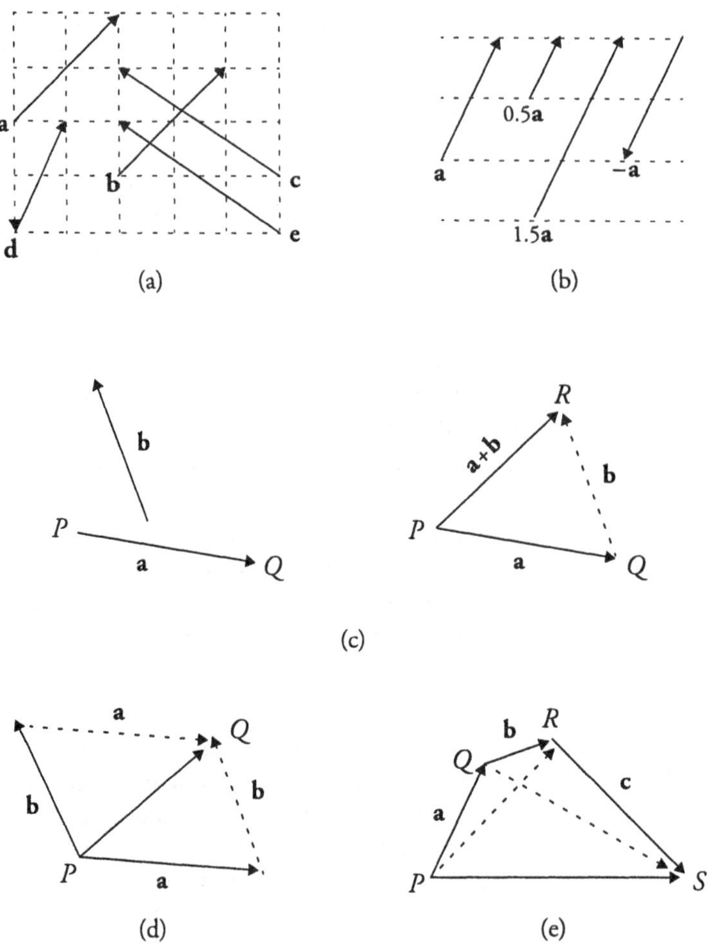

Figure 4.4
(a) Vector equality; (b) Vector multiplication; (c) Vector addition
(d) Commutativity; (e) Associativity

called the resultant vector, is found by completing the triangle defined by the starting point of the first vector, their common end/start point and the end point of the second vector. See Figure 4.4(c). So vector addition is commutative, just like the addition of ordinary numbers: $\mathbf{a}+\mathbf{b}=\mathbf{b}+\mathbf{a}$. The commutative property of vector addition is made clear by the parallelogram law illustrated in Figure 4.4(d). Since we get the same resultant vector whether we move **a** up to start at the end of **b** or move **b** to start at the end of **a**, we see why all vectors with the same direction and length are equal. Any number of vectors may be added, and again the order does not matter. Vector addition is associative: $(\mathbf{a}+\mathbf{b}) + \mathbf{c} = \mathbf{a}+(\mathbf{b} + \mathbf{c})$; see Figure 4.4(e). A vector space over the set of real numbers is a set of vectors that is closed under the operations of scalar multiplication and vector addition. A vector space includes the zero vector (0: $\mathbf{v} + 0 = 0 + \mathbf{v} = \mathbf{v}$), and the inverse of every vector ($-\mathbf{v}$: $\mathbf{v} + (-\mathbf{v}) = 0$). Additionally scalar multiplication is distributive over vector addition, $s(\mathbf{a}+\mathbf{b}) = s\mathbf{a}+s\mathbf{b}$, and scalar addition is distributive over scalar multiplication of vectors, $(r+s)\mathbf{v} = r\mathbf{v} + s\mathbf{v}$.

In vector space semantics prepositions have a richer structure than that given in Figure 4.1. Figure 4.5 is a vector space version of Figure 4.1. The denotation of *in arca* is now the set of vectors that start at any point on the edge of the box and proceed at any angle to end at some point inside the box: $V^{IN}\sigma(y)$. In addition to a preliminary eigenspace function σ we have a vector function that generates for every space in its domain the set of vectors projecting in some direction from the boundary of that space (in this case the object of the preposition, *arca*). The preposition accesses this function, lexicalizes the direction of the vectors and places the vectors in a relation to the points in the eigenspace of the subject argument (*aurum*): for all points in the space occupied by the gold there exists a vector (actually many vectors) projected inwardly from the boundary of the box and ending at that point (EP stands for 'End Point').

The space around or inside the reference object is assumed to be convex and topologically simple. Convexity means that any two points in a region can be joined by a straight line that is entirely within that region. This is not an unrealistic assumption. Even nonconvex objects are conceived as having a convex space around them, called their convex hull. The *dolium* is a large earthenware storage vessel, and the *seria* is probably a somewhat smaller one

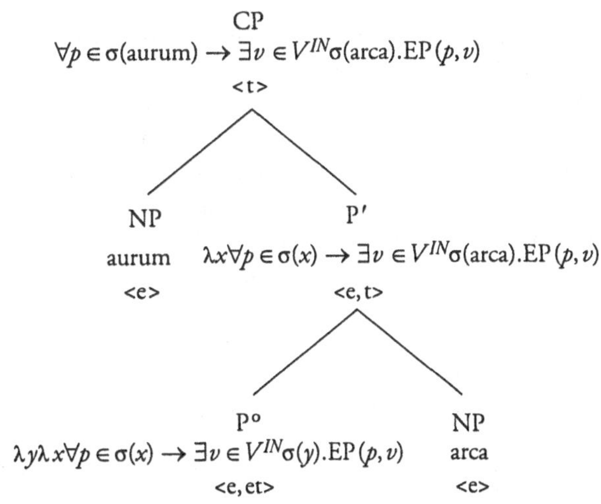

Figure 4.5
Vector space analysis of a prepositional phrase
Id aurum est in arca (cp. Pl Aul 823)

(30) Pernas sallire sic oportet *in dolio* aut *seria*... in fundo dolii aut seriae sale sternito (Cato 162).

When uncovered the *dolium* and the *seria* technically occupy a nonconvex space, because a straight line connecting any two points on the opening of either vessel would pass outside the space of the vessel itself. Nevertheless the eigenspace of each is treated as convex, because when sealed the vessel does occupy a convex space. So it is true that the hams are inside the vessel. Cato says *in fundo dolii aut seriae* rather than just *in dolio aut seria* in accordance with the Gricean maxim of informativeness. The *calix* 'wine cup' is topologically complex, typically having its bowl connected by a stem to a footed base and upward curving, open handles attached below a flared lip. The convex hull of such a vessel will not sufficiently restrict its eigenspace

(31) Largius effuso madeat tibi mensa Falerno, spumet et aurato mollius *in calice* (Prop 2.33b.39).

If some drops of Cynthia's spilled wine were adhering to the foot, stem or handle, they would be in the convex hull of the *calix*, but they would certainly not be *in calice*. In cases such as this, functional characteristics of the reference object need to be considered. Here it is only that part of the cup that affords physical containment for the wine that is salient.

As we have seen, strict vertical alignment is not a necessary condition for a located object to be *supra* the reference object. Compare the following examples

(32) isque clupeus *supra fores* aedis Capitolinae usque ad incendium primum fuit (NH 35.14)
in Nova Via ubi nunc sacellum est *supra aedem Vestae* (Livy 5.32.6).

In the first example (NH 35.14) *supra* has the sense of strict vertical alignment. This is illustrated in Figure 4.6(a), where *supra* selects just those vectors projecting upwards from the top of the doors and parallel to the vertical axis. The representation of the vectors as not extending above the ceiling of the temple reflects the conversational implicature that the space above the doors ends there. In the second example (Livy 5.32) the shrine of Aius is on the Via Nova, which runs behind the Atrium Vestae and the Aedis Vestae uphill to the Palatine. Figure 4.6(b) represents the sense of *supra* which selects all vectors projecting from the top of the temple whose endpoints have an elevation higher than the top, that is those vectors whose projection on the *up* axis is greater than 0: $|\mathbf{v} \perp up| > 0$. In most contexts the end points of the longer and smaller-angled vectors would be too far to one side or another and/or not high enough to

(30) Hams should be salted in a large or small jar as follows: spread salt on the bottom of a large or small jar (Cato 162.1).

(31) May your table be wet with more generously poured Falernian wine and may it foam more softly in your gilded cup (Prop 2.33b.39).

(32) And this shield was above the doors of the temple on the Capitol until the first fire (NH 35.14). In the Nova Via where the shrine now stands above the temple of Vesta (Livy 5.32.6).

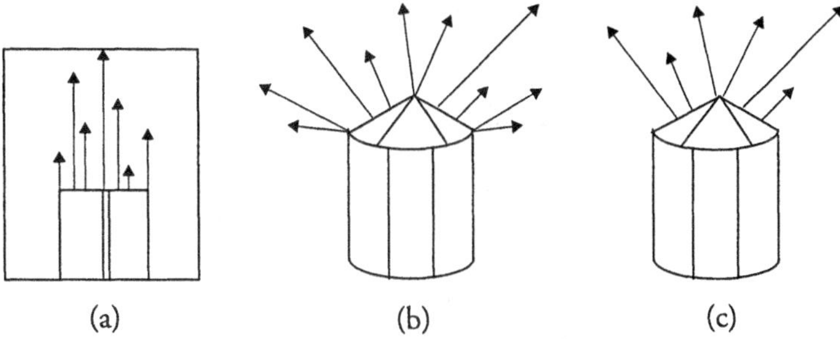

Figure 4.6
Vector selection for *supra*
(a) parallel to vertical: *supra fores aedis* (NH 35.4)
(b) $|\mathbf{v} \perp up| > 0$, (c) $|\mathbf{v} \perp up| \geq |\mathbf{v} \perp side|$: *supra aedem Vestae* (Livy 5.32.6)

count as being above the reference object. A better approximation is achieved by requiring the vectors to rise at an angle between 45° and 90°, so that they go more up than aside. The projections of these vectors on the vertical axis will be greater than their projections on the horizontal axis. The denotation of these vectors would be $\{\mathbf{v}$: $\mathbf{v}$ starts from the upper surface $\wedge\ |\mathbf{v} \perp up| \geq |\mathbf{v} \perp side|\}$. This is illustrated in Figure 4.6(c). This denotation could be further restricted by a contextually determined factor that would tell you how much greater than 1 the ratio of the vertical to the horizontal projections has to be. There will also be an absolute distance standard appropriate to the context that will set a limit on how far to one side or the other a vector can end and still count as being above: $|\mathbf{v} \perp side| \leq c$. If there are contextually salient objects to the left and/or right and front and/or back of the reference object, the pragmatics of the situation will impose a further requirement. If there is a bird above and to the left of your house, but your neighbour's house is to the left of yours and to the right of and below the bird, it would not be maximally informative to locate the bird as above your house. Let C be your house, B your neighbour's house, A the bird, and $\mathbf{v}_C$ and $\mathbf{v}_B$ vectors locating the bird from your house and from your neighbour's house respectively. Then you would say that A is above C rather than above B if and only if $\forall \mathbf{v}_C \forall \mathbf{v}_B . |\mathbf{v} \perp side(C)| < |\mathbf{v} \perp side(B)|$. The denotation of *infra* is obtained by replacing the upward projection parameter by the downward projection parameter $|\mathbf{v} \perp down|$. The denotations of *ante* and *post* are obtained by switching the projection criterion to the front half axis and the back half axis. Figure 4.7 illustrates this for *ante Castoris* in (24). All the vectors lying within the two lines at 45° angles to the front axis are more to the front of the temple than to either side.

Entailment patterns

The locative prepositions *ab, ante, pro, post, extra, supra, infra, sub, cis, citra, secus, trans, ultra,* to mention only the most common, are upwardly entailing in

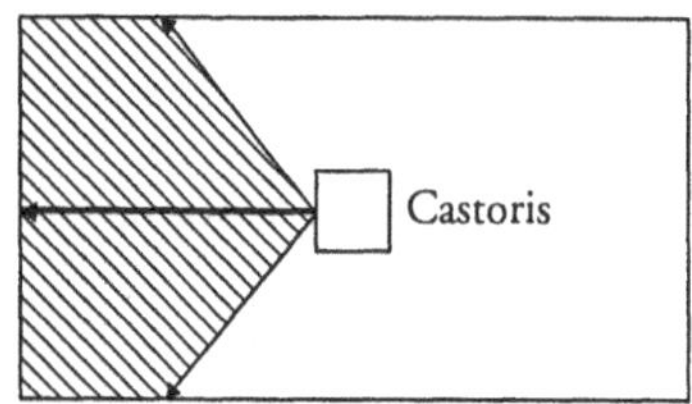

Figure 4.7
Denotation of *ante*: $|\mathbf{v} \perp \mathit{front}| \geq |\mathbf{v} \perp \mathit{side}|$
Ante Castoris (Phil 6.13)

the sense that they still hold true as the located object moves away from the reference object in the same direction. More formally, a preposition is upward entailing if it returns a set of vectors that is closed under scalar multiplication by a number $s > 1$. For example, in (24) if you move the statue farther away from the temple, but in the same direction, so that its locating vector becomes $s\mathbf{a}$, it is still in front of the temple, assuming of course that in the process it does not become 'more in front of' any other contextually salient object. Prepositions such as *ad* 'at,' *in* 'on,' *in/intra, iuxta, ob, prope* are not upward entailing. If a preposition has a distance parameter in its denotation, whether set to zero as for coincidence prepositions or to a contextually defined value, it cannot be upward entailing. If you extend the vectors these prepositions denote far enough the contact will be broken, the boundary of the enclosing object crossed, or the distance parameter exceeded.

A preposition is transitive if and only if A P(B) and B P(C) imply A P(C). Prepositional transitivity is independent of upward entailment. *Extra* is upward entailing, but not transitive; if A *extra* B and B *extra* C, A can still be *in/intra* C. *In/intra* is not upward entailing, but it is transitive: if A *intra* B and B *intra* C, then A *intra* C. The transitivity of *in/intra* follows from the transitivity of the subset relation and the fact already noted that *in/intra* is definable settheoretically. For the projective prepositions, prepositional transitivity corresponds to closure under vector addition. A projective preposition is transitive if and only if it denotes vectors such that the sum of each vector **a** locating A relative to B and each vector **b** locating B relative to C belongs to the set of vectors denoted by P(C): $\mathbf{a} + \mathbf{b} \in$ P(C) whenever $\mathbf{a} \in$ P(*end point* **b**) and $\mathbf{b} \in$ P(C). Broadly speaking this will be the case for prepositions which project axes from the erstwhile located object B that are parallel to the axes projected from the original reference object C. Examples of such prepositions are *ultra* and *pro*. In the case of *ultra* there is the single deictic centre of the speaker, so that there is a single frame of reference for both *ultra* C and *ultra* B. In the case of *pro* the axes projected by *pro* B may be shifted parallel to those projected by *pro* C, but *pro* requires the front of B to face in the same direction as the front of C, so that the axes projected by *pro* B are parallel to those projected by *pro* C. Without special qualifications other projective prepositions such as *ante, post, sub,* and *supra* are not transitive. For example, unlike *pro*, *ante* locates an object with respect to an axis which is projected from inherent features of the reference object or from the speaker's point of view. This means that the axis projected from the erstwhile located object B may be rotated with respect to the axis projected from reference object C, and as a result A may be in front of B and B in front of C, but A may not be in front of C.

All basic prepositions (probably all single word locative expressions) are downward entailing. Consider Vitruvius' water organ

(33) *Intra ar(c)am* quo loci aqua sustinetur inest pnigeus ut infundibulum inversum (Vitr 10.8.2).

As you shorten the vectors that end in the air-vessel back through the water chest, you are still inside the water organ itself. Remember that shortening a vector is defined by scalar multiplication by a nonnegative number, $0 \leq s < 1$. The direction of the vector remains the same. Going outside of the water organ is not a shortening of the vectors inside the water organ, but a reversal of their directions. Requiring all prepositions to be downward entailing rules out distal prepositions. *Procul* and *penitus* are distal adverbs, but, as we have noted, they are not basic prepositions.

All prepositions share an entailment property called point continuity. If three reference objects are so ordered that one is contained in the other, $A \subseteq B \subseteq C$, then any located object that is P(A) and P(C) is also P(B). Consider the first three levels of seating in the Flavian amphitheatre. Senators sit just above the arena, knights above them, and the plebeians above the knights. The inference 'If the arena is below the senators and the plebeians, then it is below the knights' is obviously true. This entailment property is distinct from transitivity. It also holds for prepositional relations that are not transitive, such as *prope*. If, say, in contrast to the uppermost level, the arena is near the senators and the plebeians, it is also near the knights. Point continuity may seem obvious, but it is interesting that it has a counterpart among quantifiers: if the conjunction of a downward entailing quantifier, such as more than x, and an upward entailing quantifier, such as less than y, is true on an interval $x' < y'$ and on an expanded interval $x'' < x' < y'' < y'$, then it is true on all intermediate intervals $x < y$, such that $x'' < x < x'$ and $y'' < y < y'$. If one messenger truthfully reports that in a battle Caesar lost more than 100 but less than 600 soldiers and another messenger truthfully reports that the casualties were more than 300 but less than 400, it is valid to infer that Caesar lost more than 200 but less than 500 soldiers.

Modification

All the upward entailing prepositions form prepositional phrases that can be modified by measure phrases

(33) Inside the chest where the water is kept there is an air-vessel like an upside-down funnel (Vitr 10.8.2).

(34) Hic locus ab hoste circiter *passus sescentos*... aberat (BG 1.49)
erat... citra Veliam *mil. pass.* III (Ad Att 16.7.5)
milibus passuum duobus ultra eum castra fecit (BG 1.48)
triginta milibus passuum infra eum locum (BG 6.35)
Caesar *paulo* ultra eum locum castra transtulit (BC 3.66).

In/intra also licenses measure phrase modification, see *penitus in Lusitania* in (16), but none of the other non-upward entailing prepositions do. Figure 4.8 is a diagram of a prepositional phrase with measure phrase modification, based on

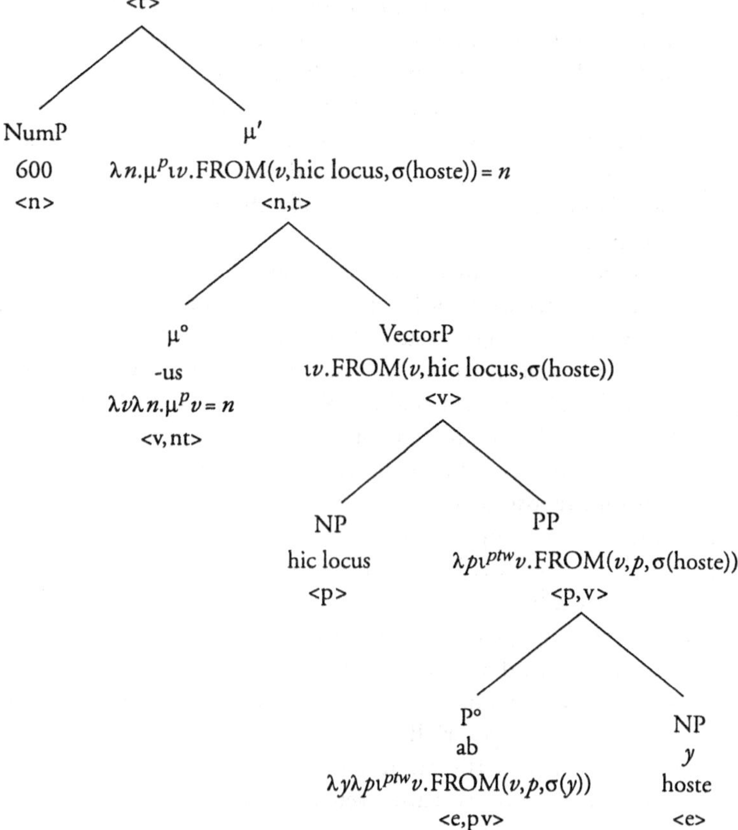

Figure 4.8
Measure phrase modification of a prepositional phrase
Hic locus ab hoste passus sescentos aberat (cp. BG 1.49)

(34) This place was about six hundred yards away from the enemy (BG 1.49). He was three miles north of Velia (Ad Att 16.7.5). He pitched camp two miles beyond him (BG 1.48). Thirty miles below that place (BG 6.35). Caesar moved his camp a little beyond that spot (BC 3.66).

the first example (BG 1.49). It gives the semantics for the closely related sentence 'The distance between this place and the enemy was six hundred yards,' which is a specificational sentence (a type of identity sentence). At the level of granularity of the narrative here, the disposition of the enemy forces and the constituent parts of 'this place' are not visible: they are both treated as points. The former has to be shifted from an object to a point by application of the sigma function, as indicated in the figure. ι^{ptw} is a pointwise definite: for every point there is just one vector that goes from the enemy to that point. Once the point is specified by *hic locus*, the definite changes from a pointwise operator into an ordinary definite operator: VectorP denotes that vector which has the location of the enemy as its startpoint and this place as its endpoint. μ^{p} is a measure function: it takes a vector to give a function from a number to a truth value. The suprascript *p* indicates that the unit of measurement is the pace. The linguistic incarnation of the head of the measure function is the accusative case ending. While the accusative simply measures the vector, the ablative, which occurs in the second (BG 1.48) and third (BG 6.35) examples, measures the degree to which the end of the vector exceeds its starting point. Dimensional adjectives and comparatives behave like upward entailing prepositional phrases in licensing measure phrase modification (see Chapter 7). The basic intuition is that only measurable expressions license measure phrase modification. At first sight this appears vacuous, but the idea is that measure phrase modification is only licensed where it could never produce a tautology or a contradiction, that is only when it is informative. In vector space semantics this idea is formalized by the requirement that the intersection of the set of vectors **V** denoted by a prepositional phrase and the set **M** of measured vectors be nonempty: $\mathbf{M} \cap \mathbf{V} \neq \varnothing$. **V** will meet this requirement for all **M** if it is closed under lengthening, closed under shortening and nonempty. Since all prepositions are downward entailing, it is upward entailment that is the main factor in licensing measure phrase modification. The permissibility of measure phrase modification of *in*/*intra*, which is not upward entailing, is explained by the fact that it is not the status of the preposition as upward entailing but the closure of the set **V** under lengthening that licenses measure phrase modification. It is possible that some reference objects, such as provinces or large geographical regions, are conceived of as unbounded. Then a set of vectors **V** such as that given by *in Lusitania* in (16) would have no upper limit on length and measure phrase modification would always be noncontradictory and informative.

Only the projective prepositions license modification by adverbs such as 'straight,' 'perpendicularly,' 'diagonally,' 'obliquely'

(35) Deinde supra epistylium *ad perpendiculum* inferiorum columnarum inponendae sunt minores quarta parte columnae (Vitr 6.3.9)
signiferi... *oblique* inter eos siti (NH 2.63).

(35) Then above the architrave columns a quarter shorter should be placed perpendicular to the lower columns (Vitr 6.3.9). Of the zodiac, which is situated obliquely between them (NH 2.63).

Such projective modifiers are defined by the unique axis projected by the preposition. In the first example (Vitr 6.3) *supra* uniquely projects the up axis, and the modifying *ad perpendiculum* denotes the set of vectors that are parallel to the up axis, that is those whose entire length falls on the up axis: $\{\mathbf{v}: |\mathbf{v}| = |\mathbf{v} \perp up|\}$. In the second example (NH 2.63), where Pliny describes the zodiac as situated obliquely between the poles, he is locating it with respect to the celestial axis. *Oblique* selects the subset of vectors which are neither parallel to the celestial axis nor perpendicular to it. If a preposition does not project any axis (and the topological ones do not) or if it selects more than one (like *beside*, which projects both left and right half axes), projective modifiers are meaningless.

Two reference objects

Inter in the sense of 'between' is unique in denoting a ternary relation. *In* and *inter* in the sense of 'among, amid' denote binary relations, just like the other prepositions; they differ only in requiring plural reference objects, the analysis of which is beyond the scope of this chapter. For *inter* 'between' the connectives *et*, *-que* etc. do not form a plurality or set containing the two reference objects. The connective serves only to mark argument places in a polyadic construction. It is the existence of separate argument positions which licenses the repetition of *inter* with each of its objects

(36) Deinde *inter matrem* deus ipse *interque sororem* Pythius... carmina.. sonat (Prop 2.31.15).

If the located and reference objects are restricted to atomic regions, that is if they are not allowed to contain other objects, *inter* 'between' has three nontrivial entailment properties. The first is reflexivity; if y is between x and z, then y is between z and x: $B(x,y,z) \rightarrow B(z,y,x)$

(37) Euganeisque qui *inter mare Alpesque* incolebant (Livy 1.1.3).

If the Euganeans live between the sea and the Alps, they also live between the Alps and the sea. The second is transitivity: if y is between x and w, and z is between y and w, then y is between x and z: $B(x,y,w) \wedge B(y,z,w) \rightarrow B(x,y,z)$

(38) una ex parte flumine Rheno latissimo atque altissimo, qui agrum Helvetium a Germanis dividit; altera ex parte monte Iura altissimo, qui est *inter Sequanos et Helvetios* (BG 1.2).

Since the Jura is between the Sequani and the Rhine and the Helvetians are between the Jura and the Rhine, the Jura is between the Sequani and the Hel-

(36) Then between his mother and his sister the Pythian god himself performs songs (Prop 2.31.15).

(37) And the Euganei, who lived between the sea and the Alps (Livy 1.1.3).

(38) On one side by the very broad and deep Rhine river, which separates the Helvetian territory from the Germans, on another side by the very high Jura mountains, which are between the Sequani and the Helvetii (BG 1.2).

vetians. The third property is connectivity; if y and z are between x and w, then either y is between x and z or z is between x and y: $B(x,y,w) \wedge B(x,z,w) \rightarrow B(x,y,z) \vee B(x,z,y)$. From the fact that both the Jura and the Helvetians are between the Sequani and the Rhine, we can without any further information conclude that either the Helvetians are between the Sequani and the Jura or that the Jura is between the Sequani and the Helvetians (as is in fact the case).

When the reference and located objects can be conceived as points, for y to be between x and z means that y lies on the straight line connecting x and z. Since a straight line is the shortest distance between points, two consequences arise that are, initially at least, quite surprising. First, if y is between x and z, then there can be no other point, no matter where it is, that is both closer to x and closer to z than y is. Second, if there is no other point ($u \neq y$) closer to x and closer to z than y, then y must be between x and z. Together these make a biconditional (if and only if) statement which defines betweenness solely and independently of context in terms of distance. Letting $d(x,y)$ stand for the distance between x and y, we have the definition: $B(x,y,z) \leftrightarrow \neg\exists u.d(u,x) < d(y,x) \wedge d(u,z) < d(y,z) \wedge u \neq y$. The 'if' part of the definition is readily visualized: in Figure 4.9(a) the circle centred at x and passing through y contains the set of points that are closer to x than y is, and the circumference contains those points as close to x as y is; similarly for the circle centred on z. Since the circles do not overlap but are tangent at y, every point other than y will be either farther from x or farther from z or both than y is. The 'only if' part of the definition is more easily visualized in its contrapositive form: if y is not between x and z, then there are points that are both closer to x and closer to z than y is. In Figure 4.9(b) the circles centred on x and z overlap. All the points in the overlap (including those on the overlapping arcs) are both closer to x and closer to z than y is. *Inter* 'between' is the only preposition whose denotation can be formulated solely in terms of contextually independent distance relations. For example, the denotation of *prope* involves distance, but that distance is a contextually determined parameter. For soldiers in a battle line to be near one another the parameter is set much smaller than for cities in a province.

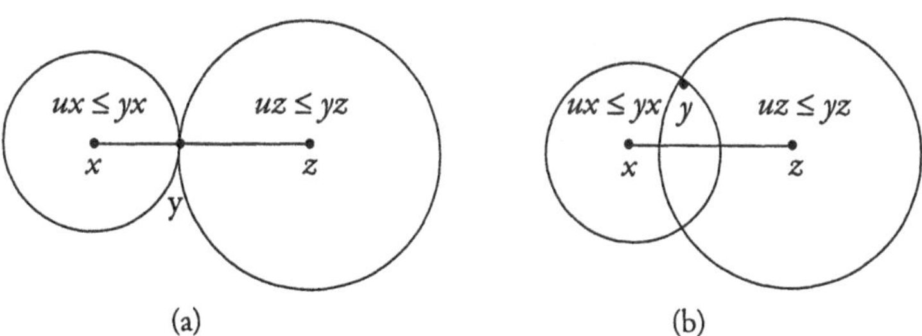

Figure 4.9
Inter
(a) y is between x and z; (b) y is not between x and z

In ordinary discourse contexts there is a deictic centre, implicit or explicit, in relation to which the three arguments of *inter* 'between' are located. In this regard, vector space semantics has an intuitively appealing advantage. The reference objects x and z and the located object y are the end points of vectors projected from the deictic centre. You can give a formal definition of the straight line connecting them without shifting your point of view to either x or z. Figure 4.10 illustrates how this is done. The end point of the vector $\mathbf{x}$ locates object x and the end point of vector $\mathbf{z}$ locates object z. The start point of the vectors is the deictic centre. Any object y is between x and z if and only if it lies on the line joining them. Consider the vectors that locate the points on this line. As y gets closer to x, its locating vector $\mathbf{y}$ more and more approximates $\mathbf{x}$, and similarly as y gets closer to z, $\mathbf{y}$ more and more approximates $\mathbf{z}$. These vectors are all vector sums of scalar products of $\mathbf{x}$ and $\mathbf{z}$. The scalar tells you how the vectors $\mathbf{x}$ and $\mathbf{y}$ are weighted in the sum. Let s be the scalar; it is never negative and never greater than 1: $0 \leq s \leq 1$. The vectors $\mathbf{y}$ that end at the points between x and z will always then be of the form $\mathbf{y} = s\mathbf{x} + (1-s)\mathbf{z}$. Such weighted vector sums are known as convex linear combinations. When $s = 1, \mathbf{y} = \mathbf{x}$, when $s = 0, \mathbf{y} = \mathbf{z}$, and when $s = ½$, y is the midpoint between x and z. Accordingly *inter*(x,z) 'between x and z' denotes the set of such convex linear combinations: $\{\mathbf{y}: \forall s.0 \leq s \leq 1 \rightarrow \mathbf{y} = s\mathbf{x} + (1-s)\mathbf{z}\}$. It is simply a matter of algebra to express the properties of reflexivity, connectivity and transitivity in terms of vector sums of scalar products of $\mathbf{x}$ and $\mathbf{y}$.

Of course the located and reference objects are quite often not conceived as points

(39) Eburones, quorum maxima pars est *inter Mosam et Rhenum* (BG 5.24)
Erat *inter oppidum Ilerdam et proximum collem*... planities passuum CCC (BC 1.43)

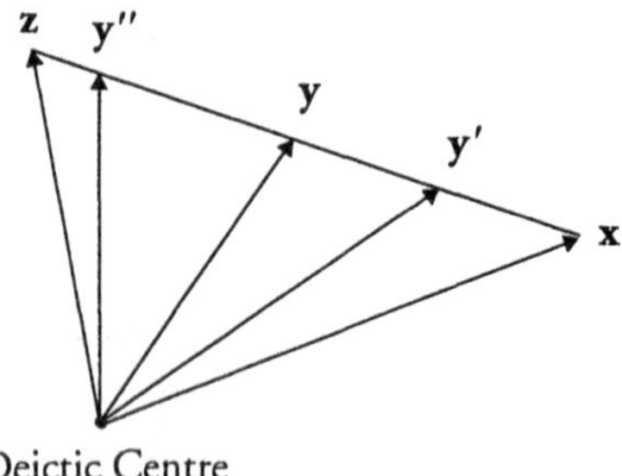

Figure 4.10
Vector analysis of *inter*

(39) The Eburones, most of whose territory lies between the Meuse and the Rhine (BG 5.24). There was between Ilerda and the nearest hill a plain of about three hundred yards (BC 1.43).

(40) forum Iulium et basilicam quae fuit *inter aedem Castoris et aedem Saturni*, coepta profligataque opera a patre meo, perfeci (Res Gest 20.3)
Fuit denique hactenus statua in pede montis Romulei, hoc est ante sacram viam *inter templum Faustinae ac Vestam* (Hist Aug Gall 19.4: app. crit.).

For objects conceived of as two- or three-dimensional, *inter* 'between' can be defined in terms of the space inside the convex hull around the two reference objects, the reference objects themselves being excluded. Topologically this is the complement of the convex hulls of x and z relative to the complex hull (H) surrounding x and z; y is dimensionally between x and z if and only if it is inside the convex hull surrounding x and z but not inside either x or z: $\mathrm{B}(x,y,z) \rightarrow \mathrm{Inside}(y, [\mathrm{H}(x \cup z)\backslash x\backslash z])$. In the case of Gallienus' statue (Aug Gall 19.4) this definition works absolutely. In the case of the Basilica Julia (Res Gest 20.3), the fact that it extends beyond the rear of the Temple of Saturn and thus falls partly outside H(Castoris ∪ Saturni)\Castoris\Saturni, is simply not relevant to the context: it is invisible at the level of granularity assumed at this point in the text. In the second example in (39) (BC 1.43) Caesar allows for an overlap but mentions only the salient greatest part.

Sometimes *inter* 'between' has to be defined in terms of positions ordered along a path

(41) is queretur Brundisium me non venisse cum *inter me et Brundisium* Caesar esset? (Ad Att 9.2a.2)
Innumeri montes *inter me teque* viaeque fluminaque et campi nec freta pauca (Ov Trist 4.7.21).

In the first example (Ad Att 9.2a) it would be absurd to model Cicero's meaning in terms of a convex hull stretching from the Tyrrhenian (he is writing at Formiae) to the Adriatic. Caesar is besieging Brundisium, but if he were at a place on the Via Appia (such as Tarentum) that lies outside the space so defined, he would still be between Cicero and Brundisium relative to a route along the Via Appia. As we will see, paths can be modelled as functions from the unit interval [0,1] to positions on the path. Here we are interested in the inverse function which maps path positions back onto the unit interval. If $\mathbf{p}(y)$ is the path position of object y on path $\mathbf{p}(\cdot)$, the inverse function $\mathbf{p}^{-1}(\cdot)$ maps $\mathbf{p}(y)$ onto a number in the unit interval. Without loss of generality we can take the reference objects as the end points of the path, assigning them to $\mathbf{p}(0)$ and $\mathbf{p}(1)$ as required by the context. Then y is between x and z on path $\mathbf{p}(\cdot)$ if and only if the

(40) I completed the forum Julium and the basilica which was between the temple of Castor and the temple of Saturn, works which had been begun and well advanced by my father (Res Gest 20.3). There has been up till this day a statue at the foot of the Mons Romuleus, that is before the Via Sacra between the Temples of Faustina and Vesta (Hist Aug Gall 19.4).

(41) Is he going to complain that I did not come to Brundisium when Caesar was between me and Brundisium? (Ad Att 9.2a.2). There are countless mountains, roads, rivers and plains between you and me and not a few seas (Ov Trist 4.7.21).

position of *y* is mapped from a number greater than 0 and less than 1: $B(x,y,z) \leftrightarrow 0 < \mathbf{p}^{-1}(\mathbf{p}(y)) < 1$. An interesting special case of the path sense of *inter* arises with cardinal directions and positions on the circumferences of circles and polygons or surfaces of spheres and polyhedra

(42) Aquitania... spectat *inter occasum solis et septentriones* (BG 1.1)
in singulis angulis octagoni, cum a meridie incipiemus, *inter eurum et austrum* in angulo erit littera G, *inter austrum et africum* H... (Vitr 1.6.13)
Septimo die sol sit ad occidentem, luna autem *inter orientem et occidentem* medias caeli teneat regiones, quod dimidia parte caeli spatio distet a sole, item dimidiam candentiae conversam habere ad terram. (Vitr 9.2.2: app. crit.).

In these cases the path is defined in terms of polar coordinates. Let $\theta(\cdot)$ be the function which maps a path position onto its polar coordinate angle. The length of the radius vector **r** is a contextually determined parameter. In the first example (BG 1.1) it is irrelevant: Aquitania is oriented to the northwest, no matter how far you look. For Vitruvius' wind dial it is the radius of the circumscribing circle. In his model of the phases of the moon, the length of **r** is the radius of the moon's orbit; *y* is angularly between *x* and *z* if and only if, for a contextually determined length of radius, the angular coordinate of *y* is greater than that of *x* but less than that of *z* or vice versa (depending on how the path is directed): $B(x,y,z) \leftrightarrow \theta(x) < \theta(y) < \theta(z) \vee \theta(z) < \theta(y) < \theta(x) \wedge |\mathbf{r}| = c$. Paths themselves may be located between other paths. For example this is how Vitruvius locates the orbit of the planet Jupiter

(43) Iovis stella *inter Martis ferventissimam et Saturni frigidissimam* media currens temperatur (Vitr 6.1.11).

Here the paths are planetary orbits. It is the relation of the norms of their radius vectors at every angular position, $|\mathbf{r}_x(\theta)|$, $|\mathbf{r}_y(\theta)|$ and $|\mathbf{r}_z(\theta)|$ that defines *inter*. The orbit of Jupiter is between the orbits of Mars and Saturn, although Jupiter is not itself always between Mars and Saturn (the three planets do not have to be lined up along the same radius vector). The path of *y* is between the paths of *x* and *z* if and only if, all along their circuits, they never cross: $B(x,y,z) \leftrightarrow \forall\theta.|\mathbf{r}_x(\theta)| < |\mathbf{r}_y(\theta)| < |\mathbf{r}_z(\theta)| \vee |\mathbf{r}_z(\theta)| < |\mathbf{r}_y(\theta)| < |\mathbf{r}_x(\theta)|$.

The status of *inter* as a projective preposition is sometimes overlooked. In two dimensions, with objects conceived as points, whether or not one object is between two others does not depend on our point of view; it is a question of

(42) Aquitania is oriented to the northwest (BG 1.1). In the individual angles of the octagon beginning from the south, in the angle between Eurus and Auster there will be the letter G, between Auster and Africus H (Vitr 1.6.13). On the seventh day let the sun be towards the west; the moon occupies the mid region of the sky between the east and the west; because it is distant from the sun by a space that is half of the sky, it likewise has half of its shining area turned towards the earth (Vitr 9.2.2).

(43) The planet Jupiter is balanced by running half way between the very hot planet Mars and the very cold planet Saturn (Vitr 6.1.11).

whether they lie on a common line or path. In three dimensions, however, whether an object can be described as between two other objects may depend on our perspective. This is why Pliny specifies the deictic origin for the consular orderly's line of sight when he announces the noon hour

(44) post aliquot annos adiectus est et meridies, accenso consulum id pronuntiante cum *a Curia inter Rostra et Graecostasin* prospexisset solem (NH 7.212).

If the orderly were not looking from the Senate House but from somewhere sufficiently far away on one side or the other of it, he would not see the sun between the Rostra and the envoys' platform at noon, and, if he did see it there, it might not be at noon. The point is that in three dimensions 'betweenness' can be computed from the configuration of objects on a deictically determined projection plane.

Directional prepositions

While locative prepositions determine static positions, directional prepositions determine change of location. They denote paths. A path can be modelled as a function from the unit interval [0, 1] to a sequence of vectors. Figure 4.11 illustrates how the function **p**(·) maps points in this interval to sequences of vectors that yield a curving path. **p**(0) is the source or beginning of the path, **p**(1) is the end or goal. In and of themselves, directional prepositions do not involve time, as is clear from their atemporal uses, which abound in Vitruvius

(45) Deinde insuper erectae mammatae tegulae *ab imo ad summum parietem* figantur (Vitr 7.4.2: app. crit.)
et per ea signa et centrum A lineae *ad extrema lineae circinationis* sunt perducendae (Vitr 9.7.5: app. crit.).

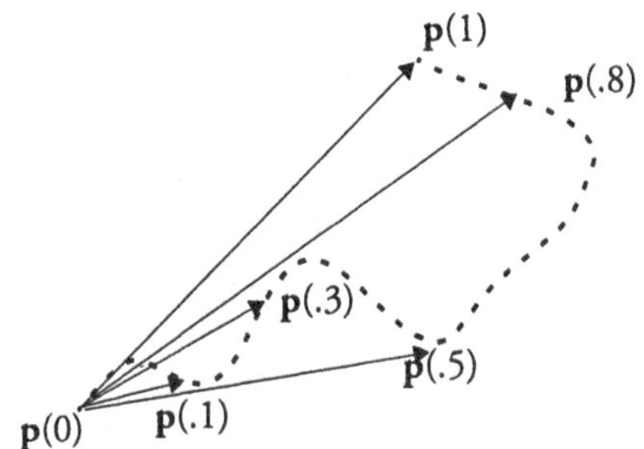

Figure 4.11
Vectors for a curving path

(44) A few years later noon was added, with the consuls' orderly announcing it when from the Curia he saw the sun between the Rostra and the envoys' platform (NH 7.212).

(45) Then tiles with spouts should be fixed vertically from the bottom to the top of the wall (Vitr 7.4.2). And through these letters and the centre A, lines should be extended to the circumference (Vitr 9.7.5).

The first example in (35) (Vitr 6.3.9) is another case in point. In these examples no motion is described: rather the path locates plural objects or indicates a line of sight. Directional prepositions may be classified as source prepositions like *ab*, *de*, *ex*, *extra*, as goal prepositions like *in* (accusative), *intra*, or as route prepositions like *adversus*, *secundum*, *circum*, *cis*, *citra*, *per*, *praeter*, *super*, *trans*, *ultra*. Source prepositions determine the starting point of the path, goal prepositions determine its end point, and route prepositions specify some interior part of the path or the entire path (as do *adversus* and *secundum*).

The entailments that can be observed between directional and locative prepositions

(46) exactos *ex urbe* reges (Livy 6.37.10) → reges in urbe erant
gladium... *in vaginam* recondidit (De Inv 2.14) → gladius in vagina erat
ab Hermandica profugi (Livy 21.5.7) → ad Hermandicam erant
per media Romana castra nocte egressus (Livy 26.4.2) → in mediis Romanis castris erat
castra *de planitie* convertit in montes (Sisenna 51) → castra in planitie erant
plebem *de sacro monte* deduxit (CIL 1.189) → plebs in sacro monte erat

suggest a mapping between them. We can define an operator *dir* that directionalizes a locative preposition in the following way. It picks out the set of paths which are the closest to the reference object of the preposition, Closest[P(A), ($\mathbf{p}(x)$)]. For source prepositions *dir* will specify the beginning of the path $\mathbf{p}(0)$, for goal prepositions the end of the path $\mathbf{p}(1)$, and for route prepositions some point or subinterval $[0 < r < 1]$. Using the corresponding abbreviations *dir0*, *dir1*, and *dirr*, we get the following directionalizations

ab = *dir0* (ad)	ex = *dir0* (in-abl)	de = *dir0* (in-abl)
ad = *dir1* (ad)	in 'into' = *dir1* (in-abl)	in 'onto' = *dir1* (in-abl)
praeter = *dirr* (ad)	per = *dirr* (in-abl)	trans = *dirr* (in-abl).

So *per* is the function that maps any set of points A to the paths which are closest to A and which satisfy *In*($\mathbf{p}(r)$,A). A few other locative prepositions can be directionalized by the *dir* operator to give route prepositions, for instance *super* = *dirr* (*supra*), and as a first approximation *secundum* = *dirr* (*prope*). It is clear that the topological prepositions *ad* and *in* have a special status: all source and goal prepositions are derived from them. This rule (and probably language universal) makes a testable prediction concerning *desuper*

(46) That the kings had been driven out of the city (Livy 6.37.10). He put the sword back in its scabbard (De Inv 2.14). The fugitives from Hermandica (Livy 21.5.7). Having made his way out through the middle of the Roman camp at night (Livy 26.4.2). He moved his camp from the plain into the mountains (Sisenna 51). He brought the plebeians down from the Mons Sacer (CIL 1.189).

(47) ingerunt *desuper* Othoniani pila (Tac Hist 2.22)
praecipiti grandine *desuper* verberatur (Apul Mun 3)
nunc *desuper* Alpis nubiferae colles atque aeriam Pyrenen abripimur (Lucan 1.688).

If a source or a goal preposition is always derived from a topological preposition, then it can never denote paths whose start or end points are above, below, beyond etc. the reference object. Thus when *desuper* means 'from above,' it will be not a preposition but an adverb, as in the first two examples (Hist 2.22; Mun 3). Similarly when it does function as a preposition, its denotation will be restricted, as in the last example where it means 'over,' and not 'from above.'

Prepositional aspect

Both source and goal prepositions can have the effect of telicizing basically atelic verbs (see Chapters 2 and 3)

(48) Quam mox navigo *in Ephesum...*? (Pl Bacch 775)
Properas ire... *ab his regionibus...*? (Pl Trin 983)
a Vestae ad Tabulam Valeriam ducta esses (Ad Fam 14.2.2).

Some route prepositions like *adversus* and *secundum* are always atelic: they leave atelic situations atelic and have no effects on telic ones

(49) calcari quadrupedo agitabo *advorsum clivum* (Pl Asin 708)
venter... cum venerit *adversus clivum* (Vitr 8.6.5)
iter *secundum mare superum* faciunt (Ad Att 16.8.2)
nomadum Aethiopum *secundum flumen Astragum* ad septentrionem vergentium gens (NH 7.31).

In the first two examples (As 708; Vitr 8.6) *adversus clivum* means 'uphill,' not 'to (the top of) the hill.' The adverb *versus* detelicizes telic *ad* and the telic goal meaning of names of towns and small islands in the accusative

(50) iubet omnes legiones... se consequi *ad oppidum Ruspinam versus* (BAfr 37)
eos cis Lirim amnem *Romam versus...* emovendos censuerunt (Livy 26.34.9).

(47) Otho's men showered javelins onto them from above (Tac Hist 2.22). It is battered by precipitating hail from above (Apul Mun 3). Next I am carried away over the peaks of the cloudy Alps and the high Pyrenees (Lucan 1.688).

(48) How soon am I sailing for Ephesus? (Pl Bacch 775). Are you going to get out of this district quickly? (Pl Trin 983). You were brought from the temple of Vesta to the Tabula Valeria (Ad Fam 14.2.2).

(49) I will drive you galloping uphill with my spurs (Pl Asin 708). When the bend in the pipe goes uphill (Vitr 8.6.5). They are marching along the Adriatic (Ad Att 16.8.2). The tribe of Ethiopian nomads stretching north along the river Astragus (NH 7.31).

(50) He ordered all the legions to follow him in the direction of the town of Ruspina (BAfr 37). They voted that they should be moved this side of the Liris towards Rome (Livy 26.34.9).

In contrast other route prepositions such as *cis*, *citra*, *trans* and *ultra* are always telic. In fact *trans* is usually paired with verbs having the telicizing prefix *trans-*

(51) Naevius... *trans* Alpes usque *transfertur* (Pro Quinct 12)
vexillum *trans* vallum hostium *traiecit* (Livy 25.14.4).

Even in the absence of the prefix it is still telicizing

(52) caelum, non animum mutant, qui *trans mare* currunt (Hor Ep 1.11.27).

Horace means 'go abroad' not 'go sailing.' Still other prepositions are aspectually ambiguous. This applies to *circum*

(53) Ego Arpini volo esse prid. Kal., deinde *circum villulas* nostras errare (Ad Att 8.9.3)
Armillas IIII facito, quas *circum orbem* indas (Cato 21.4).

In the first example (Ad Att 8.9) *circum villulas* means 'round about my villas,' not 'around the perimeter of my villas.' In the second (Cato 21.4) *circum orbem* supplies the telos for *indas*: 'encircle the circumference (of the stone).' Similarly with *per*

(54) cum *per eorum fines* triduum iter fecisset (BG 2.16)
qui non bis *per agmen hostium* perequitasset (BG 7.66: app. crit.).

The extent of time adverbial *triduum* in the first example (BG 2.16) proves that the situation is atelic; after three days of marching Caesar is still inside the territory of the Nervii. On the other hand in the second example (BG 7.66) the quotientative adverb *bis* (missing in some manuscripts) shows that the situation is telic, not a divisive and cumulative activity: the aim is to ride through the enemy column, then repeat the accomplishment in the opposite direction. Likewise with *praeter*

(55) profectus ab urbe sexaginta longis navibus *praeter oram Etruriae* (Livy 21.26.3)
praeter Caesaris castra copias traduxit (BG 1.48).

In the first example (Livy 21.26) the route is along the coast of Etruria, not over the beach to the sea. In the second example (BG 1.48) Ariovistus moved his

(51) Naevius was moved all the way across the Alps (Pro Quinct 12). He threw the banner across the enemy rampart (Livy 25.14.4).

(52) Those who rush across the sea change the sky above, not the heart within (Hor Ep 1.11.27).

(53) I want to be at Arpinum on the 28th and then to wander around my country houses (Ad Att 8.9.3). Make four rings to put around the stone (Cato 21.4).

(54) When he had marched through their territory for three days (BG 2.16). Who had not ridden through the enemy line twice (BG 7.66).

(55) Having set out from the city along the coast of Etruria with sixty warships (Livy 21.26.3). He led his forces past Caesar's camp (BG 1.48).

troops to a point two miles past Caesar's forces. Finally, here are some examples with *super*

(56) volitat *super aequora* classis (Fur Ant 4 ap. Gell 18.11.4)
super occisorum corpora vadere (Sall Jug 94.6)
lapso equo *super caput eius* humi prostratus est (Val Max 1.6.6).

In the second example (Jug 94.6), since *vado* does not mean 'step so as to avoid or surmount an obstacle,' *super corpora* means 'on (top of) the corpses' not 'over each corpse individually.'

We saw in Chapter 2 that atelic situation types are divisive and cumulative, whereas telic types are neither divisive nor cumulative. These notions can fruitfully be extended to directional prepositional phrases when we examine the algebraic structure of the paths they denote. Paths are partially ordered by a subpath relation: here is a fuller version of the second example in (55)

(57) milibus passuum sex a Caesaris castris sub monte consedit. Postridie eius diei Ariovistus *praeter castra Caesaris* suas copias traduxit et milibus passuum duobus ultra eum castra fecit (BG 1.48).

If **q** is the path from the hill to Caesar's camp and **r** is the path from Caesar's camp to Ariovistus' new camp two miles away, then **q** and **r** are subpaths of the whole path **p** from the hill to Ariovistus' new camp (as schematically represented in Figure 4.12). Paths can be added together by a concatenation operation if the end point of one path **q**(1) is the start point of the other **r**(0): in Figure 4.12 **p** = **q** + **r**. Obviously concatenants are subpaths of their concatenation. Concatenation however is not a commutative operation. Consider the stars in their courses, particularly the genus of fixed stars

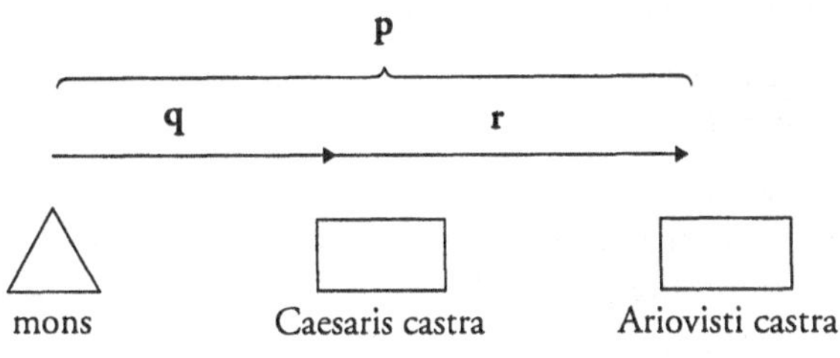

Figure 4.12
Subpaths
Sub monte... praeter castra Caesaris... ultra eum (BG 1.48)

(56) The fleet flies over the surface of the sea (Fur Ant 4). They advanced over the bodies of the fallen (Sall Jug 94.6). When his horse stumbled he was thrown over its head onto the ground (Val Max 1.6.6).

(57) He encamped at the foot of a mountain six miles from Caesar's camp. On the following day Ariovistus led his forces past Caesar's camp and pitched camp two miles beyond him (BG 1.48).

(58) alterum spatiis inmutabilibus *ab ortu ad occasum* commeans nullum umquam cursus sui vestigium inflectat (ND 2.49).

The path **p** from east to west may be concatenated with the path **q** from west to east to give back the path **p** + **q**, and vice versa to give the path **q** + **p**, but the concatenation **p** + **q** puts a star back rising in the east, while the concatenation **q** + **p** puts a star back setting in the west. So **p** + **q** ≠ **q** + **p**.

The divisivity and cumulativity of paths is defined in terms of the subpath relation and the concatenation operation. A set of paths **X** is divisive if and only if for every path **p** in **X** any subpath **q** < **p** is also in **X**. A set of paths **X** is cumulative if and only if there are paths **p** and **q** in **X** that can be concatenated and their concatenation **p** + **q** is also in **X**. Notice that there are two ways a set of paths can fail to be cumulative. The set may not contain any paths that can be concatenated, or, if it does, their concatenation may not remain in the set. No telic prepositional phrase is divisive. A source prepositional phrases like *de sacro monte* in the last example in (46) (CIL 1.189) denotes a set of paths whose start points must be on the sacred hill. But these paths have subpaths which do not have start points in the city or on the hill. Therefore those subpaths are not in the denotation of the prepositional phrase. A goal prepositional phrase such as *ad curiam*

(59) qui cum facibus *ad curiam* concurrerunt (Pro Mil 91)

will have subpaths that do not reach the senate house. Although divisivity is a sufficient condition for atelicity, it is not a necessary one. An atelic path 'up hill' is not necessarily a straight line; it may involve curves, zigzags and switchbacks. Since a switchback is not 'up the hill,' the overall path is not actually divisive, although the switchback might be discounted for pragmatic purposes. An atelic path like *secundum flumen*

(60) sex ipse in Arvernos ad oppidum Gergoviam *secundum flumen Elaver* duxit (BG 7.34)

is not divisive, because *secundum* is defined according to a criterion of nearness to and alignment with an axis of the reference object. This criterion is an average taken over the entire path and judged according to a standard determined by the scale and degree of granularity appropriate to the context. As illustrated in Figure 4.13, the overall path *p* can be 'along the river' even if a subpath such as *r* does not track along a major meander. Divisivity likewise fails to be a necessary condition for mass nouns and activity verbs: *vinum* 'wine' is divisive, *supellex* 'furniture' is not; *traho* 'drag' is divisive, *salio* 'jump' is not. Cumulativity does, however, provide the necessary and sufficient condition to distinguish

(58) One type travels from east to west on fixed paths without deviating even a step from its course (ND 2.49).

(59) Who ran with torches to the senate house (Pro Mil 91).

(60) He himself led six along the river Elaver towards the town of Gergovia in the territory of the Arverni (BG 7.34).

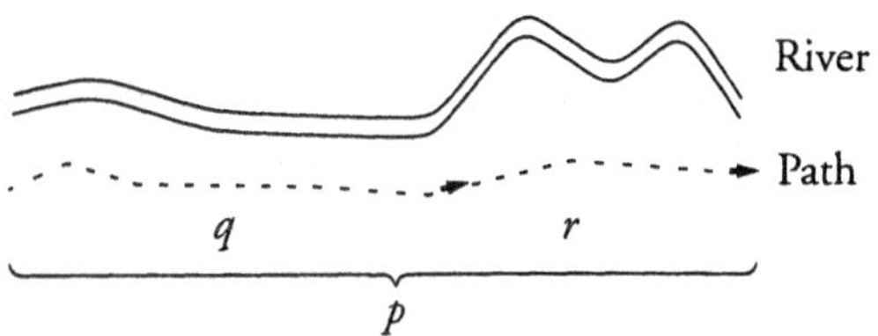

Figure 4.13
Subpath not the same as overall path
Secundum flumen (BG 1.48)

telic from atelic prepositional phrases. A prepositional phrase is atelic if and only if it is cumulative; a prepositional phrase is telic if and only if it is not cumulative

(61) *praeter oram* Etrusci maris (Livy 40.41.3)
Verti igitur me a Minturnis *Arpinum versus* (Ad Att 16.10.1).

If two paths **p** and **q** are each along the shore of the Etruscan sea and they are such as can be concatenated, then **p** + **q** is also a path along the shore, just one longer than each of its concatenants. Similarly if **p** and **q** are two paths toward Arpinum and can be concatenated, then **p** + **q** is a longer path toward Arpinum. In contrast, source prepositional phrases denote paths whose start points are at or in the reference object, and goal prepositional phrases denote paths whose end points are at or into the reference object. Different paths that share only the same start or end points obviously cannot be concatenated. There are many paths by which people can run to the senate house, but, since those paths have different start points, they cannot be joined head to tail. (We will deal with telic *circum* below.)

Source and goal prepositional phrases have a two-phase structure, an initial phase and a final phase with a single transition between the two. The two phases are also called the negative and the positive, the positive being the one that specifies the source or, respectively, the goal. Let $0 < t < 1$ be a partition of the closed unit interval $[0, 1]$; let the initial phase $I = [0, t)$ and the final phase $F = (t, 1]$. Source prepositional phrases are then defined as follows: *ab* x denotes the set of paths that are at x during their initial phase: $\{\mathbf{p}: I = \{i: \mathbf{p}(i) \text{ is at } x\}\}$; *de* x denotes the set of those that are in or on x during their initial phase: $\{\mathbf{p}: I = \{i: \mathbf{p}(i) \text{ is in/on } x\}\}$. Goal prepositional phrases are defined as follows: *ad* x denotes the set of those that are at x during their final phase: $\{\mathbf{p}: F = \{i: \mathbf{p}(i) \text{ is at } x\}\}$; *in* x denotes the set of those that are in or on x during their final phase: $\{\mathbf{p}: F = \{i: \mathbf{p}(i) \text{ is in/on } x\}\}$. In contrast atelic *adversus* and *secundum* have only a single phase. Atelic *adversus* relates to telic *ad* in a way that resembles part to whole and comparative to superlative. *Adversus* denotes the set of subpaths denoted by

(61) Along the shore of the Tuscan sea (Livy 40.41.3). So I am turning towards Arpinum from Minturnae (Ad Att 16.10.1).

ad which get closer and closer to the goal but never reach it. Letting $d(\mathbf{p}(i),x)$ be the distance from path point $\mathbf{p}(i)$ to object x, *adversus* x ≡ $\{\mathbf{p}\colon \exists \mathbf{q}.\ \mathbf{q} \in$ *ad* x. $\mathbf{p} < \mathbf{q} \wedge 0 < d(\mathbf{p}(1),x) < d(\mathbf{p}(0),x)\}$. *Secundum* denotes paths that are aligned with an axis of the reference object and close to the reference object. As noted above, 'aligned with and close to' means that there is some average measure taken over the whole path length that does not exceed some contextually assigned critical value. We denote this by $Av(\mathbf{p}(i),x) \leq c$: *secundum* x ≡ $\{\mathbf{p}\colon \forall i.i \in [0,1] \rightarrow Av(\mathbf{p}(i),x) \leq c\}$. The telic route prepositions *cis, citra, trans* and *ultra* have a three phase structure, a source-like initial, a specially constrained medial and a goal-like final phase. Let $0 < a < b < 1$ be a partition of the closed unit interval $[0,1]$ which divides it into three subintervals, $I = [0,a)$, $M = [a,b]$ and $F = (b,1]$. *Ultra* denotes the set of paths which are at x in their medial phase, but on either side of x during their initial and final phases: $\{\mathbf{p}\colon M = \{i\colon \mathbf{p}(i)$ is near $x\} \wedge$ on opposite sides of $x(\mathbf{p}(0),\mathbf{p}(1))\}$. *Cis, citra* and *trans* lexicalize the deictic distinction between 'this, nearer side' and 'that, farther side.' *Cis, citra* x denote the set of paths which are near x during their medial phase, begin in the deictically determined region on the farther side of x and end in the region on the nearer side of x: $\{\mathbf{p}\colon M = \{i\colon \mathbf{p}(i)$ is near $x\} \wedge \mathbf{p}(0)$ that side of $x \wedge \mathbf{p}(1)$ this side of $x\}$. *Trans* x denotes the set of paths which are near or on x during their medial phase, begin in the deictically determined region on the nearer side of x and end in the region on the farther side of x: $\{\mathbf{p}\colon M = \{i\colon \mathbf{p}(i)$ is near/on $x\} \wedge \mathbf{p}(0)$ this side of $x \wedge \mathbf{p}(1)$ that side of $x\}$.

The aspectually ambiguous route prepositions *circum, per, praeter* and *super* resemble verbs with semelfactive phases like *curro* 'run,' *salto* 'jump,' *tussio* 'cough,' *verbero* 'beat,' which vary between activity and achievement readings. Such verbs have a special three-phase structure: the initial and final phases are the same. A jump starts out on a surface, goes up off the surface, and finishes back on the surface. Because the initial and final states are the same, such semelfactive events can be concatenated into iterative activities. The paths denoted by *circum* in the telic sense of '360° around' can be concatenated when the next circuit begins where the previous one finished. In this way we get iterative or plural readings

(62) *terque novas circum* felix eat hostia *fruges* (Verg Georg 1.345).

Notice that this plural reading remains noncumulative. The concatenation of two circuits of 360° into one circuit of 720° falls outside the telic denotation of *circum*. So telic *circum* is noncumulative, not because concatenable paths fail to exist, but because their concatenation no longer belongs to the (360°) denotation. The plural reading of *per* as in the second example in (54) (BG 7.66) is represented schematically for a single cavalryman in Figure 4.14, where the start point of his return $\mathbf{p}_2$ is concatenated at the end point of the initial penetration of the enemy column $\mathbf{p}_1$ and *bis* is taken to denote a single round trip.

(62) Let the victim that brings good fortune go three times around the new crops (Verg Georg 1.345).

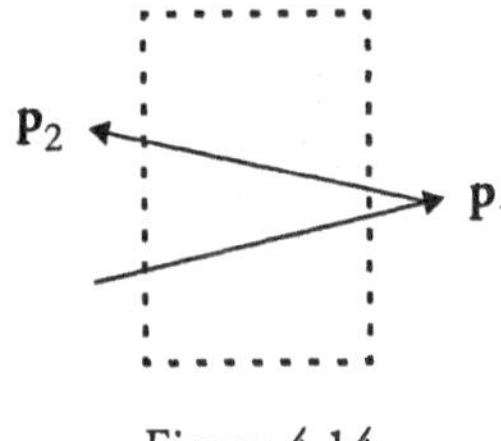

Figure 4.14
Plural *per*
Qui non bis per agmen hostium perequitasset (BG 7.66)

The atelic denotations of the aspectually ambiguous prepositions seen in the first examples of (53-56) have only a single phase. The paths remain, respectively, round about the villas, within the territory of the Nervii, along the coast of Etruria, and over the sea. A schematic representation of the singular telic *per agmen* and atelic *per fines* is given in Figure 4.15(a-b). The atelic denotations can be derived from the telic ones in the following way. First we get rid of the subpaths of the telic denotations that are outside the reference object, like the dashed lines in Figure 4.15(b). This leaves only subpaths within the reference object, the solid lines *in finibus*. Let **p**(M) denote such a path. The set of these subpaths {**p**(M)} is not yet what we need, since it is not cumulative, as is required for atelicity: we need to construct the set of subpaths of **p**(M). This set is cumulative. Figure 4.16 illustrates the concatenation of subpaths **sq** + **sr** + **sp** into a new path that is *in finibus*, thereby satisfying the definition of cumulativity. In a slightly more complicated way the atelic reading of *circum* exemplified by *circum villulas* (Ad Att 8.9 in (53)) can be derived from the plural reading exemplified by *terque novas circum... fruges* (Verg Georg 1.345 in (62)) by taking subpaths of concatenations of single circuits or concatenating subpaths of multiple circuits. The relation of the atelic to the telic reading of the aspectually ambiguous prepositions is analogous to the relation between mass and count nouns, and the truncating and chopping up of noncumulative telic paths into sets

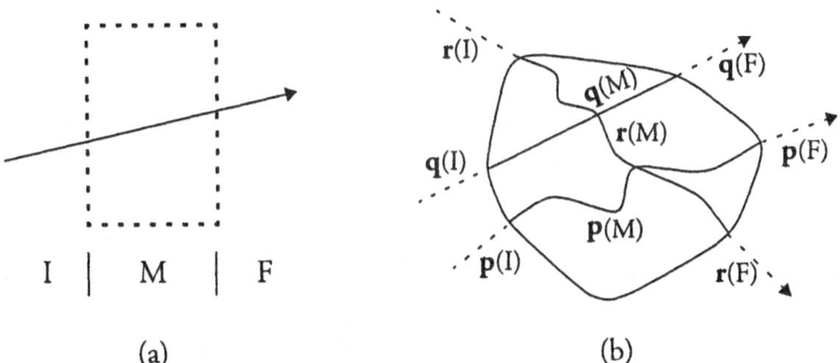

Figure 4.15
Telic (a) and atelic (b) paths
(a) *per agmen hostium perequitasset* (BG 7.66); (b) *per eorum fines* (BG 2.16)

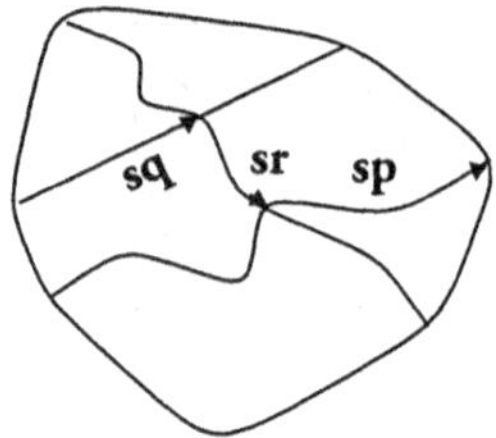

Figure 4.16
Subpaths of atelic paths are cumulative: **sq**+**sr**+**sp** ∈ *per fines*
Per eorum fines (BG 2.16)

of cumulative subpaths resembles the grinding operation which derives mass nouns from count nouns (see Chapter 6). The telic reading may be regarded as primary for all three-phase prepositions. Those that impose additional restrictions on the initial and final phases, such as *cis, citra, trans* and *ultra* cannot be truncated to their medial phase and so are unambiguously telic. Those which do not impose such restrictions can receive plural and atelic readings.

Compositional semantics

Locative and directional prepositions have a wide syntactic distribution and correspondingly show a prima facie polymorphism of semantic type. As recognized in notional and historical grammars, the local sense is basic for all proper prepositions except *cum*. The temporal, circumstantial, causal, concessive, partitive and purpose senses, to name the more prominent, are transferred from the local. Our purpose here is neither to catalogue these transferred senses nor to review the conceptual analogies and metaphorical extensions that lead to them. Rather we shall explore more formally the compositional semantics of locative prepositional phrases in their various functions. The compositional semantics of directional prepositional phrases has already come up for discussion in Chapter 3.

Locative prepositional phrases may be predicates

(63) Erat *in exercitu Vari* Sextus Quintilius Varus (BC 2.28)
Erat vallis *inter duas acies* (BC 2.34).

Here the preposition itself is a function which takes an argument of type <e>, like *exercitu* in the first example (BC 2.28), returning a prepositional phrase. The prepositional phrase, in turn, is a locational property; its type is <e,t>. It takes an argument of type <e>, like *Sextus Quintilius Varus* in the first example, and returns a truth value (type <t>), as illustrated in Figure 4.17 which abstracts away from the details in Figures 4.1 and 4.5 (eigenspaces and vectors). Locative prepositional phrases may also be secondary or covert predicates, which target some participants in an event but not the event as a whole

(63) There was in the army of Varus Sextus Quintilius Varus (BC 2.28). There was a valley between the two battle lines (BC 2.34).

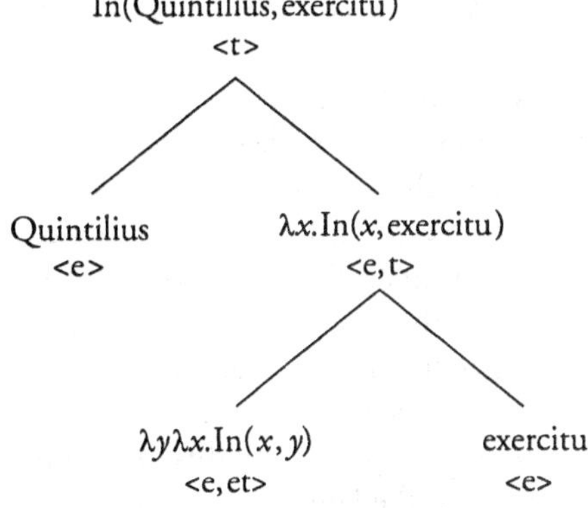

Figure 4.17
Predicative locative
Erat in exercitu Quintilius (cp. BC 2.28)

(64) prima legio... hanc *sub sarcinis* adoriri (BG 2.17)
equites nostri... fugientes perterritosque *sub sarcinis* in itinere adgressi (BG 8.27)
milites sub onere ac *sub sarcinis* defatigatos pugnare non posse (BAfr 75).

Covertly predicational prepositional phrases function like depictives. They denote sets of events or states which are intersected with the set of events denoted by the main clause. On this analysis the second example (BG 8.27) could be represented as follows: $\lambda x \lambda e'$.Sub-sarcinis$(e', x) \wedge \lambda x \lambda e$.Adgressi$(e, x)$. Prepositional phrases also locate events

(65) pugnatur acriter *ad novissimum agmen* (BC 1.80)
nuntius *victoriae ad Cannas* Carthaginem venerat Mago (Livy 23.11.7)
Iamque Caesaris *in Hispania res secundae* in Africam nuntiis ac litteris perferebantur. (BC 2.37)
locus, auctoritas, *domi splendor*, *apud exteras nationes nomen et gratia*, toga praetexta, sella curulis, insignia, fasces (Pro Clu 154).

In the first example (BC 1.80) the impersonal verb denotes an event which is located by the prepositional phrase. In the second example (Livy 21.15) *victoria* is a noun that denotes an event, in the third (BC 2.3) *res secundae* has an event reading in context, and in the last (Pro Clu 154) the state *domi splendor* is a

(64) The first legion... to attack it while loaded down under full pack (BG 2.17). Our cavalry, having attacked them fleeing and terrified on the march under full pack (BG 8. 27). That soldiers tired out under full pack and loaded down could not fight (BAfr 75).

(65) There was a fierce fight at the rear end of the line (BC 1.80). Mago had come to Carthage bearing the news of the victory at Cannae (Livy 23.11.7). And by now Caesar's success in Spain was being reported in Africa by messengers and letters (BC 2.37). Rank, authority, magnificence at home, fame and influence among foreign peoples, the toga praetexta, the sella curulis, the insignia, the fasces (Pro Clu 154).

nominalization of *domi splendebat* and *apud exteras nationes... gratia* of *apud exteras nationes gratus erat.*

Event external prepositional phrases fit easily into an event semantics that postulates event identification as the mode of combining them with the rest of the verb phrase. In such an analysis the preposition is a function of type <e,εt>, where <ε> is the type of an event and <ε,t> is a function from an event to a truth value (a property of events). The object of the preposition saturates its internal argument, returning the set of events taking place in the location that the prepositional phrase specifies. Accordingly the prepositional phrase has the type <ε,t>. This set of located events is then intersected with the set of events denoted by the verb. The process producing this intersection is known as event identification: the variable *e* in the lambda formula of the prepositional phrase is identified with the variable *e* in the lambda formula of the verb, as illustrated in Figure 4.18. Since it is assumed that the agent of an event is an external argument, a tree structure results in which the prepositional phrase is attached below the agent. It follows that the compositional semantics says nothing about the location of the agent. This seems to be what is needed: the location of an event's agent is dependent on individual verb meaning and real world knowledge. Consider

(66) Ligna *in torculario* ne caedant (Cato 67.1).

Cato is proscribing all events of wood cutting from the olive press room. Under normal circumstances, given the sorts of tools customarily used to cut wood, an axe-wielding agent would be in the same room as the wood, but if he has an axe

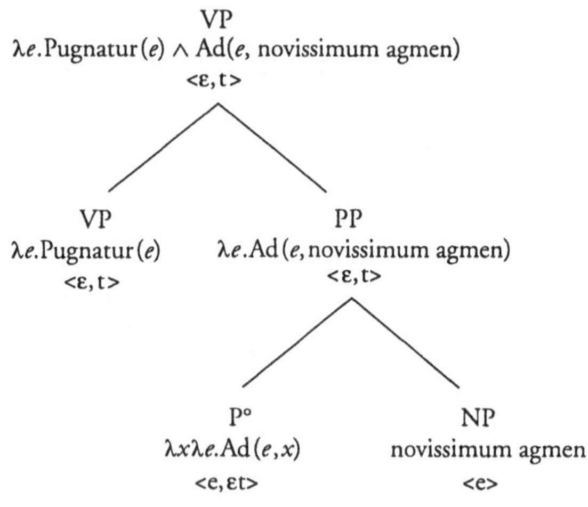

Figure 4.18
Event external prepositional phrase
Pugnatur ad novissimum agmen (cp. BC 1.80)

(66) They should not cut wood in the olive press room (Cato 67.1).

with a sufficiently long handle, he might be outside the door and only the blade and part of the handle would be in the press room with the wood: this scenario too is prohibited. So in the following example

(67) Alfenus interea *Romae* cum isto gladiatore vetulo cotidie pugnabat (Pro Quinct 29),

the semantics does not need to make Alfenus the target of the locative *Romae*: Alfenus is in Rome because the meaning of *pugno cum* requires the agent to be physically present in the (legal) fight, not just managing it from a distance like a drone operator. It is often more revealing, however, to analyze event external prepositional phrases as arguments of a functional head which augments the argument structure of the event. All events occur in some location. When not left to be inferred from the discourse context but expressed overtly, the location constitutes an additional predication. The head of this predication is the locative case ending or the preposition. Its internal argument is a set of events, denoted by the expression $\lambda e.\text{VP}(e)$, which is of type $<\varepsilon,t>$, and its external argument is the entity that is the location of the event or subevent, denoted by the variable *x*, where *x* is of type $<e>$. Consequently the locative inflection or the preposition has the type $<\varepsilon t,<e,\varepsilon t>>$, a function from a set of events to a function from an entity to a set of events. Although this approach may strike you as a semanticist's Duke of York gambit, it is well adapted for handling events that are not monadic, especially when there are two different locatives

(68) *ibi* arbores... *in lapide* statuito (Cato 18.4)
tota Tarracina tum *omnibus in parietibus* inscriptas fuisse litteras LLLMM (De Or 2.240).

In the first example (Cato 18.4) *statuito* is causative: (*x* CAUSE (there *y* GO-TO (*y* BE-IN *z*))). As is clear in Figure 4.19, the process subevent is located by the adjunct *ibi* and the state subevent is located by the argument *in lapide*.

Other locative prepositional phrases locate neither the event nor an event participant, but relate to the proposition expressed by a sentence. This type is seen for instance in ethnographic descriptions

(69) *in Gallia* a potentioribus... vulgo regna occupabantur (BG 2.1)
mulieres vero *in India*, cum est cuius earum vir mortuus, in certamen veniunt quam plurumum ille dilexerit; plures enim singulis solent esse nuptae (Tusc 5.78).

(67) Meanwhile at Rome Alfenus was fighting with this veteran gladiator every day (Pro Quinct 29).

(68) In this place fix the posts in the stone (Cato 18.4). That after that the letters LLLMM were inscribed on every wall throughout Tarracina (De Or 2.240).

(69) In Gaul the kingship was commonly seized by the more powerful leaders (BG 2.1). But the women in India, whenever the husband of one of them dies, enter into a competition as to which wife he loved the most; for multiple women are usually married to a single man (Tusc 5.78).

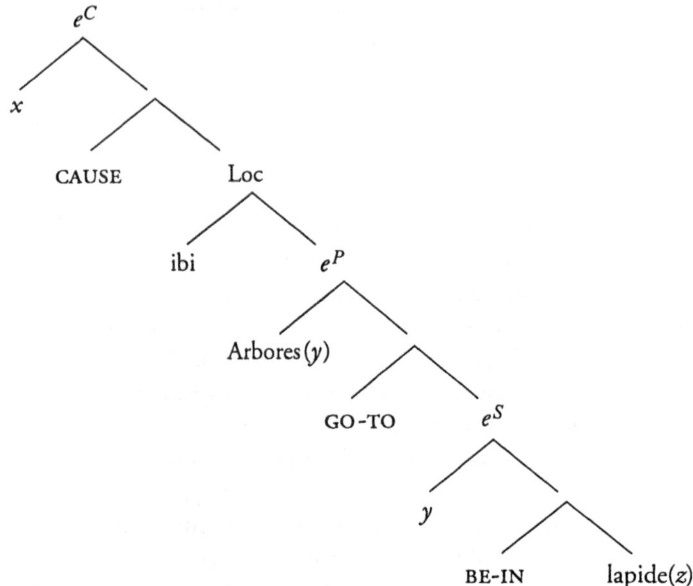

Figure 4.19
Locatives and subevents
Ibi arbores in lapide statuito (cp. Cato 18.4)

There is a test for such frame-setting prepositional phrases. Dropping them does not preserve truth. In the first example (BG 2.1), if you drop 'in Gaul,' it does not follow that powerful men commonly try to get royal power everywhere. Likewise in the second example (Tusc 5.78) it is not possible to drop *in India* and still keep a true proposition: the customs of women in India are not necessarily the customs of women worldwide. Contrast the entailment pattern of event internal locatives

(70) castraque *ad flumen Apsum* ponit (BC 3.13).

If you drop *ad flumen Apsum*, it is still true that Caesar pitched camp. It follows that frame-setting prepositional phrases are not part of the nucleus of the assertion but rather restrict the speaker's claim in some way. In both examples in (69) the prepositional phrase resembles the restrictor of a quantifier. *In Gallia* in the first example (BG 2.1) could be taken as the restrictor of *vulgo*, an adverb of quantification over events. A tripartite structure would result at logical form, as illustrated in Figure 4.20. *In India* in the second example (Tusc 5.78) could be taken as the restrictor of the generic quantificational modal covert in *veniunt*. These frame-setting prepositional phrases bear a close resemblance to domain adverbials ('Geometrically, those figures are not similar')

(70) And he pitched camp beside the river Apsus (BC 3.13).

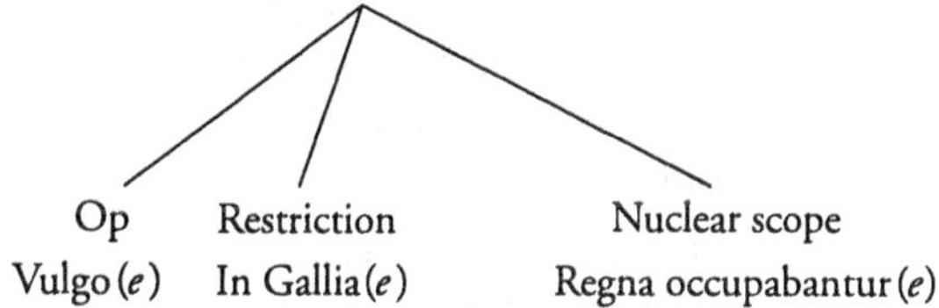

Figure 4.20
Frame-setting prepositions in a tripartite structure
In Gallia vulgo regna occupabantur (cp. BG 2.1)

(71) *in geometria*, si prima dederis, danda sunt omnia (De Fin 5.83)
in pictura, lumen non alia res magis quam umbra commendat (Pliny Ep 3.13.4).

In the first example (De Fin 5.83) *in geometria* does not belong exclusively to either the antecedent or the consequent, but restricts the condition as a whole. Since the semantic type of a condition is a truth value, the prepositional phrase must be an operator that takes a truth value as its argument, having the same type <t, t> as sentence adverbs. It is not entirely clear how the salient reading of such a frame-setting prepositional phrase is computed, particularly when it is not literally locative.

As we have seen, adnominal prepositional phrases are common with nouns denoting events or states, but they also occur with at least some object-denoting nouns not only in socalled closed word order but also in open word order. The following examples all involve individual level modification

(72) ut sibi insulam *in lacu Prilio* venderet (Pro Mil 74)
montes *supra Massiliam* incolebant (BC 1.34)
cum Piliae nostrae villam *ad Lucrinum*, vilicos, procuratores tradidissem (Ad Att 14.16.1)
Capuam et urbes *circa Capuam* occuparint (De Leg Agr 1.22).

In the first example (Pro Mil 74) it is not the event of selling the island that is located on Lake Prilius but the island itself; the transaction could take place anywhere. Purely in terms of truth conditions the second example (BC 1.34) could be analyzed as 'there is an event of mountain dwelling, and this event is located above Marseille,' but this won't work for the third example (Ad Att 14.16) where *ad Lucrinum* is sandwiched in after the first member of a list of things handed over. In the last example (De Leg Agr 1.22) *circa* is not reflexive, and an event of seizing Capua cannot be located *circa Capuam*.

(71) In geometry, if you grant the premises, you have to grant everything (De Fin 5.83). In painting, nothing enhances light more than shade (Pliny Ep 3.13.4).

(72) To sell him an island in Lake Prilius (Pro Mil 74). They inhabited the mountains above Massilia (BC 1.34). After I had handed over to our dear Pilia the villa at the Lucrine lake, its stewards and agents (Ad Att 14.16.1). They have seized Capua and the cities around Capua (De Leg Agr 1.22).

One of the commonest configurations for prepositional phrases that are not event locating is after the universal quantifier *omnis*, whether in a null head structure (*omnis* + prepositional phrase) or in the closed, left node word order (*omnis* + prepositional phrase + noun)

(73) *omnia*, iudices, *in hac causa* sunt misera (Pro Rosc Am 78)
quam sint *omnia in hominis figura* non modo ad usum verum etiam ad venustatem apta (ND 1.47)
mente consilioque divino *omnia in hoc mundo* ad salutem omnium conservationemque admirabiliter administrari (ND 2.132)
Socrates... *omnes ante eum* philosophi (Acad 1.15).

The semantics of all such examples is the same. The prepositional phrase supplies the restriction for the quantifier or an additional intersective qualification to its restrictor set: $\lambda Prep \lambda y \lambda Q \forall x. Prep(x,y) \rightarrow Q(x)$ or $\lambda Prep \lambda y \lambda P \lambda Q \forall x. P(x) \wedge Prep(x,y) \rightarrow Q(x)$.

Another notable function of prepositional phrases that are not event locating is to specify the comparison class for relative, gradable adjectives. This is very common with the superlative

(74) ipse *honestissimus inter suos* numerabatur (Pro Rosc Am 16)
Thales, qui *sapientissimus in septem* fuit (De Leg 2.26).

For another case see the first example in (15) (BG 7.13). In closed word order with a final light noun the status of the prepositional phrase as an argument of the superlative is particularly clear

(75) Hic *summo in Arvernis* ortus loco (BG 7.77)
Themistocles ille *summus Athenis* vir (Pro Arch 20).

Contrast an example like

(76) omnium rerum quae ad bellum usui erant summa erat *in eo oppido* facultas (BG 1.38),

which means that there was a very great supply of arms in Besançon, not that the greatest supply facility in Besançon was a military one.

FURTHER READING

Asbury et al. (2008); Carlson & van der Zee (2006); Herskovitz (1986); van der Zee & Slack (2003); Zwarts (2005); Zwarts & Winter (2000).

(73) Everything in this case, gentlemen of the jury, is pitiable (Pro Rosc Am 78). How everything in the human figure is designed not only for utility but also for beauty (ND 1.47). All things in this world are wonderfully regulated by the divine mind and intention for the safety and preservation of all (ND 2.132). Socrates... all the philosophers before him (Acad 1.15).

(74) He was reckoned to be the most honourable among his fellow citizens (Pro Rosc Am 16). Thales, who was the wisest among the Seven Sages (De Leg 2.26).

(75) He was born into the highest nobility among the Arverni (BG 7.77). The well-known Themistocles, a famous man at Athens (Pro Arch 20).

(76) There was in that town a very great supply of all types of military equipment (BG 1.38).

5 | QUANTIFICATION

The ability to make quantificational generalizations adds very significantly to the economy and expressive power of language. If speakers were limited to referential expressions, communication would be much more cumbersome and sometimes outright impossible. There are three main ways we can represent the meaning of quantified sentences. One is by undoing the quantification, unpacking it into conjunctions and disjunctions of referential sentences. Another is by use of a pronominal-like variable element bound by a quantifier. The third is in terms of relations between sets. Natural language arguably uses syntactic devices analogous to all three.

Consider the case of the notorious consular elections of 53 B.C.

(1) Candidati consulares *omnes* rei ambitus (Ad Att 4.18.3).

It doesn't matter for our present purposes whether we take the quantifier *omnes* as part of the subject noun phrase or as floated ('all the consular candidates are' or 'the consular candidates are all'). One way of representing the universal quantification in this sentence is simply by listing all the members of the set of consular candidates in a string of conjoined propositions (cp. Ad Qfr 3.2.3): *Dom(itius) reus est* ∧ *Mess(alla) reus est* ∧ *Sc(aurus) reus est* ∧ *Mem(mius) reus est*. The universal distributive force of the suffix *-que* 'and' in *quisque* 'everyone' and *undique* 'from everywhere' is evidence that conjunction and universal quantification are related in language. Similarly *nullus candidatus* could be represented by a disjunction inside the scope of a negative: ¬[*Dom reus est* ∨ *Mess reus est* ∨ *Sc reus est* ∨ *Mem reus est*]. But things are not always that simple

(2) *Tres* candidati rei fore putabantur (Ad Att 4.17.5).

To get the meaning of the indefinite cardinal we need [Dom ∧ Mess ∧ Sc] ∨ [Mess ∧ Sc ∧ Mem] ∨ [Dom ∧ Mess ∧ Mem] ∨ [Dom ∧ Sc ∧ Mem]. Since Cicero goes on to tell us who will prosecute each candidate, the disjunction is

(1) All the candidates for the consulship are being accused of bribery (Ad Att 4.18.3).
(2) It is thought that three candidates will be prosecuted (Ad Att 4.17.5).

resolved in favour of the first possibility; Memmius was added shortly after. Obviously, the larger the domain of quantification, the more cumbersome this system gets, even if we know exactly how many individuals are contained in the domain of quantification and if we are in a position to name all the referents, which is the case for examples like

(3) *Tres* nobilissimi Haedui... capti ad Caesarem perducuntur (BG 7.67)
Senatus... *quinque* viros misit (Livy 45.13.11).

The indefinite cardinal phrases are being used specifically here, and the authors actually go on to name the individuals in question: Cotus, Cavarillus and Eporedix in the first example (BG 7.67), and Buteo, Blasio, Musca, Balbus and Saturninus in the second (Livy 45.13).

The problems we have just seen with the referential representation of quantification are completely eliminated in the variable binding approach. Say that instead of naming the candidates for your representation of *candidati consulares omnes rei* you substituted a pronoun and imagined yourself pointing to each one in turn: *Ille reus est* ∧ *ille reus est* ∧ *ille reus est* ∧ *ille reus est*. You could abbreviate this string of propositions by using a variable element x to represent each pronoun in turn: then the resulting single open proposition *reus(x)* could be assigned sequentially to each individual in the domain of quantification, and for each assignment it would or would not be the case that the individual in question was being prosecuted. Now we can add a separate statement of universal ($\forall x$) or existential ($\exists x$) quantification, an appropriate connective and a binding relationship between the two x variables, and we get the familiar quantificational representations of predicate logic. Given a sentence like

(4) Lugent *omnes* provinciae (Verr 2.3.207)

(where again *omnes* can be adnominal or floated), instead of launching into a long series of conjoined sentences (*Luget Hispania Citerior* ∧ *Luget Macedonia* ∧ *Luget Cilicia* etc.), we simply say $\forall x.\text{provincia}(x) \rightarrow \text{Luget}(x)$: for all entities x, if x is a province, x is in mourning. $\forall$ is a propositional operator (type <t, t>), which takes a propositional formula with an open variable and binds it: see Figure 5.1. Similarly for existential quantification

(5) ad *aliquod* oppidum venit (cp. Verr 2.5.27),

instead of launching into a long disjunction of all the cities of Sicily (*Hennam venit* ∨ *Halaesam venit* ∨ *Panhormum venit* ∨ *Lilybaeum venit* etc.), we can quantify existentially over the cities of Sicily: $\exists x.\ \text{oppidum}(x) \wedge \text{venit}(\text{Verres}, x)$. This type of representation mirrors a verification procedure in which one ranges through all the individuals in the set denoted by the noun (the set of Roman provinces or the set of Sicilian towns) and checks them one by one (pointwise)

(3) Three Aeduans of the highest rank were captured and led to Caesar (BG 7.67). The senate sent five men (Livy 45.13.11).
(4) All the provinces are unhappy (Verr 2.3.207).
(5) He has come to some town (cp. Verr 2.5.27).

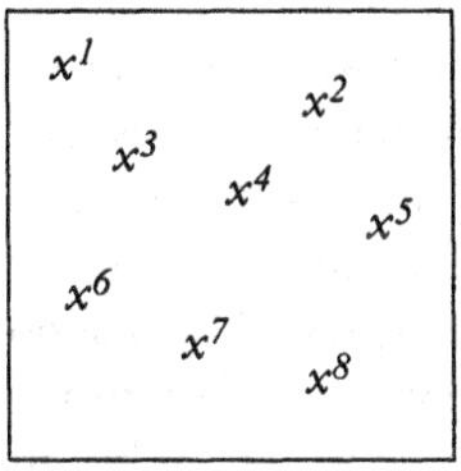

x^1 x^2 x^3 x^4 x^5 x^6 x^7 x^8

	A(x)	B(x)		A(x)	B(x)
x^1	T	T	x^2	F	F
x^3	T	T	x^4	F	T
x^5	F	T	x^6	T	T
x^7	T	T	x^8	T	T

Figure 5.1
First order quantification
Lugent omnes provinciae (Verr 2.3.207)

to see if they are also in the set denoted by the verb phrase. Use of the variable allows us to abstract away from the identity of the individual members of the set denoted by the noun and consequently to express explicitly the quantificational generalization that is not directly expressed but only implicit in the referential representation. Quantification with first order variables, while hardly homomorphic with the typical adnominal quantification of English and Latin, does have some sort of natural language analogue in English floating quantifiers and in Latin hyperbaton

(6) ut... *aliquam* Caesar ad insequendum facultatem haberet (BC 3.29)

where the quantifier is in an initial position separate from and scoping over the rest of the clause. However it can degenerate into a sort of listing with variables: one way of dealing with an example like

(7) *utraque* acies pro vallo stetit (Livy 28.14.2)

would be to say that there is a line x and there is a line y and x is not the same as y and x stood in front of the rampart and y stood in front of the rampart: $\exists x \exists y.\text{acies}(x) \wedge \text{acies}(y) \wedge x \neq y \wedge \text{stetit}(x) \wedge \text{stetit}(y)$. This is not very satisfactory: it makes an assertion out of a presupposition (the existence of the two lines) and glosses over the function that maps each army onto its own rampart. First order quantification is also not suitable for examples like

(8) Longe *plurimos* captivos ex Etruscis ante currum duxit (Livy 6.4.2),

for which we need a function to measure the cardinality of the set intersections and a function to compare different cardinalities. The point is not how many individuals in general were Etruscan captives led in front of Camillus' chariot, but what proportion of the captives were Etruscans. To get this meaning, it is no longer sufficient to look at individuals; we need to consider quantificational relations between whole sets of individuals: the cardinality of the intersection of

(6) So that Caesar might have some means of pursuing him (BC 3.29).
(7) Each line stood in front of its rampart (Livy 28.14.2).
(8) By far the most of the captives that he led in front of his chariot were from the Etruscans (Livy 6.4.2).

the set of captives from all three wars with the set of Etruscans is greater than that of the intersection of the set of captives from all three wars with the complement of the set of Etruscans, or greater than that of the set of captives less the set of Etruscan captives, or simply greater than half of the set of all captives, depending on how exactly you define *plurimi*. Not only quantificational expressions of this type but also those that can perfectly well be expressed by first order quantification can also be represented in terms of settheoretical relations rather than in terms of the individuals that are members of the sets. This third approach to quantification is called generalized quantifier theory after its mathematical model; 'generalized' means 'generalized from ∀ and ∃.'

Generalized quantifiers

Generalized quantifier theory comes in two flavours so to speak, curried and uncurried. The curried version as usual takes its arguments one at a time and provides in the generalized quantifier expression an exact analogue to the quantified noun phrase; so in an example like

(9) *omnes* hostes terga verterunt (BG 1.53)

the generalized quantifier *omnes hostes* is interpreted as the set of sets to which all the enemy belong (the set of properties that all the enemy have), and *terga verterunt* is a member of this set of sets (one of those properties). Functional application of the generalized quantifier expression (*omnes hostes*) to the verb phrase expression (*terga verterunt*) gives us the meaning of the complete sentence: <<e, t>,<t>> <e, t> → <t>. Since the subject noun without the quantifier is topical and the verb phrase is focal, in an example like this the compositional process tends to be pragmatically counterintuitive. We expect the topic to correspond to the argument and the focus to the function. In the uncurried version of generalized quantifier theory, the quantifier is seen as a second order relation between two sets. In the example just given, *omnes* is a quantificational relation between the set denoted by *hostes* and the set denoted by *terga verterunt*. This relational perspective on generalized quantifiers provides a less close fit with adnominal quantification than the set of sets perspective; on the other hand it gives a better fit with floated quantifiers and hyperbaton. The relational perspective is conceptually less complex, so that is the one we will use.

Let us look at the definitions of some Latin quantificational expressions in this perspective. We are not concerned here with their syntactic category or structure, nor with the details of the compositional semantics. The latter is often more complex than the preliminary truth-conditional characterization that we will provide, not only for syntactically complex quantifiers like *tot... quot* but also for basic quantifiers which may have nondeterminer as well as determiner readings. Many of these issues will receive more detailed attention in subsequent sections. Yet another question is the degree to which a posited set

(9) All the enemy turned tail (BG 1.53).

relation is explicit and directly accessible. Part-whole expressions, for instance, (*partim, universi*) do not behave like quantifiers either syntactically or semantically, but since they express the degree to which an event is exhaustive or every part of an entity is affected, they involve some form of implicit quantification. Take for instance

(10) Sabini... *maxima* pars... ab equitibus in flumen acti sunt (Livy 1.37.4).

This is tantamount to saying that most of the Sabines were driven into the river, but even with plural agreement (*acti sunt*) the expression chosen is partitive rather than properly quantificational.

In the following, 'A' represents the set denoted by the noun phrase of the generalized quantifier and 'B' the set with which it is related. The symbols represent a number of elementary set operations, most importantly intersection but also taking complements and cardinality measures and constructing relations on those measures.

NONNULLI: $A \cap B \neq \varnothing$

(11) temporibus illis in Hispania *non nullae* civitates rebus Cassii studebant (BAlex 62).

The intersection between the set of Spanish states (A) and the set of supporters of Cassius (B) is not empty (the two sets are not disjoint). Consequently the denotation of the quantifier *nonnulli* is $\lambda A \lambda B. A \cap B \neq \varnothing$: $\{x\text{: Civitas}(x)\} \cap \{y\text{: Studebat}(y, \text{Cass})\} \neq \varnothing$. This is illustrated schematically in Figure 5.2. Note that the supporters of Cassius that are not Spanish states ($B - A$, the part of B not in the intersection) and all entities that are neither Spanish states nor supporters of Cassius ($E - (A \cup B)$, the area outside the two circles) are not relevant to the computation; this applies to all quantifiers listed in this section except

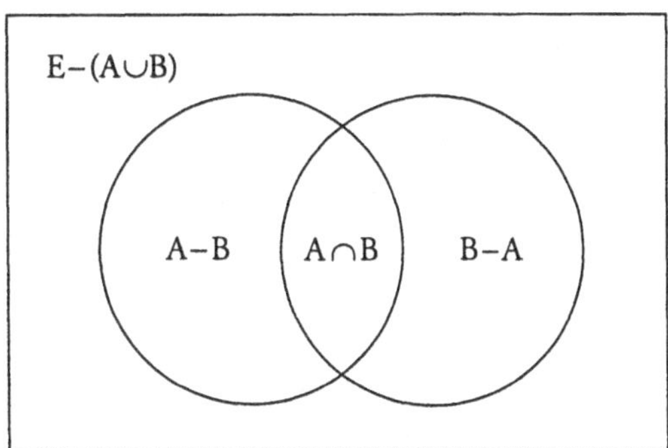

Figure 5.2
Generalized quantifier
Non nullae (*civitates* (A)) (*rebus Cassii studebant* (B)) (BAlex 62)

(10) The Sabines... The majority were driven into the river by the cavalry (Livy 1.37.4).
(11) At that time in Spain some states supported Cassius' side (BAlex 62).

soli. The irrelevance of B – A is termed conservativity, and the irrelevance of E – (A ∪ B) is termed extension; all that matters is A and A ∩ B. Finally, the identity of the states that supported Cassius is not relevant, all that matters is that there be some. The truth of the sentence is not affected if A and B are changed by a one-to-one mapping (bijection) so that they are differently populated. This is variously termed the principle of quantity, isomorphism or permutation invariance. The negative in *non nullae* is best taken not as a sentential negative operator but as a narrow scope negative operating on the quantifier; note that *interdum*, which occurs with *non nullos* in (29) below (Ad Att 15.26.2), is a positive polarity item ('sometimes does... some,' not 'doesn't ever... none') and so outside the scope of the negative.

OMNES: $A \subseteq B$

(12) cum *omnes* milites naves conscendissent (BC 1.27).

The set of soldiers is a subset of the set of those who boarded the ships. This is illustrated in Figure 5.3.

SOLI: $B \subseteq A$

(13) *soli* Aetoli decretum... carpebant (Livy 33.31.1).

The set of critics of the decree is a subset of the set of Aetolians. This is the mirror image of *omnes* above. Since $B - A = \varnothing$ and $E - (A \cup B) = E - A$, as already noted conservativity and extension are not true of *soli*.

NULLI: $A \cap B = \varnothing$

(14) *nullae* eum urbes accipiunt, nulla moenia (Livy 22.39.13).

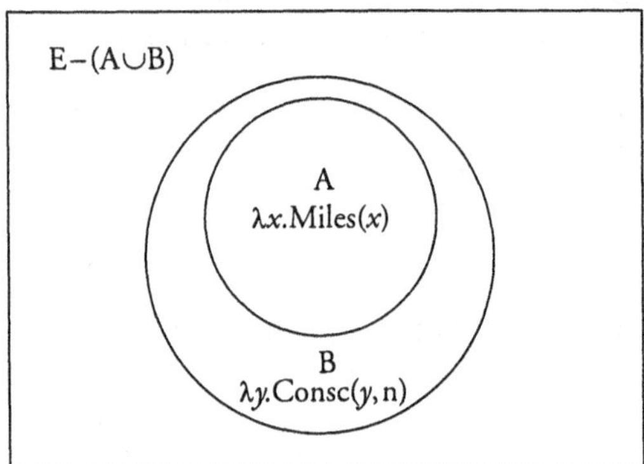

Figure 5.3
Universal generalized quantifier
Omnes milites naves conscendissent (BC 1.27)

(12) When all the soldiers had embarked (BC 1.27).
(13) Only the Aetolians criticized the decree (Livy 33.31.1).
(14) No cities receive him nor do any walls (Livy 22.39.13).

The intersection between the set of cities and the set of Hannibal-receivers is empty. This is illustrated in Figure 5.4.

TRES: $|A \cap B| = 3$

(15) Caesar legiones *tres* Massiliam adducit (BC 1.36).

The intersection of the set of legions with the set of entities led to Marseille has three members. This is the exact reading; the scalar implicature is discussed in the section on cardinals. See Figure 5.2 again, with the additional condition that the cardinality of the set resulting from the intersection is three.

AMPLIUS DUCENTI: $|A \cap B| \geq 200$

(16) cum *ducenti amplius* in ipsis faucibus portae cecidissent (Livy 44.31.9).

The intersection of the set of Illyrians with the set of casualties has at least two hundred members (taking *ducenti amplius* in its original appositional meaning as 'two hundred or more' rather than 'more than two hundred'): see the section on modified numerals. ≥ can be interpreted as a relation between the number two hundred and a set of numbers (one of which is the actual number of casualties).

NON AMPLIUS DUCENTI: $|A \cap B| \leq 200$

(17) In eo proelio *non amplius ducentos* milites desideravit (BC 3.99).

The intersection of the set of Caesar's soldiers with the set of the casualties in that battle has at most two hundred members (in principle any number from zero to two hundred).

ALIQUOT: $|A \cap B| \geq n$

(18) Accepi a te *aliquot* epistulas uno tempore quas tu diversis temporibus dederas (Ad Fam 7.18.1).

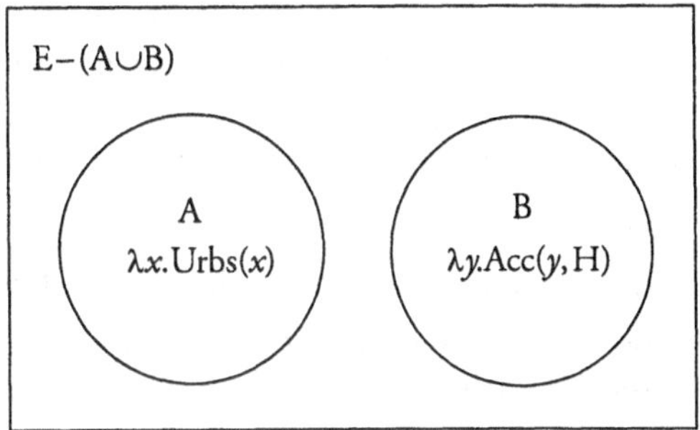

Figure 5.4
Negative universal generalized quantifier
Nullae eum urbes accipiunt (Livy 22.39.13)

(15) Caesar brought three legions to Massilia (BC 1.36).
(16) When at least two hundred had fallen right at the gate opening (Livy 44.31.9).
(17) In that battle he lost no more than two hundred regular soldiers (BC 3.99).
(18) I received several letters from you all at once which you had sent at different times (Ad Fam 7.18.1).

The intersection of the set of letters and the set of things I received has at least *n* members, where the interpretation of *n* depends on world knowledge and contextual factors. The example is interesting in requiring the same quantifier phrase to be read collectively for the delivery of the letters (a single event, *uno tempore*) and distributively for the posting of the letters (multiple events, *diversis temporibus*).

COMPLURES: $|A \cap B| \geq n$

(19) Reperti sunt *complures* nostri milites qui... scuta manibus revellerent (BG 1.52).

The definition is the same as for *aliquot* except that *n* is a larger number.

PAUCI: $|A \cap B| \leq n$

(20) perterritis omnibus... *pauci* lenunculi ad officium imperiumque conveniebant (BC 2.43).

The intersection of the set of small boats with the set of those assembling under orders has at most *n* members (*n* being a small number). Another way of interpreting this example is to assign a proportional reading to *pauci*: $|A \cap B| \leq n\% \, |A|$, only a small proportion of the boats assembled. In both cases the quantifier is interpreted relative to a standard of comparison depending partly on world knowledge and partly on the context. In this example we probably need to interpret *pauci* relative to the number of ships that might have been expected to assemble under normal, less panic-struck conditions, which introduces an intensional component into its meaning. For further details see the section on vague cardinals.

NEUTER: $|A| = 2 \wedge |A \cap B| = \varnothing$.

(21) *Neutra* acies laeta ex eo certamine abiit (Livy 1.2.2).

The cardinality of the set of battle lines is two and the intersection between the set of battle lines and the set of happily departing ones is empty. The cardinality clause is best taken as a presupposition rather than as part of the assertion.

TOT... QUOT: $|A \cap B| = |C \cap D|$

(22) *Tot* mala sum passus *quot* in aethere sidera lucent (Ov Trist 1.5.47).

The cardinality of the intersection of the set of evils with the set of things I have suffered is equal to the cardinality of the intersection of the set of stars with the set of things that shine in the sky.

(19) Several soldiers of ours turned out to have the courage to tear their shields from their hands (BG 1.52).

(20) With everyone terrified, just a few boats assembled to do their duty as commanded (BC 2.43).

(21) Neither army left that battle satisfied (Livy 1.2.2).

(22) I have suffered as many misfortunes as there are stars that shine in the sky (Ov Trist 1.5.47).

PLURES QUAM: $|A \cap B| > |C \cap B|$

(23) Haud ferme *plures* Saguntini cadebant *quam* Poeni (Livy 21.7.8).

The cardinality of the intersection of the set of Saguntines with the set of the fallen is hardly greater than the cardinality of the intersection of the set of Carthaginians with the set of the fallen. In addition to the pure cardinality reading just illustrated, there may also be a proportional reading according to which relatively more Saguntines fell than Carthaginians: $|A \cap B|/A > |C \cap B|/C$.

The default assumption is that a quantifier is a function that applies to a set to yield a function from a set to a truth value, and consequently has the type <<e,t>, <<e,t>,t>>>. This works fine for some examples but less well for others

(24) *omnis* surculus rigore torpet (Col 4.29.3)
omnes naves naufragarunt (Petr 76).

It is straightforward to assign the type <e,t> to (generic) *surculus* in the first example (Col 4.29), compare English 'every twig,' but less so to the (episodic) definite *naves* in the second example (Petr 76) ('all the ships'). One solution is to typeshift the latter from <e> (the individual entity that is the maximal contextually available set of ships) to <e,t>, another is to assign the alternative type <<e>, <<e,t>,t>>> to some quantifiers, a third is to say that 'all' and 'only' are not quantifiers at all but modifiers of definite noun phrases. The two examples are illustrated in Figures 5.5-6 on the alternative type approach.

We will finish this brief review of some quantifiers by noting one further form of representation called restricted quantification, which combines some features

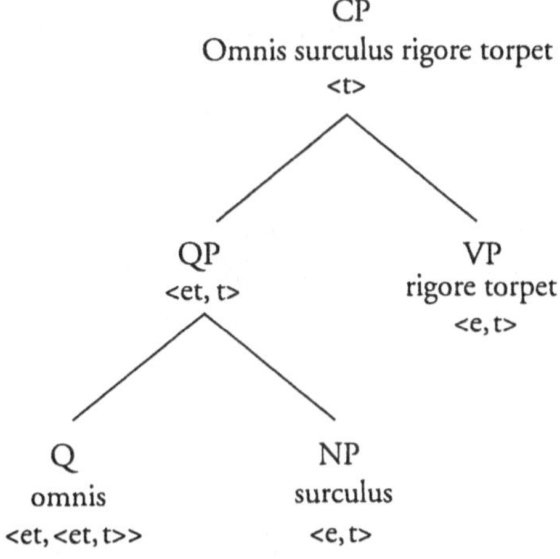

Figure 5.5
Quantifier in type <et, <et, t>>
Omnis surculus rigore torpet (Col 4.2.93)

(23) Hardly more Saguntines fell than Carthaginians (Livy 21.7.8).
(24) Every twig is numb with frost (Col 4.29.3). All the ships got wrecked (Petr 76).

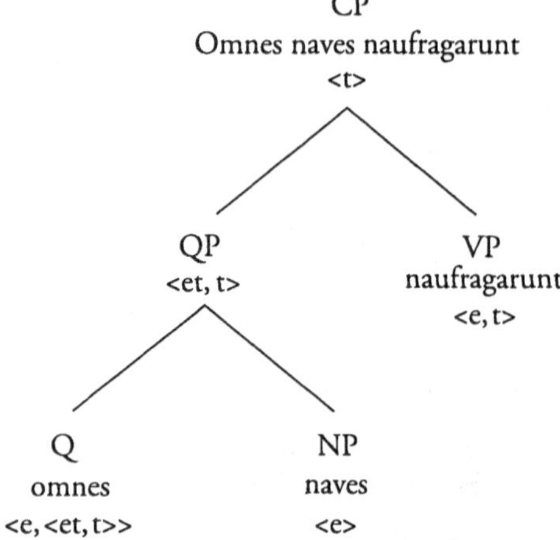

Figure 5.6
Quantifier in type <e, <et, t>>
Omnes naves naufragarunt (Petr 76)

of generalized quantifiers with others of first order quantifiers. In an example like (12) above (*omnes milites naves conscendissent*), the quantifier *omnes* was defined as a relation between sets, contributing the meaning $A \subseteq B$. The first set (A) is based on the noun (*milites*) and the second set (B) is based on the verb phrase (*naves conscendissent*), and the resulting overall structure is tripartite, that is it has three fields: Q (A, B), where (A, B) is a member of the set of pairs of sets that stand in the Q relation. Instead of representing A and B as sets, we can also represent them as open formulae: so for A, instead of the set λx.Miles (x), we can write the open formula Miles (x) 'x is a soldier,' and likewise for B. In this formalism quantification is not over all individuals in the universe of discourse but is restricted to individuals that are members of the set A (whence the term "restricted quantification"). The quantifier takes two arguments: the first argument (A) is called the restriction, and the second argument (B) is called the nuclear scope. The quantifier binds the variables in the two open formulae: Q(x). A(x). B(x), for instance OMNES (x). miles (x). conscendissset (x, navem) 'for every assignment of the variable x to a contextually relevant soldier, x boarded a ship.'

Strong and weak

As we saw in the preceding section, the idea that quantification involves a relation between two sets gives us a general framework for the definition of a wide range of natural language quantifiers. However, when it comes to the assignment of the two sets to their respective fields in the tripartite structure, there is arguably less uniformity. The problem is not limited to a quirky case like that of *solus* 'only,' which requires the A set to be mapped to the nuclear scope and the B set to the restriction, as opposed to vice versa

(25) *soli* Aetoli decretum... carpebant (Livy 33.31.1);

cp. (13) above: SOLI(x). Carpebat(x, decretum). Aetolus(x). It shows up as a systematic difference in interpretation (and consequently in compositional semantics) across quantifiers in general, relating to how the meaning of a quantifier interacts with the structure of information in discourse. This is a manifestation of the context sensitivity of quantifiers; we will discuss related issues (domain selection, context sensitivity of gradable quantifiers) in later sections. Consider a pair of examples like the following

(26) Ab eo coloniae *aliquot* deductae (Livy 1.3.7)
uniuscuiusque civitatis... provinciam... quibus in rebus *nonnullae* civitates sua sponte auxilia mittebant, item *nonnullae* portas contra cludebant (BHisp 1).

In the first example (Livy 1.3) the quantifier gets an existential interpretation, as in the existential reading of 'Some students were in the library,' where *some* tends to be pronounced *sm* (as in *sm more*); this is called the weak reading. The sentence serves to establish the existence of colonies founded by Latinus Silvius. In the second example (BHisp 1) the quantifier gets a proportional interpretation, as in 'Some students were in the library, some were out playing soccer,' where *some* tends to be pronounced like the noun *sum*. The sentence says that some Spanish states cooperated with the younger Pompey and some closed their gates; this is called the strong reading. The first example contains a verb of creation, so if you discard *ab eo* and try to interpret it with a strong quantifier rather than a weak one, you get both an understatement and a tautology: if a colony already exists, it must have been founded, and that applies not just to some but to all of the colonies. In the second example the Spanish states are already established in the previous discourse, so they should not be introduced as new discourse referents by a plural indefinite; the fact that the quantifiers are contrastive also makes an existential interpretation less likely.

Here are some examples of quantifiers that have only a strong reading

(27) uti... *omnes* Germani Rhenum transirent (BG 1.31)
dux *uterque* suos adhortatur (Livy 3.18.7)
duobus anguibus... Si *neuter* anguis emissus esset (De Div 2.62)
in dicendo leviter *unus quisque* locus plerumque tangitur (Rhet Her 4.10)
unus quisque eorum locorum quos exposui sua quaedam habet membra (Top 26).

(25) Only the Aetolians criticized the decree (Livy 33.31.1).

(26) Several colonies were founded by him (Livy 1.3.7). Of each state... the province... In these circumstances, some states sent reinforcements of their own accord, while some shut their gates to him (BHisp 1).

(27) All the Germans would cross the Rhine (BG 1.31). Each leader urged on his men (Livy 3.18.7). Two snakes... If neither snake had been released (De Div 2.62). In speaking each subject is usually touched upon lightly (Rhet Her 4.10). Each of the subjects that I have set out has some subdivisions of its own (Top 26).

In the last two examples (Rhet Her 4.10; Top 26) the distributive universal quantifier *unus quisque* appears with a regular and a partitive restriction respectively; it ranges through each member of a bounded set. The standard handy diagnostic for strong quantifiers is their ungrammaticality in the English existential construction ('There are some cats in the garden'). The empirical details of existential constructions are quite intricate and vary from one language to another; the Latin existential construction is less constrained than its English counterpart, at least in that it allows definites. In any case the examples in (27) have strong readings and are ungrammatical in most contexts in the English existential: '*There were all the Germans, *There was each leader, *There was neither snake, *There was each topic'; partitives are not quite so bad. Another diagnostic is failure of symmetry. A quantifier is symmetric if its A and B arguments can be flipped without affecting the truth of the assertion

(28) *Aliquot* publici sacerdotes mortui eo anno sunt (Livy 25.2.1).

If some state priests died that year, then some of the people who died that year were state priests. So *aliquot* is symmetric. But if all the state priests died that year, it does not follow that all of the people who died that year were state priests, so 'all' is not symmetric. When symmetry fails, the quantifier is mostly strong. However, while both *most* and *more than half* are asymmetric, only the former is excluded from the English existential construction; the latter is a type of counting expression.

Some quantifiers have both a strong (S) and a weak (W) reading

(29) si... priorum regum *alicui* regnum extorsisset (Livy 2.1.3) (S)
aliqua inveniemus blandimenta quibus saporem mutemus (Petr 141) (W)
orationes scripsit *aliquot* (Brut 286) (W)

insulas quae barbaros adiuverant... plerasque ad officium redire coegit, *nonnullas* vi expugnavit (Nepos 1.7.1) (S)
Sed tamen *non nullos* interdum iacit igniculos viriles (Ad Att 15.26.2) (W)

cum Eumenis beneficiis muneribusque omnes Graeciae civitates et *plerique* principum obligati sunt (Livy 42.5.3) (S)
In hoc erant numero *complures* Pompei milites (BC 3.103) (W)

"*duos*," inquit, "fratrum manibus dedi; tertium..." (Livy 1.25.12) (S)
Erant aenea praeterea *duo* signa (Verr 2.4.5) (W)

(28) Some state priests died that year (Livy 25.2.1).

(29) If Brutus had deprived one of the earlier kings of royal power (Livy 2.1.3). We will find some condiments with which to change the flavour (Petr 141). He wrote some speeches (Brut 286). The islands that had helped the barbarians... He forced several of them to return to allegiance and he took some by storm (Nepos 1.7.1). Every now and again he shows some sparks of virility (Ad Att 15.26.2). Although all the states of Greece and many of their leading citizens were under an obligation to Eumenes because of his kindnesses and generosity (Livy 42.5.3). Among these were many soldiers of Pompey (BC 3.103). "I have given two to the shades of my brothers," he said; "the third..." (Livy 1.25.12). There were in bronze also two other statues (Verr 2.4.5).

(30) *multi* exsulum caede sua foedavere templum (Livy 3.18.10) (S)
Erant enim circum castra Pompei *permulti* editi atque asperi colles (BC 3.43) (W)

nulla praecipitia saxa, nullae rupes obstabant (Livy 38.23.1) (S)
Illic te *nulli* poterunt corrumpere ludi (Prop 2.19.9) (W).

The last set of examples with *nulli* illustrates the strong–weak distinction particularly clearly. The strong reading of the Livy example says that none of the rocks they encountered hindered their flight; the mountainous and rugged nature of the terrain is established in the context. The weak reading says that there were no rocks or cliffs to hinder their flight. The weak reading, but not the strong reading, can be used when there were no rocks or cliffs at all (which is at odds with the context). The weak reading of the Propertius example says that Cynthia won't be corrupted by any theatrical shows because there won't be any; the strong reading says that none of the theatrical shows to be given there will be of the type to corrupt her; they will all be of the type that strengthens moral fibre. So in extensional contexts weak quantifiers assert (or in the case of *nulli* negate) the existence of the intersection of the A and B sets (and consequently the existence of the A set), whereas strong quantifiers presuppose the existence of the A set. Both of these generalizations need some qualification. Particularly for strong quantifiers making a universal claim, the presupposition is actually just a strong implicature, since it can be cancelled in facetious remarks like 'None of the shows will corrupt Cynthia because there aren't going to be any,' or 'Every student in Prof. Jones' verse composition class is nine feet tall,' which is true when there are no students in the class. This doesn't work with weak quantifiers, since they assert existence ('(There are) three students in Prof. Jones' verse composition class (who) are nine feet tall'). The restriction of a universal quantifier is downward entailing, and the more restrictive the modification of the noun, the greater the likelihood that few or no entities will match the description; this effect is particularly noticeable with postmodifiers like relative clauses. *Si quis* can be used to explicitly cancel the existential presupposition. In intensional contexts strong quantifiers continue to presuppose the existence of the A set, but weak quantifiers assert only the possible existence of the $A \cap B$ set ('If you find three mistakes, I'll buy you a beer'). Compare the strong and weak readings of the quantifiers in the following intensional examples

(31) Ex quattuor consulibus *duos* occidisse (Livy 23.11.9)
Quid titulum poscis? Versus *duo* tresve legantur (Mart 12.2.16)

(30) Many of the exiles stained the temple with their blood (Livy 3.18.10). For there were very many high, rugged hills around Pompey's camp (BC 3.43). No steep rocks and no cliffs could stop them (Livy 38.23.1). There no shows will be able to corrupt you (Prop 2.19.9).
(31) That of the four consuls he had killed two (Livy 23.11.9). Why do you ask for a title? Let two or three verses be read (Mart 12.2.16).

(32) Marcellus... si Syracusas cepisset *duo* templa se Romae dedicaturum voverat (Verr 2.4.123)
teque puta cunnos, uxor, habere *duos* (Mart 11.43.12).

The two consuls and the two verses are real, while the two *templa* and one of the two *cunni* are only possible objects.

To verify the weak reading one needs only to check the intersection of the A and B sets, to verify the strong reading one needs to check the whole of the A set, which consequently has to be accessible in the discourse context. So the strong (proportional) reading is appropriate when the A set is already established in the discourse or easily accommodated into the discourse and can be infelicitous in out-of-the-blue sentences. For the strong reading the A set belongs to the restriction in the tripartite quantificational structure: NONNULLAE (x). Civitas (x). Mittebat (x, auxilia). But the weak (existential) reading is appropriate when the existence of the A set is not presupposed but rather asserted. In this case the A set belongs to the nuclear scope: ALIQUOT (x). Colonia $(x) \wedge$ Deduxit (Silvius, x). For the strong reading quantification is restricted to the members of the A set; for the weak reading quantification is over the (contextually restricted) universe of discourse: A = 'exists.' Since this latter domain of quantification is trivial, the restriction is left empty. Then strong quantifiers are tripartite (in the sense that they have two arguments, the restriction and the nuclear scope), and weak quantifiers are bipartite (in the sense that they have just one argument, the nuclear scope). This is the same distinction as that between *who?* and *which child?*, and between *someone* and *some child*, a distinction that is sometimes referred to as "discourse linking." Consider again a couple of examples

(33) *omnes* milites naves conscendissent (BC 1.27)
Is enim *tres* libros scripsit (Tusc 1.77).

The first example (BC 1.27) has a strong quantifier: the soldiers (the A set) are the restrictor set and those who boarded the ships (the B set) are in the nuclear scope: $\forall x.$Miles$(x) \rightarrow$ Conscendit$(x,$ navem$)$. The second example has a weak quantifier; it introduces a set of books each of which was written by Dicaearchus and then counts the set (gives its cardinality): $\exists X. \forall x \in X \rightarrow$ Liber$(x) \wedge$ Scripsit(Dicaearchus, $x) \wedge |X| = 3$. X consists of the intersection of the A and B sets, the two conjoined predicates. Even those quantifiers that have a weak reading as well as a strong one do not license it when the predicate is an individual level (permanent) property: 'Three students are in the library' can mean either 'Three of the students are in the library' (strong) or 'There are three students in the library' (weak), but 'Three students are Norwegian' can only have a strong reading. This is the case for indefinites generally. There is a third reading (meaning 'The number of students in the library is three'); it is bipartite and

(32) Marcellus had vowed that if he captured Syracuse he would dedicate two temples at Rome (Verr 2.4.123). Think of yourself as having two cunts, wife (Mart 11.43.12).

(33) All the soldiers boarded the ships (BC 1.27). For he wrote three books (Tusc 1.77).

serves to count a set already established in the discourse or easily accommodated. This reading is discussed in the section on cardinals; since the set is definite, there is no existential quantifier in the count reading.

An analysis of the distinction between weak and strong quantifiers needs to refer to quite a number of different concepts (domain restriction, discourse linking, partitivity, proportionality, scalar implicature, definiteness, specificity): these are partly related to each other but not overlapping. We will briefly comment on a few of them. Domain restriction is associated with strong quantifiers and strong readings of weak quantifiers, but in a sense weak quantifiers are also domain restricted, since they are interpreted relative to the spatiotemporal context of the event

(34) aut ipsum sua manu fecissse... aut per *aliquos* liberos aut servos (Pro Rosc Am 79).

Although the quantifier is weak, its domain is implicitly limited to the spatiotemporal context of the murder, as Cicero goes on to argue that Roscius couldn't have got any free men to murder his father at Rome since he was always on his farm in the country. In principle strong 'some' triggers a scalar implicature ('some, but not all, of A'), whereas weak 'some' has nothing to say about the proportion of A that are in B. But in some contexts there may still be an implicature of nonexhaustivity

(35) impositis copiis in naves... Naves quoque *aliquot* Poenorum disiectae in alto a classe Romana... capiuntur. (Livy 30.19.5)
Erant in Romana iuventute adulescentes *aliquot*... adsueti more regio vivere (Livy 2.3.2).

In the first example (Livy 30.19) the quantifier is strong and the implicature is 'some but not all of the Carthaginian ships were captured by the Romans.' The second example (Livy 2.3) is existential and the quantifier is weak: the proportion of Roman youth that had royalist tendencies is not an issue, but there is an implicature that not all of them were royalists. On the other hand, with a verb of creation as in the third example in (29) (Brutus 286: 'he wrote some speeches'), there is no such implicature. The set $A \cap B$ associated with a weak quantifier may be specific or nonspecific

(36) In hoc erant numero *complures* Pompei milites (BC 3.103)
Erant apud Caesarem in equitum numero Allobroges *duo* fratres, Raucillus et Egus (BC 3.59).

(34) That either he committed the deed with his own hand or through some others, free men or slaves (Pro Rosc Am 79).

(35) Putting his troops onto ships... Also some of the ships of the Carthaginians, scattered on the open sea, were captured by the Roman fleet (Livy 30.19.5). There were among the Roman youth some young men accustomed to live in the royal style (Livy 2.3.2).

(36) Among these were many soldiers of Pompey (BC 3.103). There were with Caesar among his cavalry two Allobrogian brothers, Raucillus and Egus (BC 3.59).

The same applies to strong readings of weak quantifiers, as in the first example in (35) (Livy 30.19): the contextually supplied restriction (the ships of the Carthaginians) is a definite set, but the $A \cap B$ intersection (the ones captured by the Romans) need not be specific. Strong quantifiers typically involve a proportion of a definite set recoverable from the discourse; but proportionality is not restricted to episodically associated discourse-linked sets, since it is also needed for quantifiers in generic sentences

(37) aves... ambulant *aliquae* ut cornices, saliunt aliae ut passeres (NH 10.111).

Cardinals

Cardinality is a dimension of sets, and numbers are degrees on the scale that measures that dimension. The cardinality function measures a set in terms of how many atomic members it contains; it is usually written $|X|$, but $\delta^{Num}(X)$ would do as well. It maps a set X onto a numerical degree. While the adjectival degree function δ maps individuals to degrees and consequently has the type <e, d>, if plurals are treated as sets rather than as complex individuals, cardinality is a function from sets to degrees and consequently has the type <<e, t>, d>. Numbers, as noted, are degrees, and degrees are individuals, like definite descriptions, so they have type <d>. A number can be used with this type as the specificational predicate of a definite subject

(38) Eius partes sunt *quattuor* (De Inv 2.71)
C.F. Orationis quot sunt partes? C.P. *Quattuor.* (De Part Or 4).

Cicero's answer in the second example (De Part Or 4) says that a speech has four parts: discounting the genericity, $|\iota X.\forall x \in X \rightarrow \text{Pars}(x, \text{orationis})| = 4$. More often cardinals are used with one of a range of higher types. We have already given examples of cardinals as strong and weak quantifiers in (29) and (31) in the preceding section. The weak reading is an existential, which introduces a plural discourse referent

(39) In his inventae sunt *quinque* imagunculae matronarum, in quibus una sororis amici tui (Ad Att 6.1.25).

The sentence introduces a set of statuettes of Roman ladies of cardinality five: $\exists X.|X| = 5 \wedge \forall x \in X \rightarrow \text{Imaguncula}(x) \wedge \text{Inventa}(x)$. The A set that is intersected with the B set (combines with it by predicate modification) is not already in the discourse domain but is introduced into the discourse by existential quantification. Problems with this analysis, which treats the cardinal as a quantificational adjective, will be discussed below. There is another reading that simply serves to count a set

(37) Some birds walk, like crows, others hop, like sparrows (NH 10.111).

(38) Its subdivisions number four (De Inv 2.71). C.F. How many parts does a speech have? C.P. Four. (De Part Or 4).

(39) Five small busts of married women were found in it, among which one of your friend's sister (Ad Att 6.1.25).

(40) *nonaginta* vixit annos (Luc 16)
In eo proelio ex equitibus nostris interficiuntur *quattuor et septuaginta* (BG 4.12).

Unlike the existential reading, the count reading does not assert the existence of the A set: both the A set and the B set represent presupposed or easily accommodated information. The first example (Luc 16) just says that the number of years that Carneades lived was 90, the second (BG4.12) that the number of Roman cavalry the Gauls killed was 74. The existence of the Roman cavalry is part of the presupposition (like the years in the obviously nonproportional first example); if they were involved in a battle, then it is natural to think that some of them got killed; and the assertion is simply that the intersection of *equites nostri* and *interficiuntur* has a cardinality of 74: $|\{\text{equites nostri}\} \cap \{\text{interficiuntur}\}| = 74$. Like the existential reading, the count reading is bipartite; in the former both sets are typically new information, in the latter both sets are given information. It is a semantically slightly more complicated version of the specificational predicate numeral in (38): to take the second example again, the cardinality of the set X, all members of which were Roman cavalrymen and were killed, is 74: $|\iota X. \forall x \in X \rightarrow \text{Eques}(x) \wedge \text{Interficitur}(x)| = 74$. Leftward movement of the topical material in the syntax leaves only the numeral in the focus position, so the syntactic structure reflects the semantic partition typical of the count reading. Compare the following examples

(41) Haec partes habet *tres* (De Inv 1.15)
Fluminis erat altitudo pedum circiter *trium* (BG 2.18).

Numerals can also be used as attributive modifiers, mostly in definite phrases

(42) His *quattuor* causis (De Or 2.339)
quattuor hos versus (Ov Trist 2.246)
ex *quattuor* urbanis tribubus (Livy 45.15.5).

Both normally have the exactly reading (see below). Attributive numerals can be a type of intersective adjective, in which case they are quantitative modifiers. A number *n*, for instance *quattuor*, would restrict the set X to the subset of X having cardinality 4 ('the four students,' not 'the five students'). However, as in the examples cited, they are normally descriptive rather than restrictive adjectives, so they serve to add cardinality information to the description of a single given set rather than to pick out one of a number of different sets. The cardinality function is not inside the scope of the definite iota operator; rather its argument is anaphoric to the definite description. So the last example (Livy 45.15) is not dis-

(40) He lived to be ninety years old (Luc 16). In that battle the casualties among our cavalry were seventy-four (BG 4.12).

(41) It has three parts (De Inv 1.15). The depth of the river was about three feet (BG 2.18).

(42) To these four causes (De Or 2.339). These four verses (Ov Trist 2.246). Of the four city tribes (Livy 45.15.5).

tinguishing between two sets of city tribes having different cardinalities but means 'out of the set of city tribes, which you will recall numbered four.'

The interpretation of cardinals is complicated by two factors, monotonicity and scalar implicature. Consider the following examples

(43) Accepi Idibus Sextilibus *quattuor* epistulas a te missas, unam... alteram... tertiam... quartam... (Ad Att 3.15.1)
Si memini, fuerant tibi *quattuor*, Aelia, dentes: expulit una *duos* tussis et una duos. (Mart 1.19.1).

Since Cicero received four letters from Atticus, it is also literally true that he received three, so what would be wrong with him saying 'I received three letters'? And if he had received five letters, he could still have truthfully said 'I received four letters' or 'I received three letters.' In the Cicero example *quattuor* is a weak existential quantifier; in the Martial example *quattuor* is a count quantifier (it serves to count (all of) Aelia's teeth), but *duos* is a strong quantifier ('two of them'), which shows that a similar problem of interpretation affects strong quantifiers too. If the first cough expelled two of Aelia's four teeth, it is literally true that it also expelled one; but if it had expelled just one, that would have ruined the point of Martial's epigram. The problem arises because numerals are intrinsically associated with a scale; cardinality is a type of degree measure function. Asserting a higher number entails the assertion of lower numbers. This is known as (downward) monotonicity. The direction of monotonicity is reversed in negative contexts: I received four letters entails that I received three, but I didn't receive four letters entails that I didn't receive five. Monotonicity with collective predicates involves participation in the collaborative effort, not single-handedly achieving the goal ('Five legions defeated the Helvetii'). Speakers choose the highest number on the scale for the truth of which they are willing to take responsibility: choosing a lower number would not be maximally informative, and choosing a higher number would lead to possible or known falsehood. Listeners are aware of this strategy and interpret the sentence accordingly. This is termed a scalar implicature: the computation of the implicature is in terms of the relevant scalar alternatives, not in terms of any other ways in which the speaker could conceivably have phrased the sentence. For instance, scalar implicature leads the reader to interpret Martial as saying that Aelia had no more than four teeth prior to the unfortunate coughing episodes and that no more than two teeth were expelled in each coughing episode. If the speaker chooses a nonmaximal number ('equal to or more than'), the result is called an 'at least reading'; if, as in the examples in (43), the speaker chooses the maximal number ('no more than and no less than'), it is called an 'exactly reading.'

According to one view the at least reading is the basic meaning of the cardinal, and the exactly reading is derived from it by applying the scalar implica-

(43) On the Ides of August I received four letters you sent, one... another... a third... a fourth (Ad Att 3.15.1). If I remember right, you used to have four teeth, Aelia: one cough expelled two, another cough the other two (Mart 1.19.1).

ture. On the other, more intuitive, view which we will adopt here, the basic meaning is the exactly meaning; the scalar implicature is not a modification to the basic meaning but part of it. (The socalled at least reading may actually be the exact reading of a subset.) The cardinality measure function takes the complete A set, intersects it with the complete B set and returns the maximal resulting number. The count reading of numerals only has the exact reading; it is related to the predicate numeral. As already suggested, count sentences are probably semantically specificational, so that 'Aelia has four teeth' means 'The number of teeth that Aelia has is four,' the same sort of construction as 'The height of the tower is 25 feet' and 'The lady with the handbag is Mrs Thatcher.' The existential reading is more complicated. Asserting the existence of a set with cardinality = (exactly) 4 does not preclude the existence of a superset with cardinality 5 or 6, so the at least reading is automatically available. For the exactly reading to go through we have to ensure that there exist no other sets that are also intersections of A and B: the assertion has to be exhaustive. One way of doing this for the example of Cicero's four letters in (43) is to add a clause to the effect that any set of letters Cicero received from Atticus on the Ides of August is a subset of the set of four letters whose existence is asserted in the sentence.

Although cardinals typically have the exactly reading, the scalar implicature does not always click in. If someone asks you whether Bill has two kids, you can answer either 'Yes, he has three,' or 'No, he has three,' according as you interpret the quantifier with an 'at least' or an 'exactly' reading (perhaps reflecting a variation between an existential and a count reading). A nonmaximal number may be used because it is linked to a separate subevent rather than to the overall event ('Three hostages were killed; in fact five were, because they killed some more later'). It is also perfectly possible for the scalar implicature to be cancelled by a numerical modifier (see the next section). There are discourse contexts in which the exactly reading is inappropriate, for instance the borrowing context of 'Have you got two spring onions?' (if you've got two, you probably have six, so this is just existential quantification without a maximality provision). The object of the speaker is not to get an exhaustive count of how many spring onions you have, but to find out if you have available at least the number he needs (threshold reading): on one scenario he needs exactly two, and you have at least two. Similar nonexhaustive readings are common with singular indefinites ('I've got a blue shirt'), which is not surprising since weak cardinal arguments are plural indefinites, and with tell-me-some questions ('Who was killed in the battle?'). On the other hand the exactly reading is natural in answers to 'How many?' questions, since they are count readings

(44) EP. quanti eam emit?... Quot minis? TH. Tot: *quadraginta* minis. (Pl Ep 52).

(44) EP. How much did he buy her for? For how many minae? TH. This many: for forty minae (Pl Ep 52).

Questions that ask for a minimum number have a lower bound rather than an upper bound

(45) MED. I, arcesse homines qui illunc ad me deferent. SEN. Quot sunt satis? MED. ....*quattuor, nihilo minus.* (Pl Men 952).

Satis sunt is a sufficiency predicate and upward monotonic: if four are enough, then five are enough but three is not enough. Strong focus allows only the exactly reading

(46) *duas* in castris legiones retinuit, reliquas... praemisit (BC 3.75);

the hyperbaton gives syntactic confirmation of the contrastive focus, and the only possible interpretation is 'exactly two.' Similarly in English 'A bicycle has two wheels and so does a car' is all right as a sort of weak joke provided one does not put strong stress on the numeral, since cars do not have exactly two wheels.

At least readings easily arise in sentences that use a minimum to generalize over habitual or modally accessible situations ('Students always take / have to take three courses, but they often take more'). Contextual information helps to distinguish such at least readings from exactly readings and from at most readings ('Students can take six courses, but they usually take three'). In the following examples with the modal verb *debeo* the intended interpretation is overtly spelled out

(47) Elocutio commoda et perfecta... *tres* res in se *debet* habere, elegantiam, conpositionem, dignitatem (Rhet Her 4.17)
Non plures autem super terram eminere *debet* truncus quam tres aut *quattuor* pedes (Sen Ep 86.18)
minimum *duo* esse *debent* verba in quibus sit similitudo (Varro LL 9.53).

The first example (Rhet Her 4.17) has a broad scope indefinite plural object: there is a set of exactly three things, specifically elegance, composition and dignity, and in all teleologically accessible worlds these are components of good style. In the second example (Ep 86.18) the at most reading is spelled out by *non plures*: in all teleologically accessible worlds the degrees of height of the trunk are less than or equal to four feet. In the last example (LL 9.53) *minimum* spells out the threshold reading: in all worlds the cardinality of a set of words that are alike is equal to or greater than two. Here are a couple of examples with *licet* 'it is possible' to illustrate existential quantification over possible worlds

(48) ut X servorum domino *quinque* liberare *liceret*, quia usque ad dimidiam partem eius numeri manumittere ei conceditur (Gaius Inst 1.45)
pro equite uno *tres* pedites *liceret* dare (Livy 29.15.7).

(45) MEN. Go and fetch some men to bring him to my house. SEN. How many are enough? MED. Four, no less (Pl Men 952).

(46) He held back two legions in camp and sent the others ahead (BC 3.75).

(47) An appropriate and polished style should have three properties: elegance, composition and distinction (Rhet Her 4.17). But the trunk should not project above the ground more than three or four feet (Sen Ep 86.18). It takes at least two words for there to be likeness (Varro LL 9.53).

(48) For a master of ten slaves to be allowed to free five, since he is permitted to manumit up to half that number (Gaius Inst 1.45). That it should be permissible to furnish three infantrymen in place of one cavalryman (Livy 29.15.7).

The first example (Inst 1.45) says that there exist deontically accessible worlds in which the master of ten slaves manumits five or less slaves by will (but, by scalar implicature, not more than five). The second example (Livy 29.15) says that there exist deontically accessible worlds in which the colonies furnished three infantrymen in place of one cavalryman; less than three was not acceptable (more than three was unlikely but acceptable), so this is an at least reading. In the paraphrases we have just provided, we have assumed that the cardinality function has an inbuilt maximality operator: it is a function from a set to the maximum value on the cardinality scale for that set. The (maximal) cardinality for the set in question varies from one world to another, and this is captured by the numeral modifier (≥ for at least readings, ≤ for at most readings). In some worlds compatible with the law the master manumits five slaves, in others four and in others three, etc. If, on the other hand, you admit nonmaximal cardinalities into the computation, you can use variable scope to formalize the difference between maximum and minimum readings: the minimum number is defined as the maximum number that is true in all accessible worlds. For instance, the colonies in the Livy passage were required to furnish 120 cavalrymen. If this means exactly 120 cavalrymen, then 121 would not be in compliance with the senatorial decree: in all accessible worlds the maximal degree on the numerical scale of cavalrymen furnished was 120: $\forall w \textsc{max} \lambda n{=}120$. If it means at least 120 cavalrymen, then the maximal number of cavalrymen furnished in all accessible worlds would have been 120 (in some worlds many more): $\textsc{max} \lambda n \forall w{=}120$. The scope inversion approach is not available if maximality is built into the cardinality function, since in that case worlds in which 135 cavalrymen are furnished are not also worlds in which 120 cavalrymen are furnished. On this latter approach, the universal quantifier over worlds scopes above the cardinality function, just as it does for the exact reading: $\forall w.n(w) \geq 120$. More generally, the issue boils down to how you paraphrase the at least reading of a sentence like 'All the colonies furnished 120 cavalrymen.' Is it 'The maximum number for which it is true that all the colonies furnished that number of cavalrymen is 120' or is it 'All the colonies furnished a total of 120 or more cavalrymen'?

Modified numerals

We have seen that the interpretation of a cardinal involves a Janus-like process of reasoning whereby numbers lower on the scale are entailed but not asserted and numbers higher on the scale are usually excluded by scalar implicature. Both of these effects can be cancelled by use of numerical modifiers like *(non) amplius, (non) plus, (non) minus*

(49) cum *ducenti amplius* in ipsis faucibus portae cecidissent (Livy 44.31.9)
In eo proelio *non amplius ducentos* milites desideravit (BC 3.99)

(49) When at least two hundred had fallen right at the gate opening (Livy 44.31.9). In that battle he lost at most two hundred regular soldiers (BC 3.99).

(50) *plus trecentos* captos (Livy 40.50.5)
ex victoribus ceciderunt *non plus centum* (Livy 44.42.8)
minus centum militum iactura (Livy 23.36.1)
cum in senatu *centum non minus* adessent (Livy 39.18.9).

In this construction the numerical modifier is originally an appositional amplification (nonconfigurational syntax), therefore semantically disjunctive ('two hundred or more') like

(51) dies *triginta aut plus eo* in navi fui (Ter Hec 421)
Mox subrutus Piraei portus *sex aut amplius* muris cinctus (Flor 1.40.10)
Quattuor hic aestate togae *pluresve* teruntur (Mart 10.96.11)
Tu *centum aut plures* inter dominabere nymphas (Ov Am 3.6.63).

It is not clear to what extent the original appositional status remained transparent in classical Latin. Number modifiers are a function from the number in the sentence to a set of numbers standing in the relation specified to the number in the sentence. *Amplius, plus* and *non minus* cancel the exclusion of numbers higher on the scale than the cardinal in the sentence. In the case of the strong quantifier the scalar implicature is cancelled: *plus ducenti* for instance means $|A \cap B| \geq 200$ rather than $|A \cap B| = 200$. If $|A \cap B| = 200$ is p, $|A \cap B| > 200$ is q, and $|A \cap B| < 200$ is r, then *ducenti ceciderunt* with scalar implicature and maximality is $p \wedge \neg q \wedge r \neq$ MAX; *ducenti ceciderunt* without scalar implicature is $p \vee q \wedge r \neq$ MAX; *ducenti amplius ceciderunt* is likewise $p \vee q \wedge r \neq$ MAX. In the case of the weak quantifier, the maximality clause is removed: if X is the set of casualties, it is no longer the case that any set Z of casualties has to be a subset of X; Z can now also be a superset of X. The correct number is now one of a disjunction of numbers higher than or equal to the number in the sentence: 200 or 201 or 202 or 203 etc.

Conversely *non amplius, non plus* and *minus* cancel the entailment of numbers lower than the number in the sentence; the correct number is one of a disjunction of numbers lower than or equal to the number in the sentence: 200 or 199 or 198 or 197 etc. The meaning of the strong quantifier is accordingly changed from $|A \cap B| = 200$ to $|A \cap B| \leq 200$. The latter potentially includes zero

(52) *Non amplius ter* bibere eum solitum super cenam in castris apud Mutinam (Suet 2.77.1)
Quei... pequdes maiores *non plus* X pascet (CIL I.2.585).

(50) At least three hundred were captured (Livy 40.50.5). Of the victors at most a hundred fell (Livy 44.42.8). With the loss of less than a hundred soldiers (Livy 23.36.1). When at least a hundred members were present in the senate (Livy 39.18.9).

(51) I was on the ship for thirty days or more than that (Ter Hec 421). Next the harbour of Piraeus, surrounded by six or more walls, was demolished (Flor 1.40.10). Here one wears out four or more togas in one summer (Mart 10.96.11). You will be mistress among a hundred or more nymphs (Ov Am 3.6.63).

(52) That in camp at Mutina he normally did not have more than three drinks at dinner (Suet 2.77.1). Anyone who pastures not more than ten larger cattle (CIL I.2.585).

The first example (Suet 2.77) is a count cardinal: it does not exclude possible occasions in which Augustus did not drink at all, although there is an implicature that he drank every day. The meaning is that he may not have drunk every day, but on all those occasions when he did drink the number of drinks did not exceed 3. The second example is existential; it generalizes over situations in which there is a set of no more than ten larger cattle that someone puts out to pasture. This is problematic, since it is trivial if not incoherent to assert the existence of a set that is empty. One option is just to live with a disjunctive meaning: either no cattle are put out to pasture or, if they are, a maximum of ten. Another way of getting around the difficulty is to use universal quantification in place of existential quantification: you can pasture cattle tax free for all sets of ten or fewer cattle. The maximality clause has to be retained, since we don't want people circumventing the Lex Agraria by putting out multiple sets of no more than ten cattle in a single event.

Note that while the number modifiers change the scalar implicatures, they do not cancel them altogether, and their use carries with it a range of possible pragmatic effects. A scalar implicature is still involved in the choice of the upper and lower limits respectively: 'at least 200' suggests that the speaker is not in a position to assert 'at least 201' and 'at most 200' that he is not in a position to assert 'at most 199.' Particularly for single episode sentences, the further a number is from the minimum/maximum asserted, the less likely it is to be true. A large upper bound strongly implicates that zero is not a possible alternative

(53) *non amplius* CCL desideratis (BAlex 40).

Numeral modifiers can also be used as "slack" regulators, limiting interpretations to an approximation around the numeral

(54) *Septingenti* sunt *paulo plus aut minus* anni (Enn Ann 4.154)
aut minus aut certe non plus tricesima lux est (Mart 6.7.3),

and to correct possible listener expectations of a higher or lower numeral, where the speaker himself is perfectly aware that the number asserted is the exact one

(55) *Sedecim non amplius* eo anno legionibus defensum imperium est. (Livy 30.27.10).

An indefinite quantifier can be used to give an attributive cardinal an approximate reading

(56) ubi cenaveris, comesto *aliqua* V folia (Cato 156.1)
Elleborum potabis faxo *aliquos viginti* dies (Pl Men 950).

(53) With casualties of not more than 250 men (BAlex 40).

(54) It is now a little more or less than seven hundred years (Enn Ann 4.154). It is either less than thirty days or certainly not more (Mart 6.7.3).

(55) The empire was defended that year with no more than sixteen legions (Livy 30.27.10).

(56) After dinner eat five or so leaves (Cato 156.1). I'll make you drink hellebore for twenty days or so (Pl Men 950).

The appositional construction just analyzed competes with various types of comparative construction

(57) neve... virei *plous duobus*... arfuise velent (CIL I.2.581.21)
Ab neutra parte *sescentis plus peditibus*... cecidit (Livy 21.59.8)
paean... *plures* habeat syllabas *quam tres* (Orat 218)
nervos... quos *plures quam septem* haberet (De Leg 2.39)
non amplius cum plurimum *quam septem* horas dormiebat (Suet 2.78.1).

As in English, the meaning of the competing numerical modifier expressions is not exactly the same, so they are, at least in principle, not fully interchangeable. To start with, in origin *sescentis plus peditibus* (Livy 21.59) means >600, while *ducenti amplius* in (49) means ≥ 200. The appositional construction with *plus*, *amplius* in (49) leaves the listener a pragmatically and contextually constrained but otherwise open choice among the numbers equal to or greater than *n*. Every number in the disjunction is an epistemic possibility. The constructions in (57) refer to some unspecified number greater than *n* (note the shift from the degree modifier *plus* to the individual modifier *plures*). The appositional construction corresponds more closely to English 'at least,' the comparative constructions to English 'more than.' In the third example (Orat 218) for instance we are told that the paeon has some specific number of syllables that is greater than three. Saying that the paeon has more than three syllables is like saying that a square has more than three sides, for the paeon is a cretic with one of the longa resolved and consequently has just four syllables, as the author and readers of the Orator are well aware. The issue of whether a structure is a foot or a rhythm is formulated so as to generalize over various structures having more than three syllables (like the downward monotonic last example (Suet 2.78) generalizes over Augustus' sleep times). This is quite different from some of the appositional comparatives like *ducenti amplius* in the first example in (49) (Livy 44.31), where Livy does not know or does not care to convey the exact number of casualties.

Cardinals other than 'one' measure plural sets, and plural sets can be represented by powerset lattices (see Chapter 6). The principle of quantity (isomorphism) tells us that only the rows of the lattice are relevant, not the individual elements in the same row, so it may seem like overkill to use lattices, but a brief look at this perspective is quite instructive. Consider the following passage from Livy

(58) (Postumius) *quinque* equites iubet intrare urbem et modicum spatium progressos *tres* manere eodem loco... *duos* explorata ad se referre. (Livy 10.34.9).

(57) And let no more than two men be present (CIL I.2.581.21). Not more than six hundred infantry fell on either side (Livy 21.59.8). The paeon... on the grounds that it has more than three syllables (Orat 218). The strings that it had in excess of the number seven (De Leg 2.39). He slept no more than seven hours at most (Suet 2.78.1).

(58) He ordered five cavalrymen to enter the city and to advance for a short distance; three were to remain in the same spot, while two were to report back their findings to him (Livy 10.34.9).

The discourse domain includes a set of five cavalrymen; the powerset lattice for this set is given in Figure 5.7. Conservativity means that the lattice is limited to cavalrymen (the A set); three horses presumably remained in the city too, but that is not relevant to the evaluation of the quantifier *tres equites*. In all worlds in which Postumius' orders are carried out (which includes the actual world, as it turns out), exactly two of the cavalrymen (strong quantifier) report back to him. Since *duos equites* is indefinite, Postumius does not specify any particular two cavalrymen who have to report back. The bold elements in the figure represent the deontically accessible alternatives for the exactly reading of *duos*. One of these alternatives (and no more than one) will turn out to be true in the actual world. If we don't find out which two individuals reported back, the bold elements will then be epistemically accessible alternatives. It is also true by monotonicity that one cavalryman reported back, but it is not true that the maximal number of cavalrymen reporting back was one, so the atoms are not represented by bold elements. Maximality requires the cardinal to give the cardinality of the supremum of the set of all subsets whose members share the properties of being a cavalryman and of reporting back, in symbols $|\cup\{X_i: \forall i \forall x \in X_i \rightarrow P(x) \wedge Q(x)\}|$. Elements that are not bold may be true for other predicates (perhaps three cavalrymen were tall), but not for the predicate 'reported back.'

Now say that Postumius' had been less specific in his instructions, and had ordered at least two cavalrymen to report back. Then any world in which a bold element in the lattice in Figure 5.8 was true would be a world in which Postumius' orders were carried out. This includes the supremum (in which case none of the cavalrymen decided to stay in Feritrum and they all came back). Finally suppose Postumius had ordered at most two cavalrymen to report back: then any world in which a bold element in the lattice in Figure 5.9 was true would be a world in which his orders were carried out. This includes the infimum (in which case all the cavalrymen decided to stay in Feritrum and none of them reported back). The cavalrymen were presumably smart enough to realize that while this was a logically permitted course of action, it was excluded by implicature; so if noone reported back, there would surely be trouble. It is interesting that predicates that lexically require a plural subject having a certain cardinality cannot be used with these numeral modifiers at all (*'Exactly/at least/at most four students sang a quartet'). 'Exactly' is tautologous and the others make a contingency out of a logical impossibility.

Vague cardinals

The vague cardinals *multi* 'many' and *pauci* 'few' differ from ordinary cardinals in a number of ways. Most obviously they give an approximate rather than a precise indication of cardinality. They are also gradable (*plures, pauciores, plurimi, paucissimi*), while ordinary cardinals are not, and they share with gradable adjectives the property of contextual sensitivity, which interacts with informational structure to produce a variety of different meanings. (*Aliquot* 'some' can

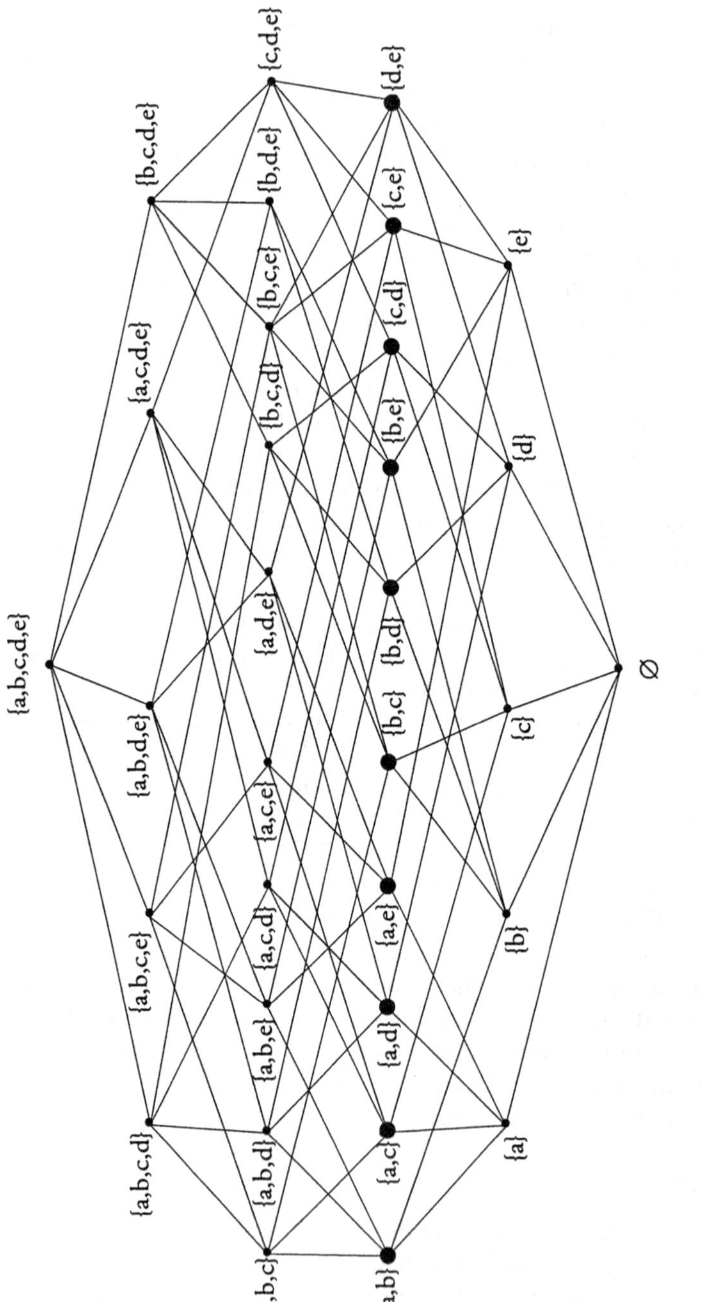

Figure 5.7
Exactly two cavalrymen are to report back
(cp. Livy 10.34.9)

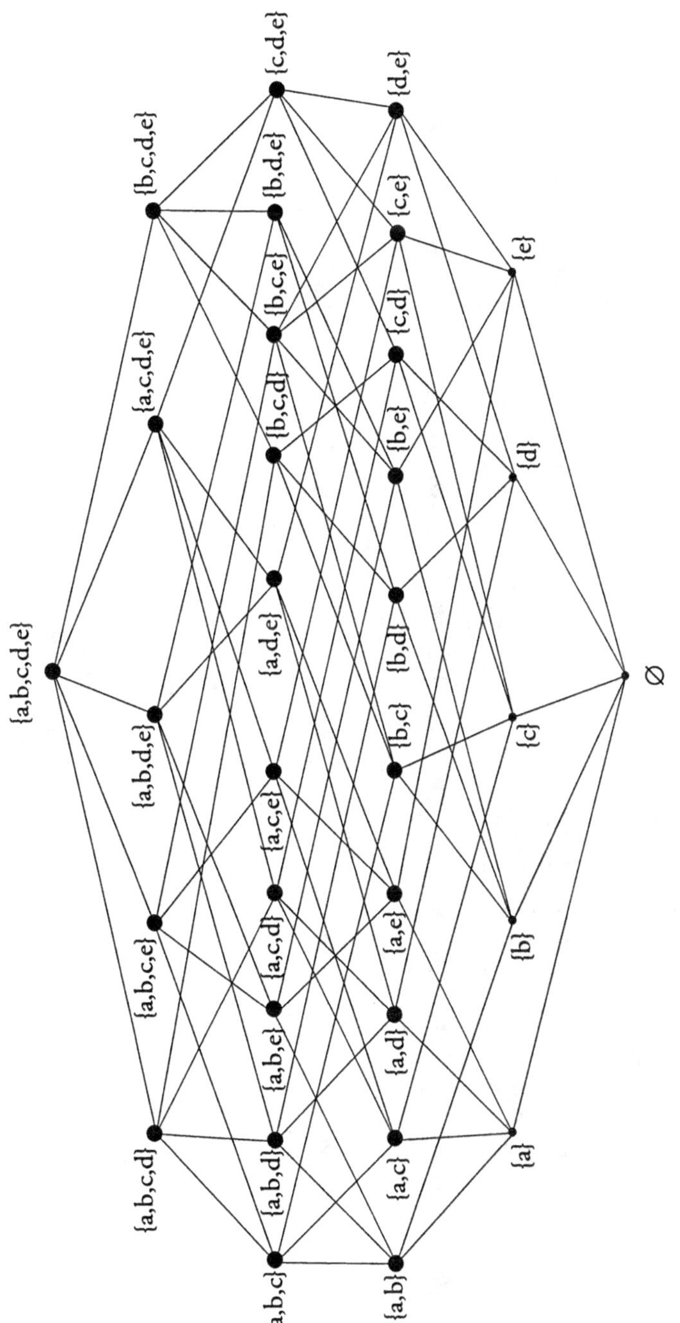

Figure 5.8
At least two cavalrymen are to report back
(cp. Livy 10.34.9)

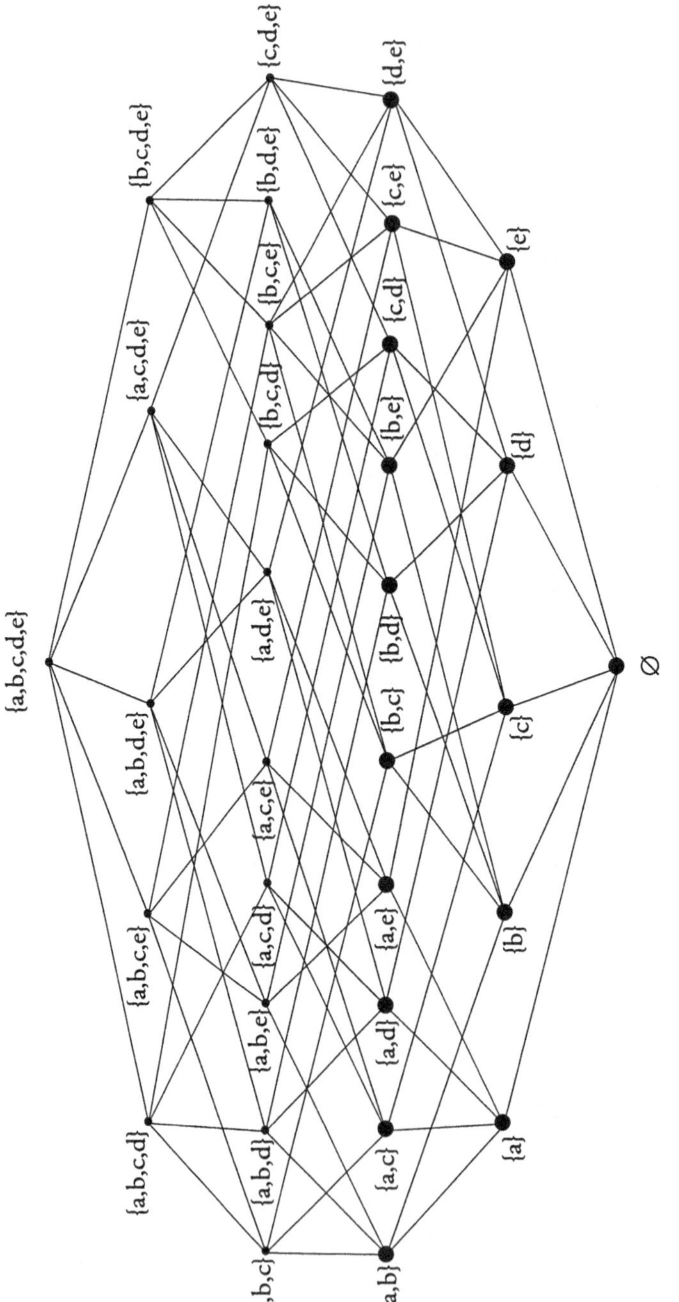

Figure 5.9
At most two cavalrymen are to report back
(cp. Livy 10.34.9)

also be considered a vague cardinal: it is context sensitive but not gradable.) We find the same three readings as with ordinary cardinals, although they can again be difficult to distinguish; we will illustrate with *pauci*. The following probably have the strong reading

(59) Aetoli... caeduntur; *pauci* armis abiectis pars Tegeam pars Megalen polin perfugiunt; ibi... sub corona venierunt (Livy 35.36.10)
Itaque primo... *pauci*... ad mare decurrunt, dein plures, postremo prope omnes (Livy 41.2.8).

The weak reading fits the following quite well

(60) *Pauci* tamen boni inerant (Ad Att 1.16.5)
in Euripo castellum Romani milites *pauci*... communiebant (Livy 35.51.8).

Finally there is the pure count reading

(61) Posset agi lege necne *pauci* quondam sciebant (Pro Mur 25)
militem a multa caede est tutatus; nec fere quisquam in ipso certamine, *pauci* in turba fugae extremae... caesi (Livy 8.19.8)
ita fecistis quo modo *pauci* nobiles in hac civitate consules facti sunt (De Leg Agr 2.3).

The count reading translates as 'few,' while the strong and weak readings translate as 'a few.' They are quite different

(62) est enim locus quem vel *pauci* possent defendere (Verr 2.5.84)
cum *pauci* pingere egregie possint (Brut 257).

The first example (Verr 2.5) says not that few men could defend the Island at Syracuse (upper bound), but that even a few men could defend it (lower bound). The second example (Brut 257) does not introduce a set of outstanding painters into the discourse in order to continue with a narration of their accomplishments ('They held an exhibition in Paris'); rather it gives an exhaustive count of the whole set of outstanding painters. While the strong and weak readings of *pauci* license anaphora, it is quite difficult with the pure count reading: 'A few students passed the test: they celebrated with a beer'; (*)'Few students passed the test: they celebrated with a beer.' This is because the count

(59) The Aetolians were killed; a few threw away their arms and fled, partly to Tegea and partly to Megalopolis; there they were sold at auction (Livy 35.36.10). So at first a few ran down to the sea, then more, and finally almost all of them (Livy 41.2.8).

(60) There were a few good men among them (Ad Att 1.16.5). A few Roman soldiers were building a fort on the Euripus (Livy 35.51.8).

(61) Originally few people knew whether it was possible to do legal business or not (Pro Mur 25). He protected his soldiers from much slaughter; hardly anyone was killed in the battle itself and only a few in the crush at the very end of the flight (Livy 8.19.8). You elected me in a manner in which few nobles have been elected consul in this state (De Leg Agr 2.3).

(62) For it is a place that even a few men could defend (Verr 2.5.84). There are few really good painters (Brut 257).

reading of *pauci* is downward entailing, while the other readings, like *multi*, are not

> (63) dentibus... aut enim *paucos* aut *nullos* habent (NH 8.116)
> quorum aut *pauci* aut... *nemo* (Fronto Aur 3.17.3)
> *multae* res vel *omnes* (Vitr 1.1.16):

'few if any, few or none,' *'a few if not any, a few or none.' 'A few' cannot downward entail to none, because the weak reading is existential and so asserts that there are not none, and the strong reading presupposes that a few already exist, so both readings result in a contradiction.

Unlike ordinary cardinals, vague cardinals are context sensitive. We will concentrate on *multi*, but the analysis can generally be extrapolated to *pauci*. While it is possible to fix a lower bound in absolute terms ('two' is not 'many' for anything), beyond that what qualifies as 'many' depends on the A and B sets and on the context in general

> (64) multi *legati* (Pro Flacc 63)
> multi *captivi nobiles* (Livy 40.49.5)
> multosque *captivos* (Curt Ruf 9.8.15)
> multi *Siculi* (Verr 2.2.80)
> multi *populi* (NH 3.133).

In any fixed area what qualifies as 'many captives' is going to be a higher number than what qualifies as 'many noble captives,' and 'many Sicilians' than 'many Alpine tribes.' And what qualifies as 'many captives' will also vary according to the size of the armies involved in the engagement, information that is not available in the sentence itself but comes from the context in which it is embedded. If necessary, the comparison class can be spelled out

> (65) *Multae* etiam *ut in homine Romano* litterae (De Sen 12)
> *Multum ut in Germanos* rationis ac sollertiae (Tac Ger 30.1).

Vague cardinals are used to measure the extent of a set, just as other measure adjectives are used to measure the dimensions of an object. One consequence of this context sensitivity is that vague cardinals do not have the same monotonicity properties as ordinary cardinals

> (66) *Tres* nobilissimi Haedui capti ad Caesarem perducuntur (BG 7.67)
> *multos* utrimque cecidisse (Livy 40.50.3)
> *multos* illustres viros in acie cecidisse (Livy 33.25.9).

(63) By their teeth... for they have either few or none (NH 8.116). Few or none of whom (Fronto Aur 3.17.3). Many or all things (Vitr 1.1.16)

(64) Many representatives (Pro Flacc 63). Many noble captives (Livy 40.49.5). And many captives (Curt Ruf 9.8.15). Many Sicilians (Verr 2.2.80). Many peoples (NH 3.133).

(65) He was also very well read for a Roman (De Sen 12). They are highly intelligent and adroit for Germans (Tac Ger 30.1).

(66) Three Aeduans of the highest rank were captured and led to Caesar (BG 7.67). That many men fell on both sides (Livy 40.50.3). That many distinguished men had fallen in battle (Livy 33.25.9).

Tres in the first example (BG 7.67) is not context sensitive and is left upward entailing: if three noble Aeduans were brought to Caesar, three Aeduans were brought to Caesar. *Multos* in the other two examples is context sensitive and this interferes with monotonicity: 'many famous men fell' does not entail 'many men fell' because the comparison class has been changed.

The meaning of vague cardinals is sensitive not just to the general discourse context but also to the way in which information is structured in the sentence, so that it is quite a tricky task to spell out exactly how the meaning is computed. We will consider four ways of interpreting *multi*. On its first reading *multi* simply denotes the cardinality of the intersection of A and B: $|A \cap B| > n$. This reading occurs in pure count sentences and in existential sentences; n can be established in absolute terms or by some contextual standard. On its other readings *multi* is a focus-sensitive proportional quantifier. The second reading counts the number of A in B: $|A \cap B| > |A \cap \neg B|$ or $|A \cap B| > i\%$ of $|A|$; this works like a generalized quantifier. The third reading counts the number of B in A: $|A \cap B| > |\neg A \cap B|$ or $|A \cap B| > i\%$ of $|B|$; this is like a nonconservative generalized quantifier. The fourth reading compares the proportion of A in B with the proportion of relevant classes other than A (focus alternates to A) in B: $|A \cap B|/|A| > |\text{ALT}A \cap B|/|\text{ALT}A|$, or the ratio of the two fractions is greater than $i{:}j$. The introduction of ALTA violates the principle of extension. The definition of n, i, j is contextually determined and reflects the norm for comparable situations. Using the norm as a standard of comparison introduces intensionality.

First let's consider some examples in which only the cardinal reading seems appropriate (first reading: existential or count)

(67) *Multi* obviam prodierunt de provincia decedenti (Pro Mur 68)
multi artifices ex Graecia venerunt (Livy 39.22.2).

The first example (Pro Mur 68) means that the number of people who went to meet Murena on his return from his province was either high in absolute terms or above the norm for *decessiones* of this type. It doesn't mean that more (or relatively more) people came out to meet him than stayed at home (which would be the second reading): the comparison class is simply the norm for events of this type. The second example (Livy 39.22) says that there were some visiting Greek actors at the games and their number was above the average for similar *ludi*. The whole sentence is a broad scope focus. Restricting the focus to the verb phrase would give the second reading: more (or relatively more) Greek actors came to Rome than stayed in Greece. Putting a strong narrow focus on the subject noun would give the third reading: more of the people who came to Rome from Greece were actors than other classes of participant in the *ludi*. In the same way, narrowly focusing the prepositional phrases in both examples causes other material in the verb phrase to shift from the nuclear scope into the

(67) Many people went to meet him on his return from his province (Pro Mur 68). Many performers came from Greece (Livy 39.22.2).

restriction. Focus on *de provincia* in the first example could evoke a comparison set of other source locations on returning from which Murena was met by relatively fewer people. Focus on *e Graecia* in the second example would evoke a comparison between the number of actors that came from Greece and the number that came from other places.

In other examples it is quite clear that what is at issue is the proportion of A in B (second reading)

(68) *Multi* exsulum caede sua foedavere templum, *multi* vivi capti (Livy 3.18.10)
cum... *multi* cecidissent Romanorum (Livy 27.1.10)
Itaque *multis* interfectis *reliquos* infecta re in oppidum reppulerunt (BC 2.14)
Multi occisi capti, *reliqui* dissipati (Ad Fam 2.10.3).

Both the partitive genitives *exsulum, Romanorum* in the first pair of examples (Livy 3.18, 27.1) and the appearance of *reliqui* in the second pair of examples point to the partitioning of A: for instance in the last example (Ad Fam 2.10) the number of enemy killed or captured is greater than the number dispersed or higher than normal for this type of engagement. *Multi* in its proportional reading may, but need not, be simply the equivalent of *maior pars*

(69) *Multae* quassatae armamentisque spoliatae naves, quaedam fractae (Livy 30.39.3)
multae fractae, *multae* naves eiectae, *multae* ita haustae mari ut nemo in terram enarit. (Livy 33.41.7).
multi ex iis occisi, plures capti (Livy 31.27.8).

In the first example (Livy 30.39) *multae* could be more than half, but in the second example (Livy 33.41) at least two of the occurrences of *multae* have to be less than half, and in the third example (Livy 31.27) since *plures* is greater than *multi, multi* must be less than half (even if very few escaped).

In another set of examples, if *multi* has a proportional reading, it is not a proportion of A

(70) Eodem anno censuram *multi* et clari viri petierunt (Livy 37.57.9)
Creatus inde pontifex maximus M. Aemilius Lepidus, cum *multi* clari viri petissent (Livy 40.42.12).

(68) Many of the exiles stained the temple with their blood, many were captured alive (Livy 3.18.10). When many of the Romans had fallen (Livy 27.1.10). So they killed many and drove the rest back into the town without letting them accomplish their goal (BC 2.14). Many were killed or captured, the rest scattered (Ad Fam 2.10.3).

(69) Many ships were damaged and deprived of their rigging, some were wrecked (Livy 30.39.3). Many ships were wrecked, many were beached, and many were swallowed up by the sea with noone swimming ashore (Livy 33.41.7). Many of them were killed, and more were captured (Livy 31.27.8).

(70) In the same year many distinguished men were candidates for the censorship (Livy 37.57.9). Then M. Aemilius Lepidus was elected pontifex maximus, although many distinguished men had been candidates (Livy 40.42.12).

These examples do not mean that a large proportion of the well-known men of Rome were candidates. The simplest reading is the pure cardinal reading (first reading), according to which the number of well-known candidates was above the norm for elections of the type in question. To get a viable proportional reading you have to take the proportion of candidates that are well-known rather than the proportion of well-known men that are candidates (third reading) or compare the rate at which well-known men are running as candidates with the rate at which ordinary men are running (fourth reading). The third reading (called the reverse reading) arises when focus on the subject (*multi clari viri*) flips the material in the restriction and the nuclear scope: instead of the well-known men being the restriction and the candidates for office being the nuclear scope, it is the other way around. This reverse reading is blocked in sentences in which the A-set is strongly topical, like partitives ('Many of the notables were running for election' ≠ Many of those running for election were notables) and subjects of individual level properties ('Many candidates were famous' ≠ Many famous men were candidates). But 'Many NOTABLES were running for election' can mean that many of those running for election were notables. The fourth reading arises because strong focus evokes a set of alternates, here other classes of candidates in the election, and these are used as a basis for the comparison.

Domain selection

We saw that in order to verify a sentence with a strong quantifier, the listener needs to be able to identify the A set. What information does he need to do so successfully? If quantification is over everything or everyone in the whole world, not very much

(71) ex quibus *omnia* constare dicuntur (Tusc 1.42)
omnesque qui ubique sunt consentiunt (Tusc 1.35).

In both cases the restriction is trivial: in the first example (Tusc 1.42) it is implicit, in the second (Tusc 1.35) it is spelled out by the relative clause. Usually quantification is not over everything in the world but is restricted to a set denoted by the noun

(72) quotiens *quaeque* cohors procurreret (BG 5.34)
cum sua *quisque* miles circumspiceret (BG 5.31);

the nominal restriction ensures that quantification is not over everything but over every cohort and every soldier respectively. In some sentences the nominal restriction may be all that is needed to verify the sentence, because the domain of quantification can still be the whole world; this includes generic sentences

(71) Of which all things are said to consist (Tusc 1.42). Everyone everywhere agrees (Tusc 1.35).

(72) Every time each cohort ran forward (BG 5.34). Since each soldier was inspecting his equipment (BG 5.31).

(73) Militat *omnis* amans (Ov Am 1.9.1)
frigoribus *omnis* surculus rigore torpet (Col 4.29.3),

lawlike sentences

(74) Pullos autem non oportet singulos, ut *quisque* natus sit, tollere (Col 8.5.15),

and quantification over sorts or kinds of things

(75) posse nocere animis carminis *omne* genus (Ov Trist 2.264)
omne genus tormentorum machinarumque ex Sicilia arcessierat (Livy 27.25.11).

Although we need the context to interpret *surculus* (Col 4.29) relative to a particular plant and *pullus* (Col 8.5) relative to a particular animal, the domain of quantification is not situation specific. Normally however, in addition to the nominal restriction, we need to access a contextually given domain of quantification: so in (72) above *quaeque cohors* does not mean every cohort in the universe but every Roman cohort fighting in the battle against Ambiorix that is being described at this point in the text, and *quisque miles* does not mean every soldier in the world but every soldier in the camp of Sabinus and Cotta. The distinction between domain universal and domain specific quantification is obviously truthconditionally significant: substituting the former for the latter will usually make a true sentence false. The same goes for the distinction between one contextually relevant domain and another. If *quisque miles* is interpreted to mean 'every soldier in the army of the Belgae,' the wrong truth conditions result. And although *quisque miles* means 'every Roman soldier' both at BG 5.31 and at Livy 27.14.10, it refers to different sets of Roman soldiers, those fighting the Belgae in 54 B.C. and those fighting Hannibal in Southern Italy in 209 B.C.

Domain selection does not apply generally in the overall context established by a text but is specific to each strongly quantified noun phrase

(76) Initio orto *plures* cum *pluribus* conloqui (Livy 24.47.7);

here the quantifiers refer to groups of Arpini and groups of Romans that are talking to each other. Sometimes the contextual domain is more or less spelled out in a relative clause

(77) *omnes* eos qui in monte consederant (BC 3.98),

(73) Every lover is a soldier (Ov Am 1.9.1). In cold weather every twig is numb with frost (Col 4.29.3).
(74) The chickens should not be removed individually upon birth (Col 8.5.15).
(75) That every kind of poem can be harmful to the soul (Ov Trist 2.264). He had ordered every kind of artillery and siege-machine from Sicily (Livy 27.25.11).
(76) Once a beginning had been made, more people spoke to more people (Livy 24.47.7).
(77) All those who had taken up position on the mountain (BC 3.98).

but mostly it has to be retrieved from the context like the referent of a pronoun. This can be done in the same three ways it is done for pronouns. One way is by deixis from the speech situation

(78) paucis suos adhortatus... virtute sua *quemque* fretos ire in aciem debere (Livy 7.32.6);

here *quemque* means each member of the assembly of soldiers that Valerius was addressing. It is also possible for the domain of a lower quantifier to depend on a higher quantifier like a bound or dependent pronoun

(79) in quod adeo intenti *omnium*... animi...fuere... ut *nemo*... senserit captam urbem (Livy 26.46.4);

nemo means *nemo omnium*. In the most common case, the contextual domain is anaphorically reconstructed from material in the preceding context in much the same way as the antecedent of an E-type pronoun

(80) *reliquos omnes* equitatu consecuti nostri interfecerunt (BG 1.53);

reliquos omnes means 'all the rest of the army of German tribes under Ariovistus that had just lost a battle against Caesar.' Nonuniversal strong quantifiers can easily be paraphrased by partitives

(81) Plures Samnitium cecidere, *plures Romani* volnerati sunt (Livy 8.36.4).

Plural partitive genitives normally have definite or specific referents (although accommodated weak quantifiers also occur), which means that they are presupposition inducing expressions; this property of *plures Samnitium* should carry over to *plures Romani*, even though it does not contain a definite expression. The necessary domain information is easily accessed from the currently updated file for the plural discourse referent. We have seen that if a quantified phrase is interpreted without its contextual domain or if the wrong domain is selected, the sentence will usually be false; so clearly domain selection is part of the interpretation process. Whether the domain is actually part of the message itself or just part of the background contextual information accessed by the listener for the interpretation of any message is a controversial issue. In the former case truthconditions depend only on what is encoded in the sentence, and what is communicated is just what is said; in the latter case the sentence underdetermines the meaning of the message, and contextual enrichment is required for full interpretation. One way or another, the information contributed by domain selection has to be integrated into the interpretation of the quantified

(78) Having encouraged his men with a few words... that each of them should go into battle relying on his own courage (Livy 7.32.6).

(79) Everyone's minds were so focused on it that noone realized that the city had been captured (Livy 26.46.4).

(80) Our men pursued all the others on horseback and killed them (BG 1.53).

(81) More of the Samnites were killed, more Romans were wounded (Livy 8.36.4).

phrase, so as to anchor it to the relevant participants in the situation. Presumably this happens via intersection of the set denoted by the noun restriction with the set denoted by the contextual domain: Q(A)(B) means $Q(A \cap C)(B)$. Consider the following examples

(82) ne... *omnes* puberes interficerent (BC 2.13)
omnes puberes interfecit (Livy 9.31.4)
ut *omnes* puberes interficerentur (Livy 21.14.3).

The A-sets are actually interpreted as $\lambda x.$puberes$(x) \wedge$ Massilienses(x) (BC 2.13), $\lambda y.$puberes$(y) \wedge$ Cluviani(y) (Livy 9.31), and $\lambda z.$puberes$(z) \wedge$ Saguntini(z), the set of adult Massilians, adult Cluvians and adult Saguntines respectively. Sometimes the antecedent property is less directly accessible

(83) Classis postero die foedissima tempestate lacerata *omnesque* naves... in litora nostra eiectae sunt (Livy 29.18.5)
multae naves eiectae, multae ita haustae mari ut *nemo* in terram enarit (Livy 33.41.7).

In the first example (Livy 29.18) *omnes naves* means 'all the ships in the fleet,' so we need to use a function from a fleet to the ships it contains; in the second example (Livy 33.14) *nemo* means 'none of the sailors on the inundated ships,' so we need to use a function from ships to the sailors they contain.

Exceptives

Sometimes it is necessary to qualify a quantificational generalization by excluding an individual or set of individuals

(84) quartae cohortis *omnibus* centurionibus occisis (BG 2.25)
omnibus primae cohortis centurionibus interfectis *praeter* principem priorem (BC 3.64).

In the first example (BG 2.25) the set of centurions (A) is a subset of the set of casualties (B), in the second example (BC 3.64) the set of centurions (A) minus the princeps prior (X) is a subset of the set of casualties (B). This is illustrated in Figure 5.10. The preposition *praeter* (sometimes also *extra*) serves to exclude its complement from the generalization. Most examples involve an overt quantifier of some sort, typically a universal (*omnis*, *nullus*), but exceptives can also be used with negative adjectives and with superlatives

(82) So that they didn't kill all the adults (BC 2.13). He killed all the adults (Livy 9.31.4). That all the adults be killed (Livy 21.14.3).

(83) The next day the fleet was battered by a terrible storm and all the ships were thrown onto our shores (Livy 29.18.5). Many ships were beached, and many were swallowed up by the sea with noone swimming ashore (Livy 33.41.7).

(84) All the centurions of the fourth cohort having been killed (BG 2.25). All the centurions of the first cohort having been killed except for the princeps prior (BC 3.64).

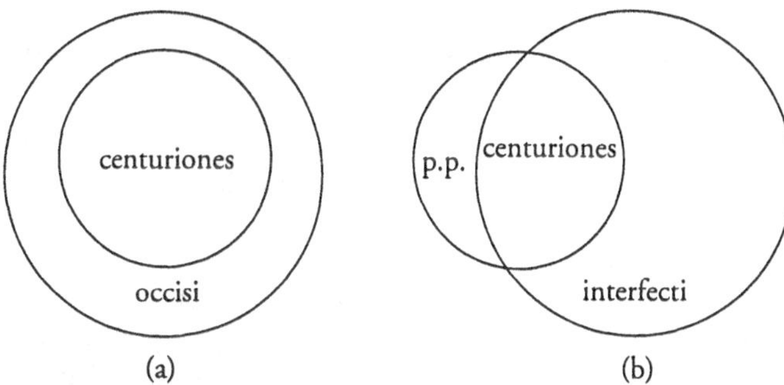

Figure 5.10
Exceptive
(a) *Omnibus centurionibus occisis* (BG 2.25)
(b) *Omnibus centurionibus interfectis praeter principem priorem* (BC 3.64)

(85) Gallus quidam *nudus praeter* scutum et gladios duos (Quadrig. ap. Gell 9.13.6)
inermis eques, *praeterquam* quod iacula secum portat (Livy 35.11.7)
III flumina tota India *praeter* Gangen *maxima* (Curt Ruf 9.4.8).

In the last example (Curt Ruf 9.4) the Ganges is removed from the domain of the superlative operator. The most usual reason for excluding an individual is that the generalization is not true of that individual (exceptive *praeter*), but there are also nonexceptive exclusions due to various pragmatic motives or to epistemic uncertainty

(86) Ariovistus... *praeter* se *denos* ut ad colloquium adducerent postulavit. (BG 1.43)
cum *praeter* pastores *plurimi* etiam ex stationibus milites concurrissent (Suet 1.32.1).

Exceptive exclusion is the default with positive and negative universal quantifiers (which make the strongest generalizations), nonexceptive exclusion with other quantifiers (like *denos, plurimi* above)

(87) segregat ab se *omnis extra* te unam (Pl Mil 1232)
Extra eam in Myrtoo *multae* (insulae) (NH 4.65).

(85) Some Gaul who was naked except for a shield and two swords (Gell 9.13.6). Their cavalrymen were unarmed except that they carried javelins with them (Livy 35.11.7). The three biggest rivers in all India besides the Ganges (Curt Ruf 9.4.8).
(86) Ariovistus demanded that they should bring ten men each besides themselves to the parley (BG 1.43). When apart from the shepherds also very many soldiers from the guard-posts had gathered (Suet 1.32.1).
(87) He keeps them all away from him except for you (Pl Mil 1232). There are many islands besides that one in the Myrtoan sea (NH 4.65).

Note the English hierarchy 'All/No/Most/*Half/*Three/*Some of the students except two.' Syntactically, exception phrases appear in a variety of different modifier positions

(88) praedaque *omnis praeter* libera corpora militi concessa est (Livy 6.13.6)
cum *praeter* libera capita *omnem* praedam militibus concessisset (Livy 27.19.2)
omnes praeter eum Stoici (Luc 107)
cum *omnibus praeter* Thracas auxiliis (Livy 33.7.11)
omni parte corporis rasa *praeter* caput et labrum superius (BG 5.14)
quia *praeter* aegros lixarum in modum *omnes* per agros vicinasque urbes negotiabantur (Livy 5.8.3).

When the informational focus after a negative quantifier is on the exception rather than on the quantifier itself, *nisi* is mostly used rather than *praeter*

(89) qui hunc honorem statuae nemini tribuendum censuit *nisi* ei qui ferro esset in legatione interfectus (Phil 9.3).

Exceptives have been analyzed as components of complex quantifiers, as quantifier modifiers (type <<et,ett><et,ett>>) and as generalized quantifier modifiers (type <<et,t><et,t>>), but the closest syntax-semantics fit is achieved by treating them where possible as noun phrase modifiers, an analysis which seems to be required when the exception phrase is the complement of a pronominal non-identity adjective

(90) neque *quemquam alium... praeter* Homerum et Archilochum reperiemus (Vell Pat 1.5.2)
praeter mundum *cetera omnia* aliorum causa esse generata (ND 2.37)
Nam *praeter* oppido propinqua *alia omnia* vasta, inculta (Sall Jug 89.5).

Irrespective of their syntactic location, the semantic effect of exception phrases is to remove entities in the denotation of the complement of the preposition (*praeter*) from the domain of the quantificational generalization. According to one theory this simply means subtracting them from the restriction set (A): instead of Q(A)(B) we get Q(A−X)(B). To see exactly how the process works, let's look more closely at the properties of the exception set (X) where Q is the universal quantifier *omnis*. In felicitous exception sentences, the remnant set

(88) All the booty except for the free men was handed over to the soldiers (Livy 6.13.6). When he had handed over to the soldiers all the booty except for the free men (Livy 27.19.2). All the Stoics except for him (Luc 107). With all the auxiliary troops except for the Thracians (Livy 33.7.11). They shave every part of the body except for the head and the upper lip (BG 5.14). Because apart from the sick they were all trading in the countryside and nearby cities like camp merchants (Livy 5.8.3).

(89) Who has argued that this honour of a statue should be given to noone except one who has met a violent death while on an embassy (Phil 9.3).

(90) Nor will we find anyone else besides Homer and Archilochus (Vell Pat 1.5.2). Everything else besides the world was created for the sake of something else (ND 2.37). For everything else besides the area near the town was a vast desert (Sall Jug 89.5).

(A−X) is typically larger than the exception set X = (A−B); 'Except for 94% of the electorate, everyone voted for the Tory candidate' is only felicitous as a facetious remark by a Labour Party supporter. There should be no members of X that are not also members of A: $X = (A \cap X)$, X is conservative on A:

(91) Adhibent omnes tribunos pl. *praeter* Saturninum (Pro Rab Perd 20)

requires that Saturninus be a tribune, otherwise we get a presupposition failure. X should contain all the exceptions, not just some of them: Q (A−X) (B) should be true

(92) *praeter* Aletrinatem Ferentinatemque et Verulanum omnes Hernici nominis populo Romano bellum indixerunt (Livy 9.42.11).

The sentence would not be true if the inhabitants of Ferentinum had been omitted from the list of exceptions. Removing the exception phrase, that is changing Q (A−X) (B) into Q (A) (B), makes the sentence false (this does not apply to nonuniversal quantifiers): *omnes Hernici nominis populo Romano bellum indixerunt*) is false. However Q (A−X) (B) is also true when X contains more than just the set of exceptions: it is literally true that, not considering the inhabitants of Aletrium, Ferentinum, Verulae and Anagnia, all the remaining Hernicans declared war on the Romans. But this is an incomplete generalization: to render it fully informative X should contain (all and) only the exceptions. So all members of X are in the complement of B; the inhabitants of Aletrium, Ferentinum and Verulae all did not declare war on the Romans, whereas those of Anagnia did. The application of this rule to plurals, definite or indefinite, is more complicated

(93) Incredibile est omnium civium latronibus *exceptis* odium in Antonium (Ad Fam 10.5.3).

All the citizens do hate Antony and at least some robbers don't, but it is not necessarily the case that each and every last robber doesn't hate Antony. If *latronibus* is indefinite, the meaning is 'except some who are robbers'; if it is definite, it has access to the normal partial reading of definites (as in 'The Romans invaded Britain,' where 'the Romans' does not mean all the Romans but rather certain sections of the Roman military). So the meaning of exceptives falls into two parts. First, there is an assertion of pure exclusion, covering both exceptive and nonexceptive exclusion: the denotation of the universal generalized quantifier is changed from the set of properties that all members of A have to the set of properties that all members of A apart from X have. Second, there are two inferences, that the exclusion is exceptive and that X contains no nonexceptions. In the expression $\lambda B.(A-X) \subseteq B \wedge X \cap B = \varnothing$, the first conjunct covers the pure exclu-

(91) They summoned all the tribunes of the people with the exception of Saturninus (Pro Rab Perd 20).

(92) All those of Hernican nationality except for the people of Aletrium, Ferentinum and Verulae declared war on the Roman people (Livy 9.42.11).

(93) The hatred of all citizens except robbers for Antony is incredible (Ad Fam 10.5.3).

sion and ensures that all exceptions are included in X, the second conjunct covers the exceptiveness and ensures that X does not contain nonexceptions.

So far all the examples we have given involved the positive universal quantifier (*omnes*); but exception phrases are also common with negative universal quantifiers (*nemo, nullus, non... quisquam*). Compare the following examples

(94) *Omnes* iam nostri *praeter* Tullium tuum venerunt. (Ad Att 5.14.2)
Ego mecum *praeter* Dionysium eduxi *neminem* (Ad Att 4.11.2).

In the case of *omnes*, subtracting the exception *Tullius* from the A set (*nostri*) involves also subtracting it from what would otherwise have been a larger B set (*venerunt*); without the exception B would have included A. In the case of *nemo*, subtracting the exception *Dionysius* from the A set ('people') involves adding it to what would otherwise have been a smaller B set (*educti*); without the exception A and B would have been disjoint, in fact B would have been the empty set. For *omnes*, X is in the complement of B relative to A (A–B), as illustrated in Figure 5.10 above; for *nemo*, X is in the complement of 'not B' relative to A, therefore in the intersection of A and B. Here are some more examples

(95) Obstabat eius cogitationibus *nemo praeter* Milonem. (Pro Mil 88)
nulla Thessaliae fuit civitas *praeter* Larisaeos... quin Caesari parerent (BC 3.81)
nec *quisquam praeter* Philippum... cum rege relictus (Livy 45.6.9)
Eam intrare haud fere *quisquam praeter* ducem ipsum audebat (Livy 9.36.1).

The second example (BC 3.81) is illustrated in Figure 5.11: *nulla A praeter X* denotes the set of properties $\lambda B.(A-X)\cap B=\varnothing \wedge X\subseteq B$. The first conjunct accounts for the occurrence of negative polarity items like *quisquam* in the last

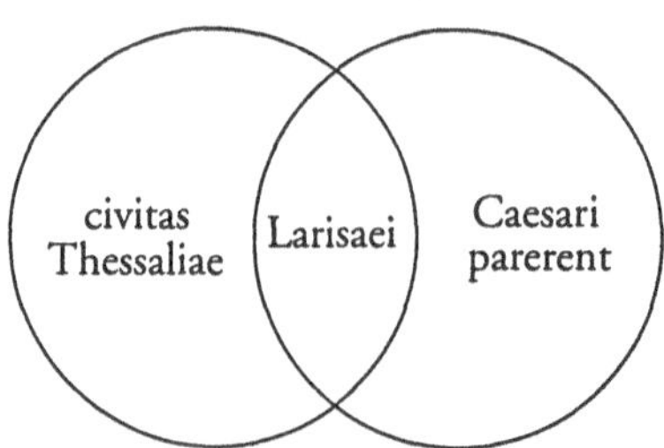

Figure 5.11
Exceptive with negative universal quantifier
Nulla Thessaliae fuit civitas praeter Larisaeos quin Caesari parerent (BC 3.81)

(94) All of my people except for your Tullius have already arrived (Ad Att 5.14.2). I did not bring anyone with me except for Dionysius (Ad Att 4.11.2).

(95) Noone stood in the way of his intentions except Milo (Pro Mil 88). There was no state of Thessaly except for the Larisaeans that did not obey Caesar (BC 3.81). And noone was left with the king except Philip (Livy 45.6.9). Hardly anyone other than the general himself dared to enter it (Livy 9.36.1).

two examples, the second conjunct for the fact that these quantifier expressions are not downward entailing on their B arguments: noone except the leader dared to enter the Ciminian forest does not entail that noone except the leader dared to enter the Ciminian forest unarmed. Exceptives with other downward entailing quantifiers are rare

(96) *Praeter* mulierem *pauca* animalia coitum novere gravida (NH 7.48).

Women are a salient exception to the generalization about the behaviour of most animals: subtracting women does not result in the empty set, and the sentence remains true even if the exception is omitted, although the proportion changes slightly. *Pauci* is just one step up from a negative universal with an exceptive

(97) oratores veteres, quorum aut *pauci* aut *praeter* Catonem et Gracchum *nemo* tubam inflat (Fronto Aur 3.17.3).

As before plurals can indicate a kind or the set from which the exceptions are drawn

(98) glans... quam *praeter* sues nullum attingat animal (NH 16.24)
Neque enim temere *praeter* mercatores adit ad illos quisquam (BG 4.20)
per eos annos... quibus *praeter* patricios nemo tribunus militum fuerit (Livy 6.37.8).

Only some merchants go to Britain and only some patricians had been military tribunes.

Sometimes the exceptive itself (X) is quantified; in the simplest case one quantifier has a null head associated with the restriction of the other

(99) naves longas *praeter* viginti omnes tradant (Livy 30.16.11)
naves omnes tectas tradere *praeter* quinque (Livy 33.30.5)
ut *praeter* quattuor equites omnes ad unum interfecerit (Livy 29.32.6).

The cardinality of (A−B) in the first two examples, the set of ships minus the set to be handed over, is twenty (Livy 30.16) and five (Livy 33.30) respectively; they were allowed to subtract some set of twenty/five ships, just which set is not specified, presumably they got to choose. X is required to be not just a subset of the lexically specified set A (cavalrymen in the last example (Livy 29.32)), but a subset of the contextually restricted set A∩C (Masinissa's cavalry in the battle with Bucar); X has the same domain restriction as A too. The restriction of X can also be a subset of the restriction of A

(96) Few animals except women have intercourse when they are pregnant (NH 7.48).

(97) The orators of old, few or none of whom except Cato and Gracchus blow a trumpet (Fronto Aur 3.17.3).

(98) Its acorns, which no animal other than pigs touches (NH 16.24). Nor does anyone apart from merchants go there without good reason (BG 4.20). During those years in which noone except patricians had been a military tribune (Livy 6.37.8).

(99) That they hand over all their battle ships except for twenty (Livy 30.16.11). That they should hand over all their decked ships except five (Livy 33.30.5). That he killed all his cavalry to a man except for four (Livy 29.32.6).

(100) cum ibi... nulla subsidia cerneret *praeter* quattuor turmas equitum (Livy 37.42.7)
neve ipse navem ullam *praeter* duos lembos... haberet (Livy 34.35.5)
Praeter duo nos loquitur isto modo nemo (Ad Fam 7.25.2).

In the third example (Ad Fam 7.25) the cardinal is part of a definite expression ('the two of us'). There are also examples of X with other quantifiers

(101) in foro *praeter* paucos seniorum nemo esset (Livy 3.52.5)
nemo adire *praeter* paucas feminas (Tac Ann 13.19).
nec erat iam quisquam mecum tuorum *praeter* omnes meos (Ad Fam 3.11.5).

Distributives

Consider first the following example

(102) mollitudo vocis in *tres* partes divisa est, et eae partes ipsae sunt in *octo* partes alias distributae (Rhet Her 3.24).

It contains two cardinal numbers, *tres* and *octo*. The correct interpretation is cumulative: there is a set of three main divisions and there is a set of eight subdivisions; the total number of subdivisions is eight (not twenty-four). Each division contains one or more subdivisions and each subdivision belongs to one of the main divisions. But now consider the following set of examples

(103) Cicerae... modii *quattuor* operas bubulcorum *tres* postulant (Col 2.12.4)
Duo iugera *tres* operae commode occabunt (Col 11.2.82)
(unus homo) *quaternis* operis *singula* iugera (confodere) possit (Varro RR 1.18.2)
Factus *tres*... a *quaternis* hominibus nocte et die premi iustum est (NH 15.23).

The first example (Col 2.12) is again cumulative: it says that a total of four modii of cicera require a total of three days' work. If the object had been distributive, each modius would have required three days' work, giving a total of twelve days' work. Similarly for the second example. But the third example (RR 1.18) has distributive numerals instead of cardinals (four days are required for

(100) Since he saw no auxiliary forces there except four troops of cavalry (Livy 37.42.7). That he himself should not have any ship apart from two small boats (Livy 34.35.5). Nobody apart from the two of us talks like that (Ad Fam 7.25.2).
(101) There was noone in the forum apart from a few of the old men (Livy 3.52.5). Noone came except for a few women (Tac Ann 13.19). And there is now noone of your people with me except all my people (Ad Fam 3.11.5).
(102) Vocal flexibility is divided into three parts, and those parts themselves are distributed into eight subparts (Rhet Her 3.24).
(103) Four modii of cicera require three days' work of the ploughmen (Col 2.12.4). Three labourers will comfortably rake two iugera in a day (Col 11.2.82). One man can dig a iugerum in four days' work (Varro RR 1.18.2). It is right for three factus to be pressed by four men in twenty-four hours (NH 15.23).

each iugerum), while the last example (NH 15.23) combines a cumulative cardinal for the total twenty-four hour output of oil with a distributive for the number of men in each shift. In eventive sentences distributives are pluractional markers, they express (sub)event iteration

(104) naves... *duae* regiae *unam* circumsistunt (Livy 36.44.6)
cum singulas *binae* ac *ternae* naves circumsteterant (BG 3.15).

The first example (Livy 36.44) describes a single incident, the second (BG 3.15) a replicating pattern. But to keep things simple, we will start with a purely stative example

(105) ad viginti milibus civium quibus *terni* pluresve liberi essent (Suet 1.20.3).

Sets of three or more children (the distributive share) are distributed over around twenty thousand citizens (the distributive key). One idea is to capture this meaning with a polyadic generalized quantifier (of type <<e×e,t>,t>): for every pair of sets consisting of a single citizen (X) and three or more children (Y), members of X are in a possession relation to members of Y. Another idea is to use a separate function to match sets of children with citizens; there is a function that maps each citizen onto the set of three or more children that he possesses: $\exists f.\forall x.\text{Civis}(x) \rightarrow \text{Tres-liberi}(f(x)) \wedge \text{Poss}(x,f(x))$. But we probably don't need this additional machinery: since quantifiers are scopal, distributivity is built into the $\forall\exists$ order, and we already have a function for assigning cardinality to sets.

Let's begin with examples in which an argument or adjunct further to the right in the default word order (S > DO > Oblique) is distributed over an argument further to the left, for instance an object or other argument over a subject

(106) singula iugera vinearum *sescenas* urnas vini praebuisse (Col 3.3.2)
cornua *trinis* firmabantur subsidiis (BAlex 37)
duo fasces *septenos* habuere libros... septem Latini... septem Graeci (Livy 40.29.6)
cum *centenis* hostibus singulos pugnaturos (Livy 6.7.2)
Nutricare *octonos* porcos parvulos primo possunt (Varro RR 2.4.19)
uxores... *denas* alii habebant (Sall Jug 80.6).

In the second example (BAlex 37: *trinis* is distributive here) each wing of Pharnaces' army had three support lines, so that there was a total of six support lines on the wings; this is illustrated in Figure 5.12. If we draw a powerset lattice for

(104) Two of the king's ships surrounded one of the Carthaginian ships (Livy 36.44.6). When each ship had been surrounded by a pair or a triple of ships (BG 3.15).
(105) To around twenty thousand citizens who had three or more children (Suet 1.20.3).
(106) That one iugerum of vineyard yielded six hundred urnae of wine (Col 3.3.2). The wings were reinforced by three support lines (BAlex 37). There were two bundles containing seven books; seven were in Latin and seven in Greek (Livy 40.29.6). That they would be fighting one against a hundred (Livy 6.7.2). A sow can feed eight piglets to start with (Varro RR 2.4.19). Some have ten wives (Sall Jug 80.6).

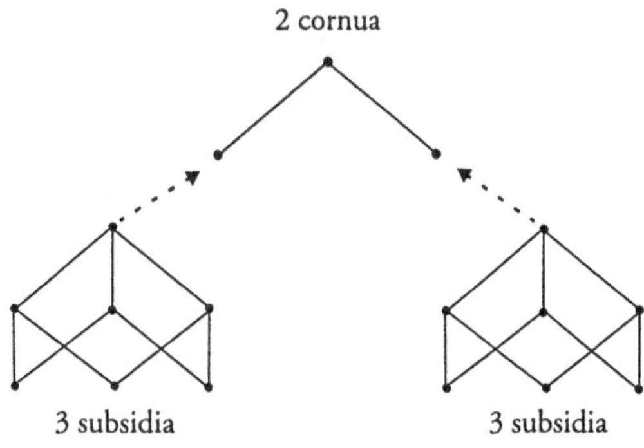

Figure 5.12
Distributive numeral
Cornua trinis firmabantur subsidiis (BAlex 37)

just the set {a,b,c,d,e,f} of these six support lines on the wings (there were also support lines in the centre, but we will exclude those), and go to the line of trials in the lattice, we will find 20 different subsets, according to the formula provided in Chapter 6. Some of these subsets are disjoint (for instance {{a,b,c}, {d,e,f}}), others overlap (for instance {{a,b,d}, {d,e,f}}). Each pair of disjoint subsets represents a different way of partitioning the set of six support lines into two non-overlapping sets of three, and one pair will correspond to the facts on the ground. In the third example (Livy 40.29) each bundle contained seven books, as is clear from the following context. The property of possessing seven books is predicated of each member of the set of two bundles: $\exists Y.\ \text{Fasces}(Y) \wedge |Y| = 2 \wedge \forall y \in Y \rightarrow \exists X.\ \text{Libri}(X) \wedge |X| = 7 \wedge \text{Habet}(y, X)$. As explained in Chapter 6, the formalism Libri(X) means that the set X is a member of the powerset of the set of books ($\mathcal{P}$Libr-) excluding singleton sets and the null set.

It is also possible for an argument further to the left in the default word order to be distributed over an argument or adjunct further to the right, for instance a subject over an object or an object over an oblique. In this class of examples scope inverts the default linear order of the quantified phrases

(107) auctores tantum seditionis (erant ii numero haud plus quam quinque et triginta)... Tribunis septem... *quina* nomina principum seditionis edita sunt (Livy 28.26.5)
Senos Charinus omnibus digitis gerit... anulos (Mart 11.59.1)
ut in singulas colonias *ternos* cives Romanos facere posset (Pro Balb 48).

In the first example (Livy 28.26) five names are distributed over the members of the set of seven tribunes, i.e. each of the seven tribunes is given a different set of

(107) Only the ringleaders of the mutiny (these were no more than thirty-five in number)... To each of the seven tribunes were assigned five names of the ringleaders of the mutiny (Livy 28.26.5). Charinus wears six rings on each finger (Mart 11.59.1).That he should be able to create three Roman citizens for each colony (Pro Balb 48).

five names, yielding a total of thirty-five names (which equals the number of leaders of the conspiracy). The five names constitute a group. On the other hand, in the last example (Pro Balb 48) there might presumably be three separate grants of citizenship in each colony. Inverse scope is illustrated in Figure 5.13 for the second example in (104) about the naval battle between the Romans and the Veneti (BG 3.15). The fact that distributivity is morphologically marked in Latin may make inverse scope easier to access than in English: it is quite difficult to get an inverse reading from English 'Five names were given to seven tribunes.' Examples with an indefinite are easier: 'A sword was given to seven tribunes.'

By definition a distributive is distributed over elements of a plural key, usually individual members (atoms, as often specified by the addition of *singuli* to the key), although double distributive sentences are also possible

(108) sextarios singulos adicere salsae aquae in *binas* musti urnas, quamvis multi etiam *binos*, nonnulli etiam *ternos* immisceant (Col 12.21.5).

Some people mix two or three sextarii of salt water for each two urnae of wine. Distributives can also iterate, but that is not the same thing

(109) *septenum* pedum stipites recti ab utroque latere *quaterni* applicantur (Col 6.19.2).

Each side had four posts seven feet high each. An atomic distributive key cannot be the subject of a collective predicate

(110) *cum *singulae* binas ac ternas naves circumsteterant (cp. BG 3.15),

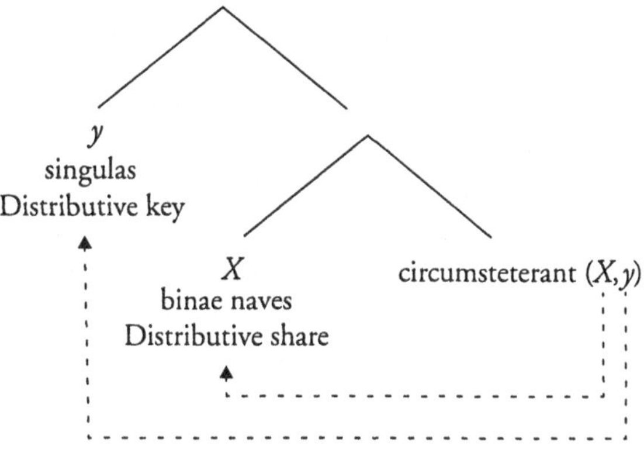

Figure 5.13
Inverse scope with distributive numeral
Singulas binae naves circumsteterant (BG 3.15)

(108) To add one sextarius of salt water for every two urnae of must, although many mix in two and some even three sextarii (Col 12.21.5).
(109) Four seven feet high upright posts are attached on each side (Col 6.19.2).
(110) When each ship had surrounded a pair or a triple of ships (BG 3.15).

nor can there be distributivity over a unique entity (without iteration). Consider the following examples

(111) Summa legionum trium et viginti ita per provincias divisa: *binae* consulum essent, *quattuor* Hispania haberet, *binas* tres praetores... *duas* C. Terentius in Etruria, duas Q. Fulvius in Bruttiis (Livy 27.36.12)
legiones decem effectae: *ternae* inde datae consulibus, *quattuor* dictator usus. (Livy 2.30.7).

The plural subjects have distributive numerals (the three praetors each get two legions and the two consuls each get three), the singular subjects have cardinal numerals: a distributive with the singular subjects would be uninterpretable ('Q. Fulvius each had two legions,' 'The dictator each had four'). In iterative, habitual and generic sentences a distributive phrase can be distributed over a singular or collective plural noun (an entity or a measure): the latter often restricts a variable bound by an implicit universal quantifier

(112) Ecfodiebam in *die denos* scrobes (Pl Aul 834)
trinisque in *die* sacrificiis (Suet 6.56)
primae vineae *centenas* amphoras *iugeratim* praeberent (Col 3.3.3)
Cenam ternis ferculis aut cum abundantissime senis praebebat (Suet 2.74).

The last example (Suet 2.74) says that Augustus typically served three courses per dinner (for every *x*, *x* a dinner, he serves three courses in *x*). Sometimes distribution involves an event implicit in the context

(113) *binis* ternisve summum ex manipulis aquandi causa missis (Livy 31.42.4)
quaterni quinive exercitus saepe per eos annos in Etruria, in Umbria... in Samnio, in Lucanis gerebant bellum. (Livy 9.19.3)
Quini aut *seni* adveniunt ad scorta congerrones (Pl Truc 99).

Distribution is over events, not over another entity in the sentence. The second example (Livy 9.19) means that on all given occasions during those years there were four or five armies in the field. The third example (Truc 99) says that five or six pals show up on each occasion ('five at a time'), not that there are five or six pals for each girl ('five per girl'). In the polyadic theory, the quantifier would

(111) The total number of legions was twenty-three, divided as follows among the provinces: two each were to be for the consuls, Spain was to have four, the three praetors two each, C. Terentius was to have two in Etruria, Q. Fulvius two among the Bruttii (Livy 27.36.12). Ten legions were formed; three of them were given to each of the consuls and the dictator got to use four (Livy 2.30.7).

(112) I used to dig ten ditches a day (Pl Aul 834). With three sacrifices a day (Suet 6.56). Prime vineyards produced a hundred amphorae per iugerum (Col 3.3.3). He served a dinner of three courses or on the most sumptuous occasions six (Suet 2.74).

(113) With two or three at the most from the maniples being sent to get water (Livy 31.42.4). Four or five armies would often be fighting simultaneously during those years in Etruria, in Umbria, in Samnium and in the territory of the Lucanians (Livy 9.19.3). Five or six pals show up to see the girls (Pl Truc 99).

be over pairs of events and sets of pals, not over pairs of sets of pals and girls. Distributives are typically subject to some form of distinctness condition: the sets in the distributive share should be totally, or at least partially, distinct. So either it is a different set of pals each time (there is a partition of the overall set of pals), or some of the same pals come more than once (there is a cover of the overall set of pals), but not a single set of pals repeatedly. Distributive pluractionality does not reduce to iteration. In the following stative example

(114) patri matrique communes liberi sunt, quibus cum duo sunt, non *singuli singulos* habent sed *singuli binos* (Sen De Ben 7.12.1),

each member of a parental couple has the same pair of children, but all parents with two children do not generically have the same single pair of children (although they may have the same king and queen).

The distributive numerals we have been analyzing so far are also used as collective numerals (except that collective *uni* and *trini* are used in place of distributive *singuli* and *terni*). The distributives are said to be derived from earlier collectives, and the two are clearly semantically related. Distributives tend to represent episodic partitions: for instance, there were two bundles of books and each bundle contained seven books, or five pals typically show up on each occasion. But it can also happen that things appear in sets of a certain cardinality regularly or intrinsically, like shoes in pairs, in which case distributivity is more dependent on lexical than on contextual factors. The pattern of co-occurrence causes the atomic objects to lose the component of individuative meaning that depends on separability. The distributive is then used to quantify over these intrinsic sets (where the cardinal would quantify over the individual members of the sets). While some examples seem to count the individuals in the collective set

(115) scyphos... *binos* (Verr 2.4.32)
frenaque *bina*... aurea (Aen 8.168),

others count the collective sets themselves

(116) triumviros *binos* creari iussit, alteros... alteros (Livy 25.5.6)
triumviri *bini*, uni... alteri (Livy 25.7.5).

The discussions of Cato and Varro about what is required for an olive orchard are good illustrations of this type

(117) boves *trinos*, asinos... qui stercus vectent *tris* (Cato 10.1)
Saserna ad iugera CC arvi boum iuga duo satis esse scribit , Cato in olivetis CCXL iugeris boves *trinos*... asinos... *tres* (Varro RR 1.19.1).

(114) Children belong to father and mother alike; when parents have two children, they do not each have one but they each have two (Sen De Ben 7.12.1).

(115) A pair of cups (Verr 2.4.32). A pair of golden bits (Aen 8.168).

(116) It ordered two committees of three men to be created, the one... the other (Livy 25.5.6). Two committees of three men, the one... the other (Livy 25.7.5).

(117) Three yoke of oxen, three donkeys to transport the dung (Cato 10.1). Saserna writes that two yoke of oxen are sufficient for 200 iugera of land, Cato that in olive orchards three yoke of oxen are sufficient for 240 iugera... three donkeys (Varro RR 1.19.1).

For the donkeys you go to the line of trials in the lattice and pick one element, for the oxen you go to the line of duals and pick three disjoint elements. This type of collective quantification is also found in derived forms like *senio* 'six on the dice,' *grex centenarius* 'a flock of a hundred birds,' *denarius* 'a coin worth ten asses,' *senarius* 'a verse with six feet'; compare the last with the distributive

(118) Sibylla, abdita quae *senis* fata canit pedibus (Tib 2.5.15).

In the same way distributives are used to quantify over collective pluralia tantum, in which the constitutive atomic objects can be reanalyzed as a single collective entity

(119) non dicimus biga una, quadrigae duae, nuptiae tres, sed pro eo *unae* bigae, *binae* quadrigae, *trinae* nuptiae (Varro LL 10.67: app. crit.).

Where a cardinal can be used, it quantifies over the individual entities of which the collectives are comprised: *binae litterae* 'two epistles,' *duae litterae* 'two letters of the alphabet.' English solves the problem of pluralizing pairs and pluralia tantum by a sort of classifier construction: *calceos binos* 'two pairs of shoes.'

Quantifier scope

For indefinites and indefinite quantifiers other than numerals distributivity is not morphologically marked in Latin, so scopal ambiguities can arise: we find the same sort of ambiguities as in English sentences like 'Every student read some book,' which can be followed by either 'It was Aeneid VI' (narrow scope subject) or 'They were all on Roman religion' (wide scope subject); similarly 'Some student took every book out of the library,' which can be followed by either 'He was totally exhausted' (wide scope subject) or 'They all returned them in good condition' (narrow scope subject). The likelihood of scopal ambiguity depends on a number of factors including the lexical meaning of the quantifiers and their monotonicity properties, the pragmatic likelihood of the two different readings, the syntactic structure of the sentence (particularly grammatical relations and islands) and the informational structure of the sentence (topic-focus partition). For instance, there are two readings for 'Several praetorian guards were standing watch over every conspirator,' but only one is readily accessible for 'Most praetorian guards / Less than three praetorian guards were standing watch over every conspirator.' The former cannot mean that for every conspirator there was a different majority set of praetorian guards standing watch over him (narrow scope subject). The latter can hardly mean that there was a single group of two (or one or zero) praetorian guards that was assigned to stand watch over all the conspirators (wide scope subject). Similarly, two readings are available for 'A praetorian guard was standing watch over every conspirator,' but only one for 'A praetorian guard was standing watch over more than three conspirators.' If

(118) The Sibyl who sings the secrets of fate in verses of six feet (Tib 2.5.15).

(119) We don't say *biga una, quadrigae duae, nuptiae tres,* but instead *unae bigae, binae quadrigae, trinae nuptiae* (Varro LL 10.67).

you replace a quantifier with a definite, the number of scopal readings automatically drops from two to one, e.g. 'Macro was standing watch over every conspirator'; different praetorian guards can be assigned to each conspirator, but there is only one Macro, so he cannot vary relative to the conspirators (although he can watch over every conspirator collectively in a single event or event-distributively in sequential events).

The following data set illustrates how scope interacts with word order and obliqueness in Latin for sentences containing both a universal (∀) and an existential (∃) quantifier. Sentences having a wide scope existential (∃∀), i.e. sentences in which the universal quantifier is contained within the scope of the existential quantifier, do occur but they are comparatively rare

(120) veritatis argumentum est *aliquid omnibus* videri (Sen Ep 117.6)
Contemnere *aliquis omnia* potest, omnia habere nemo potest. (Sen Ep 62.3).

The first example (Ep 117.6) means that there is something that everyone believes ($\exists x \forall y.\text{Videtur}(x,y)$), not that everyone believes something (possibly) different ($\forall y \exists x.\text{Videtur}(x,y)$); the first formula entails the second, but the second allows for all sorts of possible situations in addition to that described by the first. The second example (Ep 62.3) means that someone can be universally contemptuous, not that everything is such that it can be despised by someone or other. Both the word order and the obliqueness hierarchy match the scope: the existential quantifier precedes the universal quantifier in the surface linear order and is the subject in both examples. Examples with a wide scope universal quantifier (∀∃) are more common

(121) *omne* nomen ex *aliquibus*, non ex omnibus litteris scribitur (De Inv 2.16)
Omnes aliquid belli dixerunt illo loco quo deprensi sunt adulteri (Sen Con 1.4.10).

The first example (De Inv 2.16) means that every word is spelled with a different set of letters of the alphabet ($\forall x.\text{Nomen}(x) \rightarrow \exists Y.\text{ Litterae}(Y) \wedge \text{Scribunt}(z,Y,x)$), not that there is a set of letters that is used to spell every word ($\exists Y.\text{Litterae}(Y) \wedge \forall x.\text{Nomen}(x) \rightarrow \text{Scribunt}(z,Y,x)$). The ∀∃ scope of this example is compared with the ∃∀ scope of the first example of (120) in Figure 5.14, and its tripartite structure is set out in Figure 5.15: the narrow scope quantifier *aliquibus* is mapped into the nuclear scope of the wide scope quantifier *omne*. The second example (Con 1.4) means that everyone had a different clever comment, not that there was some clever comment that everyone repeated. In these ∀∃ examples, like the ∃∀ ones cited in (120), the word order and the obliqueness hierarchy (S > Obj/Obl) match the scope: the universal quantifier precedes the existential quantifier in the surface linear order and is the subject in

(120) The fact that something is agreed upon by everyone is evidence of its truth (Sen Ep 117.6). Someone can despise everything, but noone can possess everything (Sen Ep 62.3).

(121) Every word is spelled with some letters, not with all of them (De Inv 2.16). Everyone said something clever at the point where the adulterers were caught (Sen Con 1.4.10).

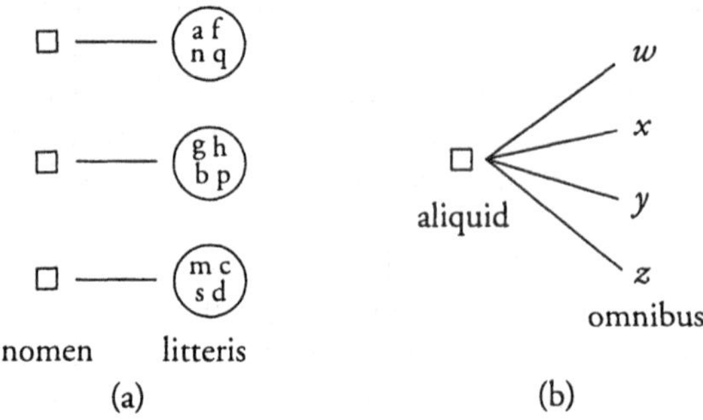

Figure 5.14
Wide scope (a) and narrow scope (b) universal quantifiers
(a) *Omne nomen ex aliquibus litteris scribitur* (De Inv 2.16);
(b) *Aliquid omnibus videri* (Sen Ep 117.6)

both examples. But this is not necessarily the case. In the following examples the obliqueness hierarchy matches the scope but the word order does not

(122) Quoniam igitur *aliquid omnes*, quid Lucius noster? (De Fin 5.5)
non quo non in *aliqua* constitutione *omnis* semper causa versetur (De Inv 2.155).

Both examples have ∀∃ scope but ∃∀ word order: focus on the universal quantifier has caused the existential to scramble to its left. Conversely scope may correlate with the word order but be inverted relative to the obliqueness hierarchy

(123) cum *omnibus* horis *aliquid* atrociter fieri videmus (Pro Rosc Am 154)
in *omnes aliquid* ex his cadit (Quint 7.2.50).

The first example (Pro Rosc Am 154) says that a different (not the same) atrocity occurs every hour: scope and word order are ∀∃, but the obliqueness hierarchy is ∃∀ because the existential quantifier is the subject. Finally it is also possible for neither the word order nor the obliqueness hierarchy to match the scopal relation

(124) Aures... cervis tantum scissae..., sorici pilosae; sed *aliquae omnibus* (NH 11.136)
exponemus locos quorum pars *aliqua* in *omnem* coniecturalem incidit controversiam... non omnes in omnem causam convenire (De Inv 2.16).

(122) So since everyone has something, what about our friend Lucius? (De Fin 5.5). Not because it is not the case that every speech always involves the formulation of some issue (De Inv 2.155).

(123) When we see some act of savagery taking place every hour (Pro Rosc Am 154). Something like this applies to all of them (Quint 7.2.50).

(124) Only deer have split ears; the shrew has hairy ears; but all species have some sort of ears (NH 11.136). We will set out the arguments, of which some part or other will be relevant to every inferential controversy... that not all of them apply to every case (De Inv 2.16).

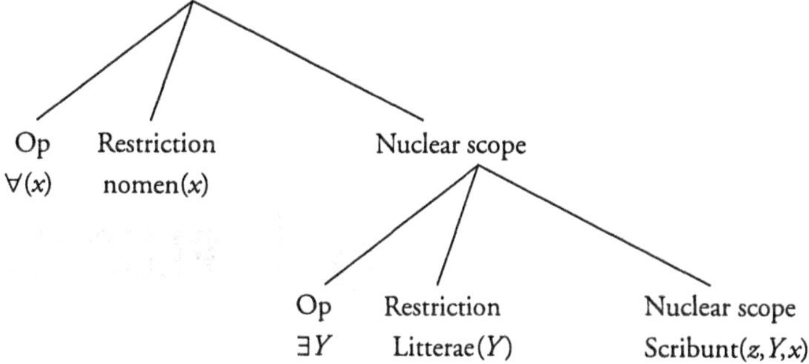

Figure 5.15
Tripartite structure with two strong quantifiers
Omne nomen ex aliquibus litteris scribitur (De Inv 2.16)

The first example (NH 11.136) says that every animal has some type of ear, not that there is a type of ear that every animal has. The second example (De Inv 2.16) says that different groups of arguments apply to different cases, not that there is a group of arguments that applies to all cases. So they both have $\forall\exists$ scope, but in both examples the word order and the obliqueness hierarchy is $\exists\forall$. The word order inversion is again explained by focus on the universal quantifier.

FURTHER READING

Bach, Jelinek, Kratzer & Partee (1995); Gil (1982); Peters & Westerståhl (2006); Tunstall (1998); Zimmermann (2002).

6 | PLURALITY

Like quantification, which it partially overlaps, plurality is a basic mechanism of the expressive economy of human language. It does not necessarily have to be encoded by morphological number (singular, dual, plural etc.), but it does have to exist as a semantic category. If a language lacks a morphological plural, the interpretation of semantic number has to rely on other components of the message (numerals, for instance) and on pragmatic information. But if a language lacked semantic number, plurality would not be a part of its semantics, and plural situations would have to be communicated in terms of sequenced or conjoined singular predications. So, like quantification, plurality greatly enriches the power of language to convey complex information in a succinct format.

Morphological plural

In Latin plurality is marked on referential, quantified and predicative noun phrases; it spreads throughout the noun phrase by agreement rules

(1) hoc nostrum consilium (Ad Fam 4.4.5)
omnia haec nostra praeclara studia (Pro Mur 22).

The number of the subject phrase is also marked on the verb by agreement rules

(2) consul *iussit* (Livy 24.9.1)
patres *iusserunt* (Livy 32.26.14).

Verbal agreement is computed off the entire subject phrase and not just off its head noun: so coordinated and even sometimes comitative subjects can trigger plural agreement on the verb

(3) Cornelius et Baebius *statuerunt* (Livy 40.38.2)
Iuba cum Labieno *capti* in potestatem Caesaris *venissent* (BAfr 52).

Number marking on the verb does not encode verbal plurality, in other words it is not used to denote repetition of the event (like an imperfect or iterative

(1) This advice of mine (Ad Fam 4.4.5). All these splendid studies of ours (Pro Mur 22).
(2) The consul ordered (Livy 24.9.1). The senators ordered (Livy 32.26.14).
(3) Cornelius and Baebius decided (Livy 40.38.2). Juba along with Labienus would have been captured and come into Caesar's power (BAfr 52).

form) nor even the subevents that arise from distributivity (since collective plural subjects take plural verbs too). Rather it is an indirect mark of the plurality of the participants in the event that have been chosen as the subject of predication in the sentence. In much the same way the personal endings on verbs encode information about a participant in the event and not about the event itself. It is not clear whether number inflections on the verb are purely formal and semantically uninterpreted syntactic features, or whether they do have their own semantic interpretation. On the former view, a plural verb has the same semantics as a singular verb, and the ungrammaticality of e.g. *milites discedit* 'the soldiers departs' in place of *milites discedunt* (BC 1.22) is due to a mismatch at the syntactic level only; it is just bad grammar. On the latter view, singular and plural verbs have different denotations: a singular verb denotes a set of singular individuals, and a plural verb denotes a set of pluralities. Ungrammaticality then results from a mismatch at the semantic level: a plurality like 'the soldiers' cannot be a member of a set of singularities like 'departs.' The semantic approach is complicated by number agreement in oratio obliqua

(4) ii qui se decemviros sperant *futuros* (De Leg Agr 2.63)
Alii ab indice nominati esse se *Christianos* dixerunt et mox negaverunt (Pliny Ep 10.96.6).

The additive (cumulative) operation that creates the distributive plural spills over into the reported speech. The Christians said "I am a Christian," not "We are Christians": what has been pluralized is an expression representing a complex predicate including a bound variable ($\lambda x.$ x dixit x esse Christianum). Compare an English sentence like 'All the candidates thought they would be elected president.'

That the verbal number agreement rule is not a purely mechanical replication of the morphological number of the subject is clear from instances of mismatch between the morphological number of the subject and that of the verb. In some examples of mismatch the noun is a semantically singular part or amount that consists of a subset of the set denoted by the genitive

(5) si pars navium adversariorum Euboeam *superasset* (Nepos 2.3.3)
Pars navium haustae *sunt* (Tac Ann 2.24)

Silvanum magna vis accusatorum *circumsteterat* (Tac Ann 13.52)
immensamque vim mortalium spectaculo *intentos* (Tac Ann 4.62)

ut quibus iumentorum calonumque turba *abesset* (Livy 7.37.6)
turba lixarum calonumque *impleverant* regiam (Curt Ruf 6.8.23).

(4) Those who hope that they will be decemviri (De Leg Agr 2.63). Others, who had been named by an informer, said that they were Christians and later denied it (Pliny Ep 10.96.6).

(5) If part of the ships of their opponents got past Euboea (Nepos 2.3.3). Part of the ships were engulfed (Tac Ann 2.24). A large number of accusers had surrounded Silvanus (Tac Ann 13.52). A vast crowd of people intent on the spectacle (Tac Ann 4.62). Since they did not have with them the crowd of beasts of burden and servants (Livy 7.37.6). A crowd of camp-followers and servants had filled the royal quarters (Curt Ruf 6.8.23).

In each pair the first example has singular agreement with the morphological (and semantic) number of the subject phrase, the second example has plural agreement with the subject's constituent plurality. For the purposes of agreement *pars navium* can be tantamount to *aliquot naves* and *turba calonum* to *multi calones,* as though the head of the phrase were not the group but the (pseudo)partitive genitive (which is either properly partitive or expresses membership constituency); compare English 'A bunch of students were reading Vergil in the library.' Number agreement mismatch is not confined to examples with overt partitive genitives but occurs also with simple collective nouns like terms of military organization

(6) ipsas fauces exercitus Ligurum *insedit* (Livy 35.11.2)
exercitus... penetrandam Caledoniam... *fremebant* (Tac Agr 27.1)
dextrum cornu hostium in fugam *inclinabat* (Livy 37.24.3)
cornu sinisterius... pedem referre *coeperunt* (Ad Fam 10.30.4).

The greater the distance from the agreement controller to the target, the more likely the morphology is to convert to plurality. Distance can be measured in terms of the number of syllables or words or/and in terms of the agreement hierarchy that likewise governs gender agreement: attributive < predicative < relative < anaphoric. Mismatch is not possible with attributive adjectives (**generi humanis* for *generi humano* (ND 2.18 in (9) below), so within the noun phrase agreement is local (syntactic). Nonlocal agreement can occur sometimes with secondary predicate adjectives and participles (*spectaculo intentos* Tac Ann 4.62 in (5)) and with relatives

(7) Caesar alteram alam mittit qui satagentibus celeriter *occurrerent* (BAfr 78)
L. Sulla quaestor cum magno equitatu in castra venit, *quos* uti ex Latio cogeret... Romae relictus erat (Sall Jug 95.1),

anaphoric pronouns

(8) cohortes sinistrum cornu... circumierunt *eosque* a tergo sunt adorti (BC 3.93)
omnem equitatum et cum *eis* velocissumos pedites (Sall Jug 91.4)

and null subjects in subordinate and conjoined clauses

(9) populus convolat, *tumultuantur*, clamant, pugnant de loco (Ter Hec 40)
hoc idem generi humano evenerit quod in terra... conlocati *sunt* (ND 2.17)

(6) An army of Ligurians sealed off the mouth of the pass (Livy 35.11.2). The army clamoured that they should invade Caledonia (Tac Agr 27.1). The right wing of the enemy was turning to flight (Livy 37.24.3). Our left wing began to retreat (Ad Fam 10.30.4).

(7) Caesar sent a second wing of cavalry to quickly support the hard-pressed men (BAfr 78). The quaestor L. Sulla came to the camp with a large group of cavalry which he had been left at Rome to collect from Latium (Sall Jug 95.1).

(8) The cohorts surrounded the left wing and attacked them from the rear (BC 3.93). The entire cavalry and with them the fastest-moving infantry (Sall Jug 91.4).

(9) The people flocked together, they created chaos, shouted and fought for seats (Ter Hec 40). The same thing happened to the human race because they are located on the earth (ND 2.17).

(10) iuventus... in castris per laborem usum militiae discebat, magisque in decoris armis... quam in scortis... lubidinem *habebant* (Sall Cat 7.4).

The converse rule, namely pluralia tantum (lexically specified plurals like *insidiae* 'ambush,' *castra* 'camp') taking singular verb agreement, is not allowed: *ubi castra posita erant/*positum est* 'where the camp had been pitched' (BG 2.8); similarly in (British) English we can say 'The committee are discussing the issue' but not *'My pants is grey.'

A collective noun like *cohors* 'cohort' is a grammatically and semantically singular entity: it denotes a group, which is an atomic object and which can itself be pluralized (*cohortes* 'cohorts'). It does not simply denote a plurality: for instance *magnus equitatus* ≠ *magni equites* (think of a large detachment of pygmy cavalry). However it is semantically related to a plurality, which is a set or a sum: you can map from a cohort onto the set of soldiers it comprises at any particular point in time and vice versa. Agreement may be with the singularity or, under the conditions just specified, with the plurality. In the case of anaphoric pronouns in the next sentence, plural agreement may be due to a processing mechanism, a tendency for the grammatical number of the first sentence to be replaced as it is processed for storage in memory. But intraclausally a singular collective with plural verb agreement presumably already stands for its constituent members. For instance, *sinistrum cornu* may stand for a singular individual entity, but it may also stand for *ei qui erant a sinistro cornu*, in which case it can take plural verb agreement, just as in

(11) capitaque coniurationis... securi *percussi* (Livy 10.1.3)

the subject noun stands for *ei qui erant capita coniurationis* and so can trigger masculine gender agreement in the predicate. Collective nouns with inanimate constituent members, like *silva* 'forest (of trees),' show less constituent transparency because inanimate pluralities are less individuated (more mass-like); this also explains why neuter plurals take singular number agreement in Ancient Greek.

Structure of plurality

According to the view adopted here, the extensional meaning or denotation of the nominal root *milit-* is just the set of individuals in the discourse domain that are soldiers (λx.Milit-(x)). (Other theories take the denotation of the nominal root to be a kind, which is turned into a count noun by a covert classifier, others again take it to include pluralities as well as singularities.) The denotation of the singular noun *miles* is likewise the set of individual soldiers in the discourse domain (λx.Miles(x)). If the noun *miles* is used in a definite noun phrase, it refers to a specific discourse salient soldier (ιx.Miles(x)); if it is used in a nonspecific indefinite noun phrase, it could be any soldier ($\exists x$.Miles(x)). The deno-

(10) The youth learned military discipline in camp through hard work and took more pleasure in beautiful arms than in call-girls (Sall Cat 7.4).

(11) The ringleaders of the conspiracy were beheaded (Livy 10.1.3).

tation of the plural noun *milites* is the set of sets of soldiers (λX.Milites(X) $\wedge$ $|X| > 1$) for the exclusive plural; a decompositional analysis in which the root *milit-* is the complement of a plural functional head *-es* is given in Figure 6.1. Apart from the cardinality restriction, the expression Milites(X) is equivalent to $\mathcal{P}$Milit-(X), which in turn is equivalent to $X \in \mathcal{P}$Milit-: the set X is a member of the powerset of the set Milit-. If the noun *milites* is used in a definite noun phrase, its referent is the plural set containing all the discourse salient soldiers (ιX.Milites(X)); if it is used in an indefinite noun phrase, it could be any plural set of soldiers ($\exists X$.Milites(X)). In this section we will look more closely at what the sets are that comprise a given plurality and see how they relate one to another. Compositional and typetheoretic issues are left for later.

The denotation of the combined singular and plural forms of a nominal root is the powerset of the set X that is the denotation of the nominal root (less the null set): $\mathcal{P}^+(X)$. The powerset of *milit-* is the set of all the subsets of *milit-*. Since soldiers tend to come in large numbers, which would produce horribly complicated examples, let's use the much more manageable root *iiiivir-*. (The *quattuorviri* were the four chief magistrates of a municipium.) A powerset is a partially ordered set, and the structure of partially ordered sets is most clearly revealed by diagrams. A diagram approximating the powerset of the set *iiiivir-* is given in Figure 6.2; the diagram deviates from the powerset (as represented in Figures 5.7-9) in that the null set has been omitted and singleton sets have been replaced by their corresponding individual members. Diagrams like this are very similar to the order-theoretic or algebraic operational structures known as free join semilattices; they clearly represent two basic properties of plural count nouns, namely cumulativity and distributivity. Cumulativity says that if *a* is a *iiiivir* and *b* is a *iiiivir*, then *a* and *b* are *iiiiviri*: join/union of any two elements of the lattice is also an element of the lattice. Informally, this means that it is always possible to create a plural (or a larger plural) by adding up subjects of the same predicate. Cumulative sentences like 'Three Romans killed five Gauls' arise because you can sum the agents and patients of the various subevents. Distributivity follows from atomicity (see below): every set of *iiiiviri* consists of individual *iiiiviri*, since every element in the lattice is built out of atomic ele-

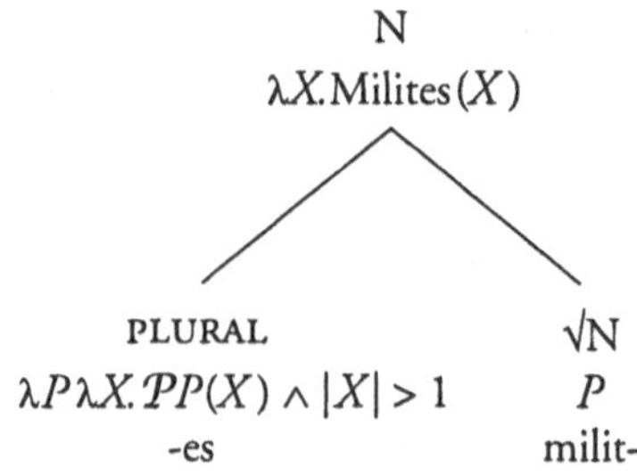

Figure 6.1
Decompositional analysis of plural *milites*

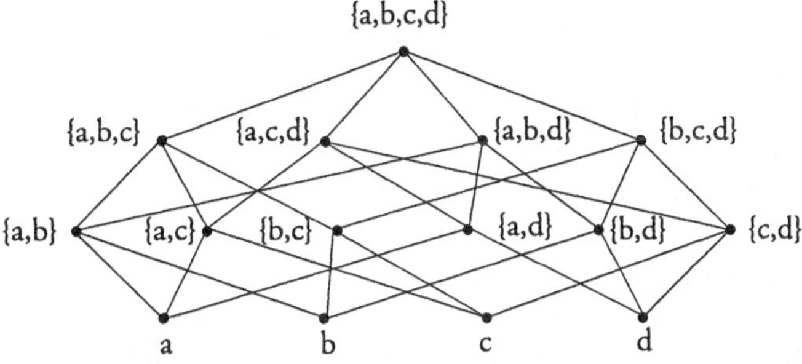

Figure 6.2
Structure of plurality

ments of the lattice: the property of being a *iiiivir* distributes from the larger elements down to the atoms.

Let's look at the diagram in more detail. If A is a superset of B, it is placed higher on the page than B and connected to B by a line or a sequence of lines. So the lowest line in the diagram represents the singulars (*a, b, c* and *d*, the four *iiiiviri*), the next line up the duals, and then the trials. (We are using these number categories semantically, although Ancient Greek has a morphological dual and some languages have morphological trials.) The singulars are the minimal elements of the structure, also called atoms; as just noted, every element of the structure that is not an atom is ultimately generated from a combination of atoms. The top line (called the supremum) is the set from which the powerset is generated. So the top line contains just one element and the bottom line contains the same number of elements as the cardinality of the generating set. The number of elements at the intervening levels is just the number of combinations of size r that can be taken out of a set containing n objects, $C(n,r)$, which is calculated by the formula $n! \div (n-r)!r!$. The sum of $C(n,r)$ for a given n over all values of r from 1 to n gives 2 to the n power minus 1, which is the number of sets in the whole powerset less the null set. Each dual joins two singulars, each trial joins three duals, and so on; more generally, n-tuples join n $(n-1)$-tuples, because there are n ways of reducing by one the cardinality of a set A where $|A| = n$. For instance a trial can be reduced to a dual by dropping the first element or by dropping the second element or by dropping the third element. Each of the three sets obtained in this way is a proper subset; so each line on the lattice contains proper subsets of the line above. Although lattices are defined in terms of weak order (greater than or equal to) rather than strict order (greater than) so as to achieve maximum algebraic generality, it is more intuitive for us to define the singular as a proper subset of the dual than as a subset of or equal to the dual. The set from which the powerset is generated (in our example the *iiiiviri*) is an unordered set. They may turn out to be ordered by some extrinsic property (e.g. 'is taller than' or 'is older than'), but that is not a relevant issue. The powerset itself is partially ordered: some sets are related to each other by inclusion, others are not. Sets on the same line are partially or completely disjoint (mutually exclusive); they are related to each other by the equivalence relation 'has the same cardinality as.' Sets on different lines are related by inclusion if the subset is the intersection of the superset with the subset. In the diagram as presented singulars are joined into duals by the operation of set formation (which takes two elements that are individuals and makes out of them an element that is a set), and from then on the different levels are related by the operation of set union (which takes two elements that are sets and forms out of them an element that is a third set containing all the members of both). If singulars are interpreted as sets containing only one member, then join is union for the whole structure. Join is a binary operation, and every pair of elements has a unique join (although, as already noted, different pairs of elements may have the same join). If any of these lattice-theoretic properties of the structure of plurality were lacking, there would be situations in the world which could not be described in language. If a given pair of elements had two (or more) different joins, the lattice structure would be destroyed, and the singulars would no longer be atoms, but some sort of fissiparous entities. If there were no supremum, then we could not interpret a sentence like

(12) *quattuorviros* quos municipes fecerant sustulit (Pro Clu 25),

since a definite picks out the supremum. Or say the sentence was 'There were two *iiiiviri* of Larinum in the forum': this means that $\{a,b\}$ or $\{a,c\}$ or $\{b,c\}$ or $\{a,d\}$ or $\{b,d\}$ or $\{c,d\}$ were in the forum. But if some pair of atoms lacked a two-member join, then the dual set resulting from that join would be excluded from the denotation of 'two *iiiiviri*,' and the sentence would describe a narrower range of possible situations. In general, if the lattice were not a free lattice, that is if one or more of the subsets of the powerset of the atoms were missing, not only would that set be excluded from the denotation of some plural expression, but the least upper bound of the two elements whose join would have produced the missing element would fall together with the least upper bound of some higher level elements. Since least upper bound and join are the same, joins of pairs of elements at two different levels would merge, so that for instance the join of two singulars could be the same as the join of two duals. For example if $\{a\}$ and $\{c\}$ did not have the join $\{a,c\}$, their least upper bound would be $\{a,b,c,d\}$, which is the join of $\{a,b\}$ and $\{c,d\}$. Also, if one or more elements of the lattice were missing, the lattice would cease to be complemented: for example, if there were no $\{a,b\}$, there would be no denotation for 'everyone except $\{c,d\}$.'

Most of the time we know whether we are talking about a singularity or a plurality, but sometimes the number of a referent is indeterminate: the resulting epistemic alternatives create a problem for the rules of number agreement. In the following examples number agreement is with the closest of two disjuncts

(12) He removed the quattuorviri that the people of the town had appointed (Pro Clu 25).

(13) si quis mihi filius *genitur* unus pluresve, *is* mihi heres esto (De Inv 2.122)
Si quis mihi filius unus pluresve in decem mensibus *gignantur, ii*... exheredes sunto (Varro in Aul Gell 3.16.13)
cum eam consonantes una pluresve praecedunt (Quint 9.4.85: app. crit.).

Notice that the number of the anaphoric pronouns (*is, ii*) in the first two examples (De Inv 2.122, Varro) agrees with the number of the verb in the antecedent clause. The same sort of indeterminacy arises with negative existentials, which, like the conditional protases in the examples in (13), are downward-entailing environments (see Chapter 8)

(14) Pontifices, augures Romulo regnante *nulli* erant; ab Numa Pompilio creati sunt (Livy 4.4.2)
nulli parietes nostram salutem, nullae leges, nulla iura custodient (Pro Reg Deiot 30).

Augures nulli erant in the first example does not mean 'there were no plural sets of augurs' but rather 'there were no singular or plural augurs.' You can't say 'There were no augurs, there was just one.' Augurs and laws come in plural sets, so the plural is used in these examples. But the singular is fine too

(15) *Nullus* erat custos, *nulla*... ianua (Tib 2.3.73)
quippe quis hostis *nullus* erat (Sall Jug 14.10).

In Cicero's time the question for an agnostic was *di utrum sint necne* (ND 3.17) 'whether the gods exist or not,' whereas by the time of Theodosius it was *deus sit necne*: the presupposed issue addressed is different, but semantically the negation covers the possible instantiation of any atom or set in the semilattice, irrespective of the morphological number. For a singular, negation spreads up through the semilattice from the atoms all the way to the supremum, which is the direction of entailment, since negation of a smaller number entails negation of a larger number. For a plural it spreads down to include the atoms. With downward entailing quantifiers like *non amplius n*, 'not more than *n*,' *minus n* 'less than *n*,' the number indeterminacy extends down through zero: 'no more than three cavalrymen' means either a plural (3 or 2), or a singular (1) or zero. This has been taken as grounds for including the null set in the structure, thereby changing it into a full lattice. According to one theory, the denotation of the plural excludes singulars, so the plural means 'more than one.' Supporters of this theory have to explain why a negative plural existential is understood as negating a singular too rather than implicating the truth of the singular (*Non erant augures* ≠ 'There was an augur'). According to a competing approach, the

(13) If one or more sons is born to me, he is to be my heir (De Inv 2.122). If one or more sons is born to me within ten months, they are to be disinherited... (Aul Gell 3.16.13). When one or more consonants precede it (Quint 9.4.85).

(14) There were no pontiffs or augurs during the reign of Romulus; they were created by Numa Pompilius (Livy 4.4.2). No walls, no laws and no rights will guard our well-being (Pro Reg Deiot 30).

(15) There was no guard and no door (Tib 2.3.73). Since we had no enemy (Sall Jug 14.10).

denotation of the plural includes singulars, so the plural means 'one or more': this theory has to explain why a positive plural existential cannot be used in a singular situation (*Erant augures* ≠ 'There was an augur'). We shall adopt the first theory, which seems the most intuitive and preserves the markedness relation between singular and plural. The plural is assigned two readings: a basic exclusive reading (true plural only), and an inclusive reading (plural or singular) which shows up in downward entailing contexts.

Distributive predication

Most expressions in language come with some degree of inherent vagueness. (We are using this word nontechnically to cover different types of underspecification and ambiguity.) Singular predicates are no exception, since they leave much about the structure of the event and its progression through time to be filled in from the context and the lexical meaning of the verb. But plurality adds a whole additional dimension of vagueness arising specifically from the interaction of plurality with predication. We can recognize a number of different modes of plural predication depending on (i) whether, and, if so, how far down the nominal lattice the verbal predicate distributes from the plural set denoted by the subject noun phrase to the atoms from which that set is generated, and (ii) what sort of distributive relation obtains between the subject and the event structure and between the subject and any other participants in the event. Both categories of information are often not encoded in the sentence; this leaves a considerable degree of inbuilt vagueness, which is only partially constrained by the lexical meanings of verbal and nominal predicates.

In examples like the following the lexical semantics of the verb ensures atomic distributivity of the predicate

(16) Tum nostri... universi ex navi *desiluerunt* (BG 4.25)
Pudor movit primos centuriones qui inter tela hostium praetorem *conspexerunt* (Livy 39.31.9)
Tres interim iatraliptae in conspectu eius Falernum *potabant* (Petr 28)
Et collegae quidem mei *riserunt* (Petr 29).

You can't jump or drink or laugh collectively; each person does it for himself. Of course it is perfectly possible for a group of people to jump, drink or laugh together (at the same time and in the same place), but, on a narrow definition of collectivity, that does not amount to true collectivity; it is still a distributive event. Adding a measure can give you a potential collective: 'drink a bottle of wine.' Intrinsically distributive predicates like *surgere* 'stand up' can shift to a sort of weak collectivity involving joint action

(16) Then our men all jumped down from the ship (BG 4.25). Shame moved the senior centurions when they saw the praetor amidst the weapons of the enemy (Livy 39.31.9). Meanwhile three masseurs were drinking Falernian wine right in front of him (Petr 28). My friends laughed (Petr 29).

(17) ipse populus qui... *surrexit* universus (Tac Dial 13.2)
consurrexit senatus cum clamore ad unum (Ad Qfr 3.2.2);

note the modifiers *universus, ad unum*, the prefix *con-* and the collective noun subjects. If the subevents are not just coincident but collaborative, that is a form of secondary collectivity.

Atomic distributivity amounts to universal quantification over the members of the set in question: so in the last example of (16) (Petr 29) every individual that was a companion of Encolpius laughed: $\forall x.\ \text{Collega}(x, \text{Enc}) \rightarrow \text{Risit}(x)$. If the property expressed by a verbal predicate is distributive, it can be represented in a lattice diagram just like a count noun. For instance we can construct a lattice for *riserunt* in the last example in (16) (Petr 29) representing all the sets of individuals who laughed on that occasion (which would include, but not necessarily be limited to, all of Encolpius' friends). One of the elements in this verbal lattice would contain the same individuals as the supremum of the lattice of Encolpius' friends. So the set of Encolpius' friends would be a member of the set of sets denoted by the plural verb *riserunt*. There is one qualification, namely that, unlike overt universal quantifiers, plurals tend to allow for some degree of exceptions. This is particularly the case if the subject phrase is definite and the number of individuals involved is fairly large. So *nostri ex navi desiluerunt* in the first example of (16) (BG 4.25) does not by itself entail that each and every last member of Caesar's men jumped off the ship into the Channel: a few could have been scared or not feeling well or whatever; so *universi* is added to rule out the possibility of exceptions. In the third example on the other hand we have an indefinite phrase with a low number (*tres iatraliptae*), a reading with exceptions is not possible and an overt universal quantifier would have been overkill: there was a set of masseurs with cardinality three and each member of that set was drinking Falernian. Notice that, although we posit a plural set of masseurs (a trial on the semilattice of masseurs), the mechanism of distributive predication applies pointwise to the singular members of that set, like saying 'Each masseur, he was drinking Falernian': $\exists X. \text{Iatraliptae}(X) \wedge |X| = 3 \wedge \forall x. \in X \rightarrow \text{Potabant}(x)$. In this analysis the plural *iatraliptae* does not have to be an autonomous semantic object but could be simply a set of singular objects; the nominal plural is a morphosyntactic mechanism for simultaneously predicating the same property of each member of the set it denotes. In fact, for each member of the set there is a subevent of the event described by the verb: for instance there is a separate jump for each of Caesar's soldiers. The universal quantifier introduced by the distributivity scopes over an existential quantifier associated with the subevents (but not over the existential quantifier associated with the overall event): $\exists E \forall x \exists e$. A lattice can be constructed to represent the sets of subevents too, and one can map between the participant lattice and the subevent lattice on a one-to-one basis (so long as noone jumped twice).

(17) The people itself who rose to their feet together (Tac Dial 13.2). The senate to a man stood up with a shout (Ad Qfr 3.2.2).

If the sentence contains other noun phrases in addition to the subject phrase, a distributive relationship may also be set up between the two sets of entities denoted by the noun phrases

(18) Sed nostri milites... *pila* miserunt celeriterque... *gladios* strinxerunt (BC 3.93).

There is an atomic distributive relationship between soldiers and swords, and also a possessive dependency that ensures that each soldier draws his own sword, not someone else's sword. The soldiers also hurled two javelins each; since the number is standard, it doesn't need to be specified. Where the cardinality of the distributed set does need to be specified, this is done by a distributive numeral

(19) Equi *binos* armatos vehunt (Curt Ruf 7.7.32).

For each horse there is a pair of armed men that it carries. The fact that distribution is over the atoms of the plural can be made explicit by use of the distributive *singuli*

(20) Summa virium in curribus: senos viros *singuli* vehebant (Curt Ruf 8.14.3).

If we construct two lattices, one representing the powerset of Spitaces' chariots and one the powerset of his men, then we can represent the distributive relation by connecting each atom in the former with a set of cardinality six in the latter. (The sets of six have to be disjoint, because one man cannot be in two chariots at the same time.) Both cardinals and distributive numerals count atoms; they do not count higher elements in the lattice: *octo cohortes* means 'eight cohorts,' not 'eight sets of *n* cohorts.' In order to count plural sets, you have to use a construction with a quotientative adverb like *bis quaternae cohortes*. Under certain conditions *quisque* (and for duals *uterque*) can be used to force (simple or relational) atomic distributivity

(21) in suas *quisque* provincias proficiscuntur (Livy 25.12.2).

Collective predication

All the verbal predicates in the preceding section were atomically distributive. Each member of the set *gladios strinxerunt* in (18) drew his sword, there were no pairs of individuals who jointly drew a single sword, and no parts of an individual drew a sword independently of the rest of that individual. The operation of predication said that each individual in the plural nominal set was a member of the set of individuals in the verbal set. This nice simple picture is complicated by the phenomenon of collectivity (broadly defined here). Collectivity appears in both nominal and verbal predicates: people can be joined together into

(18) But our men threw their javelins and quickly drew their swords (BC 3.93).
(19) Their horses carry two armed men (Curt Ruf 7.7.32).
(20) His main strength lay in his chariots; they each carried six men (Curt Ruf 8.14.3).
(21) They each set out for their own duties (Livy 25.12.2).

groups (for instance musicians can comprise a band), and people can collaborate in joint activities (for instance soldiers can surround a city). In this section we are concerned with the latter.

The lexical semantics of some verbs precludes distributivity. Some actions can only be undertaken jointly with others or reciprocally (like 'coalesce, conspire') or can only be done to a plurality of objects (like 'join, heap together'); often but not always the verb has the prefix *con-*

(22) reguli in unum *convenerunt* (Sall Jug 11.2)
Nam duodecim adulescentuli *coierunt* ex iis qui exilio erant multati (Nepos 16.2.3)
concurrendum ad curiam putaretis... *convolaretis* ad rostra. (Pro Rab Post 18)
Hi duo amnes *confluentes* incidunt Oriundi flumini (Livy 44.31.4)
Tigna bina... inter se *iungebat* (BG 4.17)
Fusi hostes... in ultimam castrorum partem *conglobantur.* (Livy 10.5.9)

Omnes mortales una mente *consentiunt* (Phil 4.7)
ex iis tredecim fere nobiles iuvenes Tarentini *coniuraverunt* (Livy 25.8.3)
conferunt sermones inter sese (Pl Curc 290).

None of these examples would make any sense with a singular subject (maintaining the intransitive sense of the verb): *'the prince met,' *'the man agrees unanimously,' *'the enemy soldier gathered.' Other cases involve comparison, classification and counting

(23) Sunt gemini fratres... *dissimiles* sunt magis an *similes*? (Mart 3.88.1)
similitudines *comparat* (De Off 1.11)
aetates *comparate.* (Quint Decl 322.2)

numerando lapides (Livy 25.23.11)
Vere prius flores, aestu *numerabis* aristas (Ov Trist 4.1.57).

Again the plural nouns in the first set of examples cannot be replaced by a singular without adding or understanding another argument phrase: *'the brother is unlike,' *'draw a comparison between his age.' Likewise in the second set the basic meaning of 'count' (compute the cardinality of a set) precludes a singular object: *'He is counting a stone.' Collectivity is not incompatible with distrib-

(22) The princes met together (Sall Jug 11.2). For twelve young men out of those who had been punished by exile came together (Nepos 16.2.3). You would think that you had to rush together to the senate, you would fly together to the rostra (Pro Rab Post 18). These two rivers merge and flow into the River Oriundes (Livy 44.31.4). He joined together pairs of beams (BG 4.17). The routed enemy collected in the far part of the camp (Livy 10.5.9). Everyone agrees unanimously (Phil 4.7). Of these about thirteen noble young men of Tarentum formed a conspiracy (Livy 25.8.3). They converse with one another (Pl Curc 290).

(23) They are twins: are they more unalike or alike? (Mart 3.88.1). He evaluates similarities (De Off 1.11). Compare their ages (Quint Decl 322.2). By counting the stones (Livy 25.23.11). You will sooner count the flowers in spring or the ears of corn in summer (Ov Trist 4.1.57).

utive subevents: you can count the stones one by one, and the soldiers can gather one by one; the subevents are isomorphic with the atoms of the argument plurality.

In another category of examples atomic distributivity is possible but not required, which consequently makes two readings available. For instance verbs meaning 'carry' like *portare, ferre* are often distributive

(24) Praecipuus erat labor eorum qui humeris onera *portabant* (Curt Ruf 4.9.19)
Alii scalas, alii ignem, alii alia... *portabant* (Livy 34.38.4)
ceteri ut quemque casus armaverat sparos aut lanceas, alii praeacutas sudis *portabant.* (Sall Cat 56.3),

but are normally collective when the body of a dead man is being carried

(25) Quattuor inscripti *portabant* vile cadaver (Mart 8.75.9)
haud secus quam ducem suum attollunt... et ex valle devia in viam *portant* (Livy 39.49.5)
Interea exanimem maesti super arma Sychaeum *portabant* Poeni corpusque in castra ferebant. (Sil It 5.585; cp. *referunt* Aen 10.506).

Similarly for a large dead animal

(26) *inferentes* aprum duo iuvenes (Livy 25.9.13).

Situations in which several men collectively carry a single lance or each man carries a different body (or the same body back and forth) tend to be Pythonesque, so these readings are marginalized by world knowledge and context. On the other hand, when it comes to carrying ladders (*scalae* plur. tant., cp. Livy 34.38 in (24)), both distributive and collective readings are more readily available, depending on the size of the ladder. Where an author thinks it necessary, he can use various modifiers to make clear which reading is intended or to shift from a default to a marked reading

(27) *singuli* introducebantur (Livy 10.38.7)
Equitum milia erant sex, totidem numero pedites... quos... *singuli singulos*... delegerant (BG 1.48)

(24) Those who were carrying burdens on their shoulders had the most trouble (Curt Ruf 4.9.19). Some were carrying ladders, others torches, others various things (Livy 34.38.4). The others were carrying javelins, lances or sharpened stakes, whatever arms they happened to find (Sall Cat 56.3).

(25) Four branded slaves were carrying a pauper's body (Mart 8.75.9). They lifted him up as though he were their own leader and carried him from the out-of-the-way valley to the road (Livy 39.49.5). Meanwhile the Carthaginians were sadly carrying the dead Sychaeus on his shield and bringing his body to the camp (Sil It 5.585).

(26) Two young men carrying the boar (Livy 25.9.13).

(27) They were brought in one by one (Livy 10.38.7). There were six thousand cavalrymen and the same number of infantrymen; each one of the former had chosen one of the latter (BG 1.48).

(28) Et tum *universis*... opem tuli et nunc *singulis* feram (Livy 6.15.11)
ex tuis litteris intellexi et eis quas *communiter* cum aliis scripsisti et eis quas *tuo nomine* (Ad Att 11.5.1).

In the first example of (27) (Livy 10.38) the leading Samnites could have been brought in all together or in groups or one by one (distributively), and *singuli* tells us that the distributive reading is the correct one. In the second example of (28) (Ad Att 11.5) Atticus wrote at least two letters, one or more collectively with other correspondents, and one or more individually; here collectivity is expressed by a singular subject with an associative phrase.

Distributivity and collectivity are not mutually exclusive (even with a single uncoordinated predicate), since distributivity may not extend down to the atomic level but just to subsets, leaving the subsets open to collective predication

(29) Servitia urbem ut *incenderent* distantibus locis *coniurarunt* (Livy 4.45.1)
Ipse idoneis locis funditores *instruxit* (BC 3.46)
Armati locis patentibus *congregantur* (Livy 24.21.9).

In the first example (Livy 4.45) the whole set of slaves conspired collectively that several subsets of slaves should each collectively set fire to the city in a different place; *coniurarunt* is fully collective, *incenderent* is collective for each partition of the set of slaves that was to ignite a different part of the city. In the other two examples the locative expressions create partitions of the noun phrase denotation, and each partition takes part in a collective predication: groups of slingers were drawn up in different places (BC 3.46) and groups of men that were armed gathered in different open areas (Livy 24.21). *Armati* denotes the union of the various sets of armed men that gathered in different open spaces. This operation of set union results in a loss of information: we no longer know which men comprised each group. If the antecedent of the pronoun in 'They kissed' is a set $\{a, b\}$, we know that *a* and *b* kissed, but if it is a set $\{a, b, c, d\}$, we no longer know who kissed who, although that may become clear from the context.

Note finally that, unlike distributive predication, collective predication cannot be reduced to atomic predication. Consider 'Four slaves carried a body to the pyre' (a telic and perfective version of Mart 8.75 in (25), cp. Suet 1.82 in (34)). On its distributive reading this means that each of four slaves carried a (possibly different) body. On its collective reading it does not mean that each of four slaves participated in carrying a single body (although it subentails that); otherwise the singular could be used to say that a slave participated in carrying a body to the pyre, and sentences like 'Jack built the Golden Gate bridge' could be interpreted without pragmatic enrichment by an implicit comitative. Collec-

(28) Then I helped the people as a whole, now I will help them individually (Livy 6.15.11). I learn from your letters, both those which you wrote in common with others and those which you wrote in your own name (Ad Att 11.5.1).

(29) The slaves conspired to set fire to the city in different spots (Livy 4.45.1). He himself drew up his slingers in appropriate places (BC 3.46). The men that were armed gather in open areas (Livy 24.21.9).

tive predication is used for joint involvement of the members of the plurality as a group ('a group of four slaves carried a body to the pyre together'). While distributive predication gives plural events, collective predication just gives a single event. This single event has its own part-whole structure, but the latter is inaccessible to the atoms of the subject: the individual slaves each presumably carried a different corner of the load, but that separate involvement is not part of the predication. Consequently nominal predicates are distributive down to atoms, but verbal predicates in collective sentences are not: the property of being a slave distributes down to the atomic individuals in the set of slaves, but the property of having carried a body to the pyre does not distribute down to the atomic individuals who collectively carried the body. Therefore while distributive verbal predicates like 'laugh' can be represented by verbal lattices of participants and of the correlated subevents, pure collective verbal predicates like 'carry the body to the pyre together' cannot: there is just one set. One way of getting around this is to assume that the plural subject of a collective sentence functions as a type of complex singular individual, a secondary atom. This would make collective predication atomic too; the set of four slaves in the denotation of the predicate would just be another type of singular individual, and the denotation of predicates would not include pluralities at all but just a set of singularities. Although the individuals comprising the derived atom are inaccessible to atomic predication and there is no event pluralization, agreement with the plural subject still requires plural morphology on the verb. We used a telic and perfective version of the Martial example because the status of the progressive in the original is less clear. Split subject quantifiers in Japanese normally have only a distributive reading, but when a telic verb phrase is in the progressive, a collective reading is also possible. This suggests that atomic predication is possible in the process phase, but the resultant state has to be a joint responsibility of the participants and therefore collective.

At this point, the available theoretical choices multiply, and the story becomes rather intricate. Is there one operator responsible for distributive readings (a universal quantifier coming from a covert 'each') and another for collective readings (an existential group-creating quantifier coming from a covert 'together')? or are collective readings the default, and distributive readings generated by a distributive operator? or are distributive readings the default, and collective readings generated by a collective operator? and where is either of these operators located, on the noun phrase, or on the verb phrase, or on both? Is 'carrying a body' always the same action, which can be done either by a single individual or by a group (noun phrase operator)? or is 'four slaves' always the same entity which can act either individually or collectively (verb phrase operator)? or are distributive and collective readings not generated by a localized operator at all, arising rather from the compositional process of predication or from variable scope relative to event arguments? The answers we choose for questions like these will determine how we are to formalize the descriptive analysis presented so far: this is the subject of the next section. Note that both predicate logic and generalized quantifier theory are primarily designed for distributive quantification only. Predicate logic uses individual variables to express quantification pointwise ('for every individual *x*, if *x* is a slave, then *x* (by himself) carried the body'), and generalized quantifier theory uses relations between sets of individuals ('the set of individuals that are slaves is a subset of the set of individuals that each carried the body').

Types for plurality

Since there are so many variable factors, it would be too long and complicated for us to set out all the different compositional theories of plurality, so we will just present the theory we ourselves use and mention some alternative options in passing. This is not meant to dismiss the study of different typing systems as just a technical exercise in the manipulation of formalism: each system of types expresses a slightly different understanding of plurality.

Let's start by assigning types to the various denotations already posited in our discussion of plural lattices above. Here are a couple of simple examples with a plural definite subject phrase

(30) dum milites... convenirent (BG 1.7)
nostri milites... gladios strinxerunt (BC 3.93).

The first (BG 1.7) is collective, the second (BC 3.93) is distributive; for present purposes we will leave the verb phrase in the latter unanalyzed. The denotation of the common noun *milit-* is a set (type <e, t>), that subset of the universe of discourse that has the property of being a soldier. The denotation of the singular noun *miles* is the set of individuals that are soldiers, also of type <e, t>; if the atoms are treated as singleton sets, the type is <et, t>. The denotation of the plural common noun *milites* is the set of all sets of soldiers except for singletons and the empty set, the powerset lattice for *milit-* limited to sets of cardinality two or more (POW$_{\geq 2}$), so of type <et, t>. POW$_{\geq 2}$ can be applied as an operator to pluralize a common noun: POW$_{\geq 2}$ *milit-* → *milites.* The plural suffix *-es* encodes a function PLUR from a set to a set of sets; if PLUR is interpreted as excluding singularities, it can be written POW$_{\geq 2}$. The inverse operation is carried out by generalized set union: $\cup$*milites* → *milit-*, since the supremum of a powerset lattice is the same as its generating set. A third operator, ATOM, gets you from the set denoted by the common noun to the set of singleton sets corresponding to its members: ATOM *milit-* → $\{\{x\}: x \in$ *milit-*$\}$ (or from a powerset to its singleton set members). The denotation of the plural definite noun phrase *milites* 'the soldiers' in the examples is the supremum of the lattice of contextually salient soldiers, a single set of type <e, t>. This set is generated when the plural iota operator (semantic definite article, type <<et, t> <e, t>>) composes with the plural common noun (<<et, t> <e, t>><et, t> → <e, t>), picking the largest set out of all the sets in the plural lattice. Treating plurals as sets is intuitively attractive, but it creates some complications. We are now using sets not only for predicates

(30) For the soldiers to gather (BG 1.7). Our soldiers drew their swords (BC 3.93).

and in generalized quantifiers but also for referential plurals. It is not problematic for a set to be a referential object in argument noun phrases. Unlike soldiers, sets can't gather (*convenirent*), but neither can sums or joins or impure atoms. However it could be argued that sets only have the type <e, t> when they are predicates, and shift to higher or lower types when used as arguments. Now we turn to the verb phrase. The denotation of a singular verb phrase is a set: for instance *gladium strinxit* denotes the set of individuals who drew their swords, type <e, t>. Correspondingly, the denotation of a plural verb phrase is a set of sets: *convenirent* is the set of all sets of cardinality two or more that gather, type <et, t>. This composes with the definite subject phrase *milites* of type <e, t> to give a truth value: the set of soldiers is a member of the set of sets of individuals that gathered. So the individuals that comprise the set of soldiers in question are the same individuals as those who comprise one of the sets of gatherers.

While treating plurals as sets does complicate the compositional process, it is interesting to note that the practical consequences of this move are somewhat limited. As we have seen, full distributivity can be reduced to a type of universal quantification over atoms. In principle this applies to any predicate, verbal, nominal or adjectival, and it is important not to conflate them: in 'The numerous tall soldiers gathered,' 'numerous' is collective, 'tall' is distributive, 'soldier' is distributive and 'gathered' is collective. It is not even clear what role is played by distributivity in nominal predicates: apart from a few pluralia tantum

(31) non dicitur una *scopa* (Varro LL 10.24)

(the singular of 'scissors' and 'pincers' does not appear without its twin), count nouns are inherently distributive, even relational nouns like 'colleague' and collective nouns like 'team.' If we insert a distributive operator DIST everywhere possible in the second example in (30) (continuing to leave the verb phrase unanalyzed), the only actual plural in the resulting formula will be the variable X, since distributive predication is pointwise: DIST *milites* DIST *strinxerunt-gladios* means $\forall x \in (\iota X. \forall y \in X \rightarrow \text{Miles}(y)) \rightarrow \text{Strinxit-gladium}(x)$. This can be simplified by taking inherent nominal distributivity for granted: $\forall x. \text{Miles}(x) \rightarrow \text{Strinxit-gladium}(x)$. We are not interested in how the property of soldierhood is distributed over X, only in how the members of X participate in the event of sword-drawing. By contrast, in the first example of (30) the soldiers participate collectively in the event of gathering: $\text{Convenirent}(\iota X.\text{Milites}(X))$. Here we do need real plural predication, since, as we have already said, collective plural predication does not reduce to singular predication:

(32) Bruttii... urbem cinxerunt (Livy 24.2.10)

does not entail $\forall x. \text{Bruttius}(x) \rightarrow \text{Cinxit-urbem}(x)$; it just subentails that each Bruttian (or at least most of them) was involved (in potentially different ways) in the process phase of surrounding the city; no single Bruttian by himself

(31) One does not say *una scopa* (Varro LL 10.24).
(32) The Bruttians surrounded the city (Livy 24.2.10).

achieved the telos. In fact the ungrammaticality of 'The Bruttian soldier gathered' could be formalized as a type clash between the verb (type <et, t>) and the subject (type <e>). So subentailments of the collective are not grounds for reducing plural predication to singular predication. The only remaining strategy for eliminating plural predication with collectives is the idea, mentioned at the end of the preceding section, of interpreting plural collective noun phrases as groups. *Bruttiorum cohortem* in the same passage of Livy (24.1.5) is a collective denoting the sort of nontransitory property that one expects a noun phrase to have. The collective plural *Bruttii* would be interpreted as a transitory singular group, a socalled impure atom, created just by collective participation in an event. This would be done by means of an operator (↑) of type <et, e>, which takes a plural noun phrase and returns a singular one (which will then compose with a verb phrase of type <e, t> rather than <et, t>). The group operator could be used not only for subjects of collective events but also for subjects of collective states ('they are similar,' 'they weigh seven pounds in all'), which need not be transitory. Empirical evidence for this idea is not entirely lacking: eventuality-related groups of individuals are also created by distributive numerals, and collective plurals can be referents of *uterque*

(33) *utrisque* satis facere non posset, *et Siculis et togatis* (Verr 2.2.154)
Peditum erant V milia, equites M; *utrisque* Platon Atheniensis praeerat (Curt Ruf 5.7.12).

There is also a mereological theory of plurality which treats plurals not as sets ($\{a, b\}$) but as singular objects made up of parts ($a \oplus b$); in this theory plural as well as singular definites have type <e>, and the complications associated with the use of the type <e, t> for plurals do not arise. We should note in passing that there also exists a diametrically opposed view which says that there is no such thing as a plural object or a singular object made up of several objects, and that the plural is just a grammatical device for simultaneous multiple singular reference and predication.

So far we have assumed that event-related distributivity involves a distributive operator attached to the verb phrase; distributivity (like collectivity) is a mode of participation in the event. The plural set of soldiers is a member of the set of sets of atomic sword-drawers: DIST *strinxerunt-gladios* translates as $\lambda X.\forall x \in X \rightarrow$ Strinxit-gladium (x). This is like using floated 'each': the soldiers each drew their swords. But it is also possible to attach the event-related distributive operator to the noun phrase; distributivity limits application of the predicate to singleton sets in the denotation of the noun phrase. DIST *milites* translates as a quantifier $\lambda P.\forall x \in$ Milit- $\rightarrow P(x)$. This is like using adnominal 'each': drawing his sword is one of the set of properties that each member of the set of soldiers has. Evidence from coordination does not help us to decide between these two options:

(33) He was unable to satisfy both parties, the Sicilians and the Romans (Verr 2.2.154). They consisted of five thousand infantry and a thousand cavalry, both under the command of Platon, an Athenian (Curt Ruf 5.7.12).

you can say 'The consuls entered the camp by different gates and met at the praetorium' (conjoining a distributive with a collective verb phrase), but you can also say 'The consuls and the praetor both won victories' (conjoining a collective and an atomic subject). Some Latin examples are given in the section on coordination at the end of this chapter. Verb phrase ellipsis also allows mixed readings: 'The consuls won a victory (together) and so did the praetor.'

Standard generalized quantifier theory as presented in Chapter 5 does not cater to the distinction between singular and plural quantifiers: for instance no distinction is made between *nulla ianua* in (15) and *nulli parietes* in (14). A number of different ways have been suggested for introducing plurality into generalized quantifiers. The results tend to be quite intricate and we will limit ourselves to a couple of examples of one way of doing it with numerals

(34) tres... perierunt rhetores (Mart 2.64.5)
tres servoli domum rettulerunt (Suet 1.82.3).

The first example (Mart 2.64) is lexically distributive, the second (Suet 1.82) is collective in context. If both plural noun phrases and plural verb phrases denote sets of sets (<et, t>), then a plural generalized quantifier will denote a set of sets of sets (<ett, t>: $\lambda \mathbf{B}.\mathcal{A}(\mathbf{B})$). On a count reading, *tres perierunt rhetores* in the first example could be taken to say that the intersection of the singleton sets in the set of sets of rhetoricians (**A**) with the set of sets of those who died (**B**) has a cardinality of three: $|\text{ATOM}\,\mathbf{A} \cap \mathbf{B}| = 3$ (applying distributivity to the noun phrase). A weak existential reading of the second example (Suet 1.82) could be taken to say that there exists a set that is a member of the set of sets of slaves (**A**) and of the set of sets of those who (collectively) carried Caesar's body back home (**B**), and the cardinality of that set is exactly 3: $\exists X \in \mathbf{A} \wedge X \in \mathbf{B} \wedge |X| = 3$ (plus the usual maximality rider). One could get a distributive version of this by changing X into its singleton sets, giving $\text{ATOM}\,\mathbf{X} \subseteq \mathbf{B}$ in place of $X \in \mathbf{B}$. We will leave the cumulative reading for later.

Further distributive and collective readings

As already noted, distributive readings involve subevents, whereas collective readings do not

(35) quae *singuli universique* eo bello hostiliter dixerant fecerantque (Livy 45.10.7).

Singuli generates subevents for the individual actions of each member of the plural subject set on each occasion ($\exists E \forall x.\text{Rhodius}(x) \rightarrow \exists e \in E.\text{Dixit-hostiliter}(e,x)$), *universi* generates a single collective event on each occasion ($\exists e.\text{Dixerunt-hostiliter}(e, \text{Rhodii})$). However, particularly with transitive verbs (more precisely verbs in clauses having two or more arguments or adjuncts), the situation is often more complicated. A whole range of different readings becomes available,

(34) Three rhetoricians have died (Mart 2.64.5). Three slaves carried him home (Suet 1.82.3).
(35) The hostile things that they had individually and collectively said and done during that war (Livy 45.10.7).

depending on the semantics of the verb and the semantics of the two argument phrases, and scopal dependencies arise not only between individuals and events but also between different individuals. In this section we will look at these readings in greater detail than we did in our overview above, although we won't be able to cover all of them. To keep things simple, event arguments will be omitted when possible, and plural nominal and collective verbal predication will be written as $\boldsymbol{P}(X)$.

When both arguments are collective, distributivity of any sort is precluded, as it is with singulars

(36) consul currum conscendit (Livy 45.1.7)
Galli Tuscos expulerant (Livy 37.57.8)
ad eum centuriones tres legatos miserunt (Livy 24.48.3).

The first example (Livy 45.1) has two singular arguments; consequently there is a single event with no subevents; even though the foot of the consul touched a part of the chariot first, there is no distributivity below the level of the atom. In the second example (Livy 37.57) both arguments are definite collectives; in the last example (Livy 24.48, illustrated in Figure 6.3), the null subject is a definite collective and the object is an indefinite collective: $\exists X.\text{Centuriones}(X) \wedge |X| = 3 \wedge \text{Miserunt}(\text{Cornelii}, X)$. Again there is a single event with no distributivity: it is not the case that individual Etruscans were expelled from Bologna in different subevents, or that the Scipio brothers sent the centurions off one by one or that each brother issued separate orders. On the contrary, the Etruscans were expelled as a group and the Scipio brothers acting as joint commanders sent the centurions as a legation (*ea legatio* ibid.). In this respect collective plurals behave like atomic individual entities.

When one argument is interpreted collectively and the other distributively (like a distributive key), the former is involved as a group with the individual members of the latter, and the result is simple event distributivity

(37) Milites positis scalis muros ascendunt (BC 1.28)
Primo ab amicis... libri lecti (Livy 40.29.7).

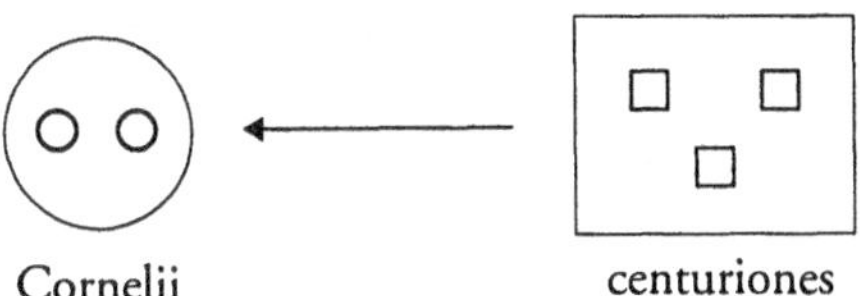

Figure 6.3
Two collective plurals
Cornelii ad eum centuriones tres miserunt (cp. Livy 24.48.3)

(36) The consul got onto his chariot (Livy 45.1.7). The Gauls had expelled the Etruscans (Livy 37.57.8). They sent three centurions to him as envoys (Livy 24.48.3).

(37) The soldiers placed the ladders and climbed the walls (BC 1.28). The books were first read by his friends (Livy 40.29.7).

There is a separate subevent for each soldier climbing up the walls and for each friend reading the books, as illustrated in Figure 6.4. Both phrases are definite and there is no entity distributivity: it is not the case that each friend read a different book, just that each friend x had the property 'x read the books' (the subeventual structure is not known): $\forall x$.Amicus (x, Petilius) $\rightarrow$ Legit(x, ιY.Libros (Y)). The set of 14 books results from the union of the set of seven Latin books with the set of seven Greek books. In the following example the distributive phrase is indefinite

(38) Aeolii.... *clarasque urbes* condiderunt (Vell Pat 1.4.4).

Here a different city is founded collectively by the Aeolians on different occasions, not a different city for each Aeolian.

Finally we have the situation in which both arguments are interpreted distributively. Members of one set Y, the distributive share, are distributed over members of the other set X, the distributive key. There are several different ways in which this can happen, ranging from one-to-one mapping of members of Y onto members of X through various possible intermediate stages to all-to-all mapping. In one-to-one mapping, each member of X is related to a different member of Y in a separate subevent

(39) Numidae equos conscendunt (Livy 35.11.6)
Sed nostri milites... gladios strinxerunt (BC 3.93)
folliculos... aestate cicadae linquunt (Lucr 5.803).

In these examples the Y phrases are definite and there is a pre-existing possessive dependency between the individual members of X and Y: each Numidian mounted his own horse (see Figure 6.5): $\forall x$. Numida (x) $\rightarrow$ Conscendit(x, EQ(x)), where EQ is a function of type <e, e> from Numidians onto the horses they possess. Similarly in the other examples, each soldier drew his own sword and cicadas generically leave their own shells. (This dependency is not a requirement for the one-to-one reading with definites.) Distributive indefinites can be singular: compare the following examples

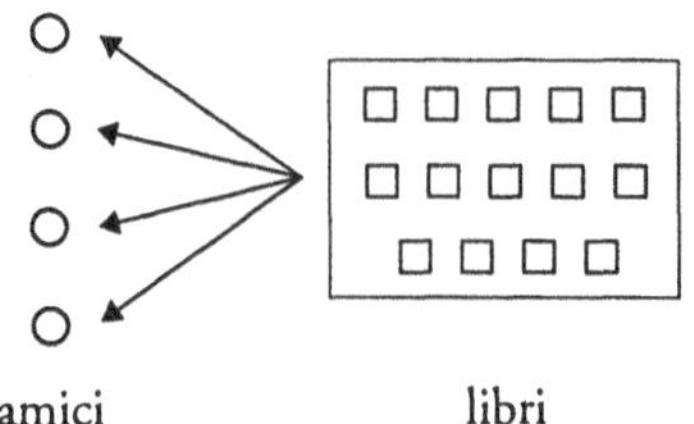

Figure 6.4
Event distributive plural
Ab amicis libri lecti sunt (Livy 40.29.7)

(38) The Aeolians... and they founded famous cities (Vell Pat 1.4.4).
(39) The Numidians mounted their horses (Livy 35.11.6). But our soldiers drew their swords (BC 3.93). Cicadas leave their shells in the summer (Lucr 5.803).

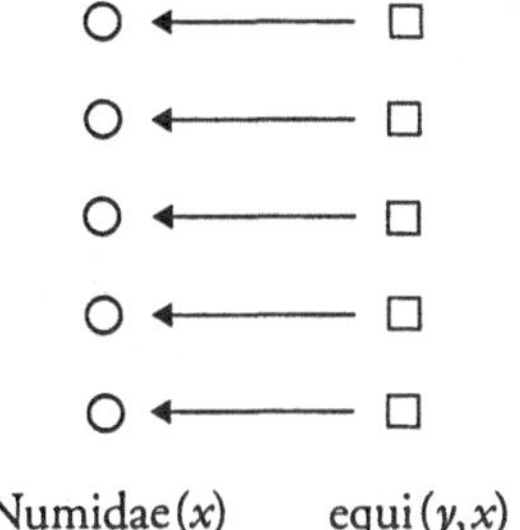

Figure 6.5
One-to-one dependent distributive plural
Numidae equos conscendunt (Livy 35.11.6)

(40) Imprudentes legis, cum exissent, *vitulum* immolaverunt (De Inv 2.95)
non fuisse armatos eos qui praetereuntes *ramum* defringerent arboris (Pro Caec 60)
Elephanti plures ab ipsis rectoribus quam ab hoste interfecti. Fabrile *scalprum* cum malleo habebant (Livy 27.49.1).

In the first example (De Inv 2.95) the subject is collective and so the indefinite direct object *vitulum* does not distribute over the members of the subject phrase: $\exists y$.Vitulus(y) $\wedge$ Immolaverunt (ιX.Nautae(X),y). In the second example (Pro Caec 60) each man broke off a branch to serve as his own weapon, so the direct object *ramum* (the *Y* phrase) does distribute over the subject of *defringerent* (the *X* phrase): $\forall x$.Praeteriens(x) $\rightarrow$ $\exists y$.Ramus(y) $\wedge$ Defringit(x,y). This produces the same distributivity as already illustrated in Figure 6.5 but without the pre-existing dependency: the dependency between each man and his branch is created by the event. In the third example (Livy 27.49) each elephant driver had a chisel. The first example licenses only a singular anaphor: 'they were accused of having sacrificed *it/*them* to Diana.' The other examples can also license a plural anaphor: 'they sharpened *their* tips.' In fact the *Y* phrase itself can be pluralized (as were the definite distributives in (39))

(41) Subito intraverunt duo servi... in collo adhuc *amphoras* habebant... neuter sententiam tulit decernentis sed alterius amphoram fuste percussit (Petr 70).

Each slave had an amphora. Quite often it is not clear whether *Y* distributes a singularity or a plurality (see below) or a mixture; the indeterminacy may be resolved by world knowledge or the context

(40) Being ignorant of the law, when they landed they sacrificed a calf (De Inv 2.95). That those who broke off the branch of a tree while passing were not armed (Pro Caec 60). More elephants were killed by their own drivers than by the enemy. They had a carpenter's chisel with a mallet (Livy 27.49.1).

(41) Suddenly two slaves came in; they still had amphoras around their necks. Neither one accepted the judge's decision but hit the other's amphora with a stick (Petr 70).

(42) quattuorque... centuriones *oculos* amiserunt (BC 3.53)
qui... proprie *libros* huic operi dedicaverunt (Quint 9.3.89)
cameli... His insidebant *Arabes sagittarii* (Livy 37.40.12).

We know that two of the centurions lost one eye each (τὸν ὀφθαλμὸν... ἐκκοπῆναι Appian 2.60). It is not per se clear whether there were single Arab archers or pairs of archers on each camel. The issue can be resolved by use of a distributive numeral

(43) si singuli *singulos* adgressuri essetis (Livy 6.18.6)
tribunis militum centurionibusque quibus *singulae* naves erant attributae (BG 3.14).

At the other end of the scale from one-to-one mapping is all-to-all mapping: each member of the *Y* set is mapped onto each member of the *X* set

(44) tot *amnes* superavimus, tot montium *iuga* transcucurrimus (Curt Ruf 6.3.16).

Each member of the set of rivers had been crossed by each member of Alexander's army (not a different river by each soldier). This reading is called the double distributive reading. It is available where members of the *Y* set can be serial objects of separate actions by members of the *X* set, like 'The students read the books,' but not of course with once only predicates like 'The Romans killed the Gauls,' since once a Gaul is dead he can't be killed again by another Roman. Where focus is on the double distributivity, universal quantifiers can be used

(45) ne confundantur opera familiae sic ut *omnes omnia* exsequantur (Col 1.9.5)
nec vero terrae ferre *omnes omnia* possunt (Verg Georg 2.109)
non enim *omnibus* litoribus *omne* genus haberi potest (Col 8.16.7).

The last example (Col 8.16) has double distributivity over kinds: it denies that every kind of coast is suitable for farming every kind of fish: $\neg\forall x \forall y.\text{Piscis}(x) \wedge \text{Litus}(y) \rightarrow \text{Haberi-potest}(x,y)$ (socalled branching quantification: see Figure 6.6).

So far, apart from the indeterminacy in (42), we have been dealing with distributive readings that are purely atomic: atoms of set *Y* are distributed over atoms of set *X*, so the atoms of one semilattice are associated with the atoms of the other. But it is also possible for plural sets of *Y* to be distributed over atoms

(42) Four centurions lost their eyes (BC 3.53). Those who have devoted books specifically to this topic (Quint 9.3.89). Camels... On these were mounted Arab archers (Livy 37.40.12).
(43) If you were going to attack them one to one (Livy 6.18.6). The military tribunes and centurions who were in charge of the individual ships (BG 3.14).
(44) We have crossed so many rivers, climbed over the peaks of so many mountains (Curt Ruf 6.3.16).
(45) The duties of the slaves should not be merged to the point that everyone does everything (Col 1.9.5). For not all lands can produce all things (Verg Georg 2.109). It is not the case that every kind of fish can be kept on every type of coast (Col 8.16.7).

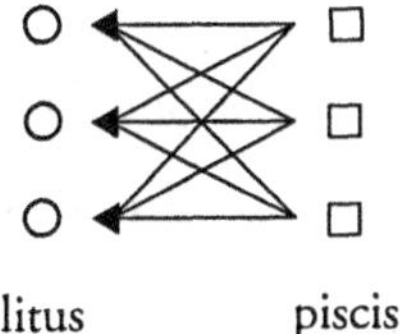

Figure 6.6
All-to-all distributivity
Omnibus litoribus omne genus haberi potest (cp. Col 8.16.7)

of X, so the atomic elements of one semilattice are associated with the non-atomic elements of the other. The indefinite distributive numeral phrases discussed in Chapter 5 are a case in point

(46) cum *centenis* hostibus singulos pugnaturos (Livy 6.7.2)
iuvenes... eis... *septena* iacula... data (Livy 26.4.4).

The distributive numeral requires each Y set to have the same cardinality, a hundred in the first example (Livy 6.7) and seven in the second (Livy 26.4), as illustrated in Figure 6.7: $\forall x.\text{Iuvenis}(x) \rightarrow \exists Y.\text{Iacula}(Y) \wedge |Y| = 7 \wedge \text{Data}(Y,x)$, assuming the javelins were handed to the youths in bundles. The object is distributive, but not down to atoms, only down to sets of seven. Each Y set comes from the same line in the semilattice. Without the distributive numeral that need not be the case. As just noted, simple indefinite objects are often indeterminate between singular and plural

(47) equites Ariovisti... *lapides telaque* in nostros conicere (BG 1.46)
hostes... *lapides gaesaque* in vallum conicere (BG 3.4).

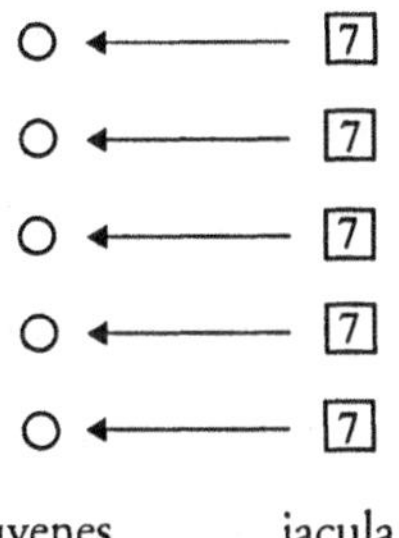

Figure 6.7
Distributive numeral
Iuvenibus septena iacula data (cp. Livy 26.4.4)

(46) That they would be fighting one against a hundred (Livy 6.7.2). Young men... they were given seven javelins each (Livy 26.4.4).

(47) That Ariovistus' cavalrymen were throwing stones and weapons against our men (BG 1.46). The enemy threw stones and javelins onto the rampart (BG 3.4).

It does not follow that each German and each Gaul threw only one stone and only one weapon. The *Y* sets may all be plural but have different cardinalities

(48) *nobiles Campani...* per sociorum Latini nominis urbes in custodias dati (Livy 26.16.6).

Each of the Latin cities may have held a different number of Capuan nobles in custody; all that is required is that at least one noble be in every city and that every noble be in one or another of the cities; see Figure 6.8. This reading arises quite naturally from combining subevents into a plural when subsets of *Y* have different cardinalities. *Y* (the set of Capuan nobles) is partitioned into a number of subsets, each of which is mapped onto one city *x*: $\forall x.\text{Urbs}(x) \rightarrow \exists Z \in \text{Part}(\iota Y.\text{Nobiles}(Y)) \wedge \text{Dati}(Z, x)$. Partitions can be spelled out explicitly

(49) legati ex Asia... deorum simulacra... itemque cetera signa et ornamenta... *alia alio in loco* lacrimantes intuebantur (Verr 2.1.59)
Barbari... *alii* in medios ignes, *alii* petris praecipitavere se (Curt Ruf 6.6.31).

The sets chosen from the Capuan noble semilattice in (48) have to be disjoint because no Capuan noble can be in more than one city at the same time. But it is also possible for the *Y* sets to overlap: 'The students read the books' has a reading in which each student read some of the books and the sets of books read are not mutually exclusive. In that case the *Y* sets comprise what is called a cover rather than a partition; a cover for a set *Y* is a set of sets from the powerset semilattice for *Y* whose union is the supremum. This type of reading is quite common in ordinary discourse

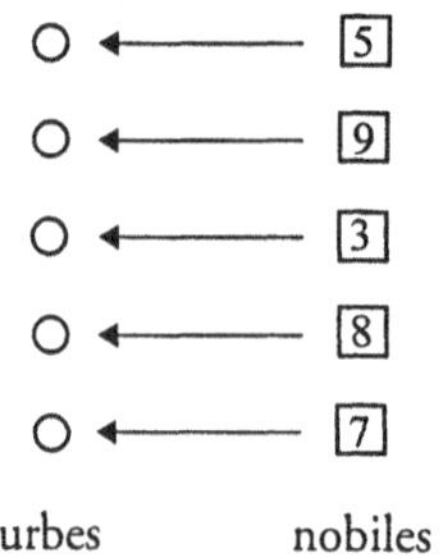

Figure 6.8
Many-to-one distributivity
Nobiles per sociorum urbes in custodias dati (cp. Livy 26.16.6)

(48) Campanian nobles who had been handed over into custody among the cities of the Latin allies (Livy 26.16.6).

(49) Envoys from Asia looked in tears at the images of the gods and the other statues and works of art distributed in different places (Verr 2.1.59). Some of the barbarians threw themselves into the middle of the flames, others threw themselves down from the rocks (Curt Ruf 6.6.31).

(50) Numidae... omnia propinqua viae tecta incendunt (Livy 35.11.11)
alii fossas complerent (BG 3.25).

There is a cover for the salient set of Numidians and another one for the set of houses, the cells of the cover are typically based on subevent structure, each cell of both covers can be the subject of atomic or collective predication, and how many houses each Numidian set fire to individually or collectively is omitted as superfluous detail. A possible scenario is illustrated in Figure 6.9; this scenario is one of a number of different, and potentially quite complex, factual situations that make the sentence true, it is not part of the meaning of the sentence as uttered. While distributivity could be restated as an atomic cover and collectivity as a monocover, they both feature in the lexical definition of predicates, whereas true covers depend principally on pragmatic variability.

Finally, sometimes all that matters is the cardinality of the *X* and *Y* sets

(51) ad singulas urbes circumferendo bello unum et *triginta* oppida intra dies *quinquaginta*... ceperunt (Livy 9.45.17)
Duobus his unius diei proeliis Caesar desideravit milites *DCCCCLX* (BC 3.71)
quippe qui *centum* equitibus adversus *sescentos* pugnaturum cerneret (Livy 37.20.7).

In the first example (Livy 9.45) a total of 31 towns was captured in a total of 50 days (combined into an interval), as illustrated in Figure 6.10: this is called the cumulative reading. *Singulas* tells us that there is a series of temporally sequenced subevents in the overall event (the Aequian campaign), each subevent corresponding to the attack and capture of an Aequian city (compare the similar scenario in the Latin campaign, Livy 1.38.4). The issue is how many towns in

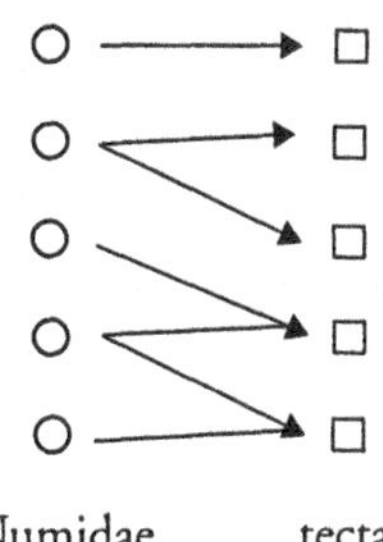

Figure 6.9
Double cover reading of plurals
Numidae tecta incendunt (Livy 35.11.11)

(50) The Numidians set fire to all the buildings close to the road (Livy 35.11.11). Some were filling up the ditches (BG 3.25).

(51) By attacking the cities individually they captured thirty-one within fifty days (Livy 9.45.17). In these two battles on one day Caesar lost 960 men (BC 3.71). Seeing that he was going to fight with a hundred cavalry against six hundred (Livy 37.20.7).

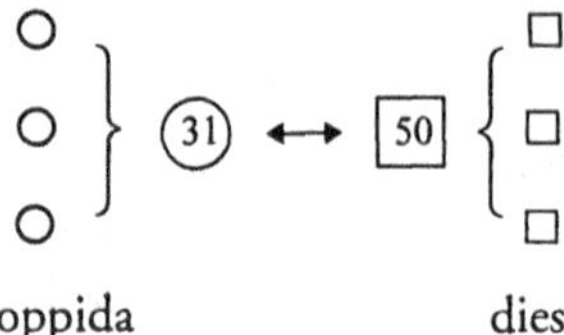

Figure 6.10
Cumulative reading
Unum et triginta oppida intra dies quinquaginta ceperunt (Livy 9.45.17)

total were captured in a total of how many days; how many days it took to capture each town is not an issue. More generally, given a transitive verb $R(x,y)$, the cumulative reading is concerned with the cardinality of the set $\{x{:}\exists y.R(x,y)\}$ relative to that of the set $\{y{:}\exists x.R(x,y)\}$. In our Livy example we have a direct object and a temporal adjunct, which gives us a cover-pair, each cell of which corresponds to a city and the number of days it took to capture it. We get the two cumulative sets by taking the union of the sets of cities in the cover of the cities captured in the campaign (in case some city had to be captured twice because it was temporarily liberated) and the union of the set of days in the cover of the days occupied by the campaign (in case two different cities were captured on the same day); then we take the cardinality of each resulting set. If we omit to take the union of the sets of cities, we will be counting city-capturing events rather than just cities (which is a different reading of the sentence). These cumulative readings are a bit like cricket scores: the quantifiers in cumulative readings only convey the desired information if they are interpreted relative to each other, just as the number of runs in a cricket innings is only informative relative to the number of wickets. The two quantified expressions are not scoped relative to each other; they are not introduced into the compositional process one after the other. Rather they are scopeless; they are introduced into the compositional process in parallel. The town–day capture score is 31 for 50. This is why some formalisms for cumulative readings use polyadic quantification (see Chapter 5) over pairs of sets.

Count, mass and collective

Up to now we have been talking about nouns that have plurals (*eques* 'cavalryman,' *equites* 'cavalrymen') and can be used with numerals (*tres equites* 'three cavalrymen') and distributive and plural quantifiers (*quisque eques* 'each cavalryman,' *complures equites* 'several cavalrymen'). Such nouns are called count nouns. They come prepackaged from the lexicon as discrete, bounded, individuated and countable entities. You can always tell whether you have one horse or two and one soldier or two; this can get more difficult when it comes to walls and ditches, but the latter are none the less count nouns for that. As we have seen, the singular forms of count nouns are represented as the atoms in the semilattice and their plural forms as the nonatomic elements in the semilattice. But there is another category of nouns which does not have a plural (in its basic, unshifted meaning) and has none of the other properties just mentioned either. This second category of nouns is called mass nouns. Mass nouns are linguistically nonatomic: they denote a substance without reference to its minimal component parts. Consider *scobis* 'sawdust': it is not used in the plural with unshifted meaning (**scobes* 'sawdusts'), nor with numerals (**tres scobes* 'three sawdusts') nor with distributive and plural quantifiers (**quisque scobis* 'each sawdust,' **complures scobes* 'several sawdusts'). There are no stable sawdust objects to count. In order to be counted, a mass noun has to be used in the (pseudo)partitive genitive with a measure expression

(52) *frumenti* denos modios ac totidem *olei*... libras (Suet 1.38.1)
selibram *tritici* puri (Cato 86.1)
Casei ovilli p. XIV... in aquam indito (Cato 76.2)

or (less commonly than in English) with a classifier expression

(53) *lardi* frusta (Hor Sat 2.6.86: app. crit.)
cum *farris* pugillo (NH 20.242)
quinque dies in os suum non coniecit... micam *panis* (Petr 42).

Measures shift the noun from a mass into countable amounts by identifying an appropriate scale of measurement; classifiers shift a mass into countable atoms, which can form sets. Both devices exploit the intrinsic part-whole structure of a mass noun to make it countable; they create bounded objects out of an unbounded mass. While these objects are discrete, they lack identity (individual identifiability): when referring to specific animals (e.g. Lucy, Belle and Miranda), we say 'three cows' rather than 'three head of cattle.' On the other hand, count nouns, as we have seen, come prepackaged into countable objects

(54) dato *salis micas tres, folia laurea* III (Cato 70.1).

There is a quantity of salt and its measure in grains is three ($\exists x.\text{Sal}(x) \wedge \mu^{mic}(x) = 3$); there is a set of laurel leaves and its cardinality is three ($\exists X.\text{Folia}(X) \wedge \mu^{\#}(X) = 3$). So comparative *plures* with count nouns compares cardinalities

(55) plures pampinos (Col 5.6.36)
plura sarmenta (Col De Arb 3.5),

whereas comparative *plus* with mass nouns compares some other measure like volume or weight

(56) plus olei (Cato 64.2)
plus vini (Petr 38).

(52) Ten modii of grain and the same number of pounds of oil (Suet 1.38.1) Half a pound of clean wheat (Cato 86.1). Put fourteen pounds of sheep's cheese in water (Cato 76.2).
(53) Scraps of bacon (Hor Sat 2.6.86). With a handful of wheat (NH 20.242). He didn't put a crumb of bread in his mouth for five days (Petr 42).
(54) Three grains of salt, three laurel leaves (Cato 70.1).
(55) More shoots (Col 5.6.36). More shoots (Col De Arb 3.5).
(56) More oil (Cato 64.2). More wine (Petr 38).

The count–mass distinction obviously reflects our perception of objects in the physical world around us. Relevant properties that have been identified include physical discreteness, identity and spatial and functional cohesion. Fluids tend to be mass (*aqua* 'water,' *vinum* 'wine,' *lac* 'milk,' *sapa* 'must'), because they do not consist of perceptible countable entities; the existence of water molecules is not a linguistically relevant fact. So *oleum* 'oil' is mass but *olea* 'olive' is count, and not vice versa. Grains (*granum*) and seeds (*semen*) are in principle countable, but when they are ground into a very fine granular substance like flour (*farina*) or cooked into a viscous substance like porridge (*puls*), the result is a mass. Animals (*asinus* 'donkey,' *palumbes* 'pigeon') and trees (*robur* 'oak tree') are countable, but when they are killed or cut down they become materials like meat and timber and are mass (*caro asinina* 'donkey meat,' *caro palumbina* 'pigeon meat,' *materies roborea* 'oak wood'). However perceptual accessibility and communicative needs can vary, and the result is a considerable lack of uniformity both between languages (Latin *lens*, English 'lentils') and within one and the same language

(57) mille *fabae* modiis (Hor Ep 1.16.55)
septem nigras... *fabas* (Ov Fast 2.576)

multamque *frondem* habet (Col De Arb 16.1)
nullas habent *frondes* (Sen Ep 12.2).

Beans belong to a class of granular aggregates that is intermediate between count and pure mass: extensional identity does not preclude different conceptualization. Some differences persist. For instance mass conceptualization suggests spatial proximity; and the truth conditions of comparatives can differ, reflecting the different relevant dimensions of comparison just noted: if you have 'more seed' (*plus seminis* Col 11.3.24) than me, you might not also have 'more seeds' (*plura semina*) than me (my seeds could be poppy seeds and yours pumpkin seeds). Languages can also have two different (related or unrelated) words, one for mass and one for count. Latin *pinna* 'feather' is count, *pluma* is count or mass ('plumage'); *vestimentum* can be count ('garment'), *vestitus* is mass ('clothing'). Clothing, like luggage and furniture, represents another intermediate category, namely collective aggregates; their component parts cooccur without being granular and are accessible to distributive adjectival predication and to count-based comparison.

Although they take singular verb agreement, in a number of ways mass nouns are more like plurals. Like plural count nouns and unlike singular count nouns, mass nouns can be used (in the singular) with collective predicates

(58) captivaque vestis *congeritur* (Aen 2.765)
laticem pertusum *congerere* in vas (Lucr 3.1009).

(57) A thousand modii of beans (Hor Ep 1.16.55). Seven black beans (Ov Fast 2.576). And it has much foliage (Col De Arb 16.1). They have no leaves (Sen Ep 12.2).

(58) And captured raiment is heaped up (Aen 2.765). Collecting water into a vessel full of holes (Lucr 3.1009).

Mass nouns also share some of the same vague quantifiers with plural count nouns (like English 'a lot of' and unlike 'much/many, a large number of/a great deal of')

(59) aqua calida *multa* (Cato 157.3)
gallinas *multas* (Cato 143.3)

magnum numerum frumenti (BG 8.34)
magnum numerum obsidum (BG 7.90).

The semantic structure of bare mass nouns is comparable to that of bare plurals in a number of ways. Both have cumulative reference and are distributive/divisible

(60) quod *vinum* bibisset e dolio (NH 14.89)
testes ursinos edisse (NH 28.224).

If you drink wine or eat bear testicles and then you drink/eat some more, it is still the case that you have drunk wine or eaten bear testicles; and if you had only drunk half as much or eaten half as many, you would still have drunk wine and eaten bear testicles. When you quantize the object by adding a measure phrase for the mass noun ('a pint of wine,' cp. 'a pound of apples') or a cardinal for the count noun plural ('three bear testicles'), the resulting phrase is no longer cumulative (or distributive): if you drink a pint of wine and then another pint, you have drunk two pints, and if you eat three bear testicles and then another one, you have eaten (exactly) four. The parallelism breaks down outside the domain of the plural, because count nouns are atomic while mass nouns are conceptualized by the language as nonatomic. So for count nouns, distributivity comes to a halt at the level of atoms: if you eat part of a bear testicle, you have not eaten a bear testicle, although you have eaten the substance (mass) known as 'bear testicle.' Number marking accords special status to atomic elements or, in languages which have a dual, to atomic elements and to pairs of atomic elements. For mass nouns, on the other hand, there is no specific point at which distributivity fails, even sometimes with aggregates: the leg of a chair might not qualify as 'some furniture,' but one can say 'You've got some rice on your tie' if the addressee has half a grain of rice on his tie. (Remember that what is at issue is how masses are conceptualized in language, not whether mass term referents actually have minimal parts.) The parallelism between bare mass nouns and bare plurals suggested that mass nouns too should be represented by some form of join semilattice. We could just use the same powerset lattice that we used for plurals: each element of the lattice for 'wine' would then be a set of minimal quantities of wine, the denotation of 'wine' would be a set of sets of minimal quantities, and 'the wine that she drank' would be the supremum of the lattice for the contextually relevant wine. This might make it easier to account for the

(59) With a lot of hot water (Cato 157.3). A lot of hens (Cato 143.3). A large amount of corn (BG 8.34). A large number of hostages (BG 7.90).

(60) Because she had drunk wine from a jar (NH 14.89). Eating bear testicles (NH 28.224).

coordination of mass and count phrases ('apples and cheese'), but it would pretty much neutralize the distinction between mass and count nouns which language goes out of its way to encode by lexicalizing individuation in count nouns and disregarding or even failing to recognize the existence of minimal quantities in mass nouns. The intuitively natural way to think about the plural of count nouns is in terms of sets, which we can represent with powerset semilattices. The intuitively natural way to think about masses, which don't have plurals, is in terms of part-whole relations. The only linguistically relevant properties of the internal structure of mass nouns can be spelled out by three conditions. The first is that the mass substance does not have atoms. Count noun sets are built up from atoms, which do not overlap; but as far down as you can (or at least need to) see into the structure of a mass, there are always overlapping quantities: for linguistic purposes, you can keep splitting masses into smaller and smaller parts indefinitely, so the mass is atomless. The second property is distributivity: if you package any two parts b and c of a mass substance (that is, form the join $b \vee c$), then any part of a of $b \vee c$ will be either wholly a part of b or wholly a part of c or overlap parts of b and c ($a = b' \vee c'$: $b' < b$, $c' < c$). So the mass substance that is in both b and c distributes down to all the parts of their join. The third condition is called witness: if a part b of the mass has a proper part a ($a < b$ and $a \neq b$), then there is always another part c of b that does not overlap a ($\neg (c \circ a)$). It follows that pairwise joins of nonoverlapping parts will be distinct. Nonatomic mereological structures satisfying distributivity and witness have the structure of free join semilattices. No matter how you divide the mass into packages, you can take subpackages and repackage them and always get a package of the same substance. However it is hardly feasible to devise a satisfactory diagram for mereological semilattices. While one could find a way to represent nonatomicity, only one partition of the mass can be represented at a time, although there is an unlimited number of partitions that could be made. Consider for instance different partitions of the mass noun *pulvis* 'dust.' The supremum corresponds to the maximum available amount of dust salient in the discourse context, the sum of all the smaller available amounts

(61) Domitiani exercitus *pulvis* cerneretur (BC 3.36).

If this sum is an object of type <e>, it is not surprising that the verb appears in the singular. The dust in question may of course consist of a number of smaller dust clouds (just as a plural count noun may consist of a number of groups of individuals), and these smaller portions are accessible in cover readings ('In many places the dust obscured our view'). A different partition might involve a comparatively large but undetermined amount of dust in some situation (comparable to 'many soldiers' in a plural semilattice)

(62) eodemque tempore vis magna *pulveris* cernebatur (BC 2.26)

(61) The dust of Domitius' army was seen (BC 3.36).
(62) At the same time a large amount of dust was seen (BC 2.26).

(63) Romani ex improviso *pulveris* vim magnam animadvortunt (Sall Jug 53.1),

or a comparatively small but undetermined amount of contextually available dust (comparable to 'a few soldiers' in a plural semilattice)

(64) cui miscuit *pulveris* paulum (Cels 5.28.14E).

The bare mass noun is used either for an unspecified amount of dust

(65) cum *pulvis* est (Cato 155.1)

or as a predicate

(66) altaque cum Licini marmora pulvis erunt (Mart 8.3.6).

Now it is perfectly true that each amount of dust in the semilattice consists of a countable number of dust particles (*corpora*)

(67) parvaque quot siccus *corpora* pulvis habet (Ov Trist 1.5.48)
Ego pulveris hausti ostendens cumulum, quot haberet *corpora* pulvis, tot mihi natales contingere vana rogavi (Ov Met 14.144).

But these particles are normally irrelevant, which is why the concept of dust is lexicalized as a mass noun. It is only for the poor Sibyl that the exact count of dust particles matters at all; for everyone else dust comes in larger (measured or unmeasured) quantities corresponding to the nonminimal elements of the lattice. The language adopts the same stance not only towards mass nouns that do not have perceptible minimal elements at all (fluids like *vinum*, solids like *materies*) but also, as we have seen, towards mass nouns that have much more clearly perceptible minimal elements than dust (*faba* and *lens*, for instance). These granular aggregate mass nouns have perfectly recognizable atomic constituents, but they are not part of the denotation of the mass noun. However they do remain accessible to distributive predication ('The rice is ⅛ inch long'). Note that a count noun like *malum* 'apple' has a subatomic mereological structure: it has detachable parts (the stalk, the peel) and nondetachable parts ('some of the apple'), but once we get to a whole apple, we start counting atoms.

Under certain conditions it is possible for nouns to shift their meaning from mass to count and vice versa. When mass nouns are used to denote kinds rather than objects, they become countable and so can appear in the plural: *vina* 'types of wine,' *frumenta* 'types of grain,' *pices resinaeque* 'different types of pitch and resin.' In their basic object meaning, they can be packaged by an implicit classifier into countable entities (like 'two coffees, please') which appear in an aggre-

(63) The Romans suddenly noticed a large amount of dust (Sall Jug 53.1).
(64) Into which he has mixed a bit of powder (Cels 5.28.14E).
(65) When there is dust (Cato 155.1).
(66) When the high marbles of Licinus are merely dust (Mart 8.3.6).
(67) As many as are the particles of dry dust (Ov Trist 1.5.48). Showing him a handful of dust that I had scooped up, I foolishly asked to have as many birthdays as there were grains of dust (Ov Met 14.144).

gate: *sales* 'lumps of salt,' *nives* 'snowdrifts,' *fumi* 'plumes of smoke,' *cineres* 'embers,' *arenae* 'sands.' An event-based type of packaging is illustrated by *grandines* 'hailstorms,' *calores* 'heatwaves,' *siccitates* 'droughts,' and by instantiations of properties (which are abstract mass nouns) like *amores* 'love affairs,' *deorum cupiditates, aegritudines, iracundiae* 'instances of desire, sorrow and anger on the part of the gods.' Pluralization can mean iteration and iteration can function as an intensifier. These shifted meanings can appear freely alongside the regular basic meaning of mass nouns

(68) Ex hoc lacte *casei* qui fiunt maximi cibi sunt bubuli... secundo ovilli, minimi cibi... caprini. Et est etiam discrimen utrum *casei* molles ac recentes sint an aridi et veteres... *caseum* facere incipiunt (Varro RR 2.11.3).

The first occurrence of *casei* denotes plural kinds (cowmilk cheese, sheepmilk cheese and goatmilk cheese), the second denotes plural objects (the individual rounds of cheese), and the third (*caseum*, possibly neuter) is a nonreferential mass noun ('make cheese'). The opposite of packaging is grinding, which shifts count nouns to mass nouns: *abies* 'fir tree' and *fagus* 'beech tree' can be used as mass nouns for their respective timber; similarly *radix* 'a root' and *iris* 'an iris plant' can be used to denote derived substances

(69) faeniculi *radicem* puram contusam minam (Cato 127.1)
iris aridae contusae heminam (Cato 107.1).

In these examples the grinding is actually lexicalized (*contusam, -ae*). Grinding in English is responsible for coerced mass readings of count nouns like 'There was cigarette all over the carpet.'

We saw that in the category of collective/granular mass nouns an atomic denotation was available for the noun, but it was ignored: 'rice' can be counted, but there doesn't seem to be much point in doing so. Animates, and particularly humans, tend to resist this sort of deindividuation: 'rice' is mass, but 'lice' is count. But in the context of military or agricultural functions animate count nouns can shift to collective mass nouns: *eques* 'the cavalry,' *pedes* 'the infantry,' *porcus* 'pigs as livestock,' *haedus* 'goats as livestock.' Abstract nouns, on the other hand, mostly behave like concrete mass nouns in the language, so presumably they are conceptualized in terms of some form of abstract cumulativity and divisivity; but some have plurals representing kinds and/or instantiations

(70) nimia longinquitate (Pro Leg Man 23)
nimiae voluptates (Tac Hist 1.10).

(68) Of the cheeses made from this milk the most nutritious are those of cow's milk, next those of sheep's milk; the least nutritious are those of goat's milk. It also makes a difference whether the cheeses are soft and fresh or dry and aged. Cheese production starts (Varro RR 2.11.3).

(69) A mina of clean crushed fennel root (Cato 127.1). A hemina of dry crushed iris (Cato 107.1).

(70) By the excessive distance (Pro Leg Man 23). His pleasures were excessive (Tac Hist 1.10).

Sometimes mass abstract nouns denoting a property or an activity can be used as concrete mass nouns to denote the animates bearing the property in question without individuating them: *nobilitas* 'nobility, nobles,' *iuventus* 'youth, young men,' *venatio* 'hunting, game'

(71) cum omnes praetores, cum cuncta *nobilitas* ac *iuventus* accurreret (Pro Rab Perd 21)
Ferocissimus quisque iuvenum... adest, sequitur et cetera *iuventus* (Livy 1.59.5)
aliquantum Romanae *iuventutis* morbo absumptum erat (Livy 4.26.5).

Animates can also be packaged into groups by use of 'bunch'-type classifiers

(72) cum latronum *manu* in Galliam inruperit (Phil 6.3)
incendere illa coniuratorum *manus* voluit urbem (In Pis 15).

These groups are themselves atoms and so countable, and, if they are not nonce creations but recurrent groups, they can be lexicalized as collective count nouns: *pecus* fem. 'farm animal,' *pecus* neut. 'flock, herd' with implicit classifier. In some cases deindividuation is triggered simply by spatial contiguity (*turba* 'crowd'), in others the group has a specific function (*collegium* 'society'). Military units are typically collective count nouns: *acies* 'battle line,' *agmen* 'line of march,' *turma* 'troop,' *equitatus* 'cavalry' (*equitatūs* plural 'bodies of cavalry'). The structure of a collective count noun is illustrated in Figure 6.11: a collective count noun like *collegium* has the same powerset semilattice as any other count noun, but underlying each atom is an associated powerset lattice representing its constituent members (the deindividuated *collegiarii* in each *collegium*); the diagram represents three *collegia* each consisting of three *collegiarii*. Two collective nouns do not necessarily have different constituent members; for instance two committees

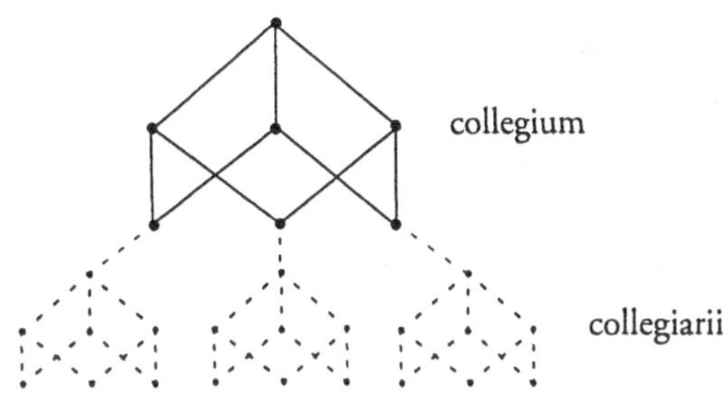

Figure 6.11
Collective count noun: *collegium*

(71) When all the praetors and all the young aristocrats were rushing to help (Pro Rab Perd 21). All the most courageous young men presented themselves; they were followed by the rest of the young men (Livy 1.59.5). A considerable number of young men had been overcome by the plague (Livy 4.26.5).
(72) He has burst into Gaul with a handful of bandits (Phil 6.3). That bunch of conspirators wanted to burn down the city (In Pis 15).

can be made up of the same people while functioning independently. The subsidiary semilattice is semantically active in the sense that there is a function mapping from a group to its constituent members, and this function is responsible for the phenomenon of number mismatch

(73) *cuneusque* is hostium qui in confertos circa ducem impetum fecerat... per totam aciem... *discurrunt* (Livy 25.34.11);

further examples have already been cited in (5)-(9) above.

Mapping from a collective to its members is also required to interpret predication with collectives. First of all, singular collective nouns can be used with collective predicates that otherwise are used with plural rather than singular subjects (compare the examples for mass nouns in (58))

(74) legati... *convenerunt* (BG 1.30)
*legatus convenit
haec multitudo quae ad audiendum *convenit* (Verr 1.15)
classis... ubi *convenit* (BG 3.14)
gratulandi causa turba *coiret* (Livy 26.22.3).

There is even an example with reciprocal predication

(75) vix mille iuvenum manus... mutuis ictibus *inter se concucurrit* (Flor 2.13.33).

Noncollective singulars cannot map to a subjacent part-whole structure in order to license collective predicates unless that structure is somehow salient

(76) Fibrenus... divisus... cito in unum *confluit* (De Leg 2.6)
ipsum <os> coit atque *concurrit* (Quint 10.7.8)
*Ariovistus coit atque concurrit.

The same applies to verbs requiring plural objects

(77) Alexandrini classem... *instruunt* (BAlex 14)
antequam rex manum *colligeret* (BAfr 92).

Navem instruere means to fit out a ship, not to arrange one in battle order; *manum colligere* means to collect a force of soldiers, not normally to collect together the fragments of a hand. Secondly, collective nouns can be used with

(73) That wedge of enemy soldiers that had attacked those who were crowded around the leader ran this way and that along the battle line (Livy 25.34.11).
(74) Envoys gathered (BG 1.30). This crowd that has gathered to hear the trial (Verr 1.15). The fleet... When it had assembled (BG 3.14). A crowd was gathering to congratulate him (Livy 26.22.3).
(75) A band of scarcely a thousand young men fought each other with reciprocal blows (Flor 2.13.33).
(76) The Fibrenus is divided and quickly comes together again (De Leg 2.6). The mouth itself closes and clams up (Quint 10.7.8).
(77) The Alexandrians drew up their fleet (BAlex 14). Before the king could collect a force of men (BAfr 92).

predicates that distribute over their members. Consider the object nouns in the following set of examples

(78) *milites* cum in duas partes divisisset (Livy 36.24.8)
caules... in duas partes dividito (Col 12.7.4)
ad... *vinum*... dividendum in naves (Livy 37.29.1)
exercitum in duas partes divisit (BG 7.34)
in duas partes *iuventutem* dividunt (Livy 10.2.9).

The first two examples involve division of a plurality: in the first example (Livy 36.24) the predication is collective (the soldiers as a group are divided into two parts), in the second example (Col 12.7) it is distributive (each stalk is split into two parts). In the third example (Livy 37.29) a noncollective mass noun is divided; only collective predication is possible because there are no atoms of wine to which the predicate could distribute (although different amounts of wine could be divided up in different subevents). The last two examples (BG 7.34, Livy 10.29) illustrate collective predication with a collective noun. However it is also possible to have distributive predication with a collective noun

(79) Tityre, *coge* pecus (Verg Ecl 3.20)
numerare pecus (Tib 1.5.25; Ov Met 13.824)
tondere pecus, non *deglubere* (Suet 3.32.2).

While the first two examples again have collective predication, the last example (Suet 3.32) has distributive predication: animals get shorn and skinned one at a time, but you cannot count or round up singular animals. The distinction emerges particularly clearly with some adjectival predicates and attributes. *Magna classis* 'a big fleet' need not consist of *magnae naves* 'big ships,' and big ships need not be members of a big fleet. So the adjective of measure does not modify the component parts of the collective noun *classis* nor does it modify *naves* collectively. On the other hand *gravis* 'heavy, weighed down' modifies *classis* distributively, so *gravis classis* does consist of *graves naves*

(80) iam praeda *gravis* ad Longunticam pervenit classis (Livy 22.20.6)
iam enim et *graves* praeda naves habebant (Livy 31.45.16).

It is the weight of each individual ship, not the overall weight of the fleet, that is evaluated, as the second example (Livy 31.45) confirms. Where both collective and distributive modification give sensible readings, there is the potential for ambiguity: 'Those books are heavy' (plural subject) is collective for fifty copies of Sallust's Catiline, but could be distributive for four copies of the Oxford

(78) When he had divided the soldiers into two parts (Livy 36.24.8). Split the stalks into two parts (Col 12.7.4). To divide the wine among the ships (Livy 37.29.1). He divided the army into two parts (BG 7.34). They divided their young men into two parts (Livy 10.2.9).

(79) Tityrus, round up your flock (Verg Ecl 3.20). To count the flock (Tib 1.5.25). To shear his flock, not to skin it (Suet 3.32.2).

(80) The fleet now heavy with booty arrived at Longuntica (Livy 22.20.6). For their ships were by now heavy with booty (Livy 31.45.16).

Latin Dictionary; similarly for 'That luggage is heavy' (collective mass subject). A distributive reading is easier when the noun phrase is indefinite ('three books are heavy') and perhaps when the adjective is attributive and restrictive ('the heavy books').

When the collective noun itself is plural, the situation becomes even more complicated. Consider first the following set of examples

(81) Naupactum concurrisse *Aetolos* (Livy 36.30.1)
cum *populus* armatus concurrisset (Nepos 19.2.5)
ut *populus* concurreret. (Verr 2.2.47)
eoque in concilium omnes *populi* conveniebant (Livy 33.17.1).

The first example (Livy 36.30) has a collective predicate with a plural subject: the individuals that meet are the members of the subject plurality *Aetoli.* The next two examples (Nepos 19.2; Verr 2.2) have a singular collective subject: we map from the collective to its constituent members, so the individuals that meet are the members of the *populus.* The last example (Livy 33.17) has a plural collective subject, and the individuals that meet are the individual *populi*; predication is collective and works just as it did for the plural count noun *Aetoli* in the first example, so there is a single joint meeting on each occasion. But this is not always what happens. Here is another set of examples

(82) iam *hostes* ante castra instructi stabant (Livy 27.47.1)
utraque *acies* pro vallo stetit instructa (Livy 28.14.2)
priusquam concurrerent *acies* (BC 3.86)
extemplo instructae *acies* (Livy 25.19.15).

The first example (Livy 27.47) has a plural subject: *instructi* is collective, so a singular subject is impossible in this sense unless the subject is a singular collective

(83) ad portas *miles* instructus erat (Livy 42.64.4).

The second example in (82) (Livy 28.14) has a singular collective subject with a distributive quantifier. The third example (BC 3.86) has a plural collective subject with collective predication as with *populi conveniebant* in (81). But the last example has a plural collective subject with distributive predication: each member of the set of battle lines was separately drawn up, they were not drawn up collectively into a single line. Distributivity can penetrate down to a singular collective in a set of collectives like *acies*, but, if the verb is collective, it cannot pen-

(81) That the Aetolians had quickly assembled at Naupactus (Livy 36.30.1). When the people had taken up arms and quickly assembled (Nepos 19.2.5). That the people quickly assembled (Verr 2.2.47). All the peoples used to assemble there for meetings (Livy 33.17.1).

(82) The enemy were already standing drawn up in front of the camp (Livy 27.47.1). Each line stood drawn up in front of its rampart (Livy 28.14.2). Before the battles lines could meet (BC 3.86). The battle lines were immediately drawn up (Livy 25.19.15).

(83) The soldiers were drawn up at the gates (Livy 42.64.4).

etrate down to the atomic members of each collective (in this case, the individual soldiers making up each battle line). If we change *eo... populi conveniebant* in (81) to *diversis / idoneis locis... populi conveniebant*, we elicit the distributive reading in that example too.

Coordination and plurality

Plural nouns define sets in terms of their characteristic functions: *duces* is the set of pluralities each member of each set of which is mapped to true by the function 'leader,' and *tutores Hieronymi* is the set of pluralities each member of each set of which is mapped to true by the function 'guardian of Hieronymus.' We can also define a plural set by spelling out its members: this is most practical if the set is quite small and consists of named individuals. The equivalence is obvious in cases of apposition

(84) Ibi diversis partibus duo duces, *Eupolemus et Nicodemus*, pugnantes hortabantur (Livy 38.6.5)
tutoribus... Tres ex iis... *Adranodorus et Zoippus... et Thraso* quidam (Livy 24.5.7).

The first example (Livy 38.5) is definite: the apposition spells out the individuals that are the members of the supremum in the semilattice for *dux*. In the second example (Livy 24.5) the denotation of *tres ex tutoribus Hieronymi* is any set of three of the guardians of Hieronymus (any element on the trial line of the semilattice: $\lambda X.|X| = 3 \wedge X \in \text{Tutores H.}$), so here the apposition serves to pick out the correct element from the available alternative elements. Of course conjoined names can be used instead of, rather than in addition to, a functional description, both in the singular and in the plural

(85) *Marcius et Atilius* Romam cum venissent (Livy 42.47.1)
Consentini et Tauriani in fidem populi Romani redierunt (Livy 25.1.2)
Antiochum et Aetolos (Livy 35.49.4).

Comitatives can also be used to spell out the members of a plurality with singular or plural agreement

(86) Caesar *cum Antonio* in Cassium Brutumque succingitur (Flor 2.17.6)
ipse dux *cum aliquot principibus* capiuntur (Livy 21.60.7).

Conversely definite and indefinite descriptions can themselves be conjoined

(84) There the two leaders, Eupolemus and Nicodemus, were urging on the fighters in different areas (Livy 38.6.5). The guardians... Three of them, Adranodorus, Zoippus and a certain Thraso (Livy 24.5.7).

(85) When Marcius and Atilius reached Rome (Livy 42.47.1). The Consentini and the Tauriani returned to allegiance to the Roman people (Livy 25.1.2). Antiochus and the Aetolians (Livy 35.49.4).

(86) Octavius with Antonius prepares for war against Cassius and Brutus (Flor 2.17.6). The general himself with several chiefs was captured (Livy 21.60.7).

(87) Quid *vallum et castra* spectatis? (Livy 6.24.6)
praeter *cyathum et cantharum* (Pl Pseud 957)
Papirium... *victoriam et triumphum* petere (Livy 8.33.13).

In the first example (Livy 6.24) two definite descriptions are conjoined, in the second (Pseud 957) two indefinites (the denotation of the conjunct is any pair of entities one of which is a ladle and the other a cup); the last example (Livy 8.33) illustrates indefinite conjuncts in an intensional context. Proper names can be conjoined with descriptions

(88) Eumenem regem et decem legatos (Livy 38.37.11)
Brutus et Cassius aliique patres (Flor 2.13.93).

In these examples, the denotation of the whole conjoined phrase is a single set containing all the individuals involved, in the first example (Livy 38.37) the set containing Eumenes and the ten *legati,* in the second (Flor 2.13) the set of those who collectively conspired against Caesar. Sometimes a sentence taken out of context allows both a reading with set union and a reading in which the conjuncts denote unjoined groups

(89) cotidie *sponsores et creditores* L. Trebelli convenire (Phil 6.11)
supplicatum *Volcano et Cereri Proserpinaeque* (Tac Ann 15.44)
vidisti ad bucinam inflatam certo tempore *apros et capreas* convenire ad pabulum, cum... apris effunderetur glas, capreis vicia (Varro RR 3.13.1)

On one reading (not necessarily a likely or even possible one in the context), the *sponsores* and the creditors held separate meetings (Phil 6.11), a prayer was offered to Vulcan and another collectively to Ceres and Proserpina (Ann 15.44), and the boars gathered to feed on acorns and the roes gathered to feed on vetch (RR 3.13). These readings involve distribution that is not atomic but only reaches intermediate sets (plurals or conjuncts), which are then open to collective predication. Distribution to subgroups arises easily with counting predicates

(90) Si *titulos annosque* tuos numerare velimus, facta prement annos. (Ov Met 7.448).

A separate count is made of Theseus' accomplishments and his years, not a single total covering both, as the apodosis confirms. The denotation of *titulos*

(87) Why are you looking at the rampart and the camp? (Livy 6.24.6). Except for a ladle and a cup (Pl Pseud 957). That Papirius was seeking a victory and a triumph (Livy 8.33.13).
(88) King Eumenes and the ten commissioners (Livy 38.37.11). Brutus and Cassius and other senators (Flor 2.13.93).
(89) That L. Trebellius' guarantors and creditors are meeting every day (Phil 6.11). Prayers were offered to Vulcan and to Ceres and Proserpina (Tac Ann 15.44). You have seen that when a horn was blown at a specific time boars and deer gathered to feed, when acorns were thrown down to the boars and vetch to the roes (Varro RR 3.13.1).
(90) If we wanted to count your honours and your years, the deeds would outnumber the years (Ov Met 7.448).

annosque is not a simple set like {*a, b, c, d, e, f, g*} but a nested set like {{*a, b, c,*}, {*d, e, f, g*}}. Subgroups are the correlate in the count domain of packages in the mass domain.

Not all *N et N* sequences create pluralities in the way just described. Consider the following

(91) qui *sodalis et familiarissimus* Dolabellae eram (Ad Fam 12.14.7)
Allienus, *familiaris et necessarius* meus (Phil 11.32)
Et ait etiam meus *familiaris et necessarius* (Pro Rab Post 32).

These are not examples of individuals being combined into a set but of properties being combined into a complex property. So from an extensional perspective they involve not set formation but set intersection. The first example (Ad Fam 12.14) is a predicate, the second (Phil 11.32) is an apposition (which is a type of predication). The third example is an argument; no plurality is created by this conjunction; rather the set *familiaris* is intersected with the set *necessarius* and the definite description containing the resulting complex property, $\iota x.\text{Familiaris}(x) \wedge \text{Necessarius}(x)$ 'the salient person who is my friend and close associate,' serves to identify a singular individual (Memmius). Often it is quite clear that two conjuncts are joined by set formation (x et $y \rightarrow \{x, y\}$) and not by set intersection ($\lambda x.P(x)$ et $\lambda y.Q(y) \rightarrow \lambda x.P(x) \wedge Q(x)$)

(92) *matrem et patrem* (Pl Capt 549)
quae L. Antonius in Parmensium *liberis et coniugibus* effecerit (Phil 14.9).

Since the sets 'mother and father' and 'wives and children' are disjoint, their intersection is empty, leaving set formation as the only possible reading. Contrast

(93) *eius matrem suamque uxorem* (Pl Trin 111),

which denotes a single individual: $\iota x.\text{Matrem}(x, y) \wedge \text{Uxorem}(x, \text{Charmides})$. But other cases may require both simultaneously

(94) agrum Campanum... *compransoribus tuis et conlusoribus* dividebas (Phil 2.101)
addite Antoni *conlusores et sodales*, Eutrapelum, Melam, Pontium... (Phil 13.3)
ut locus... daretur *amicis et tribulibus* (Pro Mur 72).

(91) Who was once a companion and great friend of Dolabella (Ad Fam 12.14.7). Allienus, a close acquaintance and friend of mine (Phil 11.32). My dear friend says so too (Pro Rab Post 32).

(92) His mother and father (Pl Capt 549). The things that L. Antonius is responsible for in the case of the women and children of the people of Parma (Phil 14.9).

(93) Her mother and his wife (Pl Trin 111).

(94) You wanted to divide up the Campanian land among your dinner companions and fellow-gamblers (Phil 2.101). Add Antony's fellow-gamblers and companions, Eutrapelus, Mela, Pontius (Phil 13.3). For seats to be given to our friends and fellow-tribesmen (Pro Mur 72).

Here we want to allow for some individuals possibly being members of both sets and others only of one: in the last example (Pro Mur 72) some of the people getting seats at shows may be friends and fellow-tribesmen, others just friends and others again just fellow-tribesmen. This is a reflection of the cumulative nature of conjunction and plurality that we have already seen with cover readings.

On the other hand, there are also cases in which it is not clear whether prima facie noun phrase coordination could in fact be coordination of some larger structure, for instance a clause for subjects and a verb phrase for objects. The rules for agreement of the predicate with a coordinated subject are quite complicated and variable; as in other languages animacy and verb precedence are conditioning factors. Conjoined inanimate subjects (particularly abstract nouns) prefer singular agreement

(95) Virtus et honestas et pudor cum consulibus esse *cogebat* (Pro Rab Perd 24)
quorum usque ad nostram memoriam disciplina navalis et gloria *remansit* (Pro Leg Man 54)
mors et cruciatus *erat constitutus* (Verr 2.5.153),

conjoined animate subjects prefer plural agreement

(96) cum Carneades et Stoicus Diogenes ad senatum in Capitolio *starent* (Luc 137)
C. Fannius et Q. Mucius ad socerum *veniunt* (De Amic 5)
Consulum Sulpicius in dextro, Poetelius in laevo cornu *consistunt* (Livy 9.27.8).

The last example (Livy 9.27) is asyndetic. However singular agreement with animates is preferred when the verb precedes either or both conjuncts and with *et... et* (which is distributive in English: *'Both Jack and Sue met')

(97) *Condemnatur* enim perpaucis sententiis Philodamus et eius filius. (Verr 2.1.75)
ut hoc Balbus *sustineat* et Oppius (Ad Att 11.7.5)
Hac ratione et Chrysippus et Diogenes et Antipater *utitur*. (De Div 1.84).

Participial gender agreement, as in the last example in (95) (Verr 2.5), indicates that singular agreement is not due to the conjuncts forming a sort of singular group (like *senatus populusque Romanus*, cp. 'Bacon and eggs makes you fat'). It could be that singular agreement is a purely mechanical rule of syntactic locality

(95) Courage and honourability and decency compelled him to side with the consuls (Pro Rab Perd 24). Whose naval skill and renown is still remembered today (Pro Leg Man 54). Death and torture were imposed (Verr 2.5.153).

(96) When Carneades and the Stoic Diogenes were at the senate on the Capitol (Luc 137). C. Fannius and Q. Mucius are visiting their father-in-law (De Amic 5). Of the consuls Sulpicius stationed himself on the right wing and Poetelius on the left (Livy 9.27.8).

(97) Philodamus and his son were convicted by a very small majority of the jury (Verr 2.1.75). That Balbus and Oppius should withstand this (Ad Att 11.7.5). Chrysippus, Diogenes and Antipater use the same line of argument (De Div 1.84).

(agreement only sees one conjunct), but it could also be that singular agreement and plural agreement are structurally different; for instance singular agreement could involve ellipsis of the verb (which certainly works quite well with the examples in (97)). In that case no plurality would be formed, since coordination would be clausal. Because clausal coordination entails distributivity ('Jack smiled and Sue smiled,' *'Jack met and Sue met'), a straightforward prediction of this theory is that singular agreement is impossible with collective predicates (as in some varieties of Arabic)

(98) Labor voluptasque... societate quadam inter se naturali *sunt iuncta* (Livy 5.4.4)
ubi ira et aegritudo *permixta sunt* (Sall Jug 68.1)
dissimillimique tamen inter se Zeuxis, Aglaophon, Apelles (De Or 3.26).

Exceptions occur with predicates of comparison (cp. *alius ac* 'other than')

(99) ea res quam ego dico et ea quam tu fecisti inter se... *differat* (Verr 2.3.203)
haudquaquam similis pugna in dextro laevoque cornu *erat* (Livy 10.28.1)
dissimilis *est* pecuniae debitio et gratiae (Pro Planc 68).

If the singular is not a semantically empty concord feature, this construction may derive from an earlier biclausal structure like the paraphrases used by early generative grammarians to reduce all conjunction to underlying sentential conjunction: 'the battle on the left wing was not similar to the battle on the right wing, and vice versa.' For object conjuncts, verb phrase rather than noun phrase conjunction is indicated when a modifier applies to just one of the conjuncts

(100) circum vias ulmos serito et *partim* populos (Cato 6.3);

this means *ulmos serito et partim populos serito*.

Conjunct pairs can be interpreted distributively or collectively (provided the predicate permits either reading) just as plurals can

(101) *L. Quinctius et Cn. Domitius* consules in provincias profecti sunt, Quinctius in Ligures, Domitius adversus Boios (Livy 35.40.2)
Titinius Genuciusque tribuni militum profecti adversus Faliscos Capenatesque (Livy 5.18.7).

Furthermore coordination of distributively with collectively interpreted constituents is not problematic. In the following examples a singular subject is coordinated with a collective noun (not interpreted distributively)

(98) Work and pleasure are joined with one another by a sort of bond of nature (Livy 5.4.4). When anger was mixed with sorrow (Sall Jug 68.1). But Zeuxis, Aglaophon and Apelles are quite unlike one another (De Or 3.26).

(99) What I am talking about and what you did are different (Verr 2.3.203). The fighting was quite different on the left and on the right wings (Livy 10.28.1). Owing money and owing a favour are quite different things (Pro Planc 68).

(100) Around the roads plant elms and in some cases poplars (Cato 6.3).

(101) The consuls L. Quinctius and Cn. Domitius set out for their provinces, Quinctius to the Ligurians and Domitius against the Boii (Livy 35.40.2). The military tribunes Titinius and Genucius, having set out against the Faliscans and Capenates (Livy 5.18.7).

(102) secutum id esse Neronem et eius *consilium* (Verr 2.1.72)
Quod anno ante frater Metellus et concors etiam tum *senatus*... excluserat (De Har Resp 45).

Conversely, a plural argument phrase can be associated with a distributive and a collective predicate, in conjoined or subordinate structures

(103) Reges amici et socii et singuli in suo *quisque* regno Caesareas urbes condiderunt et *cuncti simul* aedem Iovis Olympii... perficere communi sumptu destinaverunt (Suet 2.60)
Lampsaceni, simul ut hoc *audierunt*,... ad aedes noctu *convenerunt.* (Verr 2.1.67)
Accepi a te aliquot epistulas *uno tempore*, quas tu *diversis temporibus* dederas. (Ad Fam 7.18.1).

So coordination probably does not provide safe evidence for locating distributivity or collectivity operators rigidly and exclusively in the noun phrase or in the verb phrase.

FURTHER READING

Acquaviva (2008); Landman (2000); Lasersohn (1995); Schwarzschild (1996); Winter (2001).

(102) That Nero and his court based themselves on the following fact (Verr 2.1.72). What a year before his cousin Metellus and a still united senate had prevented (De Har Resp 45).
(103) The kings who were his friends and allies both individually in their own kingdoms founded cities called Caesarea and jointly all contributed funds towards the completion of the temple of Jupiter Olympius (Suet 2.60). As soon as the people of Lampsacum heard this, they gathered at his house during the night (Verr 2.1.67). I have received several letters from you all at once, which you sent at different times (Ad Fam 7.18.1).

7 | MODIFICATION

Nouns are modified by adjectives

(1) *gravi* volnere (Livy 2.47.2)
longum iter (Livy 27.48.12),

while verbs, adjectives and prepositions are modified by adverbs (often morphologically related to adjectives)

(2) si *graviter* eos lugeant (Tusc 3.72)
graviter saucius (Pro Tull 22)
longe citra aemulum (Quint 12.10.9).

This is a matter of grammar, not of meaning. When an event is lexicalized as a verb it is modified by an adverb, when it is lexicalized as a noun it is modified by an adjective

(3) *maxime* admirabar (De Or 1.47)
maximam admirationem (Phil 10.4).

Similarly, when a gradable property is lexicalized by an adjective it is modified by an adverb, when it is lexicalized by a noun it is modified by an adjective

(4) semina... ne *minus* crassa (Col De Arb 20.1)
ne *minore* crassitudine (Vitr 7.1.3).

Our analysis in this chapter will be confined to adjectival modification.

The most common classes of adjectives in the languages of the world (the core adjectives) are adjectives of dimension (*magnus* 'large,' *longus* 'long'), age (*novus* 'new,' *vetus* 'old'), colour (*viridis* 'green,' *ruber* 'red'), and evaluation (*bonus* 'good,' *pulcher* 'beautiful'). Also common are adjectives of physical state (*durus* 'hard,' *umidus* 'wet') and mental state (*laetus* 'happy,' *cupidus* 'eager').

(1) By a serious wound (Livy 2.47.2). A long march (Livy 27.48.12).

(2) If they mourn them deeply (Tusc 3.72). Seriously wounded (Pro Tull 22). By far without a rival (Quint 12.10.9).

(3) I admired most of all (De Or 1.47). The greatest amazement (Phil 10.4).

(4) Seedlings not less thick (Col De Arb 20.1). Of no less thickness (Vitr 7.1.3).

Such properties are evidently distinct from properties like canine and feline. The latter represent easily recognizable kinds and are consequently lexicalized as nouns ('cat,' 'dog') rather than adjectives; the former are properties (permanent or temporary) that are widely distributed over many different kinds. In addition to being attributive (adnominal) modifiers, adjectives can also function as predicates

(5) aliis *gravis* erat, plerisque non ingrata militia (Curt Ruf 7.2.36)
morbi... qui modo acuti, modo *longi* sunt (Cels 3.1.2).

In some languages adjectives can only be attributive modifiers, while in others they can be predicates but they cannot directly modify a noun.

Simple intersective combinations

In many cases adjectival modification amounts to predicate conjunction

(6) fabulos *albos* iii (Cato 70.1).

One of the ingredients of the ox medicine is three white beans. White beans are entities that combine the property of being beans with the property of being white: $\lambda x.N(x) \wedge A(x)$, where N represents the noun property and A the adjective property. This conjunction is achieved by intersecting the set of bean things with the set of white things. Various different settheoretical relations can result from this process. To start with, set intersection can create both restrictively modified phrases and descriptively modified phrases

(7) locis *calidis* hibernas serotinas serito (Col De Arb 21.1)
semen eius locis *calidis* mense Ianuario, frigidis Februario seritur (Col 11.3.32)
per *calidas* Libyae sitientis harenas (Lucan 1.368)

(8) perdices vero a domitis *feros*... iniri promiscue (NH 10.101)
quique *feros* movit Sertorius exul Hiberos (Lucan 2.549)
sola *feros* Hecates perdomuisse canes (Tib 1.2.54).

In the first two examples in (7) (De Arb 21.1; Col 11.3) some sowing areas are warm and some are cold. The adjective *calidis* is used restrictively: it serves to restrict the set of areas to those that are warm. In the third example the sands of Libya are generically hot. The adjective *calidas* is used descriptively: it serves to express a set to which the referents belong in addition to the set of Libyan sands.

(5) For some military service was burdensome, for most it was not unpleasant (Curt Ruf 7.2.36). Diseases which are at times acute and at times chronic (Cels 3.1.2).

(6) Three white beans (Cato 70.1).

(7) In warm areas plant late winter figs (Col De Arb 21.1). Its seed is sown in the month of January in warm areas and in February in cold ones (Col 11.3.32). Across the hot sands of desert Libya (Lucan 1.368).

(8) That wild partridges are indiscriminately covered by tame ones (NH 10.101). And Sertorius who as an exile stirred up the fierce Hiberians (Lucan 2.549). That she alone succeeded in taming Hecate's wild dogs (Tib 1.2.54).

In the first example in (8) (NH 10.101) some partridges are tamed and some are wild, so the adjective *feros* is being used restrictively. In the other two examples in (8) (Lucan 2.549; Tib 1.2) the adjective *feros* is being used descriptively: all the Hiberians are fierce and all the dogs are fierce. When the adjective is used restrictively, the noun set is not a subset of the adjective set; when the adjective is used descriptively, the noun set is a subset of the adjective set. (Nonvacuous) restrictive modification is illustrated in Figure 7.1, descriptive modification in Figure 7.2. Whether the adjective is used descriptively or not can depend not only on the presence of an overt restriction (like the possessive in the case of Hecate's dogs or the sands of Libya just cited) but also on the implicit domain of quantification

(9) tetigit *fulvi* saetis hirsuta leonis vellera (Ov Fast 2.339).

Being tawny is a permanent property of lions throughout the real world, so it would take an imaginary world to create a restrictive reading; but if African lions were tawny and Indian lions were grey, then the adjective would only be descriptive in a context in which the domain of the adjective was limited to African lions. This narrowing effect shows up clearly when a set is contextually established in prior discourse

(10) inveni duos solos libellos... haec paucorum mensium ratio...ex his *parvis* libellis (Verr 2.2.182-84)
pelliculis *haedinis*... his *haedinis* pelliculis praetura deiectus est (Pro Mur 75-76).

In the second example (Pro Mur 75) first the set is established by a restrictive adjective in an indefinite noun phrase, then it is reactivated by a descriptive adjective in a definite noun phrase. The descriptive adjective need not be vacuous but can redirect attention to the contextually given property or highlight its affective connotation. As in French and Spanish, a postmodifier (*pelliculis*

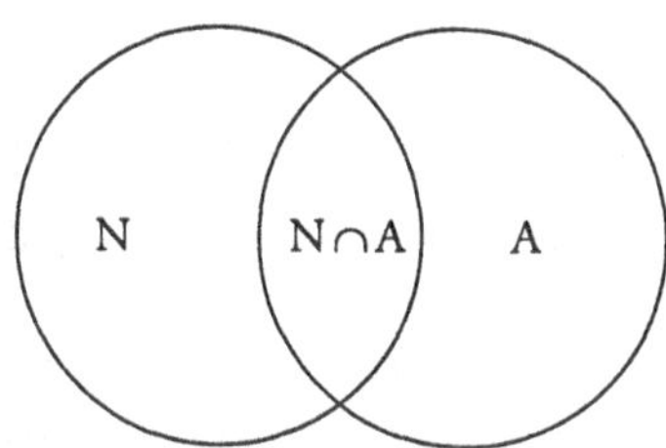

Figure 7.1
Restrictive modification: $N \not\subseteq A$
Locis calidis serito (Col De Arb 21.1)

(9) He touched the fleece of the tawny lion, hairy with bristles (Ov Fast 2.339).
(10) I found just two account books, this record for a few months... from these small account books (Verr 2.2.182-84). With goat skins... he was rejected for the praetorship because of these goat skins (Pro Mur 75-76).

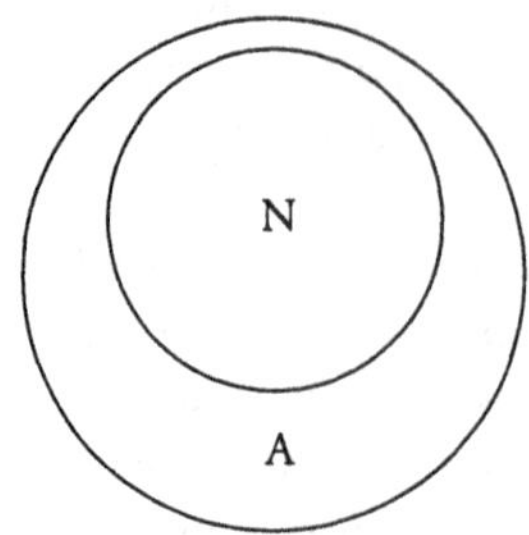

Figure 7.2
Descriptive modification: N $\subseteq$ A
Calidas Libyae harenas (Lucan 1.368)

haedinis) is preferred for the restrictive use, but a premodifier (*haedinis pelliculis*) can occur in the descriptive type (also in the absence of a preceding demonstrative). It has been observed that if a postmodifier is used in the second (descriptive) phrase in French, it sounds repetitious; once the operation of set intersection has created a new set, this set can be directly referred to; it does not need to be recreated for each subsequent reference. Note also that where English uses a descriptive adjective in definite phrases, particularly with proper names, Latin prefers an appositional phrase with a restrictive adjective

(11) collega, vir *clarissimus* (Phil 11.24)
Albicos, *barbaros* homines (BC 1.34);

these could correspond to English 'your illustrious colleague' and 'the barbarian Albici.'

Further settheoretical relations arise when, conversely, the adjective set is a subset of the noun set, whether it is used restrictively

(12) ceteraeque *pomiferae* arbores (Col 11.2.37)

or descriptively

(13) nisi di *immortales*... prope fata ipsa flexissent (Cat 3.19).

In (12) not all trees are fruitbearing, but all orchard-fruit-bearing plants are trees, so the adjective set is a subset of the noun set. In (13) all gods are immortal and all immortal beings are gods, so the adjective set is coextensive with the noun set. These two conditions are illustrated in Figure 7.3. Whether the adjective set is a subset of the noun set or not is much less important than whether the noun set is a subset of the adjective set. From a purely semantic point of view there is no difference between N$\cap$A and A$\cap$N, since intersection is symmetrical. But from a procedural point of view, first the noun set is established, then it is restricted by the adjective. The aim is to define a subset of the noun set, not

(11) Your illustrious colleague (Phil 11.24). The barbarian Albici (BC 1.34).
(12) And the other fruit-bearing trees (Col 11.2.37).
(13) Unless the immortal gods almost changed the course of fate itself (Cat 3.19).

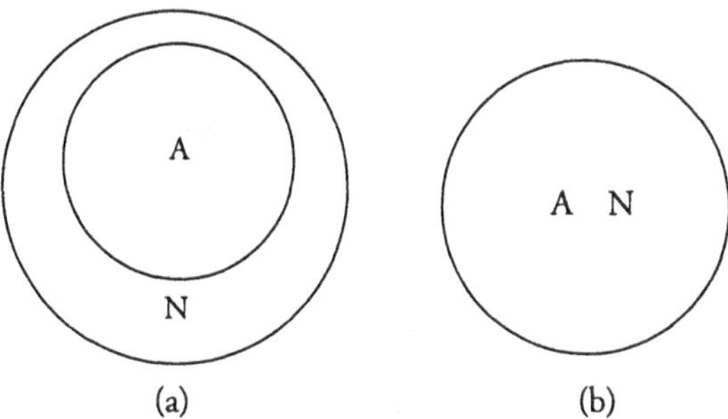

Figure 7.3
(a) Restrictive modification: $A \subset N$. *Pomiferae arbores* (Col 11.2.37)
(b) Descriptive modification: $A = N$. *Di immortales* (Cat 3.19)

of the adjective set. It may be that what is logically symmetrical is cognitively predicational. Take *fabulos albos* in (6): Cato is defining a subkind of beans, not a subset of white entities having fabaceous properties. While it is important not to pick out beans of a colour other than white to make the ox medicine correctly, the issue of using white entities other than beans never arises; so whether there actually are any such entities is not important. What we have just said is true in a pragmatically unmarked context, when neither the noun nor the adjective has narrow focus ('white beans'), and in a pragmatically marked context when the adjective has narrow focus ('WHITE beans'; small caps mean stress). It is not true when the noun has narrow focus ('white BEANS'), since that reverses the focus-presupposition values: the issue now really is which white things are beans rather than which beans are white.

If the noun set and the adjective set are disjoint, the adjective is neither restrictive nor descriptive but simply vacuous (like 'female centurions,' which is the empty set). However it is possible for the noun set and the noun plus adjective set to be disjoint without the latter being empty, in which case the combination is nonintersective and the adjective is called privative

(14) *subditivum* archipiratam (Verr 2.5.69)
quae *falsam* gremio credula fovit avem (Ov Her 17.56)
simulato transfugae (Flor 1.46.6)
effigiem nullo cum corpore *falsi* fingit apri (Ov Met 14.358).

In the last example (Met 14.358) the set of boars in the real world is disjoint from the set of hallucinatory bodiless boars (unless imaginary boars can be coerced into a type of real boar). This is illustrated in Figure 7.4. Here is an example involving different times rather than different worlds

(15) nivesque *solutas* (Ov Am 3.6.93).

(14) Fake pirate captain (Verr 2.5.69). Who unsuspectingly caressed the fake bird in her lap (Ov Her 17.56). A pretended deserter (Flor 1.46.6). She created the bodiless fake image of a boar (Ov Met 14.358).
(15) And the melted snow (Ov Am 3.6.93).

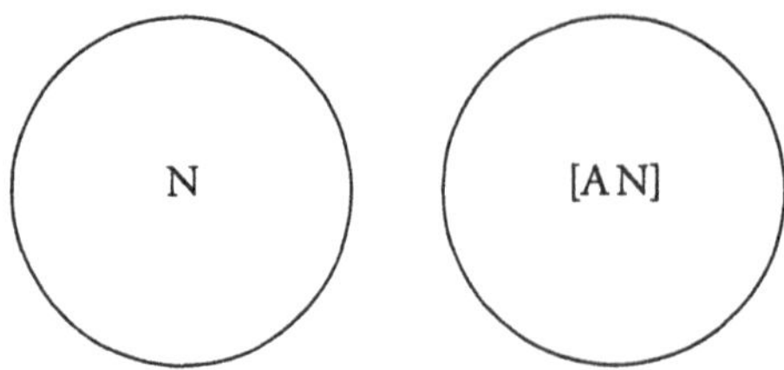

Figure 7.4
Modification with $[AN] \cap N = \varnothing$
Falsi apri (Ov Met 14.358)

The melted snows that feed the torrent were previously snows and are now no longer snows.

Nonintersectives

In the simplest conceivable scenario, any adjective could modify any noun, and all nouns would denote sets of objects. Predictably, actual language is much more complicated. Selectional restrictions prevent some adjectives from modifying some types of nouns: for instance, without coercion, inanimate nouns cannot be modified by animate adjectives (*'intelligent stone'), and, because they are unbounded, mass nouns cannot be modified by adjectives of shape (*'triangular milk'). In addition to objects, adjectives can modify other individuals in the semantic ontology like events and degrees, and, as we saw at the end of the last section, adjectives can also be used to shift the world in which a noun is evaluated to one other than the real world and the time at which it is evaluated to one other than the present. We will start by looking more closely at this latter effect.

Consider the following set of examples

(16) ferramenta *vetera* (Cato 2.7))
veterem belli gloriam... recuperare (BG 7.1)
qui *veteres* inimicitias cum Caesare gerebant (BC 1.3)
quidam *vetus* adsectator (Verr 2.2.29)
vetus tamen senator et aetate iam gravis (Livy 5.12.11).

In the first example (Cato 2.7) the adjective modifies an individual (the tools are old); in the second example (BG 7.1) it says that a state (the Gauls' glory) is in the past; the third example (BC 1.3) assigns a perfect (extended now) semantics to an event (their hostile behaviour is longstanding); the fourth example (Verr 2.2) does the same for the eventive component in the meaning of an agent noun (the man in question was a longstanding follower of Scipio); that he was not necessarily an old man is clear from the last example (Livy 5.12), where *aetate*

(16) Old tools (Cato 2.7). To regain their old military glory (BG 7.1). Who had longstanding disagreements with Caesar (BC 1.3). A certain longtime follower (Verr 2.2.29). Merely a senator of long standing and now advanced in age (Livy 5.12.11).

gravis would be tautologous if entailed by *vetus*. The temporal adjective *futurus* can likewise modify not only a noun denoting an event but also the eventive component inside the meaning of an agent noun

(17) pallida morte *futura* (Aen 4.644)
tam docendus est *futurus* vilicus quam *futurus* figulus aut faber (Col 11.1.9)

In the first example (Aen 4.644) the time of the event of Dido's death is in the future, in the second example (Col 11.1) the time (*t*) at which a person (*x*) will perform the role of bailiff (*e*) is in the future; the individual (*x*) himself already exists at the present time.

Modal adjectives work in much the same way

(18) *inopinato* classis adventu (Vell Pat 2.79.4)
Seleuci mathematici... qui... ultro *inopinatus* advenerat (Suet 7.Oth4.1).

In the first example (Vell Pat 2.79) the modal adjective modifies an event (the arrival of the fleet), in the second example (Suet 7.Oth4.1) it is a secondary predicate modifying an individual. In both cases the semantics is arguably propositional: the fleet/Seleucus arrived and, prior to the event of arrival, in every world compatible with people's predictions the proposition 'the fleet/Seleucus arrives' was not true. Here are a couple of similar examples with *insperatus*

(19) *Insperata* pax Cephallaniae adfulserat (Livy 38.28.7)
Salve, mi pater *insperate* (Pl Rud 1175).

In the first example (Livy 38.28) the adjective modifies a state, in the second (Rud 1175) a relation between individuals (fatherhood). Note that in the latter the modal adjective takes scope over both arguments of the relation: in every world compatible with my expectations, the proposition 'you are father to me' was not true. If *mi* had been outside the scope of the adjective, Daemones would have had to be the father of someone else (existential quantification over the child argument).

This ability of an adjective to take scope wider than the noun phrase it modifies emerges clearly with frequency adjectives. The meaning of *frequens* and *rarus* varies depending on the semantics of the modifiee and on whether they are used attributively or as secondary predicates (for the latter see the last section in this chapter)

(20) *frequentibus* pilis (Varro RR 2.5.8)
arbores... *rarae* (Nepos 1.5.3)

(17) Pale with the thought of her imminent death (Aen 4.644). A future bailiff needs to be taught his job no less than a future potter or a future craftsman (Col 11.1.9).

(18) Due to the unexpected arrival of the fleet (Vell Pat 2.79.4). Of the astrologer Seleucus, who had appeared of his own accord unexpectedly (Suet 7.Oth4.1).

(19) Cephallania was basking in unexpected peace (Livy 38.28.7). I am finally greeting the father I never expected to meet (Pl Rud 1175).

(20) With thick hair (Varro RR 2.5.8). Trees dotted around (Nepos 1.5.3).

(21) *frequens*... arbustum (Col 5.6.1)
raro pectine (Ov Rem 192)
usus *frequens* (De Or 1.15)
rarior usus (Juv 11.208).

The examples in (20) and the first pair in (21) have the meaning 'tightly/loosely distributed in space,' the former with the atoms of a plurality, the latter with the parts of an individual (Rem 192) or collective (Col 5.6). In the second pair in (21), the nouns do not denote objects but events, so the meaning is 'tightly/loosely distributed in time.' If the noun lacks an event component in its meaning, the temporal reading is not available when the adjective is used attributively, but it re-emerges when the adjective is used as a secondary predicate (often syntactically preceding the verb)

(22) Aurum et opes et rura *frequens* donabit amicus (Mart 8.18.9)
rarus venit in cenacula miles (Juv 10.18)
Ante *frequens* sed nunc *rarus* nos donat amicus (Mart 14.122.1).

As a secondary predicate the adjective has clausal scope and consequently modifies the clausal event like an adverb: the second example (Juv 10.18) means that the number of events in which a soldier enters a garret is few. With agent nouns both wide and narrow scope are available

(23) sit certaminis cui destinatur *frequens* spectator (Quint 10.5.19)
Cur te tam *rarus* cupiat repetatque fututor (Mart 7.18.3).

In the first example (Quint 10.5) what is frequent is the event encoded by the agent noun (he should be a frequent spectator, taking *frequens* as the modifier in a predicative noun phrase), in the second example (Mart 7.18) it is the event encoded by the verb, not the event encoded by the agent noun: the meaning is not 'rarely has sex' but 'rarely comes back for more.' English has two readings for adjectives of infrequency ('An occasional tourist greeted us': there were few pairs of different tourists and greeting events vs. a single individual who tours seldom) but only one reading for adjectives of frequency ('A frequent tourist greeted us': a single individual who tours often).

Modification of the event component inside an agent noun is also an issue for manner adjectives

(24) *vehemens* lupus (Hor Ep 2.2.28)
vehementissimo cursu (BG 8.15)

(21) A thick plantation of trees (Col 5.6.1). With wide-toothed rake (Ov Rem 192). Frequent practice (De Or 1.15). Infrequent indulgence (Juv 11.208).

(22) Many friends will give gold and wealth and land (Mart 8.18.9). Few policemen go to a garret (Juv 10.18). Many friends used to give me presents but now only a few do (Mart 14.122.1).

(23) He should be a frequent spectator of the struggle which he is destined to take part in (Quint 10.5.19). Why so few lovers desire you and come back to you (Mart 7.18.3).

(24) Like a fierce wolf (Hor Ep 2.2.28). At great speed (BG 8.15).

(25) *vehementis* accusatoris (Pro Mur 13)
T. Postumius... de re publica vero non minus *vehemens* orator quam bellator fuit (Brut 269).

In the first example in (24) (Ep 2.2) the adjective modifies the whole individual (*x*): the behaviour of wolves is fierce in general. In the second example it modifies an event (*e*). In the first example in (25) (Pro Mur 13) it modifies the event component of an agent noun: someone who is fierce in his role as prosecutor may be quite a sweet character in other respects. Since modification is linked to the event, it is also limited to the time of the event: a successful governor of Cilicia may be unsuccessful before and after his governorship. The last example (Brut 269) illustrates how modification of a role expressed by one agent noun does not entail that the property applies to the same person when performing a different role: Postumius could just as well have been a fierce orator and a meek warrior or vice versa. Here is another set of examples

(26) *divino* ac singulari viro (De Fin 3.6)
divine poeta (Verg Ecl 5.45)
ille *divinus* orator (Quint 4.3.13).

Cicero was a divine orator, perhaps not a divine man and certainly not a divine poet (at least not in the estimation of Juvenal 10.124). When an adjective is (or is used) intersectively as in *fabulos albos* in (6), the following entailment applies: if AN(*x*), then A(*x*) and N(*x*). But for *divinus orator* in the last example (Quint 4.3), we have the following entailment: if AN(*x*), then N(*x*) but not necessarily A(*x*). Adjectives used in this way are called subsective. Subsectivity in (25) and (26) is due to the ability of a manner adjective to modify just the event component inside an agent noun.

Adjectives of measure can modify degrees directly

(27) *magna* altitudine (BC 3.112)
in *magnam* longitudinem (NH 11.256),

but they can also activate a scale associated with a noun and modify a degree on that scale

(28) fur *magnus* (Ad Fam 9.21.3)
magnus es ardalio (Mart 2.7.8)
magnus moechus mulierum (Pl Mil 775)
tu *magnus* amator mulierum es (Pl Men 267).

(25) Of a forceful prosecutor (Pro Mur 13). T. Postumius... he was no less vigorous a public orator than a warrior (Brut 269).

(26) A divine and outstanding man (De Fin 3.6). Divine poet (Verg Ecl 5.45). The divine orator (Quint 4.3.13).

(27) Of great height (BC 3.112). To a great length (NH 11.256).

(28) A big thief (Ad Fam 9.21.3). You are a great busybody (Mart 2.7.8). Such a great adulterer (Pl Mil 775). You are a great lover of women (Pl Men 267).

In the first example (Ad Fam 9.21) M. Carbo was a big thief: *magnus* is interpreted like an intensifier superlative; it says that the interval on the scale of intensity or severity of thievery between the average degree for thieves (in this context) and the degree for Carbo is great. *Magnus* does not modify the individual but the degree on a scale associated with the individual in a role; contrast

(29) anseris... *magni* (Juv 5.114)
magnus homo (Nepos 4.1.1)
magnus imperator (Nepos 24.3.1).

What was big about Carbo was not (necessarily) his physical size (a big idiot can be a short and thin guy) nor his importance in society but his degree of thievery: unlike the first two examples in (29) (Juv 5.114; Nepos 4.1), *magnus fur* is subsective. So is *magnus imperator* in the last example in (29) (Nepos 24.3), but while the latter involves a scale of importance, the former involves a scale of intensity (Cato was a famous general, Carbo was a large-scale thief). Adjectives like *mirus, mirabilis* 'amazing' can also be used to modify degrees; they additionally say something about people's expectations, attitude and reactions to the degree

(30) Quintus frater, homo *mirus* (Ad Att 3.18.2)
muros in *miram* altitudinem eductos (Sen Ep 94.61)
mira longitudine crescunt (NH 19.66)
mirabili celeritate (BAfr 22)
mirumque amorem adsecutus erat (Tac Ann 6.30).

In the first example (Ad Att 3.18) *mirus* simply modifies an individual, in the other examples the adjective modifies a degree. For instance, in the second example (Ep 94.61) the interval on the scale of height between the average degree for walls (in this context) and the degree for the walls in question is great, and people are amazed at the proposition that it is so great. In the last example (Ann 6.30) the noun does not directly denote a degree, but the adjective evokes a scale for the state (*amor*) denoted by the noun; compare the agent nouns in (28); it is not the type of love that was wonderful, but its degree of intensity.

There is nothing wrong with degree and event adjectives being used predicatively with degree and event subjects: 'Its height was great,' 'Her singing was beautiful.' However subsective predicate readings, while not completely excluded ('The mezzosoprano was beautiful,' i.e. 'sang beautifully': the stage level past tense triggers an eventive reading), are usually very difficult (*'The thief was big,' *'The friend was old'), and this presumably applies to Latin too. In other words, it is much easier for an adjective to be predicated of the individual that

(29) Of a large goose (Juv 5.114). A great man (Nepos 4.1.1). A great general (Nepos 24.3.1).

(30) My brother Quintus, a great guy (Ad Att 3.18.2). Walls built to an extraordinary height (Sen Ep 94.61). They grow to a extraordinary length (NH 19.66). With astonishing speed (BAfr 22). He had achieved extraordinary popularity (Tac Ann 6.30).

is the referent of the subject noun phrase than of a scalar degree or an event that is associated with the meaning of the subject noun.

Relational adjectives

So far we have been paying attention mostly to underived adjectives, often core adjectives denoting properties like dimension, colour and evaluation. This section is devoted to adjectives derived from nouns via a derivational suffix like *-inus, -anus, -osus.* So long as the adjective is used in its original transparent meaning (like *urbanus* 'from the city' as opposed to *urbanus* 'sophisticated, witty'), the derivational suffix expresses a relation between the noun from which the adjective is derived and the noun that it modifies; consequently such adjectives are called relational adjectives. Relational suffixes include

-inus

(31) stercus *columbinum* (Cato 36.1)
columbino... ovo (Hor Sat 2.4.56)
leporini fimi (NH 28.204)
stercore *caprino* (Cato 151.2),

-anus

(32) *montana* pascua (Col 6.27.2)
fontana... numina (Ov Met 14.327),

-osus

(33) litus *harenosum* (Aen 4.257)
caespite *herboso* (NH 33.77)
robiginosam strigilim (Pl Stich 230),

and *-ulentus*

(34) *lutulenta...* sus (Hor Ep 2.2.75)
pulverulenta via (Ad Att 5.14.1)
fluore *sanguinolento* (Scrib Larg 121).

For instance in the second example of (31) a relationship is established between *ovum* 'egg' and *columba* 'pigeon'; the source of the egg is a pigeon. Most relational adjectives are not gradable. There is no scale of pigeon-derivedness: either the egg comes from a pigeon or it comes from some other bird

(35) ova *anserina* (Petr 65)
ova... *pavonina* (Varro RR 3.9.10).

(31) Pigeon dung (Cato 36.1). With pigeon egg (Hor Sat 2.4.56). Of hare dung (NH 28.204). With goat dung (Cato 151.2).

(32) Mountain pastures (Col 6.27.2). The goddesses of the springs (Ov Met 14.327).

(33) The sandy shore (Aen 4.257). Grassy turf (NH 33.77). A rusty strigil (Pl Stich 230).

(34) A muddy sow (Hor Ep 2.2.75). On a dusty road (Ad Att 5.14.1). By a bloody discharge (Scrib Larg 121).

(35) Goose eggs (Petr 65). Peacock eggs (Varro RR 3.9.10).

Unlike many gradable adjectives, relational adjectives likewise do not usually come in antonymous pairs (like *bonus* 'good,' *malus* 'bad')

(36) in agro *Nolano* (De Div 1.72)
in agro *Tusculano* (Livy 3.31.3)
in agro *Syracusano* (Livy 26.21.11).

There is no antonym to *Nolanus*: if the territory doesn't belong to Nola, it could belong to any other city in the discourse context. Adjectives in *-osus* are an exception to these rules. Since they contain a measure component in their meaning ('with a great deal of'), they are gradable

(37) nebulosior (Cato 6.4)
fructuosior (Col De Arb 20.2)
sucosior (Col 4.29.1)

and can have antonyms (*periculosus* 'dangerous,' *tutus* 'safe').

The precise nature of the relationship depends in part on the choice of suffix and in part on the nouns that are the arguments of the suffix and on the general context. For the suffix meaning compare

(38) crates *stercerarias* (Cato 10.3)
stercoroso loco (Col 11.3.43)
stercus... *asininum* (Varro RR 1.38.3)
molas *asinarias* (Cato 10.4)
asinum *molarium* (Cato 11.1).

Taking the examples in order, the baskets are for use with dung, the planting area is full of manure, the dung is derived from donkeys, the mill is for use with donkeys and the donkey is for use with a mill. The last pair show that the *-arius* relation can be symmetrical. In the examples cited above the adjective serves to fill in variables in the complex of default lexical knowledge we have about an object noun: we know that eggs and dung have a source (*columbinus*), that pastures have a location (*montanus*), that objects can have a substance covering their surface (*pulverulentus*), that utensils have a purpose (*stercorarius*) and are made from a material (*ferreus* 'iron'), and so on. These components of lexical knowledge are sometimes called 'qualia.' They are often not sufficient by themselves to fix the interpretation of the phrase but have to be integrated with contextual information. The identification of the adjectival suffixes with different components of the qualia structure is illustrated in Figure 7.5. Metaphorical uses are also quite common

(36) In the territory of Nola (De Div 1.72). In the territory of Tusculum (Livy 3.31.3). In the territory of Syracuse (Livy 26.21.11).

(37) More foggy (Cato 6.4). More fruitful (Col De Arb 20.2). Having bark that is richer in sap (Col 4.29.1).

(38) Baskets for dung (Cato 10.3). In a well-manured area (Col 11.3.43). Donkey dung (Varro RR 1.38.3). Donkey mills (Cato 10.4). A mill donkey (Cato 11.1).

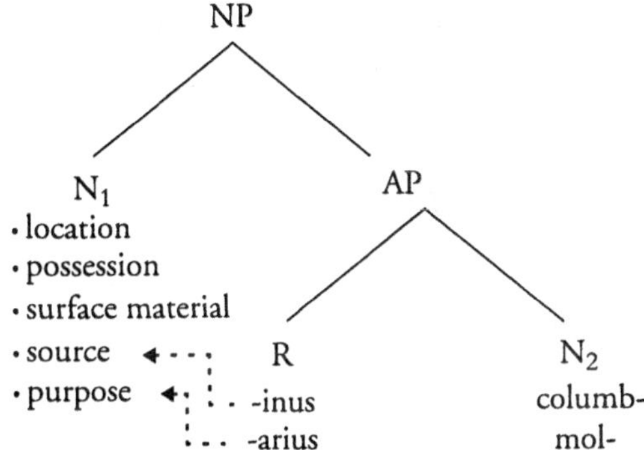

Figure 7.5
Relational adjectives and qualia
Ovum columbinum (cp. Hor Sat 2.456); *asinus molarius* (cp. Cato 11.1)

(39) *ferrea* vox (Verg Georg 2.44)
mens *ignea* (Sil It 3.136).

Conversely, a salient component of the qualia structure of the noun from which the relational adjective is derived (N_2) has to be chosen to correspond with the modified quale of N_1

(40) uncos *ferreos* (Cato 10.2)
sanguineis... bacis (Verg Ecl 10.27).

Ferreus is not used to convey that the hooks are grey-coloured nor *sanguineus* to convey that the berries are made out of blood.

Now let's consider the compositional structure. The derivational transparency of these adjectives calls for a decompositional analysis. It is simplest to start with a relational adjective used predicatively

(41) eaedem (pluviae) si *austrinae* fuere (NH 17.230)
si regio frigida et *pruinosa* est (Col 7.9.2).

The meaning of the suffix *-osus* in the second example (Col 7.9: *pruinosa*) is: $\lambda Q \lambda x$.-osus(x, Q) (type <<e,t>,< e,t>>), a function from a predicate Q 'frost' to a predicate 'frost-endowed.' Q (the complement of *-osus*, written to its right in Figure 7.6) is absorbed as a simple predicate without existential quantification (as arguably happens with incorporated or compounded nouns like 'frost-bite': no particular quantity of frost is introduced as a discourse referent), giving the expression λx.-osus(x, Pruin-), the set of things that are endowed with frost, which is then predicated of the area (*regio*). Similarly *columbinus* is λx.-inus(x, Columb-) 'the set of things that are pigeon-derived.' Abstracting over the different relational

(39) A voice of iron (Verg Georg 2.44). A heart of fire (Sil It 3.136).
(40) Iron hooks (Cato 10.2). With the blood-red berries (Verg Ecl 10.27).
(41) If the rains are brought by a south wind (NH 17.230). If the area is cold and frosty (Col 7.9.2).

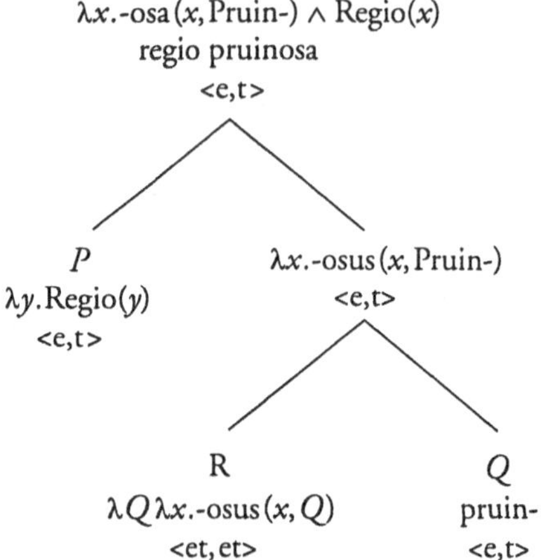

Figure 7.6
Attributive relational adjective
Regio pruinosa (cp. Col 11.3.22)

suffixes we get the general expression $\lambda R \lambda Q \lambda x. R(x, Q)$. When a relational adjective is derived from a proper name, like *Caesarianus* 'belonging to Caesar,' the type of the suffix is just <e,<e, t>>. The attributive use

(42) Regionibus... *pruinosis* (Col 11.3.22)

is a bit more complicated. Modification of nouns by intersective postmodifiers is most simply handled by a special compositional rule that directly mimics the intersective process: it is called predicate modification or intersective modification. As its name implies, it composes two predicates of type <e, t> into a single predicate of type <e, t> that denotes the conjunction of those two predicates (the intersection of their sets). In our example $\lambda x.$-osus (x, Pruin-) and $\lambda y.$Regio(y) compose by predicate modification into a single conjoined predicate $\lambda x.$-osus (x, Pruin-) $\wedge$ Regio(x) 'the set of things that are regions and are frost-endowed'; see Figure 7.6. This expression is then either predicated of an entity ('Thule is a frosty region') or referentialized ('this frosty region') or quantified ('every frosty region') in the usual way.

Turning from object nouns to event nouns, we find the picture complicated by the fact that events have participants, and relational adjectives can be used to express these participant roles as well as the sort of oblique roles we encountered with object nouns. Here are some examples of both

(43) *Apronianis...* rapinis (Verr 2.3.109: agent subject)
fraterna morte (Verg Georg 3.518: unaccusative subject)
frumentaria... largitio (De Off 2.72: direct object)

(42) In frosty areas (Col 11.3.22).
(43) In the plundering of Apronius (Verr 2.3.109). At the death of his brother (Verg Georg 3.518). The free distribution of corn (De Off 2.72).

(44) *militarem* largitionem (Tac Hist 2.82: indirect object)
novercalibus odiis (Tac Ann 1.6: psych subject)
metu *Parthico* (Ad Fam 2.17.1: psych object)
de Alexandrinorum pulsatione *Puteolana* (Pro Cael 23: locative)
adceleratio *clamosa* (Rhet Her 3.23: manner).

It is sometimes difficult to decide whether the modified noun is an object noun or an event noun, since object nouns can be associated with modifiable events (*celerisque sagittas* Aen 1.186 'swift arrows') and event nouns can be used to denote the product resulting from an event (*orationem... legit* Ad Att 3.15.3 'read the speech')

(45) *Fabriciani* veneni (Pro Clu 189)
hereditatem *Turianam* (Ad Fam 12.26.2).

Venenum is an event of attempted poisoning, *hereditas* is the property transmitted in an event of inheritance. In addition to modifying event nouns, thematic relational modifiers can sometimes be used to modify the event component in agent nouns

(46) *rhetoricae* praeceptionis (Rhet Her 4.69: event)
rhetoricis exercitationibus (ND 2.168: event)
rhetoricus artifex (Gell 17.5.9: agent)
rhetorici... doctores (De Or 1.86: agent).

This latter type of adjective combination is subsective. Agent nouns can also be modified by nonthematic relational adjectives

(47) *officiosum* salutatorem (Sen Con 2.7.3: manner)
studiosissimum Platonis auditorem (Tac Dial 32.5: manner)
fures *nocturnos* (Livy 3.58.2: time),

evaluative subsectives

(48) Isocrates doctor *singularis* (De Or 3.36)
doctoris *intellegentis* (Brut 204)

and nonsubsectively in regular individual-modifying combinations

(49) doctores *Graios* (Pers Sat 6.38)
ingens ianitor (Aen 6.400).

(44) Largesse towards the military (Tac Hist 2.82). A stepmother's malice (Tac Ann 1.6). Fear of the Parthians (Ad Fam 2.17.1). About the assault at Puteoli on the Alexandrians (Pro Cael 23). A loud and rapid delivery (Rhet Her 3.23).
(45) The poisoning of Fabricius (Pro Clu 189). Turius' legacy (Ad Fam 12.26.2).
(46) Of the teaching of rhetoric (Rhet Her 4.69). Rhetorical exercises (ND 2.168). Rhetorical expert (Gell 17.5.9). Teachers of rhetoric (De Or 1.86).
(47) An overly attentive greeter (Sen Con 2.7.3). A most studious listener of Plato (Tac Dial 32.5). Nighttime thieves (Livy 3.58.2).
(48) The outstanding teacher Isocrates (De Or 3.36). Of the discerning teacher (Brut 204).
(49) The Greek teachers (Pers 6.38). The huge doorkeeper (Aen 6.400).

These possibilities are depicted in terms of different sets of qualia for individuals and events in Figure 7.7. Thematic relational adjectives are particularly resistant to predicative use: *'The invasion was Carthaginian,' *'The critic was textual.' Apparently the predicative use requires a bona fide property, and arguments are more difficult than adjuncts to construe as properties of events. Thematic adjectives are unproblematic as postmodifiers

(50) navemque *frumentariam* (BC 3.96: entity)
inopiae *frumentariae* (BG 5.24: state)
istum praedonem *frumentarium* (Verr 2.3.76: agent).

Stacking

When a noun is modified by multiple attributive adjectives, they do not normally appear in random order but are stacked in an order that turns out to be pretty much the same from one language to another: for instance in pragmatically neutral contexts we say 'small round red Italian cushion,' not 'Italian red round small cushion.' If each adjective is treated as a separate prosodic phrase (socalled comma intonation), the order is more easily permuted ('red, round, small cushion'), as it is when adjectives are added as an amplification ('small red cushion, Italian,'). Adjectives from the same semantic class can be conjoined ('small, round, red and blue cushion'), but adjectives from different classes are often impossible to conjoin (*'red and Italian cushion'). Conjoined adjectives can be interpreted either by predicate intersection or by set union

(51) *frigido* loco et *sicco* (Col 12.47.1: intersection)
locis *siccis* et *umidis* (Col 5.9.15: union).

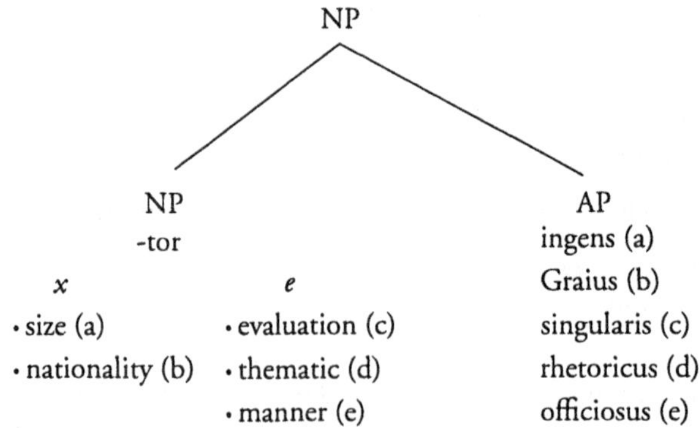

Figure 7.7
Individual (*x*) and event (*e*) modification with agent nouns

(50) A grain ship (BC 3.96). The shortage of grain (BG 5.24). This grain pirate here (Verr 2.3.76).
(51) In a cool and dry place (Col 12.47.1). In both dry and moist areas (Col 5.9.15).

Let's look at the evidence for stacking order in Latin and consider what it tells us about the semantics of attributive modification.

Relational adjectives of purpose, material and provenance are typically the closest to the modified noun, that is leftmost in the case of a postmodifier string and rightmost in the case of a premodifier string. This means that they are internal relative to adjectives belonging to classes such as

SHAPE

(52) mensa vinaria *rotunda* (Varro LL 5.121)
cavea ferrea *rotunda* (Amp 8.16),

AGE

(53) aquam caelestem *veterem* (Col 12.39.4)
aquae marinae *veteris* (Cato 24.1; 104.2)
figuras... ligneas ac fictiles *antiquas* (Varro LL 5.121),

WEIGHT and TEMPERATURE

(54) patera aurea *gravis* (De Div 1.54)
calida bubula urina (Col 6.11.1),

SIZE

(55) tumulus terrenus satis *grandis* (BG 1.43)
cella frigidaria *spatiosa* (Pliny Ep 2.17.11)
magnos regios commeatus (Livy 36.20.7),

EVALUATION

(56) culinam rusticam *bonam* (Varro RR 1.13.6)
hydrias argenteas *pretiosas* (Verr 2.2.47)
eculeos argenteos *nobiles* (Verr 2.4.42).

The relational adjectives in question tend to establish subkinds, and it makes sense to define a kind before giving its dimensions or evaluating its worth. Apart from anything else, adjectives of dimension and evaluation are scalar and so require a comparison class. But no comparison class is available until the kind has been defined: a tall dwarf myrtle is not as tall as a tall (regular) myrtle. There is also a difference in anaphoric potential. Compare 'He bought an electric car' with 'He bought a nice car': 'I bought one too' following the former means (on its default reading) that I bought an electric car, following the latter just that I bought a car, not necessarily a nice one. The evaluative adjective is less likely to

(52) A round wine table (Varro LL 5.121). A round iron cage (Amp 8.16).
(53) Old rain water (Col 12.39.4). Of old sea water (Cato 24.1). Old-fashioned wooden and pottery shapes (Varro LL 5.121).
(54) A heavy gold dish (De Div 1.54). With hot ox urine (Col 6.11.1).
(55) Quite a large earth mound (BG 1.43). The spacious cooling room (Pliny Ep 2.17.11). A large amount of supplies belonging to the king (Livy 36.20.7).
(56) A good farm kitchen (Varro RR 1.13.6). Precious silver water pots (Verr 2.2.47). His famous silver horses (Verr 2.4.42).

be part of the anaphora than the relational adjective, because it is not part of the descriptive content of the item purchased.

At the other end of the string (excluding quantifiers and demonstratives) are adjectives denoting temporary properties, which occur external not only to the categories of relational adjectives just noted

(57) ovum gallinaceum *crudum* (Cato 71.1)
cribrum farinarium *purum* (Cato 76.3)
orbiculos ligneos *pertusos* (Cato 22.2)
arida populnea vel abiegnea scobe (Col 12.44.4)

but also to other adjectives as well

(58) Testam de tegula crassam *puram* (Cato 110.1)
orcites nigras *aridas* (Varro RR 1.60)
mala cydonea grandia *expurgata* (Col 12.42.1).

This reflects the natural scope: dry black olives are a subkind of black olives, not the other way around. Sometimes a colour adjective is used as here to define a subkind (like red wine, green tea), sometimes it just characterizes a member of a kind like *canem nigrum* 'black dog' (Sen Apoc 13.3); similarly

(59) *albi* generis myrti (Col 12.38.5)
foliis *albis* (NH 27.88).

White leaves are just leaves, but white myrtle is a kind (*generis*). If there are two adjectives both from the above categories of relational adjectives, the more restrictive one is external

(60) Fiscinas olearias *Campanicas* (Cato 153.1)
statuam pedestrem *aeneam* (Phil 9.16).

Campanian olive baskets are considered a subkind of olive baskets rather than the other way around. The same applies when one or both the adjectives is non-relational

(61) vini nigri *austeri* (Cato 126.1)
vini atri *duri* (Cato 156.6)
lana sucida *nigra* (NH 24.180).

If there are two adjectives of temporary state, the order tends to replicate the temporal order of the causative events

(57) A raw chicken egg (Cato 71.1). A clean flour sieve (Cato 76.3). Perforated wooden disks (Cato 22.2). Dry poplar or fir sawdust (Col 12.44.4).

(58) A clean thick piece of tile (Cato 110.1). Dry black orcite olives (Varro RR 1.60). Well-cleaned large quinces (Col 12.42.1).

(59) Of myrtle of the white kind (Col 12.38.5). White leaves (NH 27.88).

(60) Campanian olive baskets (Cato 153.1). A bronze pedestrian statue (Phil 9.16).

(61) Of dry red wine (Cato 126.1). Of strong red wine (Cato 156.6). In black oily wool (NH 24.180).

(62) iris aridae *contusae* (Cato 107.1)
brassicam erraticam aridam *tritam* (Cato 157.15)
vasa inania *opturata* (NH 31.70).

The iris is crushed after it has dried, not before.

Adjectives of shape and colour are stacked outside the relational adjectives just analyzed and inside the scalar adjectives, which are themselves stacked in the order: size > length > width > weight (> means 'to the left of' in the prenominal order, 'to the right of' in the postnominal order). However in Latin these adjectives often conjoin with each other like predicate adjectives rather than stack

(63) acus *tenuis longa* (Varro RR 1.48.1: stacked)
in corpore *tenui longoque* (Cels 2.7.4: conjoined).

Depending on the adjectives involved, a semantic distinction may arise between stacked and conjoined adjectives, since stacking changes the comparison class when both adjectives are restrictive

(64) duas... *et magnas et nobiles* domos (De Dom 115).

Great noble homes (unlike great, noble, homes) are noble homes that are great relative to the standard size of noble homes, great and noble homes are homes that are great relative to the standard size of homes in general: they exceed the standard for homes in both size and nobility. Even when scalar adjectives conjoin, they tend to preserve the hierarchical stacking order, which suggests that they are not merged into a single large class

(65) *magnis et pretiosis* orbibus (Sen Ep 86.6)
amplae et glandulosae cervicis (Col 7.9.1)
pulchris et latis orbibus (Juv 1.137).

While the semantic basis for the stacking order of these adjectives is not always immediately obvious, the same general scopal principles already noted seem to apply to this segment of the hierarchy too. Shape and colour are less likely to be kind defining than the lower ranked relational adjectives; they apply more easily to individuals of a broad range of kinds. On the other hand, to compare the size of different shaped objects (like a triangle and a circle) requires computation; size is easier to evaluate relative to a comparison class of entities which have the same shape. When focus disturbs the neutral stacking order, this can likewise be understood as a scopal feature

(66) cavea *ferrea* rotunda (Amp 8.16.5: from (52))
rutabulo ligneo et *ferrea* curvata radula (Col 12.18.5).

(62) Of crushed dry iris (Cato 107.1). Ground dry wild cabbage (Cato 157.15). Sealed empty vessels (NH 31.70).

(63) A long thin needle (Varro RR 1.48.1). In a tall, thin body (Cels 2.7.4).

(64) Two great and noble homes (De Dom 115).

(65) With large and expensive mirrors (Sen Ep 86.6). A large and glandulous neck (Col 7.9.1). Beautiful wide tables (Juv 1.137).

(66) A round iron cage (Amp 8.16.5). With a wooden ladle and an iron curved scraper (Col 12.18.5).

In the first example (Amp 8.16) the material adjective is closer to the noun than the shape adjective, which is the default order. In the second example (Col 12.18) it is raised to a focus position external to the rest of the phrase, presumably because it contrasts with *ligneo*. The type of curved scraper to use is one made of metal: in the structured meaning focus format $\lambda P.\text{Radula}(x) \wedge P(x) \wedge \text{Curvata}(x)$, Ferrea.

The fact that multiple adjectives tend to be stacked in a fairly fixed order rather than in random order needs to be included in a compositional theory of adjective semantics. Consider examples like the following

(67) brassicam *erraticam aridam tritam* (Cato 157.15)
in vas *fictile novum picatum* (Col 12.42.3)
mala *cydonea grandia expurgata* (Col 12.42.1).

The adjectives are all intersective: that should mean that if we call the noun set A and the adjective sets B, C and D respectively, the semantics should be: A ∩ B ∩ C ∩ D. Since intersection is commutative, this is equivalent to e.g. D ∩ A ∩ C ∩ B. Logically that is so, but stacking shows us that from a compositional point of view it is wrong: adjective order is not permutable in stacking structures. The general scopal basis of the stacking order indicates that structure is built hierarchically: the adjectives are not serialized in some linguistically irrelevant order like alphabetical order. This is particularly clear with privative adjectives: a fake fake gun is a real gun disguised as a toy gun, with scope working like a negative operator ([¬ [¬ gun]]). First A is intersected with B, giving [A B]; then [A B] is intersected with C, giving [[A B] C]; finally [[A B] C] is intersected with D giving [[[A B] C] D]: [[[mala cydonea] grandia] expurgata]. Furthermore the process of intersection is pragmatically directional. As noted at the beginning of this chapter on *fabulos albos*, *Cydonea* restricts the set of apples to the kind that comes from Cydonea, namely quinces, (not the set of things that come from Cydonea to apples); in the same way *grandia* serves to restrict the set of quinces to those that are large in size (not the set of large things to quinces), and *expurgata* to restrict the set of large quinces to those that have been well cleaned (not the set of well-cleaned things to large quinces). All this is represented for postmodifiers in Figure 7.8. The tree can be seen as representing a sort of compacted recursive predication: the last adjective is predicated of the entire preceding structure. However the modifiers may need to have access to nominal qualia which they can hardly access in regular predication: as we have seen, a textual critic is someone who does textual criticism, not a critic who is textual. It is also possible for the tree structure to get disturbed when a relational adjective is narrowly modified by another adjective

(67) Ground dry wild cabbage (Cato 157.15). A new earthenware vessel treated with pitch (Col 12.42.3). Well-cleaned large quinces (Col 12.42.1).

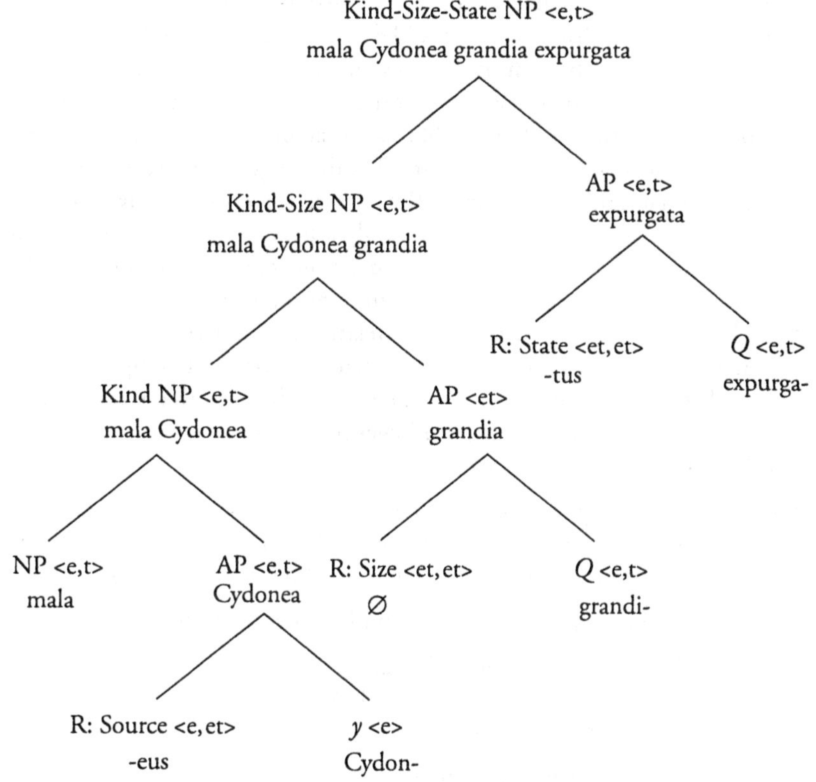

Figure 7.8
Multiple stacked postmodifiers
Mala Cydonea grandia expurgata (Col 12.42.1)

(68) scopas *virgeas ulmeas aridas* (Cato 152.1)
statuas marmoreas *muliebres stolatas* (Vitr 1.1.5).

The brushes were made of dry elm twigs (*virgae ulmeae aridae*) and the women (not the statues) wore a stola (*mulieres stolatae*).

A final point to note about Figure 7.8 is that simple, underived adjectives like *grandis* or *novus* in the third example (Col 12.42) are treated in the same way as relational adjectives, that is they are assigned a functional head *R*: they are taken to be morphologically different from but semantically similar to relational adjectives. The alternatives are to treat all adjectives as simple predicates *P*, or to treat relational adjectives as relations *R* and underived adjectives as simple predicates *P*. An argument in favour of the choice we made is that position in the stacking order by itself can express the class of the adjective, which is what *R*

(68) Brushes made of dry elm twigs (Cato 152.1). Marble statues of women wearing a stola (Vitr 1.1.5).

denotes. Since adjectives of evaluation are outside most other adjectives, we know that 'a cool cool drink' is a nice cold drink, not a cold nice drink; similarly with 'a hot hot sandwich,' 'a neat neat design,' 'a poor poor waif.' Since adjectives of temporary state are outside most other adjectives, we know that 'the visible visible stars' are the regularly visible stars that are currently visible, not vice versa. Since subsective adjectives are inside other adjectives, we know that 'a criminal^1 criminal^2 lawyer' is a criminal^1 who practices criminal^2 law and that 'a tall heavy drinker' is a tall but not necessarily a heavy person. When the same adjective is used in both positions, each position represents a different class. Class order is not permutable, and dropping one adjective can produce ambiguity (subject to context and prosody). Relational adjectives need a suffix to express adjectival category and to narrow down the class, while simple adjectives do not need an overt expression of *R*: speakers already know that red is a colour, large is a size and round is a shape. However overt expression of the class is needed for questions and relatives

(69) neque se *quo* quid *colore...* sit scire (Luc 76)
arvorum... *quis color...* sit (Verg Georg 2.177)
qui color albus erat nunc est contrarius albo (Ov Met 2.541),

and shows up in adverbials, modifier noun phrases and compounds

(70) ramuli nigro *colore* nitent (NH 22.63)
bacae puniceo *colore* in ea (NH 24.114)
atricolor (Ov Met 11.611).

So both *atricolor* and *ater* are taken to mean 'having black as its colour property,' and *grandis* is taken to mean 'having large as its size property,' analyzing colour and size as properties of properties (in other terminology, as determinable rather than determinate properties).

We have already noted a number of factors that favour premodifier position for adjectives in Latin (as well as some other languages): broadly speaking adjectives are more likely to precede the noun if they are (used as a) subsective (rather than intersective), descriptive (rather than restrictive), evaluative (rather than e.g. relational), modal (rather than extensional). Beyond that, the syntactic and semantic differences between prenominal and postnominal modifiers, if any, remain a difficult issue

(71) medulla *bubula liquefacta* tepensque infusa. (Scrib Larg 39)
calefacta bubula urina (Col 6.15.2).

(69) And they do not know what colour something is (Luc 76). Of soils... what its colour is (Verg Georg 2.177). The colour which was white is now the opposite of white (Ov Met 2.541).

(70) Their twigs shine with a black colour (NH 22.63). The scarlet berries on it (NH 24.114). Black-coloured (Ov Met 11.611).

(71) Beef marrow liquefied and poured in lukewarm (Scrib Larg 39). With heated ox urine (Col 6.15.2).

It is technically possible to generate one order from the other by recursive autonomous syntactic ("snowballing") movements with no consequences for the composition of meaning. But given the semantic distinctions just listed, it would be reasonable to assume that premodifiers and postmodifiers have different semantic types, and that the semantic type of postmodifiers was less suitable for non-intersective adjectives. For instance, postmodifiers might be more like reduced relative clauses and have the type of simple predicates <e, t>, while premodifiers might be operators having the type <<e, t><e, t>>: this would fit the examples in (71), and in turn would mean that, in one way or another, premodifiers and postmodifiers compose differently with the nouns they modify. For instance postmodifiers might compose by the rule of predicate modification (as in Figure 7.8), while premodifiers might use functional application (illustrated in Figure 7.9). Adjectives that can appear in either position are those that can be interpreted with either compositional strategy. Postnominal adjectives can become prenominal under narrow focus

(72) farre hordeaceo... vel *adoreo* farre (Col 8.5.17).

When this happens, the pragmatic status of the noun changes from local subject (topic) to tail. Ordinary prenominal adjectives are not narrowly focused and are presumably in a lower position than focused adjectives.

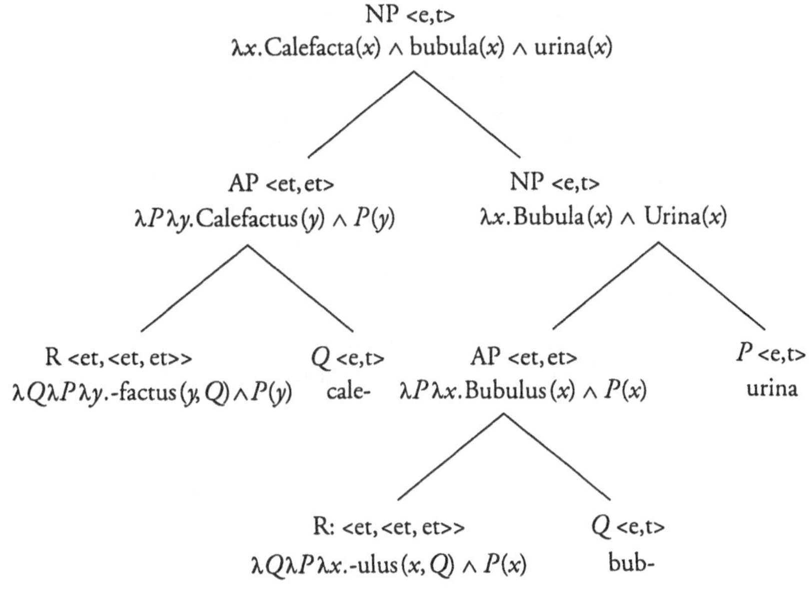

Figure 7.9
Multiple stacked premodifiers
Calefacta bubula urina (Col 6.15.2)

(72) With barley flour or with wheat flour (Col 8.5.17).

Gradability

Some adjectives do not have a comparative or a superlative because they are not gradable; they are not associated with a scale but express an all or nothing property, like *geminus* 'twin-born,' *quadratus* 'square,' *equester* 'equestrian,' *Nolanus* 'from Nola.' Either you are a twin or you are not; either you come from Nola or you don't. Other adjectives are associated with a scale, but each degree of the scale is lexicalized; this is what happens in compounds with cardinals, like *tricuspis* 'having three prongs,' *tripes* 'having three feet,' *quadrupes* 'having four feet.' But many adjectives are gradable: they have a comparative and a superlative, which can pick out different degrees on a scale associated with the adjective. We will start with the comparative. Here are a couple of concrete examples for a preliminary sketch of the analysis (to keep things simple, we will not distinguish between attributive and predicative uses at this stage)

(73) Xenophontis... cuius sermo est... melle *dulcior* (Orat 32)
omnes sapientes semper esse beatos, sed tamen fieri posse ut sit alius alio *beatior* (De Fin 5.95).

In the first example (Orat 32), the scale in question consists of an ordered set of degrees (abstract measurements) in the dimension of sweetness; a function assigns a maximum degree of sweetness to each entity in the domain of the adjective (things that evoke a sensation of sweetness or bitterness); more than one entity can be mapped to the same degree of sweetness, but each entity has a unique maximum degree on the scale. The degree of sweetness assigned to the style of Xenophon (the subject or item of comparison) is higher on the scale than the degree of sweetness assigned to honey (the standard of comparison). Figure 7.10 illustrates the second example (De Fin 5.95): five wise men are mapped onto different degrees in a scale of happiness in such a way that *sit alius alio beatior*. The positive is not entailed by the comparative ('the longer of the two short articles'), although it may be implicated, or computed from world knowledge as in the first example (*melle dulcior*), or separately asserted as in the second (*semper essse beatos*). In both examples the comparative causes the interpretation of the nouns to be shifted from entities to degrees: what seems to be a comparison of individuals is actually a comparison of degrees

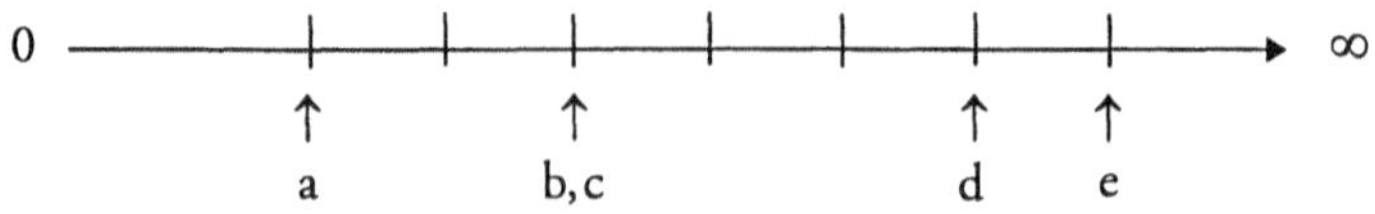

Figure 7.10
Mapping of individuals to degrees
Alius alio beatior (De Fin 5.95)

(73) Xenophon, whose style is sweeter than honey (Orat 32). That all wise men are always happy, but it is nevertheless possible for one to be happier than another (De Fin 5.95).

(74) altiores *quino semipede* (NH 17.80)
altiores *palmo* (NH 25.144)
altiores *platanis populisque altissimis* (NH 13.141).

In the first two examples (NH 17.80; 25.144) the standard of comparison is an overt degree, in the last example (NH 13.141) it is shifted from an entity to a degree ('exceeds the height of the tallest plane trees').

Some theories try to account for gradability without introducing degrees as a separate type of entity into the semantic ontology. One idea is that gradable adjectives denote a set of properties of different intensity. According to another theory (the delineation theory), the individuals in the domain of the adjective are intrinsically ordered on the dimension of the adjective and there are different ways of partitioning them into positive (true), negative (false) and undefined; *dulcior* then tells you that, relative to honey, Xenophon's style is sweet (and honey is not, although it is in other partitionings), so Xenophon's style is sweeter than honey. This allows gradable and nongradable adjectives to have the same type (<e, t>), and comparatives to express a relation between individuals rather than between degrees (whereas, one way or another, degree-based analyses have to build in a function that maps individuals onto degrees). But it is awkward when the different partitionings cooccur

(75) melle *dulci dulcior* (Pl Asin 614),

and it involves a less direct account of measure phrases

(76) latum *pedes* CCCXXX, altum *pedes* LXXX (BG 7.24)
Actus quadratus, qui et latus est *pedes* CXX et longus totidem (Varro RR 1.10.2)

and comparison with degrees

(77) tota cohors *pede* non est altior *uno* (Juv 13.173)
urtica... saepe altior *binis cubitis* (NH 21.92.1).

Also by in effect recalibrating the positive (it mimics the paratactic comparative construction found in some languages, for instance the nonconfigurational Hixkaryana), it tends to reduce explicit comparison to implicit comparison

(78) *prae nobis* beatus (Ad Fam 4.4.2) ⇒ nobis beatior
prae nostris rustica (Ov Am 2.4.19) ⇒ nostris rusticior.

(74) Deeper than two and a half feet (NH 17.80). Taller than a palm's width (NH 25.144). Taller than the tallest planes and poplars (NH 13.141).

(75) Sweeter than sweet honey (Pl Asin 614).

(76) 330 feet wide and 80 feet tall (BG 7.24). The square actus, which is 120 feet wide and equally long (Varro RR 1.10.2).

(77) The whole brigade is no taller than one foot (Juv 13.173). The nettle, often taller than three feet (NH 21.92.1).

(78) Happy as compared to us (Ad Fam 4.4.2). Unsophisticated compared to mine (Ov Am 2.4.19).

Exactly how degrees function in the compositional semantics of the comparative is a controversial and intricate issue. One approach is quantificational. While the basic type for gradable adjectives is taken to be <d,<e,t>> (functions from degrees to properties of individuals: $\lambda d \lambda x.A(x,d)$ means that x is A to degree d), quantificational theories work with sets of degrees, which can be created by lambda abstraction. Consider the levers (*vectes*) for the wine press that Cato describes (19.1): some are 18 feet long and some 15 (we are ignoring the 16-foot ones), so some are 18-foot-sized degrees on the scale of length, others 15. Since a scale is an ordered set of degrees, you could say that the comparative compares sets of degrees (the set of degrees from the bottom of the scale up to the maximum for each object measured): then the set of degrees of the shorter lever is a proper subset of the set of degrees of the longer lever, which is a generalized quantifier analysis. Correspondingly, to return to our example in (73) about Xenophon's style being sweeter than honey, the set of degrees of sweetness of honey (h) is a proper subset of the set of degrees of sweetness of Xenophon's style (x): $\lambda d'.S(h,d') \subset \lambda d.S(x,d)$, or MORE $(\lambda d'.S(h,d'))(\lambda d.S(x,d))$. MORE is the comparative morpheme *-ior* and has the type <<d,t>,<<d,t>,t>>, a relation between two sets of degrees: $\lambda P \lambda Q.P \subset Q$. In a variation on this analysis, MORE activates a silent maximality operator which takes a set of degrees as its argument and maps it onto that degree which is greater than all the other degrees in the set. Then the comparative means that the maximal degree in the set of sweetness degrees for Xenophon's style is greater than the maximal degree in the set of sweetness degrees for honey: $\text{MAX}(\lambda d.S(x,d)) > \text{MAX}(\lambda d'.S(h,d'))$. This is now a relation between points on the scale rather than between sets of points; the points are definite descriptions. A third possibility is to use the set maximum for the standard of comparison and existential quantification for the subject, thereby asserting the existence of some degree for the subject that exceeds the maximum for the standard of comparison: 'There is in Xenophon's style a degree of sweetness that exceeds the maximum degree of sweetness of honey,' $\exists d.d > \text{MAX}(\lambda d'.S(h,d')) \wedge S(x,d)$. Instead of using MAX for the standard of comparison, some analyses use negation (as suggested by the appearance of pleonastic negatives and negative polarity items in clausal comparisons in some languages). This gives 'The maximum degree to which Xenophon's style is sweet (MAX Q) is a member of the set of degrees to which honey is not sweet (P, where P exceeds the degree of sweetness attained by honey)' for the generalized quantifier version ($\lambda P \lambda Q.\text{MAX}\, Q \in P$), and 'There is a degree to which Xenophon's style is sweet and honey is not sweet to that degree' for the existential quantification version, equivalent to $\lambda P \lambda Q.P \cap Q \neq \varnothing$.

Despite their popularity, these set-based approaches to the analysis of the comparative are not entirely intuitive. The introduction of some or all of the nonmaximal degrees (see below on monotonicity) seems rather superfluous and can create problems. The subset and the existential versions do not express the presupposition that the degree measure function returns a unique value for each entity in its domain. Differentials ('This lever is three feet longer than that one') measure the interval between two maxima and are consequently difficult to handle in theories that use existential quantification, particularly when combined with negation. Set-based approaches can also produce unwanted readings for distributive adjectives when the standard of comparison is quantified or plural

(79) Issa est blandior *omnibus* puellis (Mart 1.109.3)
tanto formosis formosior *omnibus* illa est (Ov Her 18.73)
unus ramus *ceteris* aliquanto est laetior (Col 5.9.18).

The first example (Mart 1.109) can only mean that for every girl *x*, Issa the lapdog has a higher degree of cuteness than *x*. The universal quantifier has to be read with broad scope. A narrow scope reading (or its equivalent) is only available in a situation where all the girls in some domain of quantification have the same degree of cuteness: Issa has a higher degree of cuteness than the unique degree of cuteness that all the girls in the domain share. However if degrees of cuteness come in sets, then it should be possible to get a narrow scope reading (with the degree operator scoping over the quantifier) by intersecting these sets and finding the maximal degree of cuteness attained or exceeded by all the girls (which would be the maximal degree of cuteness of the least cute girl). But this reading is not available. This is the case not only for the clausemate ablative of comparison but also for the syntactically more complex distributive comparatives in a separate *quam* clause, like the first example in the following set

(80) villa... sumptuosior quam *omnes* omnium (Varro RR 3.2.5)
ut minus capiat quam *omnibus* heredibus relinquatur (De Leg 2.53)
Tamen hoc me magis sollicitat quam *omnia*. (Ad Att 11.25.3).

The first example is distributive (broad scope), the second collective-cumulative (narrow scope), the third is ambiguous. Using degree intervals rather than points does give you a sort of narrow scope reading: you construct the minimal interval that includes the maximal degree of the cutest girl and covers all the others too. Issa is no longer compared with each girl individually, but a comparison is made between an interval covering Issa and an interval covering all girls. This amounts to a collective maximum reading and is quite easy to get for *ceteris* in the last example in (79) (Col 5.9: one branch achieves better growth than the best growth attained by the others), but strongly distributive examples are less amenable to this interpretation

(81) Sed *omni* membrorum damno maior dementia (Juv 10.232)
consuetudo vitae, *omni* lege valentior (Sen De Ben 5.21.1).

(79) Issa is cuter than every girl (Mart 1.109.3). By so much is she more beautiful than all beauties (Ov Her 18.73). One branch grows a bit better than the others (Col 5.9.18).

(80) Villa... more luxurious than all those of everyone (Varro RR 3.2.5). To take less than is left to all the heirs (De Leg 2.53). But this worries me more than everything (Ad Att 11.25.3).

(81) But more serious than every type of physical damage is dementia (Juv 10.232). The conventions of human life, which are stronger than every law (Sen De Ben 5.21.1).

Another problem involves existential quantification and cardinals (on their usual exact reading) in the standard of comparison

(82) urtica... saepe altior *binis* cubitis (NH 21.92).

Since existential quantification covers nonmaximal degrees too, this sentence would be true if nettles were often as tall as California redwood trees. Degree intervals are no help: 'There is an interval of height (set of degrees of height), the maximum degree of which is two cubits, and the nettle often grows to that height.' This would be seriously underinformative if nettles were as tall as redwoods. We need a reading in which the maximum scopes over the existential quantifier: 'The maximum interval of height for which there is a degree such that the nettle grows to that degree is two cubits.' But this is just a long-winded way of saying that the value for the nettle on the height measure function is two cubits.

Nonquantificational approaches are simpler and more intuitive. Every entity in the domain of a gradable adjective has a unique maximal degree of the property in question; this degree is the value assigned to that entity by the degree measure function specified by the adjective. So lever A in the Cato wine press example is mapped to the length degree 15 feet and lever B to 18 feet. The way measure phrases are used shows that in principle gradable adjectives are (downward) monotonic, in the sense that if lever B is 18 feet long, it is also 14 feet long. Threshold contexts license such nonmaximal degrees ('The levers have to be 15 feet long: lever B is 15 feet long, in fact it's 18 feet long'). The modal 'have to' sets a minimum requirement which is satisfied by lever B. Equatives lend themselves quite well to threshold readings: lever A is not as long as lever B, but lever B is (at least) as long as lever A. But in most contexts we are only interested in the maximal degree that is the value of the measure function. Comparatives only work in terms of maximal degrees: despite what has just been said, lever A is not longer than lever B. It is not informative to say of lever A that its maximal degree of length exceeds a degree of length that lever B has; that would be true of any lever longer than say a sixteenth of an inch. Being the unique values of a measure function, degrees are definite descriptions, regular definites or pointwise (dependent) definites, although they may need to be relativized to times and worlds

(83) Nam benevolentior quam semper *fui* esse non possum (Ad Fam 13.60.1)
Neque enim hoc homine sanctior neque probior... esse quisquam *potest* (Pro Clu 133).

Of course you don't have to know what the degree actually is to refer to it with a definite description (just as you can talk about the vicar of Dibley without knowing who it is). On this approach the existence of a unique maximal degree is presupposed; contrast approaches discussed above that use existential quantification for the assertion of a nonspecific degree.

(82) The nettle, often taller than three feet (NH 21.92).
(83) For I cannot be more friendly to him than I have always been (Ad Fam 13.60.1). For noone could be more moral or more honest than this man (Pro Clu 133).

If we ask what colour an object is, we get a property as an answer (for instance 'red'); if we ask what width it is, we get a degree as an answer (for instance 'very wide' or 'three feet wide'). Asking whether a physical object has redness makes sense, asking whether it has a simple dimensional property like width is vacuous; the issue is what degree of width it has. Conversely it is felicitous to presuppose that an object has a degree of width but not that it is red, and you can deny that an object is red but not that it has a degree of width. Of course, once it is established (via assertion or accommodation) that the object in question is red, one can go on to talk about degrees of redness

(84) folio... *rubriore* (NH 20.231)
uva Aminea... est autem *ruberrima* (Scrib Larg 249: app. crit.).

Colour adjectives can be treated as either gradable or nongradable, unlike nationality adjectives, for instance, which can only be gradable with a nonliteral or coerced reading

(85) nihil *Latinius* legi. (Fronto Aur 2.3.1).

Different adjectives have different sets of entities in their domain: swords can be long but not tall, centurions can be tall but not long (in English). Both adjectives are gradable, so swords are ordered on the dimension of length and centurions on the dimension of height. We saw in Chapter 1 that there is a temporal trace function τ that maps events onto time lines, and a measure function μ that computes the duration of an event's time line in temporal degrees like hours. Similarly objects in the domain of a gradable adjective occupy a (possibly abstract) extent on the dimension of the adjective, and this extent is measured by the degree function δ. Adjectival degrees come in sorts depending on the meaning of the adjective: for any object x in the domain of the adjective P, $\delta^P(x)$ is a measure function on the position of x on the dimension of P. For the adjective 'wide' $\delta^P(x)$ is equivalent to $\mu(\text{width}(x))$, for 'hot' to $\mu(\text{thermal energy}(x))$. On the theory being presented here, there is a functional projection above the adjective (a Degree Phrase) whose head Deg° activates the degree function for the individuals being compared. Nongradable adjectives like *columbinus* 'pigeon-derived' do not need degree heads (or have empty ones), but, as already noted, gradable adjectives tend to be insufficiently informative unless they are arguments of a degree operator.

In the phrasal comparative the standard of comparison appears in the ablative, either preceding or following the adjective

(86) nobilior *Metello*, *Pompeio* fortior (Sen Con 10.1.8)
Quis *Q. Considio* constantior? (Pro Clu 107)
notior *Aufidio* (Juv 9.25).

(84) With a redder leaf (NH 20.231). The Aminean grape; it is very red (Scrib Larg 249).
(85) I have never read anything more Latin (Fronto Aur 2.3.1).
(86) Nobler than Metellus, braver than Pompey (Sen Con 10.1.8). Who is more consistent than Q. Considius? (Pro Clu 107). More notorious than Aufidius (Juv 9.25).

A simple logical form for the first example (Con 10.1) is given in Figure 7.11. The analysis is decompositional: the adjectival root P denotes the property of having a bravery dimension, something that is true of all humans and many animals. It has the type <e, t> (rather than <d, <e, t>> or <e, d>, as in other theories) and is true of both heroes and cowards but not of pluperfect subjunctives, for instance. The degree head is encoded by the comparative ending *-ior*. It does a lot of work: first it combines with P to establish the relevant dimension of measurement, then it activates the degree measure function and applies it to variables for the subject and for the standard of comparison, and finally it says that the value for the former ($\delta^P(x)$) is greater than the value for the latter ($\delta^P(y)$). So long as they are bound by lambdas, $\delta^P(y)$ and $\delta^P(x)$ are pointwise definites; when Pompey is substituted for y and *hic* for x, we get δ^P(Pompey) and δ^P(*hic*), which are regular definites. The degree measurement function (type <e, d>) is a preliminary function that generates degree values for the individual arguments of the degree head (x and y). If x or y or both are assigned to individuals who are not members of the set denoted by P (like the pluperfect subjunctive), the result is a presupposition failure: the measure function cannot find the individual in its domain. Treating the degree measurement function as a preliminary function allows one to have a single type for all adjectives (<e, t>) and allows the measure function to apply in a parallel fashion also to potentially gradable nouns of type <e, t>, as in *fur magnus* 'a big thief,' *magnus moechus* 'a big adulterer' cited in (28).

Degrees are organized into scales; P gives the dimension of the scale. Scales can be dense (like a line) or discrete (like steps). Degrees can be understood as points on the scale, and their granularity can vary with the context. Scalar intervals are sets of degrees. Some scales are associated with degrees that can be speci-

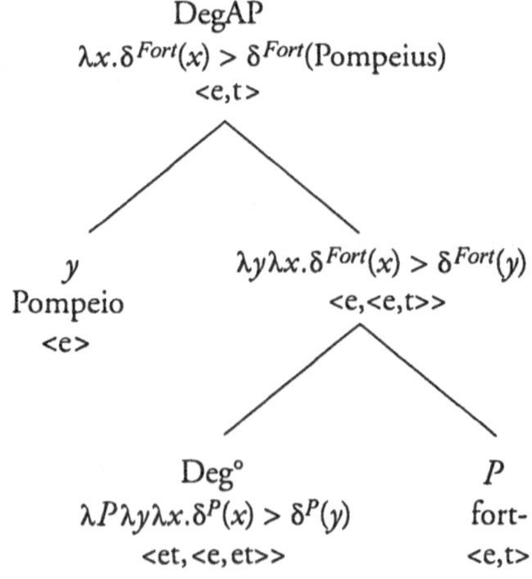

Figure 7.11
Phrasal comparative
Pompeio fortior (Sen Con 10.1.8)

fied by measure phrases as in (76), others are more abstract or not associated with scales in ordinary language

(87) *splendidior* vitro... aestiva *gratior* umbra... matura *dulcior* uva (Ov Met 13.790).

Pleasantness (*gratia*) doesn't have a dedicated scale, and sucrometric degrees (*dulcedo*) are a technical measure. Nonstandard or specialized scales can be derived from the measurement of physical objects ('two soccer pitches long')

(88) novellus palmes, non longior *tribus gemmis* (NH 17.181).

Sometimes contextual information (particularly the noun) is needed to determine the dimension of the scale; *longus* for instance is associated with a scale of spatial extent and a scale of temporal extent

(89) *sulcum*... longiorem (Col 2.2.27)
haec... *nox* est facta longior (Pl Amph 113).

These scales are incompatible: you can't say **Nox erat longior quam sulcus*; it would have the same problem as **ante noctem et vallum* or 'Nine inches is longer than twenty minutes.' If the adjective takes a complement, the *P*-node in Figure 7.11 will branch

(90) *laudis* et *honoris* cupidior (Verr 2.3.43)
avidior *poenae* (Livy 39.50.7).

The clausal comparative is introduced by *quam*, as in the following predicative examples

(91) cui patriae salus *dulcior quam* conspectus fuit (Pro Balb 11)
Philippus in acie *tutior quam* in theatro fuit (Curt Ruf 9.6.25)
Neptuni *levior quam* Iovis ira fuit (Ov Trist 3.11.62)
si ora Italiae *infestior* hoc anno *quam* Africae fuit (Livy 24.8.16).

The *quam* clause can be understood as a definite description taking the form of a free relative over degrees: Philip was safer in battle than what/how safe he was in the theatre. The second occurrence of the adjective is deleted and various other material can be ellipsed, *patriae* in the first example (Pro Balb 11), *ora* in the last (Livy 24.8). Attributive comparatives are not interchangeable with predicative comparatives for ellipsis in English (*'She's a taller girl than my brother

(87) Shinier than glass, more pleasing than the shade in summer, sweeter than ripe grapes (Ov Met 13.790).

(88) A young branch, not longer than three buds (NH 17.181).

(89) A longer furrow (Col 2.2.27). This night has been made longer (Pl Amph 113).

(90) More desirous of praise and honour (Verr 2.3.43). Keener for punishment (Livy 39.50.7).

(91) Who was willing to go into exile to save his country (Pro Balb 11). Philip was safer in battle than in the theatre (Curt Ruf 9.6.25). The anger of Neptune was milder than that of Jupiter (Ov Trist 3.11.62). If the shore of Italy has been more dangerous this year than the shore of Africa (Livy 24.8.16).

is'). Clausal comparatives (and more rarely phrasal comparatives, cp. Col 5.9.18 in (79)) can be modified by a differential measure phrase

(92) turres *denis pedibus* quam murus altiores sunt (Curt Ruf 5.1.26)
ut plaga *paulo* maior quam calculus sit (Cels 7.26.2H).

The measure phrase is a functional projection of the Degree Phrase. If the clausal comparative contains a modal verb, we can have a set of values for $\delta^P(x)$ (delta values), since different worlds can have different delta values. Comparison can then be with the maximum or the minimum delta value in this set

(93) Vitanda macrologia, id est *longior quam oportet* sermo (Quint 8.3.53)
Nec Popilius *securior quam debebat esse* inter tam mobilia ingenia erat (Livy 43.22.6)

si non *longius quam quo opus est* in narrando procedetur (De Inv 1.28)
neque id *crebrius quam opus esset* fundo (Varro RR 1.16.5).

In the first pair of examples comparison is with the maximum, in the second pair it is with the minimum. For instance, the first example (Quint 8.3) says that for all worlds w compatible with the goals of the writer, the delta value for length of the (macrologic) language in the actual world is greater than the delta value for length of the language in w: $\forall w.R^{Tel}(w^*,w) \rightarrow \delta^{Long}(w^*, \text{sermo}) > \delta^{Long}(w, \text{sermo})$. The third example (De Inv 1.28) says that (it is not the case that) the delta value for length of the narration in the actual world is greater than the lowest of the values in the worlds compatible with the goals of the orator: $\delta^{Long}(w^*, \text{narr}) > \delta^{Long}(w_0 \in R^{Tel}(w^*,w), \text{narr})$. $\forall w.R^{Tel}(w^*,w) \rightarrow \delta^{Long}(\text{ALT}w_0, \text{narr}) \geq \delta^{Long}(w_0, \text{narr})$. In this example, the minimum is also the optimum: the teleologically accessible worlds are ordered in such a way that the greater the distance between the minimum delta value and the value in w, the lower ranked w is. In other contexts the ordering source might give a different ranking; for instance if the narrative goals were prolixity and exhaustiveness, that would result in an inverse correlation between length of narration and ranking of the world, rather than vice versa. Quantificational theories do not work exclusively with delta values but have access to non-maximal degrees of length for any individual; so they can treat the difference between these examples as a scopal variation, $\forall w \text{MAX}\lambda dw^* > \text{MAX}\lambda dw$ versus $\text{MAX}\lambda dw^* > \text{MAX}\lambda d\forall w$. The broad scope universal quantifier over worlds gives the maximum delta value, the narrow scope universal quantifier gives the minimal degree shared by all members of the set, equal to the minimum delta value, the smallest delta value in any accessible world.

When the standard of comparison is a result clause

(92) The towers are ten feet higher than the wall (Curt Ruf 5.1.26). So that the wound is a little bigger than the stone (Cels 7.26.2H).

(93) Prolixity, that is a longer expression than is necessary, is also to be avoided (Quint 8.3.53). Nor was Popilius less cautious than he ought to be in a situation with such fickle characters (Livy 43.22.6). If the narrative does not proceed further than is necessary (De Inv 1.28). And that not more frequently than is necessary for the farm (Varro RR 1.16.5).

(94) motu terrae leniore *quam ut* alioqui sentiretur (Livy 35.21.6)
quaedam crassiores *quam ut* solem transmittant, aliae imbecilliores *quam ut* excludant (Sen NQ 1.3.1)
Ab his proconsuli venenum inter epulas datum est apertius *quam ut* fallerent (Tac Ann 13.1),

there is a modal component that complicates its interpretation. Quite often this is overtly encoded by a modal verb in the standard of comparison clause

(95) Alexander... urbem corona circumdedit, munitiorem *quam ut* primo impetu capi *posset.* (Curt Ruf 7.6.19)
Substringebat caput loro altius *quam ut* prioribus pedibus plane terram *posset* attingere (Nepos 18.5.5: app. crit.)
suspicionem praebuit regi nobiliorem esse *quam ut* inter convivales ludos *deberet* ostendi. (Curt Ruf 6.2.6).

The first example (Curt Ruf 7.6) says that all circumstantially accessible worlds w in which Alexander attacks the city and the city is captured on the initial assault are such that the delta value for strength of fortification of the city in the actual world is greater than the delta value for the same in w: $\forall w.R^{Circ}(w^*,w) \wedge \text{Opp}(w,\text{A},\text{urbs}) \wedge \text{Cap-PI}(w,\text{A},\text{urbs}) \rightarrow \delta^{Mun}(w^*, \text{urbs}) > \delta^{Mun}(w, \text{urbs})$. The strength of the fortifications by themselves preclude capture on the first assault in all accessible worlds (so excluding inaccessible worlds, such as those in which the walls collapse due to an earthquake or the defenders fight less bravely than normal). The last example (Curt Ruf 6.2) has deontic modality: in all deontically accessible worlds women with the degree of nobility of Hystaspes' wife are not put on show at dinner entertainments. This construction carries an implicature that the *ut*-clause is not true in the actual world

(96) Res est ineptior *quam ut* coarguenda sit; itaque transeo. (Sen Con 7.4.3).

Seneca says that Buteo's argument is too silly to merit refutation, and in fact he does not provide a refutation (*transeo*). Similarly in the last example in (94) (Ann 13.1) the poisoning did not in fact go undetected. However the implicature can be cancelled: Hystaspes' wife was in fact included in the dinner show.

In the comparative of superiority the degree relation is 'more than,' in the comparative of inferiority it is 'less than' and in the equative it is 'at least as much as' or 'equal to'; multiplicative equatives are based on the comparative with a differential

(94) By an earthquake too small to be felt elsewhere (Livy 35.21.6). Some too thick to transmit the rays of the sun, others too weak to shut them out (Sen NQ 1.3.1). The proconsul was poisoned by these men at dinner, too openly to escape notice (Tac Ann 13.1).

(95) Alexander surrounded the city, which was too well fortified to be taken on an initial assault (Curt Ruf 7.6.19). He would draw up its head with a thong too high for it to be able to fully touch the ground with its front feet (Nepos 18.5.5). She made the king suspect that she was too noble for it to be proper for her to be shown among the dinner entertainments (Curt Ruf 6.2.6).

(96) The point is too silly to merit refutation; so I pass on (Sen Con 7.4.3).

(97) ut sit alius alio *beatior* (De Fin 5.95): $\delta^P(x) > \delta^P(y)$
Si est aliquis *minus beatus* quam alius (Sen Ep 85.21): $\delta^P(x) < \delta^P(y)$
tam beati quam iste est non sumus (Verr 2.4.126): $\delta^P(x) \geq \delta^P(y)$
Ter tanto peior ipsa est quam illam tu esse vis. (Pl Pers 153): $\delta^P(w^*,x) \geq 3 \cdot \delta^P(w,x)$.

If you abstract over the degree relation, you get an expression that generalizes over the different types: $\lambda R \lambda P \lambda y \lambda x.\delta^P(x)\ R\ \delta^P(y)$. In the true equative $\delta^P(x) = \delta^P(y)$, in the threshold ('at least') equative $\delta^P(x) \in \{d\text{: } d \geq \delta^P(y)\}$. The threshold reading is blocked in contexts where a modal sets an upper bound

(98) *tam vehemens* fui *quam cogebar,* non quam volebam (Pro Mur 6)
Ipse *tantum* itinerum faciebat *quantum satis esse...* existimabat (BG 8.52)
sed his rebus *tantum* temporis tribuit, *quantum erat* properanti *necesse* (BC 3.78).

Sometimes the same degree difference that generates a comparative in one context can generate an equative in another, since the granularity of the scale depends on the context; it makes a difference whether you are weighing sacks of coal or checking a letter for postage due.

Many gradable adjectives come in complementary antonymous pairs of positive and negative adjectives

(99) Ergo ades et *longis* versibus adde *breves* (Ov Am 3.1.66)
Nam vigilare *leve* est, pervigilare *grave* est (Mart 9.68.10)
ut cuique *laeta* aut *tristia* nuntiabantur (Livy 22.7.12)
ita magis *tutum* neque umquam *periculosum* est (Cels 2.11.5).

(Unfortunately the term 'positive' is used both for the unmarked member of an antonymous adjective pair and for the unmarked degree of a gradable adjective.) The scales associated with these pairs of adjectives go in opposite directions

(100) binis pedibus *altiores* (Cato 19.1)
xx pedibus *brevior* (NH 16.201).

The Cato example means two feet more (than the standard of comparison) on the scale of height, the Pliny example means twenty feet less on the scale of length. *Altus* works on a scale that starts with zero and goes to infinity, *brevis* works on a scale that starts with infinity and goes to zero. The standard of comparison is located at some point along the scale and the differential measure

(97) For one to be happier than another (De Fin 5.95). If someone is less happy than another (Sen Ep 85.21). We are not as fortunate as he is (Verr 2.4.126). She's three times as bad by herself as you want her to be (Pl Pers 153).

(98) I was as tough as I had to be, not as I wanted (Pro Mur 6). He himself marched as much as he thought sufficient (BG 8.52). He dedicated as much time to these matters as was sufficient given the hurry he was in (BC 3.78).

(99) So come and add short verses to long ones (Ov Am 3.1.66). It doesn't matter if one is awake for a bit, but to be awake all night is a problem (Mart 9.68.10). Depending on whether each person got happy or sad news (Livy 22.7.12). It is correspondingly a safer procedure and never dangerous (Cels 2.11.5).

(100) Two feet higher (Cato 19.1). Twenty feet shorter (NH 16.201).

phrase measures up, or respectively down, from that point. In the following examples, differential ablative measure phrases express identical degrees of deviation from a standard of comparison

(101) quanto, nox, fuisti *longior* hac proxuma, tanto *brevior* dies ut fiat faciam (Pl Amph 548)
alia signa... quae quo *leviora graviorave* subsecuta sunt, eo vel *seriorem* mortem vel *maturiorem* denuntiant. (Cels 2.6.9).

In the first example (Amph 548) Jupiter shortens the day by the same amount on the scale of time as he has lengthened the night; this is illustrated in Figure 7.12. The second example (Cels 2.6) is more complex since it quantifies generically over situations: increasingly low degrees on the scale of symptomatic gravity are correlated with increasingly high degrees on the scale of time before death and vice versa. This bidirectional deviation from a standard that we have just seen in the comparative is also found with the antonymous adverbs *ante* and *post*

(102) duobus fere *post* mensibus (Livy 36.38.5)
tribus *ante* mensibus (NH 21.42).

Ordinary antonymous adjectives, if they accept measure phrases at all, do so in the positive member of the pair but not in the negative member

(103) *longi* pedes binos (Cato 41.4)
**breves* pedes binos.

Measure systems can measure up from zero to a specified degree, but measuring down from zero gives a negative degree, and since scales mostly have no upper limit, no fixed upper point is available for measuring down towards zero. Contrast the antonymous adjectives *plenus* and *vacuus*, which, although they are gradable

(104) *plenior* aliquanto animorum irarumque quam antea fuerat (Livy 6.18.3)
quodam liberiore quam solebat et *magis vacuo* ab interventoribus die (De Fat 2),

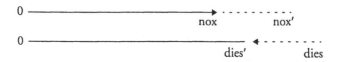

Figure 7.12
Same differential measure on opposing scales
Quanto nox longior, tanto brevior dies (Pl Amph 548)

(101) I will make the day be as much shorter as you, night, were longer than the previous one (Pl Amph 548). Other symptoms follow which, according as they are milder or more serious, bring the prognosis of a later or earlier death (Cels 2.6.9).
(102) About two months later (Livy 36.38.5). Three months before (NH 21.42).
(103) Two feet long (Cato 41.4).
(104) Somewhat fuller of courage and anger than he had been before (Livy 6.18.3). On a day that was more free than usual and more empty of interrupting visitors (De Fat 2).

are not used with measure phrases outside the comparative (*'seven ounces full') because they lexicalize the endpoints of their scale.

Instead of comparing the degrees on a single dimension attained by two different objects, one can compare the degrees attained by a single object on two different dimensions (interdimensional comparison). One way of expressing this is by the double comparative construction. In the simplest situations the two dimensions in question share the same scale (as shown by the measure phrases in the first of the following examples)

(105) At si *longior* fuerit quam *latior*, ut exempli causa iugeri forma pedes habeat longitudinis CCXL, latitudinis pedes CXX (Col 5.2.3)
sed *longior* quam *latior* acies erat (Livy 27.48.7)
ubi *latior* quam *altior* plaga est (Livy 38.21.10)
Africa... brevior est quidem quam Europe... *longior* tamen ipsa quam *latior* (Mela 1.20).

If we adopt a theory that takes both comparatives at their face value, then we get a comparison of comparisons. So the second example (Livy 27.48) means that the degree (on the shared scale) to which the battle line was long exceeded that to which it was wide rather than vice versa: $(\delta^P(x) > \delta^Q(x))$ rather than $(\delta^Q(x) > \delta^P(x))$. The first comparison is true in the actual world, the second is true in a set of epistemically accessible worlds not including the actual world: it might have been wider than it was long, but it wasn't. The positive is not entailed for either adjective: the line was not necessarily either long or wide in an absolute sense, although there is an implicature that it was not wide. An ellipsed standard of comparison is understood for each comparative, as it is for double comparatives in alternative questions

(106) Multique dubitavere *fortior an felicior* esset (Sall Jug 95.4)
utrum *fortior* esset *an felicior* (Sen Con 10.2.16)
perincertum *stolidior an vanior* (Sall ap. Gell 18.4.4),

and *quam* is interpreted as 'rather than': it compares the facts in two otherwise similar sets of possible worlds and orders the subject set higher than the standard set

(107) claris maioribus *quam* vetustis (Tac Ann 4.61).

In a few cases the comparatives are antonymous (they have opposite polarity)

(105) If it is longer than it is wide, so that for example the shape of the iugerum is 240 feet long and 120 feet wide (Col 5.2.3). But the battle line was longer than it was wide (Livy 27.48.7). Where the wound is wider than it is deep (Livy 38.21.10). Africa is narrower than Europe but it is itself longer than it is wide (Mela 1.20).

(106) And many are unsure whether he was braver or more fortunate (Sall Jug 95.4). Whether he was braver or more fortunate (Sen Con 10.2.16). It is quite unclear whether he was more dumb or more silly (Sall ap. Gell 18.4.4).

(107) Of distinguished rather than ancient ancestry (Tac Ann 4.61).

(108) ut *calidior* terra sit quam *frigidior*, *siccior* quam *umidior* (Col 3.12.4)
saluberrimum ver est... *periculosior* quam *salubrior* aestas, autumnus longe periculosissimus (Cels 2.1.1).

The adjectives in question share the same scale going in opposite directions (like 'sooner rather than later' in English). Simple comparatives cannot be crosspolar in this way ('Jack is taller than Bill is tall/*short'). The meaning seems to be that those degrees are preferable that come closer to degrees qualifying for the positive *P* than to degrees qualifying for the positive *Q*, rather than vice versa. So degrees that fall in the neutral interval between antonymous *P* and *Q* are included in the comparison, which is based on a cutoff point inside the neutral interval. In a third type the adjectives are not literally commensurable

(109) Quis est istorum... qui non *comptior* esse malit quam *honestior*? (Sen De Brev 12.3)
orator quoque *melior* quam *frequentior* habitus est (Asc Ped Pis 14)
qui alia bella *fortius* semper quam *felicius* gessissent (Livy 5.43.8)
acrius tamen quam *diutius* pugnatum est (Livy 22.47.3)
pestilentia coorta, *minacior* tamen quam *perniciosior* (Livy 4.52.3).

The context licenses a comparison between the two adjectives, which is carried out in terms of a nonspecific or abstract scale covering them both. As before, the set of worlds in which the degree for *P* exceeds that for *Q* (which includes the actual world) is ordered higher than the set of worlds in which the degree for *Q* exceeds that for *P*: $\{w: w \in p\} >^{g} \{w: w \in q\}$, where *p* is a proposition for the first comparison, *q* is a proposition for the second comparison, and *g* represents the ordering source (see Chapter 9). The latter varies: it is bouletic in the first example (Brev Vit 12.3: 'preferable') and doxastic in the second (Asc Pis 14). The last three examples have epistemic modality; they involve a sort of preventive counterassertion, since the second adjective is negated by implication. For instance in the last example (Livy 4.52) the writer fears that the mention of a plague will lead the reader to assume widespread destruction, and he uses the double comparative to pre-empt this imputed discourse development. He says in effect that the adjective 'threatening' is more appropriate to the facts of the case than the adjective 'destructive.' Because it seems to involve a choice between two terms, this type of comparison is often called metalinguistic or metacomparative, and fits in well with early theories of the comparative based on degrees of truth or applicability.

(108) So that the land should be warmer rather than colder, drier rather than wetter (Col 3.12.4). Spring is the healthiest, summer is more unhealthy than healthy, autumn is by far the most unhealthy (Cels 2.1.1).
(109) Who is there of these men who would not prefer his hairdo to be smarter than his character is honourable? (Sen De Brev 12.3). The quality of his oratorical performance was thought to have exceeded its frequency (Asc Ped Pis 14). Who had always fought other wars with greater bravery than success (Livy 5.43.8). The severity of the battle was greater than its duration (Livy 22.47.3). A plague arose, more threatening, however, than dangerous (Livy 4.52.3).

The superlative

While the comparative says that the subject of comparison has a higher degree of the gradable adjective property than the alternate specified by the standard of comparison, the true superlative (corresponding to English *-est*) says that it has a higher degree than all the contextually relevant alternates

(110) mons Scordus, longe *altissimus* regionis eius (Livy 44.31.5)
Hierosolyma, longe *clarissima* urbium orientis (NH 5.70).

Just as for instance there are two ways of expressing the meaning 'two thousand' (*duo milia* and *bis mille*), so languages use different strategies for expressing the (true) superlative; we will illustrate them with more or less close Latin analogues. One strategy simply picks the maximal degree out of the range of degrees in the degree function: $\iota x.\delta^P(x) = \text{MAX}\,\{\delta^P(y)\text{: } y \in \text{C}\}$, where C is the domain of the degree function, which depends partly on the noun (so *mons* in the first example (Livy 44.31), *urbs* in the second (NH 5.70)) and partly on the context and/or a partitive genitive (*regionis eius* in the first example, *orientis* in the second). y represents any member of the set that is the domain of the degree function including x; superlatives are always interpreted relative to such a set, since MAX cannot be calculated without one

(111) *omnium mortalium* turpissimus (Phil 10.22)
iris... Africana, amplissima *inter omnes* gustuqe amarissima (NH 21.41)
L. Crassus, homo sapientissimus *nostrae civitatis* (In Pis 62).

Another strategy is to spell out the definition of the superlative using the comparative and universal quantification over the domain of the degree function excluding x: $\iota x \forall y.x \in \text{C} \wedge y \in \text{C} \wedge y \neq x \rightarrow \delta^P(x) > \delta^P(y)$

(112) *omnibus aliis* maior (Sen NQ 3.28.6)
plura... quam *ceteri omnes* (NH 35.79).

A third strategy, the ordinal strategy, exploits the fact that the degree function on the dimension of the adjective induces a ranking, with the top ranked degree being the maximal degree in the range, that is the degree that exceeds all other degrees in the range

(113) eques Romanus *cum primis* honestus (Brut 205)
eques Romanus *imprimis* splendidus (Verr 2.2.69)
artifices ceteri... *apprime* boni (Nepos 25.13.3).

Like 'first' in English, *primus* has a superlative suffix.

(110) Mount Scordus, by far the highest of that region (Livy 44.31.5). Jerusalem, by far the most famous of the cities of the east (NH 5.70).
(111) The most disgraceful of all men (Phil 10.22). Iris... the African one, the largest of all and the most bitter in taste (NH 21.41). L. Crassus, the wisest man of our state (In Pis 62).
(112) Higher than all others (Sen NQ 3.28.6). More than all the others (NH 35.79).
(113) One of the most honourable Roman knights (Brut 205). One of the most illustrious Roman knights (Verr 2.2.69). The other workmen were first-rate (Nepos 25.13.3).

The true superlative is not limited to the singular: it can also denote a plurality. In fact the cardinality of the superlative set can be implicit in a conjunction or explicitly stated

(114) Sunt alii multi diserti... Eorum quos viderim Domitius Afer et Iulius Africanus longe praestantissimi (Quint 10.1.118)
Hae *omnium arborum* altissimae ac rectissimae. (NH 16.195)
Thracas Gallosque, *ferocissimas* gentium (Livy 42.52.11)
omnium *ferocissimi* ad hoc tempus Achaei atque Tauri sunt (Sall Hist 3.74)
duos omnium mortalium impudicitia ignavia luxuria *deterrimos*... electos (Tac Hist 1.50).

The first example (Quint 10.1) has a conjunction of individuals, the second (NH 16.195) a conjunction of kinds, the third (NH 16.195) the plural of a collective noun, the fourth (Hist 3.74) a conjunction of groups. The last example (Hist 1.50) has an explicit cardinal: it can be understood in three ways. It could be that, given a sensible level of granularity, Otho and Vitellius have the same degree of the vices in question and share the first prize (they form an equivalence class). In that case Otho and Vitellius are the worst persons but neither by himself is the worst person; the next worst person has the second worst degree of vice but is the third most vicious person. Or it could be that Otho was the worst and Vitellius the second worst (the worst excluding Otho), or vice versa. In that case there is a unique worst person, and the next worst person after Otho and Vitellius has the third worst degree of vice and is the third worst person. Finally, in a different context, each villain might be evaluated in his own degree domain, so that for instance Vitellius was the worst person north of the Alps and Otho the worst person south of the Alps. Note that the plural superlative cannot be read distributively, because the result would be a contradiction: it cannot be true that Otho is the worst person alive and Vitellius is the worst person alive, since that would make them worse than each other. More generally, what the superlative does is to partition the set of individuals in the domain of the degree function (C) into two sets, X and its complement in such a way that the members of X are at the top of the range: $\exists X \subset C \forall x \in X \forall y \in X^{-} \rightarrow \delta^{P}(x) > \delta^{P}(y)$. This formula can be used in place of one of those above for singular superlatives too, if we allow X to be singleton set. Whether X is a singleton (emphasized by *unus* in the following)

(115) qui est *unus suavissimus* pastus animorum (Tusc 5.66)
qui illi *unus inimicissimus* esse debuerat (De Har Resp 45),

(114) There are many other eloquent speakers. Of those whom I have seen Domitius Afer and Julius Africanus are far the most outstanding (Quint 10.1.118). These are the tallest and straightest of all trees (NH 16.195). Thracians and Gauls, the fiercest of all peoples (Livy 42.52.11). The fiercest of them all are still the Achaei and the Tauri (Sall Hist 3.74). The two worst men in the world for immorality, idleness and luxury had been chosen (Tac Hist 1.50).

(115) Which is absolutely the sweetest food for the mind (Tusc 5.66). Who ought to have been absolutely his worst enemy (De Har Resp 45).

or a plurality (and if the latter what its cardinality is), depends on a contextually derived cut-off point *k* on the degree scale: domain members with a degree at or above *k* belong to the superlative set *X*, those with a degree below *k* belong to the complement set. It follows that one and the same person may qualify for inclusion in the superlative set in one context but not in another. *X* cannot exhaust the domain of the degree function and is usually infelicitous if it is the majority; the proximity of degrees in the range may also affect the location of *k*.

Let us turn our attention back to singular superlatives and consider further the first example in (110) (Livy 44.31). If the variables *x* and *y* are (different) mountains in (that region of) Illyria (not anywhere in the world), then Mt. Scordus is that mountain *x* such that, for all *y*, the degree of height of *x* exceeds the degree of height of *y*: $\iota x \forall y . x \in \text{Mons-Illyr} \wedge y \in \text{Mons-Illyr} \wedge y \neq x \rightarrow \delta^P(x) > \delta^P(y)$. Note that the universal quantifier has to have wide scope: one checks the height of each mountain in the region against the height of Mt. Scordus; the superlative doesn't require all the other mountains in question to have the same height. In the absence of an explicit restriction like *regionis eius*, a restriction needs to be derived from the context, otherwise the superlative phrase will refer to Mt. Everest. There is no purely intersective reading in which, for instance, the tallest boy is the tallest entity in the domain (including adults and towers); as already noted, the true superlative is always understood relative to a comparison class (the set of alternates in the domain of the degree function). Conversely we have seen that purely intersective adjectives do not have (literally used) superlatives. The superlative ending (*-issimus*) picks out the maximal degree in the range of the degree measure function, the adjective root (*alt-*) specifies the dimension of the measure function, and the noun (along with some contextual restriction) specifies the domain of the measure function. The intensifier (elative) superlative (*altissimus* 'very high') differs from the true superlative (*altissimus* 'highest') in a number of important ways. First the true superlative definitionally involves the maximal degree, the intensifier does not

(116) *miserior* sum quam tu, quae es *miserrima* (Ad Fam 14.3.1)
Curius... et Fabricius et Coruncanius, *antiquissimi* viri, et his *antiquiores* Horatii illi (Gell 1.10.1).

These examples yield a contradiction when the superlatives are read as true superlatives rather than as intensifiers. Second, the true superlative does not entail the positive, whereas the intensifier does. A very high mountain is also a high mountain, but the highest mountain in some area could just be the least low of a set of low mountains. Third, while (as just noted) the true superlative cannot exhaust the domain of the degree function, the intensifier superlative can: consequently the true superlative is always restrictive ({the tallest students}

(116) You are very miserable, but I am even more miserable than you (Ad Fam 14.3.1). Curius, Fabricius and Coruncanius, men of a very long time ago, and the famous Horatii from an even earlier period (Gell 1.10.1).

$\subset$ {the students}), but the intensifier can be restrictive or descriptive ({the very tall students} $\subseteq$ {the students}).

The examples in (110) illustrate the socalled absolute reading of the superlative. There is also another reading, which is called the relative reading or the comparative reading; we will use the former term, since it is awkward to talk about comparative superlatives. In the relative superlative, the variable is restricted not merely by the noun (*mons*) but also by further material from the rest of the sentence (in addition to contextual material). The relative reading emerges clearly in subject focus sentences with a superlative in the object phrase. Say that three Illyrians (Gentius, Teuticus and Bellus) climbed three different mountains, and Gentius climbed the highest one. (Each climber could have climbed more than one mountain and the highest mountain could have been climbed by more than one climber, but to keep things simple we will consider the scenario in which each climber climbed a single mountain and Gentius climbed the highest one.) This does not necessarily mean that Gentius climbed the highest mountain in the absolute sense, namely Mt. Scordus, just that he climbed a higher mountain than the others. For all mountains *y* climbed by an alternate to Gentius, the height of the mountain climbed by Gentius was greater than the height of *y*. The domain of the measure function is not 'mountains in Illyria' but 'mountains in Illyria climbed by one of the relevant climbers.' Gentius is semantically focused and associates with the superlative in the object phrase. Here are some actual examples to illustrate how the superlative can associate with focus

(117) Brassica *erratica* maximam vim habet (Cato 157.12)
maximam vim *natura* habet, fortuna proximam (De Off 1.120)
is pede saucio relictus longe plurimos hostium occidit (Livy 41.4.6)
longe plurimos captivos *ex Etruscis* ante currum duxit (Livy 6.4.2).

In the first example (Cato 157.12) focus is on the modifier of the subject: the type that has greater strength than all other types of cabbage is the wild one. In the second example (De Off 1.120) focus is on the subject again: the factor that has greater importance for the choice of a career than all other factors is nature. The third example (Livy 41.4) also has subject focus, while in the last example (Livy 6.4) focus is on the prepositional phrase *ex Etruscis*: the number of captives from the Etruscans was far greater than the number from the other conquered peoples.

Although it is possible to come up with an analysis that interprets the relative superlative in situ, it is more likely that for its interpretation the superlative moves to the left to scope over the expression that supplies the domain of the degree measure function (the restriction or presupposition). In fact, even absolute superlatives can be shown to move within their phrase in English to scope

(117) Wild cabbage has the greatest strength (Cato 157.12). Nature exerts the most powerful influence, fortune comes next (De Off 1.120). Although he had been left behind because he was wounded in the foot, he killed by far the largest number of the enemy (Livy 41.4.6). By far the largest number of captives led before his chariot were from the Etruscans (Livy 6.4.2).

over higher stacked adjectives: 'small round white stone,' '*small round whitest stone,' 'whitest small round stone.' Intensifier superlatives can move but don't have to: 'small round very white stone,' 'very white small round stone.' Sometimes movement seems to be discernible from the surface syntax of the relative superlative in Latin

(118) quae civitas in Gallia *maximam* habet opinionem virtutis (BG 7.59)
longe *maximam* ea res attulit dimicationem (BC 3.111)
qui *laudatissimum* dedit citrum (NH 13.95).

Exactly what moves in the logical form is unclear: it could be just the superlative operator (*-imam*), or the whole adjective (*maximam*). Moving just the superlative suffix requires some additional device to make sure it attaches to the correct adjective in stacked examples. Moving the whole adjective preserves lexical integrity (apart from inversion of the root and the suffix) and is a type of hyperbaton. Relative superlatives in hyperbaton are probably null head definite noun phrases; the noun becomes a nonreferential part of the presupposition. When superlatives appear in hyperbaton in Hungarian, they can only have the relative reading and they appear with the definite article and their own case ending.

The positive

Let's start by reviewing some facts that were established in our discussion of comparatives and measure phrases in the preceding sections. First, the comparative does not entail the positive: this applies to both members of an antonymous pair of adjectives

(119) stipites arboresque binis pedibus *altiores* facito (Cato 19.1)
trabs... xx pedibus *brevior* (NH 16.201).

In the first example (Cato 19.1), the posts are not tall for a wine-press, since they are the prescribed height (so presumably average). In the second example (NH 16.201) the log was not short at all, since the paragraph is about exceptionally tall trees. The effect is stronger with dimensional adjectives than with other gradable adjectives like 'hot' or 'sweet'; this applies to the other points noted in this paragraph too, so we will confine our examples to dimensional adjectives. Second, when the positive is used with a measure phrase, the scale is set to start at zero

(120) Eos surculos facito sint *longi* pedes binos (Cato 41.4)
**breves* pedes binos.

(118) The state that has the greatest reputation for courage in Gaul (BG 7.59). This event brought by far the biggest fight (BC 3.111). Which once produced the most famous citrus-wood (NH 13.95).

(119) Make the guideposts and the anchorposts two feet higher (Cato 19.1). A log twenty feet shorter (NH 16.201).

(120) Make these shoots be two feet long (Cato 41.4).

The degree interval on the scale of length goes from zero to two feet; it is not entailed that the shoots are particularly long qua shoots, nor is it excluded. The negative member of the antonymous pair cannot be used with a measure phrase: see (103). Entailment is likewise absent in degree questions, but only for the positive member of an antonymous pair

(121) incertum est *quam longa* cuiusque nostrum vita futura sit (Verr 2.1.153)
Hi si volent scire *quam brevis* ipsorum vita sit (Sen De Brev 19.3)
si illos *breviores... quam longi* sint ignores (Varro LL 10.29).

The first example (Verr 2.1) implicates that in fact some people will not have long lives, the second (De Brev 19.3) entails that the lives of the people in question count as short. In the last example (LL 10.29) we don't know if any of the brothers was tall (or short). The same effect appears in nominalizations

(122) Tricliniorum quanta *latitudo* fuerit, bis tanta *longitudo/*brevitas* fieri debebit (Vitr 6.3.8).

But now consider the following example about the suitability of the fourth paeon in the clausula

(123) paeana qui dixit aptiorem in quo esset *longa* postrema vidit parum, quoniam nihil ad rem est postrema *quam longa* sit (Orat 218).

The first occurrence of *longa* is a simple positive: it serves to pick out that type of paeon that has a long final syllable; the second occurrence is in an indirect degree question and does not entail the positive (it is the phonetic equivalent of the phonological *brevis an longa sit* ibid. 217). Evidently the simple positive does not mean 'having a degree of length,' which would be a vacuous assertion for a physical object, except in geometry talk

(124) Planum est quod in duas partes solum lineas habet, qua latum est et qua *longum* (Gell 1.20.2).

Normally the positive means not 'having a degree of length' but 'having a significant degree of length'; so the issue is how to define this significant degree and where it comes from in the semantics, since, unlike the comparative and the superlative, the positive is not overtly marked by the morphology.

A pair of nongradable antonymous adjectives like *equester* 'cavalry-' and *pedester* 'infantry-' is complementary: either a land battle is fought on foot, or it is fought on horseback; it can be partly one and partly the other, but it cannot

(121) It is uncertain how long the life of each one of us will be (Verr 2.1.153). If they wish to know how short their life is (Sen De Brev 19.3). If you don't know how long those shorter ones are (Varro LL 10.29)

(122) The length of dining rooms has to be twice their width (Vitr 6.3.8).

(123) The person who said that the paeon in which the final syllable was long was more suitable missed the point, since it makes no difference how long the final syllable is (Orat 218).

(124) The plane is the one which has its lines in two dimensions only, where it is wide and where it is long (Gell 1.20.2).

be neither. But many pairs of gradable antonymous adjectives are not complementary; rather the scale is divided into three parts, a part for which the positive adjective is true, a part for which the negative adjective is true, and a part for which neither the positive nor the negative is true

(125) flumina *lata* (Verg Georg 3.213)
flumen intercedebat *angustum* (BAlex 29)
clavo *nec lato nec angusto* (Suet 2.73.1).

As illustrated in Figure 7.13, Augustus' purple stripe in the third example (Suet 2.73) had a degree of width that lay in the neutral gap on the scale between the top of the narrow interval and the bottom of the wide interval. This distinction between the bipartite structure of *equester/pedester* and the tripartite structure of *latus/angustus* has consequences for entailments under negation. 'It wasn't a cavalry (land) battle' entails that it was an infantry battle, but 'It wasn't broad' entails that it was either narrow or neither broad nor narrow and 'It wasn't narrow' entails that it was either broad or neither broad nor narrow. (We are talking about wide scope negation here; narrow scope negation ['un-broad'] gives just the antonym.) This applies equally well to many gradable adjectives that do not express a measurable physical dimension

(126) prudentiam... quae constat ex scientia rerum *bonarum* et *malarum* et *nec bonarum nec malarum* (ND 3.38).

Antonymous pairs of adjectives on this approach are contraries rather than contradictories. They do not exhaust the semantic space occupied by the scale but fill each end of it, leaving a neutral interval in between. If the boundary between the antonyms is taken to be a degree rather than an interval, then the neutral area has to be treated as an area of vagueness in which speakers have difficulty classifying borderline cases. Conjoined negatives suggest that antonyms are contraries, alternative conditionals that they are contradictories

(127) *neque* amicum recipio *neque* inimicum respicio (Gell 7.11.3)
sive amicus... *sive* inimicus (BAlex 36).

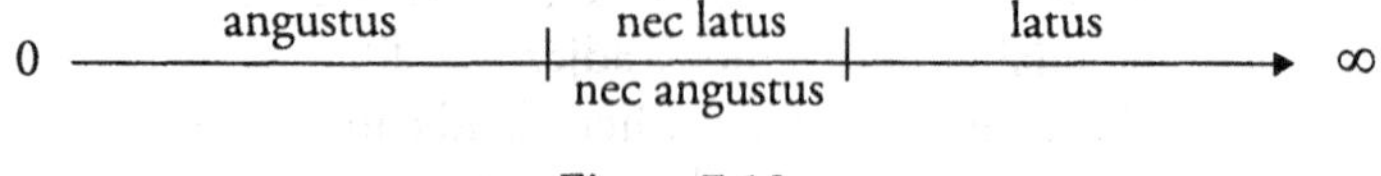

Figure 7.13
Tripartite scale for gradable adjectives
Clavo nec lato nec angusto (Suet 2.73.1)

(125) Wide rivers (Verg Georg 3.213). A narrow river stood between (BAlex 29). His purple stripe neither broad nor narrow (Suet 2.73.1).

(126) Wisdom, which consists in the knowledge of things that are good and things that are bad and things that are neither good nor bad (ND 3.38).

(127) I do not count him a friend and I discount him as an enemy (Gell 7.11.3). If as a friend... or if as an enemy (BAlex 36).

It may be that the neutral area is logically present in alternative conditionals but pragmatically discounted. The neutral interval on the scale for the examples in (125) is the range surrounding the average for width; we will call this interval the standard (S). If a river x is broad, there exists a degree higher than the standard interval and equal to the width-degree of the river: $\delta^P(x) > S$ (or $\exists d.d > S \wedge \delta^P(x) = d$). If a river y is narrow, $\delta^P(y) > S$ on the same scale running in the opposite direction. While the comparative tells us that the width degree of x is higher than the width degree of y, the positive tells us that it is higher than the standard. It follows that not only the comparative but the positive too has a degree operator (>) and a standard of comparison (S) in its semantics, as illustrated by the logical form in Figure 7.14. So while we usually simply translate scalar adjectives as $\lambda x.P(x)$, they are actually $\lambda x.\delta^P(x) > S$.

The positive is said to be norm-related or evaluative. Evaluativity also appears with antonyms in degree questions as in (121) and equatives ('as short as'), where $\delta^P(x) > S$ is added as a presupposition or an accommodation rather than being an assertion. As we have seen, this is not necessarily the case for equatives with nonantonyms ('as long as') nor for comparatives of any sort, but it is possible that $\delta^P(x) > S$ could be added to them too in the appropriate contexts. The effect of this modification is to cut off the bottom of the scale (the top of the scale for antonyms). In the same way *quam longa* in a degree question may in principle be ambiguous between nonevaluative 'What is the length of?' and evaluative 'To what degree does it exceed the standard of length?'.

Just which degree interval on the scale is covered by the standard does not depend on the gradable adjective so much as on the noun it modifies and on the wider context. It is certainly true that nongradable adjectives too, like most

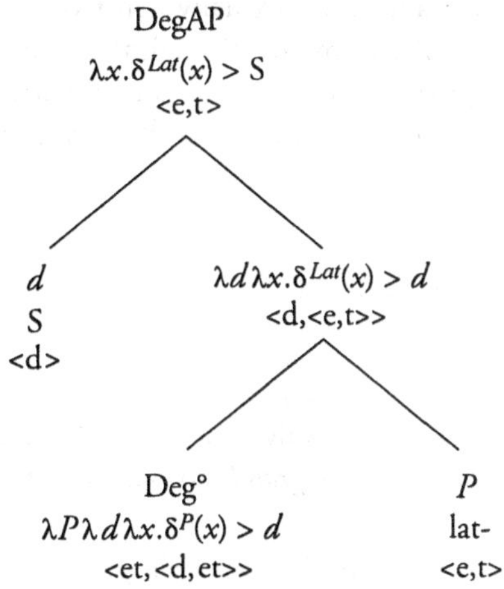

Figure 7.14
Positive degree
(*Flumen*) *latum* (cp. Verg Georg 3.213)

other linguistic expressions, are sensitive to context. For instance nongradable readings of colour adjectives still denote different shades depending on the noun they modify

(128) albam esse *nivem* (Luc 100)
album acre *acetum* (Col 12.57.1)
quattuor *ovorum* albus *liquor* (Col 6.38.2)
plumbum album (BG 5.12).

But context sensitivity is far more salient and pervasive with gradable adjectives

(129) grandi *acino* (Col De Arb 3.1)
grandibus *saxis* (BG 7.46)
grandis *ilex* (Sall Jug 93.4).

Obviously a big grape is not the same size as a big stone, let alone a big oak tree; see Figure 7.15. What counts as big for grapes depends on the average for grapes and has nothing to do with what counts as big for oak trees. The modified noun is not the only factor involved

(130) Hic nos frugilegas adspeximus *agmine longo* grande onus exiguo formicas ore gerentes (Ov Met 7.625)
regia classis... *longo agmine* veniens (Livy 37.29.8).

The dimensions of the long line in the first example (Met 7.625) are quite different from those in the second (Livy 37.29), since the former is a line of ants and the latter a line of ships; the *grande onus* is also smaller than any of the big entities in (129). Context sensitivity can vary among the members of a plurality: if 'all the animals carried a heavy load,' that does not mean that the mules and the elephants carried the same size loads. Note that while the comparative does not entail the positive, it does admit contextually sensitive (as well as literal) readings ('The child is fatter than the woman, although they are both quite slim').

Not all gradable adjectives use a contextually sensitive standard interval for the interpretation of the positive. Some lexically denote an upper or lower endpoint of the scale

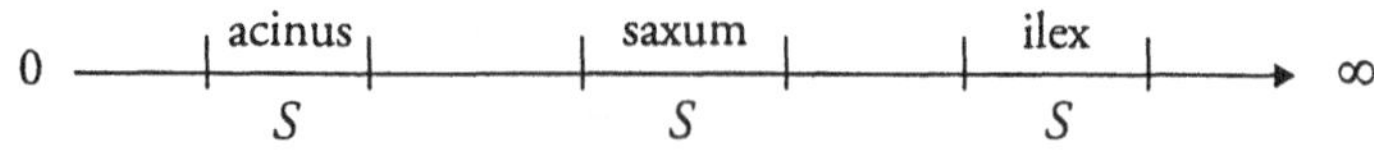

Figure 7.15
Contextual sensitivity of standard interval
Grandis acinus, grande saxum, grandis ilex

(128) That snow is white (Luc 100). Sharp white vinegar (Col 12.57.1). The whites of four eggs (Col 6.38.2). Tin (BG 5.12).

(129) With large berries (Col De Arb 3.1). Large stones (BG 7.46). A large oak tree (Sall Jug 93.4).

(130) Here we saw some graingathering ants carrying their great load in their tiny mouths in a long line (Ov Met 7.625). The king's fleet, advancing in a long line (Livy 37.29.8).

(131) huius omnino generis pugnae *imperiti* (BG 4.24)
omnino omnis eruditionis *expertem* (De Or 2.1)
omnino *certum* est (NH 18.161)
is ex toto *tutus* est (Cels 2.8.9).

The fact that these adjectives refer to or approximate an endpoint of their scale is indicated by their compatibility with maximality modifiers like *omnino* 'completely.' You can say 'completely ignorant' or 'completely safe' but not 'completely tall' or 'completely wide.' ('Issa is completely cute' probably just means that she is very cute.) The following examples show that they are gradable adjectives

(132) propter quosdam *imperitiores* (Quint 1.10.28)
adeo mali *expers* (Tac Hist 2.45)
Quae pax potest esse *certior*? (Phil 8.5)
tutiorem nostris receptum dat (BC 1.46).

If one member of an antonymous pair of gradable adjectives denotes the high endpoint of the scale and the other the low endpoint, then the scale is closed on both ends

(133) poculo *pleno*... reddito (Curt Ruf 7.5.12)
in *vacuum* pontem (Livy 7.9.8).

For the gradability of these adjectives see (104). One cup can be fuller than another; just as 'taller' does not entail 'tall,' so 'fuller' does not entail 'full.' However a full cup is not a cup that is fuller than some contextually determined standard interval, which is different from the standard interval of fullness for, say, amphorae. Rather a full cup and a full amphora are both completely full. They are mapped to the same degree on the scale of fullness, whereas a big cup and a big amphora are mapped to quite different degrees on the scale of bigness.

The positive is not the only form that often has to be interpreted relative to an implicit standard; sometimes this happens with the comparative too

(134) haec soror quam dixi ad flammam accessit *imprudentius* (Ter Andr 130)
Sed elatus studio vereor ne *longior* fuerim (ND 1.56).

Here the maximum degrees of negligence (Andr 130) and prolixity (ND 1.56) that are permitted in accessible worlds are exceeded in the actual world. Like-

(131) Completely without experience of this type of fighting (BG 4.24). Completely devoid of all learning (De Or 2.1). It is absolutely certain (NH 18.161). He is completely safe (Cels 2.8.9).

(132) For the sake of some who are less knowledgeable (Quint 1.10.28). So free from misfortune (Tac Hist 2.45). No peace could be more certain (Phil 8.5). Provides a safer withdrawal for our men (BC 1.46).

(133) Giving back the cup full (Curt Ruf 7.5.12). Onto the empty bridge (Livy 7.9.8).

(134) The sister I mentioned was too careless and got close to the flames (Ter Andr 130). But I'm afraid that in my enthusiasm for my subject I've gone on too long (ND 1.56).

wise *parum* is used when the degree attained in the actual world falls short of the degree required in accessible worlds

(135) cur *parum* amplis adfecerit praemiis (Pro Mil 57)
scuta... ad amplitudinem corporum *parum* lata (Livy 38.21.4).

The intensifier (elative) superlative ('very') works in terms of an extended standard interval

(136) oppidum *altissimis* moenibus oppugnare (BC 3.80)
transire *latissimum* flumen, ascendere *altissimas* ripas, subire *iniquissimum* locum (BG 2.27)
angustissimis semitis (De Leg Agr 2.96).

Roughly speaking, *altis moenibus* means 'taller than the average for town walls' and *altissimis moenibus* means 'taller than the average for tall town walls.' For negative antonyms the scale is read in the opposite direction as usual: very narrow alleys (De Leg Agr 2.96) are even less wide than the average for narrow alleys. Exclamations with *quam* indicate that the difference by which the degree of the adjective exceeds the standard is remarkable

(137) *Quam longum* spatium amandi amicam tibi dedi! (Ter Hec 683)
Quam longa nobis cum modestia tua pugna, quam tarde vicimus! (Pliny Paneg 21.1).

Secondary predicates

In this section we consider adjectives that are used neither as attributive modifiers nor as main predicates. We will start with resultatives, which are less common in Latin than in English. Consider the following examples

(138) *altae* nives premunt terram (Curt Ruf 7.3.11)
ita sunt *altae* stirpes stultitiae (Tusc 3.13)
dimidiatum digitum terram *altam* succernito (Cato 151.3)
patiens terrae quam *altam* iniciunt (Curt Ruf 5.1.33).

In the first examples (Curt Ruf 7.3) the adjective is used attributively; in the second example (Tusc 3.13) it is a main predicate; in the last two examples (Cato 151.3; Curt Ruf 5.1) it is a resultative secondary predicate. Earth should be sieved over the seeds to a depth of half a finger; they pile the earth on high in the

(135) Why he gave them insufficiently large rewards (Pro Mil 57). Their shields, not wide enough for the size of their bodies (Livy 38.21.4).

(136) To attack a town with very high walls (BC 3.80). To cross a very wide river, to climb up very steep banks, to advance over very difficult ground (BG 2.27). Very narrow alleys (De Leg Agr 2.96).

(137) How much time I gave you for loving your girlfriend! (Ter Hec 683). What a long struggle I had with your modesty, how much delayed was my victory! (Pliny Paneg 21.1).

(138) Deep snows cover the ground (Curt Ruf 7.3.11). So deep are the roots of foolishness (Tusc 3.13). Sieve earth over it to a depth of half a finger (Cato 151.3). Strong enough to hold the earth which they pile on deep (Curt Ruf 5.1.33).

hanging gardens. Resultative secondary predicates are tightly integrated into the event structure of the clause. In our examples the resultative expresses a property of the theme that increases incrementally during the process subevent; the process ceases when it reaches a telos denoted by the endpoint on the adjectival scale; the adjective modifies the resultant state subevent, restricting it to subevents whose argument has the property in question. So in the third example (Cato 151.3) the earth is sieved on progressively until it reaches a state of being sieved on to a depth of half a finger (see Figure 7.16); in the last example (Curt Ruf 5.1) the earth is piled on to a depth exceeding the standard. Whereas *terram succernere/inicere* is atelic (since *terram* is indefinite), the addition of the resultative adjective renders the event telic: when the earth reaches the depth specified, the event is over. In the following example the verb is punctual and the resultative adjective correspondingly nonscalar

(139) *immobiles* parumper eos defixit (Livy 21.33.3).

Resultatives are internal to depictives ('He broke the bottle open dirty'), and while (as we shall see presently) depictives can be predicated of agent subjects and obliques as well as themes, resultatives are only predicated of themes–direct objects as in (138) or passive/unaccusative subjects

(140) sic *alta* peculia crescent (Ov Am 2.2.39)
altaque nativo creverat herba toro (Prop 3.13.36).

In these examples the resultative adjective serves to specify the end point of an incremental process lexicalized in the verb. The familiar English type of resultative which adds a resultant state onto an activity verb ('wipe the table clean') is not used in Latin. As its name implies, the resultative is designed to modify the resultant state, although depending on the type of scale it may incidentally be true also at pretelic incremental stages (as in piling earth high or digging a hole deep). Depictives are quite different: if you wipe the table nude, you are nude during the wiping event, not just at its completion. Resultatives make an atelic sentence telic, depictives do not: you can eat oysters raw for hours on end with

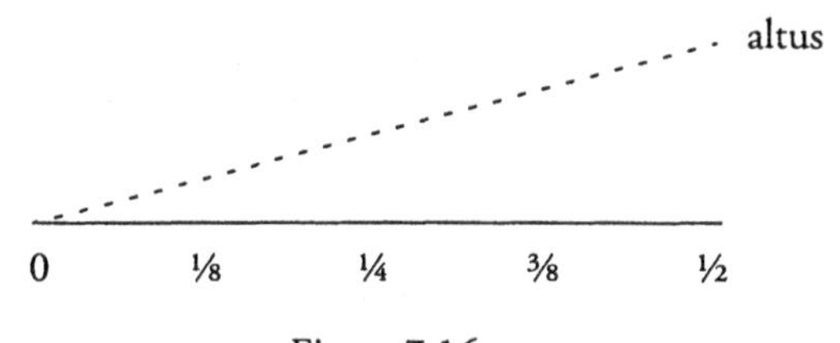

Figure 7.16
Scalar resultative adjective
Dimidiatum digitum terram altam succernito (Cato 151.3)

(139) Froze them in their tracks for a short while (Livy 21.33.3).
(140) In this way your savings will grow large (Ov Am 2.2.39). And the grass had grown tall to make a natural bed (Prop 3.13.36).

no telos in sight. In its default reading the depictive is true throughout the run time of the event: the interval on the time line occupied by the depictive state properly includes the interval occupied by the event. But it is also possible for the lefthand or righthand boundaries (or both) of the state interval and the event interval to coincide: so $\tau(s) \supseteq \tau(e)$

(141) saltare in convivio *nudus* (Verr 2.3.23; cp. Pro Reg Deiot 26)
nudus, unctus, *ebrius* est contionatus (Phil 3.12).

The first example (Verr 2.3), in which the verb is a clear activity and so atelic, asserts that Apronius' state of being naked obtained during his dance (see Figure 7.17); it is noncommittal about his state of dress before and after the dance, which depends on how the events of undressing and dressing correlate with the run time of the dance. One has to make the usual pragmatic allowances for fuzzy boundaries and for gaps. Apronius would still have danced naked if he had taken his clothes off just after the beginning of the dance and put them on again just before the end of the dance. Both lexical and perspectival aspect can affect the interpretation. Since dancing is an activity, 'Apronius danced naked' could be true of a dancing subevent without also being true of the entire event; this would not be the case with an accomplishment like 'dance the Dance of the Hours naked.' If someone is crossing a bridge naked, just as there is no guarantee that he will reach the other side successfully, so there is no guarantee that he won't put his clothes back on before he gets to the other side. Some examples deviate from the default definition of depictives above, in that the depictive is true only of the initial portion of the event, giving a sort of antiresultative

(142) qui te *vivum* comburere conatus est (Verr 2.1.83)
te *vivum* comburam (Petr 78)
vulpem decoctam *vivam* donec ossa tantum restent (NH 28.220).

In these examples, the interval occupied by the depictive strictly overlaps (overlaps but is not included in) the interval occupied by the event. So for the Apronius example we would say $\exists e.\text{Saltat}(e, \text{A}) \wedge \exists s.\text{Nudus}(s, \text{A}) \wedge \tau(s) \supseteq \tau(e)$,

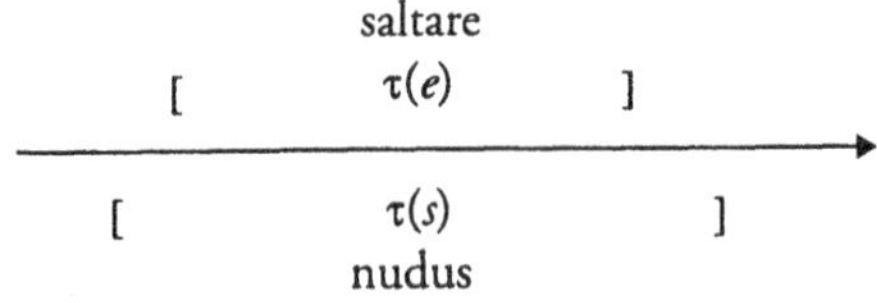

Figure 7.17
Default depictive
Saltare in convivio nudus (Verr 2.3.23)

(141) To dance naked at the party (Verr 2.3.23). He delivered a speech naked, anointed and drunk (Phil 3.12).

(142) That tried to burn you alive (Verr 2.1.83). I will burn you alive (Petr 78). A fox boiled alive until only the bones remain (NH 28.220).

meaning there is an event of Apronius dancing and there is a state of Apronius being naked and the state includes the event; whereas for the second example in (142) (Petr 78) we would say $\exists e$.Comburo(e, ego, te) $\wedge$ $\exists s$.Vivus(s, tu) $\wedge$ $\tau(s) \circ \tau(e)$. Whether a secondary predicate adjective is read as resultative, depictive or antiresultative depends on the interface of the lexical meanings of the adjective and the verb. Verbs of destruction trigger the antiresultative reading if the patient entity loses the depictive property prior to the completion of the event.

The depictive does not restrict the set of individuals denoted by the noun (English NP) but the state of the referent(s) of the whole noun phrase (English DP) during the event. Consequently, unlike attributives, depictives can modify pro-dropped subjects and anaphoric pronouns

(143) *Sobrius* a thermis nescit abire domum (Mart 12.70.8)
Eam esto vel coctam vel *crudam* (Cato 156.1).

If the state is an individual-level (permanent) property rather than a stage-level (temporary) property, the assertion becomes vacuous: one does not say of a blonde 'She went to the party blonde' unless she had intended to dye her hair. This distinction is not simply a lexical one, since some adjectives can be used in both ways

(144) *pavidumque* leporem (Hor Epod 2.35)
hostes... *pavidos* concursare (BAfr 82)
Aliquis odit filium *caecum*...? (Quint Decl Maior 1.16)
nil video, *caecus* eo (Pl Aul 714).

The hare is generically fearful (Epod 2.35: attributive), the enemy are temporarily scared (BAfr 82: depictive); the son is permanently blind (Decl Maior 1.16: attributive), I am going around as though blind temporarily (Aul 714: depictive). The constraint against individual-level adjectives ensures that the depictive is nonvacuous, but this is only a minimal requirement. The pragmatic status of the depictive is usually much stronger than that, since it is typically focused: it carries the informational nucleus of the sentence. For instance in the second example of (143) the point is not that one can eat cabbage (of course one can), but that one can eat it either cooked or raw. In the first example of (141) the point is not that Apronius danced, but that he did so nude. The depictive picks out one of the possible alternate states Apronius could have been in during his dance: in the structured meaning format $\lambda P \exists e$.Saltat(e, A) $\wedge$ $\exists s.P(s$, A) $\wedge$ $\tau(s) \supseteq \tau(e)$, Nudus. Of course other pragmatic structures can also occur: here is an example like the second one in (143) but with multiple foci

(143) He is unable to go home from the baths sober (Mart 12.70.8). Eat it either cooked or raw (Cato 156.1).

(144) A timid hare (Hor Epod 2.35). That the enemy were running around in panic (BAfr 82). Does someone hate his blind son...? (Quint Decl Maior 1.16). I can't see, I'm walking blind (Pl Aul 714).

(145) Antiqui et insanientibus dabant *crudum*, Diocles phreneticis elixum (NH 20.52).

The controller (subject of predication) of a depictive is identified by agreement; subjects and objects are the most common, but oblique depictives are also found. Languages differ as to which classes of adjectives can be used as depictives: adjectives of physical condition and mental state are the most common, followed by quantity, manner, location and time probably in that order. Latin is depictive friendly compared to English and allows depictives from the more constrained area of this hierarchy too

(146) in regio morbo *crudum* bibitur (NH 27.49: physical state)
Haec et his similia *laeti* audiere iuvenes (Curt Ruf 8.1.27: psych state)
in agmine atque ad vigilias *multus* adesse (Sall Jug 96.3: quantity)
si *citi* advenissent (Tac Ann 12.12: manner)
domesticus otior (Hor Sat 1.6.128: location)
mane forum et *vespertinus* pete tectum (Hor Ep 1.6.20: time).

In principle a subject controlled depictive gives the state of the subject during an event, while a subject oriented manner adverb gives the manner in which the event occurred. But the event-specificity of depictives extends beyond temporal inclusion

(147) primo Afraniani milites... *laeti* ex castris procurrebant (BC 1.69)
ea *laeta*... una cum viro in rogum imponitur (Tusc 5.78).

The fact that she was happy to be placed on the pyre does not mean that she was also happy about the weather or about her husband just having died. So it is quite natural for inferences to be made between adverb and depictive

(148) belli Martisque discrimen *impavidus* subibo (Curt Ruf 9.6.24)
poculum... *impavide* hausit (Livy 30.15.8).

Impavidus implies *impavide* and vice versa. This implicature can be cancelled: one can be fearless during an event while acting fearfully (pretending to be fearful) and vice versa. There may also be linguistic reasons why depictive and adverb are not interchangeable:

(149) numquam conferti sed *rari*... proeliarentur (BG 5.16)

(145) The ancients gave it raw to the insane, Diocles gave it boiled to phrenetics (NH 20.52).
(146) In the case of jaundice it is drunk raw (NH 27.49). The younger soldiers were happy to hear this and similar things (Curt Ruf 8.1.27). He was often with them on the march and on guard (Sall Jug 96.3). If they came quickly (Tac Ann 12.12). I relax at home (Hor Sat 1.6.128). Go early in the morning to the forum and return home late in the evening (Hor Ep 1.6.20).
(147) At first Afranius' men happily started running out of their camp (BC 1.69). She is happily placed on the pyre together with her husband (Tusc 5.78).
(148) I will meet the dangers of war and battle fearless (Curt Ruf 9.6.24). She drained the cup fearlessly (Livy 30.15.8).
(149) They never fought in close array but scattered (BG 5.16).

(150) nec Iliacos coetus nisi *rarus* adibat (Ov Met 11.766)
raro accidit (Col 6.24.3).

Depictive *rarus* can be used either of space (BG 5.16) or of time (Met 11.766), adverbial *raro* is specialized in a temporal meaning.

Depictives are secondary predicates. As such they need to be distinguished from attributives (first example in (138)) and from main predicates (second example in (138)). They also need to be distinguished from predicate complements

(151) Pantaleon contra *impavidus* mansit ad protegendum regem (Livy 42.15.10)
is ad nostram memoriam *fidissimus* mansit (Tac Agr 14.1).

In the first example (Livy 42.15) Pantaleon stayed in the same place fearlessly (depictive secondary predicate); in the second example (Agr 14.1) Cogidumnus remained not in the same place but in the same state of loyalty (predicate complement). Both categories need further to be distinguished from discontinuous modifiers in hyperbaton

(152) fugere *pavidos* Romanos (Livy 33.8.1: depictive)
Nec faciet *pavidos* taurus avitus equos (Ov Rem 744: predicate complement)
pavidos terre... cervos (Ov Rem 203: hyperbaton)
edidit *impavidos* ore minante sonos (Ov Fast 2.840: hyperbaton).

Since discontinuous adjectives modify entities (rather than entities during an event, like depictives), they can be individual-level properties as in the third example (Rem 203). Finally depictives need to be distinguished from adjectival circumstantials

(153) *Laetus* simplicitate barbari rex... regnum restituit (Curt Ruf 8.12.10)
Laetus his adclamationibus... protinus castra movit (Curt Ruf 9.4.23)

and from adjectival amplifications

(154) Quis porro... Germaniam peteret, *informem* terris, *asperam* caelo... ? (Tac Germ 2)
a quo aberat mons ferme milia passuum viginti... *vastus* ab natura et humano cultu. (Sall Jug 48.3).

(150) He only rarely mixed with the Trojan people (Ov Met 11.766). It rarely happens (Col 6.24.3).

(151) Pantaleon remained fearlessly to protect the king (Livy 42.15.10). He has remained most loyal right down to our own times (Tac Agr 14.1).

(152) That the Romans were fleeing in terror (Livy 33.8.1). And his grandfather's bull will not make the horses scared (Ov Rem 744). Frighten the timid deer (Ov Rem 203). He spoke these fearless words with threatening voice (Ov Fast 2.840).

(153) Happy at the sincerity of the barbarian, the king gave him back his kingdom (Curt Ruf 8.12.10). Happy at these expressions of approval, he immediately moved camp (Curt Ruf 9.4.23).

(154) Who would want to go to Germany with its ugly landscape and its harsh climate? (Tac Germ 2). About twenty miles from which was a mountain range naturally desolate and devoid of human cultivation (Sall Jug 48.3).

The circumstantials cite happiness as the state Alexander was in prior to the action and as the reason for his action, not as the state he was in during his action: contrast the depictives cited above like

(155) *laeti* ex castris procurrebant (BC 1.69).

The amplifications in (154) are entity modifiers like attributives; this explains why they can be individual-level properties. Amplifications and circumstantials are typically separate prosodic phrases, while depictives are prosodically part of the main clause. They are also typically separate focal assertions independent of the main clause, while depictives are typically the main focus of an assertion that includes the main clause. Consequently they are outside the scope of a main clause negative, while depictives often associate with a main clause negative

(156) festo semper otio *laeti* non bella novere (Mela 3.37: circumstantial)
neque enim faceres hoc *sobrius* umquam (Mart 3.16.3: depictive)
Ille numquam *nudus* est contionatus (Phil 2.111: depictive).

In the first example (Mela 3.37) the Hyperboreans are happy and they do not know wars. In the second example (Mart 3.16) you do this but you would not do it sober. In the third example (Phil 2.111) Antony's grandfather gave many speeches, but none of them without his clothes on.

It remains to say something about the semantics of adjectives in hyperbaton. If one assumes that discontinuous adjectives are moved back into contiguity with their nouns at logical form prior to semantic interpretation, then their interpretation is the same as it is for adjectives in continuous noun phrases, and you can use the semantics given earlier in this chapter or any other theory you prefer. However, at least in prose, modifiers become discontinuous because they move to pragmatically determined positions, so they should be interpreted in those positions if their contribution to pragmatic meaning is to be captured. Latin word order only makes sense on the premise that pragmatically driven syntactic structure is compositionally interpreted. Unfortunately the in situ semantics of discontinuous adjectives is a difficult issue. The simplest idea is that discontinuous adjectives are a type of secondary predicate, like depictives but without event-linking. Let's check this with some verse examples (if they are interpreted in situ in prose, presumably they are in verse too)

(157) *flavos* movet aura *capillos* (Ov Fast 5.609)
aurea purpuream subnectit *fibula* vestem (Aen 4.139)
et *laevam* tunicis inseruisse *manum* (Ov Am 2.15.12).

(155) Happily started running out of their camp (BC 1.69).

(156) Being always happy in their festive leisure, they do not experience wars (Mela 3.37). You would never do this sober (Mart 3.16.3). He never gave a speech stripped to the waist (Phil 2.111).

(157) The breeze ruffles her blonde hair (Ov Fast 5.609). A golden pin fastens her purple dress (Aen 4.139). And to put my left hand inside her dress (Ov Am 2.15.12).

In the first example (Fast 5.609) the adjective is descriptive (all Europa's hair is blonde) and the secondary predicate theory works fine ('her hair being blonde'). It is also gives satisfactory results for the indefinite restrictive *aurea* in the second example (Aen 4.129: 'a pin being gold'). But it crashes completely with the last example (Am 2.15), which is a definite restrictive. *Laevam... manum* does not mean 'my hand, being on my left side.' The problem is that the restrictive adjective has to be inside the scope of the definiteness operator, but on the discontinuous secondary predicate theory it ends up outside. The contextually salient set having just one member is not the denotation of the noun (people have two hands) but the denotation of the intersection of the noun with the adjective (people have just one left hand). The same sort of problem arises with stranded or extraposed English clauses ('Sue wore the dress to the party last night that Jack gave her for her birthday'). The solution is to create a dummy position for the adjective next to the noun and to postpone composition of the adjective until after the rest of the constituent has been composed. Since a restrictive adjective is a narrow focus, this amounts to creating a structured meaning with abstraction of the focused adjective: (omitting the tunic) $\lambda P \lambda y.$Inseruisse$(y, \iota x.$Manum$(x) \wedge P(x))$, Laevam. The direct object phrase in the cofocus means 'the hand having the property P,' the adjective substitutes for P, and the result is 'to insert the hand on the left.' Here are a couple of prose examples with split definite noun phrases comparable to the verse example just discussed (Am 2.15)

(158) hic casus... *dextram* moratur manum (BG 5.44)
equitatum... ab *dextro* locaverunt *cornu* (Livy 38.26.3).

Premodifier hyperbaton in Caesar and Cicero typically involves fairly strongly focused adjectives

(159) *pedestribus* valent copiis (BG 2.17)
gravibus acceptis vulneribus (BG 6.38)
aeneum statuerunt tropaeum (De Inv 2.69);

the same applies to one type of postmodifier hyperbaton

(160) legiones conscripsit *novas*, excepit *veteres* (Phil 11.27)
Nascitur ibi plumbum album... aere utuntur *importato* (BG 5.12).

Veteres in the first example (Phil 11.27) is a null head modifier: it is parallel to *novas*, which suggests that it might be possible to interpret focused *novas* as a null head modifier too (rather than as a secondary predicate). Null head modifiers (to be distinguished from nominalizations like *malum* 'evil,' *hiberna* 'winter quar-

(158) This accident slowed down his right hand (BG 5.44). They placed the cavalry on the right wing (Livy 38.26.3).

(159) Their strength lies in their infantry (BG 2.17). After suffering severe wounds (BG 6.38). They set up a bronze trophy (De Inv 2.69).

(160) He enrolled new legions and took over old ones (Phil 11.27). Tin is found there, but the bronze they use is imported (BG 5.12).

ters') commonly occur when contrastively focused adjectives trigger ellipsis of the noun

(161) neque nimium *calidum solum* posse tolerare vitem... neque *praegelidum* (Col 3.12.1)
ut *locis frigidis* novissime, *tepidis* celerius, *calidis* ocissime seramus (Col 2.7.2: app. crit.)
semen eius *locis calidis* mense Ianuario, *frigidis* Februario seritur (Col 11.3.32).

The null head can follow the adjective as in the first example (Col 3.12: 'very cold one') or precede it as in the other two ('in ones cold'). If we interpret strongly focused adjectives in hyperbaton as null head modifiers, we have to shift the type of the noun too, making it (rather than the adjective) the secondary predicate. With an ordinary null head modifier, the noun would be ellipsed, whereas in hyperbaton it shows up as a secondary predicate in a tail or topical position elsewhere in the sentence. For the first example in (158) (BG 5.44) the adjective is taken to mean 'the right one': $\iota x.\text{Dextram}(x) \wedge P(x)$. This mimics the colloquial Italian split focus construction 'Quelle buone si è comprato di scarpe' ('The good ones he bought for himself [of] shoes'). Focus abstraction is now over individuals rather than properties. Nonreferential *manum* is entered into the semantics either as a predicate modifier (like an incorporated noun with a stranded adjective) or as a secondary predicate of the null head. In one way or another it serves to resolve the unbound empty head P in the null head modifier.

FURTHER READING

Beck (2010); Bouchard (2002); Cinque (2010); Kennedy (1999); Morzycki (2005).

(161) That neither too hot soil can sustain the vine nor too cold soil (Col 3.12.1). That we should sow last in cold areas, sooner in mild areas and earliest of all in hot areas (Col 2.7.2). Its seed is sown in January in warm areas and in February in cool ones (Col 11.3.32).

8 | NEGATION

For the purposes of sentential negation, truth is not scalar or many-valued; truth and falsity are treated as complementary polar opposites. If the speaker asserts that Cicero was born at Arpinum, he considers that he has enough evidence to assert the proposition as true; he represents himself as knowing, believing or judging that the proposition is true. An affirmative proposition p ('Cicero was born at Arpinum') and its negative counterpart $\neg p$ ('Cicero was not born at Arpinum') are understood to occupy the whole logical space of factual possibilities; they are contradictories: $\neg(p \wedge \neg p)$ and $\neg p \vee p$. Whenever the affirmative is true, its negative counterpart is false, and vice versa; tertium non datur. The speaker may not know enough to assert the proposition as true, but he knows that in point of fact either Cicero was born at Arpinum or he wasn't. This is quite different from the situation with two affirmative propositions p and q. Obviously p and q can both be true ('Cicero was born at Arpinum,' 'Cicero wrote the Tusculan Disputations'). If one of them is false, they may be contradictories ('Cicero was male,' 'Cicero was female'), but they may also be contraries ('Cicero was born at Larinum,' 'Cicero was born at Ameria'). Contraries can't both be true ($\neg(p \wedge q)$), but they can both be false ($\neg(q \vee p)$), as is the case with our examples: Cicero was born neither at Larinum nor at Ameria. Value judgements with scalar adjectives and presupposition failures, both issues that have featured prominently in philosophical discussion of truth values, do not complicate this picture. 'Clodia is beautiful' excludes not only that part of the scale occupied by 'ugly' but also the neutral, vague or transitional segment of the scale between beautiful and ugly; 'Clodia is not beautiful' includes both those parts of the scale. Whereas 'beautiful' and 'ugly' (like antonymous pairs of adjectives with morphologically incorporated constituent negation, e.g. *felix* 'fortunate,' *infelix* 'unfortunate') are usually taken to be contraries, the affirmative assertion 'Clodia is beautiful' and its negative counterpart 'Clodia is not beautiful' are contradictories. What we have just said only holds if affirmative assertions and their negative counterparts are interpreted with the same presuppositions and the same pragmatic enrichments (including tolerance for exceptions). If you say 'Latin Loebs are red,' I cannot reply 'That's not true: they are white with black letters on them': we have to share the presupposition that Latin Loebs exist, and we both have to treat the covers as pragmatically salient. Presupposition failures ('The Australian centurion captured a Nervian') and anomalous predications ('The square root of nine captured a Nervian') are best taken to disqualify the assertion as a candidate for truth evaluation, rather than as grounds for assuming a third truth value (neither true nor false). Presuppositions that do not fail also differ from assertions, since they are unaffected by negation ('A Roman centurion captured/didn't capture the Nervian': what varies with the negation is the existence of the capture event, not the existence of the Nervian). When the negative operator (Latin *non*) has sentential scope, it is an operator of type <t,t>. It takes a proposition p, for instance *Pluit* 'It is raining,' and returns its contradictory $\neg p$, *Non pluit.* This switches the truth value of the proposition: if p is true in the context, $\neg p$ is false; and if p is false in the context, $\neg p$ is true. If p is a member of the set of true propositions, then $\neg p$ is a member of the complement set (the set of false propositions), and vice versa. In a possible worlds perspective, $\neg p$ is true in the complement of the set of worlds in which p is true; this is illustrated in Figure 8.1.

Predicate negation takes a property P and returns a property $\neg P$. It makes the subject a member of the complement of the set denoted by the predicate

(1) qui... mortem non timet (Tusc 2.2).

Mortem non timet means 'is a member of the complement of the set of those fearing death' (again excluding anomalous predication). This is illustrated in Figure 8.2. In the richer perspective of a full powerset lattice, there is a complement element $\neg x$ for each element x of the lattice. For instance, say there are five individuals (a, b, c, d, e), two of whom (d and e) fear death and three of whom (a, b, and c) don't fear death. Then the node $\{a,b,c\}$ is the complement of the node $\{d,e\}$. The union of these two elements gives the topmost node of the lattice $\{a,b,c,d,e\}$ and their intersection gives the bottommost node (the empty

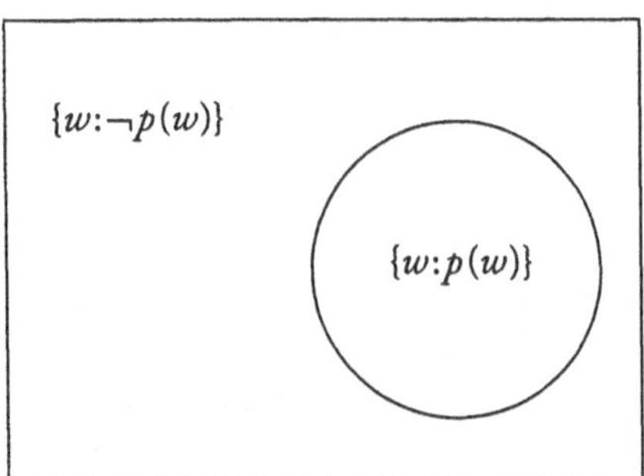

Figure 8.1
Possible worlds for polar opposites
Pluit and *Non pluit*

(1) He who does not fear death (Tusc 2.2).

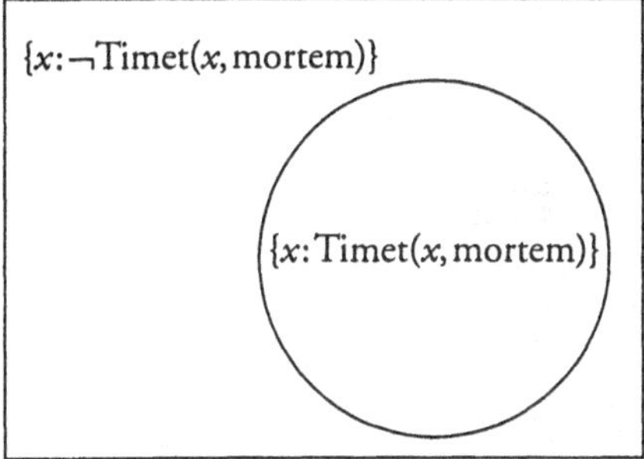

Figure 8.2
Predicate negation as complementation
Mortem non timet (Tusc 2.2)

set). In the diagram of the powerset lattice, an element x and all of its subsets and all of their subsets (and so on) are connected by lines running down from x to the empty set. This structure is called the principal ideal generated by x, written $(x]$ (= $\{y \in L: y \leq x\}$, which in the present case is equivalent to $\{y \in \wp: y \subseteq x\}$, where L means 'lattice' and $\wp$ means 'powerset lattice'). The principal ideals generated by a lattice element and its complement must necessarily be disjoint, because the set of atoms from which the elements of the one are formed is the complement of the set of atoms from which those of the other are formed. This is illustrated in Figure 8.3, where the principal ideal generated by $\{a,b,c\}$ is marked by the larger circles and the principal ideal generated by $\{d,e\}$ is marked by the squares. Any element of the lattice that belongs to neither principal ideal must contain a mixture of atoms from $\{a,b,c\}$ and its complement $\{d,e\}$, for instance $\{a,e\}$, $\{a,b,d\}$, $\{a,c,d,e\}$. Neither *mortem timent* nor *mortem non timent* is true of these sets, because they contain a mixture of members from both the positive and the negative sets. If a set is much larger than its complement, then the negative is an efficient way to convey the information exhaustively ('*a* didn't pass the test'), but if the complement is much larger, the positive is more economical ('*a* passed the test').

Scopal variation

If negation is the only operator in the sentence, there is no potential for scopal ambiguity

(2) Minucius... *non* invenit hostem. (Livy 3.30.8)
Ex eo Dinocrates ab rege *non* discessit (Vitr 2.pr.4).

'Minucius has the property that he does not find the enemy' (Minucius $\in$ $\{x: \neg\text{Invenit}(x, \text{hostem})\}$) is equivalent to 'It is not the case that Minucius has the property of finding the enemy' ($\neg$Invenit(Minucius, hostem)). The same

(2) Minucius did not find the enemy (Livy 3.30.8). From that point on Dinocrates did not leave the king (Vitr 2.pr.4).

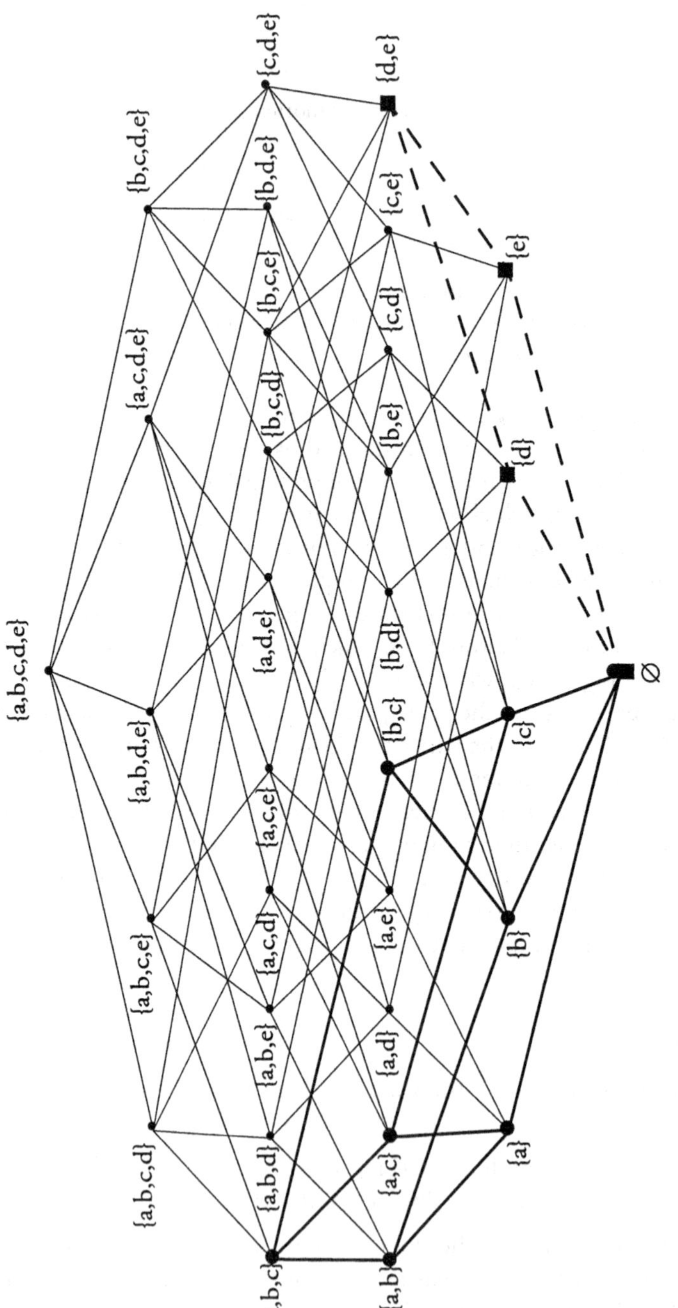

Figure 8.3
Complementation in a powerset lattice: {a,b,c} is the complement of {d,e}
● principal ideal generated by {a,b,c}; ■ principal ideal generated by {d,e}

goes for Dinocrates and the king. So in this case predicate negation amounts to sentential negation; in other words the meaning is the same whether the negative operator is to the left or to the right of the definite subject phrase. But if the sentence also contains a quantifier, scopal ambiguity can arise

(3) ex victoribus ceciderunt *non plus centum* (Livy 44.42.8)
haras... in quas *non* inducunt *plus vicenos* pullos (Varro RR 3.10.4).

The first example (Livy 44.42) means that no more than a hundred of the victors were killed ($\neg >$) rather than that more than a hundred of the victors were not killed ($> \neg$). The second example (RR 3.10) means that no more than twenty young geese were put in each coop ($\neg >$) rather than that more than twenty young geese were left outside each coop ($> \neg$). External negation is the preferred reading. This is also the case for the universal quantifier

(4) Pecunia *omnis* soluta *non* est (Div Caec 32)
Non omnis aetas, Lyde, ludo convenit (Pl Bacch 129)
Cum... uno sermone nostro *omnes* fructus provinciae *non* confero (Ad Fam 2.12.2)
id feci quod *omnes non* negant immortalitati... mandandum (De Dom 76).

The first two examples have external negation ($\neg \forall$): not all the money was paid (Div Caec 32) and not every age is suitable for games (Bacch 129). The other two have internal negation ($\forall \neg$): all the rewards of a province are not superior to a single conversation of ours (Ad Fam 2.12) and everyone does not deny the immortality of Cicero's action (De Dom 76). Switching the scopes gives the wrong reading in all four examples: all the money was unpaid, not everyone denies, etc. Often, though not always, syntactic scope (word order) is a cue to semantic scope

(5) eum cui *non omnes* placent; hoc enim malo dicere quam "*omnes non* placent." (Sen Con 2.1.7).

When this is not the case, as in the first example in (4) (Div Caec 32), some mechanism must be posited that allows the negation to be interpreted at logical form in a position other than its surface position in the syntax. The negative can also interact with a modal operator. Here are some examples involving circumstantial modality

(3) Of the victors no more than a hundred fell (Livy 44.42.8). The coops, into which they put at most twenty young geese (Varro RR 3.10.4).
(4) Not all the money has been paid (Div Caec 32). Not every age is suitable for school, Lydus (Pl Bacch 129). I do not compare all the rewards of a province with one conversation between us (Ad Fam 2.12.2). I performed an act that everyone admits should be committed to immortality (De Dom 76).
(5) One whom not everyone pleases; for I prefer to say that than "everyone displeases." (Sen Con 2.1.7).

(6) Agitur de parricidio, quod sine multis causis *suscipi non* potest (Pro Rosc Am 73)
dolorem... Si igitur deponi potest, etiam *non suscipi* potest (Tusc 3.66)
Tribus *non conduci possum* libertatibus (Pl Cas 504).

The first example (Pro Rosc 73) says that it is not possible for parricide to be undertaken without many motives: the modal is inside the scope of negation (¬◊). The second example (Tusc 3.66) says that it is possible for grief not to be entered into: only the infinitive is negated (◊¬). The third example (Cas 504) has the same word order as the second but the same scope as the first (¬◊). Deontic *debeo* further illustrates scopal variation without word order variation. In the following examples the negative scopes over the modal

(7) Si non adiutus sum, *non debui* (De Prov 43: app. crit.)
quod iam ego curare *non debui*, sed tamen fieri non moleste tuli (Ad Fam 5.2.9).

The first example (De Prov 43) says that Caesar didn't have to help Cicero (¬□), not that he ought not to have helped him (□¬). The second example (Ad Fam 5.2) says that Cicero had no need to take care of the matter (¬□), not that he ought not to have done so (□¬). Contrast the following examples with the modal scoping over negation

(8) in senatum venire... turbulento illo die *non debuisti.* (De Dom 5)
"Male iudicavit populus." At iudicavit. "*Non debuit.*" At potuit. (Pro Planc 11).

Both examples mean 'ought not to have' (□¬), not 'didn't need to' (¬□). Scopal variation with *debeo* could be due to its being a neg-raising verb (see the next section), since the negative can raise cyclically to an even higher position

(9) *non* puto Caecilium *sequi debuisse* quod assequi nequiret (Gell 2.23.22).

Non negates the highest verb (*puto*) syntactically but the lowest verb (*sequi*) semantically.

Neg-raising

We have seen that the semantic scope for the negative varies, that its syntactic scope does not always correspond to its semantic scope, and that different semantic scopes can be logically equivalent. All this complicates the semantics

(6) It is a case of parricide, which cannot be committed without many motives (Pro Rosc Am 73). Grief... So if one can put it aside, one can also not enter into it (Tusc 3.66). I couldn't be induced by three manumissions (Pl Cas 504).

(7) If I was not helped, I didn't have to be (De Prov 43). Something which I didn't have to bother with any longer but was not upset should happen (Ad Fam 5.2.9).

(8) You ought not to have come to the senate on that day of disturbances (De Dom 5). "The people made a bad judgement." But they made a judgement. "They ought not to have done so." But they had the power to do so (Pro Planc 11).

(9) I do not think that Caecilius ought to have followed what he could not emulate successfully (Gell 2.23.22).

of negation, and the problems are particularly evident with infinitival complement clauses when a negative that semantically belongs in the complement clause shows up syntactically as a negation of the matrix verb. This is called neg-raising

(10) Hunc ego cum futuit *non puto* perficere (Mart 3.79.2)
Clodiae sane placent, sed *non puto* esse venales (Ad Att 12.38a.2).

Martial is not saying that he has a different propositional attitude (or none at all) to Sertorius' sexual performance (¬Puto(*p*)), but that he thinks it is incomplete (Puto(¬*p*)). Similarly Cicero is saying that it is his belief that Clodia's gardens are not for sale (*non esse venales*). The matrix negation is understood as equivalent to complement clause negation. Like *puto* 'think that,' *opinor* 'hold the opinion that' is a neg-raising verb

(11) *Non opinor* ex eis rebus... rem ullam potuisse mutari (Pro Clu 92)
At *non opinor* fieri hoc posse hodie (Pl Cas 473)
M. Lucullus, qui se *non opinari* sed scire [Heracliae eum esse tum ascriptum]... dicit (Pro Arch 8).

The first two examples have neg-raising: the negative is inside the scope of the matrix verb. In the last example (Pro Arch 8) the matrix verb is inside the scope of negation because it is itself narrowly negated. Here is a further set of examples, with *spero* in the sense of 'expect'

(12) *non spero* esse passuros illos qui arma habent (Livy 3.47.7)
Non speraverat Hannibal fore ut tot in Italia populi ad se deficerent (Livy 28.44.4)
Dido... tantos rumpi *non speret* amores (Aen 4.292).

Dido's expectation was that such great love could not be broken.

It is important not to confuse the process of negative lexicalization with neg-raising. *Nescio* 'don't know that' lexicalizes external negation

(13) Hunc suom esse *nescit* qui domist (Pl Capt 29).

This means 'he doesn't know that the man at home is his own son.' *Nescio* is a factive verb, and as we shall see factive verbs are not neg-raising; so it cannot mean 'he knows the man at home is not his own son.' *Nego* 'say that not' and *veto* 'order that not' lexicalize internal negation

(10) When he screws I don't think he comes (Mart 3.79.2). I do like Clodia's gardens but I don't think they're for sale (Ad Att 12.38a.2).

(11) I don't think that any of the facts can have changed (Pro Clu 92). I don't think it can happen today (Pl Cas 473). M. Lucullus is present, who says that he does not just think but knows (Pro Arch 8).

(12) I don't expect those who have arms to put up with this (Livy 3.47.7). Hannibal had not expected so many states in Italy to revolt and join him (Livy 28.44.4). Dido does not expect to find that so great a love is being broken (Aen 4.292).

(13) He doesn't know that this man who is at home is his own son (Pl Capt 29).

(14) *Negat* Phanium esse hanc sibi cognatam Demipho? (Ter Phorm 352)
non dicerem hoc esse tempus quo pacem... occupare deberes (Curt Ruf 4.11.7)
Piliam angi *veta* (Ad Att 12.14.5)
lex, sicut adscribi civem alienum *vetabat*, ita eici e senatu ob hanc causam *non iubebat* (Pliny Ep 10.114.3).

If you change *negat* (internal negation) to *non dicit* (external negation) in the first example (Phorm 352), you change the meaning of the sentence, and vice versa for the second example. The first example in the second set (Ad Att 12.14) means 'Tell Pilia not to worry,' not 'Don't tell Pilia to worry'; and you cannot switch *vetabat* and *non iubebat* in the second example (Ep 10.114) without altering the sense. So neither *nego* nor *veto* is a neg-raising verb. On the other hand *nolo* 'don't want,' which in most of its forms lexicalizes (actually incorporates) negation, is neg-raising (unlike the similarly formed *nequeo* 'am unable')

(15) CLEOS. *Nolo* ames. LYS. Non potes impetrare (Pl Cas 233)
Non vult populus Romanus obsoletis criminibus accusari Verrem, nova postulat (Verr 2.5.117).

In the first example (Cas 233) Cleostrata is asserting a wish not to be loved by her husband, not denying a wish to be loved by him; *impetro* means 'get what you want,' so if there was nothing in the discourse context that Cleostrata wanted, Lysidamus' reply would trigger a presupposition failure. In the second example the unincorporated negative associates with the focus on *obsoletis* in the complement clause: the Roman people does want Verres to be prosecuted, just not on hackneyed charges.

In a few interesting examples a raised or lexicalized negation is interpreted as having scope only over the first of two conjuncts

(16) Plerique *negant* Caesarem in condicione mansurum postulataque haec ab eo interposita esse quominus... (Ad Att 7.15.3)
Qua re *non puto* Pansam et Hirtium in consulatu properaturos in provincias exire sed Romae acturos consulatum (Ad Fam 12.14.5)
Sestio... cui *non puto* suos esse concessos sed ab ipso datos (Ad Att 11.7.1).

(14) Does Demipho deny that this girl Phanium is related to him? (Ter Phorm 352). I would not be saying that this is the time when you ought to embrace peace (Curt Ruf 4.11.7). Tell Pilia not to worry (Ad Att 12.14.5). Just as the law forbade citizens of another city to become senators, so it did not require them to be forced out of the senate for this reason (Pliny Ep 10.114.3).

(15) CLEOS. I don't want you to love me. LYS. There is no way you can get what you want (Pl Cas 233). The Roman people doesn't want Verres to be prosecuted on common charges, it demands fresh ones (Verr 2.5.117).

(16) Most people say that Caesar won't stick to the agreement and that these demands were introduced by him to prevent... (Ad Att 7.15.3). So I think that Pansa and Hirtius will not be in a hurry to leave for their provinces during their consulship, but will conduct their consulship in Rome (Ad Fam 12.14.5). Sestius... I think he was not so much permitted to keep his as given them by Caesar (Ad Att 11.7.1).

This points to a "downstairs" reading of the negative. In examples similar to the last two in Danish, when the verb is changed to one that is not neg-raising, the single conjunct reading is not available.

Now that we have said what is and what is not neg-raising, three questions remain to be answered: (1) How is it possible for such a construction to arise in the first place? (2) Why is it licensed with some verbs that take infinitival complements but not with others? and (3) Why is it often preferred to simple complement clause negation?

A necessary, but not sufficient, condition for neg-raising is that complement clause negation entail matrix negation. For instance *Puto non esse venales* (Ad Att 12.38a) in (10) above entails *Non puto esse venales*, assuming that the same belief state is being described and that I am not schizophrenic. This does not work the other way around, because I might have no opinion on the matter either way. Entailment is not a sufficient condition because we find similar entailments with verbs that are not neg-raising: *Affirmavit se non indicaturum* 'He declared that he would not testify' (Sen Apoc 1) entails *Non affirmavit se indicaturum* 'He did not declare that he would testify', so long as the same claim is being described, but not vice versa, since he could have remained silent and claimed nothing at all. The problem is that there are not two but three possibilities (tertium datur): either I think/say that p, or I think/say that $\neg p$, or I think/say nothing at all about p. Neg-raising is licensed with *puto* because most of the time people can be assumed to be opinionated rather than agnostic, so the third possibility can be disregarded; hence the rarity of the reading without neg-raising. Disregarding the third possibility is the same as accepting the presupposition that the only alternatives are *Putat* (x,p) and *Putat* $(x,\neg p)$. Either p or $\neg p$ is true in all the agent's doxastically accessible worlds. If this presupposition is not triggered, we are left with the reading without neg-raising, in which case either p is not part of the doxastic modal base at all (the doxastic agent has never considered the issue of p) or both p and $\neg p$ are doxastic alternatives for him. In the latter situation p is true in some of his doxastically accessible worlds and false in others. Neg-raising is not licensed with *affirmo* because people can't be assumed always to declare their opinions, so the third possibility cannot simply be disregarded

(17) *Respondebo* me *non* quaerere... quid virtus efficere possit (De Fin 5.79)
Haruspices introducti *responderunt non* fuisse iustum comitiorum rogatorem (ND 2.10)
Non respondit tamen una facere Sullam (Pro Sull 37).

The last example (Pro Sull 37) does not have a reading 'He replied that Sulla was not working with him,' and the other examples are not equivalent to sentences with matrix verb negation (*non responderunt*). If you say 'I didn't think

(17) I will reply that I am not asking what results virtue can produce (De Fin 5.79). Soothsayers were brought in and replied that the election officer had been irregular (ND 2.10). He did not reply that Sulla was working with him (Pro Sull 37).

Sulla was working with him,' I can reasonably deduce that you thought Sulla wasn't working with him; but the most likely inference for me to make on the basis of 'I didn't say Sulla was working with him' is not that you said Sulla wasn't working with him, but that you didn't say anything at all on this issue. Factive verbs, which presuppose rather than assert the truth of the complement clause, do not license neg-raising either

(18) me *non* iam *paenitebat* intercapedinem scribendi fecisse (Ad Fam 16.21.1)
Vos *ne paeniteat* tali civi non perpercisse... providete. (Pro Flacc 104).

Obviously a sentence which presupposes that something has happened and one which presupposes that it hasn't happened have contradictory presuppositions: if I regret that I didn't pass the exam, that is quite different from my not regretting that I did pass the exam, because I didn't. The entailment from downstairs to upstairs negation required for neg-raising is absent. By and large, while neg-raising verbs in English are transparent for both weak and strict negative polarity items in the complement clause ('I don't think that Jack slept at all / a wink'), speech act verbs are transparent only for weak negative polarity items ('I don't claim that Jack slept at all / *a wink'), and factives for neither ('I don't regret that Jack slept *at all / *a wink'). Neg-raising predicates are mostly verbs of modal attitude (opinion, judgement of probability, volition, obligation). They tend to come from the mid range of a scale of modal strength: 'improbable' is neg-raising, but 'impossible' is not. The ease with which any particular verb can license neg-raising seems to depend on quite subtle factors of lexical meaning (compare English 'want' and 'desire'), syntax (nonfinite versus finite complements) and contextual use. A similar problem arises with long adjunct extraction over bridge verbs: 'Where did you say / *declare that the Gauls were defeated?'. Some sort of weak clause union may be involved.

There may also be a pragmatic reason why neg-raising is preferred to negation of the complement clause. Neg-raising attenuates the strength of the negation: it is less direct and explicit than complement clause negation, because the listener has to make an inference (tertium non datur) that is not required for complement clause negation. Instead of saying what a person believes ($\neg p$), one says what he doesn't believe and leaves the listener to infer what he does believe. Speakers like to hedge negation in this way; it is less blunt and transfers some of the responsibility for the negation from the speaker to the listener, who has to take the final inferential step to get to the intended meaning.

Structures for negation

As a working hypothesis, we can assume that predicate (verb phrase) negation is the default, particularly with referential subjects, and that negation with broader scope (sentential negation) and with narrower scope (constituent negation) are

(18) I am no longer sorry that there was an interval in which I didn't write (Ad Fam 16.21.1). Make sure you do not regret not having spared such a citizen (Pro Flacc 104).

marked. Since even nonspecific indefinite objects can appear to the left of the negative

(19) Silius *culcitas non* habet (Ad Att 13.50.5)

there was presumably some mechanism for at least some preverbal phrases to be interpreted within the semantic scope of preverbal negation. Constituent negation is transparent in structures where the negative does not c-command the verb but only the phrase it negates

(20) quod sua mandata perferre *non opportuno tempore* ad Pompeium vererentur (BC 3.57)
equites procul visi *non sine terrore* ab dubiis quinam essent (Livy 4.40.2).

Sentential negation occurs in thetic sentences that do not have an external subject, like existentials without locative inversion

(21) *Non erat* in tam immani iniuria... novae crudelitati locus (De Dom 64)
Non erat conloquii copia (Livy 25.23.5)
Non erat tum ficticium oleum, ideoque arbitror de eo nihil a Catone dictum (NH 15.24).

Sentential negation is also transparent where the negative scopes over two conjoined or asyndetic clauses

(22) *non* alio facinore clari homines, alio obscuri necantur (Pro Mil 17)
Non et legatum argentum est et non est legata numerata pecunia (Top 53)
Non igitur si L. Natta... in equitum centuriis voluit esse... gratiosus, id erit eius vitrico fraudi aut crimini, *nec* si virgo Vestalis... locum suum gladiatorium concessit huic, *non* et illa pie fecit et hic a culpa est remotus (Pro Mur 73).

Marked forms of sentential negation in English are 'It is not the case that...' and 'No way...'. This type of negation is particularly suited to denials, that is to negative sentences which are designed to correct an explicit or implicit proposition in the discourse context, but denials do not exclusively have sentential negation. Sentential negation is in principle a unary operator: we formalize *Non pluit* as $\neg p.p = Pluit.$ It has a contextually determined restriction: if it rains, it does so at

(19) Silius does not have cushions (Ad Att 13.50.5).

(20) Because they were afraid to deliver his message to Pompey at an inopportune time (BC 3.57). The cavalry seen from a distance, not without trepidation on the part of those who did not know who they were (Livy 4.40.2).

(21) There was no room for additional cruelty in so great an injury (De Dom 64). There was no opportunity for a conference (Livy 25.23.5). There was no artificial oil at that time, and I think that is why nothing is said about it by Cato (NH 15.24).

(22) It is not the case that it is one crime for famous men to be killed and a different one for ordinary folks (Pro Mil 17). It is not the case that both silver was bequeathed and coin was not bequeathed (Top 53). So it is not the case that if L. Natta wanted to be popular with the centuries of the knights, that will result in harm or prosecution to his stepfather, nor is it the case that if a Vestal virgin gave my client her seat at the gladiatorial show, both her behaviour was not that of a devoted family member and his was not beyond reproach (Pro Mur 73).

some contextually determined time and location. But this type of restriction is automatic and does not make sentential negation a binary operator. However p may have its own internal informational structure, in which case the negative can interact with the focus, thereby turning the negative into a binary operator. For instance in the third example in (22) (Pro Mur 73), what is negated by the first negative is not the whole first clause but just the words *fraudi aut crimini*.

When it functions in this way as a binary operator, the negative is like a focus particle associating narrowly with some focused constituent of the sentence and leaving the remainder (the cofocus) to go in the presupposition. As usual the focused constituent is the nuclear scope and the presupposition is the restriction, as illustrated in the following set of examples

(23) Quod non dant *proceres*, dabit histrio (Juv 7.90)
$\neg x$ | Dant(x, quod) | x = proceres (subject focus)

Colubra *restem* non parit (Petr 45)
$\neg y$ | Parit(colubra, y) | y = restem (direct object focus)

Ergo lex nobis dat praemium, *tibi* non dat (Quint Decl 345.5)
$\neg z$ | Dat(lex, z, praemium) | z = tibi (indirect object focus)

At hic nuper sororis filio infudit venenum, non *dedit* (Phil 11.13)
$\neg R$ | R(hic, filio, venenum) | R = Dedit (verb focus).

Changing the structure of any example changes its presuppositions. Take the second example (Petr 45: since it is a proverb, it is additionally in the scope of a generic operator). The presupposition is that a snake produces some offspring (which is true); the negative associates with the direct object to exclude a rope from the set of alternate possible offsprings; the proverb has nothing to say about any other animals. If you read the proverb in such a way that the negative associates with the subject rather than with the object, the presupposition is that some animal produces a rope as offspring (which is false), and the proverb says that that animal is not a snake; it has nothing to say about other types of animal progeny. If the negative is read as associating with the verb phrase, the presupposition is that snakes have some generic behaviours (which is true), and the assertion is that producing rope offspring is not one of them. Finally if the negative is read as narrowly associating with the verb, the proverb says that snakes do something with ropes (which is weird), but they don't produce them as offspring; it has nothing to say about alternatives to snakes or alternatives to ropes.

Here is another set of examples, all with the past tense of *proficiscor* 'set out,' to illustrate the negative as a binary operator

(23) An actor will bestow what the leaders of society don't (Juv 7.90). A snake doesn't beget a rope (Petr 45). Therefore the law gives the reward to us, not to you (Quint Decl 345.5). But he recently didn't just give poison to his sister's son, he poured it down his throat (Phil 11.13).

(24) praesertim cum *egomet* in provinciam non sim profectus (Ad Att 1.16.14: subject focus)
non *ad exercitum profectus est* (Verr 2.1.37: verb phrase focus)
In Britanniam te *profectum* non *esse* (Ad Fam 7.17.3: verb phrase focus with scrambling)
non *profectus* est sed profugit (Phil 5.24: verb focus)
non *eo consilio* profectus esse ut insidiaretur in via Clodio (Pro Mil 47: adjunct focus)
Legati non *ante* profecti quam impositos in naves milites viderunt (Livy 34.12.8: adjunct focus)
Profecti sunt legati non *celeri pede* (Phaedr 4.19.6: adjunct constituent negation).

The last example (Phaedr 4.19) shows that in constituent negation too the negative can associate narrowly with a subconstituent, namely the adjective *celeri.*

Negation and entailment

The effect of negation on the meaning of a sentence is not limited to switching its truth value; negation can also affect truth relations between sentences. Consider the relation of entailment. If there are two sentences, S and S′, such that whenever S is true, S′ cannot be false, and whenever S′ is false, S cannot be true, then S is said to entail S′. This happens, for instance, when S′ contains an expression in the restriction of a universal quantifier that is a hyponym of a corresponding expression in S. If it is true that

(25) Omnes vero se *Britanni* vitro inficiunt (BG 5.14),

that entails *omnes se Trinobantes vitro inficiunt*; the Trinobantes in S′ are a subset of the Britanni in S, and if all the Britanni use woad, it follows that all the Trinobantes do so too. Restrictive modification (adjectival or adverbial) generates subsets, thereby creating the potential for entailment relations between sentences

(26) Tres *nobilissimi Haedui* capti ad Caesarem perducuntur (BG 7.67)
C. Marcius... agrum... *late vastavit* (Livy 44.10.5).

'Three most noble Aeduans were captured' entails that (at least) three Aeduans were captured; 'Marcius laid waste to the territory far and wide' entails that he laid waste to the territory. In the first example the sentence remains true when

(24) Particularly since I myself have not left for a province (Ad Att 1.16.14). He did not leave to join the army (Verr 2.1.37). That you have not left for Britain (Ad Fam 7.17.3). He did not leave, he bolted (Phil 5.24). That he did not set out with the deliberate intention of ambushing Clodius on the road (Pro Mil 47). The ambassadors did not leave until they saw the soldiers embarked on the ships (Livy 34.12.8). The envoys left not at a brisk pace (Phaedr 4.19.6).

(25) All the Britons dye themselves with woad (BG 5.14).

(26) Three Aeduans of the highest rank were captured and led to Caesar (BG 7.67). C. Marcius laid waste to the countryside far and wide (Livy 44.10.5).

the denotation of the phrase 'noble Aeduans' is increased (rather than decreased as in (25) above), that is when an expression denoting a set ('Aeduans') replaces an expression denoting one of its subsets ('noble Aeduans'). This is because the set of events in which three or more noble Aeduans are captured is a subset of the set of events in which three or more Aeduans are captured. Where a quantifier is involved, we actually need to distinguish three environments: the second argument of the quantifier (B, the nuclear scope), the first argument of the quantifier (A, the restriction), and the quantifier itself. In the first example in (26) (BG 7.67), the B argument is the verb phrase (*ad Caesarem perducuntur*), the A argument is the subject noun phrase (*nobilissimi Haedui*), and the quantifier itself is *tres*. The direction of entailment (if there is any) in the A and B arguments of the quantifier depends on the semantics of the quantifier, and it need not be the same for both arguments: adding individuals to the restriction is different from adding individuals to the nuclear scope (and indeed from increasing or decreasing the quantifier itself). Upward and downward entailing functions in language are analogous to monotone increasing and decreasing functions in mathematics (the term monotonicity is sometimes used in linguistics too). A function is monotone increasing if it increases steadily as its argument increases: if $x^1 < x^2$, then $f(x^1) < f(x^2)$; and it is monotone decreasing if it steadily decreases as x increases: if $x^1 < x^2$, then $f(x^1) > f(x^2)$. For example, the reciprocal function, $f(x) = 1/x$, is strictly monotone decreasing over its entire domain, whereas the even function (the reciprocal of the square), $f(x) = 1/x^2$, is strictly monotone increasing when x is less than zero and strictly monotone decreasing when x is greater than zero.

A cardinal like *tres* '(at least) three' is upward entailing on both its A and its B arguments, in symbols A↑ and B↑: 'three noble Aeduans were captured' entails, as we have just seen, that (at least) three Aeduans were captured, and 'three Aeduans were captured near Alesia' entails that (at least) three Aeduans were captured. Cardinals modified by the numerical relation 'exactly' do not give rise to entailments on either argument; they block inference in either direction: 'exactly three noble Aeduans were captured' does not entail that exactly three Aeduans were captured (nor vice versa), and 'exactly three Aeduans were captured near Alesia' does not entail that exactly three Aeduans were captured (nor vice versa). The universal quantifier, while upward entailing on its second argument, is downward entailing on its first argument as illustrated in (25), in symbols A↓ and B↑: 'every noble Aeduan was captured near Alesia' entails that every noble Aeduan was captured, but not that every Aeduan was captured near Alesia. For the first argument of the universal quantifier the entailment goes in the opposite direction, from set to subset rather than from subset to set: 'every Aeduan was captured' entails that every noble Aeduan was captured.

A cardinal itself is an intrinsically scalar expression and so downward entailing relative to other cardinals, which we can write in symbols as Q↓: if (at least) three Aeduans were captured, then it is true that at least two Aeduans were captured and indeed that at least one Aeduan was captured. The cardinals form a scale in which each higher cardinal entails its lower cardinals (because two Aeduans is a subset of three Aeduans, etc.). As discussed in Chapter 5, whereas a cardinal *n* entails cardinals <*n*, it implicates the negation of cardinals >*n*: 'three noble Aeduans' entails 'two noble Aeduans' and implicates 'not four noble Aeduans.' Once again, when the cardinal is modified by a numerical relation (*amplius, minus*), the entailments and implications can change. This is so even if the exact cardinality is unknown:

(27) ad viduas tecum *plus minus* ire *decem* (Mart 9.100.4)

may implicate 'not fifteen' but it does not implicate 'not eleven.' Quantifiers other than cardinals also form scales, like *aliquot – complures – omnes* 'some – several – all.' 'Several Aeduans' entails 'some Aeduans' and implicates 'not all Aeduans.' Scalar particles and replacive negation can make the direction of scalar entailment explicit

(28) Semel igitur aut non saepe *certe.* (De Off 2.50)
quae *non* ex una aut duabus *sed* ex multis animi perceptionibus constat (Luc 22)
ut ille... *si non* omnem *at* aliquam partem maeroris sui deponeret (Pro Sest 7).

If you switch the quantifiers in these sentences, you end up with nonsense in the context: 'this can happen often or certainly not once,' 'that consists of not (only) many but one or two mental percepts,' 'that he might escape from all if not some of his sorrow.'

Now look what happens when we put these quantified expressions in the scope of (outer) negation: the direction of entailment and implicature is reversed. The cardinals shift from Q↓ A↑ B↑ to Q↑ A↓ B↓ and the universal quantifier from Q↓ A↓ B↑ to Q↑ A↑ B↓. Let's see how this works; to keep things simple, we will change the reading of 'three Aeduans' from the specific reading it has in Caesar's text to a nonspecific reading that just counts individuals, and we will create a universal quantifier version for comparison. First the A argument

Caesar had three or more noble Aeduan captives → Caesar had three or more Aeduan captives (A↑)
Caesar didn't have three or more Aeduan captives → Caesar didn't have three or more noble Aeduan captives (A↓)

Every Aeduan was captured by Caesar → Every noble Aeduan was captured by Caesar (A↓)
Not every noble Aeduan was captured by Caesar → Not every Aeduan was captured by Caesar (A↑).

(27) To go with you to ten widows, give or take a few (Mart 9.100.4).

(28) So it should be done once or certainly not often (De Off 2.50). That does not consist of one or two but of many mental percepts (Luc 22). That he might escape from if not all then at least some part of his sorrow (Pro Sest 7).

Now the B argument

> Caesar had three or more Aeduan captives at Alesia → Caesar had three or more Aeduan captives (B↑)
> Caesar didn't have three or more Aeduan captives → Caesar didn't have three or more Aeduan captives at Alesia (B↓)
>
> Every Aeduan was captured near Alesia → Every Aeduan was captured (B↑)
> Not every Aeduan was captured → Not every Aeduan was captured near Alesia (B↓).

If Caesar captured three or more noble Aeduans, this remains true if you add in the ignoble Aeduans that got captured. But if Caesar didn't capture three or more Aeduans, he captured less than three Aeduans, and this remains true if you throw out the captured ignoble Aeduans. Here we are using outer negation, ¬Q: 'not at least three' = 'less than three.' Inner negation (Q¬) counts the complement of B relative to A, that is the difference between A and B ($|A - B| = Q$): 'all but Q A are B.' Inner negation has no effect on the entailments of the A argument. If three or more noble Aeduans (A) weren't captured, then it is true that three or more Aeduans (A′) weren't captured. The A entailments are not reversed because $|A'| > |A|$, so that if $|A - B| > n$, $|A' - B| > n$. Inner negation does, however, reverse the entailments of the B argument. If three or more Aeduans weren't captured (escaped capture) anywhere, then it is true that three or more Aeduans weren't captured near Alesia. Here we are dealing with three subsets of A: those Aeduans captured near Alesia (B), those captured elsewhere (C), and those not captured at all (whether near Alesia or elsewhere, $D = D' \cup D''$). The set of captured Aeduans is $B \cup C$, and its complement in A is D. The complement of B in A is $C \cup D$. Obviously D is a subset of $C \cup D$, hence the reversed direction of entailment. This is illustrated in Figure 8.4. Another way to understand the reversal of entailment is to remember that as you decrease the size of a subset you increase the size of its relative complement: $|A-B| > |A-B-C|$.

The quantifier itself has scalar entailments and scalar implicatures, which are reversed by negation (see Figure 8.5). Here are the entailments

> Caesar had three or more Aeduan captives → Caesar had two or more Aeduan captives (Q↓)
> Caesar didn't have three or more Aeduan captives → Caesar didn't have four or more Aeduan captives (Q↑)
>
> Every Aeduan was captured by Caesar → Several Aeduans were captured by Caesar (Q↓)
> Several Aeduans weren't captured by Caesar → Not every Aeduan was captured by Caesar (Q↑).

If there is a set of three Aeduans each member of which got captured by Caesar, then there must also be a set of two captured Aeduans; and if there is no set of three Aeduans each member of which got captured by Caesar, then there cannot

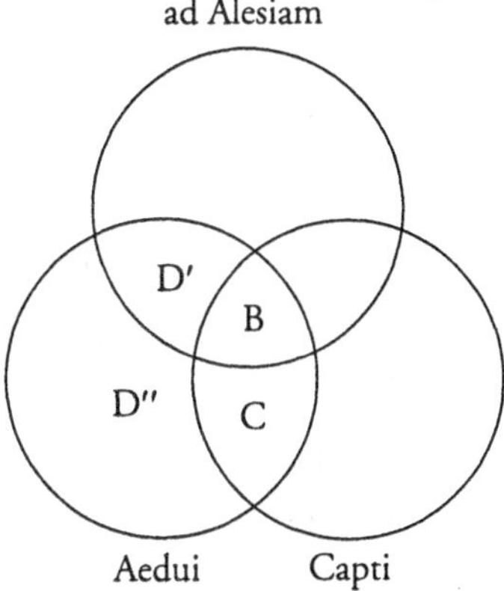

Figure 8.4
Entailments with inner negation: B = Aeduans captured near Alesia; C = Aeduans captured elsewhere; D = Aeduans not captured anywhere (D′+D″)
'Three Aeduans weren't captured (near Alesia)'

be a set of four captured Aeduans. The implicatures of quantifiers in negative sentences can be less precise and harder to compute

Caesar had three Aeduan captives ⇒ Caesar did not have more than three Aeduan captives (Q⇑)
Caesar didn't have three Aeduan captives ⇒ Caesar did have two or one Aeduan captives (Q⇓)

Every Aeduan was captured by Caesar [top of the scale]
Not every Aeduan was captured by Caesar ⇒ Several Aeduans were captured by Caesar (Q⇓).

Negation also reverses entailments with pragmatically based scales. If the dumbest student can pass the test, so can all the others; but if the dumbest student can't pass the test, it does not follow that all the others can't pass either; that would only follow if the smartest student can't pass the test. In the next example a scale of sartorial decorum is correlated with a scale of social prominence:

(29) sed etiam ipse rex... prope seminudus fugiens *militi* quoque nedum *regi* vix decoro habitu, ad flumen navesque perfugerit (Livy 24.40.13).

An outfit that is smart enough for a king is smart enough for a soldier; an outfit that is not smart enough for a soldier is not smart enough for a king (but an outfit that is not smart enough for a king may be smart enough for a soldier).

Quantifiers that are downward entailing on their B argument, and many of those that are downward entailing on their A argument, are either negative or set a quantificational upper limit (a roof). *Aliquis* 'someone' is an existential

(29) But even the king himself fleeing almost half naked in clothes hardly suitable for a simple soldier, let alone a king, escaped to the river and the fleet (Livy 24.40.13).

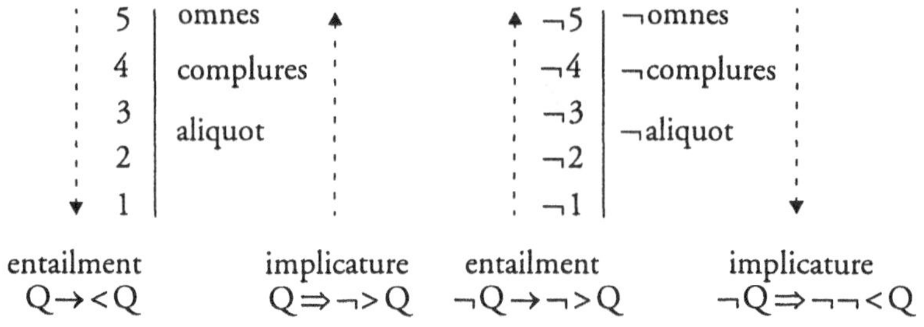

Figure 8.5
Positive and negatives scales for quantifiers

quantifier (∃*x*), and *nemo* 'noone' can be used as a negative existential quantifier (¬∃*x*), so it is not surprising that it reverses the entailments of *aliquis*

(30) quorum *nemo* propter indignitatem repudiatus est (Div Caec 63)
Dixerat *aliquis* leniorem sententiam (BC 1.2).

None were rejected entails that none were rejected on grounds of inadequacy (downward entailment), but none were rejected on grounds of inadequacy does not entail that none were rejected (upward entailment); in fact all were rejected. With *aliquis* in the second example (BC 1.2) the entailments go in the opposite direction: the expression by someone of a milder opinion entails the expression of an opinion (upward entailment) but not vice versa. While *plus* sets a lower limit to a cardinal, *minus* sets an upper limit

(31) *minus sex milia hominum* inde effugerunt (Livy 31.21.16)
Hostium plus quinque milia caesa eo die (Livy 23.46.4: app. crit.).

Let's try changing the A arguments: if less than six thousand men escaped, then less than six thousand cavalrymen escaped (downward entailment), but not vice versa. If more than five thousand enemies were killed, then more than five thousand men were killed (upward entailment), but not vice versa. The same pattern is discernible with vague cardinals, provided we abstract away from context sensitivity. Here are a couple of examples with adverbs

(32) *Raro* geminos parit. (NH 8.168)
Iuppiter... *saepe*... immoderatis tempestatibus... hominibus nocuit (Pro Rosc Am 131).

If it rarely gives birth, then it rarely (in absolute terms) gives birth to twins, but not necessarily vice versa. If Jupiter has often (in absolute terms) harmed men

(30) None of them was rejected on grounds of inadequacy (Div Caec 63). Some had expressed a milder opinion (BC 1.2).

(31) Less than six thousand men escaped from there (Livy 31.21.16). More than five thousand of the enemy were killed that day (Livy 23.46.4).

(32) It rarely has twins (NH 8.168). Jupiter has often harmed men with violent storms (Pro Rosc Am 131).

with violent storms, then he has often harmed men with storms, but not necessarily vice versa.

Subsets can also be created by verb phrase conjunction (set intersection) and supersets by verb phrase disjunction (set union). *Capti et interfecti sunt* (cp. BHisp 13) intersects the set of captured soldiers with the set of killed soldiers and gives the set of soldiers that were both captured and killed. *Caesi aut capti sunt* (cp. Livy 24.16.4) joins the set of killed soldiers with the set of captured soldiers into a superset containing all soldiers that were either killed or captured. When a quantifier is upward entailing, the direction of inference is from a single predicate to a disjunction: if at least three soldiers were killed, then at least three soldiers were killed or captured (maybe more). When a quantifier is downward entailing, the direction of inference is from a single predicate to a conjunction: if at most three soldiers were killed, then at most three soldiers were captured and killed (maybe less).

As already noted, whether a quantifier is upward or downward entailing depends on its lexical meaning. Consider the case of the B set. For an upward entailing quantifier like 'at least three,' adding individuals to the B set, whether by substituting a hypernym, removing a modifier or adding a disjunct, cannot make the new sentence untrue, because it does not change the minimum cardinality of the intersection of the A set with the B set (which is what is counted by the quantifier); subtracting individuals potentially changes the truth value. For a downward entailing quantifier like 'at most three,' subtracting individuals from the B set by substituting a hyponym, adding a modifier or adding a conjunct, cannot make the new sentence untrue because it does not change the maximum cardinality of the intersection of the A set with the B set; adding individuals potentially changes the truth value. As for the quantifier itself, changing it to a lower quantifier maintains truth ('at least two' is true if 'at least three' is true), since any property that characterizes all members of a set must also characterize some members of that set; changing it to a higher quantifier potentially changes the truth value. Negation itself, as we have seen, has the effect of reversing the direction of entailment; this is because it changes increases in the B set into decreases in the complement of B relative to the A set (A– B) and vice versa. So 'At least three soldiers were captured' does not entail 'At least three soldiers were captured and killed,' but 'At least three soldiers weren't captured' does entail 'At least three soldiers weren't captured and killed'; the intersection in the B set reduces the size of the B set and correspondingly increases the size of the set A– B.

So far we have been dealing mainly with quantifiers, but verbs, adjectives and prepositions are also functions that can create entailment relations. Most of the time these functions are upward entailing, but a few like *carere* 'lack,' *vacuus* 'free from' and *sine* 'without,' which have a negative flavour and are often used intensionally, are downward entailing. In either case, negation reverses the direction of entailment

(33) immoderatis epulis *caret* senectus (De Sen 44)
quaeque *nec* hoste fero nec nive, terra, *cares* (Ov Ex Pont 3.1.2)
in macra tenues et *vacuae* fructu veniunt (Col 3.2.21)
nec ullum... consilium periculo *vacuum* inveniri potest (Ad Att 10.8.5)
Accepi Roma *sine* epistula tua fasciculum litterarum (Ad Att 5.17.1)
Non cenat *sine* apro noster, Tite, Caecilianus (Mart 7.59.1).

Carere is downward entailing (*epulis caret* → *immoderatis epulis caret*), but in the scope of a negative it is upward entailing (*nec hoste fero cares* → *nec hoste cares*). The set of fierce enemies is a subset of the set of enemies; the set of those lacking a fierce enemy is a superset of the set of those lacking an enemy, while the set of those having (or not lacking) a fierce enemy is a subset of the set of those having an enemy; the proposition 'You lack an enemy' entails the proposition 'You lack a fierce enemy,' while the proposition 'You have (don't lack) an enemy' is entailed by the proposition 'You have a fierce enemy.' *Vacuus* is downward entailing (*vacuae fructu* → *vacuae fructu maturo*), but in the scope of a negative it is upward entailing (*nec magno periculo vacuum* → *nec periculo vacuum*). *Sine* is downward entailing (*sine epistula* → *sine epistula tua*), but in the scope of a negative it is upward entailing (*non sine apro* → *non sine venatione*). As in the multiplication of positive and negative numbers, two minuses give you a plus, but an odd number of minuses gives you a minus.

Negative polarity indefinites

The effect of negation on patterns of inference in natural language is an interesting topic in its own right (particularly for logicians), but it is also very important for our understanding of grammar, because many languages, including Latin and English, have a special series of pronouns that occur mainly (though not entirely) in downward entailing contexts, that is in the scope of negatives and other downward entailing operators. So corresponding to the indefinites *aliquis* 'someone,' *aliqui* 'some,' *aliquando* 'sometimes,' *alicubi* 'somewhere,' *aliquo* 'to some place,' Latin has the strong negative polarity indefinites *quisquam* 'anyone,' *ullus* 'any,' *umquam* 'ever,' *usquam* 'anywhere,' *quoquam* 'to any place.' The bare forms *quis, qui, quando, ubi, quo* are used as weak negative polarity indefinites (and also as simple existentials in nonepisodic contexts). The distinction between the strong and the weak forms corresponds roughly to the distinction between stressed and unstressed negative polarity *any* in English, where the stressed form tends to be more strongly scalar while the unstressed form just allows for an empty set. For clarity of exposition we prefer to use strong forms in the examples. (Do not confuse this distinction with the distinction between weak and strong, also called "strict," negative polarity items, which

(33) Old age does without excessive banquets (De Sen 44). Land which is never without wild enemies or snow (Ov Ex Pont 3.1.2). In poor soil they come up thin and devoid of fruit (Col 3.2.21). No plan free of danger can be found (Ad Att 10.8.5). I received a bundle of letters from Rome without a note from you (Ad Att 5.17.1). Our friend Caecilianus never dines without a boar, Titus (Mart 7.59.1).

classifies all negative polarity items, not just indefinites, according to the degree of negativity of their licensing contexts.)

In the following examples the downward entailing context is created by the negative operator

(34) *(Non) vetat hoc *quisquam.* (Ov Trist 3.3.67)
*(Non) novi *quemquam* cuius ingenio populus Romanus pertinacius ignoverit. (Sen Con 10.pr.2).

As indicated by the asterisk outside the parenthesis, the examples are ungrammatical without the negative, just as English 'I have known anyone' is ungrammatical. Next a couple of examples in which the negative polarity item is licensed by a negative quantifier

(35) Nemo/*aliquis apud me *quemquam* sinistris sermonibus carpit (Pliny Ep 1.9.5)
nihil/*aliquid *cuiquam* doluit (De Or 1.230).

The negative polarity item is not licensed by the corresponding indefinite; similarly in English you cannot say 'Something upset anyone.' In the last set of examples a negative polarity item is licensed by a downward entailing vague cardinal adverb

(36) raro/*saepe *unquam* nix minus quattuor pedes alta iacuit (Livy 21.61.10)
et raro/*saepe *quisquam* erga bona sua satis cautus est (Curt Ruf 10.1.40).

Similarly in English 'The snow was rarely/*often anywhere less than four feet deep.' As we have seen, if a downward entailing function is itself in a downward entailing context, the result is an overall upward entailing context, and this is reflected in the distribution of negative polarity items

(37) sine timore *ullo* (BG 8.3)
non sine tepore *aliquo* (Col 7.8.3);

$[\text{non}]^- [\text{sine}]^- \rightarrow [\text{non sine}]^+$. A biclausal context induces variation in the application of this rule, since the indefinite may be inside or outside the scope of a superordinate operator

(38) negaret *ullas* in Oceano... esse terras habitabiles (Sen Suas 1.10)
veri esse *aliquid* non negamus (Luc 73)
Non possum negare prodesse *ullam* scientiam (De Or 1.250).

(34) It is not the case that anyone forbids this (Ov Trist 3.3.67). I don't know anyone whose abilities the Roman people more obstinately made allowances for (Sen Con 10.pr.2).

(35) Noone criticizes anyone to me with adverse talk (Pliny Ep 1.9.5). Nothing upset anyone (De Or 1.230).

(36) The snow rarely ever lay less than four feet deep (Livy 21.61.10). Rarely is anyone sufficiently cautious with respect to his own success (Curt Ruf 10.1.40).

(37) Without any fear (BG 8.3). Not without some heat (Col 7.8.3).

(38) He said that there were no inhabitable lands in the Ocean (Sen Suas 1.10). We do not deny that some truth exists (Luc 73). I cannot deny that there is any knowledge that is useful (De Or 1.250).

Biclausal variation with *nego* is discussed further below: see the examples in (47). For a negative polarity indefinite to be licensed, it normally has to be not only in the semantic scope of a downward entailing function but also in its syntactic scope (therefore c-commanded by and linearly to the right of its licensor). But infinitival complements can raise to the left of the licensing verb

(39) violare *quemquam vetiti* (Livy 24.1.4)
iam novi *quidquam* exspectare *desieramus* (Ad Fam 8.4.4).

Conversely negative polarity indefinites can be quite deeply embedded below their licensor, as in the following example with neg-raising

(40) Ego... *non* existimo tam omnes deos aversos esse a salute populi Romani ut Octavius orandus sit pro salute *cuiusquam* civis (Ad Brut 24.2).

So the question that faces us is: What is it about negative polarity indefinites like *quisquam* that makes them ungrammatical in the non-downward entailing examples above? What exactly is wrong with 'I have known anyone'? (This is not the same question as: What is it about regular indefinite pronouns like *aliquis* that allows them to appear in a clause containing a downward entailing operator? We will tackle this second question later.) The most likely answer is that a negative polarity indefinite is a sort of grammaticalized minimizer, and minimizers are not adequately informative in non-downward entailing contexts. Minimizers are a class of often idiomatic expressions that denote the lowest element on a scale, a minimal quantity

(41) *neque* pertinet *hilum* (Lucr 3.830)
Ego quae tu loquere *flocci non* facio, senex (Pl Rud 782)
non habeo denique *nauci* Marsum augurem (De Div 1.132)
ne punctum quidem temporis oppugnatio respiravit (Phil 8.20)
qui fatentur se virtutis causa... *ne manum* quidem versuros fuisse (De Fin 5.93)
ab ista *non pedem* discedat (Pl Asin 603)
qui *non* valet *lotium* suum (Petr 57)
ab hac mihi *non* licet *transversum*, ut aiunt, *digitum* discedere (Luc 58).

As the examples show, minimizers are often, though not necessarily exclusively, used with negatives to express the absence of even the smallest conceivable amount. In this use they are negative polarity items: *non digitum transversum*

(39) Not allowed to injure anyone (Livy 24.1.4). I had already ceased to expect anything new (Ad Fam 8.4.4).

(40) I do not think that all the gods are so unfavourable to the wellbeing of the Roman people that Octavius needs to be begged for the safety of any citizen (Ad Brut 24.2).

(41) It doesn't matter a bit (Lucr 3.830). I don't give a damn about what you're saying, old fellow (Pl Rud 782). In short I don't give a cent for Marsian augurs (De Div 1.132). The siege did not let up even for a moment (Phil 8.20). Who admit that they wouldn't lift a finger for the sake of virtue (De Fin 5.93). He wouldn't move an inch from her (Pl Asin 603). Who's not worth the price of his own pee (Petr 57). I can't budge an inch from this, as the saying goes (Luc 58).

discedere means 'not to budge an inch,' which is the smallest amount one can budge. The idea that negative polarity indefinites are minimizers is supported by the etymology of *ullus*, which is said to be derived from the cardinal 'one' like English *any*: *(n)ullus* < **(ne)oinelos*. With a mass noun *ullus* can be paraphrased by *vel minimus* in a negative polarity context

(42) Quis hoc dixit *umquam* aut quae fuit istius rei *vel minima* suspicio? (Pro Sull 60)
Quodsi... *vel minima* res reperietur (Pro Rosc Am 8).

Negative polarity indefinites can be strengthened by the degree adverb *omnino* 'at all,' which reinforces minimizers by broadening the domain of quantification so as to exclude any possible exceptions

(43) neque *quisquam omnino* consisteret (BC 3.69)
Negabat genus hoc orationis *quidquam omnino* ad levandam aegritudinem pertinere (Tusc 3.60)
ulla omnino navis (BG 5.23)
ullam omnino veritatis notam (Luc 33).

In the third example for instance (BG 5.23), the strength of the negative assertion increases as the set of ships in the domain of quantification is increased.

Now consider a negative polarity minimizer expression like 'sleep a wink.' In a negative (downward entailing) context, it makes perfect sense to say that you didn't sleep a wink, that is you didn't have even the smallest conceivable (possibly idealized and conventionalized) amount of shut-eye. But in a positive (upward entailing) context, 'a wink' doesn't contribute any information. Hardly anyone actually sleeps just a wink: if you slept a wink, you must have slept more than a wink, so why not say so? After all, if you have three children and someone asks you how many kids you have, you don't answer 'Two.' That would be true, but insufficiently informative. Having three children entails having two children, and sleeping a bit entails sleeping a wink. So in a positive context, the contribution of a minimizer is so weak as to be vacuous; it hardly restricts the possibilities (set of possible worlds) at all. In a negative context, it makes the strongest possible claim (the least likely assertion): you did not budge even the smallest amount (an inch), which is the easiest amount for anyone to budge; any budge at all entails budging an inch. Negating the end of the scale entails negating the rest of the scale too. On the other hand, saying 'He didn't budge two inches' leaves open the possibility (or even implicates) that he did budge one inch and so is not equivalent to the simple negative 'He didn't budge.' In short, budging two inches entails, is more informative than and less likely than budg-

(42) Is there anyone who ever said that or even the slightest suspicion of such an event? (Pro Sull 60). But if even the slightest piece of evidence is found (Pro Rosc Am 8).

(43) And noone at all stopped (BC 3.69). He said that this sort of speech was not at all relevant to the relief of distress (Tusc 3.60). Any ship at all (BG 5.23). Any mark of truth at all (Luc 33).

ing an inch, whereas not budging an inch entails, is more informative than and less likely than not budging two inches.

What is important is the scalar entailment, not the physical direction of the scale. Sometimes it is the maximum end of the scale that gives the most likely event

(44) nemo umquam *post hominum memoriam* (Verr 1.32)
Nihil *post hominum memoriam* gloriosius (Ad Fam 10.16.1)
quod *post hominum memoriam* numquam est factum (BHisp 15).

To say that something has happened in a gazillion years is rather vacuous. Other examples are 'I wouldn't touch it with a barge pole' and 'Wild horses wouldn't make me do that.' So if negative polarity indefinites are a less emphatic type of minimizer that have become grammaticalized in downward entailing contexts, that would account for their not being acceptable outside those contexts. Minimizers squeak by in counterassertions ('I DID budge an inch, rather more actually'), while negative polarity indefinites are excluded in counterassertions (*'I DID see anyone'), probably because the grammar supplies a separate existential indefinite (*someone*). The presence of a negative with a positive polarity item is just as vacuous as its absence with a negative polarity item. Positive polarity items shun (are antilicensed by) a negative context. Here is an example

(45) *Croeso divitior* licet fuissem, *Iro pauperior* forem, Charine (Mart 5.39.8).

You can usefully say of someone (Bill Gates or Onassis, for instance) that he is richer than Croesus or of someone else (a beggar on the street, for instance) that he is poorer than Irus, but it is vacuous to say that someone isn't richer than Croesus or isn't poorer than Irus (except as a denial of a previous assertion or of an implicit assumption), since both are true of almost everyone.

Negative polarity indefinites are licensed not only by negatives but also by other downward entailing quantifiers, as illustrated in (36) above. These are "roofing" quantifiers like *raro* 'seldom,' *minus sex milia* 'less than six thousand,' that count the maximum number of entities for which the claim can truthfully be made (and negate the rest). Such claims are stronger if even borderline cases are included, and if the domain of quantification is as broad as possible. Consequently, like negatives, roofing quantifiers are often reinforced by expressions that widen the domain of location or time or both: *raro usquam* (Livy 3.38.10), *raro umquam* (Livy 21.61.10), *raro omnino* (Lucr 6.448). Domain widening with upward entailing quantifiers seems vacuous: 'more than six thousand men were killed anywhere.' Note that it is the direction of entailment and not merely the availability of a negative paraphrase that is significant: if *raro* can be roughly paraphrased as *non saepe*, so can *saepe* as *non raro*; but while *raro nec nisi* means 'seldom except,' *saepe nec nisi* does not mean 'often except.' An interesting piece

(44) Noone ever as far back as anyone can remember (Verr 1.32). Nothing more glorious ever (Ad Fam 10.16.1). A quite unprecedented action (BHisp 15).

(45) Even if I had been richer than Croesus, Charinus, I would be poorer than Irus (Mart 5.39.8).

of syntactic evidence is offered by inversion in English: 'Never have I seen...', 'Rarely have I seen...', *'Often have I seen...'. 'Rarely' entails 'not always' and implicates 'sometimes'; this implicature can easily be cancelled by saying 'rarely if ever,' which overtly includes a component of modality and is nonveridical. 'Rarely if ever *p*' does not entail the truth of *p*: *vel raro vel numquam* (Tac Dial 35.5), cp. *nemo aut paucissimi* (Pliny Ep 5.15.2). So while *saepe* makes an existential assertion about events (it is always veridical), *raro* involves a weaker existential commitment (it is potentially not veridical, so also a weaker form of negative) and *numquam* 'never' is an outright existential negation (it is antiveridical). Quantifiers that represent universals like 'every' and 'no' have additional entailments.

Coordinated sentences with 'no' can be turned into a single sentence with verb phrase disjunction: if 'No soldier was captured, and no soldier was killed,' then 'No soldier was captured or killed': $Q(B) \wedge Q(C) = Q(B \cup C)$. Joining the empty set (the complement of B) with the empty set (the complement of C) just gives you the empty set again. The same does not apply to a nonuniversal downward entailing quantifier like 'at most three.' 'At most three soldiers were captured, and at most three soldiers were killed' does not entail 'At most three soldiers were captured or killed.' Joining two sets of at most three soldiers could give you a set of four soldiers for instance. If the cardinality of the intersection of the set of soldiers and the set of those killed is at most three, and the cardinality of the intersection of the set of soldiers and the set of those captured is at most three, it does not follow that the cardinality of the set of soldiers that is the union of the sets of those captured and those killed should also be at most three. In this sense negation is stronger than simple downward entailment.

Although negative polarity indefinites need to be licensed, they are not in surface complementary distribution with regular indefinites: *Quicquam habeo* 'I have anything' is not a grammatical sentence, but *Aliquid non habeo* 'I don't have something' is grammatical if the indefinite can be interpreted outside the scope of the negative ($\exists x \neg$ rather than $\neg \exists x$)

(46) Dicitur enim alio modo etiam carere cum *aliquid non* habeas et non habere te sentias (Tusc 1.88)
Ratiocinatio est autem diligens et considerata faciendi *aliquid* aut *non* faciendi excogitatio. (De Inv 2.18).

Outer negation of the existential ($\neg \exists x$) equals inner negation of the universal ($\forall x \neg$). So for *non habes quicquam*, if I range through all things, I will not find anything that you have (which makes you destitute); for *aliquid non habes*, on the other hand, if I range through all things, I will find something that you don't have (which implicates that you are quite affluent). The scopal difference is correlated with a difference in licensing anaphora: 'I don't have *anything/something. It is

(46) For 'to lack' is being used in a different sense when you don't have something and are aware that you don't have it (Tusc 1.88). But premeditation is careful and considered reasoning about doing something or not (De Inv 2.18).

a Ferrari.' Since the indefinite is outside the scope of negation, its existence is not negated and it can be picked up by a pronoun in the next sentence.

It is also possible for an indefinite to be outside the scope of negation when the negation is in some sense extraclausal (that is not to the right of the existential, as in the examples just given, but somehow too far to the left). This can happen with a lexically negative verb

(47) illuc unde *negant* redire *quemquam* (Catull 3.12)
Praeterea servum qui *negat* dare *aliquando* domino beneficium ignarus est iuris humani. (Sen De Ben 3.18.2).

As we have already seen, *nego* lexicalizes the inner negation of the matrix verb (M¬); outer negation of the matrix verb (¬M) is expressed by *non dico*. In the first example (Catull 3.12) the negative is part of the complement clause and scopes over it: they say that not anyone returns from that place. The second example (De Ben 3.18) is a denial of the assertion *Servus dat aliquando domino beneficium*. The negative does not directly negate the existential quantifier *aliquando* but somehow applies to the whole proposition: 'he says that it is not the case that sometimes.' This may be truthconditionally equivalent to 'he denies that ever,' but denial is pragmatically different from simple negation, and the minimizer component of the negative polarity indefinite is absent. Notice how a nonspecific indefinite is licensed in a denial of expectation like 'She DIDN'T buy something after all' and how, conversely, a negative polarity expression is not licensed in a counterassertion like '*He did NOT budge an inch.'

The same sort of thing seems to be happening in negative purpose clauses

(48) eamque oblinito et inpicato diligenter, *ne quicquam* aquae introire possit (Col 12.29.1)
ne praeterirem *aliquid* quod ad argumentum... reperiendum pertineret (Top 100)
ne relinquatur *aliquid* erroris in verbo (Tusc 1.88).

In the first example (Col 12.29) the negative polarity indefinite *quicquam* is licensed by *ne*. In the second example the regular indefinite *aliquid* is not outside the scope of the negation: that would mean that it was Cicero's objective to have something that he failed to pass over. Rather a world or situation in which there exists something that is passed over is not one of the situations that conform to Cicero's objectives. Again the negative does not apply directly to the indefinite *aliquid* but at some higher level ('so as to avoid a situation arising in which there is something that is passed over').

(47) To that place from where they say that noone returns (Catull 3.12). Moreover he who denies that a slave can sometimes give a benefit to his master is ignorant of the laws of humanity (Sen De Ben 3.18.2).

(48) Smear it and cover it carefully with pitch, so that no water can enter (Col 12.29.1). So as not to pass over something that was relevant to the discovery of arguments (Top 100). So as to avoid some residual error in the use of the word (Tusc 1.88).

With the downward entailing quantifier *raro* a negative polarity item is licensed but not required in the description of the event

(49) *Raro* enim *quis* iterum vel ad summum tertio hoc accepto medicamento vexatus est (Scrib Larg 122)
raro quisquam ager ita situs est ut uno semine contenti esse possimus (Col 2.6.4)
Raro enim *aliquis*, priusquam se suosque tradat medico, diligenter de eo iudicat (Scrib Larg ep. 9).

According to the view adopted here, this is because, as already noted, *raro* has positive as well as negative implicatures; it is less strongly negative than *numquam*. The event does (or at least can) occur but hardly ever: 'He never says anything/*something,' 'He rarely says anything/something.'

Further contexts for negative polarity indefinites

So far we have dealt with the negative (*non*), negative quantifiers (*nemo, nihil*) and downward entailing quantifiers (*raro*) as licensors of negative polarity indefinites. We have seen that a negative polarity item ceases to be grammatical if a nonintensional episodic sentence is changed from negative to affirmative by removing the negative. For instance the minimizer *at all* is a negative polarity item: we can say 'It didn't help at all,' but not *'It helped at all.' However the contexts just noted do not exhaust the list of contexts that license negative polarity items. We can also say: 'If it helps at all,' 'Whenever it helps at all,' 'I'm surprised it helped at all,' 'Who ever helped at all?', 'Everyone who helped at all,' and so on. None of these contexts contains an overt negative, so the question is what licenses the negative polarity item, especially as regular indefinites are also fine ('Everyone who did anything/something to help'). Let us briefly look at some of the contexts in question; we don't have the space to cover them all.

Restriction of the universal quantifier

Negative polarity items are licensed in the restriction (A argument) of the universal quantifier. So we find the domain widener *umquam* 'ever'

(50) *omnium* qui *umquam* fuere Macedoniae regum (Livy 40.13.3)
omnes qui *umquam* amatores fuerunt vicisti amando (Fronto Aur 2.2.1),

and negative polarity indefinites

(49) It rarely happens that anyone who takes this medicine has symptoms twice or at the most three times (Scrib Larg 122). Rarely is any field located in such a way that we can be content with a single type of seed (Col 2.6.4). For it rarely happens that someone diligently evaluates a doctor before entrusting himself and his family to him (Scrib Larg ep.9).

(50) Of absolutely every Macedonian king there has ever been (Livy 40.13.3). You have surpassed in loving all those who have ever been lovers (Fronto Aur 2.2.1).

(51) *omnia* quae *quisquam* in illo contubernio locutus est (Sen Ep 33.4)
omnes... qui *ullam* agri glebam possiderent (Verr 2.3.28)
omnibus quae pati corpus *ullum* potest suppliciis (Livy 29.9.10).

The effect of *umquam* is to ensure that the domain of quantification includes all possible different times as well as different individuals: for all individuals x and all times t, such that x was a king of Macedonia at any time t. The negative polarity indefinites also serve to ensure exhaustive quantification, sometimes by expressing the endpoint of a scale: 'even a single clod of earth.' The listener is asked to range through the domain of quantification and to be sure to pick out each individual in the restriction, even those that only minimally satisfy it; it may even turn out that there are no such individuals. (By contrast a universal quantifier like *ambo* 'both' involves existential presupposition and does not license negative polarity items.) As already noted, the A argument of a universal quantifier is a downward entailing context: 'every Gaul' entails 'every Nervian,' but not vice versa. However it does not follow that every indefinite in the restriction of a universal quantifier has to refer to a scalar endpoint: a simple existential is also licensed

(52) *omnes* qui *aliquid* scire videntur (Parad 40)
omnia quae putes *aliquam* spem mihi posse adferre mutandarum rerum (Ad Att 3.7.3).

Apparent exceptions to downward entailment of the A argument of a universal quantifier arise from failure to recognize a covert restriction on the domain of quantification, given existential presupposition

(53) Intus autem *omne ovum volucrum* bicolor (NH 10.144).

'Every student has a laptop' entails 'Every male student has a laptop,' but 'Every egg of a bird has two colours' does not entail 'Every egg of a male bird has two colours': $\forall x. C(x) \wedge P(x) \rightarrow Q(x) \neq \forall x. C'(x) \wedge P(x) \rightarrow Q(x)$.

Comparatives

A negative polarity item is not licensed in the clausal complement of an adjective unless that adjective is downward entailing

(54) ad id tempus quo vobis *aequum* possit videri dare vos *aliquam* senectuti meae requiem (Suet 3.24.2)
etenim erat *iniquum* homini proscripto egenti de fraternis bonis *quicquam* dari (Verr 2.1.123).

(51) Everything that anyone has said in that club (Sen Ep 33.4). All those who owned any clod of land (Verr 2.3.28). With every torture that any body can suffer (Livy 29.9.10).

(52) Everyone who seems to know something (Parad 40). Everything which you think can bring me some hope of a change (Ad Att 3.7.3).

(53) On the inside however all bird eggs have two colours (NH 10.144).

(54) To that time at which it may seem fair to you for you to give some repose to my old age (Suet 3.24.2). It would of course have been totally unfair for anything from his brother's estate to be given to a proscribed man in need (Verr 2.1.123).

However a negative polarity item is licensed in a comparative phrase or clause with *quam* after all adjectives. So we find *umquam*, the negative polarity indefinite for times

(55) et *saepius* et plurium *quam* quisquam *umquam* dierum supplicationes impetravit (Suet 1.24.3),

the negative polarity pronoun *quisquam*

(56) *Latius* patet illius sceleris contagio *quam quisquam* putat (Pro Mur 78)
ut *maior* fortiorque sis *quam quisquam* (Curt Ruf 7.8.21),

and the negative polarity pronominal adjective *ullus*

(57) *libidinosior* es *quam ullus* spado (Quint 6.3.64)
maiores enim *quam ulli* insani efficerent motus somniantes (De Div 2.122).

Consider the following pair of examples from the Verrines

(58) Tu *innocentior* es *quam Metellus*...? (Verr 2.3.43)
Ac videte quanto *taetrior* hic tyrannus Syracusanis fuerit *quam quisquam* superiorum (Verr 2.4.123).

In the first example (Verr 3.43) the standard of comparison is another individual: Cicero asks if the degree on the scale of uprightness attained by Verres is greater than the (unique maximal) degree attained by Metellus. In the second example (Verr 4.123) the listener is told that if he ranges through the entire set of Verres' predecessors, he will find that the degree on the scale of tyrannical monstrosity attained by Verres greatly (*quanto*) exceeds even the degree attained by the most monstrous of his predecessors and consequently the degrees attained by all the others as well. Reference to the high endpoint of a scale entails universal quantification over all degrees lower in the scale, and so over all individuals associated with those lower degrees. If Verres had been less (rather than more) monstrous than any of his predecessors, the negative polarity indefinite would have picked out the lowest rather than the highest point on the scale. The most monstrous predecessor is the one most likely to be more monstrous than Verres; and the least monstrous predecessor is the one most likely to be less monstrous than Verres (if Verres is less monstrous than any of his predecessors). The interesting Quintilian example in (57) works in the same way; the joke lies in the inappropriate choice of comparison class (it is like 'taller than any dwarf').

(55) He managed to get victory thanksgivings more often and lasting more days than anyone ever before (Suet 1.24.3).

(56) The infection of his crime is more widespread than anyone thinks (Pro Mur 78). Even if you are greater and braver than anyone else (Curt Ruf 7.8.21).

(57) Your sex drive is greater than that of any eunuch (Quint 6.3.64). For they would behave more crazily than any madmen while dreaming (De Div 2.122).

(58) Are you more blameless than Metellus? (Verr 2.3.43). Observe how much more awful this tyrant was for the Syracusans than any of their earlier ones (Verr 2.4.123).

Instead of picking out the scalar endpoint of the comparison set, it is also possible to exclude the set as a whole

(59) *gravior* habenda *quam reliqua omnia* (De Off 3.35)
omnibus quae umquam in mari visa sunt *mirabiliorem* (NH 36.70: app. crit.)

or an arbitrarily chosen member of the set, as in the following nominal comparative

(60) *asperior quovis* aequore frater erat (Ov Fast 3.578).

Here the free choice indefinite induces universal quantification over an exceptionless domain. A simple indefinite pronoun is also licensed

(61) mundum universum *pluris* esse necesse est *quam* partem *aliquam* universi (ND 2.32).

If the standard of comparison in a *quam*-clause was in a downward entailing context, that would explain the licensing of negative polarity items and the occurrence in some Romance languages and in Cockney English of a pleonastic negative. The most likely view is that the entailments of the *quam*-clause depend on the A argument entailments of the quantifier. For instance the universal quantifier and the plural definite article are downward entailing: 'braver than (all) the soldiers' entails 'braver than (all) the Roman soldiers,' because 'The soldiers were not brave to that degree' entails 'The Roman soldiers were not brave to that degree.' 'Braver than exactly three (Roman) soldiers' is non-monotonic. 'Braver than some (Roman) soldiers' (see (61)) is upward entailing: there are some (Roman) soldiers who are not brave to that degree. 'Braver than any (Roman) soldier' is downward entailing. If there is not even a single soldier who is brave to that degree, then there is not even a single Roman soldier who is brave to that degree: in the formalism of Chapter 7, $\neg\exists x.\text{Soldier}(x) \wedge \delta^P(x) > \delta^P(y)$, equivalent to $\forall x.\text{Soldier}(x) \rightarrow \delta^P(y) > \delta^P(x)$. Some care is required with indefinites; here is a phrasal example to illustrate. The Cyclops calls Galatea

(62) *feta truculentior ursa* (Ov Met 13.803).

If this is (wrongly) given a specific reading, it means that she was fiercer than some she-bear with young that he had recently seen; in that case the context would be non-monotonic, since there is no subset of a single individual. If it is (correctly) given a generic reading, the direction of entailment depends on whether the modifier increases or decreases the typical degree of fierceness: 'fiercer than a typical bear with young' entails 'fiercer than a typical bear,' but 'fiercer than a typical bear under sedation' is entailed by 'fiercer than a typical bear.'

(59) Having greater weight than everything else (De Off 3.35). More wonderful than everything that has ever been seen at sea (NH 36.70).
(60) Her brother was harsher than any sea (Ov Fast 3.578).
(61) The whole universe is necessarily worth more than some part of the universe (ND 2.32).
(62) Fiercer than a she-bear with young (Ov Met 13.803).

Temporal clauses

Consider the following pair of examples

(63) *Postquam* consules... profecti in provincias sunt, tum T. Quinctius postulavit... (Livy 34.57.1)
Priusquam in provincias praetores irent, certamen... fuit (Livy 37.51.1).

Abstracting away from the complicating issue of (f)actuality, *postquam* is upward entailing ('after capturing a noble Aeduan' entails 'after capturing an Aeduan'), while *priusquam* is downward entailing ('before capturing an Aeduan' entails 'before capturing a noble Aeduan'): if you have already captured a member of set A, then you have already captured a member of its superset A′, but if you have not yet captured a member of superset A′, then you have not yet captured a member of set A. Note also how *priusquam* reverses the direction of entailment on the cardinality scale: after capturing four Aeduans entails after capturing three Aeduans, but before capturing three Aeduans entails before capturing four Aeduans. Like comparatives, temporal clauses of precedence can license pleonastic negation in some languages.

As is clear from examples of the corresponding prepositions with event noun complements

(64) ante *mentionem ullam* (Livy 4.59.11)
ante *ullam curationem* (Cels 5.26.25B)
post *multas preces* (Suet 4.27.2)
post *multas vomitiones* (NH 20.34)

the relation of relative earliness applies to the times of events ($\tau(e)$), not to the participants in those events: with free variables $P(e^1) \wedge Q(e^2) \wedge \tau(e^1) < \tau(e^2)$. The interpretation of this is straightforward with punctual events, which involve just a single point of time. With accomplishments, the right hand edge (culmination point) of the $\tau(e^2)$ interval is often used ('before capturing the city'), while activities elicit the left hand edge ('before besieging the city'). The fact that *prius* is a comparative form (cp. *prae*) and *quam* is the same complementizer that is used in clausal comparatives suggests that the time line is treated as a scale, with points of time as degrees: earlier times are lower on this scale than later times, so it is a scale of earliness (*prius*) and lateness (*post*). In the simplest situation there are just two single events *P* and *Q* and the time of *P* is lower on the scale than the time of *Q*. Negative polarity items quantify over sets of participants (or portions of masses), which complicates the picture: for each member of the plural set in the domain of quantification we have to map from the individual *x* to a subevent in which *x* is the participant, and then from that subevent to the interval on the timeline that it occupies. For instance, in the examples in (63), there

(63) After the consuls had set out for their provinces, T. Quinctius demanded (Livy 34.57.1). Before the praetors went to their provinces, a dispute occurred (Livy 37.51.1).

(64) Before any mention (Livy 4.59.11). Before any treatment (Cels 5.26.25B). After many entreaties (Suet 4.27.2). After multiple episodes of vomiting (NH 20.34).

may be a separate departure subevent for each consul and for each praetor. *Postquam* tells you that the time of the event described by the main clause $\tau(e^M)$ is later than the time of the last subevent of the event described by the subordinate clause $\tau(e^S)$: Quinctius' demand follows the departure of both Cornelius and Minucius. *Priusquam* tells you that the time of the event described by the main clause is earlier than the time of the first subevent of the event described by the subordinate clause: the dispute occurred prior to the departure of any of the praetors (Sempronius, Fabius Pictor, Fabius Labeo, Plautius and Baebius); this is depicted in Figure 8.6. As a departure event progresses through time, the number of departure subevents increases: *postquam* locates the event of the main clause after the highest point on the scale has been reached, *priusquam* locates the event of the main clause before the lowest point on the scale has been reached. That is why *priusquam* can license negative polarity items and *postquam* cannot

(65) *prius* mille hominum vallum intrasse *quam quisquam* sentiret (Livy 24.40.11)
priusquam ullam rem publicam ageret, liberare et se et rem publicam religione... velle (Livy 40.44.8)
priusquam inde *quoquam* procederet (Livy 34.16.10).

In the first example (Livy 24.40) all subevents of the enemy noticing, even the very first one, followed the entrance of a thousand men. So none of the subevents of *Q* (homomorphically associated with the set of participants of *Q*), not even the earliest one, was early to the same degree as the least early subevent of *P* (the entrance of the thousandth man) was early. **Postquam quisquam sentiret* 'after anyone noticed' would be ungrammatical in this context. In these examples both the event described in the main clause and the event described in the subordinate clause actually occurred; both clauses are veridical. For instance, the Romans did enter and the enemy did eventually notice. While this is always the case for *postquam*, it is often not the case for *priusquam*

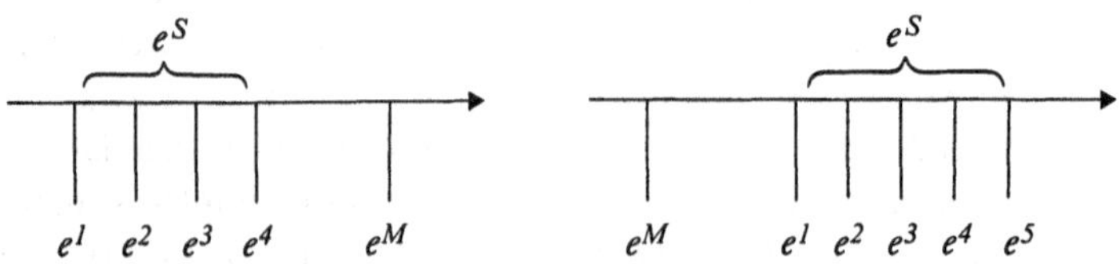

(a) Postquam in provincias praetores ierunt

(b) Priusquam in provincias praetores irent

Figure 8.6
Temporal clauses: (a) $\tau(e^M) > \tau(e^4)$; (b) $\tau(e^M) < \tau(e^1)$
Postquam/priusquam in provincias praetores ierunt/irent (cp. Livy 37.51.1)

(65) A thousand men got past the rampart before anyone noticed (Livy 24.40.11). That before he conducted any public business, he wanted to free both himself and the republic from a religious obligation (Livy 40.44.8). Before he proceeded anywhere from there (Livy 34.16.10).

(66) Et Q. Fabius Maximus augur mortuus est... *priusquam ullum* magistratum caperet (Livy 33.42.6)
priusque quam quisquam posset succurrere interfecit (Nepos 14.11.5).

In these examples the main clause is veridical, but the temporal clause is obviously not veridical, a fact that in earlier Latin is signalled by the use of subjunctive forms. In the dispute over the religious duties of Fabius Pictor (Livy 37.51 in (63): see Figure 8.6), five praetors were meant to leave, but only four actually left. In fact, it may be the case that the earlier event is performed in order to prevent the later event

(67) Caesar, *priusquam* se hostes ex terrore ac fuga *reciperent*, in fines Suessionum... exercitum duxit (BG 2.12).

In all worlds compatible with the goals of Caesar the enemy do not recover from their terror (teleological modality): $\forall w.R^{Tel,Caes}(w^*, w) \rightarrow \neg$Se-recipiunt ($w$, hostes). The occurrence of the earlier event pre-empts the occurrence of the later one, thereby determining which branch of the time line the actual world will follow. There is no time at which the later event occurs. This is illustrated in Figure 8.7. A differential ablative measuring the time between the two events consequently normally indicates factuality of the later event

(68) *Paucis ante diebus* quam Syracusae caperentur (Livy 25.31.12)
Ducentis quippe *annis ante* quam Clusium oppugnarent (Livy 5.33.5).

While the negative polarity indefinite is licensed by *priusquam*, it is not obligatory

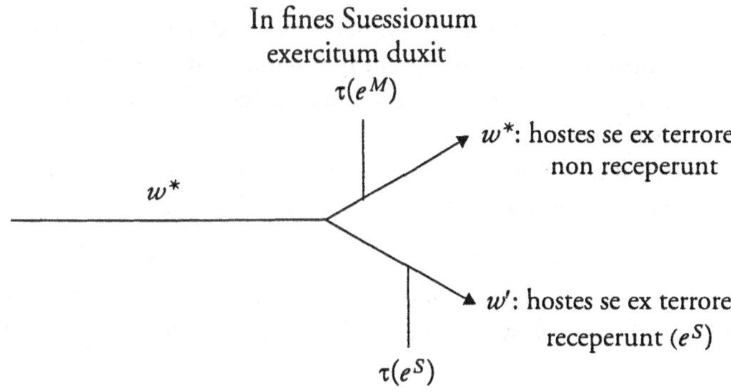

Figure 8.7
Preemptive *priusquam* with branching worlds
Priusquam se hostes ex terrore reciperent, in fines Suessionum exercitum duxit (BG 2.12)

(66) And Q. Fabius Maximus the augur died before he held any magistracy (Livy 33.42.6). And before anyone could come to his help, he killed him (Nepos 14.11.5).
(67) Before the enemy could recover from their terror and flight, Caesar led his army into the territory of the Suessiones (BG 2.12).
(68) A few days before Syracuse was captured (Livy 25.31.12). Two hundred years before they attacked Clusium (Livy 5.33.5).

(69) *prius quam quicquam* conaretur (BG 1.19)
priusquam aliquid moverent (Livy 25.8.4).

Temporal clauses expressing that the intervals occupied by the events in the main clause and in the subordinate clause are commensurate also license negative polarity items

(70) *Dum* praesidia *ulla* fuerunt, in Sullae praesidiis fuit (Pro Rosc Am 126)
nam Lacedaemonii, *quoad* lucis superfuit *quicquam*, deviis callibus medio saltu recipiebant se (Livy 35.30.10)
Quam diu quisquam erit qui te defendere audeat, vives (Cat 1.6).

These negative polarity items are licensed because they stand in the restriction of a universal quantifier over times. The second example (Livy 35.30) says that the Spartans stayed in the woods at all times that there remained even a minimal amount of light. Once again regular indefinites are also licensed

(71) *quoad* sibi spes *aliqua* relinqueretur (BG 8.55)
donec lucis *aliquid* superesset, fugientium tergis inhaererent (Curt Ruf 7.9.14).

The second example (Curt Ruf 7.9) says that they should stay on their backs at all times that there continues to be some (small) amount of light.

Conditional clauses

Negative polarity indefinites are licensed in the protasis of a conditional

(72) Quod gravius ferremus, *si quisquam ullam* disciplinam philosophiae probaret praeter eam quam ipse sequeretur (Luc 7)
si quemquam nactus eris qui perferat, litteras des antequam discedimus (Ad Att 10.15.4)
me manibus impiis eripite... per amicitiae fidem *si ulla* apud vos memoria remanet avi mei Masinissae (Sall Jug 24.10).

This is predictable if conditional clauses are interpreted as restrictions on a universal quantifier over worlds, situations or events, since the first argument of a universal quantifier is a downward entailing context. On this approach, the first

(69) Before attempting to do anything (BG 1.19). Before they took some action (Livy 25.8.4).

(70) So long as there were any lines of defence, he was in Sulla's (Pro Rosc Am 126). For so long as any light remained, the Lacedaemonians withdrew on the remote paths in the middle of the woods (Livy 35.30.10). So long as there is anyone who is bold enough to defend you, you will live (Cat 1.6).

(71) So long as some hope was left to him (BG 8.55). To press hard on the backs of the enemy so long as some light remained (Curt Ruf 7.9.14).

(72) This would bother us more if anyone approved any philosophical discipline apart from the one he himself follows (Luc 7). If you find anyone to deliver it, let me have a letter before I leave (Ad Att 10.15.4). Save me from impious hands, I beg of you by the loyalty of friendship, if you still have any memory of my grandfather Masinissa (Sall Jug 24.10).

example (Luc 7) would be interpreted to mean that in all worlds in which anyone approved of any school of philosophy other than his own, I would be more disturbed about this than I am in the real world. The second example (Ad Att 10.15) is understood to say that in all situations in which you find anyone to deliver a letter, you should let me have one. Although from a purely mechanical point of view protases are nonmonotonic, they are in fact downward entailing with the proviso that no previously excluded worlds are introduced into the set of accessible (best ranked) worlds. 'If you find a postman, give him a letter for me' does not entail 'If you find a dead postman, give him a letter for me' (so-called failure of strengthening of the antecedent). The first protasis implicitly quantifies only over worlds in which you find a live postman; compare the parallel caution above about switching the domain of the A argument of a universal quantifier over entities. Another, more obvious, constraint is that the apodosis has to be a felicitous consequent of the minimal scalar degree evoked by the negative polarity item in the protasis. 'If you find anyone to deliver it, don't give him a letter for me' only makes sense when the less likely a letter is to be delivered, the more likely it is to be written. There are examples where *si* clearly quantifies over events or times, as indicated by use of the pluperfect-imperfect iterative aspectual structure

(73) *si quicquam* caelati aspexerat, manus abstinere, iudices, non poterat. (Verr 2.4.48).

All events of Verres seeing any engraved dish at all were events of Verres being unable to keep his hands off it; each event involves one or more engraved dishes. It follows from this analysis that while negative polarity indefinites are licensed in the protasis of conditionals, they are not licensed in the apodosis

(74) Placebit *aliquod/*ullum* pretium contra amicitiam, *si ullum* in illa placet praeter ipsam (Sen Ep 9.9)
Si ulli rei sapiens adsentietur umquam, *aliquando/*umquam* etiam opinabitur (Luc 67).

However the converse does not hold: regular indefinite pronouns are licensed in the protasis too

(75) *Si* dederis *aliquid*, poteris ratione relinqui... at quod non dederis (Ov Ars Am 1.447)
Si L. Memmius *aliquem* istorum videret... utrum illum civem excellentem an atriensem diligentem putaret? (Parad 38).

(73) If he caught sight of anything engraved, members of the jury, he was unable to keep his hands off it (Verr 2.4.48).

(74) A man will be persuaded to give up friendship for some reward, if he is attracted by some reward in friendship other than friendship itself (Sen Ep 9.9). If the wise man ever assents to anything, he will also sometimes hold an opinion (Luc 67).

(75) If you have given something, you can be very reasonably dumped; but what you haven't given... (Ov Ars Am 1.447). If L. Memmius saw one of your lot..., would he think him an outstanding citizen or a diligent butler? (Parad 38).

With *aliquis*, if the event occurs at all, the existence of a referent is assumed and a minimal amount may not suffice, with *quisquam* the existence of a referent is at issue and even a minimal amount suffices. Compare 'If you do some work, you'll pass the test' with 'If you do any work, let me know.' Here is an example of *aliquis* outside the scope of a negative

(76) *si* sustinere *aliquis* aceti vim non potest, vino utendum est (Cels 5.26.23E).

Nisi, unlike *si*, does not generally license negative polarity indefinites but prefers regular indefinite pronouns

(77) Nullus es, Geta, *nisi* iam *aliquod* tibi consilium celere reperis (Ter Phorm 179)
Nisi aliquid praedixero, intellegi non poterunt quae refellentur (Sen Ep 102.6)
nisi iam factum *aliquid* est per Flaccum, fiet a me cum per Asiam decedam (Ad Fam 3.11.3).

This reflects the exceptive semantics of *nisi* in these examples. The second example (Ep 102.5) says that in all situations minus those in which I make some prefatory remarks, the arguments will be unintelligible. A negative polarity indefinite would permit subtraction of minimal amounts, which is uninformative, and subtraction of the empty set, which is vacuous.

Adversatives

Emotive factives are a class of verbs like *gaudeo* 'be happy that,' *iuvat* 'it gives me pleasure that,' *spero* 'hope that,' which express the psychological attitude of the speaker towards the fact (or what the speaker believes to be a fact) described in the complement clause

(78) In Britanniam te profectum non esse *gaudeo* (Ad Fam 7.17.3)
iuvitque me tibi cum summam humanitatem tum etiam tuas litteras profuisse (Ad Fam 5.21.3).

Although these verbs are factive, there is a modal component in their meaning: in the first example (Ad Fam 7.17) for instance, the actual world (in which Trebatius stays in Samarobriva) is compared with maximally similar possible worlds (in which he sets out for Britain); the actual world is preferable for Cicero. Adversatives are emotive factives that express a negative attitude, like *doleo* 'I'm sorry that,' *paenitet* 'it is a source of regret to me that,' *miror* 'I'm sur-

(76) If some patient cannot bear the strength of vinegar, wine should be used (Cels 5.26.23E).

(77) You're finished, Geta, unless you find yourself some plan quickly (Ter Phorm 179). Unless I make some prefatory remarks, the arguments to be refuted will not be intelligible (Sen Ep 102.6). If something hasn't already been done through Flaccus, it will be by me when I come back through Asia (Ad Fam 3.11.3).

(78) I'm happy that you didn't leave for Britain (Ad Fam 7.17.3). I was happy that your great humanity and learning helped you (Ad Fam 5.21.3).

prised that': the speaker believes that the proposition p expressed in the complement clause is true and says that all possible worlds compatible with the previous desires or, respectively, expectations of the person in question are worlds in which p is false: $\forall w.R^x(w^*, w) \rightarrow \neg p(w)$. Adversatives license negative polarity indefinites in their clausal (but not phrasal) complements

(79) ut *doleremus quicquam* esse ex illis reliquiis quod videre possemus (Phil 2.73)
et nunc *angor quicquam* tibi sine me esse iucundum. (Ad Fam 7.15.1)
inque tot adversis carmen *mirabitur ullum* ducere me tristi sustinuisse manu (Ov Trist 3.14.31)
hoc *miror*, hoc queror, *quemquam* hominem ita pessumdare alterum velle (Cic in Quint 8.6.47).

Negative emotive attitude verbs are generally more felicitous with expressions denoting minimal degrees on a scale than are positive ones, although there is a reading of 'glad' known as the "settle-for-less" reading which does license negative polarity indefinites ('I'm glad he showed up at all'). If you negate the adversative verb, a negative polarity indefinite becomes more difficult

(80) *non* inquam *miror* te *aliquid* excogitasse (Verr 2.3.17)
Nec mirum est *aliquid* ei cuius est totum posse donari. (Sen De Ben 7.5.2).

'I'm not surprised you thought up anything' is hardly possible; the same effect is produced by a downward entailing quantifier ('Few people were surprised you thought up anything'). As we know, adding a negative flips a downward entailing context into an upward entailing one. (However positive emotive attitude verbs can stay upward entailing when negated: 'I'm (not) happy Brutus stabbed someone'.) The specific semantics of emotive factives make it difficult to compute their entailment properties; we have already encountered this problem with other negative polarity contexts. Consider the first example in (78) again. Say that Trebatius had gone to Britain and Cicero had been unhappy about his decision. If I am sorry you went to England, it doesn't necessarily follow that I am sorry you went to Shropshire (downward entailment abstracting away from the issue of factuality) nor that I am sorry you went to the UK (upward entailment). In fact, I could be sorry that you went to England but happy that (given that you did) you went to Shropshire rather than to Kent and happy that you went to the UK rather than to Borneo. Emotive factives associate with focus, and if you change the focus, you also change the set of alternates to focus (the set of possible worlds being compared with the actual world), which interferes

(79) So that we regretted that there was anything of what he left for us to see (Phil 2.73). I am distressed that anything is pleasing to you without me (Ad Fam 7.15.1). He will be surprised that I have the endurance to compose any poem with sad hand under such adversity (Ov Trist 3.14.31). I am surprised and disturbed that any man should so want to ruin another (Quint 8.6.47).

(80) I am not surprised, I say, that you thought up something (Verr 2.3.17). And it is not surprising that something can be given to him who has everything (Sen De Ben 7.5.2).

with simple settheoretically based inferences. Finally, note that while adversatives license negative polarity indefinites, they do not require them; regular indefinites are also attested

(81) magis *mirari* se *aliquos* stantes cecidisse (Livy 26.2.13)
miramurque aliquos... tam multa praeterisse (NH 19.2).

Rhetorical questions

Negative polarity items are licensed in Latin rhetorical questions. What is important is for the question to be pragmatically rhetorical, irrespective of its syntax. For instance we find examples with the existential interrogative pronoun *ecquis* 'Is there anyone who?'

(82) *ecquid* ad eum *umquam* de re publica rettulisti? (Phil 2.14)
Ecquis umquam tam palam de honore... contendit...? (Div Caec 22),

with other *qu*-words

(83) *Cur* enim *quemquam* ut studeat tibi... rogas? (Pro Mur 76)
cur volumus ab industria *quemquam* removere...? (Rhet Her 3.38),

in sentential (yes-no) questions with or without the interrogative particle *-ne*

(84) Vidistine *quemquam* M. Regulo timidiorem...? (Pliny Ep 1.5.1)
Umquamne vidisti *quemquam* tam laboriosum et exercitum quam Varenum meum? (Pliny Ep 6.13.1)
Quemquam posse putas mores narrare futuros? (Mart 12.92.3).

These negative polarity items would be ungrammatical in the corresponding positive answers to the questions (**Ad eum umquam de re publica rettuli, *Vidi quemquam, *Puto quemquam posse narrare*, etc.), although they are licensed in exclamative assertions, as in the following examples with *-ne* and the accusative and infinitive

(85) *quemquamne* hominem... parare quod sit carius quam ipsest sibi! (Ter Ad 38)
Quemquamne fuisse tam sceleratum qui hoc fingeret (Phil 14.14).

It is not clear whether questions in general have entailments at all, and if they do, exactly what they are, and whether the entailments of rhetorical questions

(81) That he was more surprised that some had fallen standing their ground (Livy 26.2.13). And we are surprised that some have passed over so many topics (NH 19.2).

(82) Did you ever ask his advice about any political matter? (Phil 2.14). Has anyone ever fought so openly about a political office...? (Div Caec 22).

(83) Why do you ask anyone to support you? (Pro Mur 76). Why do we want to stop anyone making an effort...? (Rhet Her 3.38).

(84) Have you seen anyone more scared than M. Regulus...? (Pliny Ep 1.5.1). Have you ever seen anyone so distressed and harassed as my friend Varenus? (Pliny Ep 6.13.1). Do you think that anyone can predict how he will behave in the future? (Mart 12.92.3).

(85) To think that any man should take on something that is dearer to him than his own self! (Ter Ad 38). To think that anyone was so wicked as to make up this story! (Phil 14.14).

are different from those of neutral questions. Consider first a neutral question with an indefinite object phrase: 'Did he capture a (noble) Aeduan?' According to one theory, the entailments of a question are those of its true answers; in that case, since a positive answer is upward entailing and a negative answer is downward entailing, the question itself is nonmonotonic. According to another idea, if asking a question about A entails asking a question about its superset A′, the question is upward entailing: so our question is upward entailing (asking for information about the capture of a noble Aeduan involves asking for information about the capture of an Aeduan). Finally if the entailments of a question reflect ignorance space, then our question is downward entailing: if I don't know whether you captured an Aeduan, I don't know whether you captured a noble Aeduan, but not necessarily vice versa. However, we are specifically interested in sentences containing strong negative polarity items that denote the minimal degree on a scale of degrees. Since scales are downward entailing, this reverses the directions of entailment just given. To illustrate with cardinality, if he captured three Aeduans, then he also captured two; asking whether he captured three Aeduans entails asking whether he captured two; and not knowing whether he captured two Aeduans entails not knowing whether he captured three.

Rhetorical questions with negative polarity items come with two presuppositions and a resulting implicature. The first presupposition is that propositions with any degree higher than the minimal amount are known to be false; neutral questions obviously don't have this presupposition. To be sure, asking questions about a larger degree elicits a more informative response than asking questions about a minimal degree, but there is no point in asking questions about propositions that are not live possibilities in the conversational context. Secondly, there is no existential presupposition. The speaker boxes the listener in by giving him a choice between a minimal degree and zero; he challenges him to provide evidence for even a minimal degree. The result is a negative implicature; rhetorical questions with negative polarity items have a negative bias. So while ordinary polarity questions are nonveridical (they are not affirmative assertions and are compatible with a negative answer), rhetorical questions additionally have an antiveridical implicature. A positive answer would be so weak that it almost amounts to a negative response. In order to give a properly contentful positive response, the interlocutor would have to reject the minimal degree presupposition introduced by the negative polarity item. Consider again the first example in (84) (Pliny 1.5), 'Have you seen ANYONE more scared than M. Regulus?'. 'Yes, I've seen someone' is a very weak positive answer; 'Yes, in fact I've seen many more than just a single person' is a true positive answer, but it rejects the minimal degree presupposition.

FURTHER READING

Chierchia (2004); Giannakidou (1998); Homer (2011); Horn (2001); Horn & Kato (2000); van der Wouden (1997).

9 | MODALITY

Up to this point our semantics has been almost entirely extensional (with objects such as times, places and events). We have been dealing with actual individuals having actual properties involved in actual eventualities, and the sentences describing those eventualities have been true or false in the actual world. But this comes nowhere near to exhausting the expressive potential of human language. We are perfectly capable of (thinking about and) talking about the way the world might be or might have been, as well as about the way it actually is or was

(1) (Appius Claudius) Romae *mansit* (Livy 9.42.4)
in Italia fortasse *manebitur* (Ad Att 8.3.7)
Pecunia utinam ad Opis *maneret* (Phil 1.17)
Priamique arx alta *maneres* (Aen 2.56)
At tu dictis, Albane, *maneres* (Aen 8.643).

The first example (Livy 9.42) describes a state in the actual world: Appius Claudius did stay in Rome. The second example (Ad Att 8.3) describes a possibility: Cicero may stay in Italy, or he may not. The third example (Phil 1.17) describes a wish: the money is no longer in the temple, but Cicero wishes it were. The fourth example (Aen 2.50) is potential: under different circumstances Troy would still be standing; in the actual world it has been destroyed. The last example (Aen 8.643) expresses an unfulfilled obligation: Mettus should have kept his word, but in the actual world he didn't, with unfortunate consequences. If we replace the subjunctive with the indicative in the last three examples we get demodalized sentences that are false in the actual world but true in some alternative hypothetical worlds in which Cicero's wishes were fulfilled, the gods were favourable and Mettus kept his word, respectively. These alternative ways things could be (actual, possible and counterfactual) are called possible worlds. In order to handle the meaning of the examples in (1) other than the first one, we can no longer simply evaluate sentences as true or false. Rather we will need to relativize

(1) He remained in Rome (Livy 9.42.4). Perhaps Italy will not be evacuated (Ad Att 8.3.7). I wish the money had stayed in the temple of Ops (Phil 1.17). And you would still be there, high citadel of Priam (Aen 2.56). But you, man of Alba, should have kept your word (Aen 8.643).

their evaluation to possible worlds in a framework using multiple worlds rather than just a single world. The simplest way to do this is to adopt a richer semantic ontology which includes worlds (either as covert arguments or just as indices of evaluation) along with other objects like individuals, degrees, times and events. A demonstrative like *tum* can refer to worlds as well as to times

(2) *Tum* id magis faceres, si adesses (Ad Att 6.2.4)
nunc enim inopia reticere intelleguntur, *tunc* iudicio viderentur
(De Or 3.110).

Worlds can then be arguments in complex types. Instead of a sentence p (type <t>), which is simply true or false, we now have a proposition $\lambda w.p(w)$, a function from possible worlds to truth values (type <s,t>). A proposition (so long as it is contingent) is true in some worlds and false in others. Possible worlds can differ from the actual world in having sets of individuals that are differently populated

(3) Hi si Graeci fuissent (Pro Flacc 11)

(or sets that are empty in the actual world, like centaurs and dryads); for these we need a corresponding property type <s,et> ($\lambda w.P(w)$). In the actual world in (3) the set of Greeks did not include the Roman witnesses, but in the hypothetical worlds of the protasis, it did; so the truth of the sentence *Graeci erant* depends on the denotation of the predicate *Graeci* in the world of evaluation. Definite descriptions contain predicates and can vary in denotation from one world to another, so we also need a type <s,e>

(4) *praetor* Aetolorum Phaeneas (Liv 32.33.8);

it is easy to think of alternative worlds in which someone else was the leader of the Aetolians. But identity merging or switching of named individuals across worlds is a more controversial topic

(5) cum Parmenion dixisset se si *Alexander* esset usurum ea condicione,
respondit: "Et ego uterer, si *Parmenion* essem" (Val Max 6.4.ext3).

Parmenion hypothesizes worlds in which he retains his own "essence" while acquiring some pragmatically relevant properties of Alexander; Alexander hypothesizes worlds in which he retains those pragmatically relevant properties while acquiring the "essence" of Parmenion. Note the absence of the reflexive in comparable English examples like 'If I were you, I'd fire me' (≠ 'I'd fire myself').

(2) If you were here, you would be the more so (Ad Att 6.2.4). For as it is they are understood to remain silent due to lack of subject matter, whereas the other way they would seem to be doing so on purpose (De Or 3.110).

(3) If these men had been Greeks (Pro Flacc 11).

(4) Phaeneas, the leader of the Aetolians (Livy 32.33.8).

(5) When Parmenion said that if he were Alexander he would accept that offer, he replied: "I too would accept it, if I were Parmenion" (Val Max 6.4.ext3).

Informational modality

Informational modality accesses the content of some body of text or other corpus of information or of a mental state. Many instances involve imaginary worlds like the worlds of dreams

(6) Dionysii mater... praegnans... *somniavit* se peperisse Satyriscum (De Div 1.39)
somniare med ego esse mortuom (Luc 51),

delusions

(7) apud Euripidem Hercules cum *ut Eurysthei filios* ita suos configebat sagittis (Luc 89),

myths

(8) Endymion vero, si *fabulas* audire volumus... in Latmo obdormivit (Tusc 1.92),

and fiction

(9) tres albi sues in triclinium adducti sunt capistris et tintinnabulis culti (Petr 47).

World-shifting operators like *puta* 'suppose' also access imaginary worlds

(10) *Puta* venisse te Athenas, *puta* Rhodon (Sen Ep 104.8)
Puta itaque te non equitem Romanum esse sed libertinum (Sen Ep 44.6).

The eventualities described in these examples are not facts of the actual world, but they are facts of their respective imaginary worlds. Dionysius' mother was still pregnant in the actual world but gave birth to a baby satyr in her dream worlds. Epicharmus was a member of the set of live people in the actual world but of the dead in his dream worlds. Hercules assigned the property of being Eurystheus' sons to his own in his delusional worlds. Endymion (like Hercules) is a mythological character, and the three pigs at Trimalchio's dinner exist only in the fictional worlds of Petronius' Satyricon. However most facts about imaginary worlds are common to the actual world and the imaginary worlds. Neither Dionysius' mother nor Epicharmus dreamed that Syracuse was in Bactria, Hercules had no problem recognizing his arrows, and Trimalchio's

(6) Dionysius' mother when she was pregnant dreamed that she had given birth to a baby satyr (De Div 1.39). To be dreaming that I was dead (Luc 51).

(7) In Euripides when Hercules was shooting his own sons with arrows as if they were the sons of Eurystheus (Luc 89).

(8) If we want to pay attention to myths, Endymion fell asleep on Mount Latmus (Tusc 1.92).

(9) Three white pigs, decorated with muzzles and bells, were brought into the dining room (Petr 47).

(10) Suppose you are now at Athens, suppose you are now at Rhodes (Sen Ep 104.8). So suppose that you are not a Roman knight but a freedman (Sen Ep 44.6).

pigs didn't each have three ears and two tails. Imaginary worlds do not differ from the actual world arbitrarily: they are accessible from the actual world. Most facts about the actual world are carried over to imaginary worlds (even up to a point in mythology); only the pragmatically relevant facts differ, along with whatever is entailed by the new facts: Epicharmus cannot continue to breathe in his dream worlds if he is dead. We can formalize this in terms of an accessibility relation R between the actual world w^* and an imaginary world w, which we will write in prefix notation $R(w^*, w)$ ('w^* gives access to w,' 'w is accessible from w^*,' 'you can see into w from w^*'). For instance, for Petronius w^* is the base world upon which the Satyricon is founded (and in which it was written); it reflects what was taken to be common knowledge by Petronius' intended audience, as well as the conventions of Menippean satire. R is a relationship of compatibility between the actual world and the worlds of the Satyricon, reflecting the fact that the fictional elements of the Satyricon are superimposed on the circumstances of the actual world. Finally, w is any world in such a relationship with w^*. The first w doesn't have to be the actual world: Sinon's story of the construction of the wooden horse in the second book of the Aeneid involves an accessibility relation $R(w', w'')$ between fictional worlds (Sinon's story, w'') and legendary worlds (the Aeneid, w'); those parts of Sinon's story that are not lies are carried over from the legendary base worlds w' into the worlds of his story w''; the worlds of the Aeneid itself of course are accessible from the actual world by the standard accessibility relation $R(w^*, w)$.

Imaginary worlds are full of indeterminacies and can also contain inconsistencies: both have been subjects of philosophical discussion, along with the ontological status of fictional beings and associated questions of reference and transworld identity. Inconsistences arise when imaginary worlds contain explicitly contradictory propositions both of which are true, indeterminacies when they contain multiple alternative propositions only one of which could be true in any single world. Inconsistencies arise due to inattention of the author or variation in a tradition. There are various versions of the death of Hercules' children in mythology: in the one according to Euripides (*apud Euripidem* in (7)), he shoots them with his arrows. Typically inconsistencies can be eliminated by narrowing down the domain of quantification, for instance by saying 'in Euripides' version of the myth' rather than 'in mythology.' Indeterminacies are a problem because each possible world represents an exhaustive and unique list of facts describing that world. Information is not allowed to be coarse-grained and it is total; no new individuals can be added to the world and no new properties can be assigned to the individuals already there. How many grains of sand were there on the beach near Croton where the body of Lichas was washed ashore (Petr 115)? We aren't told, but for each possibility there is a separate world; no wonder the theory has been called "pedantic." Since the beach exists in the actual world too, we could get around this by saying that the exact number, whatever it was, is part of the information transferred from the actual world. We don't know the number in the actual world either, but our information about the actual world has the potential to grow to the point at which partiality is resolved and it becomes total. Purely fictional entities, however, are irredeemably incomplete or partial objects. For instance, we aren't told how many bristles each of Trimalchio's pigs had or how long their tails were. We could transfer a normal range from the actual world (invoking an ordering source to make worlds with values outside that range inaccessible), but not a single value because the pigs didn't exist in the actual world. So we are still left with a huge number of worlds. One way of avoiding this is to allow fictional worlds to be indeterminate, for instance by admitting propositions with unresolved variables ('The three-year-old pig had *n* bristles'); if *n* is replaced with an actual number, the truth value of the sentence is undefined. There may be many possible Satyricon worlds, but when we say "in the Satyricon," we are referring to just one of them, even if we don't know which one it is, just as we can refer to a set without being able to list all its members. Another way is to replace possible worlds with possible situations, narrowing the domain of objects and properties under consideration and allowing information about those there are to remain partial. Partial worlds discount pragmatically irrelevant properties like bristle numbers. The fact that in everyday speech we talk about 'the world of the Satyricon' rather than 'the worlds of the Satyricon' suggests that speakers can reduce sets of worlds to individual worlds. But for standard possible worlds theory, we have to posit a covert universal quantifier over worlds rather than a singular definite description, in order to cover all possible accessible variants. The example in (7) (Luc 89) then is analyzed as $\forall w.R^{Eur}(w^*, w) \rightarrow p(w)$: for all words w, if w is compatible with the mythological worlds described by Euripides and accessible from the actual world, then p is true in w. As already noted, w^* is the world of the author, so late fifth-century Athens, not the world of the speaker (Cicero's Rome). R^{Eur} is a specific version of R^{Inf} (the accessibility relation for informational modality): suprascript *Eur* picks the text of Euripides actually written in w^*, not some other version that Euripides might be imagined to have written (say one using Pherecydes' version of the legend, or a Hollywood version in which Hercules shoots his children with an assault rifle). The compatibility relation functions as the restrictor of the universal quantification: it is a function that maps a world onto a set of worlds ($\lambda w.R^{Eur}(w^*, w)$), with type <s,<s,t>>. The quantification $\forall w$ has the type <<s,t>,<st,t>>, a function that maps a set of compatible worlds onto a function from sets of worlds to truth values. The phrase *apud Euripidem*, then, is a function from a set of worlds to a truth value: it is a generalized quantifier over propositions viewed as the worlds in which they are true. The resulting compositional structure is illustrated in Figure 9.1. Indeterminacies not resolved by values in the actual world, like the length of each pig's tail, would require existential rather than universal quantification: 'The three-year-old pig *had/may have had a long tail.' But the issue hardly arises because they are pragmatically irrelevant, in the same category as questions about Hecuba's grandmother. If the facts in question had been relevant, they would have been explicitly stated by the author and consequently among

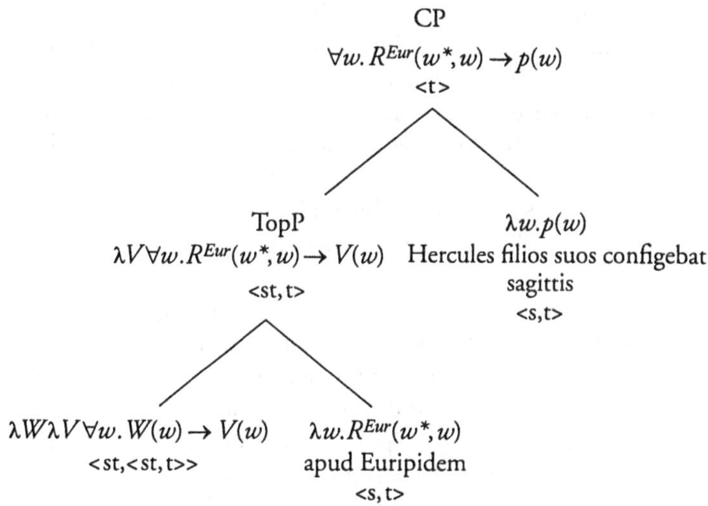

Figure 9.1
Types for fictional world modifier phrase
Apud Euripidem Hercules filios suos configebat sagittis (cp. Luc 89)

the propositions covered by universal quantification over accessible worlds as provided by the theory.

Now let's return to the worlds of the Satyricon. The corpus of explicit and implicit facts in the Satyricon (the informational content of the Satyricon) comprises a set of propositions, the set of propositions that are true in the Satyricon. This set of propositions is an example of what is called an informational modal base. It is generated by a function $f^{Sat}(w^*)$, which mirrors the composition by Petronius of the Satyricon in w^*. The informational content of the actual world is called a realistic modal base. 'The body of Lichas washed ashore near Croton' is true when evaluated against the Satyricon informational base and false when evaluated against the realistic modal base. (However, 'Petronius wrote that the body of Lichas washed ashore near Croton' is true for the realistic base and false for the Satyricon informational base.) Literary genres can be ranked according to the degree of deviation they license from a realistic base: those that allow metamorphosis are lower ranked than those that don't. Such ranking is an analogue of the ranking by ordering source that we need for other types of modality. Just as we can use the set of propositions in the common ground of a conversation to compute the set of worlds in the context set of the conversation, so we can compute a sort of derived context set for the Satyricon from the set of propositions true in the Satyricon. Every contingent proposition divides the set of all worlds W into two subsets, a set in which it is true and a set in which its contradictory is true, and every contingent proposition is true in a different set of possible worlds (if we ignore pairs of propositions that are just paraphrases of each other, like 'A vixen killed the chicken,' 'A female fox killed the chicken').

So for each proposition in the corpus of facts in the Satyricon there is a different set of worlds in which it is true. If we intersect all these different sets of worlds, we get a single set of worlds (the derived context set for the Satyricon), that in which all the propositions in the Satyricon are true, $\cap f^{Sat}(w^*)$. This is the set of worlds accessible from w^* by the Satyricon accessibility relation R^{Sat} described above: $\{w: w \in \cap f^{Sat}(w^*)\}$ and $\{w: R^{Sat}(w^*, w) = 1\}$ denote the same set. For any proposition p true in the Satyricon, $\cap f^{Sat}(w^*)$ is a subset of the set of worlds in which p is true: this is an alternative way of talking about truth in an imaginary world.

Imaginary worlds offer a convenient entry point into the rather intricate machinery of possible worlds theory. We saw that a world-shifting phrase like *apud Euripidem* could be analyzed in terms of a tripartite quantificational structure: a universal quantifier over worlds $\forall w$, a domain restriction $R^{Eur}(w^*, w)$ specifying the informational base (Euripides' version of the Hercules myth), and a nuclear scope (the proposition *Hercules filios suos configebat sagittis* in w). The universal quantifier was covert and the domain (*apud Euripidem*) was overt. Modal expressions can be analyzed in the same way, except that for modal expressions the quantifier is overt (it is the modal expression) and the domain restriction is often covert. Modality involves the interaction of a set of data (the modal base) with a set of norms (the ordering source). Modal force, which in its simplest manifestation is a binary distinction (possibility versus necessity), depends on whether the quantifier is existential or universal. The covert domain restriction comprises the modal base and the ordering source; it can be treated as the first argument of the modal. The modal base can be circumstantial (the facts in the world at some time and place) or epistemic (what someone knows about them). The ordering source (a set of norms) determines the relevant type of modality and ranks possible worlds according to the norms in question: the laws of nature for circumstantial modality, the laws of probability for epistemic modality, and the laws of the land, or morality etc. for deontic modality. The function $f(w^*)$ picks out the relevant modal base: $\cap f(w^*)$ is the set of worlds in which all the propositions in the relevant modal base are true. w in $R^f(w^*, w)$ is any world accessible from w^* by R^f, that is any world in $\cap f(w^*)$. The accessible worlds are ranked by the ordering source $g(w^*)$, giving a combined graded accessibility relation $R^{f,g}$. All this is exemplified in detail in the following sections.

Modality can be expressed in language by a wide range of categories including modal verbs (*licet* 'it is possible,' *debeo* 'ought'), modal adverbs (*fortasse* 'perhaps,' *necessario* 'necessarily'), modal adjectives and nouns (*placabilis*, *placabilitas* 'ready/readiness to forgive'), and of course verbal mood (subjunctive, gerund). While distinctions of modal force are usually expressed lexically (as in the examples just quoted), accessibility relations for unembedded bare modals are often not lexically differentiated but recovered from the context

(11) cum per leges militares effugere *liceret* iniquitatem tribuni (Pro Flacc 77)

(11) Although according to the military regulations you could have avoided a prejudiced tribune (Pro Flacc 77).

(12) *Licuit* esse otioso Themistocli, *licuit* Epaminondae (Tusc 1.33)
licet... erumpere lumen... Est etiam quoque uti... Forsitan et... (Lucr 5.595).

In the first example (Pro Flacc 77) the accessibility relation for *licet* is deontic, in the second (Tusc 1.33) it is circumstantial, and in the last (Lucr 5.595) it is epistemic. The primary meaning of *licet* is permissive and the other meanings are extensions thereof: what is permitted has the potential to occur. On the other hand, the primary meaning of *possum* 'can' is dynamic: what has the capacity to occur has the potential to occur, so *possum* also has circumstantial and epistemic uses, as well as permissive uses (what can occur legally is permitted). From a historical perspective, new meanings of modals develop through relaxation of lexical restrictions on the accessibility relation associated with the basic meaning of the verb. What was originally lexically specified now has to be recovered from the context.

Circumstantial modality

The modal base for circumstantial modality is typically a set of relevant facts or circumstances that necessitate, permit or exclude the occurrence of some eventuality by virtue of the ordering source. Since these are facts of the actual world ('the soldiers retreated,' 'the river was deep'), the circumstantial modal base is realistic. The ordering source comes from the laws of nature (physics, biology, etc.: 'what goes up comes down'). It orders the possibilities not inconsistent with the facts in the modal base: this ordering can give a binary classification of worlds (accessible and inaccessible) or a graded classification. The truth of a circumstantial modal depends on the speaker getting the facts right and taking account of all the relevant facts. The speaker can resort to an existential circumstantial modal if his imperfect knowledge state precludes simple assertion. Together, the modal base (function *f*) and the ordering source (function *g*) give us a circumstantial accessibility relation ($R^{f,g} \rightarrow R^{Circ}$). Here are some examples with universal quantification

(13) si vero interlunium incidat, omnes hibernos fructus et praecoces laedi *necesse* est (NH 18.283)
necesse erat foris et in aperto victum quaerentibus nonnumquam iniuriam propulsare (Col 12.pr.6)
Hiems frigora adducit: *algendum* est. Aestas calores refert: *aestuandum* est... Hanc vero condicionem mutare non possumus (Sen Ep 107.7).

(12) Themistocles could have led a life of leisure and so could Epaminondas (Tusc 1.33). It is possible that it emits light... it is also possible... Perhaps also... (Lucr 5.595).

(13) But if it happens to be an interlunar time, all the winter and early spring crops are bound to suffer damage (NH 18.283). It was necessary for those looking for food out of doors and in the open sometimes to repel attacks (Col 12.pr.6). Winter brings cold, so we are necessarily cold. Summer brings heat, so we are necessarily hot. We cannot change this state of affairs (Sen Ep 107.7).

The second example (Col 12.pr) says that all worlds that are circumstantially accessible from the actual world in primitive times are worlds in which men sometimes need to defend themselves when they look for food outside: $\forall w.R^{Circ}(w^*, w) \rightarrow p(w)$. Worlds in which men don't look for food are incompatible with the modal base. Worlds in which looking for food is a perfectly safe activity are theoretically possible, but they are not accessible from the actual world, given the way the actual world is: we can't change the way things are, as Seneca points out in the last example (Ep 107.7). The following examples have existential quantification over worlds

(14) fieri *potest* ut nubes summissae et humiles attritu suo ignem reddant (Sen NQ 2.26.9: app. crit.)
Idem sub terris fieri *potest* ut ex his quae impendent rupibus aliqua resoluta magno pondere et sono in subiacentem cavernam cadat, eo vehementius quo aut plus ponderis venit aut altius; et sic commovetur omne tectum cavatae vallis (Sen NQ 6.22.2).

The structure of the first example (NH 2.26) is set out in Figure 9.2. It says that some worlds circumstantially accessible from the actual world are worlds in which low clouds produce lightning: $\exists w.R^{Circ}(w^*, w) \wedge p(w)$. The second example (NQ 6.22) says that some worlds that are circumstantially accessible from the actual world and in which there is an event of a rock falling from the wall of

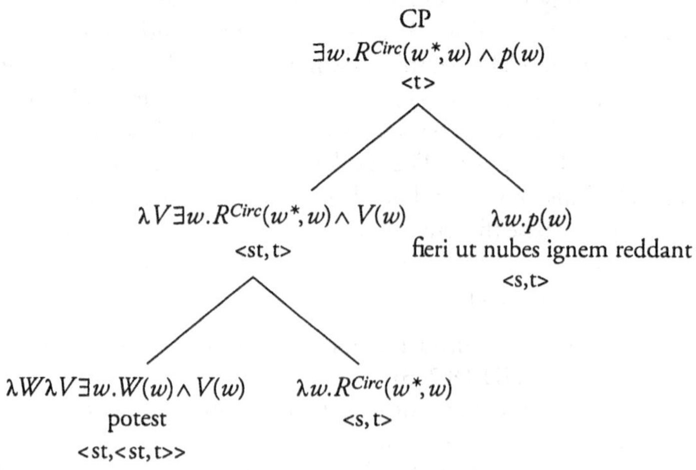

Figure 9.2
Circumstantial possibility modal
Fieri potest ut nubes ignem reddant (cp. NH 2.26.9)

(14) It is possible for clouds that are low and close to the earth to produce fire by their own friction (Sen NQ 2.26.9). The same thing can happen underground, so that an overhanging rock can come loose and fall into the cave underneath with a huge crash, the more violently so the greater its weight or the height from which it falls; and as a consequence the whole roof of the subterranean cavity shakes (Sen NQ 6.22.2).

a cave are worlds in which the roof of the cave shakes. A scalar implicature tells us that not all accessible worlds are that way: shaking is a possibility, not a necessity. The examples in (13) and (14) are generic: we have assumed that the modals are overt quantifiers akin to the normally covert generic operator, but with different modal force and therefore tolerance for exceptions (less, actually none, for *necesse* and more for *potest*). As Seneca notes, the force of impact is correlated with the physical properties of the incident, which implies that the probability of the roof of the cave shaking in any particular situation also depends on these factors. So worlds need to be ranked by the ordering source according to how closely they approximate the ideal conditions for shaking under normal circumstances. Regular dimensions and conditions give stereotypical results; worlds that combine shaking with the fall of a small, light rock are ranked very low. Different specific ordering sources can yield different accessibility judgements: what is technically possible may be stereotypically excluded.

While generic examples are typically true irrespective of time, episodic examples have to be evaluated relative to world-time pairs: they involve accessibility from the actual world at some time in its history

(15) Cum quaepiam cohors ex orbe excesserat... eam partem nudari *necesse* erat et ab latere aperto tela recipere (BG 5.35)
nonne fieri *poterat* ut populo de Cyprio rege placeret, de exsulibus Byzantiis displiceret? (De Dom 53).

In the battle between the Romans and Ambiorix (BG 5.35) in all circumstantially accessible worlds every time a cohort moved out of the formation it was exposed to missiles. In the second example (De Dom 53) the intersection of the set of accessible worlds with a positive reaction on the king of Cyprus and the set of accessible worlds with a negative reaction on the Byzantine exiles is not empty (but does not exhaust the set of accessible worlds). Logical deductions involve propositions that are true in all possible worlds in which the premises are true

(16) Num etiam una est omnium facies? nam si plures, aliam esse alia pulchriorem *necesse* est (ND 1.80)
si ortus est deorum, interitus sit *necesse* est (ND 1.68).

In all possible worlds in which the circumstances are such that the gods aren't all equally beautiful, one god is more beautiful than another (ND 1.80). If the prejacent proposition of a circumstantial necessity modal is a disjunction, then the modal quantifies over the union of the sets of worlds in which each proposition of the disjunction is true

(15) Whenever any cohort left the formation, that part was necessarily exposed and received incoming missiles on its open flank (BG 5.35). Isn't it possible that the attitude of the Roman people would have been positive in the case of the king of Cyprus and negative in the case of the Byzantine exiles? (De Dom 53).

(16) Surely they don't all look exactly alike? If not, then the appearance of one must be more beautiful than that of another (ND 1.80). If the gods have an origin, they must also have an end (ND 1.68).

(17) *necesse* sit partem pedis *aut* aequalem esse alteri *aut* altero tanto *aut* sesqui esse maiorem (Orat 188)
Necesse est enim *aut* armis urgeri rem publicam sempiternis *aut* iis positis recreari aliquando *aut* funditus interire. (Ad Fam 6.2.2).

The first example (Orat 188) says that in all worlds accessible from the actual world the phonological durational ratio of the two parts of a metrical foot is either 1 or 1.5 or 2. The disjunction is exclusive, since a ratio cannot be both 1 and 1.5 at the same time; so if any such worlds exist, they would be impossible worlds. However there are many other conceivable worlds, for instance those in which the ratio is 1.43 or 1.78; these are not impossible but just inaccessible. All this is set out in Figure 9.3.

Circumstantial modality can also be expressed by dispositional predicates, for instance adjectives in *-ilis*: *fissilis* 'that can be split,' *fragilis* 'that can be broken,' *sorbilis* 'that can be sucked up.' A wine jar is fragile (*fragiles cadi* Ov Met 12.243) because in some worlds circumstantially accessible from the actual world a jar breaks ($\lambda x \exists w. R^{Circ}(w^*, w) \wedge$ Frangitur(x, w)), particularly those in which it is dropped from a great height, hit with a blunt instrument or thrown across the room by a centaur. The ordering source gives us a correlation between the physical properties of a jar, the force applied to it and the probability of its breaking. Since the adjective is used descriptively, for all jars there are some worlds in which they break: worlds in which (ordinary) jars are unbreakable are inaccessible. The following examples illustrate circumstantial modality with the gerundive, universal in the positive and existential in a downward entailing context

(18) Discessi ab eo bello in quo aut in acie cadendum fuit... aut *consciscenda* mors voluntaria (Ad Fam 7.3.3)
sibi ipsa *toleranda* est seque includit et continet nullarum egens compagium (NH 2.5)
Ecce aliae deliciae equitum vix *ferendae*! (Ad Att 1.17.9)
intolerandus aestus existat (Curt Ruf 8.9.13).

The existential modal force in the negative is equivalent to a universal with inner negation: necessarily NOT ($\forall w \neg$) equals NOT possibly ($\neg \exists w$). Outer negation ($\neg \forall w$) would mean that it could be tolerated but didn't have to be tolerated. This creates a bracketing mismatch: the syntax gives us [*vix* [*ferendae*]], but the semantics requires [[*vix fer-*] *endae*].

(17) It is necessary for one part of the foot to be either equal to or double or one and a half times as large as the other part (Orat 188). For it is necessary that either the republic is for ever at war or it lays arms aside and recovers finally or it perishes entirely (Ad Fam 6.2.2).

(18) I withdrew from a war in which either one had to die in battle or commit voluntary suicide (Ad Fam 7.3.3). It has to hold itself up and it encloses and holds itself together without the need for any fastening (NH 2.5). Here is another piece of supercilious behaviour on the part of the knights that is scarcely tolerable (Ad Att 1.17.9). Intolerable heat arises there (Curt Ruf 8.9.13).

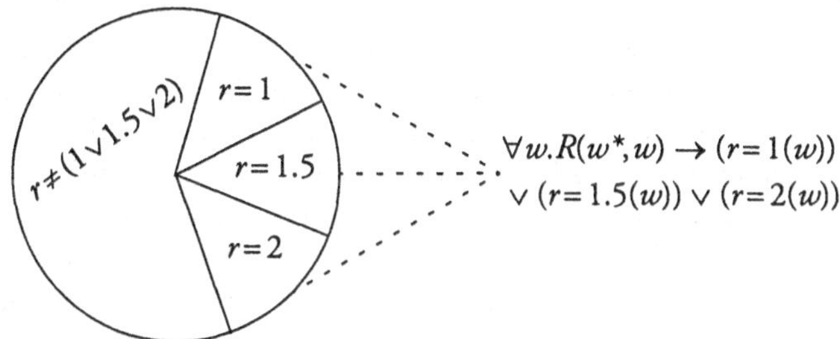

Figure 9.3
Disjunction in a circumstantial necessity: Durational ratios in the foot
Necesse sit partem pedis aut aequalem esse aut altero tanto aut sesqui esse maiorem
(Orat 188)

Epistemic modality

In the preceding section we saw that circumstantial modality was all about facts of the world, for instance the fragility of wine jars and the conditions under which they break, or the collapse of underground caves. Epistemic modality is about what facts someone knows (or thinks he knows): a sentence with an epistemic modal can be a statement of possibility given the current knowledge state, an evaluation of probability in light of the known facts, or an inference on the basis of available knowledge and evidence. The distinction is discussed with a number of good examples in Quintilian 5.9. (Both circumstantial and epistemic modals can be used either episodically or generically.) Compare the following

(19) quod... nec *potest* fieri, tempore uno homo idem duobus locis ut simul sit (Pl Amph 567)
Fieri non *potest* ut quem video te praetore in Sicilia fuisse et quem ex ipsa ratione intellego locupletem fuisse, eum tu in tua provincia non cognoveris (Verr 2.2.190).

The first example (Amph 567) says that it is a physical impossibility for someone to be in two different places at the same time. The second example (Verr 2.2) says that is impossible to believe that Verres hadn't met a well-to-do member of the Sicilian community (even though it would of course have been physically possible for them not to have met, had he existed). Circumstantial modality states what the speaker represents himself as objectively knowing, epistemic modality what he represents himself as subjectively believing on the basis of inference. In the former case, the speaker does not think that his knowledge will be subject to revision on the basis of future evidence; in the latter case the speaker does not take responsibility for the truth of the proposition, because he

(19) And which is impossible, namely for the same man at one time to be in two places at once (Pl Amph 567). It is inconceivable that you were not acquainted in your province with a man who I see was in Sicily when you were praetor and who I understand from his entry in the accounts themselves to have been rich (Verr 2.2.190).

has insufficient direct evidence to assume knowledge. It is misleading to present a fact that one knows as an inference and to present an inference as a fact that one knows. While a circumstantial modal base is realistic, an epistemic modal base is not necessarily realistic: it is based on the (possibly defective) knowledge state of the speaker (or other knowledge agent). It can be difficult to tell circumstantial and epistemic modality apart: if it is a physical fact about my wine jar that it can break, then it is a reasonable inference that it may break at some point. Moreover the speaker can only use that part of the circumstantial modal base that is represented in his current knowledge state. However speakers are clearly able to differentiate the two types of modal base. While circumstantial MUST makes a stronger claim than a simple assertion (since it serves to eliminate the possibility of exceptions), epistemic MUST makes a weaker claim (since it leaves open the possibility that the inference is mistaken): you can check this with the examples in (19). There are also scopal differences. Take a sentence like 'Every candidate could have been elected consul.' This is fine with a circumstantial modal base ('For every candidate it was objectively possible to be consul'), but it does not allow an epistemic reading ('For all we know, the candidates were all elected'): only two candidates can be elected consul, and the universal quantifier can scope over the circumstantial modal but it cannot scope over the epistemic modal. Also, a circumstantial modal is fine after a negation in sentences like 'He wasn't elected consul, but he could have been.' The epistemic counterpart of this is pragmatically defective: 'He wasn't elected consul, but maybe he was.'

We have seen that for informational modality the modal base was the set of propositions in the "text," for circumstantial modality it was the set of facts about the world. For epistemic modality the modal base is the set of all the facts of the actual world that the speaker (or other knowledge agent) knows or thinks he knows. We can call the speaker's factual knowledge state his epistemic state. For every epistemic state there is a set of worlds in which all its propositions are true: as before, the worlds that belong to this set are the epistemically accessible worlds. When Oscar Wilde's most famous character, Lady Bracknell, asks her prospective son-in-law Jack whether he knows everything or nothing, Jack, who certainly doesn't know about presupposition failure, replies after some hesitation that he knows nothing. There are no facts about the world that Jack knows, everything is possible; the set of propositions in Jack's epistemic state is the empty set, so his epistemic state is W, the set of all possible worlds. If Jack had replied that he knew everything, he would have been factually omniscient: the set of propositions in Jack's epistemic state would have been the unique set of propositions that exhaustively describes the actual world; his epistemic state would have been $\{w^*\}$, the singleton set containing the actual world. If all he knew had been a bunch of tautologies, his epistemic state would again have been W: since tautologies are true in all possible worlds, the intersection of the set of sets of worlds in which each tautology is true is the set of all possible worlds. In fact, Jack's epistemic state was none of the above, rather it was a nonmaximal and nonatomistic member of the powerset of W, namely the intersection of the set of sets of worlds in which each proposition that he knew was true.

The modal base on which an inference depends is drawn from the speaker's epistemic state, but the inference itself, once made, belongs to his doxastic state

(20) MNES. Ille... accuratum habuit quod posset mali faceret in me... PIST. Improbum istunc esse *oportet* hominem. MNES. Ego *ita arbitror*. (Pl Bacch 550).

Mnesilochus asserts that the man in question took pains to do him as much harm as he could; Pistoclerus accepts this assertion as true and adds it to his epistemic state. It can now be used in an epistemic modal base, which is just what happens when he uses this item of knowledge to make the inference that the man in question must (*oportet*) be a complete scoundrel. This inference now becomes part of Pistoclerus' doxastic state. Mnesilochus in turn accepts the inference as reasonable, and so it gets added to Mnesilochus' doxastic state too (*ita arbitror*). If a proposition in the epistemic modal base upon which the inference depends is false, then the inference may be false too

(21) "Quid? Porcus hic non est exinteratus? Non mehercules est..." "Plane... hic *debet* servus esse nequissimus" (Petr 49).

The cook had not really forgotten to gut the pig, so the inference p from the premise $\neg q$ is false. Objectively, $\neg q$ belongs to the speaker's doxastic state, but for the purposes of licensing the inference it belongs to his epistemic state. Even though $\neg q$ is not true in the actual world, it needs to be true in the worlds epistemically accessible from w^* that license strong inferences. This is illustrated in Figure 9.4: worlds in which q is true are excluded by the modal base (they are incompatible with the speaker's knowledge), and worlds in which p is false are excluded by the ordering source. Of course, to the extent that mere beliefs as opposed to factual knowledge are also used as a basis for inferential statements, the speaker is accessing his doxastic state rather than just his epistemic state.

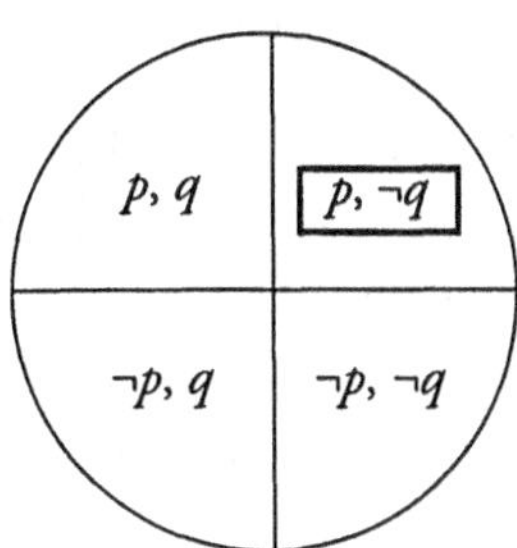

Figure 9.4
Epistemic modality
p = *Hic servus est nequissimus*; q = *Porcus est exinteratus* (cp. Petr 49)

(20) MNES. He took care to do me as much harm as he could. PIST. He must be a real scoundrel. MNES. I think so (Pl Bacch 550).
(21) "What? Hasn't this pig been gutted? It absolutely has not." "He must be a very bad servant" (Petr 49).

(Since beliefs can come in different strengths, they can function as an ordering source too.) Like other modal bases, the epistemic modal base can be narrowed down to only the relevant propositions, in which case we have the speaker's evidential state. Partial evidence can lead to the wrong conclusions, for instance 'That must be Hector' in the following epigram about a dwarf

(22) Si solum spectes hominis caput, Hectora credas: si stantem videas, Astyanacta putes (Mart 14.212).

The epistemic state that licenses the inference is normally that of the speaker: the epistemically accessible worlds are those compatible with the speaker's knowledge in the actual world at the current time. Since the speaker's epistemic state may differ from that of the hearer in relevant ways, it is possible for the speaker and the hearer to make inconsistent inferences that are both justified ('That must be Jack.' 'No, it must be Bill.'), although either or both may be false, and one of them could even be accidentally true but based on false premises. It is also possible for the speaker to draw an inference based on the common ground (the knowledge shared by the speaker and the hearer in the conversation) or for that matter on the hearer's epistemic state

(23) *Scilicet* is superis labor est, ea cura quietos sollicitat. (Aen 4.379).

The inference follows from what Aeneas has asserted but not from what Dido believes to be the case. So the epistemic accessibility relation actually has to be relativized to a contextually supplied knowledge agent (possibly a contextually bound covert argument of the epistemic modal). Substituting *quod sciam* 'as far as I know' for *scilicet* in (23) would change the value of the knowledge agent argument back to the speaker. A similar sort of covert argument seems to be needed for assertions containing aesthetic judgement expressions ('Tibullus is a good poet') and predicates of personal taste ('The soup tastes good'). There is more room for disagreement about matters of taste and inference than about matters of fact.

Weak inferences, which involve existential quantification over worlds, are used when there is less confidence in the probability of the inference, for instance when there are competing inferences

(24) Hoc ego quid sit interpretari non possum. *Potest* aliquid iratus Antonio, *potest* gloriam iam novam quaerere, *potest* totum esse σχεδίασμα (Ad Att 15.19.2).

(22) If you only looked at his head, you would think he was Hector: if you saw him on his feet, you would think he was Astyanax (Mart 14.212).

(23) I suppose this is what the gods spend their time doing, this is what they worry about when they are at leisure (Aen 4.379).

(24) I can't figure out what this means. Perhaps he is angry with Antony about something, perhaps he is looking for a new path to glory, or perhaps the whole thing is a *schediasma* (Ad Att 15.19.2).

See Figure 9.5. There are three epistemic possibilities (p^1, p^2, and p^3). Some of the worlds in which p^1 is true, namely $w^{1\text{-}3}$, are epistemically accessible, others are not (because they contain unrelated inaccessible propositions), and similarly for p^2 and p^3. Worlds in which p^1, p^2, and p^3 are all false are also epistemically inaccessible. Predictably, while a conjoined internal negation causes a contradictio in adiecto with a universal quantifier (*'He must be angry with Antony, and he must not be angry with Antony'), it does not cause a contradiction with an existential quantifier ('He may be angry with Antony, and he may not be angry with Antony'). Not all epistemic possibilities are inferential. Sometimes they are simple statements of possibility

(25) oratio... *fortasse* placebit (Pliny Ep 8.3.3)
facti *fortasse* pigebit (Ov Her 12.209).

By saying that p is possible, you raise the issue of p in the conversation, and you indicate that you don't have sufficient knowledge to deny p or to assert it, so no possible worlds are eliminated from the context set. In a disjunction ('p or q'), p and q can be understood as epistemic possibilities: in some epistemically accessible worlds p is true, in others q is true. The disjunction is then a (possibly exhaustive) conjunction of modal propositions.

Like other modals, inferential modals depend on two conversational backgrounds, a modal base comprising the facts from which the inference is drawn and an ordering source accounting for the fact that some inferences are better than others. Like the modal base, the ordering source is a body of knowledge, therefore a set of propositions used to rank the worlds in which different inferences are true. Consider the following examples

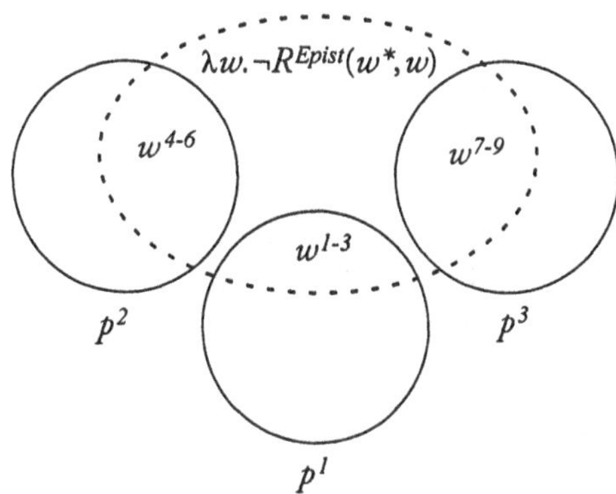

Figure 9.5
Weak inferences
Potest p^1, *Potest* p^2, *Potest* p^3 (cp. Ad Att 15.19.2)

(25) The speech... perhaps you will like it (Pliny Ep 8.3.3). Perhaps I will be sorry for my deed (Ov Her 12.209).

(26) Consilia Antoni haec sint *necesse* est (Ad Fam 11.10.4)
decemviros qui duodecim tabulas perscripserunt, quos *necesse* est fuisse prudentes (De Or 1.58)
conditoribus urbium ac legum latoribus... in quibus fuisse vim dicendi *necesse* est (Quint 3.2.4).

In the first example (Ad Fam 11.10) D. Brutus infers from his knowledge of the military facts on the ground (the epistemic modal base $f(w^*)$) that Antony has these options, which he proceeds to list. His inference depends on the assumption that Antony will behave in the way that sensible military commanders normally do (the stereotypical ordering source $g(w^*)$). In all worlds accessible on the basis of the epistemic modal base $f(w^*)$ and the stereotypical ordering source $g(w^*)$, Antony has these options (p): $\forall w. R^{Epist}(w^*, w) \rightarrow p(w)$, where R^{Epist} is the epistemic incarnation of $R^{f,g}$. There are also worlds in which Antony adopts none of the options available to him under Brutus' inference but decides to invade Scotland; these worlds are possible but inaccessible because they are excluded by the ordering source. Similarly in the other examples the ordering source serves to exclude idiosyncratic possible worlds in which unintelligent or inarticulate types are assigned the job of writing the laws of a city. The ordering source ranks the possible worlds and inserts an accessibility cut-off point, thereby narrowing the domain of quantification over worlds. If no further relevant information comes to light, the inference may never be verified; but if it is verified, it will turn out to be correct provided that the world has followed a stereotypical course. The speaker's working assumption is that it will have done so. Speakers can agree on how worlds are ranked by the ordering source but disagree on where the cut-off point between accessible and inaccessible worlds is located

(27) "*Necesse* est quoniam pallet aegrotasse," aut "*Necesse* est peperisse quoniam sustinet puerum infantem." (Rhet Her 2.39).

Universal quantification over epistemically accessible worlds (*necesse*) is licensed only if other less stereotypically likely possibilities (he is scared, her sister has had a baby) are excluded from the accessible worlds. If they are included, the modal force has to be changed from universal to existential (*dicemus potuisse* Rhet Her 2.33).

In addition to epistemic necessity and epistemic possibility, we often find inferences with a modal force intermediate between the two. This type, known as weak necessity, can be expressed by *oportet*

(26) Antony's plans have to be as follows (Ad Fam 11.10.4). The decemviri who wrote out the Twelve Tables, who must have been knowledgeable people (De Or 1.58). The founders of cities and the makers of laws, who must have possessed eloquence (Quint 3.2.4).
(27) "Since he is pale, he must have been ill," or "Since she is holding a baby boy, she must have given birth" (Rhet Her 2.39).

(28) Scire iam te *oportet* L. Caesar quae responsa referat a Pompeio (Ad Att 7.17.2)
si meis litteris obtemperavit, cum tu haec leges, illum Romae esse *oportebit* (Ad Fam 12.30.5)
Cistellam isti inesse *oportet* caudeam in isto vidulo (Pl Rud 1109, 1133)
Servum hercle te esse *oportet* et nequam et malum (Pl Poen 1030),

and *debeo*

(29) cum iam tibi Asia sicut unicuique sua domus nota esse *debeat* (Ad Qfr 1.1.45)
Celebratior quidem usus cum faenore coepisse *debet* (NH 33.28).

Strong necessity says what is true in all accessible worlds, while weak necessity says what is true just in all the highest ranked worlds among the accessible worlds. Consider for instance the second example in (28), which is illustrated in Figure 9.6. The evaluation of the available evidence in the modal base with the criteria in the ordering source leaves a number of possible inferences in play, of which the highest ranked (worlds 1-3 in the diagram) is that Lucceius is in Rome (provided he has complied with Cicero's instructions). The less likely possibilities (worlds 4-9 in the diagram) involve factors unknown to Cicero that interfere with the predicted stereotypical course of events (Lucceius falls ill, etc.); these can be evoked with 'might' ('Lucceius might still be outside Rome; he could have fallen ill'). If Cicero had simply discounted the other possibilities, he would have used *necesse* as in the examples in (26). In the following ex-

$\lambda w.R^{Epist}(w^*, w)$

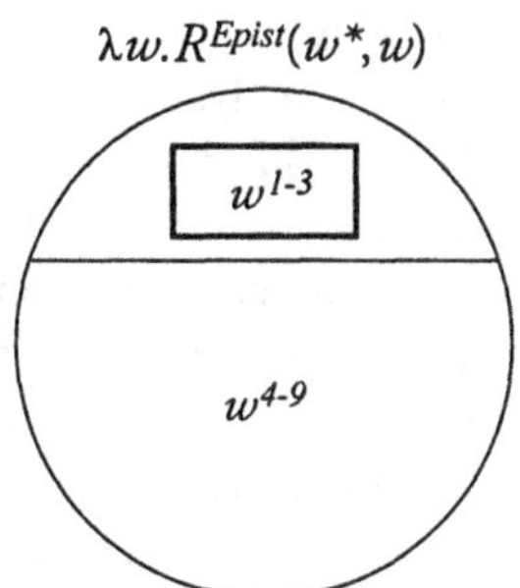

Figure 9.6
Ordering source for epistemic modality: $w^{1\text{-}3} >^{g} w^{4\text{-}9}$
Illum Romae esse oportebit (Ad Fam 12.30.5)

(28) You should know by now the nature of the response that L. Caesar is bringing back from Pompey (Ad Att 7.17.2). If he has followed the instructions in my letters, he should be at Rome when you read these words (Ad Fam 12.30.5). There in that suitcase there should be a box made of rushes (Pl Rud 1109, 1133). You really must be a bad and wicked slave (Pl Poen 1030).

(29) Since you should by now know Asia as well as everyone knows their own household (Ad Qfr 1.1.45). Its use presumably became more frequent with the introduction of loans (NH 33.28).

ample a weak epistemic necessity is rhetorically amplified by a strong teleological necessity

(30) Quem... vigilantem sic eluseritis, sopitum *oportet* fallatis, immo *necesse* est: in eo enim loco res sunt nostrae ut vobis ego magis necessitatis vestrae index quam consilii auctor sim. (Livy 7.35.6).

There are also examples of an inferential use of the future

(31) Haec *erit* bono genere nata (Pl Pers 645)
Huius motus succutientis terras haec *erit* causa: ad alteram transeo (Sen NQ 6.23.1)
Noli vexare: *quiescet* (Juv 1.126).

Haec in the second example (NQ 6.23) is anaphoric, so the future can only be inferential. The speaker uses an inferential future because he cannot verify the sentence at the present but indicates that it will be verified in the future ('will turn out to be'). In the same way (as already noted in Chapter 1) a noninferential future is used to express future verification by the hearer of a sentence that the speaker knows to be true at the present

(32) Nummi sescenti hic *erunt* (Pl Pers 437)
Tene cruminam: *inerunt* triginta minae (Pl Frag Inc 6).

If we test the inferential future with contradictio in adiecto, we find that it patterns with strong necessity modals rather than with weak necessity modals: *'That must be Jack, but it may not be,' 'That should be Jack, but it may not be,' *'That will be Jack, but it may not be.'

So far we have seen that for the analysis of epistemic modality we need a modal base, to account for the fact that you can't draw inferences from facts that you don't know (unless they are conditionalized), an ordering source, to account for the fact that some inferences are better than others, and a modal force. Possibility (*possum*) was handled by an existential quantifier covering some possible worlds and strong necessity (*necesse*) by a universal quantifier covering all possible worlds. So you might want to say that weak necessity (*oportet, debeo*) should be handled by a quantifier covering most possible worlds, but if you do, you will have to be more precise about what you mean by most worlds. The theory of probability provides one way of approaching this question. The theory of probability is founded on three basic notions which are analogous to the concepts of modal base, ordering source and modal force. The first notion

(30) The enemy that you escaped in this way when they were wide awake, you ought to be able to elude when they are asleep: for our situation has reached the point where I am telling you what you have to do rather than offering you advice (Livy 7.35.6).

(31) She must be from a good family (Pl Pers 645). This must be the cause of the motion that shakes the earth from below; now I pass on to the other one (Sen NQ 6.23.1). Don't bother her: she must be sleeping (Juv 1.126).

(32) There will be six hundred nummi here (Pl Pers 437). Take the purse: there will be thirty minae in it (Pl Frag Inc 6).

is that of possible outcome or elementary event. If you are tossing a die like the talus which has four sides, there are four possible outcomes. Outcomes in which the talus balances on an edge or a vertex are excluded as impossible. The set of possible outcomes is called the sample space, denoted by $\Omega = \{1,2,3,4\}$. The sample space is part of the modal base; worlds in which some outcome not in the sample space occurs are not accessible; they are impossible. The second basic notion is that of the family of subsets of the sample space, denoted by F. F defines what are possible events, E. When the sample space is finite, F is just the powerset of Ω. In the case of a toss of a talus, there are 16 possible events, for instance you throw a 1 or 3, or your throw is less than 4, or it is greater than 2, and so on. F can be viewed as the partitioning of worlds according to the possible alternative selections from the sample space. As such F also belongs to the modal base. The final basic notion of probability theory is that of a function which assigns each event a real number between 0 and 1, $P: E \rightarrow [0,1]$. $P(E)$ is the probability of event E. The function $\lambda E.P(E)$ belongs to the ordering source rather than to the modal base. This is so because there are accessible worlds with events whose probability is, in the limit, zero. For example, the probability of getting a 1 every time you toss a talus approaches zero the more times you toss, but a string of billions and billions of tosses all coming up 1 is not impossible in the same sense that balancing on a vertex is impossible. The modal base incorporating the sample space rules out the latter; the ordering source admits the possibility of the former but assigns it a probability effectively of zero. We can interpret the probability of a proposition φ as the proportion of possible outcomes in which φ is true: $|\{w: \varphi(w)\}| / |\{w\}|$. For circumstantial modality, probability is a property of the actual world, often called objective probability. In the case of the talus, the set of possible worlds $\{w\}$ is Ω and $|\{w\}| = |\Omega| = 4$. So if φ is the proposition that your toss comes up less than 4, $P(E < 4) = \frac{3}{4}$. Modal force can be defined in terms of probability along these lines: possibility corresponds to $P(E) > 0$, necessity to $P(E) = 1$, weak necessity to $P(E) > \frac{1}{2}$. But if your die has six sides, like the tessera, then $|\Omega| = 6$ and $P(E < 4) = \frac{1}{2}$, so that tossing less than a 4 is no longer a weak necessity. However if the die is loaded to fall most frequently on three, the number of possible outcomes remains the same, but the probabilities of the outcomes are quite different. The probability of a particular outcome is extrapolated from a very large series of throwing events, each one of which has a set of possible outcomes. So 'most worlds' does not mean most possible worlds in a set of worlds but most possible sets of worlds in a set of sets of worlds. The stereotypical ordering source used in inferential modals must have access to these probabilities. The die throwing example differs from ordinary inference in other respects too. First of all, with fair dice there is no difference between circumstantial modality and epistemic modality (for anyone who can count to six). But if the die is loaded to come up three and the speaker doesn't know this, then the proposition 'The die has a .167 chance of coming up three' is true in all epistemically accessible worlds but false in all circumstantially accessible worlds. It follows that epistemic probability is not a property of the actual world, but depends on the set of worlds epistemically accessible to the agent. The epistemic probability of a proposition can be interpreted as the ratio of the epistemically accessible worlds in which it is true to the total number of accessible worlds. If the die is heavily loaded, say $P(3) = {}^5/_6$, it won't take very many tosses before you realize that the likelihood of getting such a disproportionate number of 3's is very low on your belief that $P(3) = {}^1/_6$ and decreasing with every toss. The rational thing to do is to change your belief and assign a greater probability to getting a 3 and lesser probabilities to the other possible outcomes. Here we enter into the realm of likelihood estimation, Bayesian inference, and update logic, all of which are beyond the scope of our discussion. Secondly, the markings on the dice automatically fix the grain of information used in the inference. Normally this has to be done contextually. The finer the grain of information, the lower the probability of any particular possibility. For instance, when Caesar orders Sabinus to fortify the camp across the river Aisne with an eighteen-foot ditch (BG 2.5), the probability that the soldiers will actually dig an eighteen-foot ditch is far greater if anything between seventeen feet six inches and eighteen feet six inches counts as an eighteen foot ditch than if the width of the ditch is measured down to the last fraction of an inch and each different measurement counts as a different possibility.

We have seen that dispositional adjectives in *-ilis* like *fragilis* 'breakable' involve circumstantial modality. Since they are gradable, they denote degrees on a scale of probability

(33) salici... Finditur Graeca rubens, candidior Amerina sed paulo *fragilior* (NH 16.177)
quisquis dolor deorsum tendit *sanabilior* est (Cels 2.8.15).

The conditional probability of an Amerian willow breaking is greater than the conditional probability of the Greek red willow breaking: $P(B|Am) > P(B|G)$. Conditional probability amounts to restricting the accessible worlds to those in which the condition is fulfilled and specifying the probability as a proportion of these: $\{w\text{: } B(w) \wedge A(w)\} / |\{w\text{: } A(w)\}|$. This is the ratio of the number of worlds in which Amerian willows break to the number of worlds which have Amerian willows. That is very different from the unconditional probability of breaking. Out of all possible worlds, the unconditional probability of the Greek red willow breaking might be greater than that of the Amerian willow breaking merely because there are many more Greek red willows than there are Amerian willows. The degree of fragility, however, does not depend on the size of a variety's population but on the variety's toughness. The expression *veri similis* 'probable' is likewise a gradable adjective, but it involves epistemic rather than circumstantial modality. Here are some examples with propositional arguments

(33) To the willow... The Greek red willow is split, while the Amerian one, being lighter in colour but a bit more fragile (NH 16.177). Any pain that spreads in a downward direction is more curable (Cels 2.8.15).

(34) Nec *veri simile* est ea tum ad Galliam patuisse itinera (Livy 21.38.8)
Sunt qui hanc multitudinem captivam servorum fuisse scribant, idque *magis veri simile* est quam deditos venisse (Livy 7.27.9)
Utrum *veri similius* sit ab eo occisum qui adsiduus eo tempore Romae fuerit an ab eo qui multis annis Romam omnino non accesserit (Pro Rosc Am 92).

The first example (Livy 21.38) says that it is not the case that the degree of probability that those routes were open at that time is greater than .5. The second example (Livy 7.27) says that the degree of probability that those sold were slaves is greater than the degree of probability that they were soldiers who had surrendered: *magis veri simile* means $\lambda q \lambda p.P(p) > P(q)$.

Deontic modality

Like circumstantial modality (and unlike epistemic modality), deontic modality uses a circumstantial modal base, a set of facts in the actual world. The ordering source comprises a set of norms or obligations. The existence of the norms is also a fact of the actual world, but adherence or obedience to the norms is not necessarily a fact of the actual world: if people always behaved in a legally and morally ideal manner, one might still need laws but one wouldn't need penalties. The deontically accessible worlds are those possible worlds accessible from the actual world in which the laws or norms are not violated (just as circumstantially accessible worlds are those worlds in which the laws of nature are not violated, and epistemically accessible worlds are those in which principles of inference like stereotypicality are not violated). The following examples illustrate some of the different types of norms that can be used as ordering sources for deontic modals

(35) veterem cooptari *necesse* erat *legibus* (Verr 2.2.124)
Non *potes* tu *lege* vendere illam (Pl Merc 450)
cur... in illius legione miles fuisti, cum *per leges militares* effugere *liceret* iniquitatem tribuni? (Pro Flacc 77)
Sin autem hoc... *ex foedere licuit* (Livy 42.41.11)
Ac ne vindemiam quidem cogi *per religiones pontificum* feriis *licet* nec oves tondere... defrutum quoque facere et vinum defrutare licet (Col 2.21.4)

(34) And it is not probable that these routes to Gaul were open at that time (Livy 21.38.8). There are some who write that this multitude of captives consisted of slaves, and this is more probable than that men who had surrendered were sold (Livy 7.27.9). Whether it is more probable that he was killed by a man who was constantly in Rome at that time or by one who had not gone to Rome at all for many years (Pro Rosc Am 92).

(35) It was legally required for a member of the old class to be chosen (Verr 2.2.124). You can't sell her legally (Pl Merc 450). Why were you a soldier in his legion, although according to the military regulations you could have avoided a prejudiced tribune (Pro Flacc 77). But if it was permitted under the terms of the treaty (Livy 42.41.11). But it is not permissible either according to the regulations of the priests to pick the grapes on holidays nor to shear sheep. It is permitted to make must and to boil down wine (Col 2.21.4).

(36) *Senatus... decernit...* suo atque populi iniussu nullum *potuisse* foedus fieri (Sall Jug 39.3)
Et vidit quae *mos* ipse videre *vetat* (Ov Rem 438)
potes id *mea voluntate* facere (Ad Att 12.30.1)
tuas litteras... quibus petis ut tibi *per me liceat* quendam de exsilio reducere adiurasque id te invito me non esse facturum (Phil 2.9).

We see that the deontic ordering sources include different types of laws, treaty provisions, religious requirements, senatorial decrees, societal customs and personal permissions. The italicized phrases explicitly exclude potential nondeontic readings: for instance in the second example in (35) (Merc 450) it is physically possible for her to be sold (circumstantial *possum*) and a perfectly reasonable inference that it may turn out to be the case that she is sold (epistemic *possum*), it is just not legally possible for her to be sold (deontic *possum*). The intersection between the set of worlds accessible from the actual world in which the relevant law is obeyed and the set of worlds in which she is sold is the empty set: $\{w\text{: } R^{Deont}(w^*, w) = 1\} \cap \{w\text{: Vendis illam}(w) = 1\} = \varnothing$.

We have seen that the way in which the modal base interfaces with the ordering source can be conditionalized to different possibilities. In some scenarios a wine jar breaks, in others it doesn't; in some scenarios the correct inference is that Lucceius is in Rome, in others (e.g. he falls ill) that he isn't. The different scenarios are covered by different clauses of the laws of physics and stereotypicality respectively. For each different clause of the ordering source the modal base provides a different set of worlds to match. This is particularly clear for deontic modality

(37) Tertio loco, *si nemo sit heres*, is qui de bonis quae eius fuerint cum moritur usu ceperit plurimum possidendo. Quarto qui *si nemo sit qui ullam rem ceperit*, de creditoribus eius plurimum servet. (De Leg 2.48).

The rules for the performance of the *sacra privata* provide for various possibilities depending on the availability of heirs, legatees, creditors and debtors of the deceased in any particular situation. Each possibility is a slightly different set of facts generating a different set of accessible worlds, for each of which there is a matching clause in the ordering source. For instance for the third option the law provides that when the actual world is such that there is no heir, in all worlds in which the provisions of the law are fulfilled the familial rites are assigned to the

(36) The senate resolved that no treaty could have been made without its authorization and that of the people (Sall Jug 39.3). And saw what normal standards of decency themselves forbid one to see (Ov Rem 438). As far as I am concerned you are free to do so (Ad Att 12.30.1). Your letter... in which you ask me to allow you to recall someone from exile and swear that you will not do so without my consent (Phil 2.9).

(37) In the third case, if there is no heir, the person who obtains by possession the largest part of the property that belonged to the deceased at the time of his death [is required to perform the rites]. In the fourth case, if there is noone who acquires any part of the property, the creditor who keeps the largest part of the estate (De Leg 2.48).

person who takes over the largest part of the property by occupancy. As already noted, laws are not always observed, so they can provide penalties in the case of the actual world being one in which the law has been violated

(38) quique non paruerit, capital esto (De Leg 2.21)
poenaque est "si quis bustum... aut monimentum... aut columnam violarit, laeserit, fregerit" (De Leg 2.64).

The law is the primary obligation, the penalty is a contrary-to-duty obligation. (Examples with imperatives can be found in the Twelve Tables.) It may also happen that in the actual world someone not only fails to obey the law but also fails to get punished because he is pardoned or the authorities are corrupt

(39) Ei ignoscitur qui *puniri debuit* (Sen De Clem 2.7.1)
quod scelus *vindicare debebant*, inhonesti lucri captura invitati auctoritatibus suis texerunt (Val Max 9.4.1).

Here even the less than ideal penalty worlds fail to get actuated and become counterfactual in the past: what gets actuated is a deontically inaccessible world.

The modal force of obligations is universal: all worlds (or all the best worlds) deontically accessible from the actual world are worlds in which the norm is obeyed

(40) Aut non *suscipienda* fuit ista causa, Antoni, aut cum suscepisses *defendenda* usque ad extremum. (Phil 2.75)
Nam si violandum est *ius*, regnandi gratia violandum est; aliis rebus pietatem *colas* (De Off 3.82; Suet 1.30.5)
Imitari, Castor, potius avi *mores* disciplinamque *debebas* quam optimo et clarissimo viro... male dicere (Pro Reg Deiot 28)
Omnibus eum contumeliis onerasti quem patris loco, si ulla in te *pietas* esset, colere *debebas*. (Phil 2.99).

The examples with a past tense all illustrate an obligation that was not carried out in the actual world. A distinction can be made between people's obligations under the law or under the norms of morality (weak necessity expression) and the strict requirements of the law (strong necessity expression)

(38) If anyone fails to obey, it shall be a capital offence (De Leg 2.21). A penalty is specified for anyone who violates, damages or breaks down a tomb or burial monument or column (De Leg 2.64).

(39) Pardon is given to a man who ought to have been punished (Sen De Clem 2.7.1). Attracted by a desire for dishonest profit they covered up with their authority a crime that they ought to have punished (Val Max 9.4.1).

(40) Either you should not have taken on that cause, Antony, or, once you had taken it on, you should have defended it right up to the end (Phil 2.75). If the law is to be broken, it is to be broken for the sake of the throne; in other matters respect morality (De Off 3.82). You ought rather to have imitated the character of your grandfather, Castor, than to have slandered an excellent and outstanding man (Pro Reg Deiot 28). For you heaped every insult onto the man whom, if you had any sense of family obligation, you would have respected like your father (Phil 2.99).

(41) ex lege utrum statim fieri *necesse* sit, utrum habeat aliquam moram... nam id quod statim *faciendum* sit perfici prius *oportet* (De Inv 2.146)
Qui vinum fugiens vendat sciens, *debeatne* dicere: non *necesse* putat Diogenes, Antipater *viri boni* existimat (De Off 3.91)
tamquam ita fieri non solum *oporteret* sed etiam *necesse* esset, tamquam hoc senatus mandasset populusque Romanus iussisset (Verr 2.4.84).

At least in principle, weak necessity allows for access to less than optimal worlds in which compliance fails or is incomplete. There is a comparable distinction between weak deontic necessity and strong circumstantial necessity in the following examples

(42) Quod fieri, praeterquam quod ita *deberet*, etiam prope *necessarium* esse; ita enim esse obstinatos milites ut non ultra retineri *posse* in provincia viderentur (Livy 40.35.6)
aliquam rem quam caram esse omnibus aut *necesse* est aut *oportet* esse (De Inv 2.86)
aut *oportuerit* aut *licuerit* aut *necesse* fuerit (De Or 2.106).

In the last example (De Or 2.106) there is a three-way contrast between what is deontically required (*oportuerit*), what is deontically permissible (*licuerit*) and what is circumstantially necessary (*necesse fuerit*) for instance in self-defence. The modal force of permissions is existential: in some world deontically accessible from the actual world the norm is obeyed

(43) Si *potest* quod civili bello actum est obici (Sen Con 7.2.9)
Quis tibi id permisit? Quo *iure* fecisti?... Qui tibi id facere *licuit*? (Verr 2.5.151)
fuerisne, quod *sine senatus consulto* tibi facere non *licuit*, in regno Hiempsalis... ? (In Vat 12).

The last example (In Vat 12) asserts the existence of a prohibition: as usual, outer negation of the existential ($\neg\exists w$) is equivalent to inner negation of the universal ($\forall w\neg$). If there is no legally accessible world in which Vatinius visits Hiempsal,

(41) Whether according to the law immediate action is required or some delay is permitted; for what has to be done immediately ought to be done first (De Inv 2.146). Whether someone who is knowingly selling wine that is going off has an obligation to say so: Diogenes thinks that it is not necessary, Antipater believes that a good person ought to do so (De Off 3.91). As though it was not only proper but actually necessary, as though the senate had instructed him to do so and the Roman people had ordered it (Verr 2.4.84).

(42) Apart from the fact that it was right for this to happen, it was also almost inevitable; for the soldiers were so resolute that it didn't seem that they could be kept in the province any longer (Livy 40.35.6). Something which either must or ought to be dear to everyone (De Inv 2.86). Either it was right or it was permissible or it was necessary (De Or 2.106).

(43) If what was done in a civil war can be made the basis of a charge (Sen Con 7.2.9). Who authorized you to do so? By what right did you do so? How was it lawful for you to do this? (Verr 2.5.151). Whether you were in the kingdom of Hiempsal, something that you could not do without a decree of the senate (In Vat 12).

then all legally accessible worlds are worlds in which Vatinius does not visit Hiempsal. Also as usual $\exists$ implicates $\neg\forall$ and $\neg\exists$ entails $\neg\forall$

(44) est... aliquid quod *non oportet*, etiam si *licet*; quicquid vero *non licet*, certe *non oportet* (Pro Balb 8).

In the following examples a legal and, respectively, circumstantial possibility is contrasted with a moral obligation

(45) Si *licuit*, an *debuerit*. Nocens est iste, sed mihi frater est. (Sen Con 7.1.17)
Miror cur me accuses cum tibi id facere non liceat. Quod si *liceret*, tamen non *debebas* (Ad Fam 7.27.1).

Different subtypes of deontic ordering (legal and moral) or even different ordering sources (deontic and circumstantial) can be used in the same sentence.

In the simplest account, modals take a single argument, the proposition that provides the nuclear scope for the quantification over possible worlds. On closer inspection, we find that either the modal base or the nuclear scope or both may have to be relativized to some individual, a discourse participant or a participant in the eventuality described by the proposition. We saw that for epistemic modals the modal base has to be relativized to some knowledge agent, the speaker by default, while the stereotypical ordering source was circumstantial. For deontics, the modal base is circumstantial and the norms of the ordering source (like not breaking the rules or keeping one's promises) typically apply to communities rather than to single individuals (although, particularly in performative uses of deontics, the authority to impose an obligation can be attributed to the speaker). Rather what we commonly find in deontics is that some individual is identified as the carrier of the obligation. The modalized proposition tells us not only what the world is like if the norm is obeyed but also who bears the responsibility for seeing to it that this actually happens. Often it is the subject of the embedded proposition

(46) Frumentum, inquit, *me* abs te emere *oportet* (Verr 2.3.196)
faber haec faciat *oportet* (Cato 14.1).

In the case of a personal modal, it is also the subject of the modal itself

(47) *qui* milites dare *debebant* (Livy 34.56.5)
duae causae sunt cur *tu* frequentior in isto officio esse *debeas* quam nos (Ad Fam 15.20.2),

(44) For there are things that are not right even if they are lawful; but whatever is not lawful is also certainly not right (Pro Balb 8).

(45) If it was lawful, whether he should have done it. He is guilty, but he is my brother (Sen Con 7.1.17). I don't understand why you are accusing me when you do not have the right to do so. And even if you had the right, you ought not to (Ad Fam 7.27.1).

(46) I have to buy corn from you, he says (Verr 2.3.196). The builder is responsible for constructing the following (Cato 14.1).

(47) Who were required to provide troops (Livy 34.56.5). There are two reasons why you ought to write letters more frequently than me (Ad Fam 15.20.2).

while in the gerund(ive) construction it is a possessive dative. The subject can also be arbitrary

(48) Pullos non *oportet* singulos... tollere (Col 8.5.15)
isto bono *utare* dum adsit (De Sen 33)
Ames parentem si aequus est, si aliter *feras* (Publ Syr A8).

That there is a difference between this type of deontic subject and individual subjects of epistemic modals is evident from examples with symmetric predicates

(49) Sed me movet unus vir cuius fugientis *comes*... videor esse *debere* (Ad Att 8.14.2)
Genetivus aut *par* esse *debet* nominativo aut non plus una syllaba excedere (GL 5.536K).

Although subjects and complements of symmetrical predicates may have distinctive pragmatic properties (topicality) and even semantic properties (initiation of or involvement in the event), there is always a symmetricality entailment: if Cicero is with Pompey (Ad Att 8.14), then Pompey is with Cicero; if the genitive has the same number of syllables as the nominative (Palaemon 536), then the nominative has the same number of syllables as the genitive. This entailment survives under epistemic modalization: 'Cicero (Pompey) is very likely to be with Pompey (Cicero)'; 'The genitive (nominative) is very likely to have the same number of syllables as the nominative (genitive).' But it does not survive under deontic modalization: if Cicero has a duty to be with Pompey, it does not follow that Pompey has a duty to be with Cicero; if there is a rule for genitive formation requiring parisyllabicity with the nominative, it does not follow that there should be any rule at all for forming the nominative from the genitive. This suggests that while the subject is inside the scope of an epistemic modal, it is outside the scope of a deontic modal. On this approach, an epistemic modal takes the proposition p as its single overt argument, a deontic modal takes two arguments, an individual x and the property P that is the obligation of that individual. The nuclear scope of an epistemic gives the set of worlds in which the proposition is true ($\lambda w.p(w)$), that of a deontic the set of worlds in which some property holds of an individual ($\lambda w \lambda x.P(x,w)$). The former says that in all probable worlds Cicero is with Pompey; the latter says that Cicero is such that in all worlds in which he complies with his obligations he is with Pompey: the different structures involved are set out informally in Figure 9.7.

It is clear that this simple schema will not work in many cases. In the following examples the carrier of obligation is not a syntactic argument at all, but accessible by inference from the context

(48) Chickens should not be removed one by one (Col 8.5.15). One should enjoy this asset while it is there (De Sen 33). You should love your parent if he is just, if not you should put up with him (Publ Syr A8).

(49) There is just one man who affects me, whose companion it seems that I ought to be in his flight (Ad Att 8.14.2). The genitive should either have the same number of syllables as the nominative or be no more than one syllable longer (GL 5.536K).

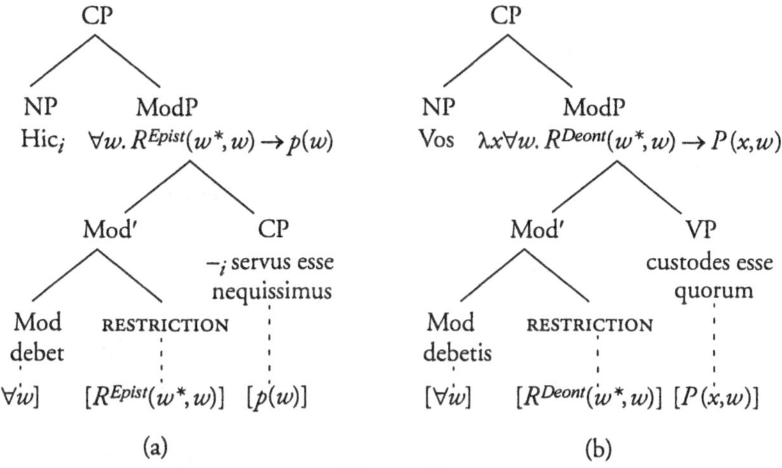

Figure 9.7
Epistemic subject raising versus deontic predication
(a) Epistemic: *Hic debet servus esse nequissimus* (Petr 49)
(b) Deontic: *quorum vos custodes esse debetis* (De Dom 37)

(50) Scrofa in sua quaeque hara suos alat *oportet* porcos (Varro RR 2.4.13) acerbum nisi ex alba olea fieri non *debet* (Col 11.2.83).

It is not the sow or the bitter oil that is the carrier of obligation but an arbitrary farmer. (There is also a teleological reading available for this example and similar ones below, according to which the farmer has a goal rather than a norm.) This also applies to passive generics that are used with a stipulative connotation

(51) fodere oportet... danda fossio est... Iisdem diebus... oleae *putantur* et *muscantur.* (Col 11.2.41)
In quadratum pedem *seruntur* grana sex eius seminis Arcturo exoriente (Col 2.10.21).

With nonagentive verbs the subject may have the obligation to experience or undergo some eventuality

(52) Si est spes aliqua rebus communibus, ea tu... *carere* non *debes* (Ad Fam 6.1.4)
Quo tempore? est enim ullum quo nocens *perire* non *debeat*? (Sen Con 9.2.20)
Ego *mori debeo*, qui amicitiae sacramentum delevi (Petr 80).

(50) Each sow should feed her pigs in her own separate sty (Varro RR 2.4.13). Bitter oil should only be made from white olives (Col 11.2.83).

(51) One should dig... must be given a good digging... During the same period olive trees get pruned and moss is removed from them (Col 11.2.41). Six grains of this seed per square foot are sown at the rising of Arcturus (Col 2.10.21).

(52) But if the political situation affords some hope, you ought not to be excluded from it (Ad Fam 6.1.4). When? Is there any time that a guilty person ought not to perish? (Sen Con 9.2.20). I ought to die, because I broke the oath of friendship (Petr 80).

Some passives can be read in the same way

(53) quisquis patrem pulsavit *puniri debet* (Sen Con 9.4.10)
Non ego nego securi quemquam *feriri debere* (Verr 2.5.133)
Rus hoc *vocari debet* an domus longe? (Mart 3.58.51).

The first example (Con 9.4) does not mean that someone has the obligation to punish him but that he deserves to be punished. But other passives cannot have this reading, for instance the following with nonspecific indefinite subjects

(54) gratiae sunt *agendae*... Curioni (Ad Fam 8.11.2)
veterani *debent intermisceri* (Col 8.10.1).

In the first example (Ad Fam 8.11) the thanks have no need or obligation: it is required that there be an event of thanks being given. Likewise in the second example (Col 8.10) the old thrushes don't need anything, it is the newly caught ones that need the company of the old ones; the carrier of obligation is again the covert agent farmer. This example is generic, but over events, not over thrushes: in all worlds in which the best farming practices are observed it typically happens under normal circumstances that old thrushes are mixed in among the new ones in those worlds. In both examples the subject is inside the scope of the modal, just as in an epistemic. Impersonals and anaphoric pronouns can introduce events as subjects of a deontic modal

(55) ita acriter... ut a viris fortibus in extrema spe... *pugnari debuit* (BG 2.33)
idque quater anno fieri *debet* (Col 6.4.1).

The pronoun in the second example (Col 6.4) might be outside the scope of the modal, but there is no overt argument to be outside the modal in the case of the impersonal (BG 2.33). We also find both scope types with event nouns

(56) huic tamen ignoranti *damnatio* patris nocere non *debuit* (Quint Decl 366.3)
Ablaqueationem deinde sequitur... putatio... Quae *putatio* non *debet* secundum articulum fieri (Col 4.9.1)
De magnitudinibus autem *finitio* nulla *debet* esse (Vitr 5.12.7).

In the first two examples (Decl 366.3; Col 4.9) the event noun is definite, which gives a categorical sentence; so the subject could be outside the scope of the

(53) Whoever has struck his father ought to be punished (Sen Con 9.4.10). I do not say that noone should ever be beheaded (Verr 2.5.133). Should this be called a country property or a townhouse far from town? (Mart 3.58.51).

(54) Curio must be thanked (Ad Fam 8.11.2). Old ones should be mixed in with them (Col 8.10.1).

(55) As fiercely as brave men in a desperate situation ought to fight (BG 2.33). This should be done four times a year (Col 6.4.1).

(56) The condemnation of his father ought not to have harmed him when he didn't know about it (Quint Decl 366.3). Pruning then follows loosening of the soil. This pruning should not be done close to the joint (Col 4.9.1). There should be no limitation on their dimensions (Vitr 5.12.7).

modal, if the semantics correlates with the syntax. But in the last example (Vitr 5.12) we have a nonspecific indefinite in a modalized thetic sentence. In this type of sentence the event noun has to be inside the scope of the modal (again like an epistemic): it is required that there not be any limitation on dimensions.

The existence of an external subject argument representing the carrier of obligation in deontic modals has some interesting consequences: especially in the second person (when the carrier of obligation is typically the addressee), modals can take on a secondary directive connotation; this is known as the performative use. In addition to their primary function of conveying information about deontically accessible worlds, they assume a secondary function of requiring, requesting or permitting the addressee to act in such a way that his actions conform to the norms in the ordering source. Assertions and directives are different types of speech act, but there are examples of modals and imperatives being used almost interchangeably

(57) *Exi*, inquam; age *exi*. *Exeundum* hercle tibi hinc est foras (Pl Aul 40).

This also emerges from the following pairs of examples

(58) vos, iudices,... penitus *perspicere debetis* (Pro Clu 95)
Hoc quod nunc vos, quaeso, *perspicite* (De Leg Agr 2.95)

Irasci nostro *non debes*, Cerdo, libello (Mart 3.99.1)
Noli, amabo, Amphitruo, *irasci* Sosiae (Pl Amph 540)

Si mihi non parcis, fortunae *parcere debes* (Ov Trist 5.6.33)
Si tibi non parcis, dilectae *parce* puellae (Ov Her 19.205).

While modalized propositions are primarily assertions and only secondarily directives, so conversely imperatives are primarily directive but can have the corresponding modalized proposition as a secondary connotation. So the second example of each pair in (58) can have the first as an implicature. That they are not actually interchangeable is clear on a number of counts. For instance the negative for deontic modals is *non* as in the third example *irasci... non debes* (Mart 3.99), while the negative for prohibitions is *ne* (*ne suscensueris* Mart 7.60.6). Modals can occur in questions, but imperatives cannot

(59) His igitur auctoribus *nonne debes* moveri? (ND 3.13),

and they take different propositional modifiers

(60) *Nisi fallor*... hoc primum *aestimare debetis* (Quint Decl Maior 16.8)
Aestimate quale sit scelus istius (Sen Con 10.4.1).

(57) Get out, I say; come on, get out. You have to get the hell out of here (Pl Aul 40).

(58) You must consider carefully, gentlemen of the jury (Pro Clu 95). What I now ask you to consider (De Leg Agr 2.95). You should not be angry at my little book, Cerdo (Mart 3.99.1). Please don't be angry with Sosia, Amphitruo (Pl Amph 540). If you have no consideration for me, you ought to have consideration for my misfortune (Ov Trist 5.6.33). If you have no consideration for yourself, have consideration for the girl you love (Ov Her 19.205).

(59) So shouldn't you be influenced by the authority of this evidence? (ND 3.13).

(60) Unless I am mistaken, you should consider this point first (Quint Decl Maior 16.8). Consider the nature of this man's crime (Sen Con 10.4.1).

Nisi fallor could hardly be used with the imperative in the second example (Con 10.4). Conversely *amabo* in the fourth example in (58) (Amph 540) could hardly be used with the modal in the third example (Mart 3.99). On the other hand, since the first example in each pair clearly expresses the speaker's wishes, the addressee could hardly respond with a propositional denial like 'That's not true.'

The same relationship between primary assertion and secondary directive that we have just seen for obligations also occurs with permissions

(61) LYS. *Licetne* amplecti te?... OL. *Licet* (Pl Cas 457).

In both constructions the speaker gives the addressee permission to do something that otherwise the addressee might have taken to be forbidden by the authority of the speaker (either the addressee is mistaken and the action was permissible all along, or the speaker has just changed his mind)

(62) Iure tuo nostris *maneas licet* hospes in hortis (Mart 5.62.1)
neglegite praeterita *si vultis* (Verr 2.3.219).

The descriptive implicature of the imperative in the second example (Verr 2.3) says that Cicero permits the judges to ignore previous incidents of provincial extortion (whether they want to or not), and the primary directive meaning says to go ahead and do so if they want (all they are required to do is condemn Verres). In both examples whether something is permitted or not depends on the speaker, whether the permission is acted upon depends on the addressee. The modal construction has the resources to keep obligations separate from permissions (*oportet* versus *licet*), while the imperative collapses them into a single form, leaving the distinction to be recovered from the context.

When the speaker is simply reminding the hearer about what is known by both to be required or permitted, the meaning of the modal can be captured in a purely static perspective: it is simply the universal or existential quantification over worlds that we have been using up to this point. The information represents a fact about the actual world that can be activated as a topic of conversation. But if the speaker is causing a change in the deontic situation, a revision in the deontic beliefs of the addressee, then we need (additionally) a dynamic perspective on meaning to capture the modification. In order to keep things simple we will forget about properties and simply talk about p (the proposition in the scope of the modal). On one approach, p is added to the set of propositions in the ordering source, just as it can be added to the modal base for suppositions (*puta* 'suppose'), concessions (*fuerit* 'granted that he was') and conditional protases (*si fuisset* 'if he had been'). The revised ordering source is used to compute the new set of deontically accessible worlds in all or some of which p is true.

(61) LYS. Can I hug you? OL. You can (Pl Cas 457).
(62) It's fine for you to stay freely as a guest at my country house (Mart 5.62.1). Ignore the past if you want (Verr 2.3.219).

Note that p has to carry its practical entailments along with it: if you learn that you must attack the enemy, you must also draw your sword; we don't want to end up with obligatory worlds in which you attack the enemy with your sword undrawn. Also, if p actually reverses a previously applicable prohibition q, then q has to be removed from the ordering source to keep the set of norms consistent. On another approach the revision is made directly to the set of deontically accessible worlds. For obligations we need to remove some previously permissible worlds, specifically to throw out all the worlds in which p (together with its entailments) are not true. Technically this is done by intersecting the old set of worlds (in some of which $\neg p$ is true) with the set of worlds in which p is true. For permissions we need to remove a pre-existing prohibition against p. We start with a set of worlds in none of which p is true and we use set union to add some worlds in which p is true, but only those in which p and its entailments are true without licensing a bunch of other irrelevant "spurious" permissions: 'you may kiss the bride' does not mean 'you may kiss the bride and the bridesmaids,' although there are possible worlds in which you do both. So we have to sort through the worlds in which p is true and order them so as to be able to pick just those that involve the minimum necessary adjustments to the pre-existing set. Finally if the speaker is using the modal performatively (with an imperative implicature), he is aiming to regulate some agent's future behaviour, typically the addressee's; that is to restrict the set of possible future worlds to those in which p is true as a result of the action of the addressee (all of them for commands, some of them for permissions). The actual world has to develop into one of the deontically accessible worlds. Assuming that the addressee has a list of things he needs to do and a list of things that are OK for him to do, the performative meaning requires p (again with its entailments) to be added to the former list in the case of commands and to the latter in the case of permissions.

Bouletic modality

The ordering source for circumstantial modality was the laws of nature, for epistemic modality the norms of stereotypicality and for deontic modality the rules of an institution or the norms of morality. Each of these different sets of norms is pretty much accepted throughout society: none of them typically varies much from one person to another. By contrast, the modals we will discuss in the next three sections require their ordering source to be relativized to some individual, since wishes, goals and abilities do vary significantly from person to person. Of course, this does not preclude assertions about the wishes, goals or abilities of a plurality (either episodic or generic), which represent the intersection of the wishes, etc., of the members of the plurality.

As its name implies, bouletic modality is concerned with people's wants, wishes, desires and preferences. It is quite complex to analyze, since it requires two ordering sources. Let's start with wishes that are realizable

(63) Te *spectem* suprema mihi cum venerit hora (Tib 1.1.58)
Quem tu nimis urbanus es nisi concupiscis; atque *utinam concupiscas* (Pliny Ep 2.17.29)
Eas litteras *volo habeas* (Ad Att 13.32.2)
Othonem *vincas volo* (Ad Att 13.29.1).

The first two examples (Tib 1.1; Pliny 2.17) are direct nonpropositional expressions of items from the speaker's wish list. The other two examples (Ad Att 13.32; 13.29) are regular assertions, therefore propositions. The relationship between the nonpropositional and the propositional expression of wishes is analogous to that between imperatives and deontic modals described in the previous section. In the third example (Ad Att 13.32) possible worlds in which Atticus receives copies of Cicero's philosophical writings are among the worlds compatible with Cicero's wishes (in w^*) and are ranked higher than possible worlds in which he doesn't; both sets of worlds represent possible future developments of the actual world. In the last example (Ad Att 13.29) possible worlds in which Atticus outbids Otho for Scapula's gardens are among the worlds compatible with Cicero's wishes and are ranked higher than possible worlds in which he doesn't; this example has a secondary directive connotation. Negation reverses the ranking

(64) Uxorem *nolo* Telesillam *ducere* (Mart 2.49.1)
alius "hoc *volo*," inquit, "*discere*, istud *nolo*" (Gell 1.9.9).

Worlds in which the poet marries Telesilla are not compatible with his wishes and are ranked lower than worlds in which he doesn't (Mart 2.49). Preferences express the relative ranking of two sets of possible worlds (without requiring that either or both of them necessarily be compatible with an individual's wishes)

(65) *malle* quod dixerim me *cum Pompeio vinci* quam *cum istis vincere* (Ad Att 8.7.2)
Sed quae faciam fecerimque pro te *ex illorum te litteris* quam *ex meis malo cognoscere* (Ad Fam 6.14.1).

The set of possible worlds in which Ligarius finds out about Cicero's efforts for his recall from exile from his brothers' letters is ranked higher than the set of possible worlds in which Ligarius finds out from Cicero's own letters (Ad Fam 6.14: $\{w: w \in p\} > \{w: w \in q\}$).

(63) May I look at you when my final hour arrives (Tib 1.1.58). You are too much of a city person if you don't long to enjoy this place, and I hope you do (Pliny Ep 2.17.29). I want you to have these works (Ad Att 13.32.2). I want you to outbid Otho (Ad Att 13.29.1).

(64) I don't want to marry Telesilla (Mart 2.49.1). Another one says "I want to learn this, I don't want to learn that" (Gell 1.9.9).

(65) My having said that I prefer to be conquered with Pompey than to conquer with Caesar's side (Ad Att 8.7.2). But I prefer you to find out what I am doing and have done for you from their letters rather than from mine (Ad Fam 6.14.1).

Only accessible worlds are included in this ranking: ideally Cicero would like to get the gardens for free ($\{w: w \in r\}$), but he does not say he wants to, because worlds in which he does are not accessible. The ideal bouletic ordering source gives the order $r > p > q$, the realistic one gives $p > q$ (with r inaccessible and so excluded from consideration). Therefore the first step in the analysis is to establish a modal base and an ordering source with which to choose the accessible worlds for wishes. Although a simple circumstantial modal base would often work fine, examples like the following show that the modal base has to be personalized to the individual who is doing the wishing

(66) Aeolis interea tantorum ignara malorum... utque foret sospes coniunx suus utque rediret optabat, nullamque sibi praeferret; at illi *hoc de tot votis* poterat contingere *solum* (Ov Met 11.573).

Alcyone in her prayers expresses her wish that Ceyx may return safely to her, although in fact he is already dead: only her last wish is for a set of circumstantially accessible worlds (*hoc poterat contingere solum*), the others are for doxastically accessible worlds. So the modal base is not circumstantial because wishes can be based on false information. It is doxastic rather than epistemic because wishes can be based not only on what the wisher knows (or thinks he knows) but also on what he merely believes ('I think it will rain tomorrow, so I want to buy an umbrella'). The doxastic modal base is filtered by a stereotypical ordering source to give just the set of accessible possible worlds (different ways the world could develop or possible candidates for actuality, as they have been called). The bouletic ordering source selects the contextually relevant subset of these possible future developments and ranks them. For instance in the last example in (63) (Ad Att 13.29), the modal base provides the information that the gardens are for sale and that Otho wants to bid for them, the stereotypical ordering source eliminates fluke scenarios like the sale being cancelled or Otho having a heart attack while retaining worlds in which Atticus outbids Otho and worlds in which he does not, and the bouletic ordering source says that worlds in which Atticus outbids Otho are ranked higher than worlds in which he doesn't. Just as the modal base has to be personalized (because different beliefs can be the basis for different wishes), so the bouletic ordering source has to be personalized, because not everything that x wishes is also something that y wishes ($\neg\forall w. R^{Boul(x)}(w^*, w) \rightarrow R^{Boul(y)}(w^*, w)$)

(67) quae ego *volo* tu *non vis*, quae ego *nolo* ea *cupis* (Naevius in GL 1.197K).

It is possible for two people to share the same beliefs without having the same desires. Some examples require quantification over different bouletic ordering sources

(66) Meanwhile the daughter of Aeolus, unaware of this terrible accident, prayed that her husband might be safe and might return and prefer no other woman to her; but out of so many prayers only this last one could come true (Ov Met 11.573).

(67) What I want you don't want, what I don't want you desire (Naevius GL 1.197K).

(68) Tertio anno domare incipiunt ad eas res quas *quisque* eos *vult* habere in usu. (Varro RR 2.6.4)
An ideonea sit in tractationes quas *quisque vult* dividit (Sen Con 1.2.14).

Different people wish to put asses to different uses (RR 2.6), each declaimer makes the thematic subdivisions he wishes to make (Con 1.2).

So far we have considered examples in which the wished for worlds are possible developments of the actual world. But of course not all wishes are realizable. For instance *utinam concupiscas* in the second example in (63) (Pliny Ep 2.17) is a realizable wish, but

(69) *utinam... reviviscat* frater aliamque classem in Siciliam ducat (Gell 10.6.2)

is not. Like 'want' in English, *volo* typically is used when the speaker thinks that his wish may be actualized but is not sure that it will be. Sometimes events prove him wrong: the highest ranked world is not actualized

(70) id quod *maxime volui* fieri non potuit (Pro Rosc Am 136)
id quod *maxime voluit* nullo modo potuit (Pro Caec 48)
occidere *nolui*, coactus sum (Sen Con 7.2.13).

Sometimes the speaker is being deliberately misleading

(71) Multa *videri* volumus *velle* sed *nolumus*... Saepe aliud *volumus*, aliud *optamus* (Sen Ep 95.2).

Gaudeo 'I am glad' is used when the speaker is sure that what he wishes will in fact occur (it is factive)

(72) Caesarem... inimicissimum mihi futurum *gaudere* se aiebant (Ad Fam 1.9.10).

They regarded it as a settled issue that Caesar would be hostile to Cicero and they ranked worlds in which he was higher than worlds in which he wasn't. At the other end of the scale is the situation in which the speaker's wishes are incompatible with his beliefs about the future

(73) *Velim* Pompeius idem faciat. Qui ut adduci tali tempore ad ullam condicionem possit *magis opto quam spero*. Sed cum... timere desierit,

(68) In the third year one begins to train them for the tasks for which each one wants them to be in use (Varro RR 2.6.4). Everyone divides the issue of whether she is suitable into the treatment he wishes (Sen Con 1.2.14).

(69) I wish my brother would come back to life and lead another fleet to Sicily (Gell 10.6.2).

(70) What I wanted most became impossible (Pro Rosc Am 136). He was quite unable to do what he most wanted (Pro Caec 48). I didn't want to kill him; I was forced to (Sen Con 7.2.13).

(71) There are many things that we wish to seem to want but actually don't want. We often want one thing and pray for another (Sen Ep 95.2).

(72) They said that they were happy that Caesar was going to be very hostile to me (Ad Fam 1.9.10).

(73) I wish Pompey would do the same. I do not expect that he can be persuaded to come to any terms in these circumstances, though that is what I pray for. But, once he has regained his selfconfidence, I will begin to have some hope that your authority will be of great influence with him (Ad Att 8.15a.1).

tum incipiam non desperare tuam auctoritatem plurimum apud eum valiturum. (Ad Att 8.15a.1).

In this example at the time of writing (t^u: *tali tempore*) future worlds in which Pompey reconciles with Caesar are bouletically accessible for Balbus but doxastically inaccessible, accessible as desire worlds but inaccessible as belief worlds; at a later time (t': *cum timere desierit*) they will become doxastically accessible too. Let us assume three sets of possible worlds, a set in which Pompey agrees to reconcile with Caesar $\{w: w \in p\}$, a set in which he refuses to reconcile with Caesar $\{w: w \in q\}$, and for the sake of argument a set in which Pompey does neither but instead capitulates voluntarily and disappears off the face of the earth $\{w: w \in r\}$. Assuming that Balbus is really on Caesar's side, r would be the optimal outcome, but it has no chance of actually happening. The ideal bouletic ordering is $r > p > q$, the realistic bouletic ordering at t^u gives only one set of accessible worlds (the undesirable q; p and r are inaccessible), the realistic bouletic ordering at t' is $p > q$ (r is still inaccessible), and the doxastic ordering is $q > p > r$, with the accessibility cut-off point above p at t^u and below p at t'. All this is set out in Figure 9.8. Although the p worlds are doxastically inaccessible at t^u, they are doxastically accessible from a conditionalized doxastic modal base

(74) Sum tamen hoc tempore occupatissimus. Ideo non eum legi, cum *alioqui* valdissime *cupiam.* (Pliny Ep 9.35.1)
Si possim, velim. Verum hic apud me cenant alieni novem (Pl Stich 486).

Worlds in which Pliny reads his correspondent's book are not compatible with his beliefs in w^*, but they are compatible with his beliefs when modified in such a way that he is no longer so busy (*alioqui*, world $w^{*\prime}$) (Ep 9.35). Worlds in which Gelasimus comes to dinner are not compatible with Epignomus' beliefs in w^*, but they are compatible with his beliefs when modified by a cancellation of the dinner with the Ambracian envoys (Stich 486). So the example in (73) can be understood as containing a covert conditional protasis shifting w^* into $w^{*\prime}$: if p were doxastically accessible, it would be ordered above q by an ordering source representing Balbus' wishes at t^u. On this approach the subjunctives are modally cumulative: *velim* gets you from w^* to $w^{*\prime}$, *faciat* gets you from $w^{*\prime}$ to

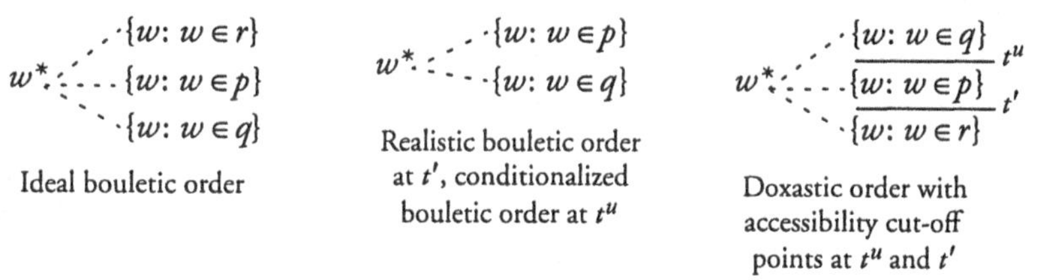

$$w^* \cdots \begin{cases} \{w: w \in r\} \\ \{w: w \in p\} \\ \{w: w \in q\} \end{cases}$$

Ideal bouletic order

$$w^* \cdots \begin{cases} \{w: w \in p\} \\ \{w: w \in q\} \end{cases}$$

Realistic bouletic order at t', conditionalized bouletic order at t^u

$$w^* \cdots \begin{cases} \{w: w \in q\} \\ \overline{\{w: w \in p\}}\ t^u \\ \overline{\{w: w \in r\}}\ t' \end{cases}$$

Doxastic order with accessibility cut-off points at t^u and t'

Figure 9.8
Bouletic modality
Velim Pompeius idem faciat (Ad Att 8.15a.1)

(74) But I am very busy right now. So I haven't read it, although otherwise I would very much like to do so (Pliny Ep 9.35.1). If I could, I would like to have you. But nine foreign guests are having dinner here at my house (Pl Stich 486).

$w^{*\prime\prime}$ ($w^{*\prime\prime}$ is a world compatible with Balbus' wishes in $w^{*\prime}$). *Velim* is also used in the following examples in which the speaker is not sure whether the bouletically highest ranked world is an open possibility or not

(75) *Velim* ante possis; *si minus*, utique simul simus cum Brutus veniet in Tusculanum (Ad Att 13.4.2)
Velim possis coram; *si minus*, litteris idem consequemur (Ad Att 15.8.2)
Huic tu libro maxime *velim* ex animo, *si minus* gratiae causa suffragere (Ad Fam 12.17.2.).

This last type seems to be the basis for the common politely tentative use of *velim* for perfectly realizable wishes (assuming the attenuative potential theory in preference to the modal attraction theory); compare the following minimal pair

(76) Syro *ignoscas volo* quae mea causa fecit (Ter Haut 1066)
ignoscas velim huic festinationi meae (Ad Fam 5.12.1).

Although a bouletic ordering source has to be personalized, bouletic modals can still be used with two different argument structures. The complement of a bouletic modal can be either a proposition

(77) Cupio... *me esse clementem* (Cat 1.4)
Cupio *eum suae causae confidere* (Pro Sest 135),

or a property

(78) Cupio... Alexandriam *reliquamque Aegyptum visere* (Ad Att 2.5.1)
pendula quod *patriae visere tecta* libet (Mart 10.13.2).

In the former case, the wisher wants a proposition to become true, in the latter case he wants to become a member of the set of individuals having a certain property. The appearance of *me* in the first example in (77) (In Cat 1.4) confirms the distinction rather than supporting the assumption of an empty pronominal subject position for the infinitives in (78).

Teleological modality

Teleological modality involves worlds in which the goals of an individual are attained. A circumstantial modal base provides the actual world w^*, which has a number of possible future developments. In some of them the individual attains his objectives in w^* and in others he does not; as usual, the former are the worlds

(75) I wish you could come earlier; if not, at least let's be together when Brutus comes to my place at Tusculum (Ad Att 13.4.2). I wish you could do so face to face; if not, we will achieve the same purpose by letters (Ad Att 15.8.2). I would like you to support this book preferably out of conviction, if not then as a favour (Ad Fam 12.17.2).
(76) I want you to forgive Syrus for what he did for my sake (Ter Haut 1066). I would like you to forgive this impatience of mine (Ad Fam 5.12.1).
(77) I desire it to be the case that I am merciful (Cat 1.4). I want him to have confidence in his case (Pro Sest 135).
(78) I desire to visit Alexandria and the rest of Egypt (Ad Att 2.5.1). That it pleases me to see the hillside roofs of my country (Mart 10.13.2).

that are accessible via the teleological accessibility relation ($\lambda w.R^{Tel(x)}(w^*, w)$). The teleological ordering source (the set of goals in question) determines which worlds are accessible and if necessary establishes an order among the accessible worlds. Purpose clauses are diachronically derived from independent sentences with bouletic modality; this shifts to teleological modality with subordination

(79) Hasdrubali occurrendum esse... *ne* Gallos Cisalpinos... sollicitaret, et Hannibalem suo proprio occupandum bello *ne* emergere ex Bruttiis atque obviam ire fratri posset (Livy 27.38.6).

The goals of the Romans in w^* are to stop Hasdrubal inciting the Cisalpine Gauls and to stop Hannibal from joining his brother; all worlds in which they attain these goals are worlds in which armies were sent to meet both enemy forces. Other purpose expressions work the same way

(80) Caesari *ad* saucios deponendos, stipendium exercitui dandum, socios confirmandos, praesidium urbibus relinquendum, necesse erat adire Apolloniam. (BC 3.78).

The use of the gerunds in (79) and of *necesse* in (80) makes them like anankastic conditionals: if Caesar is to achieve this list of objectives, he has to go to Apollonia; worlds in which he doesn't go to Apollonia are worlds in which the wounded don't get dropped off, the army doesn't get paid, etc. Often the objectives are not overtly stated but implicit in the context

(81) *terrendique* magis hostes erant quam fallendi (Livy 25.24.4)
Proxime indicari *debent* metalla ferri (NH 34.138).

It was no longer sufficient to escape the notice of the Syracusans in order to capture Epipolae (Livy 25.24); the next topic Pliny has to tackle if he is to give a complete and coherent account of metals is iron mines (NH 34.148). In the agricultural treatises, teleological modality typically describes the objectives of the generic farmer (first, second or third person: a deontic reading is also possible)

(82) *necesse* erit ad unam vel summum duas gemmas recidere surculum, ne proceriorem faciamus quam ut tempestates... pati possit (Col 4.29.6)
Agrum quibus locis conseras sic observari *oportet* (Cato 6.1)

(79) They felt that Hasdrubal should be confronted to prevent him from stirring up the Cisalpine Gauls and that Hannibal should be kept busy with his own war to prevent him from being able to come out of the territory of the Bruttii and meet his brother (Livy 27.38.6).

(80) It was necessary for Caesar to go to Apollonia to drop off the wounded, to give their salary to the army, to encourage the allies and to leave garrisons for the cities (BC 3.78).

(81) They now had to terrify the enemy rather than escape their notice (Livy 25.24.4). The next topic that has to be covered is that of iron mines (NH 34.138).

(82) It will be necessary to shorten the cutting to one or at the most two buds, so that we don't make it too long to withstand storms (Col 4.29.6). The following rule should be observed as to how you should plant the land (Cato 6.1).

(83) Eum porro an recte aretur frequenter explorare *debet* agricola (Col 2.4.3)
Si equo maxillae dolent, calido aceto *fovendae* et axungia vetere confricandae sunt (Col 6.30.6).

Our examples so far have had universal quantification: the modalized proposition is a sine qua non for goal achievement; doing nothing and just hoping or praying for the desired outcome is excluded by the ordering source. There may be other theoretically possible strategies for achieving one's objectives, but they too are excluded as impractical (their worlds are inaccessible): the fact that you can get from Rome to Naples by way of Chile is not relevant. But teleological modals with existential modal force also occur

(84) Satio autem cytisi vel autumno circa Idus Octobris vel vere fieri *potest.* (Col 5.12.2)
Sed pendent tibi crura. *Potes*, si forte iuvabit, cancellis primos inseruisse pedes (Ov Am 3.2.63).

To achieve your goals you can sow cytisus in autumn or in spring; the options given are exhaustive (sowing in summer or winter will not work) (Col 5.12). Ovid's girlfriend can rest her toes on the grating and see if that helps to achieve the objective of making her legs more comfortable (on a performative reading, this is a suggested course of action); she might also try something else (Am 3.2). A third option would be for her to just grin and bear it: the set of worlds in which she does that is teleologically inaccessible but circumstantially accessible.

Ability modality

Ability modality involves worlds in which the abilities of an individual are realized by action. A circumstantial modal base provides the actual world w^*, which has a number of possible future developments. Some of them contain events within the capability of the individual under the appropriate circumstances (the dynamically accessible worlds), others do not. The dynamic ordering source gives the capacities of the individual (physical, intellectual, sociopolitical), determines which worlds are dynamically accessible in light of those capacities, and establishes an order of accessibility among them. If the ability exists only in possible worlds rather than in the actual world ('He might be able to pass the test'), then the dynamic accessibility relation is between those possible worlds and the worlds in which the ability is actuated, because the modality is iterated. Ability modals can be used statively or eventively. The stative meaning typically expresses a stable, long-term property and means 'have the capacity to.'

(83) The farmer should check it frequently to see if it is being ploughed correctly (Col 2.4.3). If a horse has painful jaws, they should be treated with hot vinegar and rubbed with old axle grease (Col 6.30.6).
(84) The sowing of cytisus can be done either in autumn around the middle of October or in spring (Col 5.12.2). But your legs are hanging down. You can see if it helps to put your toes in the grating (Ov Am 3.2.63).

(85) An soli sumus qui flumina transnare *possumus*? (Curt Ruf 7.7.15)
Possum ego diversos iterum coniungere amantes et dominae tardas *possum* aperire fores (Prop 1.10.15)
Homines enim neque longule dissita neque proxime adsita *possumus* cernere (Apul Flor 2).

The first example (Curt Ruf 7.7: the ability is a presupposition) says that all dynamically accessible worlds in which there is a river we want to swim across and the weather is fine are worlds in which we swim across it. Some languages use different case marking in the complement phrase to distinguish abilities from events. The eventive meaning typically expresses a transient property, often depending more on the circumstances of the situation (like circumstantial modality) than on the agent's abilities

(86) Omnis populus *poterit* spectare triumphos (Ov Trist 4.2.19)
Massiliae animadvertere *possumus* sine tegulis... tecta (Vitr 2.1.5)
Sed *possumus* audire aliquid an serius venimus? (De Rep 1.20).

These examples all express opportunities rather than abilities. The stative meaning naturally tends to appear in the imperfective and the eventive meaning in the perfective. However these defaults can be overriden. A delimited, short-term ability can be perfective

(87) tenuit locum quam diu ferre *potuit* laborem (Brut 236),

and an event can be imperfective if distributed or negated

(88) qui velocitate effugere *poterant* (BAlex 76)
propter loci difficultatem neque equo neque vehiculo saluti suae praesidium parare *poterat* (BHisp 39).

The imperfective is vague about the actuation of the complement event in the real world: it may be the case that there is an opportunity in the real world to actuate the ability and that it is indeed actuated

(89) Dionysius omnia quae moveri *poterant* Dionis in naves imposuit (Nepos 10.4.2)
quantum diligentia provideri *poterat* providebatur (BG 6.34),

but there is no actuality entailment with the imperfective

(85) Are we the only ones that can swim across rivers? (Curt Ruf7.7.15). I can bring estranged lovers back together and I can open a mistress's recalcitrant door (Prop 1.10.15). We men can see neither objects that are somewhat far removed nor objects that are very close (Apul Flor 2).
(86) The whole people will be able to see the triumph (Ov Trist 4.2.19). At Massilia we can see roofs without tiles (Vitr 2.1.5). But can we hear some discussion or have we come too late? (De Rep 1.20).
(87) He held his position as long as he could carry the work load (Brut 236).
(88) Those that were able to escape due to their speed (BAlex 76). Due to the unevenness of the ground he could not effect his escape on horseback or in a vehicle (BHisp 39).
(89) Dionysius loaded all the movable property of Dion onto ships (Nepos 10.4.2). All the precautions that could be taken with due diligence were taken (BG 6.34).

(90) Hi *poterant* omnes eadem illa de Andromacha deplorare... sed iam decantaverant fortasse. (Tusc 3.53)
Poteras non flectere puppem, cum fugeres (Lucan 8.586).

One can have abilities that are never actuated and opportunities that one chooses not to actuate or not to reactuate. The perfective has two readings. The first entails actuation: it means 'manage to, successfully complete the action of.' An agent has the ability and the opportunity to see to it that *p* is actuated and he does so

(91) Ergo velocem *potuit* domuisse puellam (Prop 1.1.15)
Postume, plorantem *potuisti* linquere Gallam... ? (Prop 3.12.1).

In the second reading, which is salient when there is contrastive focus on the modal, the ability or opportunity is closed off by a failure to actuate. An agent has the ability and the opportunity to see to it that *p* is actuated but refrains from doing so

(92) Decem his annis proximis HS sexagiens honestissime consequi *potuit*: noluit (Pro Rosc Com 23)
At tamen in vostras *potuisti* ducere sedes (Catull 64.160).

At first sight the perfective meaning with actuation should entail the imperfective one (if you manage to do something, you can do it), but since this is not always the case ('It was a pure fluke that he managed to pass the test'), the relationship is an implicature. (Conversely the negated imperfective meaning would entail the negated perfective meaning if one discounted flukes.) On this view, flukes need to be distinguished from very shortlived abilities. The type of ability involved in a fluke perfective is not the same as the type of ability involved in an ordinary imperfective ability attribution. Flukes seem to be an extreme type of opportunity, where the circumstances are paramount and any contribution from the agent's ability is comparatively minor.

Negated perfectives can express failure to perform successfully ('Last night, he wasn't able to sing the high C') or just the absence of opportunity

(93) Filium tuum, ad Brutum cum veni, videre *non potui*, ideo quod iam in hiberna cum equitibus erat profectus (Ad Fam 12.14.8).

Negated imperfectives can express the simple absence of a permanent property

(90) All of them could have made the same complaint as in the Andromache. But perhaps by then they had already finished reciting their complaints (Tusc 3.53). You could have not changed course when you were fleeing (Lucan 8.586).

(91) Consequently he was able to subdue the swift girl (Prop 1.1.15). Postumus, how could you leave Galla weeping...? (Prop 3.12.1).

(92) In the past ten years he could have honourably made six million sesterces: he refused to do so (Pro Rosc Com 23). You could still have brought me into your home (Catull 64.160).

(93) I was unable to see your son when I visited Brutus, because he had already left for winter quarters with the cavalry (Ad Fam 12.14.8).

(94) *num* nescio qui ille divinus, si oculis captus sit... *possit* quae alba sint, quae nigra dicere (De Div 2.9)

or a short-term incapacity (the temporary suspension of a permanent property, whether episodic or iterated)

(95) verum *nequeo* dormire (Hor Sat 2.1.7)
non edepol bibere *possum* iam, ita animo malest (Pl Truc 365)
Illa velit, *poterit* magnes *non* ducere ferrum (Prop 4.5.9).

Negation may apply to both the activity and the telic phases of an accomplishment or to just the activity phase

(96) cum vallis aut locus declivis suberat, neque ei qui antecesserant morantibus opem ferre *poterant* (BC 1.79)
Primum Delphicum corrumpere est conatus. Cum id non *potuisset*... (Nepos 6.3.2).

In the first example (BC 1.79), presumably no attempt was made; in the second example (Nepos 6.3) an attempt was made but it was unsuccessful.

Finally, ability modals can appear in a shifted tense, whereby the imperfect expresses nonactuation in the present, and more rarely the pluperfect nonactuation in the past

(97) etsi *poteram* remanere, tamen... proficiscar hinc (Ad Att 13.26.2)
quamquam aliquid ipse *poteram*, tamen invenire malo paratiores (De Fin 2.119)
Is... vitam quam gloriosissime degere *potuerat* immatura morte finivit (Vell Pat 2.3.2).

This type is discussed in the section on tense below.

Ability modals generate pragmatically based scales of difficulty that can reverse the intrinsic scalar entailments of quantifiers

(98) cum quo Ripaeos *possim* conscendere montes (Prop 1.6.3)
decem versiculis totum conficere *potuisset* (De Or 2.327).

In the first example (Prop 1.6) the Rhipaean mountains are more distant than, say, the Alban Hills, so the distance of the destination is inversely correlated with

(94) Surely it is not the case that some diviner or other, if he is blind, can tell what is white and what is black (De Div 2.9).

(95) But I get insomnia (Hor Sat 2.1.7). I can't drink now, I feel so faint (Pl Truc 365). If she wishes it, a magnet will be able not to attract metal (Prop 4.5.9).

(96) Whenever a valley or a slope lay ahead and those who had gone on ahead could not bring help to those who delayed behind (BC 1.79). First he tried to corrupt the oracle at Delphi. When he was unable to do so... (Nepos 6.3.2).

(97) Although I could stay, I will leave here (Ad Att 13.26.2). Although I could make some points myself, I prefer to find people who are better prepared (De Fin 2.119). He ended with premature death a life which he could have led with the greatest glory (Vell Pat 2.3.2).

(98) With whom I could climb the Rhipaean mountains (Prop 1.6.3). He could have finished the thing in ten short verses (De Or 2.327).

the dynamic accessibility of the possible world (the more miles the mountains are distant, the less likely the worlds in which one is able to reach them: if you can do twenty miles, then you can do ten). In the second example (De Or 2.327) it is more difficult to compact the long background description at the beginning of the Andria into ten lines than it is into twenty, so the length of the description is positively correlated with the dynamic accessibility of the possible world (the more lines in the text, the more likely the worlds in which one is able to achieve that level of compaction: if you can do ten lines, then you can do twenty).

Subjunctives of ability modals in conditional and potential sentences are rather like their counterparts with bouletic modals

(99) Non mihi si linguae centum sint oraque centum... omnia poenarum percurrere nomina *possim* (Aen 6.624)
imitari neque *possim* si velim (Brut 287)
nec si forte roges, *possim* tibi dicere quot sint (Ov Met 13.823).

The examples are all negative: they say that the ability (and consequently its actuation) is lacking in worlds $w^{*\prime}$ derived from the actual world w^* by minimally adjusting the modal base to make the protasis true. The implicature is that the ability is also lacking in w^*, a fortiori in the first example (Aen 6.624). In the last two examples (Brut 287; Met 13.823) that is not an immediate problem, since there is no need for it to be actuated in w^*. The conditional can be hidden inside an adverbial expression

(100) CAL. Crucior. PSEUD. Cor dura. CAL. Non possum. PSEUD. Fac possis. CAL. *Quonam pacto possim*? PSEUD. Vince animum. (Pl Pseud 236).

If Calidorus exercises selfcontrol, he will become able to harden his heart. The conditional can also be completely covert

(101) quod facile intellegi *possit* (Ad Att 2.23.3)
Possem idem facere, etsi minus quam ille (Tusc 1.84).

Given the need, fancy, inclination, opportunity, an individual can actuate in $w^{*\prime}$ an ability he has in $w^{*\prime}$ and in w^*.

The subjunctive is also licensed in certain nonveridical and downward entailing contexts. So it occurs with arbitrary second person pronouns in generic contexts

(99) If I had a hundred tongues and a hundred mouths, I still could not list all the different types of punishments (Aen 6.624). I would not be able to imitate them if I wished to (Brut 287). If you happened to ask me, I would be unable to tell you how many they are (Ov Met 13.823).

(100) CAL. I'm extremely upset. PSEUD. Harden your heart. CAL. I can't. PSEUD. Force yourself. CAL. How could I be able to do that? PSEUD. Control your feelings (Pl Pseud 236).

(101) Very understandably (Ad Att 2.23.3). I could do the same, even if less than him (Tusc 1.84).

(102) non omnem frugem neque arborem in omni agro reperire *possis* (Pro Rosc Am 75)
id semen de cupresso, de pino quidvis anni legere *possis* (Cato 17.1).

It also occurs (but is not obligatory) in rhetorical questions

(103) Quae enim fortuna aut quis casus aut quae tanta *possit* iniuria omnium imperatorum de Deiotaro decreta delere? (Pro Reg Deiot 37)
tam doctas quis non *possit* amare manus? (Ov Am 2.4.28)

and in the complements of comparatives

(104) Hector... parvum navigium conscendit pluribus quam capere *posset* impositis (Curt Ruf 4.8.7)
plus impositum quam ferre *possent* (Verr 2.4.20).

Tense

Different classes of modals interact with tense in different ways. Modal constructions involve two times, the time of the modal accessibility relation and the time of the complement eventuality (either of which can be modified by a temporal adverbial). Epistemic modals are concerned with the current state of knowledge about past, present or future situations. So in default epistemic contexts the modal verb is restricted to the present tense but the complement can be present or past infinitive. By contrast other modals like deontic, ability and circumstantial modals do not restrict the tense of the modal verb; for instance an ability modal can describe past, present or future capacities and a deontic past, present or future obligations. However the event expressed by the complement of such a modal verb is (at least partially) future relative to the reference time of the modal verb; for instance, abilities and obligations typically pre-exist their instantiation. Here are some epistemic examples

(105) *potest* gloriam iam novam *quaerere* (Ad Att 15.19.2)
Corruat iste *necesse est* aut per adversarios aut ipse per se (Ad Att 10.8.8)
prodigum te *fuisse oportet* olim in adulescentia (Pl Amph 1031)
ne... praeter mea regna redires... ventos non *habuisse potes* (Ov Her 6.6).

(102) One couldn't find every crop or tree in every field (Pro Rosc Am 75). You could collect this seed from the cypress and the pine at any season (Cato 17.1).
(103) What misfortune or disaster or outrage could nullify the decrees of every general regarding Deiotarus? (Pro Reg Deiot 37). Who could fail to love such skilful hands (Ov Am 2.4.28).
(104) Hector boarded a small ship which was loaded with more men than it could carry (Curt Ruf 4.8.7). A greater burden was imposed on them than they could bear (Verr 2.4.20).
(105) He may now be looking for a new path to glory (Ad Att 15.19.2). He is bound to fall either through his enemies or of his own accord (Ad Att 10.8.8). You must have been a spendthrift once as a young man (Pl Amph 1031). It's possible that you did not have the right winds to return past my kingdom (Ov Her 6.6).

The modal verb is in the present tense expressing current information about eventualities in the present (Ad Att 15.19), the future (Ad Att 10.8) or the past (Amph 1031; Her 6.6). In the last example (Her 6.6) Hypsipyle considers the possibility that Jason may have wanted to pass by Lemnos on his way home but did not have the requisite winds to do so. *Habuisse* is a real past infinitive (not just a perfective), which triggers historical sequence. This is illustrated (very schematically) in Figure 9.9: the higher tense (present) is the time of the modal accessibility relation (formalized as an argument of R), the lower tense (relative past) is the time of the eventuality in the complement. The tense of the modal verb can be changed to future or past if the time of evaluation of the modal is shifted

(106) cum tu haec leges, illum Romae esse *oportebit* (Ad Fam 12.30.5)
cum haec scribebam v Kalend., Pompeius iam Brundisium venisse *poterat* (Ad Att 8.9a.2)
Candelabrum... erat eo splendore qui ex clarissimis et pulcherrimis gemmis esse *debebat* (Verr 2.4.65).

In the first two examples (Ad Fam 12.30; Ad Att 8.9a) the time of evaluation for the modal accessibility relation is shifted forward to the time when the letter is read and backward to the time when the letter was written respectively. In the

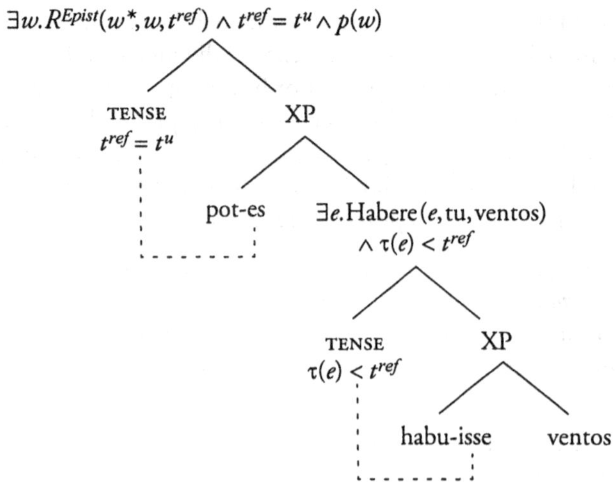

Figure 9.9
Tense with an epistemic modal
Potes habuisse ventos (cp. Ov Her 6.6)

(106) He should be at Rome when you read these words (Ad Fam 12.30.5). As I am writing this on the 25th February Pompey may already have reached Brundisium (Ad Att 8.9a.2). The candelabrum had a splendour that could only have come from the most brilliant and beautiful gems (Verr 2.4.65).

last example (Verr 2.4) the time of evaluation is the narrative time when Verres made the aesthetic judgement based on the inference cited.

As already noted, nonepistemic modals do not have such restrictions on the tense of the modal verb. For instance deontics can appear in the tense that is appropriate to the episode of obligation

(107) Compedes te capere *oportet* (Pl Cist 244)
debebunt Pompeium hortari (Ad Att 9.7c.2)
quod facere *debuisti* (Verr 2.2.116)
et casu tunc respondere vadato *debebat* (Hor Sat 1.9.36).

However the tense of the complement is more restricted than with epistemics: in each example the obligatory event is future relative to the reference time of the modal verb; see Figure 9.10. The modal is not assumed to introduce a tense itself but to condition the interpretation of the relative tense of the complement infinitive. The third example (Verr 2.2) is past perfective (the event ought to have occurred), while the last example (Sat 1.9) is past imperfective expressing a background obligation in force at the past reference time (*tunc*). The obligation terminates once the complement is actuated or when the opportunity for actuation lapses. If the infinitive expresses an eventuality that is already in progress (as it can with a state, an activity, an iterated event or the activity phase of an accomplishment), it is required to continue into the future

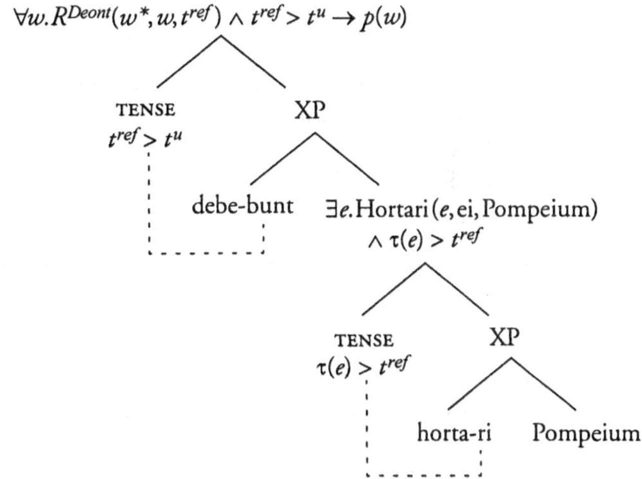

Figure 9.10
Tense with an deontic modal
Debebunt hortari Pompeium (cp. Ad Att 9.7c.2)

(107) You ought to get some fetters (Pl Cist 244). They should encourage Pompey (Ad Att 9.7c.2). Which you ought to have done (Verr 2.2.116). By chance he had to appear in court at that time (Hor Sat 1.9.36).

(108) Ego vos universos... deorum numero *colere* debeo (Post Red Sen 30)
et sum totus vester et *esse* debeo (Ad Fam 15.7.1).

In the following examples (one deontic, one ability), a present modal takes a perfect infinitive complement

(109) Tametsi statim *vicisse debeo*, tamen de meo iure decedam
(Pro Rosc Am 73)
usu tuum etiam nunc *fecisse* non *potes* (Rhet Her 4.40).

The time of the complement is not past relative to that of the modal verb but is the right boundary of the perfect XN interval, which is a resultant state, therefore present, as also in the case of the prospective ('ought to be about to'), which is its mirror image.

We have already touched on the issue of actuation in the section on ability modals, but it is relevant for other types of modality too; we will use mostly deontic examples in the following discussion. A modal verb tells us that the eventuality in its complement is actuated in some (or all) accessible possible worlds. There is nothing in the lexical meaning of a modal that either guarantees or precludes that the actual world will develop in such a way as to become one of the actuating worlds. This lexical property of modals lives on in the imperfective aspect, which is just vague about actualization

(110) Se autem tutelae rationes ut *debebat* reddidisse (Quint Decl 355.2)
illa quae gravissima *debebat* esse... fuit infirma et levis (Pro Mur 11).

In the first example (Decl 355.2) the modal is actualized, in the second (Pro Mur 11) it is not. We have chosen past tense examples because imperfective aspect is morphologically expressed in the past, but the same holds for present and future imperfectives. Focus on the modal forces the unactualized reading (see further on the perfective)

(111) Legatis quaestores sumptum quem *oportebat* dari non dederunt
(De Inv 2.87).

The perfective is more complicated. It has two (mutually exclusive) principal readings, one with actualization and one without. In the former reading the perfective aspect expresses the occurrence of the event in the actual world (like English 'had to')

(108) I ought to venerate you all together among the gods (Post Red Sen 30). I am entirely at your disposal, as indeed I ought to be (Ad Fam 15.7.1).

(109) Even though I ought to be the winner at once, I will give up my right (Pro Rosc Am 73). Even now you cannot have made it yours by prescriptive right (Rhet Her 4.40).

(110) That he had rendered the accounts for his guardianship as required (Quint Decl 355.2). The part which ought to have been the most serious was feeble and trivial (Pro Mur 11).

(111) The treasury officials did not give the ambassadors the expenses that they ought to (De Inv 2.87).

(112) hic *fecit* hominem frugi ut *facere oportuit* (Pl Capt 294)
Omnia... *praestiti* rei publicae quae *praestare debuit* is qui esset in eo quo ego sum gradu... collocatus (Ad Brut 1.2).

Putting the lexically stative modal into the perfective aspect adds a completive component to its meaning: the modal state consummates in the actualization of the complement. The other perfective reading is just the opposite: the obligation is closed off by failure to actualize (like English 'ought to have'). This reading is most salient when there is focus on the modal verb ('OUGHT to have'). A contrast is evoked between possible worlds in which p is true ($\lambda w.p(w)$) and those (in particular the actual world) in which it is not ($\lambda w.\neg p(w)$), and the latter are excluded from the set of modally accessible worlds

(113) Exigere te *oportuit* navem quae contra praedones, *non* quae cum praeda navigaret (Verr 2.5.59)
Archipiratam ipsum videt *nemo*, de quo supplicium sumi *oportuit*. (Verr 2.5.64).

Similarly, past circumstantial and dynamic possibilities become counterfactual when they are eliminated by supervening events

(114) etiam tum... opprimere *posset* hostes. Iterum ab eodem gradu depulsus est (Nepos 2.5.1).

After the battle of Salamis Xerxes could still have defeated the Greeks, but he was again thwarted by Themistocles (at any time slice of the actual world after that defeat of the Greeks was no longer a live possibility). A circumstantial modal in the present generates a set of live possibilities: with the passage of time the modal becomes past, one of the possibilities is actuated and the remainder become counterfactual.

Distinct from all of the above are the shifted tense modals, in which non-actualization in the present is expressed by the imperfect indicative

(115) quamquam languet iuventus nec perinde atque *debebat* in laudis et gloriae cupiditate versatur (In Pis 82)
in cena fit quod fieri *debebat* in ventre (Sen Ep 95.27: app. crit.)

(112) This man acted as an honest man should have acted (Pl Capt 294). I have shown towards the republic all those qualities that one placed in my high position ought to have shown (Ad Brut 1.2).

(113) You ought to have required a ship to sail against the pirates, not to sail with your pirated goods (Verr 2.5.59). Noone caught sight of the pirate captain who ought to have been brought to punishment (Verr 2.5.64).

(114) Even then he could have overwhelmed the Greeks. For a second time he was thwarted by the same man (Nepos 2.5.1).

(115) Although our young people are inert and do not exert themselves in the quest for praise and glory as they ought to (In Pis 82). What ought to happen in digestion happens at the dinner table (Sen Ep 95.27).

(116) praetereo illud quod mihi maxime argumento ad huius innocentiam *poterat* esse (Pro Rosc Am 75)
At ego tuas litteras, etsi iure *poteram*... tamen non proferam (Phil 2.9).

Occasionally nonactualization in the past is expressed by the pluperfect

(117) populusque Romanus, quam vivo iracundiam *debuerat*, in corpus mortui contulit. (Vell Pat 2.21.4)
imperator, qui in desertores saevire *debuerat*, desertor exercitus sui factus est (Vell Pat 2.85.3).

In each example in (115) and (116), by the time of the eventuality expressed by the main clause verb—stative *languet* (In Pis 82), generic *fit* (Ep 95.27) and episodic *praetereo* (Pro Rosc Am 75), *non proferam* (Phil 2.9)—actuation of the event in the complement of the modal is precluded and foreclosed. It is not the case that the modal is in the past tense because the event in its complement ought to have occurred before the event expressed by the present tense verb: the second example in (115) (Ep 95.27) does not mean that digestion ought to have happened before dinner. Rather it is the time of evaluation for the modal accessibility relation that is shifted back into the past: during a period of time prior to the mixing of the ingredients, a requirement held that this mixing be done by the diner's digestion (not by the cook). The effect of this is similar to the effect of using a past prospective

(118) arietem muris *admoturus erat*. Ceterum incepto absistere eum coegit subitus Aetolorum adventus (Livy 32.4.1).

By shifting the time of the intention, possibility or obligation back into the past, the speaker implicates that actuation is no longer a live issue: the opportunity for actuation has passed, or the agent has conclusively decided against actuation. (It may still objectively be a possibility or a requirement at the present time, but that is not relevant because the issue has already been decided: there will be no actuation unless the decision is reversed.) This again evokes a focal contrast between possible worlds in which the event is actuated and the real world in which it is not. The former and the latter share the same history up to the point in time at which actuation is foreclosed (provided the speaker gets the facts right and does not omit any relevant facts): at that point the worlds branch and go their different ways. At all times during an interval whose right boundary abuts the time of foreclosure, actuation is a live option and the modal accessibility relation applies. This is illustrated in Figure 9.11. As usual the unactuated event is (at

(116) I pass over the point that might have been my strongest argument for his innocence (Pro Rosc Am 75). I will not produce your letter, although I could rightfully do so (Phil 2.9).
(117) The Roman people directed at his dead body the anger that they ought to have directed against him when he was alive (Vell Pat 2.21.4). The general who ought to have dealt severely with deserters, himself deserted his own army (Vell Pat 2.85.3).
(118) He was about to move up his battering ram. But the sudden arrival of the Aetolians forced him to give up this project (Livy 32.4.1).

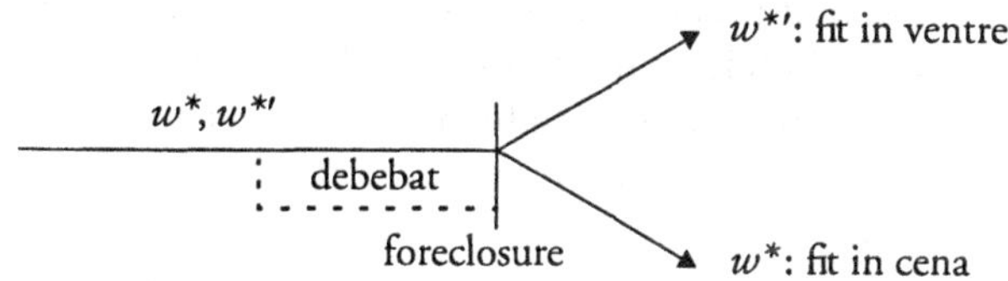

Figure 9.11
Shifted modal with branching worlds
In cena fit quod fieri debebat in ventre (Sen Ep 95.27)

least partially) future relative to the time of the modal, but its time relative to the time of utterance is not relevant: it can be past, present or future

(119) I fuge: sed *poteras* tutior esse domi (Mart 1.3.12).

Martial's book of epigrams is still at home but it has decided to leave for publication: the modal verb applies to a past time prior to this decision, while the time when the book is published and ceases to be safe at home is in the future. The same applies to past unfulfilled conditionals

(120) Si... postulassent,... brevi sententiam *peregissem* (Livy 22.60.6);

if the envoys of the prisoners had demanded their ransom, Manlius would have quickly finished his speech later than the narrative reference time. Compare 'If Jack had taken the test tomorrow, he would have passed,' where both protasis and apodosis refer to future events. If actuation is neither achieved nor foreclosed (if the obligation is thought of as still applying at the time of utterance, even in the absence of current compliance), the present is used

(121) quod non aut is agit quem *oportet* aut cum eo quicum *oportet* (De Inv 2.57; cp. 1.10)
eam molestiam quam *debent* capere non capiunt... quod contra *oportebat* delicto dolere, correctione gaudere (De Amic 90).

The second example (De Amic 90) illustrates both types: the first modal (*debent*) says what they ought to be doing even while they are not doing it, the second (*oportebat*) what they ought to have decided to do but chose not to.

Shifted tense modals raise three questions: (1) Why is the tense past rather than present? (2) Why is the aspect imperfective rather than perfective? and (3) Why is the mood indicative rather than subjunctive, given that the event is unactuated and therefore counterfactual? The foreclosure theory provides an answer to the first of these questions: the modal accessibility relation is evaluated

(119) Off with you! But you could have been safer at home (Mart 1.3.12).
(120) If they had asked, I would have completed my speech briefly (Livy 22.60.6).
(121) Because the case is not being brought by the person who ought to bring it or not against the person against whom it out to be brought (De Inv 2.57). They are not annoyed at what they ought to be annoyed about; on the contrary they ought to be sorry about their misdeed and happy about having it corrected (De Amic 90).

at a past time. Tense shift probably also underlies the use of the imperfect subjunctive for present unfulfilled conditions (and the pluperfect subjunctive for past ones). The conditional is evaluated for all times in a past interval up to the time of foreclosure of the eventuality in the protasis. The two types co-occur in the following example

(122) Nec me turpitudo deterret, etsi maxime *debebat*... Ac vellem quidem (*essem* enim qui esse *debebam*) (Ad Att 13.28.1).

This use of the imperfect can be extended to situations in which a literally temporal interpretation is not appropriate, like fictional events or roles in games and plays in Italian or counterfactuals about permanent situations

(123) si nihil animus *praesentiret* in posterum (Pro Arch 29).

In such cases the imperfect is a fake past, a direct mark of modal ($w \neq w^*$) rather than temporal ($t < t^u$) distance. As far as the second question is concerned, the obligation applies throughout the interval prior to foreclosure, so the modal appears in the imperfective; the perfective would have meant that the obligatory event actually either occurred or failed to occur at some point during that interval. The answer to the third question is that the obligation exists in the actual world w^*, even though the obligatory event belongs only to a possible world $w^{*\prime}$ that is like the actual world in most respects other than the issue of the event.

This picture is complicated by the fact that the indicative of modal verbs is found also in the apodoses of present and past counterfactual conditions, in some of which a deontic or circumstantial necessity could not have existed in w^*

(124) "Non *potuit*," inquies, "fieri sapiens nisi natus esset." (De Fin 2.103)
Si ita esset, hac lege accusatum *oportuit* qua accusatur Habitus. (Pro Clu 90)
ob ea quae si propriis gessisset auspiciis, triumphare *debuerat* (Vell Pat 2.115.3).

(In the last example (Vell Pat 2.115) the additional past marking of the pluperfect encodes the counterfactuality.) The same applies to the past prospective and the gerund

(125) si P. Sestius... occisus esset, *fuistisne* ad arma ituri? (Pro Sest 81)
ubi *erat* mansurus, si ire perrexisset (De Div 1.26)
si unum diem morati essetis, moriendum omnibus *fuit* (Livy 2.38.5).

(122) It is not shame that prevents me, although it definitely ought to. I wish it were (for then I should be the man I ought to be) (Ad Att 13.28.1).

(123) If the soul had no premonition of posterity (Pro Arch 29).

(124) "He could not have become wise," you will say, "if he had not been born" (De Fin 2.103). If that had been so, he ought to have been prosecuted under the same law as Habitus is being prosecuted (Pro Clu 90). For these achievements, for which, if he had accomplished them under his own auspices, he would have deserved a triumph (Vell Pat 2.115.3).

(125) If P. Sestius had actually been killed, would you have been ready to take up arms? (Pro Sest 81). Where he was going to stay, if he had continued on his journey (De Div 1.26). If you had stayed one more day, you would all have been killed (Livy 2.38.5).

Examples like these are usually understood as arising from a semantically unmotivated grammatical extension of the indicative construction to situations in which the modal was not true in the actual world. This rests on an oversimplification. In principle every world has its own set of norms; but the worlds that are closest to w^* except that the protasis is true in them are close enough to w^* to share the same set of norms with w^* (unless of course the protasis introduces a counterfactual norm). Although the modal base is modified by the counterfactual protasis, the ordering source still quantifies over worlds accessible from w^*: norms and plans in w^* may be designed to cover different possibilities (possible outcomes in the future, actual or counterfactual outcomes in the past). For instance, indicative prospectives like those in (125) follow naturally if the conditional is understood as a restriction inside the scope of a bouletic or circumstantial ordering source: was it your intention (in w^*) to rush to arms (in w') in the event of Sestius' murder (in w')? A similar scopal interpretation is possible for the modals in (124): it was not a circumstantial possibility given the laws of nature in w^* that Epicurus would have become a wise man (in w') if he had not been born (in w'). The subjunctive for the apodosis is so to speak hidden inside the infinitive governed by the modal. Due presumably to its greater simplicity, the broad scope modal is the norm in the accusative and infinitive (e.g. *oportuisse* rather than *futurum fuisse ut oporteret*). But otherwise the modal can appear either in the indicative or in the subjunctive, depending on quite subtle factors of speaker perspective

(126) in qua quid facere *potuissem*, nisi tum consul fuissem? Consul autem esse qui *potui*, nisi eum vitae cursum tenuissem... ? (De Rep 1.10).

In the subjunctive version the first argument of the accessibility relation for the ordering source is not w^* but only the counterfactual worlds derived from w^* in which the protasis is true. The semantics for an indicative modal in a counterfactual apodosis says that all worlds w that are accessible by the ordering source g from w^* and accessible from a modal base f that is derived from the facts in w^* modified (only so far as is necessary) by the protasis are worlds in which p is true: $\forall w.R^g(w^*, w) \wedge R^{fProt}(w^*, w) \rightarrow p(w)$. The semantics for a subjunctive modal in a counterfactual apodosis is more complicated: it says that all worlds w' accessible by the ordering source g from those worlds w accessible from a modal base f that is derived from the facts in w^* modified (only so far as is necessary) by the protasis are worlds in which p is true: $\forall w \forall w'.R^{fProt}(w^*, w) \wedge R^g(w, w') \rightarrow p(w')$. Note finally that this would not cover an indicative deontic modal in the apodosis where the protasis introduces a counterfactual norm. The following example has the subjunctive

(127) quorum tibi si esset illa lex nihil *liceret* (De Dom 70; cp. 68).

(126) What could I have done in that crisis, if I had not been consul then? But how could I have been consul, if I had not adhered to that course of life...? (De Rep 1.10).

(127) None of which would have been legal for you to do, if that law existed (De Dom 70).

Other subjunctive contexts show a similar sensitivity to veridicality (inter alia)

(128) testis erit tibi ipsa quantae mihi curae fuerit ut Quinti fratris animus in eam esset is qui esse *deberet.* (Ad Att 1.5.2)
Sed illum eum futurum esse puto qui esse *debet.* (Ad Att 6.3.7).

The first example (Ad Att 1.5) deals with obligations in the worlds of Cicero's objectives (in Pomponia's evidence), the second (Ad Att 6.3) deals with real world obligations in Cicero's beliefs.

FURTHER READING

Bradley & Swartz (1979); Kratzer (1991); Portner (2009); von Fintel & Heim (2005).

(128) She herself will tell you how much effort I have spent ensuring that my brother Quintus' attitude towards her should be what it ought to be (Ad Att 1.5.2). But I think he will behave as he ought to (Ad Att 6.3.7).

SYMBOLS

(1) Variables and types

	Default Variable	Type
Individual	x, y, z	<e>
Event	e, f	<ε>
State	s	<ε>
World	w	<s>
Time (instant/interval)	t	<i>
Point (spatial)	p	<p>
Region	r	<p, t>
Degree	d	<d>
Number	n	<n>
Vector	v	<v>
Declaration	p, q	<t>
Proposition	p, q	<s, t>
Property of individuals	P, Q	<e, t>
Property of events	P, Q	<ε, t>
Relation between individuals	R	<e, <e, t>
Relation between worlds	R	<s, <s, t>
Quantifier	Q	<et, <et, t>
Generalized quantifier	T	<et, t>
Set of individuals	X, Y	<e, t>
Set of sets of individuals	$\boldsymbol{P}, \boldsymbol{Q}$	<et, t>
Set of events	E	<ε, t>
Set of worlds	W	<s, t>
Set of vectors	V	<v, t>
Cause subevent	e^C	<ε>
Process subevent	e^P	<ε>
State subevent	e^S	<ε>
Poststate of event	s^e	<ε>
Runtime function for event	$\tau(e)$	<ε, i>
Lifetime function for individual	$\tau^l(x)$	<e, i>
Path function for event	$\sigma(e)$	<ε, pt>
Eigenspace function	$\sigma(x)$	<e, pt>
Degree function	$\delta^P(x)$	<e, d>
Measure function	$\mu(x)$	<e, n>

(2) Logical forms

°	Head symbol
′	Bar symbol
VP	Verb Phrase
NP	Noun Phrase
AP	Adjective Phrase
PP	Preposition Phrase
CP	Complementizer Phrase
XP	Unspecified Phrase
DegP	Degree Phrase
DegAP	Comparative Adjective Phrase
TnsP	Tense Phrase
AspP	Aspect Phrase
ModP	Modal Verb Phrase
FinP	Finite Phrase
VectorP	Vector Phrase

BIBLIOGRAPHY

Acquaviva, P. 2008. *Lexical Plurals.* Oxford.

Allwood, J., L. Andersson and O. Dahl. 1995. *Logic in Linguistics.* Cambridge.

Arsenijević, B. 2006. *Inner Aspect and Telicity.* Utrecht.

Asbury, A., J. Dotlačil, B. Gehrke and R. Nouwen. 2008. *Syntax and Semantics of Spatial P.* Amsterdam.

Bach, E., E. Jelinek, A. Kratzer and B. Partee. 1995. *Quantification in Natural Languages.* Dordrecht.

Beck, S. 2010. Quantifiers in *than*-clauses. *Semantics and Pragmatics* 3:1-72.

Borer, H. 2005. *The Normal Course of Events.* Oxford.

Bouchard, D. 2002. *Adjectives, Number and Interfaces.* Amsterdam.

Bradley, R. and N. Swartz. 1979. *Possible Worlds.* Oxford.

Cann, R. 1993. *Formal Semantics. An Introduction.* Cambridge.

Cann, R., R. Kempson & E. Gregoromichelaki. 2009. *Semantics. An Introduction to Meaning in Language.* Cambridge.

Carlson, L. and E. van der Zee. 2006. *Functional Features in Language and Space.* Oxford.

Chierchia, G. 2004. Scalar implicatures, polarity phenomena, and the syntax-pragmatics interface. *Structures and Beyond,* ed. A. Belletti: 39-103. Oxford.

Cinque, G. 2010. *The Syntax of Adjectives.* Cambridge, Mass.

Copley, B. 2009. *The Semantics of the Future.* New York.

Detlefsen, M., D. McCarty and J. Bacon. 1999. *Logic from A to Z.* London.

Giannakidou, A. 1998. *Polarity Sensitivity as (Non)Veridical Dependency.* Amsterdam.

Gil, D. 1982. *Distributive Numerals.* Ph.D. diss. University of California, Los Angeles.

Giorgi, A. and F. Pianesi. 1997. *Tense and Aspect.* Oxford.

Heim, I., and A. Kratzer. 1998. *Semantics in Generative Grammar.* Oxford.

Herskovitz, A. 1986. *Language and Spatial Cognition. An Interdisciplinary Study of the Prepositions in English.* Cambridge.

Homer, V. 2011. *Polarity and Modality.* Ph.D. diss. University of California, Los Angeles.

Horn, L.R. 2001. *A Natural History of Negation,* ed.2. Stanford.

Horn, L.R. and Y. Kato. 2000. *Negation and Polarity.* Oxford.

Kamp, H. and U. Reyle. 1993. *From Discourse to Logic.* Dordrecht.

Kempchinsky, P. and R. Slabakova. 2005. *Aspectual Inquiries.* Dordrecht.
Kennedy, C. 1999. *Projecting the Adjective.* New York.
Klein, W. 1994. *Time in Language.* London.
Kratzer, A. 1991. Modality. *Semantik,* eds. A. von Stechow and D. Wunderlich: 639-650. Berlin.
Landman, F. 1991. *Structures for Semantics.* Dordrecht.
Landman, F. 2000. *Events and Plurality.* Dordrecht.
Lasersohn, P. 1995. *Plurality, Conjunction and Events.* Dordrecht.
Levin, B. and M.R. Hovav. 2005. *Argument Realization.* Cambridge.
Matellán, V.A. 2010. *Argument Structure and the Syntax-Morphology Interface.* Ph.D. diss. Barcelona.
Morzycki, M. 2005. *Mediated Modification.* Ph.D. diss. University of Massachusetts, Amherst.
Partee, B., A. ter Meulen and R. Wall. 1990. *Mathematical Methods in Linguistics.* Dordrecht.
Peters, S. and D. Westerståhl. 2006. *Quantifiers in Language and Logic.* Oxford.
Portner, P. 2009. *Modality.* Oxford.
Portner, P. and B. Partee. 2002. *Formal Semantics. The Essential Readings.* Oxford.
Ramchand, G.C. 2008. *Verb Meaning and the Lexicon.* Cambridge.
Rothstein, S. 2004. *Structuring Events.* Oxford.
Sider, T. 2010. *Logic for Philosophy.* Oxford.
Smith, C. 1997. *The Parameter of Aspect,* ed. 2. Dordrecht.
Schwarzschild, R. 1996. *Pluralities.* Dordrecht.
Tonhauser, J. 2006. *The Temporal Semantics of Noun Phrases.* Ph.D. diss. Stanford.
Tunstall, S.L. 1998. *The Interpretation of Quantifiers.* Ph.D. diss. University of Massachusetts, Amherst.
van der Wouden, T. 1997. *Negative Contexts.* London.
van der Zee, E. and J. Slack. 2003. *Representing Direction in Language and Space.* Oxford.
von Fintel, K. and I. Heim. 2005. *Intensional Semantics. Lecture Notes.* MIT.
Winter, Y. 2001. *Flexibility Principles in Boolean Semantics.* Cambridge, Mass.
Zimmermann, M. 2002. *Boys Buying Two Sausages Each.* Utrecht.
Zwarts, J. 2005. Prepositional aspect and the algebra of paths. *Linguistics and Philosophy* 28:739-779.
Zwarts, J. and Y. Winter. 2000. Vector space semantics: a model-theoretic analysis of locative prepositions. *Journal of Logic, Language and Information* 9:169-211.

INDEX